THE VERB IN CLASSICAL HEBREW

The Verb in Classical Hebrew

The Linguistic Reality behind the Consecutive Tenses

Bo Isaksson

UNIVERSITY OF CAMBRIDGE
Faculty of Asian and Middle Eastern Studies

OpenBook Publishers

https://www.openbookpublishers.com

All external links were active at the time of publication unless otherwise stated and have been archived via the Internet Archive Wayback Machine at https://archive.org/web

Any digital material and resources associated with this volume will be available at https://doi.org/10.11647/OBP.0414#resources

Semitic Languages and Cultures 27

ISSN (print): 2632-6906
ISSN (digital): 2632-6914

ISBN Paperback: 978-1-80511-350-8
ISBN Hardback: 978-1-80511-351-5
ISBN Digital (PDF): 978-1-80511-352-2

DOI: 10.11647/OBP.0414

Cover image: Fragments of Hebrew Bible manuscripts from the Cairo Genizah. Left: Cambridge University Library, T-S A20.16 (Ruth 1.18–2.9). Right: Cambridge University Library, T-S A18.4 (Ezra 3.2–4.2). Courtesy of the Syndics of Cambridge University Library.
Cover design: Jeevanjot Kaur Nagpal

The main fonts used in this volume are Charis SIL and SBL Hebrew.

To my wife Greth

CONTENTS

Acknowledgements xiii

Abbreviations xv

1. Introduction 1
   1.1. Aim 1
   1.2. Method and Terminology 4
   1.3. Previous Research 45

2. The Conjunction *Wa* in CBH 79
   2.1. PS **Wa* and the Concept of Natural Language Connective 79
   2.2. Some Reflexes of PS **Wa* in Semitic Languages 81
   2.3. The Reflex of PS **Wa* in CBH 96
   2.4. Summary 134

3. The Short *Yiqṭol* as a Separate Verbal Morpheme in CBH 155
   3.1. The Semitic Background of the CBH Short *Yiqṭol* 156

3.2. The Short *Yiqṭol* in the Archaic Hebrew Poetry 191

3.3. The Short *Yiqṭol* in the Pre-exilic Hebrew Inscriptions..201

3.4. The Short *Yiqṭol* in CBH 205

3.5. Summary: The Independent Status of the Short *Yiqṭol*..245

4. The Imperfective Long *Yiqṭol(u)* in CBH............293

4.1. The Semitic Background of the CBH Long *Yiqṭol* 293

4.2. The Long *Yiqṭol* in the Archaic Hebrew Poetry 312

4.3. The Long *Yiqṭol* in the Pre-exilic Hebrew Inscriptions..316

4.4. The Meanings of the Long *Yiqṭol* in CBH....317

4.5. Summary: The Independent Status of the Long *Yiqṭol* (< **yaqtulu*)...........................324

5. The Perfective Formation *Qaṭal* in CBH.............337

5.1. The Semitic Background of *Qaṭal* 337

5.2. *Qaṭal* in the Archaic Hebrew Poetry...........358

5.3. *Qaṭal* in the Pre-exilic Hebrew Inscriptions 367
5.4. The Meanings of *Qaṭal* in CBH 369
5.5. Why *Qaṭal* Came to Alternate with *Wa(y)-yiqṭol*: *Qaṭal* as Intruding Morpheme in CBH 382
5.6. Summary: The Identity of *Qaṭal* as Perfective Gram in CBH 384

6. The Construction *Wa-qaṭal* in CBH 395
6.1. The Construction Concept 395
6.2. Precursors of the CBH Construction *Wa-qaṭal* in Northwest Semitic 399
6.3. Parallels of the CBH Construction *Wa-qaṭal* in Iron Age Northwest Semitic 408
6.4. Survey of Modal Sequences with Internal *Wa-qaṭal* in CBH 413
6.5. Result Functions of *Wa-qaṭal* in Other Domains in CBH 418
6.6. The Significance of the Result Meaning in the Development of *Wa-qaṭal* in CBH 424
6.7. Survey of Conditional Sentences with *Wa-qaṭal* as Apodosis in CBH 427

6.8. Discussion about the Birthplace of the Construction *Wa-qaṭal* 435

6.9. Temporal or Causal Clause with *Wa-qaṭal* 436

6.10. Topics and their *Wa-qaṭal* Comments 445

6.11. First Clause and *Wa-qaṭal* Being of Equal Status 450

6.12. The Linking *Wa-qaṭal* + *(Wa)-X-yiqṭol(u)* 458

6.13. The Linking *Wa-qaṭal* + *(Wa)-lō-yiqtol(u)* 461

6.14. Summary: The Identity of *Wa-qaṭal* as Imperfective Construction in CBH 461

7. The Linguistic Reality behind the Consecutive Tenses 479

7.1. A New Terminology 479

7.2. Tenet 1a: *Wa-VX // Wa-XV* 486

7.3. Tenet 1b: *Wa-VX // Ø-(X)V* 492

7.4. Tenet 1c: *Wa-VX // (Wa)-(X)-qoṭel* 511

7.5. Tenet 1d: *Wa-VX // (Wa)-XØ* 523

7.6. Tenet 1e: The Aspectual Interruption 533

7.7. Tenet 2a: // *Wa-XV* + (1a, 1b, 1c, or 1d) + *Wa-VX* 549

7.8. Tenet 2b: // *Ø-(X)V* + (1a, 1b, 1c, or 1d) + *Wa-VX* 554

7.9. Tenet 2c: // *(Wa)-(X)-qoṭel* + (1a, 1b, 1c, or 1d) + *Wa-VX* 560

7.10. Tenet 2d: // *(Wa)-XØ* + (1a, 1b, 1c, or 1d) + *Wa-VX* 565

7.11. Tenet 3: The Prototypical Discourse-continuity Clause-type *Wa-V(X)* 570

7.12. Tenet 4: The Prototypical Negated Discourse-continuity Clause-type *Wa-NEG-V(X)* 574

8. Did This Book Achieve Its Aim? A Summary 609

References 613

Indices 685

ACKNOWLEDGEMENTS

This book is the final result of a monograph project funded by a grant from the Swedish Research Council (project-ID: 2015-01168) and hosted by the Department of Linguistics and Philology, Uppsala University. I am very grateful to the Research Council for this grant.

First and foremost, I remember with gratitude my Doktorvater, the late Frithiof Rundgren, who opened my eyes to the problems and intricacies of the Hebrew verbal system and always had the attitute that it was an enigma that could be and should be solved.

The research presented in the book is based on several previous research projects also funded by the Swedish Research Council. The published books include *Circumstantial Qualifiers in Semitic: The Case of Arabic and Hebrew* (2009, by B. Isaksson, H. Kammensjö, and M. Persson), and *Clause Combining in Semitic* (2015, ed. B. Isaksson and M. Persson). This was the starting point, and I would like to express my gratitude to Heléne Kammensjö and Maria Persson for many inspiring discussions during those early projects. Other scholars to whom I owe a debt of gratitude are Eran Cohen, Michal Marmorstein, and Jan Retsö.

I also would like to thank Geoffrey Khan, who invited me to Cambridge and the conference *Biblical & Rabbinic Hebrew: New Perspectives in Philology & Linguistics*, 8th-10th July 2019, where I could present some of the main tenets in the present book.

Last but not least, my gratitude goes to my wife Greth, who made this research possible by her never-ending support, love, and encouragement.

ABBREVIATIONS

1	1st-person
2	2nd-person
3	3rd-person
I*wy*	verb(s) with first radical *w* or *y*
II*wy*	verb(s) with second radical *w* or *y*
III*wy*	verb(s) with third radical *w* or *y*
«…»	marks a relative clause
«REL-…»	marks a syndetic relative clause
!	morphologically distinctive form
n / *n*	line break (in Ugaritic)
+	marks a linking between two clauses
-A	ventive/cohortative suffix (paragogic *heh*)
ADV	adverb; adverbial
BH	Biblical Hebrew
BHS	Biblia Hebraica Stuttgartensia
c	common (gender)
CBH	Classical Biblical Hebrew
ch.	chapter
CJB	Complete Jewish Bible
CONJ	conjunction
d	dual
ESV	English Standard Version
f	feminine
IMP	imperative (morpheme)
INT	interrogative particle
l.	line

m	masculine
MSA	Modern South Arabian
MT	Masoretic Textual Tradition
-N	ventive/energic suffix
n.	endnote or footnote
NAB	New American Bible
NEG	negation
NET	New English Translation
NIV	New International Version
NJB	New Jerusalem Bible
-Npar	paragogic *nun*
NRSV	New Revised Standard Version
OB	Old Babylonian
O.noun	object noun phrase
O.pron	object pronoun
p	plural
p.	page
PREP	preposition
PrP	prepositional phrase
PS	Proto-Semitic
REL	relative particle
s	singular
S.noun	subject noun phrase
S.pron	subject pronoun
TAM	Tense, Aspect, Mood
-V	ventive suffix (verbs II*wy*, III*wy*)
VN	verbal noun; infinitive construct
VNabs	infinitive absolute

VOC	vocative; vocative phrase
WS	West Semitic
X	non-verbal clausal constituent (not merely negation)
XØ	verbless clause
yiqṭol(Ø)	short *yiqṭol* (preterite or jussive)
yiqṭol(u)	long *yiqṭol*

1. INTRODUCTION

1.1. Aim

The traditional system of consecutive tenses in Biblical Hebrew has three hallmarks:[1]

1. The syntactic distributional opposition between clause-initial *waw*-consecutive forms and the corresponding non-initial *waw*-less forms. *Wayyiqṭol* and *wə-qaṭal* are clause-initial, while long *yiqṭol* forms and *qaṭal* forms must be non-initial.
2. The explicit opposition in temporal, aspectual, and modal semantics between two pairs of constructions: *wayyiqṭol* / *qaṭal* and *wə-qaṭal* / long *yiqṭol*. In short terms: *wayyiqṭol* 'equals' *qaṭal* (past meaning), and *wə-qaṭal* 'equals' long *yiqṭol* (present/future meaning).
3. Certain semantic, pragmatic, or discourse-conditioned notions associated with the '*waw*-consecutive' constructions *wayyiqṭol* and *wə-qaṭal*, in contrast to their '*waw*-less' counterparts *qaṭal* and long *yiqṭol*. Usually, the difference between the pairs is described as one of (temporal or logical) sequentiality (or foregrounding) for the *waw*-consecutive clauses in contrast to the non-consecutive verb forms.

At the heart of the matter stands the role of word order, with a conspicuous alternation of clauses with initial verb (type *wa-VX*) and clauses with non-initial verb (Isaksson 2015d; 2021a, 204).

 https://doi.org/10.11647/OBP.0414.01

Grammars of Classical Biblical Hebrew (CBH) describe an alternation of 'forms' in double pairs: *wayyiqṭol* alternates with its 'equivalent' *qaṭal*, and *wə-qaṭal* alternates with its 'equivalent' long *yiqṭol*.[2] "This standard treatment is problematic and unsatisfactory" because it places "too much semantic weight on the *waw* conjunction" (Cook 2012a, 313f.). Especially problematic is the nature of the *waw* conjunction in the *wayyiqṭol* type of clauses.

It is commonly held in comparative Semitic linguistics that the short *yiqṭol* in Biblical Hebrew has an historical background in an old short prefixed conjugation *yaqtul* with perfective meaning (Isaksson 2021, 197).[3] This short *yiqṭol* is attested in freestanding form in the Archaic Hebrew poetry and with two basic meanings, indicative (past) and jussive (Notarius 2013, 307, 313). In classical prose, the indicative meanings of short *yiqṭol* are found only with word order restriction, in *wayyiqṭol* (Smith 1991, 6; Hasselbach and Huehnergard 2008, 416; Blau 2010, 150). In comparison with the relatively free usage of short *yaqtul* in Amarna Canaanite, the indicative short *yiqṭol* in Classical Hebrew has been replaced by *qaṭal* in most positions and functions; the only exception is the *wayyiqṭol* syntagm (Rainey 1986, 5; Baranowski 2016a, §4.2).[4] By contrast, the jussive short *yiqṭol* is retained in freestanding form (Isaksson 2021a, 198). It is "fairly frequent that perfective categories may have non-past reference in non-indicative moods or (which is the same thing) certain non-assertive contexts" (Bybee and Dahl 1989, 84; also Tropper 1998, 168; Palmer 2001, ch. 8; Isaksson 2021a, 198).

Table 1: Short *yiqṭol* for past and jussive meanings (Tiberian vocalisation)

	Indicative (past)	**Jussive**
Archaic Hebrew poetry[5]	*Ø-yiqṭol, wayyiqṭol*	*Ø-yiqṭol, wə-yiqṭol*
Classical prose	*wayyiqṭol*	*Ø-yiqṭol, wə-yiqṭol*

A problem with the theory of consecutive tenses is that it contains assumptions about verbal morphology ('tenses' with *waw*) that belong to the realm of macro-syntax (continuity and discontinuity in a text). There is certainly a 'truth' contained in the theory, but this 'truth' is macro-syntactic, not morphological.[6]

It is a thesis of this book that the basic suppositions of Tropper (1996; 1998), Van de Sande (2008, 206–39) and Cook (2012a, 315) accord with the linguistic reality in the CBH texts: there was only one single conjunction -ו *wa* 'and' in Biblical Hebrew (Isaksson 2021a, 205f.). It is a principle of economy—"a proposed development that accounts for the most data with the least effort is usually to be preferred" (Huehnergard 2006, 3).

To prove this thesis, Classical Hebrew linguistics must be able to account for the following issues in CBH (Isaksson 2021a, 206f.):

1. why *wa* has two formal variants (*wə-* and *way-*) in the Masoretic text;
2. the status of the short *yiqṭol* (with both past and jussive meanings) as a separate verbal morpheme distinct from long *yiqṭol*;
3. how long *yiqṭol* was distinguished from short *yiqṭol*;
4. why *qaṭal* came to alternate with the inherited *wayyiqṭol*;

5. why *wə-qaṭal* acquired imperfective meanings and came to alternate with the inherited long *yiqṭol* (< **yaqtulu*);
6. the linguistic reality behind *wa* in the 'consecutive tenses'.

The first point, about the Tiberian variants of the conjunction *wa*, will be treated already in this introductory chapter (§1.2.5). The second, about the status of short *yiqṭol* in CBH, is treated in §3. The third, on how long *yiqṭol* was distinguished from short *yiqṭol*, is discussed in §3.4 and §4. The fourth point is treated in §5, which discusses the emerging *qaṭal* morpheme in relation to the indicative short *yiqṭol* (in the *way-yiqṭol* clause-type). The fifth, about the much-discussed origin of the *wa-qaṭal* clause-type, is treated in §6. Finally, the sixth point is treated in §2 and §7.

These are the questions to be treated in the book. The answers will constitute an account of the linguistic reality behind the 'consecutive tenses'. Since it is these that are in focus, less attention will be paid to the jussive meaning of the short *yiqṭol*.

1.2. Method and Terminology

The description of CBH will be both descriptive and reconstructive. In recent linguistic research, it has become obvious that a purely synchronic description of an ancient language is not sufficiently illuminating. An understanding of the diachronic processes is necessary in order to fully grasp a verbal category in the extant texts (Givón 1979, 271; Cook 2012a). For this reason, I will use the methods of historical linguistics: internal reconstruction and comparative Semitic reconstruction.[7] They will be supplemented by other approaches: diachronic typology and grammaticalisation. On this point, the work on comparative Semitic linguistics by Kouwenberg (2010a; cf. Kogan 2012) has been an inspiration. It is truly philological, based on knowledge of the texts, and at the same time linguistically sound. Another source of inspiration has been the standard work on grammaticalisation by Bybee, Perkins, and Pagliuca (1994).[8] It is data-driven, not theory-driven, and based on empirical data from languages representative of all the major genetic groups in the world. A third inspiration has been the sharp evaluation of previous research found in Cook (2012a).

1.2.1. Diachronic Typology and Grammaticalisation in a Comparative Semitic Setting

"Historically, the study of the BHVS has suffered from idiosyncratic analyses that find no support among the recent typological classifications (e.g., the *waw hahippuk* theory of the *waw*-prefixed verbal forms)" (Cook 2012a, 185). Diachronic typology starts from the assumption that language variation and language change are subject to universal restrictions. Typology investigates "what is a more probable, as opposed to less probable, human language" (Song 2001, 3). "[D]iachronic developments tend to follow rather narrowly circumscribed paths that recur again and again with different lexical means" (Kouwenberg 2010a, 3). What I like most in diachronic typology is that it "intertwines the cross-linguistic with the diachronic… grammaticization paths are similar across languages" (Bybee et al. 1994, 23).

Diachronic analysis increases the explanatory power of linguistic descriptions (Cook 2012a, 178, 185).[9] It is a great achievement to be able to demonstrate how a grammatical category came to have a certain function. Establishing the forces behind a grammatical change reveals “the cognitive and communicative factors which underlie grammatical meaning” (Bybee et al. 1994, 3). Studying only a synchronic stage (if such a thing is possible at all) does not allow us to explain the meanings of specific grammatical morphemes.[10] “Viewing the synchronic slice as simply one stage in a long series of developments helps us explain the nature of grammar at any particular moment” (Bybee et al. 1994, 4). Finally, similarities between languages, not least those in the Semitic family, “are more easily seen from a diachronic perspective” (Bybee et al. 1994, 4).

Grammaticalisation is defined as (Hopper and Traugott 2003, 18):

> a term referring to the change whereby lexical items and constructions come in certain linguistic contexts to serve grammatical functions and, once grammaticalized, continue to develop new grammatical functions.[11]

Grams, or verbal morphemes, are a closed class of morphemes. There are usually only a handful of them, and they are determined by a restricted grammatical behaviour, unique for each morpheme. The TAM terminology is used for the semantic description of such morphemes. Some such morphemes are commonly called perfect, imperfect, or progressive, and often they consist of only one word with stem and affixes.[12]

Grammaticalisation theory observes how "grammatical morphemes develop gradually out of lexical morphemes or combinations of lexical morphemes with lexical or grammatical morphemes" (Bybee et al. 1994, 4).[13] An important type of grammaticalisation is semantic generalisation, whereby the meaning of a morpheme undergoes a process of bleaching (or generalisation), which is a parallel to the phonological reduction that the grammaticalised element undergoes (Bybee 1985, 17; Bybee and Dahl 1989, 56, 63). Such phonological reduction usually involves loss of independent stress, and loss of lexical status, which results in "reduction or loss of segmental material and the reduction in the length" (Bybee et al. 1994, 6) of the grammatical morpheme.[14] Such a reduction renders the resulting grammaticalised morpheme unsegmentable, and this reduction also means that the morpheme becomes more and "more dependent on surrounding material and begins to fuse with other grammatical or lexical morphemes in its environment" (Bybee et al. 1994, 6). As a parallel to the semantic and phonological reduction comes an increasing fixation of the syntactic position of the morpheme, and this fixing of the syntactic position causes the gram to gradually "fuse with other elements in its environment" (Bybee et al. 1994, 7).[15]

The source concepts that are grammaticalised are basic to human experience and "tend to be conceived of in a similar way across linguistic and ethnic boundaries" (Heine et al. 1991, 33), which "partially account[s] for the great similarities in grammaticization paths across genetically and areally unrelated languages" (Bybee et al. 1994, 10). An example is the use of the word for 'face' in a construction that means 'in front of' in a large number of unrelated languages. The substantive retains its concrete meaning 'face', but at the same time develops a generalised meaning 'front', which becomes the basis for a construction with the meaning 'in front of, before', which is grammaticalised to a preposition, such as CBH *lifnē* (preposition *lə-* + *pānɛ̄* 'face').

If structuralism in linguistics can be viewed as constituting "dramatic shifts from an essentialist to a relationalist conception of reality" (Korchin 2006, 14), the grammaticalisation theory represents a return to essentialism (Cook 2012a, 176f.). The typical concern of grammaticalisation studies is verbal morphemes, and such morphemes may possess meanings of their own, while at the same time influencing the functions and meanings of other morphemes. New verb forms develop and gradually take over the functions of older forms (Cook 2012a, 177).[16]

An important result of the investigation of grammaticalisations is that the source of the grammaticalisation, the original construction of lexical elements that undergoes a bleaching and semantic reduction, "uniquely determines the grammaticalisation path" (Bybee et al. 1994, 12).[17] This means, for example, that a construction that gives rise to a present tense morpheme cannot also give rise to a past tense. The paths for developing verbal morphemes tend to be similar around the world.[18] The grammatical morpheme develops in several steps, and the meanings it acquires during this process can be regarded as different stages on a specific cross-linguistic path. For example, resultative constructions generalise to anteriors with a strong shade of personal involvement of the subject. Anteriors evolve into perfectives or pasts with a diminished personal involvement and greater distance

distance from the subject in space and time (Bybee and Dahl 1989, 57). But past tenses do not develop into resultatives. Grammaticalisations are unidirectional.[19] It has turned out that "many languages have a general past, perfective, present, imperfective, or future whose functions are very similar," and the paths to them are similar cross-linguistically (Bybee et al. 1994, 12, 15; Hopper and Traugott 2003, 7, 17).

Certain original meanings of the source construction may be retained for a long time in the grammaticalisation process ('expansion'; Croft 2003, 262).[20] Remnants of earlier meanings "are detectable in certain contexts" (Bybee et al. 1994, 16). The grammatical meaning(s) of a morpheme can thus be considered "links on a chain, one having given rise to another" (Bybee et al. 1994, 17). Multiple meanings of a grammatical morpheme constitute the diachronically ordered links of a chain, the first link of which is the most ancient and the last link the youngest. For example, perfective grammatical morphemes may be used to indicate past events that have relevance to the current situation (anterior meaning). Such categories may have evolved from resultatives, which means that, in one specific context, a perfective morpheme exhibits perfective/past meaning; in another context, a past with personal involvement and relevance in the present situation; and in yet another context, a resultative. If a past-tense conjugation shows in some contexts a resultative meaning, then we can with confidence conclude that its grammaticalisation has been built on a stative verb as the source construction (Bybee et al. 1994, 18).

Cross-linguistic data show that a language may have more than one grammatical morpheme representing the same type of verbal category. Earlier forms (grammatical morphemes) usually coexist with later ones (Hopper and Traugott 2003, 16). In English, there are three regular futures, all used in their particular contexts: *will*, *shall*, and *be going to*. This is a typical situation. The rise of a future marker does not necessitate the loss of its predecessors, and this is a common phenomenon, not least for expressions of future and modality (Bybee et al. 1994, 21). In addition, earlier meanings may interact with and constrain later meanings (Hopper and Traugott 2003, 16). In Classical Hebrew, we encounter two new intruding verbal forms: an anterior/perfective gram (*qaṭal*), which competes with the older *wayyiqṭol*, and a present/progressive gram (*qoṭel*), which competes with the older imperfective long *yiqṭol*. It is fruitful in this instance to use the term 'renewal': the renewal of the durative meaning of the imperfective category, and the renewal of the (personal) involvement in the past perfective category (Rundgren 1963). "Where a long historical record is available, the process of renewal can be seen to occur repeatedly" (Hopper and Traugott 2003, 9). A classic formulation of the renewal of the anterior/perfective is found in Kuryłowicz (1964, 22):[21]

> As regards the so-called *perfect* the normal evolution seems to be: *derived form* (or verbal noun + auxiliary) > *perfect* > *indetermined past* ('passé indéfini') > *narrative* tense. The derivative is adopted as a regular member of the conjugation in order to replace the old form of the perfect, which, having been additionally charged with the narrative function, has lost its expressiveness.

The renewal of the durative aspect, which can also be called cursive, is formulated in this way (Kuryłowicz 1964, 20):

> The most important phenomenon which has repeated itself over and over again and has left numerous traces in the old I.E. languages, is the renewal of the *durative* character of the verbal forms denoting the moment of speaking (present-imperfect system). The durative form may easily invade other semantic spheres: general ('timeless') present, futurity, modality ('capability', 'eventuality'), etc. This expansion, involving the loss of expressiveness (i.e., of concentration on durativity), is the cause of drawing upon derived forms designed to renew the durative function. A formal split is likely to ensue: durative present (new form) and general or indetermined present (old form), present (new form) and future (old form), indicative (new form) and subjunctive (old form).

A renewal may lead to a situation when the centre (prototypical meaning) of the older gram is "invaded by the younger one, but keeps the periphery for the time being" (Dahl 2000, 10). Typical cases are progressives/imperfectives that lose their protypical progressive and imperfective meanings when a new progressive formation is introduced. Such a process may lead to "grams whose domain has been reduced by the invasion of another gram" (residual grams; Dahl 2000, 10; also Bybee and Dahl 1989, 84).[22]

Grammaticalisation always involves a moment of *reanalysis* (Hopper and Traugott 2003, 59). In reanalysis, a receiver of an utterance understands a grammatical form as having a structure and meaning that are different from those understood by the sender. The well-known example is *hamburger* 'item (of food) from Hamburg', which is heard as [*ham*] + [*burger*], a burger made of ham. "Sooner or later someone substitutes the word *cheese* or *beef* for *ham*" (Hopper and Traugott 2003, 50). When this happens, the reanalysis (*ham* + *burger*) has already occurred. Thus reanalysis could be defined as a silent rebracketing of an expression, and such a rebracketing may occur also with syntactic sequences, as the English example *be going to* > *be gonna*, and *let us* > *let's* > *lets* shows (Hopper and Traugott 2003, 50f.).[23] Another example is the Latin *dicere habeo* 'I have to say', which in certain contexts is interpreted as obligative or future orientated, until finally the user interprets the syntagm not as two underlying clauses, but as one structure (expressing the future in Late Latin) in which *dicere* is no longer subordinate to *habeo*. The reanalysis process is gradual, and the changes may occur "in different verbs at different times" (Hopper and Traugott 2003, 54f., 57).

In reanalysis, steps are taken from more concrete and specific meanings to more grammatical, more abstract, meanings (semantic bleaching), and at the same time there is an expansion of the domain of applicability of the expression (Dahl 2000, 9; Croft 2003, 261).[24]

An important type of reanalysis concerns the typologically frequent use of past tense verbal forms to express irrealis: distance in time is expressed by a past tense form, a meaning that is utilised as a vehicle for conceptualising other kinds of distance, like distance in epistemic modality. Such is the case in the reanalysed English pluperfect for the expression of modality (Heine et al. 1991, 75f.):

(1) I had helped him.

(2) I had hoped we might get together tonight.

In (1), we can interpret the pluperfect as having a normal tense–aspect meaning. In (2), however, "The speaker, via the pluperfect, distances himself... from the potential loss of face that a rebuff would entail" (Suzanne Fleischman, quoted from Heine et al. 1991, 75). The (pluperfect) verbal morpheme's property of marking temporal distance is employed as a vehicle to express modality, in this case an interpersonal distance (metaphorical extension; Croft 2003, 269).

When, in this and similar ways, a new grammatical meaning arises, the source expression usually retains its original form, at least for some time (Heine et al. 1991, 213):

> The result is a stage of asymmetry where one and the same linguistic form simultaneously offers two different meanings, a lexical or less grammatical meaning on the one hand and a (more) grammatical one on the other. Synchronically, this results in polysemy or in homonymy.

1.2.2. The TAM Categories

The primary verbal entities to be discussed in this book are (verbal) grammatical morphemes (or verbal forms, or grams), not tenses and not aspects.[25] Notions such as tense, aspect, and mood belong to the semantics of grams in a specific language, and "[m]any, if not most, grams combine elements from several domains in their semantics" (Dahl 2000, 7; also Bybee and Dahl 1989, 97). A verbal grammatical morpheme (gram) has a language-specific behaviour. It "belongs to the grammar of an individual language, rather than to the general theory of human languages" (Dahl 2000, 7). It is one of the findings of recent typological research that a large majority of the languages in the world have verbal grammatical morphemes that belong to one of six *types*, roughly characterised in the following way (cross-linguistic gram types; Dahl 1985, 33; Bybee and Dahl 1989, 55; Dahl 2000, 7; Cook 2012a, 181):[26]

a. **perfective**, indicating that the situation is viewed as bounded;[27]
b. **imperfective**, indicating that the situation is viewed as not bounded;
c. **progressive** (called **continuous** in Bybee's study), indicating that the situation is in progress at reference time;[28]
d. **future**, indicating that the speaker predicts that the situation will occur subsequent to the speech event;
e. **past**, indicating that the situation occurred before the speech event;
f. **perfect** (called **anterior** in Bybee's study), indicating that the situation is being described as relevant at the moment of speech or another point of reference.

The distinction between *perfective* and *imperfective* "is the most common inflectional aspectual distinction" in the world (Bybee 1985, 141).[29] Next in frequency comes the *progressive / habitual*. It often happens that an imperfective morpheme covers both habitual and continuous meanings (Bybee 1985, 143).

Aspect and tense have a higher relevance to the verb than mood. This is shown by the fact that aspect and tense markers tend to be closer to the stem than mood markers. Highly relevant morphemes "will be tightly fused, while less relevant morphemes will have a looser association with the verb stem" (Bybee 1985, 35f.).[30]

Bybee defines the concepts of *aspect, tense*, and *mood* in the following way. "*Aspect* refers to the way the internal temporal constituency of the situation is viewed" (Bybee 1985, 28). When *aspect* is an inflectional category (and not expressed lexically) it is used to (Bybee 1985, 21; see also 152):

> indicate how the action or state described by the verb should be viewed in the context of the whole discourse. Background information is expressed by imperfective verb forms, and the foregrounded information of the main narrative line appears in perfective verb form.

Regarding *tense* (Bybee 1985, 21; see also 28):

> *Tense* is a deictic category that places a situation in time with respect to the moment of speech, or occasionally with respect to some other pre-established point in time.

Regarding *mood* (Bybee 1985, 22; see also 28, 165):

> *Mood* distinctions express what the speaker wants to do with the proposition in the particular discourse. This will include expression of assertion (indicative), non-assertion (subjunctive), command (imperative), and warning (admonitive). It also includes other expressions of the speaker's attitude about the truth of the proposition.[31]

The so-called paragogic *heh* (cohortative suffix) in Biblical Hebrew, attached to the imperative and the short prefix conjugation, and the linking *-n-* between the verb and a following pronominal suffix (energic suffix), are analysed in this book as allomorphs of the ventive morpheme, expressing various shades of a reflexive-benefactive meaning (see Sjörs 2023, ch. 6). In this instance, it must be pointed out that, for verbs III*wy*, a formally long prefix verb form with the usual ending *-ɛ̄* must sometimes be analysed as a ventive-cohortative suffix and the verb as a short *yiqṭol* (Sjörs 2023, 105). This is illustrated in (3):

(3) *Ø-IMP + wa-IMP +* [2]*wa-yiqṭol(Ø)-A + wa-yiqṭol(Ø)-V*

הִתְהַלֵּךְ לְפָנַי וֶהְיֵה תָמִים: וְאֶתְּנָה בְרִיתִי בֵּינִי וּבֵינֶךָ וְאַרְבֶּה אוֹתְךָ בִּמְאֹד מְאֹד:

'Walk before me and be perfect, [2]and I will make my covenant between myself and you, and I will give you a multitude of descendants.' (Gen. 17.1–2)

In (3), the second of two first-person volitive forms (אַרְבֶּה) lacks a cohortative-ventive paragogic *heh*; instead, the ventive morpheme has resulted in the long final vowel *-ɛ̄*, so that the verb is formally identical to a long *yiqṭol(u)*. But the form must be parsed as short *yiqṭol(Ø)* with ventive suffix ("le *mode cohortatif*;" Joüon 1923, 307 n. 1; Kummerow 2008, 69; cf. Sjörs 2023, 105; see further §3.4.2.3).[32]

1.2.3. The Data: My Corpus and Database

There are diachronic strata also in Classical Biblical Hebrew, even within the Pentateuch (Joosten 2016). A reader acquainted with the Hebrew texts from Genesis to Numbers who turns to Deuteronomy will perceive that there are a number of features that work in a different way, or are conspicuously more frequent in this book than in the first four books of the Pentateuch. Deuteronomy is written in a slightly different language.[33] The sentences are longer and more complicated (Polak 2017, 350), as in Deut. 1.30–31.[34] It is a language created by scribes with writing as their profession, for clarity but also complexity, with a richer use of complicated relative clauses,[35] complement clauses, and appositions; extended use of infinitives for subordinate clauses[36] and main clauses;[37] and a tendency towards new idioms (Polak

2021, 324, 332f.).[38] Complement clauses are introduced by אֲשֶׁר, not כִּי (Deut. 1.31). The normal negation for participle clauses becomes אֵין instead of לֹא,[39] and more complicated conjunctions creep in.[40] The participle, which represented a renewal of the imperfective aspect in Genesis–Numbers and thus was an invasive form for the expression of progressive aspect and present tense, is pushed a step further in Deuteronomy, with extended replacement of the long *yiqṭol* morpheme,[41] exhibition of explicit future time reference,[42] and performative function,[43] but also with past time reference in an attributive/relative position.[44] We also have in Deuteronomy occasional instances of a violation of the word order rule for the long *yiqṭol* conjugation. This word order was the first syntactic defence against the potential merger of the two prefix conjugations after the dropping of short final vowels in Proto-Hebrew (see §3.2; also Hasselbach and Huehnergard 2008, 412; Isaksson 2015d).[45] The reader also encounters the first departure from the rule of the 'normal' *qaṭal* that it may not be placed directly after the conjunction *wa*.[46] In addition, there are early indications of a new analytic tense: היה + active participle (Deut. 9.7, 22, 24; 30.4).[47] Inherited and partly oral traditions such as the patriarchal stories have received a "subsequent textualization as the Deuteronomistic History" (Gzella 2018, 29).

In spite of the linguistic differences mentioned above, I regard the Pentateuch as a relatively solid representation of CBH.[48]

The present book is based on:

A *corpus* of CBH texts: the Pentateuch and the Book of Judges, with the exclusion of the archaic poems;

A *database* of classified syntactic samples, mostly clause linkings, from the corpus (6559 non-archaic records; the 628 records from the archaic poetry are treated separately).

The corpus is intentionally restricted to secure a reasonably consistent synchronic state of CBH.[49] The poetry in the Psalter, for example, is notoriously difficult to evaluate diachronically and cannot be used as evidence of CBH.[50] I have used no poetry in this study, except, for diachronic comparison, the poems commonly accepted as archaic (with the exception of late additions, such as Gen. 49.17: Notarius 2013, 205, §§13.1.10, 13.3.2).

The database has been developed in Microsoft Access. The principal goal of the database is to register clauses and their relations (linkings) to other (mostly preceding) clauses. A typical record in the database registers a clause and its relation to a preceding clause. The fields registered in each record are displayed in Table 2.

Table 2: The fields in the database

field	explanation	sample values
Source	place in text	Gn 01:01
Data	original text (for CBH: BHS)	—
Data transl	my translation of Data	—
Connective	conjunction, if any	*wa*; *way*; *Ø*; *kī*; REL[51]
1st Constit	first constituent in clause except *wa*-	ADV; *lō*; *ʾal*; *pɛn*; *ʾim*; S.noun; O.noun; S.pron; O.pron; PrP
Other constituent	other pre-verbal constituent after the first	same as 1st Constit
Clause-type	type of predicate in clause	*qaṭal*; *yiqṭol(Ø)*; *yiqṭol(u)*; *qoṭel*; *XØ*; IMP[52]

Clitic	verbal clitic, if any	nun parag. (Npar); vent./coh. -*ā*; vent./energ. -*nn*-; -*nāʾ*
TAM	aspect, temporal reference	resultative; anterior; perfective; progressive; future; habitual-past; habitual present; performative[53]
Switch	type of 'switch' in the linking	*qaṭal/yiqṭol(u)*; *qaṭal/ yiqṭol(Ø)*; *yiqṭol(u)/XØ*[54]
Person	the person–gender–number of the verb	3ms; 3fs; 2ms; 2fs;...
Sem Rel	the semantics of the linking in which the clause is involved	Consequence: purpose; Logical: comparative; Elaboration; Attendant circumstance; conditional[55]
Discourse type		Narrative; Report; Direct speech; Poetry; Legal discourse; Instruction
Special	Notable syntactic feature in the clause or in linking	Serial verb; Apposition; Left-dislocation; Ellipsis; Rightdis-location; Chiasm; Sub-structure (e.g. within protasis)
Other clause	type of predicate in other clause involved in the linking	same value list as Clause-type
Connective in Other clause		same value list as Connective
1st Constit in Other clause		same value list as 1st Constit
TAM in Other clause		same value list as TAM
Comment	my free-text philological notations, including the structure of the linking	Exod. 1.7: *wa-S.noun-qaṭal* + *wa(y)-yiqṭol* + *wa(y)-yiqṭol* + *wa(y)-yiqṭol*

Each field has a limited list of values. The database is searchable by multiple fields. A sample search could be: Sem Rel = 'Attendant circumstance'; AND Clause-type = '*yiqṭol(u)*', AND Discourse type = NOT 'Poetry-archaic', which yields all cases of circumstantial clauses coded by a *yiqṭol(u)* predicate that are not part of an Archaic Hebrew poem. With this search capacity, it is possible to filter out all types of linkings, and examine the resulting records one-by-one, while making further notations in the Comment field.

The statistics in the book are based on this Access database. When feasible, they are transferred into Excel for further processing of the data. In relevant cases, such data are copied into tables in the book. This is done when the search has resulted in a significant number of records. When a less significant number of instances of a certain verbal morpheme (gram) or linking is found in the database, the extant samples (records) are accounted for in the text and footnotes.

When absolute numbers of attestations are supplied, they refer to the number of registered forms or constructions in the database. They of course represent a selection of all forms and constructions and linkings that exist in the Masoretic text. The numbers given in the tables are not exhaustive, but they are representative. Relevant meanings and constructions and linkings are registered.

1.2.4. The Concept of Domain and the Chaining Nature of Early Semitic

"[C]haining was one of the most important syntactic features of Early Semitic" (Baranowski 2016a, 190). A domain is a specifically Semitic device for organising chains into recognisable semantic units with roughly the same function as paragraphs. As Eran Cohen (2014) has shown, the domain is a macrosyntactic entity or unit inherited from the most archaic phase of Semitic. It is a sequence of verbal clauses signalled by macro-syntactic markers.

The domain is well documented in Old Babylonian Akkadian (OB). In OB, the connective particle *-ma* plays a central role in signalling the clauses that constitute a domain. It is significant that this connective particle is asymmetrical: the sequence of clauses connected by *-ma* is non-reversible. It is also significant that *-ma* functions as a marker of the beginning of the following clause in a domain. Thus, the syntagm between two instances of *-ma* is always a clause. The final clause in the domain, however, is not followed by *-ma*. A specific domain "is bound together by a special connective, verbal forms of a particular kind, internal order, syntactic peculiarities and overall functional unity, with well-defined boundaries" (Cohen 2014, 251). There are domains in every type of text, and, according to Cohen, there are three major domain types: indicative, subordinative, and directive.[56] In a domain, verbal grammatical morphemes constitute "the major signal of grammatical and discourse structure, as well as temporal and aspectual relations" (Bybee and Dahl 1989, 51).

In the **indicative domain**, which in Cohen's corpus is always a narrative unit, the chain consists of preterite *iprus* forms, and the domain tends to end with an *iptaras*, a form that in main clauses normally fulfils the function of a perfect. The most common function of the *iptaras* form is to appear at the end of an indicative domain, which can be quite long. The *iptaras* clause marks its final boundary, as in (Cohen 2014, 239 example 5; cf. Cohen 2006, 55):

(4) Old Babylonian

ana PN ṭupp-am ***uš-ābil–ma***

to PN tablet-ACC (1)CS-CAUS-carry-PST = CONN

meḫer *ṭupp-i*

answer.NUC tablet-GEN

uš-ābil-am–ma [*u*]***š-t-ābil-akkum*** #

(3)CS-CAUS-carry-PST-DAT.1CS = CONN (1)CS-CAUS-PRF-carry-DAT.2MS

'**I sent** PN a tablet, **he sent me** a response and **I sent** (it) to you' (AbB 3, 55:30–32)

The sequence of clauses in this (reportive) narrative domain is *iprus-ma* + *iprus-ma* + *iptaras#*. The *iptaras* form in OB has two distinct functions: in domain-final position it marks the end of the domain, and in the single clause domain it has the present perfect function.

The **subordinative domain** consists of clauses forming an attribute, or annexation, to a previous nucleus. This nucleus can be a noun, a pronoun, or a preposition/conjunction. The forms in the subordinative domain are marked by the morpheme *-u* in Akkadian. Since the nucleus may be a conjunction, the subordinative domain does not only comprise what are commonly called relative clauses, but also all other explicitly (by conjunction) marked subordinate clauses.

The **directive domain** is coded by directives (expressions of will), that is, in Cohen's terminology, jussives (*liprus* in the third person), imperatives, cohortatives (*liprus* in the first person), and prohibitives.

Subordinative clauses are embedded in another domain, but do not form part of this superordinate domain and do not conform to its syntactic rules. An example is found in Cohen (2014, 241 example 7):

(5) Old Babylonian

ina *ṣāb* PN_1 *u* PN_2 100 *ṣāb-um*
from army-NUC PN_1 CONN PN_2 100 troop-NOM

ittī-šu ***l-i-llik–ma***
with-GEN.3MS JUSS-3CS-go = CONN

5 *ūm-ī* {*adi* PN_1 u PN_2
5 day-OBL.PL until PN_1 CONN PN_2

ištu GN *illak-ū-nim#*}
from GN 3MP-come-NPST

in *āl-ān-ī* ***l-i-p-tar-rik-ū–ma***
in city-PL-OBL JUSS-3MP-ITER-trouble = CONN

ḫarrān-āt-im {*ša* *ī-ten-errub-ā-nim#*} [*i*]*šteat*
caravan-PL-OBL PRON.NUC 3FP-ITER-come_in one

ū *šittā* ***l-i-dūk-ū–ma*** ***l-ī-dur-ā*** *#*
or two JUSS-3MP-strike = CONN JUSS-3FP-fear

'Let one hundred troops from the troops of PN_1 and PN_2 go with him, and let them cause continuous difficulties in the cities for five days {until PN_1 and PN_2 come from GN}, and let them strike at one or two caravans {that come in regularly} so that they be afraid' (AbB 11, 193:13–23)

The sequence of clauses in this directive domain is *liprus-ma* + *ADV* {until *S.noun PrP iparras#}* + *liprus-ma* + *O.noun {REL iparras#} liprus-ma* + *liprus#*. The example shows a directive domain in which two subordinative clauses are embedded, one temporal clause ('until PN_1 and PN_2 come from GN') and one relative ('that come in regularly'). In a directive domain, the last clause often expresses a purpose or result (in the example above, *liprus l-ī-durā #* 'so that they be afraid'). In the example, the two subordinative domains digress from the syntax of the main directive domain. Both the temporal clause and the relative clause are coded by *iparras* forms (imperfective, realised respectively as future and past iterative). Cohen's example illustrates that the directive domain may express the will of the speaker, and purpose. Clauses in the directive domain may also express an indirect command that reports the content of a command, and concessive conditionality:

(6) Old Babylonian

qibī-šum–ma ***l-i-llik–ma*** *aḫ-ā-šu*

tell-IMP-2MS-DAT.3MS = CONN JUSS-3CS-go = CONN brother-ACC-GEN.3MS

l-i-tr-am–ma ***{l [ām] a*** *attalk-u}*

JUSS-3CS-lead_forth = CONN before 1CS-leave-PRF-SUBORD

nikkass-ī-šunu ***l-ī-puš-ū***

account-OBL.PL-GEN.3MP JUSS-3MP-do

'Tell him that (lit. and) he should go and (OR: in order to) bring over his brother so they can do their accounting {b[efo]re I (will) have left}' (AbB 12, 44:16–21)

In the sequence *IMP-ma* + *liprus-ma* + *liprus-ma* + {before *iptaras*} + *liprus#*, the content of the command is coded by the switch from imperative (*qibī-šum–ma*) to jussive (*l-i-llik–ma*): "Tell him *to bring over* his brother." The last jussive is a purpose clause (*l-ī-puš-ū*). Neither the content clause nor the purpose clause is explicitly marked as subordinate. They form part of the directive domain marked by the connective particle *-ma*, and their semantic functions are signalled by the switch from imperative to jussive (the latter expressing the content of the command) and by position (last jussive in the domain is usually a purpose clause). "[T]he directive domain has its own unique complement syntax, as opposed to other domains" (Cohen 2014, 242). Thus, in a command to do something, the directive domain uses a switch to a jussive clause. In a command *not to do* something, the directive domain exhibits an asymmetric pattern, as is often the case also in other domains (Sjörs 2015, 34): when a negative content clause is intended, the jussive is replaced by a negated *iparras*, as in (7), where the imperative is followed by *lā iparras* (still connected by *-ma*). The sequence pattern is in this case *IMP-ma* + *lā iparras*:

(7) Old Babylonian

qi[b]ī–ma	***ma[mman***	*lā*	***udabbab-šu***
tell-IMP-2MS = CONN	PRON.INDEF	NEG	(3)CS-harass-NPST-ACC.3MS

'O[r]der that (lit. and) **n[o one] should harass him**' (AbB 12, 13:17–18; Cohen 2014, 242 ex. 9)

In the directive domain, infinitives and object clauses are rare, whereas in the indicative domain, a corresponding content complement is constructed with an infinitive. The main verb in the indicative domain may be a perfect *iptaras*, as in (8):

(8) Old Babylonian

mamman	*lā*	*dubbub-šu*	[*i*]*qtabī-šunūšim*
PRON.INDEF	NEG	harass-INF-GEN.3MS	3CS-tell-PRF-DAT.3MP

'[He] ordered them that no one should (lit. anyone not to) harass him' (AbB 12, 13:12–13; Cohen 2014, 242 ex. 10)

In sum, in the directive domain, a wish or command is found at the beginning, while purpose and indirect command are found after the first clause in the domain (Cohen 2014, 247).

In **conditional structures**, the protasis and the apodosis each constitute separate domains, which may in principle contain several clauses (Cohen 2012, 85). A frequent simple conditional linking is a protasis with *iparras* and an apodosis with jussive, as in (9).[57] In a protasis domain, the *iparras* form, which is otherwise indicative, has a modal, eventual, meaning. The sequential pattern in the example is (*iparras-ma*) + *precative*:

(9) (*ūmam eleppētum* [*ša*] *ana* GN [*aṭru*]*du* ***is*****[*a*]*****nniqā-ma***) [*u*]*rra*[*m*] *ina* GN ***šuṣēnšīnāti***

'Should the boats that [I se]nt to GN arrive today, load them [to]morrow in GN' (Cohen 2012, 83 ex. 145)

An example of a multiclausal protasis with *iparras* forms is (10):

(10) Old Babylonian

(u	*midde*	*annikīam*	***iba’’-ū-ka=ma***	
CONN	perhaps	here	3MP-pass-NPST-ACC.2MS=CONN	
alp-ī	*ana*	*āl-im*	*ayy-im=ma*	***inassaḫ-ū=ma***
ox-OBL.PL	to	city-GEN	some-GEN-PTCL	3MP-move-NPST=CONN
būrt-um	***iḫalliq*** *#)*		***alkam-ma***	
cow-NOM	3CS-get_lost-NPST		come-IMP-2MS=CONN	
būrt-am	***purus-ma***		***taru***	
cow-ACC	separate-IMP-2MS=CONN		lead_away-IMP-2MS	

‘But if they pass you by here and move the oxen to some town and (as a result) the cow may perish, come here, separate the cow and lead (it) away’ (AbB 9, 83:18–24; Cohen 2012, 112)

In this example, the apodosis also is multiclausal, and the pattern is (*iparras-ma* + *iparras-ma* + *iparras-#*) + *IMP-ma* + *IMP-ma* + *IMP-#*.

Circumstantials also in principle constitute separate complex domains, though they usually consist of only one clause. As with conditionals, they too are “incorporated by the chaining clause-combining strategy” (Cohen 2014, 244). An example of a circumstantial domain coded by an indicative non-verbal clause in OB is (11):

(11) Old Babylonian

u	*aššum*	PN	*ša*	*bīs-su*	*maḫrī-ka*
CONN	TOP.MARK.NUC	PN	PRON.NUC	house-GEN.3MS	front-GEN.2MS

u	***šū***	***aḫī–ma***	(indicative)
CONN	NOM.3MS	brother-GEN.1CS = CONN	⇓

arḫiš	*aššas-su…*	*[p]uṭram–ma*	(directive)
quickly	wife-GEN.3MS	release.IMP = CONN	

'And, as for PN whose house is in front of you, **he is my brother**, so release his wife…' (AbB 2, 170:10–15; Cohen 2014, 244)

In (11), the sequential pattern is (*u NVC-ma*) + *IMP-ma* (the *IMP* is followed by *-ma* because the main clauses continue). There is no conjunction that marks the NVC as circumstantial, and it clearly deviates from the clause chaining rules of the directive domain represented by *IMP-ma*. The circumstantial function of the clause is signalled by its own deviating domain, which does not conform to the syntactic rules of the superordinate directive domain.

The concept of domain and the chaining nature of verbal syntax are attested also in the Amarna letters from Canaan (Baranowski 2016a, 190). The indicative sequences of narration are reportive in this corpus and exhibit both perfective *yaqtul* and perfective *qatal* forms. It seems that *yaqtul* and verbal *qatal* could be used interchangeably in the Canaanite of the scribes. An example of a report sequence that comes close to a narrative chain is given by Baranowski (2016a, 203 ex. 5.4.1):

(12) ⸢*ù*⸣ ⸢*an*⸣-⸢*nu*⸣-*ú* ***i-še$_{20}$-me*** *a-na* ^{16}⸢*a*⸣-*wa-te*^{MEŠ}-*ka ù* ***ú-wa-ši*[*r$_4$*]‹-*šu*›** ^{17}*ù* ***uṣ-ṣa-am*** *ri-qú-tám* ^{18}***ù i-še$_{20}$-me-e*** *ú ia-nu-um* ⸢ÉRIN⸣.MEŠ ^{19}*it-ti-šu ù* ***te-né-pu-⸢uš⸣*** ^{20}URU *Baṭ-ru-na a-na ša-šu* ^{21}*ù* ÉRIN.MEŠ SA.GAZ.MEŠ *ù* GIŠ.GIGIR.MEŠ ^{22}*ša-ki-in$_4$ i-na* ⸢*lìb*⸣-*bi* ^{23}*ù* ***la*!(AD) *i-nam-mu-šu-ni$_7$*** ^{24}[*i*]*š-tu pí* KÁ.GAL URU *Gub*‹-*la*›^{KI}

‘And behold, **I heeded** your words **and I sen[t] ‹him› but he came forth** empty handed. **And he** (ʿAbdi-Ashirta) **heard** that there were no troops with him **then** the town of Baṭrôna **went over** to him and he stationed *ʿapîru* troops and chariots within (it). **And they do not depart** from the entrance to the city gate of the city of Byb‹los›.’ (EA 87:15–24, my emphasis)

This example illustrates the chaining nature of the syntax in early Canaanite. The verb forms are connected by *u* and have the same perfective aspect and temporal reference. The pattern is *u PARTICLE yaqtul* + *u yaqtul* + *u yaqtul* + *u yaqtul* + *u yaqtul* + *u lā yaqtul*. The reportive passages in the letters are not true narrative passages (where the storyteller fades away), but many passages come close to a narrative and in any case attest to the narrative style of the Canaanite scribes (Baranowski 2016a, 203, 206f.). In comparison with the OB indicative domain, there is no connective postpositional particle *-ma*. Instead, the conjunction *u* (practically always written *ù*) joins the clauses. There is a tendency to follow this conjunction with a clause-initial indicative *yaqtul* (as in ***ù i-ši-me-e*** ‘and he heard’), but, as the example shows, a deictic particle or an adverb or the negation *lā* or a subject may be inserted before the verb form (***ù*** *a*[*n-n*]*u-ú* ***i-ši-me*** ‘and [s]o I listened'). Moreover, there is no counterpart to the OB perfect *iptaras,* which was inserted as the last clause in a narrative domain and thus marked its end point. In the Amarna letters, the end of the sequence is inferred from the context.

Subordination may be coded by a digression from the pattern in the main domain. A complement clause can be expressed by means of a non-verbal clause (NVC)[58] introduced by the usual conjunction *u* and constitutes its own (subordinate) domain, as in (Baranowski 2016a, 203):

(13) *u yaqtul* + *u NVC*

ù i-še$_{20}$*-me-e* ***ú ia-nu-um*** ⸢ÉRIN⸣.MEŠ [19]*it-ti-šu*

'And he (ʿAbdi-Ashirta) heard **that there were** no troops with him' (EA 87:18–19, Baranowski's emphasis)

The verbal *qatal* in the Amarna letters is the oldest secure attestation of a past anterior and perfective suffix conjugation in Semitic (Baranowski 2016a, 208). It is apparent that this newly emerged perfective intrudes into the indicative functional domain of the old *yaqtul.* The verbal *qatal* often enters into positions where a *yaqtul* is used in similar passages. There is no geographical pattern that can explain the distribution of indicative *yaqtul* and verbal *qatal,* and in some instances *yaqtul* is even glossed by *qatal* (Baranowski 2016a, 188). When the verbal *qatal* is used in main indicative clauses, it often bears anterior meaning (Baranowski 2016a, 124 ex. 4.1.6):

(14) *ia-ši ù* [I]*Pa-ḫu-ra* [32]***a-pa-aš*** *ip-ša ra-ba* [33] *a-na ia-ši* ***uš-ši-ir*** [34]LÚ.MEŠ KUR *Su-te ù* [35]***da-ku*** LÚ *Še-er-da-\ ni* [36]*ù* 3 LÚ.MEŠ [37]***šu-ri-ib*** *a-na* KUR *Mi-iṣ-ri*

'And Paḫuru **perpetrated** a great misdeed against me. **He sent** Sutean men and **they killed** a Sherdanu and (they) **took** three men into the land of Egypt.' (EA 122:31–37, Baranowski's emphasis)[59]

The linking pattern is *u S.noun-qatal* + *Ø-qatal* + *u qatal* + *u O.noun-qatal*, and the asyndesis in this case signals a new domain (with three clauses) with the function of elaborating on the first clause: the last three *qatal* clauses specify the misdeed committed by Paḫura. It is apparent that the position of the *qatal* form does not affect its meaning: the *u qatal* has the same past perfective meaning as the clause initial *Ø-qatal* and the non-initial *u O.noun-qatal*. Within the elaboration, the conjunction *u* in this case expresses temporal succession: one action occurs after the other, as in a narrative chain. A meaning of temporal succession can also be observed in a passage with two *qatal* clauses (Baranowski 2016a, 125 ex. 4.1.12):

(15) ***ša-ma*** *a-*⸢*na*⸣ [*ia-ši*] [36]*ù* ***na-ṣa-ar*** URU.[MEŠ] [37]LUGAL EN-*šu*

'**He listened** to [me] and **protected** the cit[ies] of the king, his lord.' (EA 132:35–37, Baranowski's emphasis)

The pattern in (15) is *qatal* + *u qatal*, and the temporal succession expressed by the *u qatal* clause receives in this semantic context a nuance of result.

The modal (directive) domain in the Amarna letters exhibits some striking similarities to that found in Old Babylonian. A frequent sequential pattern is *IMP* + *u yaqtul*, as in (16):

(16) ***uš-ši-ra*** ÉRIN.MEŠ *pí-ṭá-ti* [39]*ra-ba ù* ***tu-da-bi-ir*** [40]*a-ia-bi* LUGAL *iš-tu* [41]*lìb-bi* KUR-*šu ù* [42]***ti-né-ep-šu*** *ka-li* [43]KUR.KUR.MEŠ *a-na šàr-ri*

‘**Send** a large regular army and **you can drive out** the enemies of the king from within his land and all the lands **will be joined** to the king.’ (EA 76:38–43, Baranowski’s emphasis)[60]

As in OB, the last, usually syndetic, *yaqtul* expresses a purpose, which in the example is coded by two clauses: *u yaqtul u yaqtul*. When the verb is lexically stative, a *u qatal* in a similar sequence may express a result or purpose (Baranowski 2016a, 162; also Rainey 1996, II:126):

(17) *du-ku-mi* [26]⌜*eṭ*⌝*-la-ku-nu ù i-ba-ša-tu-nu ki-ma ia-ti-nu* [27]⌜*ù*⌝ *pa-aš-ḫa-tu-nu ù ti-né-ep-šu ki-ma* [28][*a-*]⌜*wa*⌝*-te*^{MEŠ}*-šu ù i-ba-aš-šu ki-ma* [29]⌜ÉRIN⌝.MEŠ GAZ

‘“Kill your ‘lad’ and become like us, and you will be at rest.” And they have been won over in accordance with his [wo]rds and they are like the *ʿapîru* troops.’ (EA 74:25–29)

The modal sequence is a quotation, and has the pattern *Ø-IMP* + *u qatal* + *u qatal*. The *u qatal* in this sequence expresses ‘in that case you will be like us and you will be at peace’. The action of the *u qatal* clauses depends on the action in the imperative, and can be described as a result, though it is often hard to distinguish a result from a purpose. As Baranowski (2016a, 162) points out, the clauses that follow the quotation are indicative, and do not belong to the modal domain. The last verb, *ù i-ba-aš-šu* ‘and they are (like ʿApiru)’ is an indicative *u qatal* of the same stative verb in the modal sequence.

When a *yaqtula* is used in modal sequence, it usually follows directly after the initial directive form (IMP or jussive) and is part of the same wish or command, while a *yaqtul* usually follows and expresses a result or purpose (Baranowski 2016a, 164, 167):

(18) [...] ***ši-mé*** *i⌜a⌝-⌜ši⌝* [10]***qí-ba-mi*** *a-na šàr-ri* [11]*ù* ***yi-di-na*** *a-na ⌜ka⌝-ta*$_5$ [12]3 *me* LÚ.MEŠ *ù* ***ni-*****[*d*]*****a-gal*** [13]⌜URU⌝ ⌜*ù*⌝ ***ni-pu-uš***

‘**Listen** to me, **speak** to the king **that he give** you three hundred men **so that we can look after** the city and **we may restore** (it).’ (EA 93:9–13, emphasis by Baranowski)[61]

The modal sequence in (18) has the pattern *Ø-IMP. Ø-IMP* + *u yaqtula* + *u yaqtul* + *u yaqtul*. The first imperative stands alone as its own domain, but the next domain contains four clauses, of which the *u yaqtula* is part of the command and codes the content of the command: *IMP* + *u yaqtula* with the meaning ‘Tell the king to give’. The two *u yaqtul* express the purpose of the command, ‘so that we can look after the city and we may restore it’.

The concept of discourse type (discourse mode) does not coincide exactly with that of domain, but is complementary. They are closely related, though, and perhaps we can say that discourse type is a literary term that depends on language use situations (Notarius 2008, 58), while a domain is syntactically delimited. Many discourse types are coded by the same syntactical devices (instruction/procedure). Though few scholars deny the significance of some basic discourse types for Biblical Hebrew, such as narrative and instruction, the classification of *all* discourse modes according to text-types is illusory, since it “depends on situations of language use, the number of which is unlimited”

(Notarius 2008, 57–59). It is not surprising that "there is no uniformity in classifying discourse types in the scholarly literature" (Notarius 2013, §1.1.1.2).[62]

1.2.5. The Pronunciation of the Conjunction *Wa* in CBH and the Tiberian Masoretic Text

The sources for the Tiberian reading tradition and its codification in the sign system of *Biblia Hebraica* show that *shewa mobile* was read as a short vowel with the same quality as *pataḥ* (Khan 2013a, 98; 2013b; Isaksson 2021a, 208–10). The two variants *wə-* (written with *shewa mobile*) and *way-* (written with *pataḥ* and *dagesh forte*) were read with the same vowel quality (Kantor 2020, 59, 95).[63]

וְיִקְטֹל was read *wa-yiqṭōl* 'and let him kill'
וַיִּקְטֹל was read *way-yiqṭōl* 'and he killed'

The difference in the reading of the two types of clauses is just a gemination, because the vowel quality of the conjunction was the same for both variants (Khan 1991, 241 n. 17; 2013a, 98; 2013b).

Gemination (written *dagesh forte*) was sometimes utilised in the Tiberian reading tradition to create a secondary distinction between words that were originally homophonous. This phenomenon was a strategy for avoiding unclarity that probably originated in the Second Temple period ('orthoepy').[64] In the Babylonian vocalisation (Khan 2013a, 43) and the Samaritan oral tradition, it is even more widespread.[65]

In the Archaic Hebrew poetry, a free-standing past perfective short *yiqṭol* is never preceded by another distinct morpheme in order to mark it as past (Kantor 2020, 63 n. 7). *Ø-yiqṭol(Ø)* was enough, which means that *wa* + *yiqṭol(Ø)*, with a normal *wa*, was able to express a past perfective meaning. No intervening particle was needed.[66]

Khan (1991, 241 n. 17; 2020, 534) argues that *dagesh forte* in Tiberian וַיִּקְטֹל is a case of orthoepy, introduced in the Second Temple period,[67] thus well after the classical period. But in CBH there persisted a homophony between jussive short *yiqṭol* and indicative short *yiqṭol*, including when used after the conjunction *wa* (in the latter case forming a very frequent clause-type).[68] The differentiation is fairly old, indeed as old as the Second Temple period, but it was not a feature of CBH (Isaksson 2021a, 210).[69] For CBH, it is reasonable to suppose an inherited homophony between a jussive *wa-yiqṭol* and an indicative *wa-yiqṭol*, both signalling discourse continuity (but in different domains):[70]

ויקטל [wa-yiqṭōl] 'and let him kill'
ויקטל [wa-yiqṭōl] 'and he killed'

In order to avoid confusion and achieve clarity, the Tiberian reading tradition introduced a gemination of the first prefix consonant in the reading of the text.[71]

Tiberian reading:

ויקטל [wa-yiqṭōl] 'and let him kill'
ויקטל [way-yiqṭōl] 'and he killed'

The speakers and writers of CBH made no distinction between two different *wa*. Such a distinction was introduced in the reading tradition after the classical period, probably as early as the Second Temple period.[72]

Obviously, the distinction created in the reading tradition also involves a semantic interpretation of the verbal forms (Notarius 2011, 261). An example of the distinction is found already in the first chapter of the Bible. In verse six, there is a *wa* with jussive *yiqṭol(Ø)*, and verse seven includes a *wa* with gemination and a realis *yiqṭol(Ø)*, with past time reference:[73]

(19) יְהִ֥י רָקִ֖יעַ בְּת֣וֹךְ הַמָּ֑יִם **וִיהִ֣י** מַבְדִּ֔יל בֵּ֥ין מַ֖יִם לָמָֽיִם׃ **וַיַּ֣עַשׂ** אֱלֹהִים֮ אֶת־הָרָקִיעַ֒

‘Let there be an expanse in the midst of the waters **and let it separate** water from water. [7]**So God made** the expanse…’ (Gen. 1.6–7)

The meaning of the conjunction *wa* is the same in both cases. It signals discourse continuity, but in two separate domains. The *raison d’être* of the gemination is not to change the function of the *wa*, but to achieve clarity as to the meaning of two homophonous *yiqṭol(Ø)*: the short *wa-yiqṭol* with jussive meaning is distinguished in the reading from the short *way-yiqṭol* with past perfective meaning.[74] This past perfective *way-yiqṭol* is the “**yaqtul* preterite and simple *waw*” that Muraoka and Rogland (1998, 101) see in the Tel Dan and Zakkūr inscriptions,[75] but fail to recognise in the Biblical Hebrew *way-yiqṭol* (Renz 2016, 632; Isaksson 2021a, 199–201).

In consequence of this, and from now on, I will make use of a more pertinent terminology, *wa(y)-yiqṭol* and *wa-qaṭal*, for the traditional ‘consecutive’ clause-types.[76] The ‘*(y)*’ in *wa(y)-yiqṭol* is meant to indicate that the gemination was pronounced in the Tiberian reading (and thus written in our Hebrew Bibles), but that it was not a feature of CBH. In free-standing form, the short *yiqṭol* will be designated *yiqṭol(Ø)* (see §3), and the long *yiqṭol* written *yiqṭol(u)*, recalling its origin from Central Semitic *yaqtulu* (see §4).

1.2.6. The Concept of Discourse Continuity in CBH

It is one of the cornerstones of Biblical Hebrew text-linguistics that two of the principal verb forms in the central verbal system are 'consecutive'.[77] One of them is assumed to be *wa(y)-yiqṭol*, the other *wa-qaṭal*. The consecutive verbal forms tend to build series of main-line consecutive clauses (see §1.2.8). Clauses that break the main-line pattern are 'non-consecutive'. Hebrew text-linguistics is concerned with the nature of the consecution, and the function of the non-consecutive clauses. This can be summarised in a table displaying *the essence of Biblical Hebrew text-linguistics*; see Table 3.

Table 3: The essence of Biblical Hebrew text-linguistics (affirmative clauses)

	Consecutive clauses	**Non-consecutive clauses**
Narrative, report	***wa**(y)-yiqṭol*	*(wa)-X-qaṭal*
Instruction, forecasting	***wa**-qaṭal*	*(wa)-X-yiqṭol*

Characteristic features of consecutive clauses are:

1. The initial 'consecutive *waw*' (bold type in Table 3);
2. The initial position of the (finite) verb.

A non-consecutive clause is characterised by having a clausal constituent (*X*) before the verb. The alternation between the two clause-types[78] can be summarised as a central Tenet 1* of Biblical Hebrew text-linguistics, where '*' indicates a preliminary formulation:

Tenet 1*. A series of discourse-continuity ***wa***-*VX* clauses is interrupted by a clause with (*wa*)-*XV* pattern (Isaksson 2021, 212).[79]

This formula subsumes the labour of generations of Biblical Hebrew scholars, since it is the legacy of the system of 'consecutive tenses'. It contains the germ of a clause linking approach to the verbal system.[80] Tenet 1* is a confirmation that CBH has retained the old "unmarked declarative V(S)(O) word order" of Semitic syntax (Pat-El 2019, 86).

The term *discourse continuity* is borrowed from Givón. He uses the phrase "a break in the discourse continuity" (Givón 1977, 201), where a break means a syntactic interruption of the main line of continuity clauses. The notion of interruption is found also in Van der Merwe et al. (1999, 167). Discourse continuity is a broader concept than the idea of temporal or logical consecution. The semantic breadth of the concept of discourse continuity based on Givón (1977) and Buth (1995) will be of paramount importance for the following investigations in this book (see especially §2 and §7).

The '*XV*' pattern in the Tenet 1* formula represents the "practically universal strategy for realizing focus" by word order (Hopper 1979, 220); the '*X*' can be the subject, an instrumental adverb, or the direct object. "In this strategy, it is the position of the verb which is crucial" (Hopper 1979, 240).

A clause linking approach will be the central methodological procedure in this book, in order to uncover the linguistic reality behind the 'consecutive tenses' in CBH.

1.2.7. Clause Linking

"Traditional and modern grammarians alike have restricted what they call 'syntax' to the study of what goes on within the boundaries of the prosodic sentence" (Haiman and Thompson 1988, ix). As for Biblical Hebrew grammars, this approach came to an end with the introduction of text-linguistics, which forever changed the perspective of syntactic analysis from the sentence to that of the text.[81]

Clause linking is a general linguistic approach to examine how different kinds of clauses combine in a specific language.[82] It can be regarded as "a grammaticalization of a very general property of the hierarchical structure of the discourse itself" (Matthiessen and Thompson 1988, 290). The pattern of clause linking used in a text reflects the rhetorical intentions of the author or narrator (Matthiessen and Thompson 1988, 275, 299). In the present book, it is assumed that this holds also for Biblical Hebrew. The 'proof' of this assumption will be that the texts communicate meaning with this approach. The textual structure will become more understandable and more transparent (cf. Isaksson 2015a, 173).

The following example is a simple but illustrative linking of two clauses (Verstraete 2005, 619 ex. 15):

(20) Pattern: Clause_1 *and* Clause_2

Macy's advertised a sale yesterday and the whole town went crazy.

Two clauses are combined, and on the surface two actions are described that stand in a relation of temporal succession: the event in $Clause_2$ is temporally sequential to that of $Clause_1$. This (possibly unconscious) interpretation requires a certain amount of cultural knowledge. If the phenomenon of advertising were unknown to the reader, the temporal succession would possibly escape him/her. For the knowledgeable reader, however, the temporal succession is evident, and also receives a notion of a result. Macy's' advertisement *caused* the whole town to go crazy. But an even more delicate cultural understanding, on the level of a native speaker, might result in an understanding of this bi-clausal linking as having a specific illocutionary force: that of surprise or indignation or excitement. This is perhaps more apparent when the verb forms are changed to present tense (Verstraete 2005, 619, ex. 14b):

(21) Pattern: $Clause_1$ *and* $Clause_2$

Macy's advertises a sale yesterday and the whole town goes crazy.

In a linking of clauses, the clause is any syntagm containing one predication. Clause linking can be defined as "a relation of dependency or sociation obtaining between clauses in this sense" (Lehmann 1988, 182). In this definition, dependency involves the embedding of one clause X in another clause Y ("X occupies a grammatical slot of Y"); this means that the Y-clause "determines the grammatical category of the complex and thus its external relations." Embedded clauses (such as complement clauses) are relatively trivial in Biblical Hebrew. Of greater interest are non-dependency relations, which Lehmann calls "relations of *sociation*." Among them are coordination, which is "a relation of sociation combining two syntagms of the same type and forming a syntagm which is again of the same type" (quotations from Lehmann 1988, 181f.; see also Haspelmath 2007, 1). Parataxis means the coordination of clauses, which may be syndetic or asyndetic. The concept of syndesis has nothing to do with parataxis or hypotaxis; it is exclusively a question of the "presence or absence of a connective device," that is, a linking connective (Lehmann 1988, 210f.):

(22) Pattern: Clause_1 *but* Clause_2

You are very kind, **but** I must contradict you.

(23) Pattern: Clause_1 *and* Clause_2

This is right, **and** that is wrong.

This is a type of clause linking which is extremely frequent also in CBH. It is a linking structure with inferred interclausal relation (Bril 2010, 16), which can be given the pattern (Isaksson 2021a, 215f.):

Clause_1 *wa*-Clause_2

In this biclausal linking, Clause_2 is said to *be linked to* Clause_1. The proclitic conjunction *wa* puts Clause_2 *in a relation* to Clause_1 (see further §2). The order of the clauses is fundamental. Clause_2 *relates to* Clause_1.

To determine the 'main line' in a text "one must appeal to the discourse context" (Matthiessen and Thompson 1988, 275). It is a discourse-related concept. A "[*b*]*ackground* relation holds for a text span which provides for the comprehensibility of an item mentioned in another text span" (Matthiessen and Thompson 1988, 293). It "is used to provide the reader/listener with information that will enable him/her to comprehend an item" (Matthiessen and Thompson 1988, 298).

1.2.8. The Foreground-Background Distinction

The concept of a foreground-background distinction plays a major role in CBH text-linguistics and is recognised by almost all linguists as a language universal (Hopper and Thompson 1980, 280, 283; Isaksson 2021a, 220 n. 50). Foregrounding and backgrounding are psycholinguistic entities; the distinction is related to the processing of discourse (Cook 2012a, 283–88). They cannot be defined by specific clause-types (Shirtz and Payne 2015, 1f.). For example, *qaṭal* and *wa(y)-yiqṭol* clauses can be either backgrounded or foregrounded.[83] A *qaṭal* clause may, as a discontinuity clause, begin a new literary unit, and as such it can be either foregrounded or backgrounded (Tenets 2a and 2b; see §§7.7–8).

Material that supplies the main points of the discourse is foreground; the "part of a discourse which does not immediately and crucially contribute to the speaker's goal, but which merely assists, amplifies, or comments on it" is background (Hopper and Thompson 1980, 280).

In English, there is no specific marker of foregrounding; "the audience infers grounding not from a single morphosyntactic feature, but from a cluster of properties, no single one of which is exclusively characteristic of foregrounding" (Hopper and Thompson 1980, 283f.). Foregrounding is expressed by a continuum of saliency features, "along which various points cluster and tend strongly to co-occur" (Hopper and Thompson 1980, 294):[84]

Table 4: A continuum of saliency features

More salient	Less salient
temporal succession	temporal overlap
perfective aspect	imperfective aspect
dynamic	nondynamic (descriptive)
telic	durative
volitional (involvement)	nonvolitional
affirmative	negative (negated)
indicative (finite reality of the state or event described by the clause)	non-assertive (subjunctive, hypothetical, imaginary, conditional)
nonanaphoric	anaphoric
identity of subject maintained and it tends to be presupposed	frequent change of subject
human topics	nonhuman topics
total affectedness	partial affectedness
high individuation	low individuation
unmarked distribution of focus in clause, with presupposition of subject	marked distribution of focus, e.g. subject focus, instrument focus, focus on sentence adverbial

In narrative, *foreground* is "the default (or unmarked) mode of recounting events, often, but not always, marked by means of a dominant narrative verb; *background* is marked by departures from the default mode of narration" (Cook 2012a, 295).[85]

1.2.9. Bybee's Construction Theory

Bybee's construction theory (2010; 2015) has proved fruitful for the explanation of the enigmatic 'consecutive tense' *wa-qaṭal*. Khan (2021a) has shed light upon *wa-qaṭal*, with its future and habitual meanings, as a construction in Bybee's sense. This puts

Bybee's construction theory at the centre of interest for the Hebrew verbal system (Isaksson forthcoming; and §6 in this book).

A central concept for Bybee is chunking: "When two or more words are often used together, they also develop a sequential relation" (Bybee 2010, 25, 33). Constructions are sequential chunks "that sometimes have special meanings and other properties" (Bybee 2010, 36). High frequency is determinative. The more a sequence of morphemes or words is used together, the more strongly the sequence will be perceived as a unit and the less it will be associated with its component parts. This process leads to increasing autonomy of the construction (Bybee 2010, 36, 48).

Example: the English phrase *be going to* is a chunk, which because of its frequency was extended in usage and developed into a general future morpheme *gonna*.

Be going to is a construction, with many extensional steps that widen its applicability. It is a construction, since the futural/intentional meaning cannot be deduced from the parts of the construction, *be* + *going* + *to*. The original construction was: SUBJECT + BE + *going to* + VERB, where the capitalised items are schematic. This construction is still in living usage (Bybee 2010, 96; 2015, 124). In *gonna*, a construction has adopted grammatical meaning and phonetically reduced form as a future auxiliary (Bybee 2010, 106; 2015, 268). The separate parts of the construction have lost their individual functions.

Grammaticalisation represents the extreme end of the development of a construction, but it is not necessary that a construction develop into an independent morpheme. The construction may remain a construction (as *be going to*).

Khan's (2021a) idea is that Biblical Hebrew *wa-qaṭal* in apodosis position was a chunk with high frequency that became a construction (see further §1.3). This will be the basic idea behind the investigation of *wa-qaṭal* in §6.

1.3. Previous Research

The concept of 'conversive *waw*' emerged among the medieval Jewish grammarians.[86] This idea permitted the grammarians to explain why the present/future *yiqṭol* had past tense meaning when preceded by this *waw*, and it also explained why the past tense *qaṭal* with initial *waw* had present/future meaning. That the *waw ha-hippūḵ* had two different shapes, one before indicative *yiqṭol* (with gemination of the prefix vowel) and another before *qaṭal* (sometimes with change of accent), was generally ignored in this instance. It was also passed over in silence that past tense *wayyiqṭol* and jussive *yiqṭol* both had a morphologically shorter form in several instances (Cook 2012a, 80).

The idea of a 'conversive *waw*', together with a temporal view of verbal forms, was taken over by the early western scholarship,[87] and it is still alive and well in some leading grammars of the twenty-first century (Joüon 1923; Joüon and Muraoka 2006).[88] The 'conversive *waw*' was a rule of thumb intended as a remedy for an enigma—that of the strange Biblical Hebrew verbal system. But it became itself part of the enigma and an obstacle to its solution. Since it could explain only some of the usages of the verbal forms, the enigma would occupy Hebrew scholarship for centuries to come (McFall 1982).

Out of the idea of a conversive *waw* emerged the conception of a 'system' of four basic verb forms ('tenses') in Biblical Hebrew grammar, of which two were intrinsically combined with the 'conversive *waw*': *qaṭal, yiqṭol, weqaṭal,* and *wayyiqṭol.* This is a conception from which Hebrew scholarship has never entirely recovered, although the terms used for the special *waw* vary considerably in the literature: inductive, inversive, energic, strong, conservative, or consecutive (Van de Sande 2008, 198f.; Cook 2012a, 80, 83, 93).

The scholarly literature on the subject comprises an immense flood of works. For an overview of the literature up to Thacker (1954), it is necessary to refer to McFall (1982), although McFall himself uncritically presupposes the terminology that is the root of the enigma: the 'consecutive tenses', the 'consecutive *waw*'.[89] He takes for granted what he should have kept a critical distance from: the conceptual world of four basic verb forms of which two have a 'consecutive *waw*' and the other two are '*waw*-less'. If terminology contains false assumptions, raw data and statistics will only support the suppositions and block the introduction of fruitful new ideas.[90] What also characterises so many new (and old) attempts to solve the enigma is the plain belief that a fresh 'synchronic' approach to the Biblical Hebrew verbal system must be enough. This has resulted in "idiosyncratic analyses that find no support among the recent typological classifications" (Cook 2012a, 185).

Among the first attempts to resolve the enigma was the explanation of the conversive *waw* as 'relative': it was not conversive, but gave the verb form a temporal meaning in relation to the preceding verb: *wa(y)-yiqṭol* was (past) future (a true *yiqṭol*) in relation to a preceding *qaṭal* or *wa(y)-yiqṭol*, and *wa-qaṭal* was a past used for future (Schroeder 1766; see McFall 1982, 22). A similar idea is the 'inductive *waw*', which transfers the temporal or modal force of the governing verb to the verb after the *waw* (J. Bellamy; P. Gell; see McFall 1982, 24–26). The idea of a 'relative *waw*' was a little step forward, because it recognised the semantic dependence of continuity clauses (the relative 'tenses') on preceding clauses. But still there were two different *waw* in Biblical Hebrew.

It was a step forward when Hebrew and Semitic scholars introduced the concept of verbal aspect in descriptions of the Hebrew verbal system (G. H. A. Ewald 1891; S. R. Driver 1892; Brockelmann 1951; see Cook 2012a, 86–93). The *qaṭal* verb form was regarded as expressing perfective, finished action and the *yiqṭol* as expressing unfinished action ('imperfective'). This way of analysing the verbal usage in Biblical Hebrew found good parallels in Indo-European languages and supplied an explanation as to why the *yiqṭol* could in historical contexts express a past repetitive or habitual action. Verbal aspects could certainly explain many obscure verbal usages, but no aspectual theory was able to explain the conversive or consecutive 'tenses' (with initial *waw*!) and the strange phenomenon of a conversive *waw*.

Research on the Hebrew verbal system advanced considerably with the introduction of a historical-comparative perspective in the nineteenth century. It was the recovery of the Akkadian language and later also Ugaritic that gave rise to valuable comparative studies of the Classical Hebrew language. Until then, the Semitic languages available for comparison offered only texts that were considerably later than the Bible: Syriac, Arabic, Ethiopic. From then on, Hebrew could be compared with languages of a much earlier provenance, and *wa(y)-yiqṭol* (with a short *yiqṭol*) was recognised as a cognate of *iprus* in Akkadian as well as *lam yaqtul* in Arabic. The same evidence identified the Hebrew jussive short *yiqṭol* as a reflex of Akkadian *l-iprus* and Arabic jussive *yaqtul*. The Hebrew verb form *qaṭal* was analysed in the light of the Akkadian verbal adjective, the stative.[91] In the early twentieth century, the application of comparative Semitic studies to the understanding of the Hebrew verbal system was summarised and pushed forward by Hans Bauer (1910; see Finley 1981, 243). But no consensus was attained regarding the Hebrew *wa-qaṭal*, since a comparative perspective proved incapable of explaining the semantic difference between an anterior/perfective *qaṭal* in discontinuity clauses and the discourse-continuity *wa-qaṭal* clauses with imperfective/future/habitual meanings. The discovery of some very early Northwest Semitic epigraphs in the second half of the twentieth century has provided a further broadening of the comparative evidence.[92]

The majority view in comparative Semitics research has come to the conclusion that Proto-Semitic had three verbal forms (none with a preceding *waw*-conjunction): *qatal(a)* expressing states, *yaqtul* with both past perfective and jussive meanings, and an imperfective *yaqattal* (Cook 2012a, 96f.). According to this view, the Central Semitic languages share an important innovation: the imperfective *yaqtul-u/-ūna* (Huehnergard 2005; Cook 2012a, 97).[93] The morphological and semantic distinction between a short *yiqṭol* (< *yaqtul*) and a long *yiqṭol* (< *yaqtulu*) was finally confirmed by the investigation of the Amarna tablets, which displayed data from a stage of Canaanite several centuries earlier than Biblical Hebrew (Moran 1950; Rainey 1996; Cook 2012a, 114, 118).

Among the relatively recent attempts to understand the Biblical Hebrew verbal system from a comparative Semitic perspective, the book by Mark S. Smith (1991) must be mentioned for its quality and modern linguistic terminology. Smith recognises the fruitful linguistic terminology introduced by Givón (1977; 1983) and pays proper attention to the role of the two 'consecutive' verbal 'forms' in signalling discourse continuity (the flow of the text) and the role of other clause-types in signalling discontinuity. He does not study the conjunction *wa* in itself, only the '*waw* consecutive', but recognises that "the BH converted imperfect represents a survival of NWS **yaqtul* preterite" (Smith 1991, xi). The primary emphasis in the work is "the comparative evidence from the Amarna letters, the Ugaritic texts, first millennium NWS inscriptions and the Hebrew texts from Qumran" (Smith 1991, xi). It is a mistake, though, that he throughout the book uses the terms 'converted imperfect' and 'converted perfect', though he is well aware that "'converted' and 'unconverted' are improper designations for the verbal forms with and without prefix *waw*" (Smith 1991, xi). His justification is: "this study frequently uses the first set of terms for the sake of convenience... given the common acceptance of the terms 'converted' and 'unconverted'" (Smith 1991, xii). This is a methodological mistake, because without proper terminology he proves unable to arrive at a proper description of the conjunction, and all his conclusions are confined to the uses of *wa* in the clause-types *wa(y)-yiqṭol* and *wa-qaṭal*, though some of his observations, with the help of Givón's cross-linguistic research, are valid for the use of *wa* in CBH in general.[94] Smith's focus is on clauses of the type *wa-V(X)*, and his conclusions are ahead of his time: such clauses express "continued topicality" and, in narrative, the clause-type *wa(y)-yiqṭol* "controls the *flow* of the story: The opposition between *unmarked* or *sequential* narration as against *counter-sequential* narration" (Givón 1977, 188, quoted from Smith 1991, 14). Smith's study lacks a theory of grammaticalisation, but it is hard to blame him. The main works by Joan Bybee and Östen Dahl were still to be written at the time of writing of his book.[95]

A further step was taken at the turn of the new century with the introduction of a theory of grammaticalisation which enabled scholars to understand the evolution of the verbal forms ('grams') in Biblical Hebrew (thus Andersen 2000). The importance of cross-linguistic grammaticalisation studies was emphasised by John Cook (2012a, 104, 114). According to him, all new theories should be tested against a typologically reliable perspective: "a theory of the BHVS should be judged by whether it presents a 'typologically credible' model of the verbal system in light of the abundance of data on verbal systems in the world's languages" (Cook 2012a, 149).[96]

If previous research on the Biblical Hebrew verbal system has often been hampered by a lack of linguistic clarity and comparative perspective, it is a relief to turn to the critically conducted survey of research by Cook (2012a, 77–175). It partly overlaps the time period covered by McFall, and treats modern works until about 2010. Cook is sharp and linguistically up-to-date and evaluates recent research according to three principles that are fundamental for research on the Biblical Hebrew verbal system: (1) a comparative and diachronic Semitic perspective on the Hebrew verbal system (Cook 2012a, §2.3); (2) a discussion of diachronic layers within the Hebrew Bible (at least: archaic, classical, and late);[97] (3) a recognition of processes of grammaticalisation with a cross-linguistic conception of the history of verbal forms (bearing in mind that each language reveals unique paths of development).[98] In addition, Cook treats with critical distance the attempts to present the different 'grammars' of the discourse types in Biblical Hebrew, and concludes that semantics must take precedence over discourse analysis: "so also discourse-prominent analysis of the BHVS seems to serve for some as an escape from the morass of traditional semantic and (predominantly) diachronic approaches" (Cook 2012a, 150, 268, §4.1). In text *en clair*: in the various discourse types (probably unlimited in number), we encounter the same grammar and the same verbal forms, but context and text-type influence the meaning of a verb form. Discourse analysis has been valuable in many respects, including its emphasis on the text at the expense of single sentences, but as a method for understanding the verbal system it is disappointing, as Cook states about the contribution of F. J. del Barco: "the BH verbal forms do not align with discourse functions as uniformly as he expects" (Cook 2012a, 161; also Notarius 2008, 57–59; 2013, 10–11, 51–53).

The strengths of Cook's work are the methodological chapters and his critical assessment of current research. His discussion of the foreground/background concept is valuable. His own explanation of the verbal system (Cook 2012a, §4.4) is, however, hampered by a methodological mistake. He assumes that word order is signalled by the position of the subject in the clause, and that this word order is the basic signal for distinguishing realis and irrealis clauses in a text. Cook supports this conclusion by referring to generative linguistic considerations raised by Holmstedt, and proposes that a SV word order basically signals realis meaning in the clause, whereas VS word order signals irrealis. This thesis works tolerably well with *wa-qaṭal* clauses in CBH,[99] but the theory becomes less consistent when faced with the copious amount of *wa(y)-yiqṭol* clauses which by (nearly) all scholars are considered verb-initial and realis. Though *wa(y)-yiqṭol* is a clause-type[100] that is gradually declining in favour of the intruding *qaṭal*, it cannot be considered a minor verbal usage. Cook's mistakes are fourfold:

(1) He supposes that the basic word order distinction is SV // VS, instead of recognising the basic observation of Hebrew text-linguistics that the fundamental distinction of word order concerns the position of the verb. According to Biblical Hebrew text-linguistics, the fundamental word

order opposition is not VS // SV but VX // XV, where X may be not only subject, but direct object, adverbial expression, etc. In Cook's definition of word order, the subject is given too much weight in comparison with other clausal constituents.

(2) Cook supposes that "irrealis clauses exhibit verb-subject word order" (Cook 2012a, 234), which makes him incapable of explaining the subject + long *yiqṭol* clauses in instruction, which often alternate with *wa-qaṭal* clauses with the same type of irrealis meaning (obligation). He maintains that the word order opposition SV // VS signals an alternation between realis and irrealis clauses in a text, but this is obviously not the case. The fundamental word order opposition is one between discourse-continuity and -discontinuity clauses (not between realis and irrealis): *XV* expresses discourse discontinuity, and *wa-VX* is the typical pattern of macro-syntactic continuity, for example in a narrative main line (*wa(y)-yiqṭol*) or the successive steps in an instruction (*wa-qaṭal*). The inevitable conclusion is that a *VX* word order can be either realis (e.g. narrative) or irrealis (e.g. instruction/obligation), and the same holds for an *XV* word order.[101]

(3) Cook's word order supposition lacks typological evidence. He is unable to explain the linguistic forces behind such a development in Biblical Hebrew. His treatment of the *wa(y)-yiqṭol* clause-type is hard to understand, since such clauses have VS word order, which according to Cook should be analysed as irrealis, but an assumption of

this type is fundamental for Cook, because otherwise his irrealis/realis word order hypothesis would collapse.[102]

(4) Cook does not recognise the distinction between discourse-continuity (*wa-VX*) and discourse-discontinuity clauses. The reason why *wa-qaṭal* clauses are preferred for "procedural instruction" (in Exod. 25.10–14) in contradistinction to *X-yiqṭol* clauses is that *wa-qaṭal* clauses signal continuity. Cook fails to recognise the fundamental role of the conjunction *wa* in *wa-VX* clauses.[103]

Jan Joosten (2012) strives to retain a certain amount of traditional terminology and to "keep theory and technical terminology to a minimum," for the benefit of "exegetes of the biblical texts" (Joosten 2012, 7). A definite strength of Joosten's monograph is that his description of the CBH verbal system is independent of a semantic distinction between two different *wa*. Joosten is relatively consistent in calling the conjunction 'copula', irrespective of its being a traditional 'consecutive *waw*' or a traditional 'copulative *waw*'. The *waC-* (with following gemination in *wayyiqṭol*) is regarded as having retentive function (an ancient Semitic preterite *yaqtul* is preserved in *wa(y)-yiqṭol*). But at the same time, and without further explanation, two of the basic 'tenses' in Classical Hebrew are presented as verbal forms with a proclitic *wa*: *wayyiqṭol* and *weqaṭal*. This *wa* is designated by Joosten as both a 'copula' and as an intrinsic part of the 'tense' itself. In this way, Joosten has got rid of the terminology of two different *waw*, but has retained the typologically unparalleled idea of two verbal forms with an intrinsic initial 'copula'. As a consequence of this, there are two kinds of *wa* anyway: such that are constituents in a 'tense',[104] and such that are not. I presume that Joosten's defence would be that this is how a synchronic state of Biblical Hebrew works (namely the Classical Hebrew prose language), and we have to accept it as is, strange or not.[105]

The ambition to keep theory and technical terminology at a minimum comes at a price, though, because old terminology can be misleading and an obstacle to a deeper understanding (thus Cook 2014, 380). An example is Joosten's terminology "YIQTOL and the jussive," which invites the impression that there is only one *yiqṭol* in Classical Hebrew (Joosten 2012, 11). Even in Joosten's view, there are at least two *yiqṭol*, because the jussive is also a *yiqṭol*, though with a 'short' morphology, so that the most logical terminology should be long *yiqṭol* and short *yiqṭol*. The latter term invites a discussion of the nature of *wa(y)-yiqṭol* as being an indicative (short) *yiqṭol*, a terminology that was relevant at least for the state of Biblical Hebrew when poetry used the short *yiqṭol* without the conjunction *wa* as a past perfective verb form (thus also Joosten 2012, 417f.). So Joosten recognises that there are two *yiqṭols* in Biblical Hebrew, while his terminology makes the reader think there is only one.

Joosten's terminology concerning the verbal forms in Biblical Hebrew is traditional.[106] *Wa-qaṭal* and *qaṭal* are "two distinct verbal forms" and the *wa* in *wa-qaṭal* is called "the copula" (Joosten 2012, 16). This is old-fashioned and inappropriate terminology, because 'copula' in linguistics means a word used to link subject and predicate, not to link clauses. In a similar way, Joosten calls *wa(y)-yiqṭol* a verbal form, which means that Biblical Hebrew has two verbal forms with the proclitic conjunction *wa* ('copula') regarded as an intrinsic part of the verbal form. I suspect that Joosten regards this as a linguistic fact that has somehow occurred in a specific synchronic state (= Classical Hebrew). Since it is a typological anomaly, one would expect Joosten to discuss this phenomenon, but he has no comments to offer (Joosten 2012, 16, 41).[107] In all other Semitic languages, such expressions are regarded as *clauses* with an initial conjunction *wa*, not as verbal forms.

The final break-down of this unconsidered terminology occurs in chapter X ('Verbal forms in textual perspective'). In this chapter, Joosten (2012, 350) introduces the concept of a clause: "The building blocks of texts are not individual verbal forms, but clauses." Knowing from Joosten's book that both '*weqaṭal*' and '*wayyiqṭol*' are 'verbal forms' (as well as 'tenses'), it is certainly surprising to read the following in the same chapter:

> Finally, the verbal clause as a whole can be linked to the context by one or more conjunctions or sentence adverbs such as ו, או, עתה, לכן, אבל, אכן, כי. These conjunctions come at the head of the clause and do not seem to have any direct effect on its inner structure. (Joosten 2012, 351)

Since '*weqaṭal*' and '*wayyiqṭol*' according to Joosten are 'verbal forms', they should be expected to conform to the property formulated above. But there are no examples of Classical Hebrew clauses of the types ווַיִּקְטֹל or ווְקָטַל, nor או וַיִּקְטֹל or או וְקָטַל, nor עתה וַיִּקְטֹל or עתה וְקָטַל, nor לכן וַיִּקְטֹל or לכן וְקָטַל, nor אבל וַיִּקְטֹל or אבל וְקָטַל, nor אכן וַיִּקְטֹל or אכן וְקָטַל, nor כי וַיִּקְטֹל or כי וְקָטַל. How then can Joosten call the syntagms '*weqaṭal*' and '*wayyiqṭol*' verbal forms and tenses? Joosten (2012, 350) says that verbal forms "need to be incorporated in a clause or sentence." Yes, but

Joosten's *weqaṭal* and *wayyiqṭol* cannot be incorporated, because they are not verbal forms. They are in themselves clauses with a conjunction, and they are not 'tenses' (Isaksson 2021a, 221). Very often, *wa-qaṭal* and *wa(y)-yiqṭol* also constitute main clauses. The whole scheme of "the Hebrew verbal sentence in main clauses" that Joosten presents on page 352 inevitably leaves out the most frequent main-line verbal clauses in Classical Hebrew prose, the clause-types *wa-qaṭal* and *wa(y)-yiqṭol*. Such clauses are not even mentioned in his overview of Hebrew verbal sentences.

Unlike many of his predecessors, Joosten (2012, 308) recognises a comparative Semitic perspective and admits that *wa(y)-yiqṭol* has a history as a Proto-Semitic 'preterite', that *qaṭal* is a cognate of the Akkadian stative, and that *yiqṭol* (that is, the long *yiqṭol*) was originally an imperfective formation. In fact, long *yiqṭol* was even used as a present progressive in Archaic Hebrew (Notarius 2012, 194f.). But Joosten maintains that the comparative perspective is an issue of interest to the *experts*: what matters to the student and exegete of Biblical Hebrew is the synchronic state of Classical Hebrew, and this synchronic state exhibits the four traditional basic 'tenses'. To them he adds a present tense: the active predicative participle. The *yiqṭol* has a "basic modal, *irrealis* function" (Joosten 2012, 29, 32). *Wa-qaṭal* is also irrealis. The synchronic state Joosten studies remains a mystery, inexplicable in the comparative Semitic perspective.[108] It is apparent that comparative Semitic typology has little bearing on his book. Joosten makes comparisons and considers cognate verbal forms in Ugaritic and Amarna Canaanite to be relevant for *earlier* stages of Hebrew, even for the archaic biblical poetry, but such comparisons seem stunningly irrelevant for his synchronic understanding of CBH. "One of the foremost challenges to Joosten's model of the BHVS is that it is typologically unparalleled" (Cook 2012a, 141).

In spite of the research accounted for above, until recently, the verbal system of Biblical Hebrew has deserved to be called "this most mystifying domain" (Greenstein 1988, 7). This predicament has come to an end with the latest research by Geoffrey Khan, who has contributed significantly to the solution of the most mystifying facet of the consecutive 'tenses', the *wa-qaṭal* clause-type. In a recent publication, Khan (2021a) has shown that *wa-qaṭal* is a construction in Bybee's (2010; 2015) sense (see further §1.2.9 and §6 in this book). Khan's explanation of *wa-qaṭal* as a construction in Bybee's sense represents a great step forward to a linguistic understanding of the 'consecutive tenses' (Isaksson forthcoming). The basic idea behind his arguments is that the 'consecutive' *wa-qaṭal* began its specific development in the position of apodosis, which many scholars have already suggested. With this usage as a starting-point, *wa-qaṭal* was schematised by step-by-step extensions of its meanings, in accordance with the construction theory of Joan Bybee. This development took place in a stage after the archaic language (Notarius 2013, 288f., 304). Khan applies Bybee's general linguistic terminology, and argues that CBH *wa-qaṭal* was a chunk with high frequency that became a construction. "Constructions often contain explicit lexical material" (Bybee 2010, 76), and in this case the lexical material is the conjunction *wa* in *wa-qaṭal*. Constructions also "have a special form, meaning and pragmatic effect that cannot be captured by more general principles of grammar" (Bybee 2010, 76f.). This explains why the meanings of *wa-qaṭal* cannot be deduced from the separate elements *wa* + *qaṭal*. This is the reason Biblical Hebrew scholarship has failed concerning *wa-qaṭal*. In the construction, *wa* is the invariant part and *qaṭal* is schematic with multiple forms: *wa-QAṬAL*.[109] An inevitable conclusion is that *wa-qaṭal* as a construction is a clause-type with the conjunction *wa* preserved in the construction. Specifically, *wa-qaṭal* is not a 'tense' (cf. Isaksson 2021a, 218f.; forthcoming).[110] The retention of the connective *wa-* is probably the reason why *wa-qaṭal* did not grammaticalise into a verbal morpheme (Khan 2021a, 342).

Khan's argumentation is an excellent application of modern linguistic theory to an enigma in Biblical Hebrew.[111] On this, see further §6.

---

[1] See further Isaksson (2021, 201–3). On this point I follow Notarius (2013, 22); Renz (2016, 437). Cook (2012a, 313): "There is a high degree of uniformity among all these discussions, despite the long gap of time between some of them with respect to the roles they assign to the *waw* conjunction."

[2] For CBH, see Lam and Pardee (2016).

[3] See also Huehnergard (2005; 2019, 62); Kouwenberg (2010a, 126ff.); Hackett (2012); Hasselbach (2013b, 329); Baranowski (2016b, 1); Kossmann and Suchard (2018, 47, 52).

[4] Gzella (2018, 27) takes the strange position that *way-yiqṭol* "completely replaced the perfect" in a "literary usage that extended into the vernacular." In this view, the older replaced the newer.

[5] For the concept of Archaic Biblical Hebrew, see Pat-El and Wilson-Wright (2013); Gianto (2016). The initial position of the verb in the

archaic language is a tendency for which there are exceptions (Isaksson 2021, 198 n. 5).

[6] On the debate about this *waw* in relation to the Aramaic Tel Dan inscription, see Isaksson (2021, 199–205).

[7] For the classification of the Semitic languages, I follow Huehnergard and Pat-El (2019); Pat-El (2019).

[8] Here must be mentioned also the works by Östen Dahl (1985; 2000) and Bybee and Dahl (1989).

[9] "[D]iachronics (and particularly diachronic typology) remains the only truly viable external 'control' on the analysis of BH grammar" (Cook 2012a, 178).

[10] There is some bewilderment as to which term to use for a (verbal) grammatical morpheme. Hopper and Traugott use (verbal) 'form', while Bybee and Dahl have introduced the neologism 'gram' to cover also periphrastic expressions. 'Inflectional category' is too narrow and 'grammatical category' too wide. For a discussion, see Bybee and Dahl (1989, 51). In the present book I will use (grammatical) form, (grammatical) morpheme, and gram interchangeably. For a wider term, cf. 'construction', introduced by Bybee (2010; 2015); see §1.2.9; §6.1.

[11] Concerning grammaticalisation and inferring diachrony from synchrony, see Croft (2003, 253–79). A history of research on grammaticalisation is found in Hopper and Traugott (2003, 19–38).

[12] Hopper and Traugott (2003, 4) prefer the term (verbal) 'grammatical form'.

[13] Dahl (2000, 8) maintains that this definition may in some cases be too narrow, and should include also, for example, the emergence of fixed word order, and Croft (2003, 271) emphasises "that grammaticalization applies to whole constructions, not just lexemes and morphemes." On this point, cf. Bybee's concept of 'construction'; see §1.2.9; §6.0.

[14] An example is the reduction of *going to* > *gonna* in English, with its bleached grammaticalised meaning and reduction of segmental length.

[15] Grammaticalisation involves both phonological and morphosyntactic processes. Croft (2003, 257) states that the first of two major grammaticalisation processes is rigidification of word order, "the fixing of the position of an element which formerly was free" (cf. construction, §1.2.9).

[16] An influential group of Semitists has remained structuralists and rejects the grammaticalisation approach (for example Huehnergard, Pat-El). The structuralist approach, with its concept of 'markedness', leads to explanations of verb forms that are conspicuously deficient in explanatory power, as in the following quotation from Korchin (2008, 324): "As predicted by markedness theory, the paradigmatically marked forms (*yqtl-u-* and *yqtl-a-*) each evidence a functional range that is both more restricted than, and yet also encompassed by the unmarked form (*yqtl-Ø*)."

[17] Hopper and Traugott (2003, 6) use the term 'cline': "forms do not shift abruptly from one category to another, but go through a series of small transitions, transitions that tend to be similar in type across languages." Heine et al. (1991) use the term 'grammaticalisation channels'.

[18] Bybee and Dahl (1989, 52) speak of "a small set of cross-linguistic **gram-types**." Certain meanings, such as perfective/past and present/future "are commonly expressed by grams in the languages of the world" (Bybee and Dahl 1989, 53).

[19] This is a claim that Dahl (2000, 11) regards as "fairly uninteresting" and "probably untrue."

[20] This means also a refutation of a common theoretical assumption "that all uses of a word, morpheme or construction can be characterized by a single, general meaning. In fact, that is not generally the case" (Croft 2003, 262).

[21] The article is reprinted in Kuryłowicz (1975, 93–120). A similar formulation is in Kuryłowicz (1949, 49ff.).

[22] Subjunctives are often residual morphemes ('doughnut grams' with a lost centre), with originally indicative meaning (Dahl 2000, 10). Croft (2003, 260) calls such a process 'fossilisation': "Certain morphemes or phonological alternations cease to be the standard means of forming a grammatical category or construction. Instead, they become restricted chiefly to a limited specified class of words or constructions.... An extreme case of fossilization is the random retention of a former morpheme on lexical items."

[23] For the analysis of *be going to* as a construction, but *gonna* as a grammaticalised morpheme, see §1.2.9.

[24] Another aspect of the same process is a "rapid increase in token frequency which accompanies grammaticization" (Bybee and Dahl 1989, 64; Bybee 1985, 17).

[25] The idea of exclusively binary (or even privative) oppositions in TAM systems is borrowed from universal phonology and probably misguided (Dahl 2000, 13). Languages vary essentially in two respects: "(i) which categories they choose out of the set of cross-linguistic categories, (ii) how they reduce the impreciseness that these categories have in choosing among the possible secondary or non-focal uses they have" (Dahl 1985, 33).

[26] In the present book, I will follow this terminology, with the exception of item f, for which I will use 'anterior' (Bybee's term; see Bybee 1985, 159). Gram types should be thought of as "relatively stable points along the paths of development that grams take in the course of grammaticalization processes" (Dahl 2000, 7).

[27] The term 'bounded' should be understood in the sense that "a certain limit or end-state is attained" (Dahl 1985, 29).

[28] Cross-linguistically, the progressive has a strong tendency to be marked periphrastically (Dahl 1985, 91). For the concept of reference time, see Hatav (2004, §5).

[29] Both perfective and imperfective grams tend to have markers. "In structuralist terms, we cannot identify one of the members of the opposition as the unmarked one.... [There are] stem alternations between perfective and imperfective forms to an extent not found anywhere else in tense–aspect systems" (Dahl 2000, 16).

[30] "It seems to be generally true that the order of morphemes within a word reflects an earlier ordering of words within a sentence" (Bybee 1985, 38, 41, referring to Givón 1971, and Vennemann 1973).

[31] Dahl (1985, 26) has a more syntactic definition: moods "are a grammatical way of indicating that the proposition is embedded into a modal or non-assertive context." Mood distinctions are normally used "in well-defined types of subordinate clauses" (Dahl 1985, 53). Because of our focus on the consecutive tenses, modal forms are not a central issue in the present book. For a more elaborate discussion of modality, see Palmer (2001).

[32] Some other examples of ventive/cohortative forms of verbs III*wy* where a formally long *yiqṭol(u)* should be analysed as short *yiqṭol(Ø)* with ventive suffix, from the first half of Genesis: 1.26; 2.18; 6.7; 11.4 (Sjörs 2023, 105); 18.21; 19.32, 34; 22.5; 24.14, 48 (*wa(y)-yiqṭol-V*); 24.49; 26.3.

[33] This is a linguistic confirmation that Deuteronomy is to be read diachronically as an exposition of "both P and non-P legislative material" (Kilchör 2019, 102). P is written in a firmly CBH language (Petersson 2019). Eberhard Otto also regards D as a later text than P (Retsö 2017).

[34] One sentence often stretches over several verses, as in 4.45–46, 4.47–49, 6.10–11, 14.24–25. Extreme protases are found in Deut. 17.2–4, 19.8–9.

[35] There is a relative clause within a relative clause in Deut. 3.24 (Brockelmann 1956, §151); concatenated relative clauses in Deut. 4.46; a relative clause with extended meaning (purpose/result) in Deut. 6.3; rhetorical scribal syntax with repeated relative clauses in Deut. 11.4–6.

[36] The normal purpose clause in Classical Hebrew is *wa* + jussive short *yiqṭol*, but *lə-VN* functions as purpose clause in Deut. 4.36 (לְיַסְּרֶךָּ)—and in 4.38 (לְהוֹרִישׁ) with a more independent function—as do *bə-VN* in Deut. 5.28 (בְּדַבֶּרְכֶם) and *lə* + general VN in Deut. 5.29, 10.12 (לְיִרְאָה). A more independent (close to finite) function of VN is also found in Deut. 6.19 (לַהֲדֹף), 10.12 (5×). A protasis is enlarged with *lə-VN* clauses (instead of with *wa-qaṭal* clauses, as in Gen.–Num.) in Deut. 11.13, 22; 28.1, 12. Several instances of *lə-VN* function as complement clauses in Deut. 26.18–19.

[37] There is, for example, increased use of VNabs for IMP, as in Deut. 5.12, 15.2, 16.2, 24.9, 31.26.

[38] Some new idioms: a tendency to replace הִנֵּה with רְאֵה (Deut. 4.5, 11.26); the new phrase עַד־לֵב הַשָּׁמַיִם (Deut. 4.11); frequent use of a main verb with following infinitive, as in Deut. 5.25 (יֹסְפִים ׀ אֲנַחְנוּ לִשְׁמֹעַ), instead of a serial verb construction with two syntactically equal verbal clauses; a connection formed by *wa-qaṭal* of the copula verb after a frozen request particle (cf. Brockelmann 1956, §9), as in Deut. 5.29: מִי־יִתֵּן וְהָיָה. Conspicuous in Deuteronomy also is the extended use of the verb *pnh* instead of *šwb*, as in Deut. 10.5 (וָאֵפֶן וָאֵרֵד מִן־הָהָר) and 16.7.

[39] In Genesis–Numbers, אֵין expresses the non-existence of the actant in the *qoṭel*. Compare its normalisation as a means of negation before *qoṭel* in Deut. 1.32; 4.12, 22.

[40] In Deut. 3.3, the complex conjunction עַד־בִּלְתִּי occurs before a *qaṭal* clause. In Deut. 4.37, there is the complex וְתַחַת כִּי (consisting of three particles).

[41] This is seen in the protasis אִם־יֹסְפִים׀ אֲנַחְנוּ לִשְׁמֹעַ אֶת־קוֹל יְהוָה אֱלֹהֵינוּ עוֹד in Deut. 5.25, where a long *yiqṭol* would have been expected, and also in a temporal clause after כִּי in Deut. 18.9.

[42] This usage, which Joosten (2012, 241) calls *futurum instans*—a present that is used to represent imminent action—is seen in Deut. 2.4.

[43] In Deut. 11.26 (רְאֵה אָנֹכִי נֹתֵן), *qoṭel* is used as a performative instead of the expected *qaṭal*; but it can be taken as prospective.

[44] In Deut. 3.21 and 4.3, the *qoṭel* with definite article functions as a relative clause after a left-dislocated noun phrase 'your own eyes'.

[45] According to Gzella (2013c, 859) short word-final vowels disappeared in Northwest Semitic at the beginning of the first millennium BCE. Violation of word order is attested in Deuteronomy in 19.3—thus also Joosten (2012, 217 n. 19, 266, 319 n. 19), though he suggests that תָּכִין may be read as a VNabs with imperative meaning from a root *tkn*—and possibly also in Deut. 2.4 (Joosten 2015, 33).

[46] The rule has been misunderstood to mean that *qaṭal* cannot take a clause-initial position. For this, there are many counterexamples (for example, the clause-type *Ø-qaṭal*, in §7.3.3). The word order rule for *qaṭal* means that it should not be allowed to conform to the *wa-qaṭal* clause-type, which has invaded the imperfective semantic field as a replacement for clause-initial *yiqṭol(u)* (see §6.11). An example of a *wa* + *qaṭal* clause in Deuteronomy is found in 2.30 (*ki-qaṭal* + *wa-qaṭal*) in direct speech (Schulz 1900, 36; Joosten 2012, 225; Hornkohl 2014, 260, 289); it is the only *wa-qaṭal* with the function of a *qaṭal* in Deuteronomy (Gropp 1991, 48).

[47] The last three features—clause-initial *yiqṭol(u)*, 'normal' *qaṭal* preceded by *wa*, and a form of *haya* + *qoṭel* as an emerging new analytic tense—represent tendencies that forebode the gradual breakdown of the classical verbal system in LBH (Hornkohl 2016b, 1045, with references).

[48] Joosten (2016, 328) takes the same position, with the exception of the archaic poetry and some possible insertions from later layers of CBH. It is assumed that CBH represents the high literary register in a diglossic situation in the political centre of Jerusalem (Khan 2013c, 16). Of Elitzur's (2018) nine early CBH features, the first three are unconvincing, but the remaining six are probable at least. I agree with Hornkohl (2017, 55) in considering the Tiberian Masoretic tradition "sufficiently clear and authentic to permit meaningful linguistic discussion leading to sound diachronic conclusions." There are "striking patterns of historical development discernible in the case of numerous linguistic features within the MT" (Hornkohl 2017, 57).

[49] This is not to deny that some later additions can be detected; see Joosten (2019).

[50] While "linguistic verification for the alleged postexilic origins of extensive stretches of material in the Pentateuch is strikingly absent," this cannot be stated for many of the psalms (Hornkohl 2017, 75). A diachronic evaluation of the psalms on linguistic grounds is still an unfinished task, which requires a clear picture not only of LBH but also of CBH (a goal still not reached, since fundamental problems with the consecutive tenses have remained unsolved to this day).

[51] *REL* stands for a relative pronoun; *way* indicates that the Tiberian tradition reads the connective *wa-* with a following gemination (see §1.2.5); Ø means that the clause is asyndetic.

[52] *XØ* stands for a verbless clause, and IMP is imperative. A *wa(y)-yiqṭol* clause is registered as *yiqṭol(Ø)* predicate with connective *way*, and (usually) TAM perfective-past (one of the values in field TAM).

[53] The values constitute the actual meanings found in the database.

[54] The number of switch-types in the database is 193, including cases with no switch, such as *yiqṭol(u)/yiqṭol(u)*.

[55] The values of Sem Rel are 87 in number, and are based on the semantic taxonomy presented in Dixon (2009), with some additions typically

found in CBH texts, such as 'Attendant circumstance', 'Background', and '(Editorial) Comment'. This taxonomy will be used in the present book.

[56] The domain is a more precise concept than Longacre's concept of 'discourse types' (Longacre and Bowling 2015, 4–11), which partly coincides with genre; see the criticism by Notarius (2008, 58): it "is based on language use situations, the number of which is not limited."

[57] My parentheses mark the protasis.

[58] In the résumé of Baranowski's investigation, I have retained his abbreviation NVC, instead of my own (*XØ*), which is used in the rest of this book.

[59] Baranowski 2016a, 124: 'And Pạhura [*sic*] **has committed** a great misdeed against me. **He sent** Suteans and **they killed** a šerdanu. And **he brought** 3 men into Egypt.'

[60] Baranowski 2016a, 161: '**Send** me a large archer host so that **it may drive out** the king's enemies from his land and so that all lands **be joined** to the king.'

[61] Baranowski renders the last phrase "we may restore (it)" in italics, but it should be in bold.

[62] Cook (2012a, 268) criticises what are often perceived as the exaggerated conclusions of the concept of (different) discourse types: "there is not a fundamentally different TAM system at work in speech and non-speech deictic contexts." He quotes Comrie (1986, 21): "the meaning of a tense is independent of its discourse function in any particular context" (quoted from Cook 2012a, 274). For this reason, I am at variance with Longacre's position, formulated in this way (Longacre 1992, 178): "The uses of a given tense within a given cluster may differ quite well strikingly from the uses of the same tense within another cluster (discourse type)."

[63] This [a] shifted to [i] before *yod*, an assimilation in the 3m and 3p forms, in the later Tiberian tradition, so the [a] of *wayyiqṭol* must be a preservation of an original [a] vowel of the *wa-* in *wayyiqṭol*, which later

shifted to [i] (Khan 2021a, 332 n. 30, and personal communication). The Tiberian differentiation of the reading of *wa* into two variants, *wə* and *wa* + gemination, is not found in all reading traditions. It is not found in the Samaritan oral tradition of the Pentateuch (Müller 1991, 148; Florentin 2016, 126), and it is not upheld in the second column of the Hexapla or in the Latin transcription of St. Jerome (Müller 1991, 146; Yuditsky 2016, 115). In the Palestinian reading, the ו before a perfective past *yiqṭol(Ø)* is sometimes unmarked, sometimes marked as *wa* (Müller 1991, 147f.); it is unmarked in Ezek. 16.11, 13; Ps. 37.36 (see Yahalom 2016, 167). But the Babylonian tradition reflects the distinction (Müller 1991, 147), and the Karaite Arabic transcriptions generally follow the Tiberian reading (Khan 2016, 158).

[64] Yeivin (1980, 49, 294); Khan (2018a, 341, 344; 2018b; 2020, 534); *pace* Pardee (2012, 294 n. 47), who regards the gemination as "late proto-Hebrew." Pardee's conclusion (2012, 287 n. 12) is: "[i]t appears in any case likely to me that the proto-Hebrew conjunctival element was identical, i.e. */wa/*, and that the doubling of the preformative consonant of the PC is secondary."

[65] Khan (2018a, 345): "there are numerous examples of morphophonemic restructuring to distinguish homophones" in the Samaritan oral tradition. A number of scholars, like Müller (1991, 145, 155), maintain that the gemination (creating a closed syllable) was introduced in order to retain the vowel *a* in the conjunction, but the linguistic force behind this retention remains unexplained. Other scholars explain the gemination as due to a difference in stress: perfective **yáqtub* but imperfective **yaktúbu*, which, when preceded by *wa*, led to a gemination in the perfective form (Lambdin 1971a, 325 n. 16): perfective **wa* + *yáktub* > *wayyiktōb* versus 'imperfective' (thus Lambdin) *wəyiktōb* < **wayaktúbu* (this does not generally exhibit an attested stress contrast, but Lambdin argues that the stress contrast survives intact in some root types, e.g., Iwy *wayyḗšeb/wəyēšḗb*). All theories of different stress patterns are refuted by recent observations by Huehnergard (2019, 53) that word

stress was non-phonemic in Proto-Semitic. Some scholars have adduced Egyptian *ỉw* as a reflex (or loan) of Hebrew *wa* + gemination (Smith 1991, 4). Some *way-yiqṭol* forms evidently exhibit penultimate stress, but, as Revell (1984, 441) argues, "it is difficult to believe that the penultimate stress which they show is a genuine survival from an earlier stage of the language."

[66] Müller (1991, 145; also Revell 1984, 443 n. 25; Smith 1991, 4) rejects with good reason the suggestions by numerous scholars that *wə* and *wa* plus gemination represent historically distinct morphemes. *Wa* + gemination is sometimes derived from an adverbial morpheme **wan*, in which *n* is proposed to be a past tense marker borrowed from Egyptian (Young 1953, 251f.; also Sheehan 1971; Gordon 1983). Schramm (1957–58, 6) derives *wa* plus gemination from "**walyišmor*," where *l* is proposed to be the optative marker found before the jussive in Akkadian and Arabic. The position of Cook (2013, 899f.) is unacceptable and approaches linguistic mysticism: the *wa* in *wayyiqṭol* is "fused with" the verb. Cook's false assumption that *realis* and *irrealis* moods were distinguished by word order drives him to maintain that *wayyiqṭol* is a case of "triggered inversion" of the word order (which he analyses as not verb-initial) "brought about by the peculiar morphology of the enclitic conjunction with gemination (often explained as the remnants of a grammatical word)."

[67] The Tiberian Masoretes felt a need to avoid the homonymic readings of jussive ויקטל and past perfective ויקטל (Kantor 2020, 58f.). Long *yiqṭol* was not involved in this process, since it was (practically) always distinguished by its internal position in the clause. In CBH, there was no need to distinguish short *yiqṭol* from long *yiqṭol*. This does not necessarily hold for later biblical texts, and Khan (2020, 534) keeps this question open. It is quite possible that the Tiberian Masoretes, who also handled the reading of LBH texts, wanted to avoid all homonymic readings, regardless of whether they concerned the short *yiqṭol* or the (mostly homonymic) long ויקטל. "It would seem, then, that the introduction of

gemination was innovated in the reading tradition to preserve the distinct meaning of a past tense that otherwise might have been perceived as non-past/future" (Kantor 2020, 107).

68 Blum (2008, 138) also supposes a Classical Hebrew stage when the two syntagms were homophonous: "eine formale Differenzierung zwischen sog. *Waw copulativum* und *Waw consecutivum* sprachgeschichtlich für die alttestamentliche Zeit noch gar nicht anzunehmen ist" and "[g]erade unter der Voraussetzung eines formal nicht differenzierten *wayiqṭol* bewährt sich die angenommene Systematik: ein Ausdruck wie *wyktbw* kan darin entweder „und sie schrieben" oder „und sie sollen schreiben / auf dass sie schreiben" bezeichnen;" similarly Müller (1994, 166). In CBH (in contradistinction to archaic poetry), the realis *yiqṭol(Ø)* was used only after *wa* (a phrase that represents a retention). In other positions, it had been replaced by the *qaṭal* morpheme. This means that a *Ø-yiqṭol(Ø)* was unambiguous as jussive in CBH. The homophony occurred only after *wa*.

69 This is confirmed by the investigation of the transcriptions of the Secunda and Jerome by Kantor (2020, 99f., 124): in the First Temple period "the conjunction *waw* was ***pronounced identically*** before a preterite *yiqṭol* and non-preterite *yiqṭol* form, probably with the original etymological */a/ vowel" (Kantor's emphasis).

70 This is also the position of Gropp (1991, 47f.); Ben-Ḥayyim (2000, 171); Yuditsky (2017, 232); Kantor (2020, 65f., 95). For domain, see §1.2.4 and Cohen (2014). Revell (1984, 444) arrives at a similar time period for the differentiation. Thus also Tropper (1996, 636), although he is less specific concerning the age of the differentiation, which he describes as "zwischen kopulativem und 'konversivem' *Waw*."

71 This is the conclusion also of Kantor (2020, 100, §6.2). Hornkohl (2019, 556): "The signature gemination of its verbal prefix, i.e. *wayyiqṭol*, which distinguishes it from the volitional-final *we*PC, i.e., *weyiqṭol*, may well reflect a secondary, semantically driven development." Thus also Tropper (1998, 165 n. 41); Pardee (2012, 287 n. 12). This is

suggested by Khan (2013a, 43 n. 31), though his terminology implies that the verb form after the *wə* is an 'imperfect' (similarly Tropper 1996, 636), a clause-type (*wa-yiqṭol(u)*) that is rarely found in CBH. Khan (2013a, 43 n. 31) suggests an Aramaic influence: "One may perhaps identify this marking of *dagesh* to express a semantic distinction in its occurrence in the prefixes of imperfect consecutive verb forms to distinguish them from imperfect forms with conjunctive *waw*."

[72] Müller (1991, 146, 148, 156; 1994, 166) agrees with Khan that the gemination is a Masoretic feature, but regards it a case of atavism (restitution) of an archaic verbal usage. Revell (1984, 444) argues that the gemination after *wa* was introduced "near the end of the biblical period, when the use of the *waw* consecutive imperfect began to be abandoned." He does not, however, discuss the role of the reading tradition on this point (cf. Smith 1991, 4).

[73] Rainey (1986, 6) gives additional nice examples of the jussive/perfective distinction of the old *yiqṭol(Ø)* in CBH.

[74] Revell (1984, 444) concludes that the function of *wa* + gemination is not to distinguish short forms (< **yaqtul*) from long forms (< **yaqtulu*), but to mark the specific "*waw* consecutive use," that is, to clearly mark the past narrative use as against the jussive (which has the 'normal' form of the conjunction). Baranowski (2016b, 12f.) also discusses the retention of *wa* in *wayyiqṭol* as a device to mark off the preterite meaning of the syntagm, but he is unsure about the Masoretic origin of the doubling. Baranowski on this point quotes Loprieno (1980, 10) "that *wayyaqom* was an old morphological formation, specialized in Hebrew in a new function unknown before." Against this we must object that the function of indicative '*wayaqom*' is neither new nor unknown, but old and in continued use in Biblical Hebrew, and that the jussive *wa-yiqṭol(Ø)* (Masoretic *wə-yiqṭol*) is as old as the 'preterite' *wa-yiqṭol(Ø)* (Masoretic *wayyiqṭol*). They represent the same verbal grammatical morpheme.

[75] For a different view of *w-yqtl* in the Tel Dan and Zakkūr inscriptions, see Gzella (2013c, 859; 2018, 26 n. 17).

[76] In comparative Semitic discussions, a more general terminology is necessary: *yaqtul*, *wa-yaqtul* (indicative or jussive), *yaqtulu*, *qatal*, *wa-qatal*.

[77] I disregard that some scholars prefer to make use of a term other than 'consecutive', for example 'conversive', 'conservative', 'energic', etc. 'Consecutive' is, however, the term used in a majority of the Biblical Hebrew grammars.

[78] For the concept of clause-type, see Talstra (2013).

[79] This tenet was formulated with inspiration from Buth (1995) and Hornkohl (2018, 48ff.). In Tenet 1*, boldface ***wa*** indicates 'consecutive *waw*', '*V*' is a finite verb and '*X*' is any non-verbal clausal constituent except negation. The terminology with *X* used before a verb form is taken from Niccacci (1990). I have concluded from my material that *wa-lō-qaṭal* creates no break in the consecution; it takes part in the storyline (see §7.12). The '*X*' before the verb may also be a conjunction (other than *wa*), such as *kī* or *ʿal-kēn*. Givón (1977), in spite of a fundamental mistake in his identification of *wa(y)-yiqṭol* as "IMPERFECT" (and thus, in his view, *in se* an expression of discourse-pragmatic continuity), and in spite of his disregarding the role of *wa* in this continuity—but possibly because he speaks of just "the conjunction va̲- 'and'" (Givón 1977, 190, 199)—arrives at a conclusion not too far from the position in the present book, i.e., the role of SV syntax being a signal of topic shifting (Givón 1977, 240). Topic continuity correlates with VS syntax (Givón 1977, 210). Givón's (1977, 236, 202) statistics on Genesis show that his focus on the position of the subject (only) is unwarranted: object topicalisation is found in 10.6%, subject topicalisation in 11.6% of the cases when the continuity is broken. Givón (1977, 240) is right in his conclusion that there was a gradual word order shift to SV in LBH,

and this shift was completed with the replacement of *wa(y)-yiqṭol* by *qaṭal* as the dominant narrative past verbal morpheme.

[80] For a clause linking approach, see Isaksson (2014a; 2015a; 2015b; 2017; 2021; forthcoming).

[81] This is known as the 'bottom-up' approach. For a survey of research, see Talstra (2013); Hornkohl (2018). The epoch-making work by Alviero Niccacci (1990; Italian version 1986) must be mentioned. This book became an eye-opener for many biblical scholars in the 1990s. In spite of the achievements in all those books surveyed by Talstra (2013), including those by Niccacci, I dearly miss a comparative Semitic perspective and a notion of grammaticalisation (and with it a diachronic approach; see §1.2.1). This perspective is missing even in the relatively recent book by Longacre and Bowling (2015).

[82] "The *clause* ('sentence') is the basic information processing unit in human discourse. A word may have 'meaning', but only the proposition—grammaticalised as clause—carries information. Human discourse, further, is *multipropositional*. Within it, chains of clauses are combined into larger thematic units which one may call *thematic paragraphs*" (Givón 1983, 7). For a presentation of the concept of clause in a Biblical Hebrew context, see Isaksson (2015a, 173–75).

[83] *Wa(y)-yiqṭol* does not normally introduce background, but may take part in a background complex introduced by, e.g., a *qaṭal* clause (see §2.3.3).

[84] For Table 4, see Cook (2012a, 287f.); also Hopper (1979, 214–16, 220), and Hopper and Thompson (1980, 252f., 264, 277).

[85] I disagree with Heimerdinger (1999, 223–25), who works with an understanding of foreground that is less fruitful for CBH texts (see Cook 2012a, 295 n. 12). Heimerdinger (1999, 223) proposes that the "first foregrounding device consists in the use of norms and standards people assume will be obeyed in communication." I also disagree with the ideas about foreground (based on schema theory) presented in Cotrozzi

(2010). For Cotrozzi (2010, 6, 9, 50), a key factor in foregrounding is 'deviance from a norm': "foregrounded material, then, can be determined simply by setting the specific realization of a knowledge structure underlying a passage against its default."

[86] The idea seems to have come up as early as the tenth century C.E. (Van de Sande 2008, 27 n. 6; Cook 2012a, 83).

[87] Wilhelm Gesenius in the first 13 editions of his Hebrew grammar (1813–42).

[88] For a list of features in the medieval system of 'inversive tenses' that remained unexplained, see Van de Sande (2008, 54).

[89] See Van de Sande (2008, 55 n. 2) concerning the position of McFall himself (1982, vii). A defender of the conversive *waw* and a temporal interpretation of the verb forms is Blake (1951). Joosten's basic assumption in this instance is that *wa-qaṭal* and *wa(y)-yiqṭol* (with *waw* included in the syntagms) are regarded as 'verbal forms' (and 'tenses'); the special *wa* before the two verbal forms he calls '*waw* conservative' (Joosten 2012, 15). This term is misleading as regards *wa-qaṭal*, in which practically nothing of the *qaṭal* semantics is preserved (Isaksson forthcoming, and §6 in this book).

[90] For a principal discussion on this topic, see Isaksson (2015c).

[91] "The impact of historical-comparative investigations on the understanding of the BH *qatal* is no less dramatic" (Cook 2012a, 119). it is now crystal clear that the *qaṭal* developed from the predicative use of a verbal adjective *qatil* / *qatul*. And an *active* dynamic pattern *qatal* is attested at Ebla (thus Cook 2012a, 119).

[92] For example, the Tel Dan inscription (Cook 2012a, 94, 99f., 104).

[93] This is the strongest position, supported also by Kogan (2015). But it remains a mystery that the old imperfective formation *yaqattal* left seemingly no traces in Central Semitic (see Cook 2012a, 108).

[94] "[T]he consecutive *waw* links two clauses and delimits the boundary between them;" and "it is the syntax and not *waw* which 'converts'" (Smith 1991, 14).

[95] See, however, Dahl (1985) and the early article Bybee and Dahl (1989).

[96] Unfortunately, Cook forgot this methodological principle when he worked out his own word order hypothesis for Biblical Hebrew (see below).

[97] See further Garr and Fassberg (2016). It is strange that Cook (2012a) himself does not sort his own text samples according to this diachronic principle.

[98] Though I agree with Cook that Classical Hebrew is aspect-prominent, this is not a crucial question in the present book, since the concept of gram permits verb forms to show both temporal and aspectual meanings. For me, the verbal grammatical morpheme (gram) is the central concept for understanding the entities of the verbal system. Tenses and aspects are semantic descriptions of the meanings encountered in grams.

[99] The theory fails in texts close to LBH when *wa-qaṭal* is used as a narrative clause-type for past time, as in 2 Kgs 18.3–4, where *wa-qaṭal* is clearly realis; this is an example that Cook himself adduces without observing the problem with his word order theory (Cook 2012a, 282).

[100] Cook often calls *wa(y)-yiqṭol* a verb ("the narrative verb," Cook 2012a, 297).

[101] Quoting DeCaen, Cook suggests that there is an *underspecified subject* between the conjunction and the verb: "an 'underspecified' function word assimilated between the conjunction and the agreement affix (i.e., *wa-y-yiqtol*)" (Cook 2012a, 236, 258).

[102] On another page, Cook writes that "the *wa*C- prefix remains unanswered" (Cook 2012a, 120, 259) and intimates that an underspecified function word is hidden between the *wa-* and the *yiqṭol*. He tries to

prove that *wa(y)-yiqṭol* was perceived by the natives as SV word order (and thus realis). With this assumption, it is not enough just to assume a "function word" between *wa* and *yiqṭol* for his hypothesis to remain true: the function word must specifically represent the *subject* in order to create the SV word order, and this may be at the same time as an explicit subject is positioned after the verb in the same clause. Cook (2012a, 260) also discusses the archaic example 2 Sam. 22.16, with an asyndetic "archaic past form." In a case like this, Archaic Hebrew exhibits a clear Ø-VS (short *yiqṭol*) word order with explicit following subject, which according to Cook must be irrealis (at least if CBH). In the case of 2 Sam. 22.16, it is impossible to assume an "underspecified function word" before the verb.

[103] Cook's terminology concerning 'irrealis *yiqṭol*' is ambiguous and misleading: the term is used for irrealis meanings of long *yiqṭol* and in several cases also for jussive short *yiqṭol* (Exod. 9.13; Cook 2012a, 254).

[104] With Joosten's (2012, 264) wording: "WEQATAL incorporates a conjunction."

[105] The inconsistency of the synchronic state of Classical Hebrew also includes the identification of (long) *yiqṭol* and *wa-qaṭal* as 'allomorphs', because "one should disregard the etymology of the forms" (Joosten 2012, 261).

[106] Cook (2014, 380) describes Joosten's terminology as "a faulty, underdeveloped, or outdated theory."

[107] It is odd to encounter a formulation such as "WAYYIQTOL occurring in clause-initial position when the clause begins with the copula" (Joosten 2012, 41). Does Joosten not hold that *wayyiqṭol* always begins with "the copula"?

[108] A prototypical meaning of an imperfective formation, describing repeated actions in the past, is explained by Joosten (2012, 32) as an irrealis feature of *yiqṭol* and *wa-qaṭal*, though this contradicts his definition of *realis* "that a process really did come about." Joosten's (2012,

32f.) argument that such actions just "express possible actions... [not] as having come about, but as liable to happen" is simply incomprehensible. Joosten's (2012, 40) argument about the irrealis nature of *yiqṭol* and *wa-qaṭal* is a consequence of his assumption that the verbal forms in Hebrew must belong to either of two mutually exclusive *systems* of verb forms: an indicative and a modal system. This assumption is unfounded. Joosten (2012, 62) goes so far as to maintain that all questions are in some way modal ("There is something inherently modal about questions"), and he tries to prove that the relevance case of the progressive (long) *yiqṭol* in Gen. 37.15 must be modal anyway. A brief review of the development of imperfective grams shows that Joosten's efforts on this point are unwarranted (Bybee et al. 1994, ch. 5). Now, if Joosten (2012, 76) recognises that the progressive function was "formerly expressed by the long form of the prefix conjugation (*yaqtulu*, corresponding to biblical Hebrew YIQTOL)," why not reckon with a period of coexistence between the active participle and this long *yiqṭol*, even if this would contradict his thesis of its consistently modal nature? "The historical perspective explains the fact that YIQTOL expresses the real present in a number of well-defined syntactic environments, notably in questions" (Joosten 2012, 78). So it is not, after all, necessary to declare that questions are inherently modal. The real present meaning of long *yiqṭol* is retained in some syntactic environments of CBH, as is the case also in an Aramaic inscription (KAI^5 312 I:4). Examples of this in CBH: Gen. 2.6 (past progressive); 32.18 (question); 32.30 (question); 37.15 (question); 42.1 (question); 48.17 (past progressive); Exod. 17.2 (question); Num. 23.9 (possibly archaic); 23.9 (relative clause); Deut. 3.28 (relative clause); Judg. 17.9 (question); 19.17 (question); and, outside the corpus, 1 Sam. 1.10 (past progressive). Joosten (2012, 78) maintains that such uses are residual functions, and that "YIQTOL has become a modal form in biblical Hebrew." The syntagm *hinnē-yiqṭol(u)* is attested in non-archaic poetry with real present meaning, but since this meaning cannot be classified as "prospective, iterative, modal" (all meanings declared modal by Joosten), this fact is mentioned by Joosten (2012, 102) as a curiosity.

[109] Khan has not written exactly this, but as far as I can see it is an inevitable conclusion from his argumentation.

[110] *Pace* Khan (2021a), I propose that *wa(y)-yiqṭol* is not a construction (Isaksson forthcoming, n. 21). Both *wa-qaṭal* and *wa(y)-yiqṭol* are clause-types (Isaksson 2021, 218f.), but only *wa-qaṭal* is a construction. The meanings of *wa(y)-yiqṭol* can be deduced from its component parts: *wa*, which is a normal Semitic connective, and the short 'preterite' *yiqṭol*, which is inherited from Proto-Semitic (Baranowski 2016b; Isaksson 2021).

[111] A forerunner to this idea is found in Smith (1991, 8): "It would appear that the future uses of **qātal* in BH conditional sentences were extended to **qātal* in independent clauses in the form of the 'converted perfect'." For a critical evaluation of Khan (2021a), see Isaksson (forthcoming).

2. THE CONJUNCTION *WA* IN CBH

2.1. PS **Wa* and the Concept of Natural Language Connective

Chaining was a central feature of Early Semitic syntax, and in this syntax the conjunction *wa* played a fundamental role (Cohen 2014, 234; Baranowski 2016a, 190). *Wa* was monosyllabic and proclitic (Huehnergard 2008, 241f.; Kogan 2014, 42, 53). This proclitic *wa* is used in all Semitic languages as a connective element between clauses (and thus as a conjunction).

It is a thesis of this book that the PS **wa* was a natural language connective in the sense described by Van Dijk (1977, 58).[1] As a natural language connective, *wa* should *not* be expected to fulfil de Morgan's law:[2]

$$\sim(P \;\&\; Q) = \sim P \vee \sim Q$$

Instead, the meaning of *wa* was ambiguous and pragmatically determined (Brongers 1978, 273; Posner 1980, 186). As clause-linking connective, this *wa* could express readings such as '(and) at the same time', '(and) there', '(and) therefore', '(and) then', '(and) so', '[if]… then'. A comparison with the English connective *and*, the basic meaning of which is rich and asymmetric, provides a good illustration (Schiffrin 1986, 45, emphasis added):[3]

(a) Annie is in the kitchen **and** (there) she is making doughnuts. [location]

(b) Annie fell into a deep sleep **and** (during this time) her facial color returned. [simultaneity]

 https://doi.org/10.11647/OBP.0414.02

(c) The window was open **and** (coming from it) there was a draught. [source]
(d) Peter married Annie **and** (after that) she had a baby. [temporal succession]
(e) Paul pounded on the stone **and** (thereby) he shattered it. [cause]
(f) Give me your picture **and** I'll give you mine. (If you give me your picture, I'll give you mine.) [conditionality]
(g) The number 5 is a prime number **and** (therefore) it is divisible only by 1 and itself. [conclusion]

These more specific meanings were primarily derived from the context (which includes the whole paragraph; Garr 1998, lxxii–lxxiii).[4] A terminology such as 'locative *and*', or 'sequential *and*', based on one of the examples above, would be misleading. There is only one *and*.

As a natural language conjunction, *wa* sets a clause in a certain relation to a previous clause. Pattern:

(*wa*)-Clause_1 *wa*-Clause_2

The pattern illustrates the simplest linking of two clauses (cf. §1.2.7).[5] Clause_2 is *linked* to Clause_1.[6] The conjunction *wa* puts Clause_2 in a *relation* to Clause_1. The full perceived meaning of *wa* is the semantic relation between the two clauses, and the order of the clauses is fundamental. It is Clause_2 that *relates to* Clause_1:

If the action or state described in Clause_2 follows temporally after the action or state in Clause_1 the reader may perceive that *wa* is sequential (temporal succession), or even consequential.[7]

If the action or state described in $Clause_2$ is a consequence of the action or state in $Clause_1$ the reader may perceive that *wa* is consequential (*therefore*; *and so*).[8]

If the action or state described in $Clause_2$ explains something in $Clause_1$ the reader may perceive that *wa* is 'epexegetic' or 'explanative'.

If the action or state described in $Clause_2$ is concomitant with the action or state in $Clause_1$ the reader may perceive that *wa* is circumstantial or elaborative or summational.

The pragmatic meaning of *wa* is a relation: how $Clause_2$ relates to $Clause_1$. The nature of this relation is of primary importance for understanding a text. If a reader perceives that there are several different *wa*, this only proves that there are many different clausal relations between clauses connected by (one and the same) *wa*. It is impossible to prove that, for example, a 'consecutive *waw*' in CBH in itself has any deviating meanings: "these readings are no different from those of the conjunctive *waw* attached to any other word in Hebrew" (Garr 1998, lxxxvi).[9]

2.2. Some Reflexes of PS **Wa* in Semitic Languages

2.2.1. PS **Wa* in Akkadian

According to Kienast, the meaning of *wa* in Akkadian (*u* < **wa*) was "und ausserdem" (Kienast 2001, 395, 438; Kogan 2014, 42), but, for the most ancient stages of Akkadian, this is a simplification. The connective *wa* was used in early Sargonic Akkadian and at that time could express both an additive meaning ('and also') and a sequential meaning ('and then'). At this early stage, word order was still VSO and in the unmarked word order the (always proclitic) *wa* was attached directly to the verbal predicate (*wa*-verb), while other clausal constituents like subject, object, and adverbial expressions followed the verb.[10] In narrative or reports of historical events, the clauses were asyndetic (Ø) or connected by *wa* (*ù*). The following example in (1) is from a Sargonic inscription:

(1) URU^{ki} UNUG^{ki} SAG.GIŠ.RA ***ù*** BÀD-*śu* Ì.GUL.GUL **Ø** *in* ^{KASKAL}ŠUDUL UNUG[^{ki} *iš*$_{11}$*-ar* ***ù*** *lugal-z*]*ag-*⸢*ge*⸣*-si* [LU]GAL [UN]UG^{ki} *in* ^{KASKAL}ŠUDUL ŠU.DU$_{8}$.A **Ø** *in* SI.GAR-*rìm a-na* KÁ ^{d}*en-líl u-ru-uś*

'He conquered the city of Uruk **and** destroyed its walls. **Ø** [He was victorious] over Uruk in battle [**and**] captured Lugalzagesi, king of Uruk, in battle. **Ø** He led him in a neck stock to the gate of Enlil.' (Kogan 2014, 43, his emphasis)

According to Kogan (2014, 51f.), "many examples of *ù* in the inscriptions of Sargon and Rīmuš fully satisfy the idea of consecution both temporally and logically," as in (2):

(2) *in* ^{KASKAL}ŠUDUL URÍM^{ki} *iš*$_{11}$*-ar* ***ù*** URU^{ki} SAG.GIŠ.RA ***ù*** BÀD.*śu* ì.GUL.GUL

'He was victorious over Ur in battle, **and** (*then, as a consequence of this victory*) he conquered the city, **and** (*then, as a consequence of this conquest*) he destroyed its walls.' (Kogan 2014, 43, his emphasis)

When both *-ma* and *ù* are used in the same early Akkadian texts, the *ù* tends to become a minority connective marker which introduces an additive and sometimes alternative event, as in the Narām-Su'en inscriptions:

(3) [*in kiš*^{ki}] ⸢*ip-ḫur*⸣*-kiš śar-ru*$_{14}$*-súm i-śî-*⸢*ù*⸣ ***ù*** *in* UNUG^{ki} *amar-giri*$_{16}$ *śar-ru*$_{14}$*-súm-ma i-śî-*⸢*ù*

'[In Kiš] they elevated Ipḫur-Kiš to kingship, **and** (*also*) in Uruk they elevated Amar-Giri likewise to kingship.' (Kogan 2014, 52, his emphasis)

In what seems to be a Proto-Semitic syntactic feature, an adverbial subordinate clause[11] may be followed by a *wa*-clause (syndesis) with the temporal or logical meaning 'und dann',[12] especially when the subordinate clause expresses a condition or a temporal relation. An example from early Akkadian, in a Sargonic royal inscription, is (4), where I also supply the translation by Gelb and Kienast:[13]

(4) *iś-tum* ^{KASKAL}ŠUDUL.^{KASKAL}ŠUDUL *śú-nu-ti iš*$_{11}$*-ar-ru* ***ù śar-rí-śu-nu*** 3 *i-ik-mi-ma maḫ-rí-iś* ^{d}*en-líl u-śa-rí-ib in u-mi-śu li-pi*$_{5}$*-it-ì-li* DUMU-*śu* ÉNSI *már-da*^{ki} É ^{d}*lugal-már-da*^{ki} *in már-da*^{ki} *ib-ni*

'After he was victorious in those battles, **he captured** their three kings and brought them before Enlil. At that time, Lipit-ilī, his son, governor of Marad, built the temple of Lugalmarda at Marad.' (Frayne 1993, 112; quoted by Kogan 2014, 54, my emphasis)

'Nachdem er diese Schlachten siegreich bestanden hatte, **da** hat er ihrer drei Könige gefangen genommen und vor Enlil hingeführt. Damals hat Lipitilī, sein Sohn, der Statthalter von Marda, den Tempel des Lugalmarda in Marda gebaut.' (Gelb and Kienast 1990, 102f.)

This *wa* has remained in use in all West Semitic languages.

2.2.2. PS **Wa* in Gəʿəz

In Gəʿəz, *wa* is the most general connecting particle. It can connect clauses "even in those cases in which other languages, more accurate in their expression of logical relations, make use of other uniting-words or particles" (Dillmann 1907, 522; Butts 2019, 134). An example is:

(5) *wä-ʔämmä kon-ä ʕəlät-ä täwäld-ä herodəs zäfän-ät wälätt-ä herodəyada bä-maʔkäl-omu* ***wä****-ʔäddäm-ät-o lä-herodəs* [7]***wä****-mäḥäl-ä l-ati yä-häb-a zä-säʔäl-ät-o*

'When it was the day on which Herod was born, the daughter of Herodias danced among them, **and** she pleased Herod. [7](Herod) swore to her to give her whatever she asked him.' (Butts 2019, 139–40; Mt. 14.6–7)

In (5), the first *wa*-clause (***wä****-ʔäddäm-ät-o* 'and she pleased') is simultaneous with the previous clause in the narrative. The second *wa*-clause, however, describes an action that is temporally successive ('and he swore') in relation to the previous clause ('and she pleased').

2.2.3. PS **Wa* in Modern South Arabian

Jibbali is a MSA language in Oman. Its most common conjunction is *b-*, which derives from an earlier **w-* (a reflex of PS **wa*; Rubin 2014, §12.1.1). It is often followed by an epenthetic vowel *ə*, as in (6) and (7) (both from Rubin 2014, 302, my emphasis):

(6) ***bə***-*ẑēṭ ɛrḥīt* ***bə***-*ẑīṭə́s ɛūt* ***bə***-*ḳéré xaṭɔ́ḳɛ́s.* ***bə***-*zīs xáṭɔ́ḳ mənhūm* ***bə***-*šfɔ́ḳ bes*

'**and** he took the pretty one, **and** he took her to the house **and** hid her clothes. **And** he gave her some (other) clothes **and** married her'

(7) *he bek śēʿak* ***bə***-*šfáḥk ðɛ́nu*

'I am already full, **and** I have this leftover'

The Jibbali samples show the conjunction *b*- linking clauses with the meanings of temporal succession in past time narrative (first sample), and simultaneity (second sample) respectively. In the narrative sample, *b*- is prefixed to all clauses.

In the **Mehri** language of Oman, the common coordinating particle is *w(ə)*, with the free variant *u* < **əw* (Rubin 2010a, 235). As a connective it may have a variety of meanings. In the first example below, the second clause is simultaneous with the action or state described in the first clause (all Mehri examples are from Rubin 2010a, 236, my emphasis):

(8) *ṣōr* ***u*** *ġəlōk b-aġəggēn*

'he stood **and** looked at the boy' (simultaneity)

In another example, the linking with *wə* describes an action that is temporally successive in relation to the first clause:

(9) *yəġərəbay* ***wə***-*yabrə́ḳa təwalyɛ*

'he recognized me **and** ran to me' (temporal succession)

The connective *wə* can also link a clause that describes a complementary action or state which is indifferent to the temporal relation between the clauses:

(10) *ʾagbək bīs* ***wə****-sē ʾagəbōt bay*

‘I fell in love with her, **and** she fell in love with me’ (complementary action)

This linking in (10) can by classified as unordered addition or temporal succession (Dixon 2009, 26).

But *w(ə)* is also the suitable connective in narration:

(11) *śxəwəllūt bərk alang* ***w****-aġayg ḳəfūd* ***wə****-wkūb əl-ḥōkəm* ***wə****-śītəm ləhān šəh*

‘she stayed in the launch, **and** the man got out **and** went to the ruler(’s house) **and** bought all that he had’ (temporal succession)

The *wə* can also connect a focal clause after a temporal clause:

(12) *tɛ̄ ḏ̣ār bayr,* ***wə****-hərbā moh*

‘then (when they were) at the well, they drew water’ (focal clause after temporal clause)

Similar narrative chains as in Jibbali and Mehri are found in **Soqotri**, a conservative MSA language. The normal form of the conjunction is a proclitic *wa*, as in (13):

(13) *báˁad-aḷ ˁəmɛ́ro ˁáže dɛ́nˁa ḷətóˁos ˁággi* ***wa****-zaˁáyo díˀyhi ḥídho* ***wa****-žiréme* ***wa****-ṭahɛ́ro*

‘After the woman said this, the men killed her, took their roots and their berries **and** went off.’ (Naumkin et al. 2014, 102, text 4:11)

A *wa*-clause in Soqotri can also express the reason for the previous clause(s), as in (14):

(14) *wa-ˀəḳdémo ˁəy ˁáġgi wa-fizóˁo* ***wa***-*ˀaḷ-bíto ífuḷ l'išgóˀo*

'The two men looked at him and became scared, **for** they did not know what to do.' (Naumkin et al. 2014, 220, text 12:12)

2.2.4. PS **Wa* in Ancient (South) Arabian

In Ancient South Arabian also, *w- 'und'* is the most frequent conjunction (Stein 2013, §9.4.1). In Middle Sabaic, the typical narrative chain is built up by an initial *qatal* clause followed by several infinitive clauses preceded by *w*, as in (15):

(15) *¹šrḥʿṯt / yʾmn̊ / bn / ḏrnḥ / ʾbʿl / bytn / ʾḥrm / ʾqwl / šʿbn / ḏmr / ²ʾrbʿw / qšmm / brʾ /* ***whwṯr*** */* ***whqšbn*** */* ***whšqrn*** */* ***wṯwbn*** */ mṣnʿthmw ³/ tʿrmn / kl / ʾbythw / wmḥfdthw / wgnʾhw / wkryfyhw…*

'¹ŠRḤ-ʿṮT YʾMN of (the family) ḏū-RNḤ, owners of the house ʾḤRM, leaders of the tribe ḎMR, ²of a fraction of QŠMM, has built **and** founded **and** restored **and** finished **and** repaired their fortress ³TʿRMN, all its houses and its tower and its wall and its cisterns,…' (Stein 2012, B.2.3; my translation and emphasis)

The linking pattern in (15) is *S.noun-qatal + w-VN + w-VN + w-VN + w-VN* (Multhoff 2019, 336). In Old Sabaic, the narrative chain is typically constructed by clauses with finite verbal predicates. An example is found in the inscription RÉS 3945 from the early seventh century BC:

(16) [3]...***w**ywm / mḫḏ / sʾdm / **w**wfṭ / nqbtm / wkl / ʾhgr / mʿfrn / **w**hbʿl / ẓbr / wẓlmm / wʾrwy / **w**wfṭ / kl / ʾhgrhmw / **w**qtlhmw / šlṯt / ʾlf[m] # ʾ ʾ ʾ # **w**sbyhmw / ṯmnyt / ʾlfm # ʾ ʾ ʾ ʾ ʾ ʾ ʾ ʾ # **w**hṯny / ślʾhmw / **w**bḍʿ / bʿlhmw / bʿm / ślʾhmw / bqrm / wsfrtm ḏy(h)bw bʿm [4]śʾhmw*[14]

'[3]...**and** on the day when[15] he conquered SʾDM **and** burnt down NQBTM and all cities of MʿFRN, **and** seized (the territories of) ẒBR and ẒLMM and ʾRWY, **and** burnt down all their cities, **and** killed of them three thousand (3000), **and** captured of them eight thousand (8000), **and** doubled their tribute, **and** imposed on them as tribute, together with their (former) tribute, cattle and other amounts which they would have to give together with [4]their (former) tribute'[16] (Stein 2012, E.1.5, my emphasis)

The linking pattern in (16) is *ADV-qatal* + *w-qatal* + *w-qatal* + *w-qatal* + *w-qatal* + *w-qatal* + *w-qatal* + *w-qatal*, where ADV is a noun (*ywm*) in the construct state.

The *w-* may also connect two modal propositions, which is shown in a wooden stick with a Sabaic letter from the third century C.E. (Stein 2015, 198f.):

(17) ***w**-l-ʿbd-k / slymm / bn / ġṭyfm / l-thḥywnn / **w**-ʿṯtr / w-ʾlmqh / l-yhṣbḥnn / l-kmw / nʿmtm / **w**-[2]l-yšmnn / wfy-kmw / w-b-ḏt / wfym / ʿbr-n-kmw / f-hʿsm / ʿbd-k / ḥmd / w-ʿbr-n-hw / wfym*

'Von Deinem Diener Sulaymum aus (der Sippe) Ġuṭayfum seid gegrüßt! (Die Götter) ʿAṯtar und ʾAlmaqah mögen Euch Glück leuchten lassen, **und** sie mögen Euer Wohlergehen aufrichten. Dafür, daß Wohlergehen von Euch (berichtet wurde), hat Dein Diener (d.h. Sulaymum) vielfach gedankt.

Von ihm (wurde ebenfalls) Wohlergehen (berichtet).' (Stein 2015, L4/1f.; my emphasis)

In (17), three jussive clauses with the proclitic precative particle *l* (*li*) are connected by the conjunction *w*. The linking pattern is ***w**-PrP-l-yaqtul* + ***w**-S.noun-l-yaqtul* + ***w**-l-yaqtul*. The clauses have seemingly equal status. As can be seen, it is possible to place a clausal constituent before the jussive for focusing.

2.2.5. PS **Wa* in Classical Arabic

Classical Arabic has *wa*, but also the conjunction *fa*, which has a more specific sequential (temporal or logical) meaning.[17] As a result, *wa* in Arabic is more confined to non-sequential meanings, for example elaboration. After both conjunctions, Classical Arabic could use the new West Semitic perfective *qatala* in affirmative clauses in narration (cf. Isaksson 2009, 67):

(18) *fa-faʿala ḏālika* ***wa**-qatala Ǧuzihr-a* ***wa**-ʾaḫaḏa tāǧ-a-hu* ***wa**-kataba ʾilā ʾArdawān-a l-Bahlawiyy-i…*

'And this he did. He killed Ǧuzihr, seized his crown, **and** wrote to Ardawān the Pahlawī…' (Ṭab. I, 816:1)

The *wa* in Classical Arabic can also introduce a clause that is circumstantial in relation to the preceding clause, as in (25):

(19) *halaka ʾAbū ʾUmāmata* ***wa**-l-masǧidu yubnā*

'Abū Umama died **while** the mosque was being built' (Isḥ. 346, 6, quoted from Reckendorf 1921, §221.2)

The Classical Arabic *wa* may also function as a discourse marker (without being a clausal connective), signalling a certain connection to the preceding clauses. In the following example, *wa* introduces direct speech that is a reply to a previous question within the meta-context of the textual tradition, but this *wa* does not signal a linking between clauses in the text (cf. Miller 1999, 168):[18]

(20) *qāla yā Qaysu mā yaqūlu hāḏā qāla* ***wa****-mā yaqūlu*

'He said: "O Qays, what does he say!" Then he said: "**And** what does he say then?"' (Ṭab., 1857, 2, quoted from Reckendorf 1895–98, §156; my transcription, translation and emphasis)

A *wa* in Classical Arabic may also link a clause that is the result of the action or state in the preceding clause. An example is (21):

(21) *qad wallāhi rābanī ʾamru hāḏā l-ġulāmi* ***wa****-lā ʾāminuhu*

'The behaviour of this youngster has seemed to me confused, **and** I do not trust him' (Ḥam. 40, 11, quoted from Reckendorf 1895–98, 449; my translation and emphasis)

With focusing of two different subjects, a *wa*-clause can describe a contrast to the action or state in the preceding clause, as in (22):

(22) *allāhu yaʿlamu* ***wa****-ʾantum lā taʿlamūna*

'Allah knows, **but** you do not know.' (Qur. 2:212, quoted from Reckendorf 1895–98, 450; my transcription, translation, and emphasis)

The conjunction *wa* can also introduce a clause that expresses an elaboration or interpretation of the preceding clause, as in (23):

(23) *qālū wallāhi mā ʿarafnāhu* ***wa****-ṣadaqū*

'They said: By God, we did not recognize him, **and** (by that) they told the truth.' (Isḥ. 577, 17, quoted from Reckendorf 1895–98, 454; my transcription, translation, and emphasis)

2.2.6. PS **Wa* in Ugaritic

In Ugaritic, the conjunction *w* /*wa*/ is the most prominent linking connective. It connects "Wörtern, Wortgruppen, Sätzen und ganzen Textteilen" (Tropper 2012, §§83.11, 96.1). As in the Hebrew poetry, there are many examples of a so-called 'synonymous parallelism' in the Ugaritic poetry:[19]

(24) *mġy . ḥrn . l bth .* ***w*** */ yštql . l ḥẓrh .*

'Ḥôrānu ging zu seinem Haus, er begab sich zu seinem Hof' (KTU[3] 1.100:67–68, my emphasis; Tropper 2012, §83.113b)

The *wa* may also introduce a clause that describes the reason for the action or state in the preceding clause:

(25) *b ḥrn . pnm . trġn {w} .* ***w*** *tṯkl / bnwth*

'Hôrānus Gesicht wurde verstört/traurig, denn sie war daran, ihre Nachkommenschaft zu verlieren' (KTU[3] 1.100:61–62, my emphasis; Tropper 2012, §83.113f.)

A purpose clause may be introduced by *wa*, as in (26):

(26) *hm* [. iṯ . b btk . l]ḥ*m . w tn /* ***w*** *nlḥ*m . *hm . i*ṯ[. b btk . yn . w]tn . ***w*** *nšt /*

'Falls [es in deinem Haus Br]ot [gibt], dann gib (es uns), **daß** wir essen können; falls es [in deinem Haus Wein] gibt, [dann] gib (ihn uns), **daß** wir trinken können!' (KTU[3] 1.23:71–72, my emphasis; Tropper 2012, §83.113h)

2.2.7. PS **Wa* in Amarna Canaanite

In Amarna Canaanite, sequences of clauses are typically linked by the conjunction *ù* (*wa*) (Baranowski 2016a, 206). According to Baranowski (2016a, 190):

> The logical relationship between two coordinated clauses in a sequence may often require the use of subordination in the translation because other languages require explicit marking of the logical relationship between the message of the two clauses in cases where the Amarna interlanguage leaves such a relationship open to the interpretive logic of the discourse instead of marking it explicitly.

(27) […] *ma-ni* ^{45}UD. KAM^{v}.MEŠ-*ti yi-šal-la-l*[*u*]-⸢*ši*⸣ ^{46}***ù*** *in*$_4$*-né-ep-ša-a*[*t ki-ma*] ^{47}⸢*ri*⸣*-qí ḫu-bu-l*[*i*] ^{48}⸢*a*⸣*-na ša-šu* […]

'How long has he been plundering it **so that** it has become like a damaged pot because of him.' (EA 292:44–48, emphasis by Baranowski)

The typical narrative syntax in Amarna Canaanite is (Baranowski 2016a, 205f.):

> the clause-initial (usually preverbal) conjunction 'and' (*u*//*wa*), the short conjugation (*yaqtul*//historically short *yiqtol*), and their typical use in narrating successive events to advance a story. These features must reflect Canaanite syntax and semantics.

(28) ***ù yi-la-ak*** ^{I}*Ar-sà-wu-ya* ^{27}*a-na* URU *Qì-i*[*s-sà*] ⸢***ù***⸣ ***yi-il***$_5$***-qa*** ^{28}ÉRIN.MEŠ ^{I}A-⸢*zi*⸣-[*ri*] ⸢***ù***⸣ ***iṣ-ba-at*** ^{29}URU *Ša-ad-du* ***u ya-di-in***$_4$***-ši*** *a-na* ^{30}LÚ.MEŠ SA.GAZ ***u la-a ia-di-in***$_4$***-ši*** ^{31}*a-na* LUGAL EN-*ia* […]

> ‘**And** Arsawuya **went** to the town of Qi[ssa] (Qedesh) **and he took** the troops of Azi[ru] **and he seized** the town of Shaddu **and he handed it** over to the *ʿapîru* men **and did not hand it over** to the king, my lord.’ (EA 197:26–31, emphasis by Baranowski)

This short example illustrates the strong tendency in Amarna Canaanite to place the verb directly after the conjunction *wa*, but exceptions occur from time to time, as when the verb must be negated. The clause-type *wa-lā-yaqtul* (as in *u la-a ya-di-in*$_4$*-ši* above) is regular in Amarna Canaanite. An adverb or a subject may also be inserted between the *wa* and the verb (Baranowski 2016a, 207).

An example of the use of *wa* within a modal domain is (Baranowski 2016a, 161):

(29) *an-nu-ú* LÚ.MEŠ MÁŠKIM *šàr-ri* ^{31}*yu-wa-ši-ru-na š*[*à*]*r-ru* ***ù*** ^{32}*ia-aq-bi šàr-ru a-na ša-šu-nu* ^{33}***ù*** *tu-pa-ri-šu be-ri-ku-ni*

> ‘So, behold, the king is sending the king’s commissioners. **So** may he speak to them **that** they should adjudicate between you (or: us).’ (EA 116:30–33, my emphasis)

In (29), after a circumstantial or temporal clause (with *yaqtulu*), *wa* first introduces a jussive *yaqtul*; after that, a jussive *wa-yaqtul* expresses purpose or complement (‘that they should adjudicate’).

2.2.8. PS **Wa* in Phoenician

In Phoenician also, *wa* is the most common conjunction, described by Friedrich and Röllig (1999, §257) as “*u̯a-* > *u̯ə-*.” It is an “anreihende Konjunktion” (Friedrich and Röllig 1999, §319), but it can also introduce circumstantial clauses, as in (Friedrich and Röllig 1999, §319a):

(30) בשנת 11 לאדן מלכם פתלמיש... (5) אש המת לעם לפש שנת 33 **ו**כהן לאדן מלכם עבדעשתרת

> 'in the 11th year of the lord king Ptolemy,... which is the 33rd year of the people of Lapethos, **while** ʿBDʿŠTRT was priest for the lord king' (KAI^5 43:4f., my translation and emphasis)

The *wa* in Phoenician can also open an apodosis, as in (Friedrich and Röllig 1999, §319d):

(31) ומי . בל . חז . כתן . למנערי . **ו**בימי . כסי . ב(13)ץ

> 'and whoever had not seen linen from his youth, **then** in my days he was covered in Byssus' (KAI^5 24:12–13, my translation and emphasis)

2.2.9. PS **Wa* in Old Aramaic

Old Aramaic has a conjunction *p*, which, like its reflex *fa* in Classical Arabic, has "a consecutive sense ('then', or sim.)" (Fales 2009, 569).[20] Thus *wa* could be expected to have a more restricted semantic range, as it has in Classical Arabic, but this does not seem to be the case. The use of the conjunction *p* is more restricted and *wa* is used "nahezu vor jedem Satz" (Degen 1969, §89). An example of *wa* introducing a purpose/result clause is found in the inscription from Sefire (Degen 1969, §89):

(32) וא֯ל יפק חצר **ו**ליתחזה ירק **ו**לי֯[תחזה] (29) אחוה

‘May the grass not come forth **so that** no green may be seen and **so that** its vegetation is not [seen]!’ (KAI[5] 222 1A:28–29)

The Old Aramaic *wa* may also introduce a circumstantial clause, or a clause that is concomitant with the preceding clause, as in Sefire (Degen 1969, §89):

(33) לתשלח לש(18)נך בניהם **ו**תאמר לה קתל אחך

‘Do not speak up between them **in that** you say to him: “Kill your brother!”’ (KAI[5] 224:17–18, my translation and emphasis)

Another example of a *wa*-clause describing an action concomitant with that in the preceding clause is found in the Deir ʿAllā inscription (Schüle 2000, 110):[21]

(34) (3) ויקם֯ . ב֯ל֯ע֯ם֯ . מן . מ֯ח֯ר֯[..] ---[...]ל . י֯מן . -[........]-ה . ול֯ י֯כ֯[ל .
אכל ויצ[ם [.] **ו**ב֯כ֯(4)ה . יבכה֯ .

‘Then Balaam stood up in the morning… **and by that he** wept grievously.’ (KAI[5] 312, I:3)

2.2.10. PS **Wa* in Epigraphic Hebrew

In Epigraphic Hebrew, *wa* in the main functions as it does in Classical Hebrew. An example of temporal succession is found in (35):

(35) *(wa-NP)*[22] + *Ø-qaṭal* + ***wa****(y)-yiqṭol*

וסמכיהו לקחה . שמעיהו **ו**(7)יעלהו העירה .

‘As for Semachiah, Shemaiah has taken him **and** sent him up to the city’ (Lachish 4:6–7, text and translation HI 315, my transcription and emphasis; cf. Gogel 1998, 262)

Wa may also indicate temporal succession in a modal domain, as in an Arad letter:

(36) *Ø-IMP + … +* ***wa****-IMP*

> [אל אלי]שב ק[ח] שׁ̊מ̊ן 1 ו̊(2)[חתם וקח] 1 ל קמח **ו**תן . א[תם] (3)
> [לקו]ס̊ענל מהרה .
>
> '[To Elia]shib: Ta[ke] 1 (jar of) oil and [seal it and take] 2 (jars of) flour **and** give t[hem to Qau]sʿanali quickly' (Arad 12:1–2, text and translation HI 28, my transcription and emphasis; cf. Gogel 1998, 264)

Wa in a modal domain may also indicate an additional instruction that is added to an initial imperative clause, as in (37):

(37) *Ø-IMP +* ***wa****-qaṭal +* ***wa****-qaṭal*

> תן . מן . היין 1 1 1 ב\ **ו**(3)צוך . חנניהו . על ב(4)אר שבע עם . משא
> צ(5)מד . חמרם . **ו**שררת̊ (6)אתם . בצק̊ .
>
> 'Give from the wine, 3 baths, **and** Hananiah **will then** order you to Beersheba with the load of a pair of donkeys, **and you are to** bind them with dough.' (Arad 3:2–5, text HI 15, my transcription and emphasis; cf. Gogel 1998, 266)

A possible case of two concomitant main clauses connected by *wa* in a modal domain is found at Kuntillet Ağrūd:

(38) *Ø-yiqṭol(Ø) +* ***wa****-yiqṭol(Ø) +* ***wa****-yiqṭol(Ø)!*

> יב(8)רך **ו**ישמרך (9) **ו**יהי עם . אד[נ](10)י[
>
> 'May he bless **and** keep you **and** may he be with my Lord.'[23] (Kuntillet Ağrūd 19:7–9, text and translation HI 293, my transcription and emphasis; cf. Gogel 1998, 287)

2.3. The Reflex of PS **Wa* in CBH

This section will treat in some detail the semantics of the conjunction *wa* as a natural language connective in CBH.[24] Because the aim of this book is to clarify the linguistic reality behind the 'consecutive tenses', I will endeavour to recognise both what is traditionally called the 'consecutive *waw*' (discourse-continuity clauses),[25] and the so-called 'copulative *waw*' (usually discontinuity clauses).

2.3.1. *Wa*-linking as Elaboration or Summary

In an elaboration, "the second clause echoes the first, adding additional information about the event or state described" (Dixon 2009, 2, 27). A summary amounts to the opposite: it echoes the previous clauses, but supplies fewer details and less information about the event or state described in the previous clauses. Elaboration and summary clauses are frequently introduced by *wa* in Biblical Hebrew (Brongers 1978, 276).[26]

2.3.1.1. Discourse-discontinuity Clauses

In the following example, a syndetic *qaṭal* clause breaks the chain of main-line narration in a chiastic construction:

(39) *wa(y)-yiqṭol* + [16]***wa**-S.noun-qaṭal* + *wa(y)-yiqṭol*

וַיָּבֹאוּ אֶל־נֹחַ אֶל־הַתֵּבָה שְׁנַיִם שְׁנַיִם מִכָּל־הַבָּשָׂר «אֲשֶׁר־בּוֹ רוּחַ חַיִּים»׃
וְהַבָּאִים זָכָר וּנְקֵבָה מִכָּל־בָּשָׂר בָּאוּ כַּאֲשֶׁר צִוָּה אֹתוֹ אֱלֹהִים וַיִּסְגֹּר יְהוָה
בַּעֲדוֹ׃

‘Pairs of all creatures that have the breath of life came into the ark to Noah. [16]**And** those that entered went in male and female of all flesh as God had commanded him. Then the LORD shut him in.’ (Gen. 7.15–16)

In (39), the information conveyed by the *qaṭal* clause with initial *wa* (*wa-X-qaṭal*) adds more details (elaboration) about the event described by the preceding *wa(y)-yiqṭol* clause.

(40) ***wa***-*S.noun-qaṭal* + *wa(y)-yiqṭol* + *wa-lō-qaṭal*

וּמֹשֶׁ֣ה וְאַהֲרֹ֗ן עָשׂ֛וּ אֶת־כָּל־הַמֹּפְתִ֥ים הָאֵ֖לֶּה לִפְנֵ֣י פַרְעֹ֑ה וַיְחַזֵּ֤ק יְהוָה֙ אֶת־לֵ֣ב פַּרְעֹ֔ה וְלֹֽא־שִׁלַּ֥ח אֶת־בְּנֵֽי־יִשְׂרָאֵ֖ל מֵאַרְצֽוֹ׃

‘**And** Moses and Aaron, they did all these wonders before Pharaoh. But Yahweh strengthened Pharaoh’s heart, and he did not release Israel’s sons from his land.’ (Exod. 11.10; Propp 1999, 292)

Example (40) is a summary that refers to both the plagues that have hit Egypt already, and what is going to happen. The summary is a complex of three clauses, of which only the first is discontinuous.[27]

2.3.1.2. Discourse-continuity Clauses

In (41), a discourse-continuity *wa(y)-yiqṭol* clause elaborates on a preceding *qaṭal* clause:

(41) *wa-S.noun-qaṭal* + *wa(y)-yiqṭol* + ***wa***(*y*)-*yiqṭol*

וַֽיהוָ֞ה בֵּרַ֧ךְ אֶת־אֲדֹנִ֛י מְאֹ֖ד וַיִּגְדָּ֑ל וַיִּתֶּן־לוֹ֩ צֹ֨אן וּבָקָ֜ר וְכֶ֣סֶף וְזָהָ֗ב וַעֲבָדִם֙ וּשְׁפָחֹ֔ת וּגְמַלִּ֖ים וַחֲמֹרִֽים׃

‘The Lord has richly blessed my master, and he has become very wealthy. **And** (the Lord) has given him sheep and cattle, silver and gold, male and female servants, and camels and donkeys.’ (Gen. 24.35)

The second *wa(y)-yiqṭol* (וַיִּתֶּן) in this verse is not sequential, but adds additional information and more details about the blessing coded by the first verbal clause (בֵּרַךְ).[28]

Wa-qaṭal clauses too may code elaborations, as is seen in (42):

(42) *Ø-VNabs* + [11]***wa****-qaṭal* + ***wa****-qaṭal*

הִמּ֥וֹל לָכֶ֖ם כָּל־זָכָֽר׃ **וּ**נְמַלְתֶּ֕ם אֵ֖ת בְּשַׂ֣ר עָרְלַתְכֶ֑ם **וְ**הָיָה֙ לְא֣וֹת בְּרִ֔ית בֵּינִ֖י
וּבֵינֵיכֶֽם׃

‘Every male among you must be circumcised. [11]**And** you shall be circumcised in the flesh of your foreskin; **and** it shall be the sign of the covenant between Me and you.’ (Gen. 17.10b–11)

In (42), the instruction starts with an infinitive absolute (הִמּוֹל) giving the general command of circumcision. There then follow two *wa-qaṭal* clauses that detail how the command should be worked out and also explain its significance.[29]

A summary can also be introduced by a traditional ‘consecutive *waw*’ (J-M §118i), as in example (43):[30]

(43) *wa(y)-yiqṭol…* [19]*wa-ADV-qaṭal* + [20]***wa****(y)-yiqṭol*

וַיָּ֣קָם ׀ שְׂדֵ֣ה עֶפְר֗וֹן אֲשֶׁר֙ בַּמַּכְפֵּלָ֔ה אֲשֶׁ֖ר לִפְנֵ֣י מַמְרֵ֑א הַשָּׂדֶה֙ וְהַמְּעָרָ֣ה אֲשֶׁר־
בּ֔וֹ וְכָל־הָעֵץ֙ אֲשֶׁ֣ר בַּשָּׂדֶ֔ה אֲשֶׁ֥ר בְּכָל־גְּבֻל֖וֹ סָבִֽיב׃ 18 לְאַבְרָהָ֥ם לְמִקְנָ֖ה לְעֵינֵ֣י
בְנֵי־חֵ֑ת בְּכֹ֖ל בָּאֵ֥י שַֽׁעַר־עִירֽוֹ׃ 19 וְאַחֲרֵי־כֵ֡ן קָבַ֨ר אַבְרָהָ֜ם אֶת־שָׂרָ֣ה אִשְׁתּ֗וֹ
אֶל־מְעָרַ֞ת שְׂדֵ֧ה הַמַּכְפֵּלָ֛ה עַל־פְּנֵ֥י מַמְרֵ֖א הִ֣וא חֶבְר֑וֹן בְּאֶ֖רֶץ כְּנָֽעַן׃ 20 **וַיָּ֨קָם**
הַשָּׂדֶ֜ה וְהַמְּעָרָ֨ה אֲשֶׁר־בּ֔וֹ לְאַבְרָהָ֖ם לַאֲחֻזַּת־קָ֑בֶר מֵאֵ֖ת בְּנֵי־חֵֽת׃

'So Abraham secured Ephron's field in Machpelah, next to Mamre, including the field, the cave that was in it, and all the trees that were in the field and all around its border, [18]as his property in the presence of the sons of Heth before all who entered the gate of Ephron's city. [19]After this Abraham buried his wife Sarah in the cave in the field of Machpelah next to Mamre (that is, Hebron) in the land of Canaan. [20]**So Abraham secured** the field and the cave that was in it as a burial site from the sons of Heth.' (Gen. 23.17–20)

2.3.2. *Wa*-linking as Circumstantial Action or State

In view of the various semantic types of accompanying actions or states coded by *wa*-clauses discussed above, it is not surprising that a clause linked with *wa* can also describe a circumstantial or backgrounded action or state. The exact borderline between the two types is indistinct. As a rule of thumb, a circumstantial clause is concomitant with a (specific) main clause and semantically subordinate to that clause.[31] A circumstantial linking belongs to the sentence level of the text.[32] A background clause belongs to the discourse level, and its action or state may or may not be concomitant with the main line clause(s). Background is often a complex of clauses, which are semantically more independent in relation to the main line than are circumstantial clauses.[33] The present section treats syndetic circumstantial clauses. In the next (§2.3.3), I describe background with an initial *wa*-clause.

2.3.2.1. Discourse-discontinuity Clauses

There are very few syndetic circumstantial long *yiqṭol* clauses in CBH prose. In consideration of the few examples of asyndetic circumstantial long *yiqṭol* clauses in my corpus, it is tempting to assume that CBH preferred asyndesis in this case. However, circumstantial *yiqṭol(u)* clauses with the connective *wa* seem to have been functional in the Archaic Hebrew poetry (as they were in Classical Arabic),[34] and do exist in other Northwest Semitic languages, as is shown in this example from Deir ʿAllā:

(44) *wa(y)-yiqṭol* + *wa-lā-qaṭal* + *[wa-yVqtV]l* + ***wa**-VNabs-yiqṭol(u)*

ויקם . ב֯ל֯ע֯ם . מן . מח֯ר֯ [..] ---[...]ל . י֯מן . -[........]-ה . ול֯ י֯כ֯[ל .
אכל . ויצ]ם [.] ו֯ב֯כ֯(4)ה . יבכ֯ה֯ .

'And Balaam arose the next day […] days […] but he was not ab[le to eat and he fas]ted **while** weeping grievously.' (KAI[5] I:3–4)

The small number of examples (syndetic or not) of circumstantial *yiqṭol(u)* clauses in CBH is an indication that the circumstantial function of long *yiqṭol* clauses has been taken over by infinite clauses in CBH, especially the active participle (sometimes finite; see §4.1.1.1 and §7.4). Among the few circumstantial long *yiqṭol* clauses in CBH, we find some that start with asyndesis and continue with syndesis (with *wa*). In such a case, a 'continuing' circumstantial long *yiqṭol* can be introduced by *wa*, as in (45):[35]

(45) *wayhī: S.noun-qoṭel* + ***Ø****-S.noun-yiqṭol(u)* + ***wa****-S.noun-yiqṭol(u)-N*

וַיְהִי֙ ק֣וֹל הַשּׁוֹפָ֔ר הוֹלֵ֖ךְ וְחָזֵ֣ק מְאֹ֑ד מֹשֶׁ֣ה יְדַבֵּ֔ר **וְ**הָאֱלֹהִ֖ים יַעֲנֶ֥נּוּ בְקֽוֹל׃

'The blast of the shofar grew louder and louder, **while** Moses was speaking **and** God was answering him with thunder.' (Exod. 19.19, NAB)

The *wayhī* in this construction is macro-syntactic, and the first half of the verse exhibits a type of biclausal cleft construction that has developed into a monoclausal syntagm (ק֣וֹל הַשּׁוֹפָ֔ר הוֹלֵ֖ךְ) with a focus marker (וַיְהִי֙; Khan 2019, 15–18). The monoclausal construction is a participle clause, which is strengthened by another participle/adjective (HALOT: "grew stronger and stronger"). This participle clause is the main informative component of the message (cf. Khan 2019, 19). What concerns us here is the two circumstantial long *yiqṭol* clauses that form a circumstantial complex, the first clause of which is asyndetic, the second connected by *wa*.[36]

The most frequent syndetic circumstantial clause in CBH has a participle predicate (§7.4). An often quoted example is (46):

(46) *wa(y)-yiqṭol* + ***wa****-S.pron-qoṭel*

וַיֵּרָ֤א אֵלָיו֙ יְהוָ֔ה בְּאֵלֹנֵ֖י מַמְרֵ֑א **וְ**ה֛וּא יֹשֵׁ֥ב פֶּֽתַח־הָאֹ֖הֶל כְּחֹ֥ם הַיּֽוֹם׃

'YHWH appeared to Abraham by the oaks of Mamre **while** he was sitting at the entrance to the tent during the hottest time of the day.' (Gen. 18.1)

As is sometimes the case, the circumstantial clause is ambiguous as to which constituent is referred to in the main clause. Syntactically, it could have been YHWH (the last mentioned in the matrix clause) that was sitting at the entrance, but the pragmatic situation decides that it must be Abraham.

Such circumstantial clauses are often to be translated with an *ing*-form, but sometimes a prepositional phrase is a better choice, as in (47):[37]

(47) *wa-ADV-qaṭal* + ***wa****-S.noun-qoṭel* + *wa(y)-yiqṭol*

וְאַחֲרֵי־כֵן יָצָא אָחִיו **וְ**יָדוֹ אֹחֶזֶת בַּעֲקֵב עֵשָׂו וַיִּקְרָא שְׁמוֹ יַעֲקֹב

'Then his brother emerged, **with** his hand holding on to the heel of Esau. So they named him Jacob.' (Gen. 25.26)

The example shows how tightly connected a circumstantial *wa*-clause often is to the matrix clause semantically. In Hebrew, they are two separate clauses, but in an English translation, the *wa*-clause corresponds semantically to a prepositional phrase and is a constituent in the matrix.

Verbless clauses with a circumstantial relation to a previous matrix are often introduced by *wa*.[38] Such clauses always indicate a state. An example in direct speech is (48):

(48) *Ø-IMP-A* + *Ø-yiqṭol(Ø)-V* + ***wa****-XØ*

וַיֹּאמְרוּ הָבָה ׀ נִבְנֶה־לָּנוּ עִיר וּמִגְדָּל **וְ**רֹאשׁוֹ בַשָּׁמַיִם

'Then they said, Come, let's build ourselves a city and a tower **with** its top in the heavens' (Gen. 11.4)

This is a classic example of a concomitant attendant circumstance coded by a syndetic verbless clause.[39] The verbless clause in (48) belongs to the quotation and describes how the tower is intended to be.[40]

An example of a syndetic verbless clause coding an attendant circumstance in a narrative main line is (49):[41]

(49) *wa(y)-yiqtol + wa(y)-yiqtol +* **wa-XØ**

וַיִּקַּ֣ח הָעֶ֡בֶד עֲשָׂרָה֩ גְמַלִּ֨ים מִגְּמַלֵּ֤י אֲדֹנָיו֙ וַיֵּ֔לֶךְ **וְכָל־ט֥וּב אֲדֹנָ֖יו בְּיָד֑וֹ**

'Then the servant took with him ten of his master's camels and left, **loaded with** all kinds of good things from his master.' (Gen. 24.10)

2.3.2.2. Discourse-continuity Clauses

A clause that expresses a concomitant circumstance and a dependence on a previous matrix clause cannot at the same time express discourse continuity. Not surprisingly, I have found no example of a traditional 'consecutive *waw*' connecting an attendant circumstantial clause.

2.3.3. *Wa*-linking as Background

2.3.3.1. Discourse-discontinuity Clauses

Nearly two out of three background clauses or clause complexes introduced by *wa* are connecting a clause signalling discontinuity.[42] From the frequencies in my corpus, it seems that relatively few of the *wa*-clauses with background function have a long *yiqtol* predicate (8×).[43] A prose example is (50):

(50) *wa(y)-yiqtol + wa(y)-yiqtol +* [34]***wa*-PREP-VN-*yiqtol(u)!* +** *wa-qatal + wa-qatal +* [35]*wa-qatal + wa-qatal*

וַיְכַ֣ל מֹשֶׁ֗ה מִדַּבֵּר֙ אִתָּ֔ם וַיִּתֵּ֥ן עַל־פָּנָ֖יו מַסְוֶֽה׃ 34 **וּבְבֹ֨א מֹשֶׁ֜ה לִפְנֵ֤י יְהוָה֙ לְדַבֵּ֣ר** אִתּ֔וֹ יָסִ֥יר אֶת־הַמַּסְוֶ֖ה עַד־צֵאת֑וֹ וְיָצָ֗א וְדִבֶּר֙ אֶל־בְּנֵ֣י יִשְׂרָאֵ֔ל אֵ֖ת אֲשֶׁ֥ר יְצֻוֶּֽה׃ 35 וְרָא֤וּ בְנֵֽי־יִשְׂרָאֵל֙ אֶת־פְּנֵ֣י מֹשֶׁ֔ה כִּ֣י קָרַ֔ן ע֖וֹר פְּנֵ֣י מֹשֶׁ֑ה וְהֵשִׁ֨יב מֹשֶׁ֤ה אֶת־הַמַּסְוֶה֙ עַל־פָּנָ֔יו עַד־בֹּא֖וֹ לְדַבֵּ֥ר אִתּֽוֹ׃ ס

> ‘And Moses finished speaking with them, and he put a veil on his face. 34**And** in Moses’ entering before Yahweh to speak with him, he would remove the veil until he came out, and he would go out and speak to the Israelites what he would be commanded. 35And the Israelites would see Moses’ face, that the skin of Moses’ face shone, and Moses would return the veil over his face, until he went in to speak with him.’[44] (Exod. 34.33–35)

The background complex in (50) relates to a narrative main-line (*wa(y)-yiqṭol* clauses). It starts with *wa* and a verbal noun construction followed by a morphologically distinctive long *yiqṭol* with habitual past meaning. This *yiqṭol(u)* is followed by four (discourse-continuous) *wa-qaṭal* clauses that conclude the background section.[45]

Among the syndetic background clauses with finite predicate, the most frequent in the corpus are those having a *qaṭal* morpheme (75 ×). An example is (51):

(51) ***wa***-*S.noun-qaṭal* + *wa(y)-yiqṭol* + *wa(y)-yiqṭol* + *wa(y)-yiqṭol* + 57***wa***-*S.noun-qaṭal* + *kī-qaṭal*

> וְהָרָעָב הָיָה עַל כָּל־פְּנֵי הָאָרֶץ וַיִּפְתַּח יוֹסֵף אֶת־כָּל־אֲשֶׁר בָּהֶם וַיִּשְׁבֹּר לְמִצְרַיִם וַיֶּחֱזַק הָרָעָב בְּאֶרֶץ מִצְרָיִם׃ וְכָל־הָאָרֶץ בָּאוּ מִצְרַיְמָה לִשְׁבֹּר אֶל־יוֹסֵף כִּי־חָזַק הָרָעָב בְּכָל־הָאָרֶץ׃
>
> ‘The famine was over all the earth, but then Joseph opened all the storehouses and sold food to the Egyptians. The famine became more and more severe in the land of Egypt. 57Moreover all countries came to Egypt to Joseph to buy grain, because the famine was severe throughout the earth.’ (Gen. 41.56f.)

The initial copula verb *qaṭal* (הָיָה) describes the general situation. It functions as a background to Joseph's actions. The perfective past *qaṭal* clause at the beginning of verse 57 is also background, describing actions taking place in the countries outside Egypt.[46]

A frequent background clause-type is the verbless one. It is most often syndetic, with an initial *wa* (76 ×).[47] A good example is (52):

(52) *wa(y)-yiqṭol* + *wa(y)-yiqṭol* + *wa(y)-yiqṭol* + *wa(y)-yiqṭol* + *wa(y)-yiqṭol* + *wa(y)-yiqṭol* + [27]*wa(y)-yiqṭol* + ***wa****-XØ* + [28]***wa****-S.noun-qoṭel*

וַיַּעֲלוּ כָל־בְּנֵי יִשְׂרָאֵל וְכָל־הָעָם וַיָּבֹאוּ בֵית־אֵל וַיִּבְכּוּ וַיֵּשְׁבוּ שָׁם לִפְנֵי יְהוָה וַיָּצוּמוּ בַיּוֹם־הַהוּא עַד־הָעָרֶב וַיַּעֲלוּ עֹלוֹת וּשְׁלָמִים לִפְנֵי יְהוָה׃ 27 וַיִּשְׁאֲלוּ בְנֵי־יִשְׂרָאֵל בַּיהוָה **וְ**שָׁם אֲרוֹן בְּרִית הָאֱלֹהִים בַּיָּמִים הָהֵם׃ 28 **וּ**פִינְחָס בֶּן־אֶלְעָזָר בֶּן־אַהֲרֹן עֹמֵד׀ לְפָנָיו בַּיָּמִים הָהֵם

'So all the Israelites, the whole army, went up to Bethel. They wept and sat there before the LORD; they did not eat anything that day until evening. They offered up burnt sacrifices and tokens of peace to the LORD. [27]The Israelites asked the LORD (**for** the ark of God's covenant was there in those days; [28]Phinehas son of Eleazar, son of Aaron, was serving the LORD in those days)' (Judg. 20.27–28a)

In (52), a syndetic verbless clause and a syndetic participle clause together form a parenthetic background to the storyline.[48]

A participle clause with initial *wa* can also describe backgrounded information:[49]

(53) *wa(y)-yiqṭol* + ***wa**-S.noun-ADV-qoṭel*

וַיְהִי־רִ֗יב בֵּ֚ין רֹעֵ֣י מִקְנֵֽה־אַבְרָ֔ם וּבֵ֖ין רֹעֵ֣י מִקְנֵה־ל֑וֹט **וְ**הַֽכְּנַעֲנִי֙ וְהַפְּרִזִּ֔י אָ֖ז יֹשֵׁ֥ב בָּאָֽרֶץ׃

'So there were quarrels between Abram's herdsmen and Lot's herdsmen. (**Now** the Canaanites and the Perizzites were living in the land at that time.)' (Gen. 13.7)

In (53), a parenthetic piece of historical information is inserted into the storyline. The background is coded by *wa* and an active participle clause.

2.3.3.2. Discourse-continuity Clauses

Since an attendant circumstance cannot be coded by a discourse-continuity clause (as was noted above), it is striking indeed that continuity clauses (§1.2.6) may be utilised for background descriptions. There is a considerable number (18 ×) of *wa(y)-yiqṭol* clauses that either take part in background complexes or (rarely) introduce background. In 17 instances, *wa-qaṭal* clauses partake in background or introduce background. In addition, 13 cases of the so-called macro-syntactic *wa-haya* introduce background (Isaksson 1998).

The *wa-qaṭal* clause-type never enters into a storyline in CBH. The continuity function in the storyline was still fulfilled by *wa(y)-yiqṭol*.[50] While the most frequent backgrounding clause-type was marked for discontinuity (*wa-X-qaṭal*), *wa-qaṭal* on the other hand was marked for continuity (type *wa-VX*) and remained a relatively infrequent clause-type for the introduction of background descriptions in narrative.

An illustration of the complexity of both *wa(y)-yiqṭol* and *wa-qaṭal* clauses taking part in background sections is found in (54), where backgrounding is set within square brackets:

(54) *wa(y)-yiqṭol* + *"…"* + ^{5}*[wa-S.noun-qaṭal* + *kī-qaṭal* + *wa-S.noun-qaṭal* + ***wa**-qaṭal]* + ^{6}*wa(y)-yiqṭol* + ^{7}*[wa-S.noun-qaṭal* + ***wa**(y)-yiqṭol* + ***wa**(y)-yiqṭol]* + ^{8}*wa(y)-yiqṭol*

וַיֹּ֣אמֶר שְׁכֶ֔ם אֶל־חֲמ֥וֹר אָבִ֖יו לֵאמֹ֑ר קַֽח־לִ֛י אֶת־הַיַּלְדָּ֥ה הַזֹּ֖את לְאִשָּֽׁה׃ 5 וְיַעֲקֹ֣ב
שָׁמַ֗ע כִּ֤י טִמֵּא֙ אֶת־דִּינָ֣ה בִתּ֔וֹ וּבָנָ֛יו הָי֥וּ אֶת־מִקְנֵ֖הוּ בַּשָּׂדֶ֑ה **וְ**הֶחֱרִ֥שׁ יַעֲקֹ֖ב עַד־
בֹּאָֽם׃ 6 וַיֵּצֵ֛א חֲמ֥וֹר אֲבִֽי־שְׁכֶ֖ם אֶֽל־יַעֲקֹ֑ב לְדַבֵּ֖ר אִתּֽוֹ׃ 7 וּבְנֵ֨י יַעֲקֹ֜ב בָּ֤אוּ מִן־
הַשָּׂדֶה֙ כְּשָׁמְעָ֔ם **וַ**יִּֽתְעַצְּבוּ֙ הָֽאֲנָשִׁ֔ים **וַ**יִּ֥חַר לָהֶ֖ם מְאֹ֑ד כִּֽי־נְבָלָ֞ה עָשָׂ֣ה בְיִשְׂרָאֵ֗ל
לִשְׁכַּב֙ אֶת־בַּֽת־יַעֲקֹ֔ב וְכֵ֖ן לֹ֥א יֵעָשֶֽׂה׃ 8 וַיְדַבֵּ֥ר חֲמ֖וֹר אִתָּ֣ם לֵאמֹ֑ר...

'[4]Shechem said to his father Hamor, "Get me this girl to be my wife." [5][But Jacob had heard[51] that Shechem had dishonoured his daughter Dinah. At that time[52] his sons were out in the countryside with his livestock, **so** Jacob kept quiet until they came back.] [6]Hamor Shechem's father went to Jacob to discuss the matter with him. [7][Meanwhile Jacob's sons had come in from the field, having heard the news. The men were distressed **and** very angry because Shechem had done a disgrace in Israel by sleeping with Jacob's daughter—a thing never to be done.] [8]Hamor spoke with them as follows:…' (Gen. 34.4–7)

After Shechem's shameful act against Jacob's daughter, Hamor the father of Shechem visits Jacob to settle the matter and negotiate for a marriage between his son and Jacob's daughter. In this passage, the storyline is interrupted by two separate sections of background information necessary for the listener to understand the motives behind Jacob's behaviour and the actions undertaken by his sons. The background sections both consist of several clauses, and each background complex interrupts a narrative main-line coded by *wa(y)-yiqṭol* clauses.[53] The main-line is resumed with Hamor's speaking in verse 8 (*wa(y)-yiqṭol*). The great syntactic problem in this passage is the use of discourse-continuity clauses within the background sections. In the first background section, there is a *wa-qaṭal* clause (וְהֶחֱרִ֥שׁ), and the second background section contains two *wa(y)-yiqṭol* clauses (וַיִּֽתְעַצְּב֣וּ and וַיִּ֥חַר) that form part of the background. Both *wa(y)-yiqṭol* have stativic meaning (or at least may be interpreted as stativic), but the question arises as to why a *wa-qaṭal* clause is used in the first background section and why *wa(y)-yiqṭol* clauses continue from the initial (*qaṭal*) clause in the second section. Both clause-types signal discourse continuity and both have past time reference. The *wa-qaṭal* clause describes a continuative process which takes place during a specific space of time: the aspectual meaning of the verb is imperfective (past), i.e., Jacob kept quiet until his sons came back (Ges-K §112ss). That fits well with the acquired meaning of the *wa-qaṭal* construction in CBH, a meaning close to the meaning of the long *yiqṭol* gram (see §§6.11–14). A long *yiqṭol* clause could not be used here.[54] What is required in this final position of the background complex is a clause signalling continuity. That is why a *wa-qaṭal* clause must be used: it must express an imperfective meaning in temporal (or logical) succession to the fact that Jacob's sons were out in the countryside with his livestock, a succession that is also perceived as a consequence ('so Jacob kept quiet'; cf. Dixon 2009, 28, 17).[55] The second background section is introduced by a pluperfect *wa-X-qaṭal* clause and the two *wa(y)-yiqṭol* clauses describe the feelings of Jacob's sons: they were outraged already when they arrived. The continuity in this case signals temporal (or logical) succession: they came home and were outraged and infuriated.[56] In the example, none of the discourse-continuity clauses in background sections is positioned as the first in that section. They just continue a preceding discontinuity clause that signals the background. If discourse-continuity clauses are at all involved in the construction of background complexes, they most frequently do this in non-initial position of the background complex.

Nearly all examples of discourse-continuity clauses in background are disputed, controversial, or regarded as text-critically doubtful by scholarship on the Hebrew. They deserve special consideration.

2.3.3.3. *Wa(y)-yiqṭol* Clause(s) in Background

A *wa(y)-yiqṭol* clause is marked for discourse continuity (type *wa-VX*). If it is perceived as background, there are two possibilities: it constitutes a continuity clause within a narrative background complex, or, for some exceptional reason, it starts a background that should have the property of discourse continuity. The former possibility is already exemplified above.[57]

One rare example of *wa(y)-yiqṭol* introducing background is attested in my corpus, (55):

(55) *wayhī-PrP* + *wa(y)-yiqṭol* + *wa(y)-yiqṭol* + *wa(y)-yiqṭol* + [24]***wa****(y)-yiqṭol*

וַיְהִ֣י בָעֶ֔רֶב וַיִּקַּח֙ אֶת־לֵאָ֣ה בִתּ֔וֹ וַיָּבֵ֥א אֹתָ֖הּ אֵלָ֑יו וַיָּבֹ֖א אֵלֶֽיהָ׃ **וַיִּתֵּ֤ן** לָבָן֙ לָ֔הּ אֶת־
זִלְפָּ֖ה שִׁפְחָת֑וֹ לְלֵאָ֥ה בִתּ֖וֹ שִׁפְחָֽה׃

'In the evening he brought his daughter Leah to Jacob, and Jacob had marital relations with her. [24](Laban gave his female servant Zilpah to his daughter Leah to be her servant.)' (Gen. 29.24)

In (55), a *wa(y)-yiqṭol* clause is used as backtracking to the surrounding clauses and background information (Joosten 2012, 172),[58] which most translations render with parentheses. It is only the pragmatics of the situation that triggers the background interpretation of the *wa(y)-yiqṭol* clause in (55), and it is quite possible that this *wa(y)-yiqṭol* clause was perceived by a native as a storyline clause expressing an action that overlapped with a preceding complex activity (Cook 2012a, 290). The pragmatic setting presupposes knowledge about the custom of giving a rich dowry to a daughter upon marriage (Wenham 1994, 236). The problem for us interpreters is that it is impossible to insert the action of the clause into a consequent series of temporally sequential actions. Where is it to be placed? During Jacob's sleep?

2.3.3.4. *Wa-qaṭal* Clause(s) in Background

Wa-qaṭal clauses are also sometimes used to introduce background clauses in a narrative setting.

(56) *"wa-ʿattā-IMP + Ø-ʾim-yiqṭol(u) + Ø-PrP-«REL-qaṭal»-yiqṭol(u)!"* [24]*wa(y)-yiqṭol* + *"Ø-S.pron-yiqṭol(u)"* + [25]***wa-qaṭal***

וְעַתָּ֗ה הִשָּׁ֨בְעָה לִּ֤י בֵֽאלֹהִים֙ הֵ֔נָּה אִם־תִּשְׁקֹ֣ר לִ֔י וּלְנִינִ֖י וּלְנֶכְדִּ֑י כַּחֶ֜סֶד אֲשֶׁר־
עָשִׂ֤יתִי עִמְּךָ֙ תַּעֲשֶׂ֣ה עִמָּדִ֔י וְעִם־הָאָ֖רֶץ אֲשֶׁר־גַּ֥רְתָּה בָּֽהּ׃ 24 וַיֹּ֙אמֶר֙ אַבְרָהָ֔ם
אָנֹכִ֖י אִשָּׁבֵֽעַ׃ 25 וְהוֹכִ֥חַ אַבְרָהָ֖ם אֶת־אֲבִימֶ֑לֶךְ עַל־אֹד֗וֹת בְּאֵ֣ר הַמַּ֔יִם אֲשֶׁ֥ר
גָּזְל֖וּ עַבְדֵ֥י אֲבִימֶֽלֶךְ׃

> ‘[23] “Now therefore swear to me here by God that you will not deal falsely with me or with my descendants or with my posterity, but as I have dealt kindly with you, so you will deal with me and with the land where you have sojourned.” [24]And Abraham said, “I shall swear,” [25]**and at that** Abraham reproved Abimelech about a well of water that Abimelech’s servants had seized.’ (Gen. 21.23–25)

Abraham’s answer to Abimelech’s friendly proposal is terse: “I shall swear,” but not now, because I have some complaints against you that must be settled first (Wenham 1994, 92). The answer is coded as a long *yiqṭol* with its usual *XV* word order. It has future time reference. This is certainly not the usual syntax of a binding contract or covenant formula, for which we would expect a performative *qaṭal*, as in Genesis 23.11. The real covenant between Abraham and Abimelech is related in Genesis 21.27 without quotation of the contract formula. After his terse answer, Abraham is quick to put forward the reproofs about one of the water wells. This complaint is formulated as a background construction that answers the questions that have occurred in the minds of the receivers of the text: why Abraham’s answer is so terse, and why he does not immediately enter into the covenant. There is a continuity between the background description and the direct speech quotation immediately before. It is not correct to translate the *wa-qaṭal* clause with ‘Now it was so that Abraham reproved/had reproved Abimelech’, which would have required a discontinuity syntax (type *wa-XV*, for example וְאַבְרָהָם הוֹכִחַ אֶת־אֲבִימֶלֶךְ). A discontinuity clause would not have been so tightly connected (semantically) with the preceding quoted speech.[59]

In (56) above, it is hard to perceive a repetitive nuance, and the same holds for the *wa-qaṭal* clause in the much-discussed example (57):

(57) *wa(y)-yiqṭol* + *wa(y)-yiqṭol* + *"Ø-IMP* + *wa-IMP"* + *wa(y)-yiqṭol* + *"Ø-ADV-yiqṭol(u)"* + [6]***wa**-qaṭal* + *wa(y)-yiqṭol*

וַיּוֹצֵ֨א אֹת֜וֹ הַח֗וּצָה וַיֹּ֙אמֶר֙ הַבֶּט־נָ֣א הַשָּׁמַ֔יְמָה וּסְפֹר֙ הַכּ֣וֹכָבִ֔ים אִם־תּוּכַ֖ל לִסְפֹּ֣ר
אֹתָ֑ם וַיֹּ֣אמֶר ל֔וֹ כֹּ֥ה יִהְיֶ֖ה זַרְעֶֽךָ׃ **וְ**הֶאֱמִ֖ן בַּֽיהוָ֑ה וַיַּחְשְׁבֶ֥הָ לּ֖וֹ צְדָקָֽה׃

'He took him outside and said, "Look up at the sky and count the stars – if indeed you can count them." Then he said to him, "So shall your offspring be." [6]**And at that** Abram believed YHWH, and therefore YHWH counted it to him as righteousness.' (Gen. 15.5–6)

YHWH has uttered some very hard-to-believe promises of offspring—hard-to-believe, because Abram is childless and his wife Sarah is old. The utterances of YHWH are presented in direct speech quotations. Directly after the expressed promises, we expect a response, an answer from Abram. But no answer is supplied as a quotation. Instead, Abram's response is related in a background clause in direct connection to the utterance of YHWH. *Wa-qaṭal* is a continuity clause and this expresses a close connection to the preceding quoted promise. There is nothing repetitive or habitual in this verbal action. The conclusion of the passage exhibits the unusual word order *wa-qaṭal* + *wa(y)-yiqṭol*. The *wa(y)-yiqṭol* clause (וַיַּחְשְׁבֶ֥הָ) has focal-result semantics (see §2.3.6): 'therefore he counted it to him as (covenant) righteousness'.[60]

The distinguishing features of *wa-qaṭal* as an initial background clause in narrative are the continuity with the preceding clause, its background signalling, and its semantic affinity with the imperfective *yiqṭol(u)*, features that hold also for the macrosyntactic *wa-haya* (Isaksson 1998).[61]

2.3.4. *Wa-linking* as Same-event Addition and Parallelism

In not a few cases, two clauses joined by *wa* just "describe different aspects of a single event," a semantic relation that Dixon (2009, 3, 27) calls same-event addition (cf. Müller 1994, 143). Both elaboration and same-event addition describe the same event. But while elaboration "echoes the first" (Dixon 2009, 27), and usually adds more details, a same-event addition does not echo; instead, it supplies a different aspect of the event in the first clause. In the example *John telephoned, he invited us to dinner*, the second clause echoes the first and is an elaboration that adds some details. However, in *You are together with me; (and) as for me, I am together with you*, the second clause describes the same event (or state), but it does not echo the first; the two clauses just describe different aspects of the same state (Dixon 2009, 27).

The most frequent cases of same-event addition with *wa* in the Hebrew Bible are found in poetry, in the type of semantic linking that is called parallelism (Brongers 1978, 273–275). A good example is (58).[62]

(58) *kī-XØ* + ***wa**-S.noun-yiqṭol(u)!*

כִּֽי־אַתָּ֣ה נֵירִ֣י יְהוָ֑ה **וַ**יהוָ֖ה יַגִּ֥יהַּ חָשְׁכִּֽי׃

‘You are my lamp, O Lord; the Lord illumines my darkness.’ (2 Sam. 22.29)

In (58), the fact that the Lord is the lamp of the poet is another aspect of the Lord’s giving light to the poet’s darkness. The second clause does not ‘echo’ the first.

2.3.4.1. Discourse-discontinuity Clauses

Very few discontinuity clauses expressing same-event addition in the corpus begin with a *wa*. An example is (59):

(59) *wa(y)-yiqṭol* + ***wa**-O.noun-S.pron-haya* + *qoṭel*[63]

וַיִּתֵּ֞ן שַׂ֣ר בֵּית־הַסֹּ֗הַר בְּיַד־יוֹסֵ֔ף אֵ֚ת כָּל־הָ֣אֲסִירִ֔ם אֲשֶׁ֖ר בְּבֵ֣ית הַסֹּ֑הַר **וְ**אֵ֨ת כָּל־אֲשֶׁ֤ר עֹשִׂים֙ שָׁ֔ם ה֖וּא הָיָ֥ה עֹשֶֽׂה׃

‘The warden put all the prisoners under Joseph’s care. **Moreover**, he was in charge of whatever they were doing.’ (Gen. 39.22)

The clauses in (59) describe the same situation, Joseph being given the responsibility for the prisoners, but the second clause construction with *haya* and *qoṭel* is even more broad-reaching: he was in charge of everything that was going on there. This type of linking is also called same-event addition by Dixon (2009, 43, 50).[64]

2.3.4.2. Discourse-continuity Clauses

The continuity examples in prose are more numerous. One is (60):

(60) *Ø-ADV-qaṭal* + ***wa(y)**-yiqṭol*

לָ֤מָּה נַחְבֵּ֙אתָ֙ לִבְרֹ֔חַ **וַ**תִּגְנֹ֖ב אֹתִ֑י

‘Why did you run away secretly **and** deceive me?’ (Gen. 31.27a, NET, my emphasis)

In (60), the running away secretly and the deception are one and the same event. The clauses just describe different aspects of this event.

An example with a *wa-qaṭal* clause is found in (61):

(61) *wa-PrP-yiqṭol(u)* + ***wa**-qaṭal*

וּמִפָּנֶיךָ אֶסָּתֵר וְהָיִיתִי נָע וָנָד בָּאָרֶץ

'and I must hide from your presence; I will be a restless wanderer on the earth' (Gen. 4.14)

It is reasonable to evaluate the two clauses as expressing the same event. The *wa-qaṭal* clause does not echo the first. Being a restless wanderer describes another aspect of hiding from God's presence.[65]

2.3.5. *Wa*-linking as Temporal Succession

As in West Semitic in general, the proclitic *wa* in CBH may also serve as a marker of temporally successive events (Dixon 2009, 9).[66] In this case, the *wa*-clause describes an action or state that is temporally sequential in relation to the preceding clause.

2.3.5.1. Discourse-discontinuity Clauses

A clause-type *wa-XV*, where *X* is not merely a negation and *V* is a finite verb, signals discontinuity and needs explicit adverbs to describe a sequential action or state. If, for example, a temporal succession is to be expressed by an affirmative *qaṭal* clause, then a temporally explicit adverb is used, as in (62):

(62) *wa(y)-yiqṭol* + *wa(y)-yiqṭol!* + ***wa**-ADV-qaṭal*

וַיְנַשֵּׁק לְכָל־אֶחָיו וַיֵּבְךְּ עֲלֵיהֶם וְאַחֲרֵי כֵן דִּבְּרוּ אֶחָיו אִתּוֹ׃

'He kissed all his brothers and wept upon them; **only then** were his brothers able to talk to him.' (Gen. 45.15)

Without an explicitly temporal adverbial expression, the suffix-verb clause would have described a temporal indifference as to the previous clause. With the temporal adverb (אַחֲרֵי כֵן), the clause describes an emphasised temporal succession. Joseph's brothers were so shocked, so frightened, that only *after* his hugging and kissing them did they dare to talk with him (Westermann 1982, 153, 161).[67]

In a similar way, a *wa*-clause with a *yiqṭol(u)* predicate (*wa-X-yiqṭol(u)*) is not an expression of temporal succession. If such a clause must be marked as temporally sequential, an explicit temporal adverb is added. An example is (63):

(63) *Ø-S.noun-REL-yiqṭol(u)* + *wa-qaṭal* + *wa-lō-yiqṭol(u)* + [7]*wa-qaṭal* + ***wa**-ADV-yiqṭol(u)* + *kī-XØ*

נֶ֚פֶשׁ אֲשֶׁ֣ר תִּגַּע־בּ֔וֹ וְטָֽמְאָ֖ה עַד־הָעָ֑רֶב וְלֹ֤א יֹאכַל֙ מִן־הַקֳּדָשִׁ֔ים כִּ֛י אִם־רָחַ֥ץ
בְּשָׂר֖וֹ בַּמָּֽיִם׃ וּבָ֥א הַשֶּׁ֖מֶשׁ וְטָהֵ֑ר **וְ**אַחַר֙ יֹאכַ֣ל מִן־הַקֳּדָשִׁ֔ים כִּ֥י לַחְמ֖וֹ הֽוּא׃

'The person who touches any of these will be unclean until evening and must not eat from the holy offerings unless he has bathed his body in water. [7]When the sun goes down he will be clean. **Only afterward** he may eat from the holy offerings, because they are his food.' (Lev. 22.6–7)

With a constituent other than *lō* before *yiqṭol(u)*, the clause signals discontinuity and can signal temporal succession only with an explicit temporal adverb (אַחַר֙), and in such a case with a sense of emphasis (Milgrom 2000, 1855). The *wa-lō-yiqṭol(u)* clause (וְלֹ֤א יֹאכַל֙) signals continuity (§7.12) and carries over the time period indicated by the previous clause (וְטָֽמְאָ֖ה עַד־הָעָ֑רֶב, cf. §2.3.8).[68]

2.3.5.2. Discourse-continuity Clauses

In narrative and report, the conjunction *wa* and the reflex of the old Semitic perfective *yaqtul*, the CBH perfective short *yiqṭol*, often form narrative chains expressing successive actions (see §§3.4.2, 7.11; Kienast 2001, 438; Kogan 2014, 52).

(64) ***wa**(y)-yiqṭol* + ***wa**(y)-yiqṭol* + ***wa**(y)-yiqṭol* + ***wa**(y)-yiqṭol* + ***wa**(y)-yiqṭol* + ***wa**(y)-yiqṭol*

וַיַּשְׁכֵּם אַבְרָהָם בַּבֹּקֶר וַיַּחֲבֹשׁ אֶת־חֲמֹרוֹ וַיִּקַּח אֶת־שְׁנֵי נְעָרָיו אִתּוֹ וְאֵת יִצְחָק
בְּנוֹ וַיְבַקַּע עֲצֵי עֹלָה וַיָּקָם וַיֵּלֶךְ אֶל־הַמָּקוֹם אֲשֶׁר־אָמַר־לוֹ הָאֱלֹהִים׃

‘**So** Abraham rose early in the morning, saddled his donkey, **and** took two of his young men with him, and his son Isaac. **And** he cut the wood for the burnt offering **and** arose **and** went to the place of which God had told him.’ (Gen. 22.3)

In the sequence displayed in (64), “temporal succession refers to the linear portrayal of events according to the order of their occurrence in the depicted world” (Cook 2004, 251). This is the default interpretation of the discourse-continuity clauses in such a chain: “the order in which clauses are presented in discourse is semantically significant… That is, in the absence of any linguistic cues to the contrary, events are understood as occurring in the order in which they are reported in narrative discourse” (Cook 2004, 251, who refers to Fleischman 1990, 131; also Hornkohl 2018, 47, 49).

But temporal succession is of course described also by other types of *wa*-clauses. The new (West Semitic) perfective *qaṭal* has in CBH taken over some of the functions of the old past perfective *yiqṭol(Ø)*, and one such overtaken function is found in negative storyline clauses (Tenet 4, see §7.12; cf. Isaksson 2015a, 256–59):[69]

(65) *wa(y)-yiqṭol* + [9]***wa**-lō-qaṭal* + *wa(y)-yiqṭol* + *wa(y)-yiqṭol* + *wa(y)-yiqṭol* + *wa(y)-yiqṭol*

וַיְשַׁלַּ֥ח אֶת־הַיּוֹנָ֖ה מֵאִתּ֑וֹ לִרְאוֹת֙ הֲקַ֣לּוּ הַמַּ֔יִם מֵעַ֖ל פְּנֵ֥י הָאֲדָמָֽה׃ **וְ**לֹא־מָצְאָה֩
הַיּוֹנָ֨ה מָנ֜וֹחַ לְכַף־רַגְלָ֗הּ וַתָּ֤שָׁב אֵלָיו֙ אֶל־הַתֵּבָ֔ה כִּי־מַ֖יִם עַל־פְּנֵ֣י כָל־הָאָ֑רֶץ
וַיִּשְׁלַ֤ח יָדוֹ֙ וַיִּקָּחֶ֔הָ וַיָּבֵ֥א אֹתָ֛הּ אֵלָ֖יו אֶל־הַתֵּבָֽה׃

'Then he sent out a dove, to see if the water had gone from the surface of the ground. [9]**But** the dove found no place for her feet to rest, so she returned to him in the ark, because the water still covered the whole earth. He put out his hand, took her and brought her in to him in the ark.' (Gen. 8.8f.)

After Noah sent the dove, it found no place to rest, and so it returned. The negative clause implies a searching with no result, which is a successive event in relation to the sending out.[70]

Not surprisingly, the discourse-continuous *wa-qaṭal* clause-type may also describe temporal succession. Such is often the case in complex *pɛn*-constructions:

(66) *wa(y) yiqṭol* + *"Ø-hēn-S.noun-qaṭal* + *wa-ʿattā-pɛn-yiqṭol(u)* + ***wa**-qaṭal* + ***wa**-qaṭal"*

וַיֹּ֣אמֶר ׀ יְהוָ֣ה אֱלֹהִ֗ים הֵ֤ן הָֽאָדָם֙ הָיָה֙ כְּאַחַ֣ד מִמֶּ֔נּוּ לָדַ֖עַת ט֣וֹב וָרָ֑ע וְעַתָּ֣ה ׀ פֶּן־
יִשְׁלַ֣ח יָד֗וֹ **וְ**לָקַח֙ גַּ֚ם מֵעֵ֣ץ הַֽחַיִּ֔ים **וְ**אָכַ֖ל וָחַ֥י לְעֹלָֽם׃

'Then the LORD God said, "Behold, the man has become like one of us in knowing good and evil. Now, lest he reach out his hand **and** take also of the tree of life and eat, **and** live forever—"' (Gen. 3.22)

The two *wa-qaṭal* clauses in (66) are positioned after a *pɛn*-clause with initial *yiqṭol(u)* predicate. This *pɛn* construction involves both the *yiqṭol(u)* clause and the two *wa-qaṭal* clauses, and the whole *pɛn* complex can be interpreted as a subordinate sentence whose main clause is not expressed within the direct speech, but by the action verb starting Genesis 3.23.[71] The two *wa-qaṭal* clauses express temporally successive actions in a 'possible consequence' construction (Dixon 2009, 23).[72]

A *wa-qaṭal* clause may often express a temporally successive event after an imperative. In such a case, it takes part in a modal domain and expresses, for example, the intention of the actant who formulates the command (see further §6.4). In the following example, *wa-qaṭal* clauses follow three coordinated imperative clauses, and the context makes clear that the *wa-qaṭal* clauses both describe temporal sequentiality:

(67) *wa(y)-yiqṭol: Ø-hinnē-nā-VOC-IMP + wa-IMP + wa-IMP +* ***wa****-qaṭal +* ***wa****-qaṭal*

וַיֹּאמֶר הִנֶּה נָּא־אֲדֹנַי סוּרוּ נָא אֶל־בֵּית עַבְדְּכֶם וְלִינוּ וְרַחֲצוּ רַגְלֵיכֶם
וְהִשְׁכַּמְתֶּם וַהֲלַכְתֶּם לְדַרְכְּכֶם

'He said, My lords, please turn aside to your servant's house and spend the night and wash your feet. **Then** you may rise up early **and** go on your way.' (Gen. 19.2a)

The two *wa-qaṭal* clauses in (67) constitute additional instructions (intended) to be performed after the fulfilment of the first commands coded by the imperatives. Such additional instructions with *wa-qaṭal* clauses in modal domains are frequent in CBH.[73]

In a narrative setting also, *wa-qaṭal* clauses signal discourse continuity and may code temporally successive habitual events.

In such cases, the past reference is marked in a preceding clause with explicit temporal marking, such as a past perfective *wa(y)-yiqṭol* clause. An example is found in (68):

(68) *wa(y)-yiqṭol!* + *wa-hinnē-XØ* + *wa-hinnē-qoṭel* + *kī-PrP-yiqṭol(u)* + *wa-XØ* + [3]*wa-qaṭal* + *wa-qaṭal* + ***wa**-qaṭal* + ***wa**-qaṭal*

וַיַּרְא וְהִנֵּה בְאֵר בַּשָּׂדֶה וְהִנֵּה־שָׁם שְׁלֹשָׁה עֶדְרֵי־צֹאן רֹבְצִים עָלֶיהָ כִּי מִן־
הַבְּאֵר הַהִוא יַשְׁקוּ הָעֲדָרִים וְהָאֶבֶן גְּדֹלָה עַל־פִּי הַבְּאֵר׃ וְנֶאֶסְפוּ־שָׁמָּה כָל־
הָעֲדָרִים וְגָלְלוּ אֶת־הָאֶבֶן מֵעַל פִּי הַבְּאֵר **וְ**הִשְׁקוּ אֶת־הַצֹּאן **וְ**הֵשִׁיבוּ אֶת־הָאֶבֶן
עַל־פִּי הַבְּאֵר לִמְקֹמָהּ׃

'He looked up and saw a well in a field, and three flocks of sheep lying there next to it. This well was used for watering the flocks. But the stone on the well's mouth was large, [3]and only when all the flocks had gathered there would they roll the stone away from the opening of the well **and** water the sheep. **Then** they would put the stone back in its place on the well's opening.' (Gen. 29.2–3)

In this narrative passage, the temporal frame is defined by the *wa(y)-yiqṭol* (וַיַּרְא) clause, which connects what follows to the current (preceding) narration. The *kī* particle is in this case an adverb ('indeed') that introduces a background description for the information of the receiver (listener or reader) of the text. The *yiqṭol(u)* (יַשְׁקוּ) clause that follows *kī* codes a habitual past action and the same holds for the four succeeding *wa-qaṭal*-clauses. The verbless clause that closes 29.2 determines the interpretation of the first *wa-qaṭal* clause in 29.3. Formally, 29.3 consists all in all of four *wa-qaṭal* clauses, and there are no syntactic signals that inform the receiver of the semantic relations between the four clauses. But an initial *wa-qaṭal* clause in such a chain may sometimes take the meaning of a temporal clause, or, in other cases, a conditional clause (see §§2.3.10, 6.7; Ges-K §§159g, 164b; Num. 10.5). The most reasonable interpretation of the first *wa-qaṭal* clause (וְנֶאֶסְפוּ) is as a 'when'-clause, the second *wa-qaṭal* clause (וְגָלְלוּ) being the focal clause after the temporal clause. The last two *wa-qaṭal* clauses express temporally successive past (habitual) events.[74]

Wa-qaṭal clauses may also be sequential in a future chain of events. In a sense, the events in such a chain are *irrealis*, because they are predicted or expected or instructed to occur. But they can be *realis* in being depicted as real in a future moment of time. An example is (69), which is the description of a foreseen series of events in the future:

(69) *Ø-PrP-yiqṭol(u)* + ***wa**-qaṭal* + ***wa**-qaṭal*

בְּע֣וֹד ׀ שְׁלֹ֣שֶׁת יָמִ֗ים יִשָּׂ֨א פַרְעֹ֤ה אֶת־רֹֽאשְׁךָ֙ מֵֽעָלֶ֔יךָ **וְ**תָלָ֥ה אוֹתְךָ֖ עַל־עֵ֑ץ **וְ**אָכַ֥ל הָע֛וֹף אֶת־בְּשָׂרְךָ֖ מֵעָלֶֽיךָ׃

'In three more days Pharaoh will decapitate you **and** impale you on a pole. **Then** the birds will eat your flesh from you.' (Gen. 40.19)

This is pure (prophetic) prediction of a chain of events. As is frequently the case in CBH, the prediction starts with a discontinuity *yiqṭol(u)* clause (or *qoṭel* clause), and the successive events are coded by *wa-qaṭal* clauses.[75]

A *wa-qaṭal* clause may also at times describe a temporal succession within a protasis. In the typical case, the protasis is initially marked by a conditional conjunction (such as *ʾim* or *kī*) and a *yiqṭol(u)* predicate, and the *wa-qaṭal* clause then follows, extending the protasis with a sequential action. An example is (70):

(70) *(Ø-ʾim-S.noun-yiqṭol(u) +* ***wa****-qaṭal) + Ø-S.noun-yiqṭol(u)! + wa-S.pron-yiqṭol(u)*

(אִם־אֲדֹנָיו֙ יִתֶּן־ל֣וֹ אִשָּׁ֔ה **וְ**יָלְדָה־ל֥וֹ בָנִ֖ים א֣וֹ בָנ֑וֹת) הָאִשָּׁ֣ה וִילָדֶ֗יהָ תִּהְיֶה֙ לַֽאדֹנֶ֔יהָ וְה֖וּא יֵצֵ֥א בְגַפּֽוֹ׃

'(If his master gives him a wife **and** she bears him sons or daughters), the woman and her children shall belong to her master, and only the man shall go free.' (Exod. 21.4, parentheses enclose the protasis)

In (70), it is pragmatically clear that the *wa-qaṭal* clause describes an added condition that is temporally sequential in relation to the initial stipulated event in the protasis. The apodosis then follows and is asyndetically attached to the protasis.[76]

2.3.6. *Wa*-linking as a Focal Result Clause

Sometimes a *wa*-clause describes an action or state that is the result of the action or state described in the preceding clause(s) and at the same time a focal clause. The previous clause describes a certain cause or reason, and the *wa*-clause describes a natural consequence of what was previously related (Dixon 2009, 2, 6, 17). Such a result clause is in CBH usually not syntactically subordinate (see §1.2.7). It can often be translated by an initial 'therefore', or 'because of that', or just 'then'.[77]

2.3.6.1. Discourse-discontinuity Clauses

When a focal result clause is to be coded, a discontinuity clause is not the most intuitive choice for this purpose. In the examples registered in my database, a constituent in the clause is focused and thus placed before the verb (type *wa-XV*). An example is (71):

(71) *wa-XØ* + ***wa**-O.noun-lō-qaṭal*

וּפְנֵיהֶם֙ אֲחֹ֣רַנִּ֔ית **וְ**עֶרְוַ֥ת אֲבִיהֶ֖ם לֹ֥א רָאֽוּ׃

'Their faces were turned the other way **so** they did not see their father's nakedness.' (Gen. 9.23b, NET, my emphasis)

In (71), the nakedness of their father (עֶרְוַ֥ת אֲבִיהֶ֖ם) is the focused constituent and has been placed before the verb. Semantically, the verbless clause constitutes the reason for what is expressed by the *qaṭal* clause, which is the focal clause in Dixon's sense.[78]

2.3.6.2. Discourse-continuity Clauses

The most natural expression of a focal result is a continuity clause. When a *wa(y)-yiqṭol* clause is used, the temporal reference is usually past with perfective aspect, as in (72):

(72) *Ø-PrP-qaṭal* + [2]*wa-S.noun-qaṭal* + *wa-XØ* + *wa-S.noun-qoṭel* + [3]***wa**(y)-yiqṭol*

בְּרֵאשִׁ֖ית בָּרָ֣א אֱלֹהִ֑ים אֵ֥ת הַשָּׁמַ֖יִם וְאֵ֥ת הָאָֽרֶץ׃ 2 וְהָאָ֗רֶץ הָיְתָ֥ה תֹ֙הוּ֙ וָבֹ֔הוּ וְחֹ֖שֶׁךְ עַל־פְּנֵ֣י תְה֑וֹם וְר֣וּחַ אֱלֹהִ֔ים מְרַחֶ֖פֶת עַל־פְּנֵ֥י הַמָּֽיִם׃ 3 **וַ**יֹּ֥אמֶר אֱלֹהִ֖ים יְהִ֣י א֑וֹר וַֽיְהִי־אֽוֹר׃

'In the beginning God created the heavens and the earth. [2]Now the earth was without shape and empty, and darkness covered the deep and the Wind of God hovered over the water. [3]**Then** God said, "Let there be light." And there was light.' (Gen. 1.1–3)

In an initial act of creation, God created the heavens and the earth. After this act, the earth was total chaos, and there was darkness over the deep waters (see Westermann 1976; Isaksson 2021, 227f.).[79] This is the reason for the next step in creation, to command light into existence, which could have been translated, 'Therefore God said,…'.[80]

When a *wa-qaṭal* clause expresses a focal result, it usually has future time reference, sometimes with an obligatory meaning. In the next example, YHWH gives a reason for his future saving acts concerning the people of Israel (73):

(73) *Ø-ADV-IMP: Ø-S.pron-XØ* + ***wa**-qaṭal* + ***wa**-qaṭal* + ***wa**-qaṭal* + [7]***wa**-qaṭal* + ***wa**-qaṭal* + *wa-qaṭal*

לָכֵ֞ן אֱמֹ֥ר לִבְנֵֽי־יִשְׂרָאֵל֮ אֲנִ֣י יְהוָה֒ **וְ**הוֹצֵאתִ֣י אֶתְכֶ֗ם מִתַּ֙חַת֙ סִבְלֹ֣ת מִצְרַ֔יִם
וְהִצַּלְתִּ֥י אֶתְכֶ֖ם מֵעֲבֹדָתָ֑ם **וְ**גָאַלְתִּ֤י אֶתְכֶם֙ בִּזְר֣וֹעַ נְטוּיָ֔ה וּבִשְׁפָטִ֖ים גְּדֹלִֽים׃
וְלָקַחְתִּ֨י אֶתְכֶ֥ם לִי֙ לְעָ֔ם **וְ**הָיִ֥יתִי לָכֶ֖ם לֵאלֹהִ֑ים וִֽידַעְתֶּ֗ם כִּ֣י אֲנִ֤י יְהוָה֙ אֱלֹ֣הֵיכֶ֔ם
הַמּוֹצִ֣יא אֶתְכֶ֔ם מִתַּ֖חַת סִבְל֥וֹת מִצְרָֽיִם׃

'So say to the Israelites: I am YHWH. **And therefore** I will bring you out from your enslavement to the Egyptians, **and** I will rescue you from the hard labor they impose, **and** I will redeem you with an outstretched arm and with great judgments. [7]**And** I will take you to myself for a people, **and** I will be your God. Then you will know that I am YHWH your God, who brought you out from your enslavement to the Egyptians.' (Exod. 6.6–7)

In (73), YHWH, the God of Israel, states his reasons for rescuing his people from Egypt, and the reasons he gives are himself, his own personality, his nature as represented by his name. And the temporal reference is future (cf. Pedersen 1934, 190).[81]

2.3.7. *Wa*-linking as a Supporting Reason Clause

In many instances, a clause is introduced by *wa* that expresses a cause or reason as a supporting clause. In such a case, the supporting clause specifies a cause or reason for the focal clause (Dixon 2009, 3, 6). Reason is often expressed by the conjunction *kī* (or another conjunction). Such instances are not discussed here, since they are not introduced by *wa*. However, in many cases, a *wa*-clause is enough.

2.3.7.1. Discourse-discontinuity Clauses

Most discontinuity examples are verbless clauses. One with a *qaṭal* predicate is (74):

(74) *Ø-ADV-yiqṭol(u)* + ***wa****-S.pron-qaṭal*

מַה־נַּעֲשֶׂה לָהֶם לַנּוֹתָרִים לְנָשִׁים **וַ**אֲנַחְנוּ נִשְׁבַּעְנוּ בַיהוָה לְבִלְתִּי תֵּת־לָהֶם מִבְּנוֹתֵינוּ לְנָשִׁים׃

‘How can we provide wives for those who are left, **since** we have taken an oath by the LORD not to give them any of our daughters in marriage?’ (Judg. 21.7, NIV, my emphasis)

In (74), the supporting clause with *qaṭal* supplies a reason for the question. There was a difficulty providing wives for those who were left, and the supporting clause explains why.[82]

2.3.7.2. Discourse-continuity Clauses

A few *wa-qaṭal* also function as supporting clauses expressing reason (no *wa(y)-yiqṭol* has this function). An example is (75):[83]

(75) *wa-qaṭal* + ***wa****-qaṭal*

וּזְרַעְתֶּם לָרִיק זַרְעֲכֶם **וַ**אֲכָלֻהוּ אֹיְבֵיכֶם׃

'You will sow your seed in vain **because** your enemies will eat it.' (Lev. 26.16b)

2.3.8. *Wa*-linking Carrying over the Preceding Manner

2.3.8.1. Discourse-continuity Clauses

In many instances, the coded 'world' that precedes a *wa*-clause represents a procedure or method or circumstance that is presupposed in the *wa*-clause. This close relationship with the preceding clause(s), the sharing of a common 'world', seems to be coded only by discourse-continuity clauses (type *wa-VX* or *wa-NEG-VX*; see §7.11–12). In this type of semantics, the *wa*-clause can often be translated with an understood (or explicitly stated) 'in this way', or 'under such circumstances', referring back to the previous clause(s). An example is (76):

(76) *wa-O.noun-yiqṭol(u)!* + *wa-qaṭal* + ***wa**-qaṭal* + ***wa**-qaṭal*

וְאֶת־כָּל־חֶלְבָּהּ יָסִיר כַּאֲשֶׁר יוּסַר חֵלֶב־הַכֶּשֶׂב מִזֶּבַח הַשְּׁלָמִים וְהִקְטִיר הַכֹּהֵן אֹתָם הַמִּזְבֵּחָה עַל אִשֵּׁי יְהוָה וְכִפֶּר עָלָיו הַכֹּהֵן עַל־חַטָּאתוֹ אֲשֶׁר־חָטָא וְנִסְלַח לוֹ׃

'They shall remove all the fat, just as the fat is removed from the lamb of the fellowship offering, and the priest shall burn it on the altar on top of the food offerings presented to the LORD. **In this way** the priest will make atonement for them for the sin they have committed, **and** they will be forgiven.' (Lev. 4.35, NIV, my emphasis)

The clause that starts with *wə-ḵippɛr* is not a separate further action to be taken by the priest, as some translations suggest by the rendering 'and the priest shall make atonement' (thus ESV), and it is not a subordinate result or a purpose clause. This discourse-continuity clause has the same status as the preceding clauses, and it describes (together with the last *wa*-clause, *wə-nislaḥ lō*) what is achieved by the procedural steps taken in the previous clauses.[84]

The corresponding negated continuity clause, *wa-lō-yiqṭol(u)* (Tenet 4, §7.12), may also carry over the manner or procedure in the preceding clause(s). An example is (77):[85]

(77) *wa-qaṭal* + ***wa**-lō-yiqṭol(u)*

וְהָיָה הָאֹכֶל לְפִקָּדוֹן לָאָרֶץ לְשֶׁבַע שְׁנֵי הָרָעָב אֲשֶׁר תִּהְיֶיןָ בְּאֶרֶץ מִצְרָיִם **וְ**לֹא־תִכָּרֵת הָאָרֶץ בָּרָעָב׃

'This food should be held in storage for the land in preparation for the seven years of famine that will occur throughout the land of Egypt. **In this way** the land will survive the famine.' (Gen. 41.36; NIV, my emphasis)

Such continuity clauses are found also in narrative contexts. An example is (78):

(78) *wa(y)-yiqṭol* + *wa(y)-yiqṭol* + ***wa**(y)-yiqṭol*

וַיִּקַּח מֹשֶׁה אֶת־שֶׁמֶן הַמִּשְׁחָה וַיִּמְשַׁח אֶת־הַמִּשְׁכָּן וְאֶת־כָּל־אֲשֶׁר־בּוֹ **וַ**יְקַדֵּשׁ אֹתָם׃

'Then Moses took the anointing oil and anointed the tabernacle and everything in it, **and in this way** he consecrated them.' (Lev. 8.10)

In (78), the action of consecrating (**וַ**יְקַדֵּשׁ) is not a successive separate action, but summarises what was achieved by the preceding procedure.[86]

2.3.9. *Wa*-linking as Semantic Complement

Examples of *wa*-clauses functioning as semantic complements are found only with discourse-continuity syntax (*wa-VX*).[87] A complement is defined as one clause functioning semantically "as an argument (generally as a core argument) of a higher clause" (Dixon 2009, 1). This section treats *wa-IMP* as second-person complement, *wa-yiqṭol(Ø)* as third-person complement, and *wa-qaṭal* clauses as complements independent of grammatical person.

2.3.9.1. Discourse-continuity Clauses

As is well known, second-person purpose clauses may be coded by *wa-IMP* clauses in CBH (J-M §116f.). In complementary distribution, first- and third-person purpose clauses are often coded by jussive *wa-yiqṭol* clauses, the first person often with a ventive/cohortative clitic (J-M §116d; Notarius 2017; Sjörs 2019). However, when the preceding clause describes a request or prayer or admonition or instruction or learning, a discourse-continuity clause may function semantically as a simple complement. In the second person, this pertains also to a *wa-IMP* clause. An example is (79):

(79) *wa-ʿattā-IMP + kī-XØ + wa-yiqṭol(Ø) +* ***wa****-IMP*

וְעַתָּ֗ה הָשֵׁ֤ב אֵֽשֶׁת־הָאִישׁ֙ כִּֽי־נָבִ֣יא ה֔וּא וְיִתְפַּלֵּ֥ל בַּֽעַדְךָ֖ **וֶ**חְיֵ֑ה

'So now, return the man's wife, because he is a prophet, so that he may intercede for you **that** you may live.' (Gen. 20.7a)

In (79), the initial imperative clause is followed by an added third-person jussive (וְיִתְפַּלֵּל) that expresses the purpose of the imperative ('so that he may intercede for you'). The last clause before the pause describes in the second person the content of the intercession, which makes it semantically a complement clause ('that you may live'). The complement clause in the second person is expressed by a discourse-continuity clause with imperative predicate.[88]

Third-person purpose clauses may also, when the preceding clause describes a request or prayer etc., turn semantically into a complement. In such a case, a discourse-continuity clause with jussive predicate is used, as in (80):

(80) *Ø-IMP* + ***wa**-yiqṭol(Ø)!* + *wa-yiqṭol(Ø)-A* + ***wa**-yiqṭol(Ø)*

הַעְתִּ֣ירוּ אֶל־יְהוָ֗ה וְיָסֵר֙ הַֽצְפַרְדְּעִ֔ים מִמֶּ֖נִּי וּמֵעַמִּ֑י וַאֲשַׁלְּחָה֙ אֶת־הָעָ֔ם וְיִזְבְּח֖וּ
לַיהוָֽה׃

'Plead with the LORD **to** take away the frogs from me and from my people, and I will let the people go **to** sacrifice to the LORD.' (Exod. 8.4, ESV, my emphasis)

In (80), the initial imperative clause (הַעְתִּירוּ) has the lexical meaning of 'to plead' and, with this type of semantics in the first clause, the following jussive clause (וְיָסֵר) receives the connotation of a simple complement 'to take away'. The following ventive/cohortative expresses the response of the same subject (Pharaoh) as in the imperative clause, but after that, once again, a jussive in the third person with initial *wa* codes a motion purpose clause (וְיִזְבְּחוּ '**to** sacrifice'), which is semantically close to a complement (Dixon 2009, 45). In the latter case, the jussive does not show a distinctively short *yiqṭol(Ø)* form, but the preceding distinctive jussive (וְיָסֵר), and the initial position of the verb (see §3.4.3), inform us that a jussive is intended.[89]

Wa-qaṭal clauses as personal (volitive) purpose clauses are practically non-existent in CBH.[90] As we have remarked above, the normal syntax for purpose clauses is *wa-IMP* or *wa-yiqṭol(Ø)* (the latter including ventive/cohortative *wa-yiqṭol(Ø)-A*), depending on the grammatical person to be expressed.[91] But *wa-qaṭal* is now and then also used with the meaning of a complement. In this function, *wa-qaṭal* can be used in all grammatical persons. As usual, the preceding semantic context is one of request or prayer or admonition. An example is (81):

(81) *Ø-IMP* + ***wa***-*qaṭal*

צַ֚ו אֶת־בְּנֵ֣י יִשְׂרָאֵ֗ל **וְ**נָתְנ֤וּ לַלְוִיִּם֙ מִנַּחֲלַ֣ת אֲחֻזָּתָ֔ם עָרִ֖ים לָשָׁ֑בֶת

'Instruct the Israelites **to** give the Levites towns to live in from the inheritance the Israelites will possess.' (Num. 35.2a, NET, my emphasis)

In (81), the initial command is coded by an imperative clause (צַ֚ו אֶת־בְּנֵ֣י יִשְׂרָאֵ֗ל) and the *wa-qaṭal* clause gives the content of the command, that is, its complement.

An example of a *wa-qaṭal* complement clause in the second person, preceded by an imperative, is (82):

(82) *Ø-IMP* + ***wa***-*qaṭal*

שְׁמֹ֣ר **וְ**שָׁמַעְתָּ֗ אֵ֚ת כָּל־הַדְּבָרִ֣ים הָאֵ֔לֶּה אֲשֶׁ֥ר אָנֹכִ֖י מְצַוֶּ֑ךָּ

'Be careful **to** obey all these words that I command you' (Deut. 12.28a, ESV, my emphasis)

The examples (81) and (82) are the only ones registered in my corpus with *IMP* + *wa-qaṭal* linking where *wa-qaṭal* has the function of a complement. A *yiqṭol(u)* + *wa-qaṭal* linking is a more frequent way to express a complement. The following example (83) is from instructional discourse (obligation):

(83) *Ø-O.noun-yiqṭol(u)* + ***wa**-qaṭal* + *CONJ-qaṭal* + *REL-qaṭal*

מוֹצָ֥א שְׂפָתֶ֖יךָ תִּשְׁמֹ֣ר **וְ**עָשִׂ֑יתָ כַּאֲשֶׁ֨ר נָדַ֜רְתָּ לַיהוָ֤ה אֱלֹהֶ֙יךָ֙ נְדָבָ֔ה אֲשֶׁ֥ר דִּבַּ֖רְתָּ בְּפִֽיךָ׃

‘Whatever vow that passes your lips you must be careful **to** do, exactly according to what you voluntarily vowed to YHWH, your God, what you promised in words spoken aloud.’ (Deut. 23.24)

The example (83) expresses with its initial *yiqṭol(u)* an obligation, and its semantics (‘be careful to’) cause *wa-qaṭal* to function as a complement. This is possible also in a context with future time reference, as in (84):

(84) *kī-qaṭal* + *CONJ-yiqṭol(u)!* + ***wa**-qaṭal*

כִּ֣י יְדַעְתִּ֗יו לְמַ֙עַן֙ אֲשֶׁ֨ר יְצַוֶּ֜ה אֶת־בָּנָ֤יו וְאֶת־בֵּיתוֹ֙ אַחֲרָ֔יו **וְ**שָֽׁמְרוּ֙ דֶּ֣רֶךְ יְהוָ֔ה לַעֲשׂ֥וֹת צְדָקָ֖ה וּמִשְׁפָּ֑ט

‘I have chosen him so that he may command his children and his household after him **to** keep the way of the LORD by doing what is right and just.’ (Gen. 18.19, NET, my emphasis)

The complement clause in (84) is part of a complex purpose sentence explicitly signalled by a compound conjunction (לְמַ֙עַן֙ אֲשֶׁ֨ר). The purpose sentence has a *yiqṭol(u)* predicate with the lexical meaning ‘to command’ and these semantics lead the *wa-qaṭal* clause to be perceived as a complement (and not as a normal coordination).[92]

It seems obvious that *wa-qaṭal* clauses may function as semantic equivalents to complement clauses, just as discourse-continuity ventives/cohortatives (*wa-yiqṭol(Ø)-A*), imperatives (*wa-IMP*), and jussives (*wa-yiqṭol(Ø)*) can, but without the restriction to grammatical person.

2.3.10. *Wa*-linking and Conditionality without Conditional Conjunction

As in the English example *Give me your picture and I'll give you mine,* CBH can express a conditional linking without conditional conjunction but instead using *wa* as the connective between protasis and apodosis. Cases with an initial imperative clause as protasis and a *wa*-clause as apodosis are relatively frequent, as in (85):

(85) *Ø-IMP* + *wa-IMP* + [2]***wa**-yiqṭol(Ø)-A* + ***wa**-yiqṭol(Ø)-V*

הִתְהַלֵּ֥ךְ לְפָנַ֖י וֶהְיֵ֥ה תָמִֽים׃ **וְ**אֶתְּנָ֥ה בְרִיתִ֖י בֵּינִ֣י וּבֵינֶ֑ךָ וְאַרְבֶּ֥ה אוֹתְךָ֖ בִּמְאֹ֥ד מְאֹֽד׃

'Walk before me and be perfect, [2]**and** I will make my covenant between myself and you, and I will give you a multitude of descendants.' (Gen. 17.1-2)

In (85), it is understood that the imperatives state a condition for the promise to be fulfilled: 'If you walk before me and are perfect, then I will make my covenant…'. In the example, the apodosis is constituted by two jussive clauses with ventive/cohortative clitic (see §3.4.2.3), both introduced by the connective *wa*.[93] All my examples with imperative as protasis have a discourse-continuity apodosis, and this *wa* is in traditional Hebrew grammars regarded as 'copulative', not 'consecutive'.

2.4. Summary

The traditional theory of consecutive tenses with its thesis of two different conjunctions *wa* in Biblical Hebrew has disguised the fact that every *wa* has the same basic meaning.[94] This chapter has shown that both 'consecutive *waw*' and 'copulative *waw*' may have meanings of simultaneity, temporal succession, conditionality, reason, result, and conclusion. In all instances discussed above, a *wa*-clause relates to the preceding clause(s), and the meaning that *wa* is perceived to possess is determined by the semantic relation between the two clauses. A *wa*-clause may even function semantically as a complement, and such cases include instances of both traditional 'copulative *waw*' (as in *wa-yiqṭol(Ø)* and *wa-IMP*) and traditional 'consecutive *waw*' (as in *wa-qaṭal*).

It turns out that the principal syntactic distinction in CBH is not between 'consecutive *waw*' and 'copulative *waw*', but instead between discourse-continuity clauses and discontinuity clauses. In this distinction, *wa* plays a fundamental role, in the formation of the principal continuity clause-type in CBH prose: *wa-V*.

In this chapter, I have given examples of the semantics of clause linking with *wa*, and many of the semantic types can be coded by both continuity and discontinuity clauses (temporal succession, elaboration). Some semantic types require a strict discontinuity coding (attendant circumstance), and others require a continuity coding (carrying over the preceding manner; semantic complement).

---

[1] I owe this reference to Khan (1991).

[2] "That is, the negation of both P and Q is logically equivalent to the negation of either P or Q" (Schiffrin 1986, 42).

[3] Schiffrin refers to Posner (1980, 186). This is the so-called 'maximalist view', which Traugott (1986, 147) shows is supported by historical data (cf. Schiffrin 1986, 45 n. 1).

[4] In a similar way, Müller (1991, 156) compares *wa* with the German *und*. Tropper (1996, 635) defines the meaning of *wa* in Biblical Hebrew and Old Aramaic as 'und (dann)'.

[5] The '(*wa*-)' before Clause_1 indicates a possible connection backwards to previous clause(s), as is often the case. This connection can be a linking to a preceding clause and *wa* is in this case simply a clausal conjunction. But the '(*wa*-)' before Clause_1 can also be a discourse marker, in which case it fulfils a discourse-pragmatic function and does not provide a syntactic linking to a preceding clause. At the level of the discourse, such a *wa* marks "the location of an utterance with respect to its emerging context" and, at the textual level, it signals "the pragmatic relationship of an utterance to its broader context" (Miller 1999, 167f.). A discourse marker is syntactically nonessential and can be syntactically detached from the clause. For the notion of 'connection' to a previous context, see Miller (1999, 170). See further Tenet 2 (§§7.7–10).

[6] It is certainly practical in complicated text analysis to note that *wa*, in addition to linking two clauses, also "delimits the boundary between them," as Smith (1991, 14) says about "the consecutive *waw*," an observation that actually holds for all uses of *wa* as long as it is a clausal connective.

[7] Dixon (2009, 2, 9, 28): "[Mary left John]$_{\text{SC}}$ and he went into a monastery."

[8] As in 'Result linking' (Dixon 2009, 2, 17–23): "[It rained on Saturday]$_{\text{SC}}$ and so we could not hold the planned picnic" (Dixon 2009, 19).

[9] As a natural connective, *wa* is non-commutative. If the antecedent clause and the following clause change place, the complex sentence usually becomes unacceptable (Van Dijk 1977, 61). The cases of *wa* connecting two clauses in 'unordered addition' (Dixon 2009, 26) are extremely rare in CBH. Possible cases are: Gen. 4.22 (*wa(y)-yiqṭol*... + *wa-S.noun-qaṭal*, genealogy); 17.6 (*wa-qaṭal* + *wa-S.noun-yiqṭol(u)*, prediction); Exod. 3.7 (*Ø-VNabs-qaṭal* + *wa-O.noun-qaṭal*, direct speech); 34.25 (*Ø-lō-yiqṭol(u)* + *wa-lō-yiqṭol(u)*!, instruction); Judg. 7.25 (*wa(y)-yiqṭol* + *wa-O.noun-qaṭal*, narrative); and, outside the corpus, 1 Sam. 2.6–7 (*Ø-S.noun-qoṭel* + *wa-qoṭel*, poetry); Ps. 18.26f. ([26]*Ø-PrP-yiqṭol(u)* + *Ø-PrP-yiqṭol(u)* + [27]*Ø-PrP-yiqṭol(u)* + *wa-PrP-yiqṭol(u)*, archaic poetry). For further discussion of clause combining with *wa* (and all its allomorphs) in Semitic, see Isaksson (2009); Isaksson and Persson (2014; 2015).

[10] The shift to SOV word order in Akkadian changed all this. With this gradual shift of word order, the original conjunction *wa/u* came to be attached to other constituents in the clause, so that the close connection to the verbal predicate was lost. This was the driving force behind its early replacement in Akkadian by the enclitic particle *-ma*, which was attached to the verbal predicate at the end of the clause. This is an indication that the Proto-Semitic word order was VSO (Kogan 2014, 52–54).

[11] For the term, see Givón (2001, II:330–351). A subordinate clause has unequal status in relation to a main clause. Hypotaxis refers to the relation between two (or more) clauses of unequal status (Halliday 2004, 374, 489). For what it is worth, this is possibly the best definition of a subordinate clause I can offer (though it is close to being circular: Isaksson 2013, 657). A subordinate clause being embedded is a special case (see §1.2.7)

[12] Some scholars call this usage of *wa* '*wāw* of apodosis' (Kogan 2014, 54), though the linking is not conditional.

[13] To support the interpretation of *wa* as '*wāw* of apodosis', Kogan supplies the translations of two independent editors of the text, which are

quoted in Kogan. Of course there is no special '*wāw* of apodosis' in Semitic, there is only one *wa* (pseudopolysemy: Blau 2010, 285).

[14] The text is partly complemented by Stein (2011, 1064).

[15] For the phrase *(w-)ywm*, see Nebes and Stein (2008, 165).

[16] The translation is partly taken from Stein (2011, 1064).

[17] For a discussion of the linguistic entity called 'Classical Arabic', see Birnstiel (2019, 367–70).

[18] Reckendorf (1895–98, 447): "es wird nicht der Inhalt des zweites Satzes, sondern die Tatsache, dass Etwas geäussert werden soll, an den ersten Satz angeknüpft." Concerning *fa*, see Reckendorf (1895–98, §157). Miller (1999, 168): "To function as a discourse marker, the conjunction must be syntactically detachable from the sentence (i.e., syntactically nonessential)."

[19] This is Dixon's same-event addition (2009, 27); see §2.3.4. In the transcription, translation, and division of the clauses in the example, I follow Tropper (2012, 785).

[20] In later stages of Aramaic, the use of this *p* has come to an end (Segert 1975a, §7.5.2).

[21] The classification of the Aramaic of the Deir ʿAllā inscription is disputed. See the discussion in §3.1.11, and Huehnergard and Pat-El (2019, 3). For the purpose of the present book, this classification is not essential.

[22] The parentheses indicate a left dislocation.

[23] "*ybrk wyšmrk*: The formula here recalls the priestly benediction in Num. 6.24–26, where one finds the pair *ybrkk… wyšmrk*" (HI 294).

[24] Schulz (1900, 28) argues that the meaning of *waC-* as a connective is the same as the meaning of *wə-*, but takes the impossible position that the *yiqṭol* in *wayyiqṭol* is a normal 'Imperfekt' (that is, *yiqṭol(u)*) used as a historical present in the Hebrew narrative: "Das Imperfekt mit וַ setzt also niemals andere Funktionen in Kraft, als solche, welche auch dem Imperfekt an sich eigentümlich sind." For a survey of *wa* as a connective of constituents *within* a clause, see Müller (1994).

[25] As an example, Cook (2004, 259–61) shows convincingly that temporal succession is not a specific semantic feature of *wa(y)-yiqṭol*.

[26] The examples of elaboration overlap considerably with the use of the so-called '*waw* explicativum' (Baker 1980).

[27] Judg. 20.34 (*wa-S.noun-qaṭal* + *wa-S.pron-lō-qaṭal*) is a summary before the main events.

[28] The first *wa(y)-yiqṭol* in the verse (וַיִּגְדָּ֑ל) is not analysed as elaborative here. It can be interpreted as a consequence of the blessing ('result', Dixon 2009, 19, 22, 45), which is supported by the *ʾatnāḥ* that indicates the conclusion of the first hemistich: "Jahwe hat meinen Herrn gesegnet so daß er 'sehr' reich wurde" (Westermann 1981, 465). The examples in CBH of *wa(y)-yiqṭol* clauses coding an elaboration are so numerous that I restrict them to the book of Genesis and one example in Exodus: Gen. 5.7 (*wa(y)-yiqṭol* + ***wa****(y)-yiqṭol*, genealogy); 10.18b–19 (*wa-ADV-qaṭal* + ***wa****(y)-yiqṭol*); 12.16 (*wa-PrP-qaṭal* + ***wa****(y)-yiqṭol*); 14.19—according to Hornkohl (2018, 46), this is not sequential, the speaking and blessing are the same act; 18.2 (Joosten 2012, 174); 19.19; 21.1f. (*wa-S.noun-qaṭal* + ***wa****(y)-yiqṭol* + ***wa****(y)-yiqṭol*, narrative); 24.35 (*wa-S.noun-qaṭal* + *wa(y)-yiqṭol* + ***wa****(y)-yiqṭol*); 25.17 (*wa(y)-yiqṭol* + ***wa****(y)-yiqṭol* + ***wa****(y)-yiqṭol*); 26.15 (*wa-O.noun-qaṭal* + ***wa****(y)-yiqṭol*); 26.29 (*wa-CONJ-qaṭal* + ***wa****(y)-yiqṭol*); 31.26 (*Ø-O.pron-qaṭal* + ***wa****(y)-yiqṭol* + ***wa****(y)-yiqṭol*); 32.23f. (*wa(y)-yiqṭol* + [24]***wa****(y)-yiqṭol* + ***wa****(y)-yiqṭol* + ***wa****(y)-yiqṭol*)—but the elaboration has been explained as being due to different sources, namely, v. 23 is from J, 24a from E, and 24b from L (Eissfeldt 1922, 66*); 34.3 (*wa(y)-yiqṭol* + ***wa****(y)-yiqṭol* + ***wa****(y)-yiqṭol*)—concomitant clauses according to Joosten (2012, 169 n. 24); 35.16 (*wa(y)-yiqṭol* + ***wa****(y)-yiqṭol*); 37.5f.—"an event is first stated generally and then told in detail" (Joosten 2012, 174); 37.17b–18a (*wa(y)-yiqṭol* + *wa(y)-yiqṭol* + ***wa****(y)-yiqṭol*, an anticipating clause is followed by elaboration); 42.30 (*Ø-qaṭal* + ***wa****(y)-yiqṭol*, report); 48.3 (*Ø-S.noun-qaṭal* + ***wa****(y)-yiqṭol*); 50.12f. (*wa(y)-yiqṭol* + ***wa****(y)-yiqṭol* + ***wa****(y)-yiqṭol*); Exod. 19.18 (*wa-S.noun-qaṭal* + *Ø-CONJ-qaṭal* + ***wa****(y)-yiqṭol* + ***wa****(y)-yiqṭol*)—simultaneity according to Joosten (2012, 169 n. 24).

[29] Of course, an English translation may leave out the conjunction *and* in the elaboration, as most versions do. More examples of elaborative *wa-qaṭal* clauses: Gen. 9.9–11 (*wa-S.pron-hinnē-qoṭel* + ***wa***-*qaṭal* + ***wa-****lō-yiqṭol(u)* + ***wa-****lō-yiqṭol(u)*, future, direct speech); 31.7a (*wa-S.noun-qaṭal*-PrP + ***wa***-*qaṭal*, habitual anterior); 32.13; 48.4 (*Ø-hinnē-S.pron-qoṭel* + ***wa***-*qaṭal* + ***wa***-*qaṭal* + ***wa***-*qaṭal*); Exod. 4.15b–16a (*wa-S.pron-yiqṭol(Ø)* + ***wa***-*qaṭal* + ***wa***-*qaṭal*, direct speech, volitive future); 7.27b–28 (*Ø-hinnē-S.pron-qoṭel* + ***wa***-*qaṭal* + ***wa***-*qaṭal* + ***wa***-*qaṭal*, an apodosis); 12.11; 15.26a (*ʾim-VNabs-yiqṭol(u)* + *wa-O.noun-yiqṭol(u)* + ***wa***-*qaṭal* + ***wa***-*qaṭal*, in protasis); 20.9 (*Ø-ADV-yiqṭol(u)* + ***wa-qaṭal***)—the temporal frame of the *wa-qaṭal* clause is determined by the preceding *yiqṭol(u)* clause, so the *wa-qaṭal* may also be interpreted temporally, i.e., 'then you shall do all your work'; 26.3f. (*Ø-S.noun-yiqṭol(u)* + ***wa***-*qaṭal* + ***wa-***ADV-*yiqṭol(u)*); 26.24f. (*Ø-ADV-yiqṭol(u)* + ***wa***-*qaṭal*); Num. 4.24f. (*Ø-XØ* + ***wa***-*qaṭal*, elaboration of initial general instruction).

[30] More examples of a summary introduced by 'consecutive *waw*': Exod. 39.32 (***wa****(y)-yiqṭol* + ***wa****(y)-yiqṭol*, both clauses a summary of preceding narrative unit); Num. 8.15 (***wa***-*qaṭal* + ***wa***-*qaṭal*)—'So you must cleanse them and offer them like a wave offering' (NET), but Levine (1993, 277) misinterprets the summary as an interpolation; Judg. 20.46 (copula verb).

[31] Cf. Isaksson (2009); but the present definition with its 'concomitant' restriction is narrower. A circumstantial clause qualifies a specific preceding clause and usually also supplies information about a constituent in that clause (see further §7.4). Backgrounded clauses are not necessarily concomitant with the main clause, and give explanatory or other information important for the reader to understand the main events. Information in the background belongs to the world of the text. If a piece of information is added by the editor of the text, not belonging to the pragmatic world of the text (for example, information for later readers), I call such a clause comment.

[32] While the definition of a clause is fairly straightforward (any syntagm that contains one predication), I must admit that I am unable to supply a tenable definition of 'sentence' (cf. Dixon 2010, 340). For what it is

worth, I preliminarily regard such an entity as a syntagm made up of a complex of clauses with a common illocutionary function.

[33] I restrict the concept of background to cases when the author/narrator is an anonymous text creator not mentioned in the text. In the present section about circumstantial and background clauses introduced by *wa*, I have decided to exclude (editorial) added comments.

[34] On this point, I take the position of Notarius (2008, 63, 83; 2013, 143, 282f.; 2015, 242); see also Isaksson (2014a, 127). An example put forward by Notarius (2013, 165) is 2 Sam. 22.5/Ps. 18.5, with the clausal pattern (*kī*)-*qaṭal* + (***wa***)-*S.noun-yiqṭol(u)*, in which the *yiqṭol(u)* clause is asyndetic in 2 Sam. 22.5 but introduced by *wa* in Ps. 18.5.

[35] Another possible example is Gen. 2.25 (*wa(y)-yiqṭol* + ***wa***-*lō-yiqṭol(u)*), regarded as circumstantial also by Brockelmann (1908–13, II, §321b; Nyberg 1972, §86t). The long *yiqṭol* clause in Gen. 2.25 can also by analysed as background. Joosten (1999, 24) regards this *yiqṭol(u)* as a "past modal."

[36] Asyndetic circumstantial long *yiqṭol* clauses are also rare, though possibly more frequent than the syndetic ones. In my corpus, there are three examples: Exod. 8.5; 12.34; Num. 14.3 (thus also Driver 1892, §163). Outside my corpus, examples include 1 Sam. 13.17—thus Driver (1892, §163); Muraoka (2001, 390), but Joosten (2012, 133) discerns a possible prospective function; 1 Sam. 18.5 (*wa(y)-yiqṭol* + ***Ø***-*PrP-yiqṭol(u)!*)—but Driver (1892, §163) analyses the clausal boundaries incorrectly and regards it as an example of circumstantial *Ø-yiqṭol(u)*, which would be an anomaly in CBH prose.

[37] No such circumstantial active participle clauses are found in the archaic poetry, a fact that indicates their gradual diachronic take-over of circumstantial functions from the long *yiqṭol* clauses in CBH. There are about 40 syndetic circumstantial active participle clauses in my corpus (linking patterns are supplied only in Genesis): Gen. 14.13 (*wa(y)-yiqṭol* + *wa(y)-yiqṭol* + ***wa***-*S.pron-qoṭel*); 18.1 (see above); 18.8 (*wa(y)-yiqṭol* + *wa(y)-yiqṭol* + **wa**-*S.pron-qoṭel*); 18.10 (*wa(y)-yiqṭol* + "…" + ***wa***-*S.noun-qoṭel*); 18.16 (*wa(y)-yiqṭol* + *wa(y)-yiqṭol* + ***wa***-*S.noun-qoṭel*);

18.22 (*wa(y)-yiqṭol* + *wa(y)-yiqṭol* + ***wa**-S.noun-ADV-S.pron-qoṭel*); 19.1 (*wa(y)-yiqṭol* + ***wa**-S.noun-qoṭel*); 24.21 (*wa(y)-yiqṭol* + ***wa**-S.noun-qoṭel*); 24.30 (*wa(y)-yiqṭol* + ***wa**-hinnē-qoṭel*); 25.26 (*wa-ADV-qaṭal* + ***wa**-S.noun-qoṭel*); 30.36 (*wa(y)-yiqṭol* + ***wa**-S.noun-qoṭel*); 32.32 (*wa(y)-yiqṭol* + CONJ-*qaṭal* + ***wa**-S.pron-qoṭel*); 37.15 (*wa(y)-yiqṭol* + ***wa**-hinnē-qoṭel*); Exod. 2.5; 2.13; 5.13; 9.24; 13.21; 14.8; 14.27; 18.14; Num. 10.33; 23.6; 23.17; 24.18 (but archaic); 25.6; 33.4 (the matrix *qaṭal* is in 33.3); 33.40 (circumstantial clause inserted within matrix: *wa(y)-yiqṭol* + ***wa**-S.pron-qoṭel*); 35.23; Deut. 4.11; 4.42; 5.23; 22.6; Judg. 3.20; 3.25; 6.11; 7.13; 11.34 (Nyberg 1972, §86bb); 13.9; 13.20; 16.9 (circumstantial *qoṭel*-clause before matrix, cf. Judg. 16.12); 16.12 (matrix this time before the *qoṭel*-clause); 18.7 (*wa(y)-yiqṭol* + ***Ø**-qoṭel* + ***Ø**-qoṭel* + ***wa**-qoṭel*); 18.17; 19.27; 20.33.

[38] Circumstantial verbless clauses are introduced by *wa* practically twice as often as they are asyndetic. In my corpus, there are 87 examples of circumstantial *wa-XØ* and 44 of *Ø-XØ* (archaic examples exist but are excluded).

[39] The modal forms in the verse (הָבָה | נִבְנֶה) are ‘long’ (ending in *ā* or *ɛ̄*), which in both instances should be interpreted as a ventive enclitic (-*V*), but this does not concern us here (Sjörs 2019). Thus, the verb *nibnɛ̄* should be derived from **nabniy-an* rather than **nabniy-u*.

[40] My examples of syndetic circumstantial *XØ* in Genesis are: 4.7 (*Ø-PrP-S.noun-qoṭel* + ***wa**-XØ*); 8.11 (*wa(y)-yiqṭol* + ***wa**-hinnē-XØ*); 9.23 (*wa(y)-yiqṭol* + ***wa**-XØ*); 11.4; 18.10 (*Ø-VNabs-yiqṭol(u)!* + ***wa**-hinnē-XØ*); 18.12 (*Ø-PREP-VN-qaṭal* + ***wa**-XØ*); 18.14 (*Ø-PrP-yiqṭol(u)!* + ***wa**-XØ*); 24.10 (Brockelmann 1908–13, II, §321b); 24.45 ‘along came Rebekah with her water jug on her shoulder’ (NET); 25.1; 25.29 (*wa(y)-yiqṭol* + ***wa**-XØ*); 29.2 (*kī-PrP-yiqṭol(u)* + ***wa**-XØ*); 29.31 (*wa(y)-yiqṭol* + ***wa**-XØ*); 32.7 (*wa-gam-qoṭel* + ***wa**-XØ*); 33.1 (*wa(y)-yiqṭol* + *wa-hinnē-S.noun-qoṭel* + ***wa**-PrP-XØ*); 36.32 (*wa(y)-yiqṭol* + ***wa**-XØ*); 36.39 (*wa(y)-yiqṭol* + ***wa**-XØ* + *wa-XØ*; the first *XØ* is an attendant circumstantial clause, the second is background); 38.1 (*wa(y)-yiqṭol* + ***wa**-XØ*); 38.2 (*wa(y)-yiqṭol* + ***wa**-XØ*); 38.6 (*wa(y)-yiqṭol* + ***wa**-S.noun-XØ*); 41.8 (*wa(y)-yiqṭol* + ***wa**-ʾēn-XØ*; the participle is a noun here); 42.27

(*wa(y)-yiqṭol* + ***wa**-hinnē-XØ*); 44.14 (*wa(y)-yiqṭol* + ***wa**-XØ*), 44.30 (*wa-ʿattā-PREP-VN* + ***wa**-XØ* + ***wa**-XØ*, within a temporal clause); 44.34 (*kī-ADV-yiqṭol(u)* + ***wa**-S.noun-ʾēn-XØ*).

[41] There are also some uses of the infinitive that must be called circumstantial. Such infinitive clauses are always asyndetic; see Isaksson (2007).

[42] In total, 192 background clauses in the corpus are syndetic (connected with *wa-*). 58 are asyndetic. Editorial comments are mostly asyndetic and are not counted here.

[43] In addition, one such instance in the books of the corpus is archaic: Deut. 32.14 (*wa(y)-yiqṭol* + ***wa**-O.noun-yiqṭol(u)!*); see Notarius (2013, 80, 83, 85, 307; 2015, 240), who regards the *tištɛ̄* as a long imperfective form (past habitual).

[44] The translation accords relatively closely with Propp (2006, 585).

[45] Other examples of long *yiqṭol* in background: Gen. 2.10 (*wa-S.noun-qoṭel* + *wa-PrP-yiqṭol(u)* + *wa-qaṭal*, background initiated by a *qoṭel* clause); 34.7 (*wa(y)-yiqṭol* + *wa(y)-yiqṭol* + *kī-O.noun-qaṭal* + ***wa**-kēn-lō-yiqṭol(u)*) 'something that is simply not done' (CJB); Exod. 1.12 (***wa**-CONJ-yiqṭol(u)* + *Ø-ADV-yiqṭol(u)!* + ***wa**-ADV-yiqṭol(u)*, a logical-comparative construction which functions as background); 33.7 ([7]***wa**-S.noun-yiqṭol(u)* + *wa-qaṭal* + … [12]*wa(y)-yiqṭol*, the only example in the corpus with a long *yiqṭol* background clause that precedes the mainline; the *wa* in this case marks a connection with the foregoing context); 40.36 (***wa**-VN-yiqṭol(u)*, habitual past); Num. 11.9; Judg. 6.4 ([3]… + *wa-qaṭal* + [4]*wa(y)-yiqṭol* + ***wa**-lō-yiqṭol(u)*, all clauses habitual past and background).

[46] Hornkohl (2018, 49 n. 64) calls this off-line information; verse 57 is "end of scene."

[47] Only 24 backgrounded verbless clauses in the corpus are asyndetic, as in Gen. 11.29 (*wa(y)-yiqṭol* + *Ø-XØ* + *wa-XØ*).

[48] I supply the first ten backgrounding syndetic verbless clauses in the corpus: Gen. 1.2 (*wa-S.noun-qaṭal* + ***wa**-XØ* + *wa-S.noun-qoṭel*); 2.19 (*wa(y)-yiqṭol* + ***wa**-XØ*); 9.18 (*wa(y)-yiqṭol* + ***wa**-XØ*); 12.4 (*wa(y)-*

yiqṭol + ***wa**-XØ*); 13.2 ([1]*wa(y)-yiqṭol* + [2]***wa**-XØ*); 13.13 (*wa-S.noun-qaṭal* + [13]***wa**-XØ*); 14.10 (***wa**-XØ* + *wa(y)-yiqṭol*); 14.13 (*wa(y)-yiqṭol* + *wa-S.pron-qoṭel* + ***wa**-XØ*); 14.18 (*wa-S.noun-qaṭal* + ***wa**-XØ*, new paragraph beginning with main-line *qaṭal* and then a piece of historical information with *XØ*); 16.16 ([15]*wa(y)-yiqṭol* + [16]***wa**-XØ*).

[49] There are 24 other backgrounding *qoṭel* clauses introduced by *wa*. In the following list of syndetic participle clauses, I supply the linking pattern for the first ten: Gen. 1.2 ([1]*Ø-qaṭal* + [2]***wa**-S.noun-qaṭal* + ***wa**-XØ* + ***wa**-S.noun-qoṭel*); 2.10 ([9]*wa(y)-yiqṭol* + [10]***wa**-S.noun-qoṭel*); 14.12 (*wa(y)-yiqṭol* + ***wa**-S.pron-qoṭel*; *yōšēb* can also be analysed as a noun); 24.20f. (*wa(y)-yiqṭol* + ***wa**-S.noun-qoṭel* + *Ø-qoṭel*); 24.62 ([62]*wa-S.noun-qaṭal* + ***wa**-S.pron-qoṭel* + [63]*wa(y)-yiqṭol*; the *qaṭal* clause here introduces a new paragraph); 27.5 ([4]*wa(y)-yiqṭol* + [5]***wa**-S.noun-qoṭel*); Exod. 13.20f. (*wa(y)-yiqṭol* + *wa(y)-yiqṭol* + [21]***wa**-S.noun-qoṭel*); Judg. 4.2 (*wa(y)-yiqṭol* + ***wa**-XØ* + ***wa**-S.pron-qoṭel*); 4.4f. ([4]***wa**-S.pron-qoṭel* + [5]***wa**-S.pron-qoṭel* + *wa(y)-yiqṭol*, where *wa(y)-yiqṭol* belongs to the background); 7.11f. ([11]*wa(y)-yiqṭol* + [12]***wa**-S.noun-qoṭel* + *wa-XØ*); 10.1; 13.19; 14.4, 5; 16.8f.; 17.7; 18.1; 19.16; 20.28. I have found only one asyndetic background participle clause: Gen. 39.23.

[50] This holds for most of the Biblical Hebrew period. In the archaic poetry, where the semantic development of the construction *wa-qaṭal* is incomplete, there is a rare example of a very expressive report (Judg. 5.26) where the successive actions in a peak of the report are coded by *qaṭal* and *wa-qaṭal* clauses (Bergsträsser 1929, §9n; Müller 1983, 50; Notarius 2013, 134, 289).

[51] The most natural interpretation of the introductory *qaṭal* clauses in the two background sections is as anterior-pluperfect ("off-line anteriority," Hornkohl 2018, 49 n. 64).

[52] The two *qaṭal* clauses are simultaneous with past time reference (Ges-K §164b.3; Nyberg 1972, §85k; Joosten 2012, 169 n. 24).

[53] On this point, I disagree with the analysis in the excellent article by Hornkohl (2018, 49 n. 64, 52). Hornkohl argues that the *XV* clause signals a new unit.

[54] Long *yiqṭol* as a discourse-continuity clause (type **wa-yiqṭol(u)*) is avoided in CBH (see §4.4 and §6.11). It is replaced by *wa-qaṭal*.

[55] According to Gropp (1991, 48), a *wa(y)-yiqṭol* should be read instead of *wa-qaṭal*. J-M (§119z) regards this as an anomalous occurrence of *w-qatálti*. Joosten (2012, 227) argues that *wa-qaṭal* here has the same meaning as *wa(y)-yiqṭol*, and similarly Nyberg (1972, §86kk) calls it a single past action.

[56] The *wa(y)-yiqṭol* clauses are, according to Joosten (2012, 169 n. 24), concomitant with the *qaṭal*.

[57] Other examples of *wa(y)-yiqṭol* clauses within background complexes: Gen. 34.7 (*wa-S.noun-qaṭal* + ***wa****(y)-yiqṭol* + ***wa****(y)-yiqṭol*)—stativic verbs that create circumstantial semantics in relation to a preceding *qaṭal* clause, or in Joosten's (2012, 169 n. 24) terms, simultaneity; 35.16 (*wa(y)-yiqṭol* + *wayhī-ADV-lə-VN* + *wa(y)-yiqṭol* + ***wa****(y)-yiqṭol*)—stativic verb that can also be analysed as elaboration, or again, in Joosten's (2012, 169 n. 24) terms, simultaneity; 37.2 (*Ø-S.noun-qaṭal* + *wa-S.pron-XØ* + ***wa****(y)-yiqṭol*)—according to Joosten (2012, 174, 178), *wa(y)-yiqṭol* is iterative and part of the background.

[58] Wenham (1994, 233, 236) renders the verb with a pluperfect: 'Laban had given Leah Zilpah his maid to be her maid'.

[59] Gropp (1991, 48): *wə* + *qaṭal*, "[it] may signal anterior circumstance." Thus also Westermann (1981, 423): "das perf. 'zur Bezeichnung eines Zustandes, der… in die Gegenwart hineinreicht' PNeuenzeit 226 Anm. 7," but Westermann (referring to Ges-K §112tt and BHS) is also open to an emendation. Joosten (2012, 227): "*w*ᵉ + QATAL." J-M (§119z): "omission of energic Waw" so that "the form w-qatálti *and I killed* is used instead of the expected *wayyiqṭol* form required by classical usage." Schulz (1900, 37) seems to argue for a "streng aoristische Fassung" of *wa-qaṭal*. BHS suggests an emendation to a *wa(y)-yiqṭol* clause ("l frt").

[60] According to Nyberg (1972, §86kk), the *wa-qaṭal* has the same function as a long *yiqṭol* clause, and is a verbal circumstantial clause, "that is, it refers to an incidental circumstance beside the main action" (my

translation). De Boer (1974, 47) interprets the *wa-qaṭal* clause as a resumption: "Well, he was a believer in Yahweh, therefore he—Yahweh—planned righteousness—blessing—for him." Gropp (1991, 48) regards it as one of few examples of normal *qaṭal* with normal *wa* (but prefers to read *wa(y)-yiqṭol*). Normal *wa* + *qaṭal* is also affirmed by Schulz (1900, 37) and J-M (§119z). According to Ges-K (§112pp), this case of *wa-qaṭal* does not follow the usual interpretations; it expresses "A longer or constant continuance in a past state," as a variety of the frequentative perfect discussed in Ges-K (§112ss). Westermann (1981, 252): "Das perf. steht hier, weil der Satz die Erzählung nicht weiterführt;" this does not accord with Ges-K (§112ss), to which he refers.

[61] Other examples of *wa-qaṭal* clauses introducing background: Gen. 37.2–4 'und zwar als Bursche bei den Söhnen der…' (Westermann 1982, 21); 38.5 (not a macro-syntactic function, but should be regarded as a background clause as well as a straightforward verbal clause; Isaksson 1998, 16); Exod. 18.26 'So they served as judges for the people at all times'; 36.29–30; Judg. 7.13 'on which the tent lay flat' (subevent in close connection with the preceding *wa(y)-yiqṭol*; Isaksson 2009, 76; Khan 2021a, 318); 16.18 (background complex: *wa-qaṭal* + *wa(y)-yiqṭol*)—this *wa-qaṭal* cannot be analysed as frequentative (Rubinstein 1963, 64).

[62] Other examples in the archaic poetry: Deut. 33.9 (*kī-qaṭal* + ***wa**-O.noun-yiqṭol(u)*; Notarius 2013, 242); 2 Sam. 22.29 (*kī-XØ* + ***wa**-S.noun-yiqṭol(u)*!); Ps. 18.23 (*kī-XØ* + ***wa**-O.noun-lō-yiqṭol(u)*!).

[63] For the construction *haya* + *qoṭel*, see Ges-K (§116r).

[64] Another example in prose is Gen. 24.16: *Ø-XØ* + ***wa**-S.noun-lō-qaṭal* 'She was a virgin; no man had ever been physically intimate with her' (NET).

[65] I count as continuity examples also simple negated clauses of the type *wa-NEG-V*, where *V* is a finite verb (Tenet 4; see §7.12). Some continuity cases of same-event addition in prose are: Gen. 31.27 (see above); 39.15 (*kī-qaṭal* + ***wa**(y)-yiqṭol*); 39.18 (*PREP-VN* + ***wa**(y)-yiqṭol*); Exod. 19.3 (*Ø-ADV-yiqṭol(u)* + ***wa**-yiqṭol(u)!*, ellipsis?); 24.7 (*Ø-O.noun-yiqṭol(u)!*

+ ***wa**-yiqṭol(u)*, ellipsis?); Lev. 11.43 (wa-*lō-yiqṭol(u)* + ***wa**-qaṭal*); Deut. 1.21 (*Ø-ʾal-yiqṭol* + ***wa**-ʾal-yiqṭol*); 2.9 (*Ø-ʾal-yiqṭol!* + ***wa**-ʾal-yiqṭol!*); 2.19 (*Ø-ʾal-yiqṭol!* + ***wa**-ʾal-yiqṭol!*); 31.6 (*Ø-ʾal-yiqṭol* + ***wa**-ʾal-yiqṭol*); Judg. 13.2b (*wa-XØ* + ***wa**-lō-qaṭal*, 'His wife was infertile **and** had no children').

[66] "**Temporal succession.** Two clauses occurring one after the other in a sentence indicate that the actions or states they describe happened in that iconic order: 'X, and following after X, Y'. This is shown in English by marker *and* or *and then* with the Focal clause" (Dixon 2009, 9).

[67] Other examples of *wa-ADV-qaṭal* clauses with temporally explicit adverbial (including prepositional) phrases: Gen. 10.15–18 (*wa-S.noun-qaṭal* + ***wa**-ADV-qaṭal*); Gen. 23.17–19 (*wa(y)-yiqṭol* + ***wa**-ADV-qaṭal*)—it is emphasised that Abraham buried his wife only after his purchase of this piece of Canaanite land property (Westermann 1981, 460); 45.15 (*wa(y)-yiqṭol* + ***wa**-ADV-qaṭal*); Exod. 5.1; Judg. 1.8f. (*wa(y)-yiqṭol* + *wa-O.noun-qaṭal* + ***wa**-ADV-qaṭal*, complementary military campaigns of Judah: Jerusalem, and after that outside Jerusalem).

[68] Other examples of *wa*-clauses with *yiqṭol(u)* predicate and temporally explicit adverbial phrases: Exod. 16.12a (*Ø-PrP-yiqṭol(u)* + ***wa**-PrP-yiqṭol(u)*, temporally marked *PrP*); Lev. 14.8, 19, 36 (*wa-lō-yiqṭol(u)* + ***wa**-ʾaḥar-kēn-yiqṭol(u)*); 15.29; 16.26, 28; 22.7 (*wa-qaṭal* + ***wa**-ʾaḥar-yiqṭol(u)*); Num. 5.26; 6.20; 12.14b (*Ø-yiqṭol(Ø)* + ***wa**-ʾaḥar-yiqṭol(u)*); 19.7 (*wa-qaṭal* + ***wa**-ʾaḥar-yiqṭol(u)*); Judg. 7.10b–11a (*Ø-IMP* + *wa-qaṭal* + ***wa**-ʾaḥar-yiqṭol(u)*).

[69] The negated realis *lā yaqtul* attested in Amarna Canaanite—e.g., EA 254:12f. *ù la-a a-kal-li* 'and I have not withheld', analysed as preterite *yaqtul* by Baranowski (2016a, 138)—is not found in BH. It is replaced by the new *wa-lō-qaṭal* clause-type in narrative and report.

[70] More examples of *qaṭal* in negative storyline clauses are given in Isaksson (2015a, 257 n. 153). See also §7.12.1.

[71] Westermann (1976, 254) refers to Ges-K (§152w), which regards the *pɛn* to be "virtually dependent on a cohortative." But it must be admitted that an archaic meaning of the *pɛn* particle would suit the context

very well indeed: *pini* 'turn away!' (Brockelmann 1956, §133e), *pace* the suggestion in J-M (§168g), which appears artificial. In such a case, the *pɛn* complex could be analysed as being made up of main clauses: 'Far be it that he reach out his hand and take also of the tree of life and eat, and live forever!" Procksch (1913, 31) also prefers a main clause: "Und nun ist Gefahr, daß er noch seine Hand ausstrecke und nehme auch vom Baum des Lebens und esse und lebe so ewiglig."

[72] Other examples of *pɛn* constructions with temporally sequential *wa-qaṭal* clauses: Gen. 19.19 (*wa-S.pron-lō-yiqṭol(u)* + *pɛn-yiqṭol(u)* + ***wa-qaṭal***); 32.12 (*Ø-IMP* + *kī-qoṭel* + *pɛn-yiqṭol(u)* + ***wa-qaṭal***)—this could also be interpreted as 'motion purpose' (Dixon 2009, 45); Exod. 13.17b (*Ø-pɛn-yiqṭol(u)* + ***wa-qaṭal***); 19.21 (*pɛn-yiqṭol(u)* + ***wa-qaṭal***); 23.29 (*Ø-lō-yiqṭol(u)* + *pɛn-yiqṭol(u)* + ***wa-qaṭal***).

[73] Other examples of temporally sequential *wa-qaṭal* clauses after initial imperative(s): Gen. 27.9–10a (*Ø-IMP* + *wa-IMP* + *wa-yiqṭol(Ø)* + ***wa-qaṭal*** + *wa-qaṭal*, a modal domain that involves also a short *yiqṭol* with ventive morpheme); 27.44 (*wa-ʿattā-VOC-IMP* + *wa-IMP* + *Ø-IMP* + ***wa***-*qaṭal*); 37.20 (*wa-ʿattā-IMP* + *wa-yiqṭol(Ø)* + *wa-yiqṭol(Ø)* + ***wa-qaṭal*** + *wa-yiqṭol(Ø)*); Exod. 8.12 (*Ø-IMP* + *wa-IMP* + ***wa***-*qaṭal*); 9.8f. ([8]*Ø-IMP* + ***wa***-*qaṭal* + [9]***wa***-*qaṭal* + ***wa***-*qaṭal*); 12.21f. (*Ø-IMP* + *wa-IMP* + *wa-IMP* + [22]***wa***-*qaṭal* + ***wa***-*qaṭal* + ***wa***-*qaṭal*); 19.24 (*Ø-IMP* + *Ø-IMP* + ***wa***-*qaṭal*); 24.1f. ([1]*Ø-IMP* + *wa-qaṭal* + [2]***wa***-*qaṭal*); 30.34f. ([34]*Ø-IMP* + *Ø-ADV-yiqṭol(u)* + [35]***wa***-*qaṭal*); 34.1 (*Ø-IMP* + ***wa***-*qaṭal*); Lev. 24.14 (*Ø-IMP* + ***wa***-*qaṭal* + ***wa***-*qaṭal*); Num. 13.17b–20 (*Ø-IMP* + ***wa***-*qaṭal* + [18]***wa***-*qaṭal*... + [20]***wa***-*qaṭal* + ***wa***-*qaṭal*); 19.2f. (*Ø-IMP* + *wa-yiqṭol(Ø)* + [3]***wa***-*qaṭal* + ***wa***-*qaṭal* + ***wa***-*qaṭal*); 20.8 (*Ø-IMP* + *wa-IMP* + ***wa***-*qaṭal*).

[74] Other examples of *wa-qaṭal* clauses expressing temporally sequential habitual events in the past: Exod. 33.7a (*wa-S.noun-yiqṭol(u)* + ***wa***-*qaṭal* + ***wa***-*qaṭal*); 33.9 (*Ø-PREP-VN-yiqṭol(u)* + ***wa***-*qaṭal* + ***wa***-*qaṭal*, similarly in vv. 10–11).

[75] For the meanings of the construction *wa-qaṭal*, see §6. Examples of future sequential events coded by *wa-qaṭal* clauses: Gen. 24.43 (*Ø-*

S.noun-qoṭel + ***wa**-qaṭal* + ***wa**-qaṭal*, a wished-for case); 41.29–30 (*Ø-hinnē-S.noun-qoṭel* + ***wa**-qaṭal* + *wa-qaṭal* + *wa-qaṭal*, prediction, only the first *wa-qaṭal* is sequential); Exod. 3.13 (*Ø-hinnē-S.pron-qoṭel* + ***wa**-qaṭal* + ***wa**-qaṭal*, an imagined future sequence of events); 4.14b–15a (*wa-gam-hinnē-S.pron-qoṭel* + ***wa**-qaṭal* + ***wa**-qaṭal* + ***wa**-qaṭal* + ***wa**-qaṭal*, prediction); 7.17b (*Ø-hinnē-S.pron-qoṭel* + ***wa**-qaṭal*, prediction); 8.23 (*Ø-ADV-yiqṭol(u)* + ***wa**-qaṭal*); Judg. 15.18b (*wa-ʿattā-yiqṭol(u)!* + ***wa**-qaṭal*, fear of future event); 21.21 (*wa-qaṭal* + *wa-hinnē-ʾim-yiqṭol(u)* + *wa-qaṭal* + ***wa**-qaṭal* + ***wa**-qaṭal*, a planned future scenario).

[76] Other examples of *wa-qaṭal* clauses expressing temporal succession within a protasis (protases enclosed by parentheses): Exod. 21.12 (*(Ø-qoṭel* + ***wa**-qaṭal)* + *Ø-VNabs-yiqṭol(u)*); 21.33–34 ([33]*(ʾō-kī-yiqṭol(u)* + *wa-lō-yiqṭol(u)* + ***wa**-qaṭal)* + [34]*Ø-S.noun-yiqṭol(u)*); 21.37 (*(kī-yiqṭol(u)* + ***wa**-qaṭal* + *ʾō-qaṭal)* + *Ø-O.noun-yiqṭol(u)*); 22.1 (*(Ø-ʾim-PrP-yiqṭol(u)* + ***wa**-qaṭal* + *wa-qaṭal)* + *Ø-XØ*); 22.6a (*(kī-yiqṭol(u)* + ***wa**-qaṭal)*, only the protasis); 22.9 (*(kī-yiqṭol(u)* + ***wa**-qaṭal* + *ʾō-qaṭal* + *ʾō-qaṭal* + *Ø-ʾēn-qoṭel)*, only protasis); 22.13 (*(wa-kī-yiqṭol(u)* + ***wa**-qaṭal* + *ʾō-qaṭal* + *Ø-XØ)*, only protasis); Lev. 5.2 (*ʾō-S.noun-REL-yiqṭol(u)* + *wa-qaṭal* + *wa-XØ* + ***wa**-qaṭal*, alternative protasis); 13.2 (*(Ø-NP-kī-yiqṭol(u)!* + ***wa**-qaṭal)* + *wa-qaṭal*)—for the temporally sequential interpretation of וְהָיָה, see Milgrom (1991, 774); Judg. 1.12 (*(Ø-REL-yiqṭol(u)!* + ***wa**-qaṭal)* + *wa-qaṭal*).

[77] An example in English (with the focal clause in italics) is: John has been studying German for years, *thus he speaks it well* (Dixon 2009, 17). Focal clause: “One clause refers to the central activity or state of the biclausal linking” (Dixon 2009, 3).

[78] Other discontinuous focal result clauses: Gen. 15.3 (*Ø-hēn-PrP-lō-qaṭal* + ***wa**-hinnē-S.noun-qoṭel*: ‘You have given me no children; so a servant in my household will be my heir’); Lev. 11.35 (*Ø-XØ* + ***wa**-O.noun-yiqṭol(u)*, *XØ* supplies a reason); 17.11 (*kī-XØ* + ***wa**-S.pron-qaṭal*) ‘for the life of every living thing is in the blood. So I myself have assigned it to you on the altar to make atonement for your lives…’ (NET); Num. 30.13 (*Ø-S.noun-qaṭal* + ***wa**-S.noun-yiqṭol(u)*) ‘since her husband has annulled them, the LORD will release her from them’ (NAB).

[79] On Gen. 1.3, I follow Wenham (1987, 2, 15f.): "This frightening disorganization is the antithesis to the order that characterized the work of creation when it was complete... The same point is made in another powerful image in the next clause, 'darkness covered the deep'."

[80] Wenham (1987, 18) quotes Stadelmann (1970, 49), who writes, "Light manifests most adequately the divine operation in a world which without it is darkness and chaos." Wenham's translation of 1.3 is "Then God said, 'Let there be light,' and there was light." Procksch (1913, 422) also emphasises in his translation the connection between verse 2 and 3: 'Wie nun die Erde dalag, eine wüste, leere Masse,—und Finsternis lag über der Urflut, Gottesgeist aber brütete über der Wasserfläche, [3] da sprach Gott: Es werde Licht. Und es ward Licht'. Other examples of focal result clauses with *wa(y)-yiqṭol*: Gen. 3.10; 3.13, 18; 4.4b–5 '**So** Cain was very angry, and his face was downcast' (NIV); 12.19a; 15.6; 16.4, 6; 18.11–12a; 19.11; 20.12; 25.25; 25.26; 29.33; 41.10; 45.6f.; Exod. 17.12; 36.3b–4; Lev. 17.14a; 18.27; 20.23; 20.26 (*wa-qaṭal* + *kī-XØ* + ***wa****(y)-yiqṭol*)—Milgrom (2000, 1301) translates, 'You shall be holy to me, for I YHWH am holy; **therefore** I have set you apart from other peoples to be mine', and on p. 1762 he comments, "Whereas holiness is God's *nature* and is apprehensible solely from his self-revelation, separation is the result of his *act*, visible in the creation of the world (nature) and in the creation of Israel (history);" Num. 33.9b; Judg. 1.21 and similar examples in Judg. 1 (*wa-O.noun-lō-qāṭal* + ***wa****(y)-yiqṭol*) 'so the Jebusites have shared Jerusalem with Benjamin to this day' (Sasson 2014, 153); 15.2a (*kī-VNabs-qaṭal* + ***wa****(y)-yiqṭol*)—"It stands after a causal clause and expresses a consequence" (Zewi 1999, 85).

[81] Other examples of focal result clauses coded by *wa-qaṭal* clauses: Gen. 6.3 (*Ø-lō-yiqṭol(u)!* + ***wa****-qaṭal*); 20.11; 26.22b (*kī-ʿattā-qaṭal* + ***wa****-qaṭal*); 34.5 (*wa-S.noun-qaṭal* + *wa-S.noun-qaṭal* + ***wa****-qaṭal*)—many, with Gropp (1991, 48), suggest an emendation to *wa(y)-yiqṭol*, and Joosten (2012, 227) regards it as one of the cases in CBH when *wa-qaṭal* has the same function as *wa(y)-yiqṭol*; Exod. 3.20 (*wa-S.pron-qaṭal* + ***wa****-qaṭal* + ***wa****-qaṭal*); Lev. 11.44a 'For I am ADONAI your God; therefore, consecrate yourselves and be holy, for I am holy' (CJB); 16.4b;

18.4b–5 'I am the LORD your God. You shall **therefore** keep my statutes and my rules' (ESV); 19.36b–37 'I am Yahweh your God who brought you out of Egypt; **hence** you are to keep all my laws and all my customs and put them into practice. I am Yahweh' (NJB). I regard also clauses of the type *wa-NEG-V* as continuity clauses (see §7.12), and they often code focal result. They are not accounted for above. Some few instances are: Num. 14.43b (*CONJ-qaṭal* + ***wa***-*lō-yiqṭol(u)*); 25.11 (*Ø-S.noun-qaṭal* + ***wa***-*lō-qaṭal*).

[82] Other syndetic discontinuity clauses coding a cause/reason for the preceding focal clause: Gen. 15.2 (*Ø-VOC-O.pron-yiqṭol(u)* + ***wa***-*S.pron-qoṭel*); 20.3 (*Ø-hinnē-S.pron-qoṭel* + ***wa***-*XØ*); 24.31 (*Ø-ADV-yiqṭol(u)* + ***wa***-*S.pron-qaṭal*); 34.21 (*wa-yiqṭol(Ø)* + *wa-yiqṭol(Ø)* + ***wa***-*S.noun-XØ*); 39.3 (*wa(y)-yiqṭol* + ***wa***-*O.noun-S.noun-qoṭel*); Exod. 9.28 (*IMP* + ***wa***-*XØ*); 23.9 (*wa-O.noun-yiqṭol(u)* + ***wa***-*S.pron-qaṭal* + *kī-O.noun-qaṭal*); Judg. 13.18 (*Ø-ADV-yiqṭol(u)* + ***wa***-*XØ*) 'You should not ask me my name, because you cannot comprehend it' (NET).

[83] The rest of my examples of continuity reason clauses are less clear and depend on the interpretation: Lev. 25.36 (*Ø-ʾal-yiqṭol(Ø)* + ***wa***-*qaṭal* + *wa-qaṭal*, or: 'instead you shall fear…'); 25.43 (*Ø-lō-yiqṭol(u)* + ***wa***-*qaṭal*, or: 'instead…').

[84] Milgrom (1991, 228): 'Thus the priest shall effect purgation…'. Other examples of *wa-qaṭal* clauses with this type of linking semantics are (I supply the linking pattern only for the first ten): Gen. 17.13 (*Ø-VNabs-yiqṭol(u)* + ***wa***-*qaṭal*); 39.9 (*wa-ʾēḵ-yiqṭol(u)* + ***wa***-*qaṭal*); 45.19 (*Ø-O.pron-IMP* + *Ø-IMP* + ***wa***-*qaṭal* + ***wa***-*qaṭal*); Exod. 13.15f. (Ø-ADV-*S.pron-qoṭel* + *wa-O.noun-yiqṭol(u)* + ***wa***-*qaṭal*); 17.5 (*IMP* + *wa-IMP* + *wa-O.noun-IMP* + ***wa***-*qaṭal*); 19.23b (*IMP* + ***wa***-*qaṭal*); 23.25 (*kī-VNabs-yiqṭol(u)* + *wa-VNabs-yiqṭol(u)* + ***wa***-*qaṭal*, within protasis); 28.43 (*wa-qaṭal* + ***wa***-*lō-yiqṭol(u)* + ***wa***-*qaṭal*); Lev. 4.26 (*wa-O.noun-yiqṭol(u)!* + ***wa***-*qaṭal*); 4.31 (*wa-qaṭal* + ***wa***-*qaṭal*); 5.6; 5.10; 5.12–13a; 12.7a; 14.18; 14.20; 14.36; 15.15, 30, 31; 16.6, 11, 19; 19.12; 22.2; Num. 4.19 (*wa-O.pron-IMP* + ***wa***-*qaṭal* + *wa-lō-yiqṭol(u)*)—cf. Garr

(1998, lxxxiii), who assigns the *wa-qaṭal* a result value, "and [as a result] they will live," which is close to my interpretation; 8.13f.; 11.17; 20.8; Deut. 13.6; 21.8 (*wa-qaṭal* + "..." + ***wa**-qaṭal*).

[85] Other examples of *wa-lō-yiqṭol(u)* clauses presupposing the manner of preceding clause(s): Gen. 42.2 (*Ø-IMP* + *wa-IMP* + *wa-yiqṭol(Ø)-V* + ***wa**-lō-yiqṭol(u)!*, where *-V* is a ventive clitic); 43.8 (*Ø-IMP-V* + *wa-yiqṭol(Ø)-V* + *wa-yiqṭol(Ø)-V* + *wa-yiqṭol(Ø)-V* + ***wa**-lō-yiqṭol(u)*); 47.19 (*wa-IMP* + *wa-yiqṭol(Ø)-V* + ***wa**-lō-yiqṭol(u)!* + *wa-S.noun-lō-yiqṭol(u)*); Exod. 28.35 (*wa-qaṭal* + ***wa**-lō-yiqṭol(u)!*); 28.43 (*wa-qaṭal* + ***wa**-lō-yiqṭol(u)* + *wa-qaṭal*); 30.12 (*kī-yiqṭol(u)* + *wa-qaṭal* + ***wa**-lō-yiqṭol(u)!*); 30.20 (*PREP-VN-yiqṭol(u)* + ***wa**-lō-yiqṭol(u)*); 30.21 (*wa-qaṭal* + ***wa**-lō-yiqṭol(u)*); 39.21 (*wa(y)-yiqṭol* + ***wa**-lō-yiqṭol(u)*); Lev. 8.35 (*wa-ADV-yiqṭol(u)* + *wa-qaṭal* + ***wa**-lō-yiqṭol(u)*); 14.36; 15.31; Lev. 16.2, 13; 18.28, 30; 19.17, 29; 20.14, 22; 21.6, 15, 23; 22.2; Num. 5.3; 8.19; 11.17; 17.25; 18.5, 22; 35.12; Deut. 13.12; 17.13; 19.10; 22.8.

[86] Cf. the note by NET: "The expression 'and consecrated it' refers to the effect of the anointing earlier in the verse," and Milgrom (1991, 493), who translates 'thus consecrating them'. Similar examples are: Gen. 25.33; 30.38 (*wa(y)-yiqṭol* + ***wa**(y)-yiqṭol*); 31.9; Exod. 12.36 (*wa-S.noun-qaṭal* + *wa(y)-yiqṭol* + ***wa**(y)-yiqṭol*, supported by the accents, part of background); 20.25 (*kī-O.noun-qaṭal* + ***wa**(y)-yiqṭol*); Lev. 8.10, 15, 30 (*wa(y)-yiqṭol* + ***wa**(y)-yiqṭol*); Num. 7.1b (*wa(y)-yiqṭol* + ***wa**(y)-yiqṭol*); 26.10 (*wa(y)-yiqṭol* + *wa(y)-yiqṭol* + ***wa**(y)-yiqṭol*, within a relative clause complex).

[87] Jussive clauses in this function may in rare cases be asyndetic: Lev. 9.6 (*REL-qaṭal* + ***Ø**-yiqṭol(Ø)*); Deut. 32.29 (*lū-qaṭal* + ***Ø**-yiqṭol(Ø)* + ***Ø**-yiqṭol(Ø)*, archaic, counterfactual). Complements are impersonal. I have found no example of a ventive/cohortative clause (first person!) functioning as complement.

[88] For the form of the imperative, see Ges-K (§63q). Ges-K (§110i) maintains that the meaning of this *wa-IMP* is "a consequence which is to be expected with certainty, and often a consequence which is intended, or

in fact an intention," as referred to by Westermann (1981, 387), 'so daß du am Leben bleibst', and Wenham (1994, 66), 'so that you may live', and Strack (1894, 65). This is close to the truth, but does not recognise that in some semantic contexts the meaning is a plain complement. Andersen (1974, 108) misses the point and translates 'return the man's wife... and live!'. Procksch (1913, 290), however, interprets correctly 'und er wird dann für dich beten [daß du am Leben bleibest]' (although with doubt about the text). Other examples of *wa-IMP* as a complement clause: Gen. 20.7; Exod. 25.40.

[89] Other examples of third-person jussive *wa-yiqṭol* clauses in CBH with the function of a complement: Gen. 23.9 (*wa-IMP* + [9]***wa**-yiqṭol(Ø)*); 41.34 (*Ø-yiqṭol(Ø)* + ***wa**-yiqṭol(Ø)*!, Westermann 1982, 95); Exod. 6.11; 8.4 (*Ø-IMP* + ***wa**-yiqṭol(Ø)!*)—*pace* Qimron (1986–87, 152), who regards it as a purpose clause; 10.17 (*Ø-IMP* + *wa-IMP* + ***wa**-yiqṭol*!); 11.2; 10.21 (the second *wa-yiqṭol(Ø)*); 14.2, 15; 25.2; Lev. 22.2; 24.2; Num. 5.2; 17.2 (*Ø-IMP* + ***wa**-yiqṭol*!); 19.2; 21.7 (*Ø-IMP* + ***wa**-yiqṭol(Ø)!*); Judg. 13.4; 14.15 (*Ø-IMP* + ***wa**-yiqṭol*!). A corresponding negated complement: Lev. 16.2 (*IMP* + ***wa**-ʾal-yiqṭol(Ø)*).

[90] *Wa-qaṭal* clauses describing an implied result are relatively frequent. Some instances are: Gen. 29.8; 33.10—according to Rainey (2003, 26f.), apodosis; 43.14; Exod. 8.24; 10.25; 22.5 (within protasis); 26.11; 28.7; 40.9; Lev. 19.29. For the semantics of result clause linking, see Dixon (2009, 2, 19, 22).

[91] For a further discussion on this topic, see Notarius (2017).

[92] Other examples of *wa-qaṭal* clauses forming complements after *yiqṭol(u)* or *wa-qaṭal* clauses (since *wa-qaṭal* alternates with long *yiqṭol* with the same meaning, I have included also *wa-qaṭal* main clauses): Exod. 23.30 (*CONJ-yiqṭol(u)* + ***wa**-qaṭal*)—this interpretation is evident in NJB 'I shall drive them out little by little before you, until your numbers grow sufficient for you **to** take possession of the land'; Lev. 13.54 (*wa-qaṭal* + ***wa**-qaṭal*); 25.49b (*ʾō-qaṭal* + ***wa**-qaṭal*) 'Or he can afford **to** redeem himself'—*ʾō-qaṭal* is correct and is equivalent to *wa-qaṭal* (see §5.4.8), but most commentators, including Milgrom (2001, 2148), and

Hartley (1992, 422), emend the text according to LXX and translate as Milgrom's 'or if he prospers, he may redeem himself'; Num. 3.10 (*wa-O.noun-O.noun-yiqṭol(u)* + ***wa****-qaṭal*, Levine 1993, 152); 15.38; 23.27 (*Ø-ADV-yiqṭol(u)* + ***wa****-qaṭal*, Levine 2000, 165); Deut. 5.31 'teach them **to** follow'; 11.8 (*CONJ-yiqṭol(u)* + ***wa****-qaṭal* + ***wa****-qaṭal*, with generalised semantics: 'be strong enough **to** enter and possess the land'); 31.12b (*CONJ-yiqṭol(u)* + *wa-CONJ-yiqṭol(u)* + ***wa****-qaṭal* + ***wa****-qaṭal*).

[93] Other examples of conditional linking and a *wa* introducing the apodosis: Gen. 12.1f.; 24.49 (*Ø-IMP* + ***wa****-yiqṭol(Ø)-A*); 26.3 (*Ø-IMP* + ***wa****-yiqṭol(Ø)-V* + ***wa****-yiqṭol(Ø)-N*)—energic clitic is regarded as ventive (Sjörs 2019); 29.27; 30.28; 32.10; 34.12; 47.16 (*Ø-IMP* + ***wa****-yiqṭol(Ø)-A*); 47.19; 49.1; Exod. 3.10; 9.28; 24.12; Num. 16.22 (*Ø-INT-S.noun-yiqṭol(u)* + ***wa****-PrP-yiqṭol(u)*, Levine 1993, 408); Judg. 6.13 (*wa-yēš-XØ* + ***wa****-ADV-qaṭal*); 9.7 (*Ø-IMP* + ***wa****-yiqṭol(Ø)*); 9.19 (*Ø-IMP* + ***wa****-yiqṭol(Ø)*).

[94] Blau (2010, 190) rejects the term 'consecutive *waw*', "because it simply is not true that the action is represented as a consequence of a preceding action."

3. THE SHORT *YIQṬOL* AS A SEPARATE VERBAL MORPHEME IN CBH

The theory of consecutive tenses hides the true nature of the short *yiqṭol*. In one respect, it is put out of sight as the 'jussive', as if the jussive were not also a *yiqṭol*. Among the four principal 'tenses', only one *yiqṭol* is mentioned. The short *yiqṭol* is again put out of sight, because it is concealed in one of the other principal verb forms: *wa(y)-yiqṭol*, a 'tense' of its own in the consecutive system.

The purpose of the present chapter is to clarify the independent status of the short *yiqṭol* in CBH and its Semitic background (Isaksson 2021a). The *wa(y)-yiqṭol* clause-type is one of four primary constituents of the 'consecutive tenses', and a correct analysis of the short *yiqṭol* is of utmost importance for a synchronically correct understanding of *wa(y)-yiqṭol* in CBH. The false idea of only one *yiqṭol* conjugation in the synchronic state of CBH is so established in Biblical Hebrew grammars that this alone motivates a separate chapter on the issue. Did the native speakers and writers of CBH recognise two *yiqṭols* or only one?

Already in Proto-Semitic, a short prefix conjugation stood in opposition to a long prefix conjugation. In the earliest attested stages, the long prefix verb was a formation with reduplication of the second radical (type *iparras*). In Central Semitic, a probably new formation emerged as a long prefix conjugation with an enclitic imperfective marker *-u* (type *yaqtul-u*).

 https://doi.org/10.11647/OBP.0414.03

The distinguishing features of the PS short prefix conjugation (type *yaqtul*) were: (1) two meanings, perfective/past and jussive,[1] and (2) a short form, as opposed to the long imperfective prefix conjugation (Huehnergard 2019, 62; also Rabin 1984, 393). These features of the *yaqtul* gram were constitutive in the earliest attested Semitic languages, and are found in CBH as well.

3.1. The Semitic Background of the CBH Short *Yiqṭol*

Cook (2012a, 118) writes:[2]

> The historical-comparative data from Akkadian, Ugaritic, and El-Amarna Canaanite have been revolutionary with respect to the BHVS. The most important conclusion arrived at through the historical-comparative investigations is that WS originally possessed a Past prefix form *yaqtul*. Comparison of the Akkadian Past *iprus* with BH *wayyiqtol* and the Arabic syntagm *lam yaqtul* supported the supposition that a Past prefix form *yaqtul* existed in WS.

It is possible to trace the origin of an old perfective *yaqtul* back to Afroasiatic (Kouwenberg 2010a, 126ff.; Hasselbach 2013b, 329; Kossmann and Suchard 2018, 47, 52; Huehnergard 2019, 62). A plausible assumption would be that the Proto-Semitic *yaqtul* is the result of a long grammaticalisation path that began with a resultative periphrastic verbal morpheme with proclitic pronominal element + verbal adjective, *taprus* 'du (bist) getrennt habend' (Kienast 2001, 196f., 199; see also Huehnergard 2008, 238; Kossman and Suchard 2018, 41, 51).[3] The *yaqtul* gram must have been the standard perfective formation in PS, and it could also be used injunctively (Hasselbach and Huehnergard 2008,

416; Huehnergard and Pat-El 2019, 7; Huehnergard 2019, 62). However, in the individual Semitic languages, the grammaticalisation process of *yaqtul* is usually advanced. It is quite possible that *yaqtul* in individual Semitic languages represents a 'doughnut gram', in which the prototypical use as a resultative is obscured or completely lost (Dahl 2000, 10).[4]

In Akkadian, the old perfective *iprus* is primarily but not exclusively preserved as a plain past tense (Tropper 1998, 158). Anterior meanings are taken over by an innovative 'perfect' (*iptaras*), a typologically common process (Kuryłowicz 1964, 22). In the later Akkadian dialects, the use of the perfective recedes to negative clauses only, in a development similar to Arabic *lam yaqtul* (Soden 1969, §79b). In a shared single proto-language of West Semitic, the innovative perfective *qatal(a)* to a large extent replaced the perfective *yaqtul* (Huehnergard 2005, 163). The latter is retained in jussive and negated indicative clauses, as in Arabic; only as a jussive, as in Aramaic;[5] or as a receding old past perfective (*yaqtul*) competing with a new perfective (*qatal*), as in Amarna Canaanite, Ugaritic, and CBH (Kuryłowicz 1949, 49f.; Rainey 2003a, 406f.).[6]

It has been regarded as a puzzle that the old Semitic perfective *yaqtul*, side by side with its realis and usually past meanings, could be used with irrealis meanings in the Akkadian precative and the Central Semitic jussive.[7] But from a cross-linguistic perspective, there is considerable variation as to the degree to which a 'past time reference only' is manifested. In the prototypical properties of a perfective grammatical morpheme, "the aspectual properties could thus be seen as 'dominant' relative to the temporal properties: both kinds of properties characterize the prototypical instances" (Bybee and Dahl 1989, 84). It is "fairly frequent that perfective categories may have non-past reference in non-indicative moods or (which is the same thing) certain non-assertive contexts" (Bybee and Dahl 1989, 84).[8]

This fact, realis meaning side-by-side with irrealis, has resulted in a theory of two separate, but morphologically identical, *yaqtul* conjugations, one indicative and another modal.[9] But the use of perfectives in the marking of subjunctive clauses is widely attested. According to Givón (2001, I:362), it proceeds in several related developments (see also Bybee 1995).[10] It is reasonable to assume that the domain type (§1.2.4) determined the realis or irrealis meaning in Proto-Semitic.[11] In a modal domain, the irrealis meaning was understood, while in a narrative domain, the realis meaning (usually with past time reference) dominated. Such is still the case in Archaic Hebrew poetry, where the domain type determines the irrealis or realis meaning of short *yiqṭol*. Some Semitic languages have handled the dual nature of the old perfective by the use of grammatical markers, in order to explicitly mark the intended irrealis meaning (Kogan 2015, 119). In Akkadian, an irrealis marker became obligatory, as in the precative *l-iprus*[12] and the vetitive (prohibitive) *ay iprus* (Soden 1969, §81c, i; Tropper 1998, 158; Kouwenberg 2010a, 33, 130ff.);[13] in Arabic, the clitic *l-* became a facultative signal of the irrealis mood (in *li-yaqtul*).[14] If a proclitic *l-* ever existed in Hebrew, it must have been entirely optional: its alleged use as clitic before jussive *yiqṭol(Ø)* rests on extremely shaky examples (Huehnergard 1983, 591).

3.1.1. East Semitic: Akkadian

The past-tense usage of *iprus* in a narrative main line has the linking pattern *iprus-ma* + *iprus-ma* + *iptaras#* (Soden 1969, §156c). This *iprus* is neutral as to the durativity or punctuality of the event, and thus compatible with durative meanings. The essential nature of the perfective is to view the event as a bounded whole, as completed. It is not specifically a past tense (Tropper 1998, 158f.; Kouwenberg 2010a, 127):[15]

(1) *ištu mūtānī 10 šanātim abī* ***ib-lá-aṭ***

'after the plague, my father **was** (still) **alive** for ten years' (Old Assyrian ArAn. 1, 48 n. 23 kt 88/k 507b:11–12)

It is also significant that this old perfective may take anterior or pluperfect meanings (Soden 1969, §79b; Kouwenberg 2010a, 128):

(2) *x a.šà še.giš.ì ša am-ḫu-ru itbalma alpī ša ina maḫrīya* ***il-qú-ú*** *ana libbu x eqlim šuāti [iš]talal*

'he appropriated the 2 bur of sesame field that I had received and dragged the oxen which **he had taken** from me to that 2 bur field.' (AbB 11, 116:13′–14′ [OB], my emphasis)

The old perfective *iprus* in Akkadian competes with, and is restricted in its usage by, the newly formed 'perfect' *iptaras* (Soden 1969, §79b). In this competition, *iprus* is neutral, and lacks "speaker involvement, actuality, and recentness" (Kouwenberg 2010a, 128; also Tropper 1998, 157f.).

3.1.2. Ethio-Semitic

The reflex of *yaqtul* in Gəʿəz[16] is a non-indicative (irrealis) form, traditionally called 'subjunctive'. In independent position, it functions as a jussive (Butts 2019, 131): *yə́ngər* or *yəlbas* contrasts with an imperfective conjugation with geminated second radical, *yənággər* (Tropper 2002, 90; Huehnergard 2005, 157). In subordinate clauses, *yaqtul* often expresses purpose or result. This opposition between a short prefix conjugation and a long one with gemination of the second root consonant is usually regarded as a retention from Proto-Semitic, since it is compared with the Akkadian *iprus/iparras* opposition (Weninger 2011, 1131).[17] The jussive may optionally be preceded by the clitic *la* (Lambdin 1978, 150), which according to some grammars indicates an emphatic wish or command. The clitic *la* is especially frequent before third-person forms of the jussive (Tropper 2002, 150, 192):

(3) *la-yəqrab*

'let him approach'

(4) *ʾəngər*

'let me speak'

(5) *wa-kiyāhu bāḥtito* ***tāmlək***

'and him only **shall you serve**'

The jussive *yaqtul* in Gəʿəz can be used in all persons. There seem to be very few, if any, traces of a realis usage of a perfective *yaqtul* in Ethio-Semitic.[18]

The modern Ethiopian dialects generally preserve a short jussive that contrasts with an imperfective with an (originally) geminated second radical: Tigrinya *yəgbär* versus imperfective *yəgäbbər* (Voigt 2011, 1164); Amharic *yəsbär* 'may he break' (but 1cs with the *l* clitic: *ləsbär*) versus imperfective *yəsäbr* (Meyer 2011, 1193f.); Gurage *yädläs* versus imperfective *yədäls-ənā* (Meyer 2011a, 1245);[19] Harari *yasbar* versus *yisabri* (Wagner 2011, 1260).

3.1.3. Modern South Arabian (MSA)

The speakers of Proto-Modern South Arabian departed from the West Semitic speech community very early, before the time when Ethio-Semitic and Central Semitic developed into two distinct branches of the West Semitic family tree (Kogan 2015, 109, 600). This is not undisputed, of course, and some scholars prefer to speak of a Western South Semitic group (Simeone-Senelle 2011, 1074).[20] In the present book, Central Semitic, Ethio-Semitic, and Modern South Arabian (MSA) are regarded as three independent West Semitic branches, among which there is "a special diachronic unity" between Central Semitic and Ethiopian Semitic. Of the six MSA dialects, Jibbali and Soqotri form an eastern group and Mehri, Harsusi, Bathari, and Hobyot a western branch (Kogan 2015, 115, 597; also Rubin 2014, 14; 2015, 313).

The reflex of the old perfective *yaqtul* in MSA is an irrealis (jussive) category usually called the 'subjunctive': Jibbali *yɔ́sfər* 'May he travel', which contrasts with a long imperfective,[21] *yəsɔ́fər* 'He will travel' (Rubin 2014, 103). The term 'subjunctive' as used in the grammars is inappropriate, since this *yaqtul* can be used in independent jussive clauses, as in (6):

(6) ***yəfɔ́rḥək*** *ɔ̄ź bə-xár*

'**may** God **make you happy** with good things' (Jibbali, Rubin 2014, 147; also in Mehri, Rubin 2010b, 128)

The II-*y* verbs exhibit a shortening of the stem vowel in the jussive: Jibbali *yəfɔ́t* 'may he die', versus the long imperfect *yəfɔ̄t* (Rubin 2014, 190).

An *l* clitic is added before all vocalic prefixes of the jussive in the 1cs and 1cd forms in Mehri and Jibbali: *l-ɔ́ḳdər* 'may I be able', *l-əḳɔ́drɔ́* 'may we two be able', versus 3ms *yɔ́ḳdər* 'may he be able' (Rubin 2010a, 90; 2014, 103).[22]

3.1.4. Ancient South Arabian

Ancient South Arabian is probably not closely related to the Modern South Arabian dialects.[23] Ancient South Arabian is nowadays generally classified as a Central Semitic language group, whereas MSA is regarded a separate branch of West Semitic (Huehnergard and Pat-El 2019, 5). A turning point in the classification of Ancient South Arabian was a study by Norbert Nebes (1994b), who was able to show that there is no indication in any Ancient South Arabian language of an imperfective formation with geminated second root consonant, such as is found in the Ethiopian *yənaggər* (Tropper 1997a, 45f.; Huehnergard 2005, 160; Stein 2011, 1061).[24] Nebes clarified that the graphically attested prefixed conjugation had only one stem, and that this prefixed verb form functionally corresponded to two conjugations in other Semitic languages (a perfective and jussive *yaqtul* on the one hand and an imperfective *yVqattVl* or *yaqtulu* on the other): "Diese Basis lautet /qtVl/ und hat somit dieselbe Gestalt wie im Nordarabischen und in den nordwestsemitischen Sprachen" (Nebes 1994b, 74f., 78).

The defective consonantal script allows for *matres lectionis* only in final position of a word structure, marking long *ī* (by *y*) and long *ū* (by *w*). This makes a distinction between two different prefix conjugations, one short and one long, difficult to verify (Stein 2013, 77).[25] If within the Ancient Arabian prefix conjugation there is one reflex of the Central Semitic *yaqtul* and another reflex of the Central Semitic *yaqtulu*, as Huehnergard's (2005, 161, 165) hypothesis presupposes,[26] then this distinction can be verified only on the basis of typical uses and meanings of perfective verbs and imperfective verbs respectively.[27]

The jussive is marked by the proclitic particle *l* (probably /li-/; Stein 2003, 240 n. 258; 2013, 112; also Huehnergard 1983, 584). An example is (7):

(7) *w-ʾlmqhw l-ykrbn-k*

'May ʾLMQHW bless you' (X.BSB 98/1–2; Stein 2011, 1064)

An interesting feature of Sabaic syntax is the use of chains of *w-yfʿl* clauses in past contexts marking temporal succession in narratives (cf. §1.2.4):[28]

(8) *w-bn-hw f-**ygbʾw** ʿdy hgrn nʿḍ w-bn-hw f-**yhṣrn** mlkn ʾlšrḥ yḥḍb w-ḏ-bn ḫms-hw w-ʾfrs-hw ʿdy ʾrḍ mhʾnfm **w-yqmʿw** w-hbʿln hgrnhn ʿṯy w-ʿṯy **w-ylfyw** b-hw mhrgtm w-sbym w-mltm w-ġnmm ḏ-ʿsm w-bn-hw f-**ytʾwlw** b-ʿly hgrn ḍfw **w-ykbnn** b-hw ḏ-mḏrḥm w-šʿbn mhʾnfm **w-yhbrrw** šʿbn mhʾnfm b-ʿly mqdmt-hmw w-hsḥt-hmw mqdmt-hmw ʿdy ḏt ḥml-hmw hgrn ḍfw **w-yhrgw** bn-hmw mhrgm ḏ-ʿsm*

'And from there, **they returned** to the city of NʿḌ. And from there, the king ʾLŠRḤ YḤḌB and some of his troops and his cavalry **marched** against the land of MHʾNFM. **And**

they overthrew and seized the two cities ʿṮY and ʿṮY. **And they got** there trophies, captives, loot, and booty that were numerous. And from there, **they turned** to the city of ḌFW. **And they found** there the (clan) Ḏ-MḎRḤM and the tribe MH'NFM. **And** the tribe MH'NFM **came** into the open against their vanguard, but their vanguard defeated them until they drove them back into the city of ḌFW. **And they killed** a number of them that was considerable.' (J 576/7–9)

Traces of the narrative pattern in (8) are attested also in Minaic and Qatabanic. As can be seen in (8), there is a narrative pattern of the type *w-f-yfʿl* involving the conjunction *f*, corresponding to the Arabic *fa.*[29] On the basis of such narrative chains, Tropper (1997a, 39, 43) has argued that there must have existed in Sabaic a perfective short *yaqtul* with past time reference.

In Qatabanic, a short plural prefix form *yfʿlw* is found in past narrative contexts, which can be interpreted as **yifʿalū*. It contrasts with a long imperfective plural form *yfʿln* (**yifʿalūna*; Avanzini 2009, 213; Stein 2011, 1060; for Sabaic, Stein 2013, 80):

(9) ***w-ygbʾw*** *w-h[t]b Yḏmrmlk ʾbyt w-ʾrḍty w-ʾqny Qtbn*

'*Yḏmrmlk* **gathered** and returned the houses, the lands, and the possessions of Qataban' (Avanzini 2009, 213, my emphasis)

(10) ***w-yhrgw*** *w-s^{1}lqḥ Ḥḍrmwt*

'**and then they scattered death** and destruction on the Ḥaḍramawt' (Avanzini 2009, 213, my emphasis)

In many Minaic legal texts, there are prefix forms expressing past time "without the form necessarily having the *w*-prefix" (Avanzini 2009, 213):

(11) *kl ʾklh* ***ys¹ʿrbn*** *byt Wd k-s¹m*

'all comestibles **marked** in the bayt Wadd, whether belonging to them' (Avanzini 2009, 213, my emphasis)

Similar examples are found in Had'ramitic:

(12) *ḏ-ʾ****l ys³b*** *h-ḏt Ḥmym ḏt* ***ynsf***

'he who did not offer to *ḏt Ḥmym* that which he had to provide according to the rite' (Avanzini 2009, 214, my emphasis)

Though the orthography is not distinctive in most cases, Avanzini's conclusion is that all Ancient South Arabian languages had a prefix form *yaqtul/yaqtulū* for the past, and another prefix form *yaqtulu/yaqtulūna* for the 'present', a fact that is most clearly displayed in Qatabanic, where the imperfective prefix form is preceded by the particle *b* (*b-yfʿl/b-yfʿlwn*), and the jussive is distinguished by the precative particle *l* (*l-yfʿl/l-yfʿlwn*; Avanzini 2015, 18).[30] The past time prefix form is not always preceded by the conjunction *w*, as in (13):[31]

(13) *w-hgrn Ns²n* ***yhḥrm*** *bn mwfṭm*

'and the city of Nashshān, **he annihilated** with fire' (RES 3945, 16; Avanzini 2009, 215; 2015, 15f., my emphasis)

In verbs II*wy*, the long vowel is generally not indicated in the script. Only occasionally can a short, defectively written stem vowel in a short jussive form contrast with a plene spelling of the corresponding long imperfective form (as is also pointed out by Multhoff 2019, 332, 334):[32]

(14) jussive

l-yšmn wfy

'may he set up the well-being of (...)' (J 611/16–17; Stein 2011, 1061)

(15) imperfective

d̠t šym ***w-yšymn*** *wfy*

'that he has set up **and will set up** the well-being of (...)' (München VM 91–315 336; Stein 2011, 1061)

The North Sabaic idiom *Amiritic* exhibits a negation *lm*, which is followed by a prefix conjugation form with past meaning, as in Classical Arabic *lam yaqtul* (Stein 2011, 1047, 1063; see also Smith 1991, 12, who refers to Beeston 1984, 47). For example:

(16) *fa-naẓara l-laṣṣu ʾilā l-mawti wa-rāma ḥīlatan fī naqbin ʾaw manfad̠in* ***fa-lam yaǧid***

'The thief faced death and searched for an escape through a hole or an exit, **but found none**.' (Brunnow et al. 2008, 9: lines 4–5)

3.1.5. Classical Arabic

In Classical **Arabic**, *yaqtul* is used as both jussive and 'negative preterite' *lam yaqtul* (Fischer 2002, 103).[33] The indicative use of *yaqtul* is confined to negative clauses preceded by *lam* 'not' or *lammā* 'not yet' (Lipiński 1997, §39.16; Fischer 2002, §194; Blau 2010, 195; Huehnergard 2017, 7, 26):[34]

(17) *lam ya'ti*

'he did not come'

(18) *fa-***lam yaḥfil** *Bābaku bi-ḏālika wa-halaka fī tilka l-ʾayyāmi*
'but Bābak **took no notice** of this and he died in those days' (Ṭab. I.816:5)

(19) *lammā ya'ti*

'He has not yet come'

The *lam yaqtul* in Classical Arabic can take anterior meaning. It is also independent of the temporal reference of the preceding verb, as is shown by this example from *Kalīla wa-Dimna*:

(20) *mā lī ʾarā-ka l-yawma ḫabīta l-nafsi* **wa-lam ʾara-ka** *muḏ ʾayyāmin*

'Why is it that I see you today depressed **and haven't seen you** for days?!' (Marmorstein 2016, 181)[35]

In some weak verbs, the Arabic *yaqtul* exhibits a distinctively short form, as the examples *ya'ti* and *ʾara-ka* above illustrate (Lipiński 1997, §39.14). In verbs II*wy*, the long stem vowel was shortened in closed syllables, possibly already in Proto-Semitic (Brockelmann 1908, 608, 613; Kienast 2001, §324.1),[36] resulting in a change of stress, since word stress was non-phonemic (Huehnergard 2019, 53): *yáqum* < **yaqūm*, *yásir* < **yasīr*, *yánam* < **yanām*. In verbs III*wy*, a final root vowel is short in *yaqtul*: *yarmi*, but imperfective *yarmī* 'he throws'; *yadʿu*, but imperfective *yadʿū* 'he calls'; *yalqa*, but imperfective *yalqā* 'he meets' (Fischer 2002, §§244, 253b).[37]

In affirmative narrative clauses, the suffix conjugation *qatala* has completely replaced the old past perfective *yaqtul*.

An affirmative jussive *yaqtul* is practically always combined with the particle *li-*, usually in the third person (*li-ya'ti* 'Let him come!'), and only rarely in the first and second persons (Brockelmann 1977, §94):

(21) *li-tukabbirī-hi*

'make it (the tray of palm leaves) large' (uttered to a woman; Wright 1896–98, I:35D)

In Arabic poetry, the particle *li-* is optional. Originally, the *li-* must have been facultative also in prose (Wright 1896–98, I:35D–36A; Huehnergard 1983, 580).

3.1.6. Amorite

The data from the linguistic subdivision of Northwest Semitic called Amorite come from several thousand West Semitic names and loanwords in Akkadian and Sumerian sources, from the middle of the third millennium down to about 1200 BCE (Streck 2011, 452; Gzella 2011a, 427). Data also come most recently from a publication of two lexical texts from the early second millennium BCE (George and Krebernik 2022). The speakers possessing the names are called Amorites in the extant sources, and occupied roughly the same area as the first Aramaeans later came to do: the Middle Euphrates and the Syrian steppe. The lexical texts are two Old Babylonian tablets containing bilingual vocabularies in which the left-hand column presents words and phrases from a variety of Amorite dated to the early second millennium BCE. At that time, Amorite was still a living language (George and Krebernik 2022, 46). The two columns are typical of southern Old Babylonian pedagogical scholarship. These two tablets confirm that Amorite was a Northwest Semitic language with both a short prefix conjugation *yaPRuS/yaPruSū* and a long prefix form *yaPRuSu/yaPruSūna* (George and Krebernik 2022, 2, 29).

The short prefix conjugation is attested as a 'preterite' *yaqtul* and jussive *l-aqtul* with (an optional) proclitic *la-* or *li-* (Golinets 2010, 287f., 336; 2020, 192f.; Streck 2011, 455; Cook 2012a, 119; George and Krebernik 2022, 29):

(22) *Yaśmaʿ-Hadda*

'Hadda has heard'

(23) *ʾAnnu-taśmaʿ*

'Annu has heard' (fem. name)

(24) *ʾAšūb*

'I have turned' (Golinets 2010, 337; 1cs, root II*w*)

(25) *ta-aḫ-ni-šum* ***el-ḫa-ku-un-na-ni****-la-a-ka*

'The woman **sent me** to you.' (2:14, George and Krebernik 2022, 5, 21, my emphasis)[38]

In (25), the *yaqtul-N* is translated by an Akkadian *iprus* in the second column.

An example of a jussive with precative particle is (26):

(26) *li-iḫ-wi-i-ka* [DIĜIR][39]

'May the god (El) preserve your life!'[40] (George and Krebernik 2022, 14f., 30)

Example (27) exhibits a jussive *yaqtul* without precative particle:

(27) *ta-mar ḫa-aš-ti*

'Talk with me!'[41] (George and Krebernik 2022, 14, 30)

The typical Central Semitic shortening of the middle root vowel in verbs II*wy* does not seem to be attested in Amorite names:[42] *Yašūb-lîm* 'The tribe has turned to face'. In verbs III*wy*, the final root vowel does not seem to be short: *Yabnī-dagan* 'Dagan has created' (Streck 2011, 457).

3.1.7. Ugaritic

Ugaritic is now classified as a separate Northwest Semitic language.[43] It is attested in more than a thousand texts from the thirteenth century down to ca 1180 BCE. The poetic texts seem to represent a somewhat older stage (Gzella 2011a, 427).

It is possible to discern three indicative verb forms in Ugaritic: the long prefix conjugation *yaqtulu* (imperfective), the short prefix conjugation *yaqtul* (perfective, mostly past), and the (with non-stativic verbs) perfective suffix conjugation *qatal* (Tropper and Vita 2019b, 493, 495). As in PS, the *yaqtul* in Ugaritic is a category with two meanings, indicative perfective and jussive. The indicative *yaqtul* is attested as past perfective only in the corpus of narrative poetry. In that corpus, it can be used with or without proclitic *w*, probably **wa-* (Tropper 1998, 162; 2012, 454f., 696; Huehnergard 2012, 56):[44]

(28) ***tšu*** *. ilm . rašthm*

'die Götter **erhoben** ihre Häupter' (KTU[3] 1.2:I:29, my emphasis; Tropper 2012, 697)

In such contexts, the *yaqtul* can be linked with the connective *w*:

(29) *tša / ghm .* ***w*** *tṣḥ*

'Die beiden (sc. zwei Boten) erhoben ihre Stimmen **und riefen**' (KTU[3] 1.5:II:16f., my emphasis; Tropper 2012, 699)

The following is an example of a (graphically) proclitic *w*- before a perfective distinctively short *yaqtul*:

(30) w y'n . *aliyn / b'l*

'Then answered mighty Baal' (KTU[3] 1.4.VII:37f.; cf. Huehnergard 2012, 57)[45]

With stativic verbs, the perfective *yaqtul* may refer to the present. This shows that *yaqtul* in Ugaritic cannot be classified as a general past tense:

(31) *abn . brq . d l .* ***td'*** *. šmm*

'Ich weiß Bescheid über den Blitz, den die Himmel nicht **kennen**' (KTU[3] 1.3:III:26, my emphasis; Tropper 2012, 701)[46]

A jussive meaning of *yaqtul*, with preposed subject, is found in (32):[47]

(32) *ilm . tġrk / tšlmk*[48]

'may the gods protect you (ms) (and) keep you well' (KTU[3] 2.14:4–5; Huehnergard 2012, 56)

In Ugaritic prose texts, *yaqtul* is mainly a jussive.[49] As a past perfective verb, *yaqtul* is largely replaced by (1) the suffix conjugation and (2) the diegetic present function of *yaqtulu* (Tropper 2012, 700; Huehnergard 2012, 56).[50]

Ugaritic has a 'precative particle' *l*, but it is infrequent and its use is facultative.[51] An example of precative *l* with *yaqtul* is (33):

(33) *l tb*rkn

'let them (m) bless me' (KTU³ 1.19.iv:32; Huehnergard 2012, 78: /la-tvbarrikū-nī/; cf. Tropper 2012, 812)

In response to the heated discussion on the existence of a short *yqtl*, Hackett has published a number of instances of distinctively short forms in Ugaritic, some of which are displayed below (Hackett 2012, 112ff.).

Some examples of short jussive *yaqtul* are found in (34):

(34) *wa-yarid Kirta li-gaggāti ʿadbu / ʾakla li-qaryīti / ḥittata*[52] *li-Bêti Ḫubūri /* ***yaʾpi*** *laḥma dā-ḫamši / magīda ṯadīṯi yaraḫima / ʿadānu nagubu* ***wa-yaṣiʾ*** */ ṣabaʾu ṣabaʾi nagubu /* ***wa-yaṣiʾ*** *ʿadānu maʿʿu*

'Now, let Kirta come down from the roof, [let him] prepare food for the city, wheat for Bêt Ḫubūr; **let him bake** bread for five months, provisions for six. **Let** the equipped host **go forth**, the great equipped host, **let** the strong host **go forth**.' (KTU³ 1.14.ii.26–31, vocalised and translated by Hackett 2012, 112, my emphasis)

An example of short past reportive *yaqtul* is (35):

(35) *yarid/yarada Kirta li-gaggāti ʿadaba / ʾakla li-qaryīti / ḥittata li-Bêti Ḫubūri /* ***yaʾpi*** *laḥma dāḫamsi / magīda*[53] *ṯadīṯi yaraḫima, and so forth.*

'Kirta came down from the roof, prepared food for the city, wheat for Bêt Ḫubūr; **he baked** bread for five months, provisions for six (and so on).' (KTU^3 1.14.iv.8–12, vocalised and translated by Hackett 2012, 113, my emphasis)

3.1.8. Amarna Canaanite

Proto-Canaanite can be dated no earlier than 1550 BCE (Wilson-Wright 2019, 509). Data about early Canaanite dialects are found in more than 300 diplomatic letters from Canaanite vassal rulers of city-states to their overlords in Egypt, written during the thirteenth century BCE.[54] The letters are written in cuneiform Akkadian, but interesting traits of the scribes' Canaanite native language are revealed by their insufficient knowledge of standard Akkadian in this peripheral area. The language of the Amarna letters can be classified as an 'institutionalised interlanguage' which provides the data for an analysis of this early Canaanite. Dialectal distinctions are "hard to establish in this corpus" (Gzella 2011a, 428; Baranowski 2016a, ch. 2).[55]

The morphological distinction between a short *yaqtul* and a long *yaqtulu* is clearly seen in many examples:

(36) short *yaqtul*: 3fs

[4d]NIN *ša* URU *Gub-la* ***ti-din*** [5]*ba aš-ta-ka i-nu pa-ni* [6]*šàr-ri*

'**May** the Lady of the city of Byblos **grant** you honor before the king, your lord.' (EA 73:4-6; Baranowski 2016a, 74)

(37) short *yaqtul*: 1cs

ù aš-pu-ur! [31][*a*]-*na* LUGAL *be-li-ia*

'**And I wrote** to the king my lord' (EA 138:31–32; cf. EA 362:18 *ù aš-pu-ur*; Tropper and Vita 2010, 68; Baranowski 2016a, 79)

(38) short *yaqtul*: 3mp

ù i-ša-ra-pu KUR.M[EŠ *a-n*]*a* IZI

‘**and they have set fire** to the country.’ (EA 126:52, Baranowski 2016a, 80)[56]

(39) long *yaqtulu*: 3fs

a-di ***ti-ik-šu-du*** [15]*a-wa-at šàrri*

‘until the word of the king, my lord, **comes to me**.’ (EA 221:14–15, Tropper and Vita 2010, 64)

(40) long *yaqtulu*: 3mp

⌜*ù*⌝ *a*[*l-lu-ú-mi*] [122]***ta-aš-pu-ru-na***

‘And be[hold, the men of the city of Byblos **write**’ (EA 138:121–22; similarly Tropper and Vita 2010, 65)

The old *yaqtul* in Amarna Canaanite was one of three primary verbal forms and was seemingly used interchangeably with the new *qatal* gram (Baranowski 2016a, 184, 188). The *yaqtul* exhibits the same dual nature, past indicative and jussive, as the Akkadian *iprus*, except that a ‘precative particle’ *l-* is not needed to signal the jussive meaning (Baranowski 2016a, 77). The indicative use of *yaqtul* is mainly as a past verb form that forms chains of the type *ù yaqtul* + *ù yaqtul*. And there is a tendency to place the *yaqtul* in initial position in the clause (Tropper 1998, 162f.; Notarius 2015, 249; Baranowski 2016a, 137):[57]

(41) […] *ù yi-ìl-qé-šu* [31]ˡ*Sú-ra-ta ù yu-ta-šir*$_9$*-šu* [32]*iš-tu* URU *Ḫi-na-tu-na*ᴷᴵ [33]*a-na É-šu*

‘So Surata took him but he released him to his home from the town of Hannathon’ (EA 245:30–33)

Two coordinated morphologically distinctive short indicative *yaqtul* in report are attested in (42):

(42) *ù a-nu-ma i-na-an-na ši-iḫ-ṭá-at* [11]URU *Ṣu-mu-ur a-di a-bu-li-ši* [12]*ša-ḫa-aṭ-ši* ***i-le-ú*** *ù ṣa-bat-ši* [13]*la* ***i-le-ú*** (EA 106:10–13)

'And right now Ṣumur is besieged up to its city gate. They are able **to besiege** it but they are unable **to conquer** it.'[58]

The typical usage of the jussive is in a modal domain. A distinctively short jussive *yaqtul* is found in the following modal sequence:

(43) *uš-ši-ra* ÉRIN.MEŠ *pí-ṭá-ti* [39]*ra-ba ù tu-da-bi-ir* [40]*a-ia-bi* LUGAL *iš-tu* [41]*lìb-bi* KUR-*šu ù* [42]***ti-né-ep-šu*** *ka-li* [43]KUR.KUR.MEŠ *a-na šàr-ri*

'Send a large regular army and you can drive out the enemies of the king from within his land and all the lands **will be joined** to the king.' (EA 76:38–43)[59]

A focalised clausal constituent, or the negation *lā*, may be placed before *yaqtul*,[60] as in (44), where *yaqtul* has anterior meaning (Baranowski 2016a, 138):

(44) [...] *ù la-a ar-na-ku* [12]*ù la a ḫa-ṭá-ku ù* [13]*la-a* ***a-kal-li*** GÚ.UN.ḪI.A-*ia* [14]*ù la-a* ***a-kal-li*** [15]*e-ri-iš-ti$_7$* LÚ *ra-bi-ṣí-ia*

'and I am not a wrongdoer nor am I a criminal and **I have not withheld** my tribute **nor have I withheld** the request of my commissioner.' (EA 254:11–15)

With stative verbs, *yaqtul* usually refers to "the moment in which the state began" (ingressive; Baranowski 2016a, 139), as in (45):

(45) *ù i-nu-ma iš-te-mé a-wa-at* [14]LUGAL EN-*ia i-nu-ma iš-tap-pár a-na* ÌR-*šu* [15]*ù* ***yi-iḫ-di*** *lìb-bi-ia ù* [16]***yi-⸢ša⸣-qí*** SAG-*ia ù* ***in$_4$-nam-ru*** [17]2 IGI-*ia* \ *ḫe-na-ia i-na ša-me* [18]*a-wa-at* LUGAL EN-*ia*

‘And when I heard the word of the king, my lord, when he wrote to his servant, then my heart **rejoiced** and my head **was lifted up** and my eyes **shone** at hearing the word of the king, my lord.’ (EA 144:13–18)

A prohibitive meaning with *yaqtul* can have two different negations, *lā* interfering with *ul* spelled with the OB orthography (*ú-ul*). The latter use of *ul* is against Babylonian syntax and reminiscent of the Hebrew negation *ʾal* (Rainey 1996, III:221). Examples are (Baranowski 2016a, 156):

(46) *ši-mé ia-‹ši›* UGU-*‹šu-nu›* [51]***ú-ul ti-im-i***

‘Listen to m‹e›; **do not refuse** concerning ‹them›.’ (EA 122:50–51)

(47) ***la-a ta-qú-ul*** L[UGAL *a-na Gu-‹ub›-la*^{KI}] [6]URU-*ka ù* URU *a-bu-t[i-ka]* [7]*iš-tu da-ri-ti* [...]

‘**Do not keep silent**, (O) k[ing, concerning Byblos], your city and the city of [your] ancest[ors] from of old.’ (EA 139:5–7)

The jussive is attested in all three persons. As a rule, the verb occupies first position in the clause, except for the conjunction *u* and the particle *lū* (Baranowski 2016a, 156–158). Example (48) is in the second person singular (Baranowski 2016a, 156):

(48) […] *ša-ni-tam šum-ma* ^{28}*ap-pu-na-ma a-nu-ma pa-aṭ-ra* ^{29}⸢URU⸣ *Ṣu-mu-ra ù* URU *É-Ar-*[*ḫ*]*a*(?) ^{30}[***t***]***a-din-ni*** *i-na qa-at* ^{31}^{I}*Ia-an-ḫa-mi ù ia-dì-na* ^{32}ŠE.IM.ḪI.A *a-na a-ka-li-ia* ^{33}*a-na-ṣa-ra* URU LUGAL *a-na ša-a-šu*

'Furthermore, if moreover now the town of Ṣumur and the town of Bêt-Arḥa have defected, **assign me** to Yanḥamu and allot grain for my sustenance so that I may guard the city of the king for him.' (EA 83:27–33)[61]

The jussive *yaqtul* is nearly always clause-initial. There are some rare cases when a subject or object is placed in focalised position before *yaqtul* (Baranowski 2016a, 158).[62]

The indicative past *yaqtul* is often used in narrative sequences. In this type of domain also, the verb is usually placed first in the clause (type *ù yaqtul*). This is the unmarked word order of the narration. If another constituent of the clause is placed before the verb, it is a signal of a specific discourse function (here a left dislocation), as in (49):

(49) *ù* ^{I}*Sú-ra-t*[*a*] ^{25}*yi-il*$_{5}$*-qé-mì* ^{I}*La-*[*ab-a-ia*]

'But Surata took La[baʾaya]' (EA 245:24–25)[63]

3.1.9. Phoenician

The original language area of Phoenician coincided more or less with the present state of Lebanon. At the beginning of the Early Iron Age, Byblos became the centre of alphabetic writing, and the Phoenician variant of the alphabet the standard medium for writing in the adjacent linguistic areas. Soon the dialect of Tyre and Sidon "became a kind of 'Standard Phoenician' which replaced or influenced others" (Gzella 2012a, 55).[64]

The Central Semitic morphological distinction between a short prefix conjugation and a long prefix conjugation was upheld in the 2fs, 2mp, and 3mp forms by the final *-n* (< **-īna, *-ūna*) in the imperfective long *yqtl*.[65] The corresponding short forms lack this *-n*: the short prefix form ended in *ī* (2fs) or *ū* (2mp, 3mp).[66] In most forms, the morphological distinction is blurred, at least in the script.[67]

A syntactic distinction is upheld in negative clauses. The jussive is preceded by the specific 'prohibitive' negation *ʾl*, while the long imperfective form is negated (mainly) by *bal* (Friedrich and Röllig 1999, §318).

In the earliest stage of the Phoenician textual tradition, about 1000 BCE, it is possible to point to a perfective usage of the old *yaqtul* in a protasis domain (Friedrich and Röllig 1999, §324).[68] The speaker is Ittōbaʿl, son of Aḥīrōm, who threatens a possible desecrator of his father's grave:

(50) ואל . מלך . במלכם . וסכן . בס(כ)נם . ותמא . מחנת . עלי . גבל . **ויגל** .
ארן . זן . תחתסף . חטר . משפטה . תהתפך . כסא . מלכה . ונחת . תברח
. על . גבל . והא . ימח . ספרה . לפ̊ן . ג̊בל

'Now, if any king among kings, or any governor among governors, or any commander of an army has come up against Byblos **and has uncovered** this coffin, may then the sceptre of his rule be torn away, may the throne of his kingdom be overturned, and peace shall flee from Byblos!' (KAI^5 1:2, my emphasis)

The prefix form *wygl* in the example follows a suffix-conjugation form *ʿly* within the protasis (Korchin 2008, 339 n. 23; Gzella 2009, 63: *ʿalaya*). This is a construction with several parallels in CBH.[69] The structure of the whole conditional linking, with the protasis set within parentheses, is: (*w-ʾillū-S.noun-qtl* + ***w-yqtl***) + *Ø-yqtl* + *Ø-yqtl* + *wa-S.noun-yqtl*. The form *ʿly* expresses a completed action. “Das ‘Perfekt’ für den Sachverhalt in der Protasis drückt dessen relative Vorzeitigkeit gegenüber seinem Gegenstück in der Apodosis aus” (Gzella 2009, 66). And the same can be stated for the form that continues the *qtl*, namely *w-ygl*,[70] which is “wohl Kurzimpf.” (Friedrich and Röllig 1999, §324; also Segert 1975b, 90).[71] The apodosis in (47) above, with its many *yqtl* forms, expresses a wish (or possibly a prediction about the future), and at least the first two (*tḥtsp* and *thtpk*) are jussives (Friedrich and Röllig 1999, §264; Gzella 2013b, 190).

Apart from the Byblos inscription, there are only a few possible traces in the extant Phoenician texts of an indicative short prefix form *wyqtl* for narration of past events (Friedrich and Röllig 1999, §266; Röllig 2011, 477f.).[72] In such functions, the old perfective *yaqtul* is normally replaced by the suffix conjugation. The possible, but shaky, examples of perfective narrative *wyqtl* clauses are (text and translation from Friedrich and Röllig 1999, §266):

(51) מל שער ז גלב **ויפג**[ע

‘ML schor dieses Haar (?) und fleh[te an (??)’ (Kition III D 21, 1)’[73]

(52) ובארץ הׄמלך אשר **וׄיׄבׄא**

‘… und er kam’ (KAI[5] 23.4; cf. Lemaire 1983)

(53) [ג]בׄלׄ בד אורך **ויפעל** בחׄלבׄ [של]ם וׄ[ ]

‘… und er machte…’ (KAI[5] 23.5)

Krahmalkov (2001) has added a few doubtful examples of past perfective meaning of a *wyqtl* clause (with presumably short *yqtl*) in Phoenician and Punic.[74] The paucity of examples might suggest that "narrative tenses in Phoenician, including its lack of the *waw*-consecutive, apparently reflect a more highly accelerated rate of linguistic change than Aramaic and Hebrew" (Smith 1991, 20).

There are traces of a proclitic *l* before jussive forms in Punic—*l-yšmʿ qlʾ* 'May he hear (*lismaʿ*) his voice' (Krahmalkov 2001, 190)[75]—but in Phoenician, the jussive lacks this clitic:

(54) **יארך** . בעל . שמם . ובעל(ת) (4) גבל . ומפחרת . אל גבל (5) קדשם .
ימת . יחמלך . ושנתו (6) על גבל

> '**May** the Baʿal of the Heavens and the Lady of Byblos and the assembly of the holy gods of Byblos **lengthen** the days of Yaḥūmilk and his years over Byblos.' (KAI[5] 4.3–4, translated after Friedrich and Röllig 1999, §264)

3.1.10. Moabite

There is no consensus as to the internal classification of the Canaanite dialects in the Iron Age, and this concerns especially the Trans-Jordanian dialects Ammonite, Moabite, and Edomite, which from the fifth century BCE were replaced step by step with Aramaic. The debate is partly caused by the paucity of textual material.[76] Given the available data, there is no reason to regard the Trans-Jordanian spoken varieties as three distinct national languages. Rather they should be seen as located in an area with dialectal variations.[77]

Ammonite is attested from about 800 BCE to the beginning of the sixth century BCE, and the corpus consists mainly of seals and bullae, but also a number of inscriptions of up to 10 lines (Aḥituv 2008, 357–386; Lemaire 2013a). The Edomite corpus is even smaller: two ostraca,[78] and some seals, bullae, and seal-impressions. The inscriptions in Ammonite and Edomite are very short and "unrevealing of linguistic peculiarities" (Parker 2002, 47; Lemaire 2013b). The old Semitic *yaqtul* does not seem to be attested in either of the two dialects.[79]

Only the Moabite corpus of inscriptions permits a reasonable discussion of the verb forms and their meanings, and especially the Moabite stone from about 830 BCE (the Mēšaʿ stele, now in the Louvre: Smith 1991, 17–19; Parker 2002, 49).[80] The oldest inscriptions are from the ninth century BCE and written in the Hebrew script (Fassberg 2013a). Practically all linguistic features of Moabite discussed below are drawn from the 34-line Mēšaʿ inscription.[81] The inscription at el-Kerak (KAI[5] 306) by Mēšaʿ (Swiggers 1982; Aḥituv 2008, 387), or by his father Kmšyt, adds very little to our knowledge of the language (Parker 2002, 54).

The old *yaqtul* is attested both with jussive meaning and with past perfective meaning. Despite the defective spelling, it is possible to identify a short prefix form in some cases (Smith 1991, 17–19; Parker 2002, 49; Hasselbach 2013a). Several examples of a narrative short *yaqtul* are found in the Mēšaʿ inscription (Garr 1985, 138; Schüle 2000, 164; Renz 2016, 629f.):

(55) אבי . מלך . על . מאב . שלשׁן . שת . ואנך . מלכתי . אחר . אבי | **ואעש** . הבמת . זאת . לכמש . בקרחה |

'My father ruled over Moab thirty years, and I have taken over the kingship after my father, **and I have made** this high place for Chemosh in Qarchoh' (KAI[5] 181: 2–3)[82]

The syntactic structure of this quotation is *w-S.noun-qtl* + *w-S.pron-qtl* + ***w-yqtl***. We can see that the new perfective *qatal* has been utilised for establishing the narrative frame of the inscription (Dahl 1985, 30), whereas the old *yaqtul* (always with a preceding conjunction *w*) has been retained for successive narrative events.[83] The reference to a building (*hbmt zʾt* 'this high place') in the close neighborhood of the monument triggers an anterior meaning of the *w-yqtl* (*w-ʾʿś* 'and I have made').[84] Since the Trans-Jordanian scribes usually marked long final vowels with corresponding *matres lectionis*, the letters *w-ʾʿś* indicate a short form, as in the CBH form with the same consonantal orthography (*wāʾaʿaś*).[85]

A passage with past perfective meaning of *w-yqtl* is found some lines further in the same inscription:

(56) וישראל . אבד . אבד . עלם . **וירש** . עמרי . את . כ֯[ל . אר]ץ . מהדבה |
וישב . בה . ימה . וחצי . ימי . בנה . ארבען . שת . **וי֯שבה** . כמש . בימי |
ואבן . את . בעלמען . **ואעש** . בה . האשוח . **ואב֯[ן]** את . קריתן |

'But Israel is utterly destroyed forever: Omri **took possession** of the land of Medeba, **and he dwelled** in it in his days and half the days of his son, forty years. **But then** Chemosh **restored it** in my days. **And I built** Baal-Meon, **and I made** in it a reservoir, **and I bui[lt]** Qiriathaim.' (KAI[5] 181: 7–10)

The narrative frame in this case is again established by the new perfective *qatal* (*ʾbd*), in a clause that functions as a subheading or preamble, which could be followed by a colon in the translation.[86] All in all, there are 35 attested realis *w-yqtl* clauses with past time reference in the Mēšaʿ inscription.[87]

The old *yaqtul* with jussive meaning is attested in some Trans-Jordanian inscriptions, but the forms are not distinctive in the script. A semantically evident example is found in an Ammonite seal:[88]

(57) אבנדב ש נדר לעשתרת בצדן **תברכה**

'Abinadab, who has fulfilled a vow to ʿAštart in Ṣīdōn. **May she bless him**!' (Jackson 1983, 77, 101; Aufrecht 1989, no. 56)

3.1.11. Aramaic

Aramaic belongs to the Aramaeo-Canaanite group of Northwest Semitic (Huehnergard and Pat-El 2019, 5). The Aramaic discussed under this heading is Old Aramaic (inscriptions) and Imperial (or Official) Aramaic, with an emphasis on the more ancient stage.[89]

The reflex of the Central Semitic imperfective marker *-u/ -na* was retained in Aramaic after the decline of short final vowels in the form of the *-n* endings in 3mp and 2mp forms of the (imperfective) long prefix conjugation. This resulted in a preserved distinction (in forms 3mp and 2mp) between a short *yqtl* without *-n* and a long *yqtl* with *-n* in all verb classes (Degen 1969, §§49–50; Voigt 1987, 6; Kogan 2015, 162):

Table 5: Imperfective markers in Aramaic

	short *yqtl*	**long *yqtl***
3mp	*y-...-w*	*y-...-n*
3fp	*y-...-n*	*y-...-n*
2mp	*t-...-w*	*t-...-n*
2fp	not attested	not attested

The long *yqtl* (*yaqtulu*) is an imperfective formation and can be used for present and future actions (“kursiven Aspekt,” Degen 1969, §75). The short *yqtl* can be both jussive and indicative (past). The indicative past short *yqtl* occurs in clauses of the type *w-yqtl* (Degen 1969, 114; Voigt 1987, 6). It is obvious that the short *yqtl* in Old Aramaic is a reflex of the PS **yaqtul*.

The indicative past meanings of the old *yaqtul* are confined to the earliest inscriptions.[90] Some of the oldest texts exhibit a narrative past use of (*w*) *yqtl* reminiscent of the realis *yaqtul* in Amarna Canaanite and CBH *wa(y)-yiqṭol* (Tropper 1996; 1998, 163f.). Such is the case in the Zakkūr stela from the beginning of the eighteenth century (Bron 1973–79, 607; Smith 1991, 18; Rainey 2003a, 404f.; 2007, 79):[91]

(58) ושמו . כל <.> מלכיא <.> אל . מצר . על . חזר̊[ך] (10) והרמו . שר .
מן . שר . חזרך . והעמקו . חרץ . מן . חר̊[צה] (11) ו̊אשא . ידי . אל .
בעלש[מי]ן . ויענני <.> בעלשמי[ן . ויד(12)בר] . בעלשמין . אלי . [ב]יד
. חזין . וביד . עדדן̊ [. ויאמר .(13)לי .]בעלשמין

‘all these kings put up a wall against Ḥazrak and raised a siege wall higher than the wall of Ḥazrak and dug a trench deeper than its moat. **But then I lifted up** my hands to Baʿal-Šamayin, **and** Baʿal-Šamayin **answered** me… [**and**] Baʿal-Šamayin [**said** to me]’ (KAI[5] 202A:9–13)

In the example, the *w-yqtl* forms (bold in translation) express a temporal succession or a response to the activities of the enemy. Reacting to the hostile actions described by suffix conjugation forms, Zakkūr, the king of Ḥamat, lifted his hands to Baʿal-Šamayin, and as a result Baʿal-Šamayin answered him.[92]

If scholarly opinion was hesitant about the status of the *w-yqtl* clauses in the Zakkūr inscription,[93] the discussion came practically to an end with the discovery of the Tel Dan (Tel el-Qāḍi) inscription from around 800 BCE (KAI[5] 310) by A. Biran and J. Naveh (1993; 1995) and the judgement of T. Muraoka (1995a; 1995b; 1998).[94] It is now widely accepted that a reflex of the Proto-Semitic perfective **yaqtul* was used as a past perfective verb in the earliest attested stage of Aramaic (Emerton 1994; Huehnergard 2005, 165; Fales 2011, 559; Renz 2016, 631f.).[95] Lines 2–6 in (59) are a good illustration:

(59) [ב]ר֯[ה]ד֯ד֯ . אבי . **יס֯ק**[. עלוה . בה]ת֯לחמה . בא x [.](3)
וישכב . אבי . **יהך** אל[. אבהו]ה֯ .
ויעל . מלך י[ש](4)ראל . קדם . בארק . אב֯י֯[.
ו]**י֯המלך** . הדד [.] א[יתי .] (5)אנה .
ויהך . הדד . קדמי[.
ו]**אפק** . מ֯ן . ש֯בע֯[ת .] (6) י מלכי .
ואקתל . מל֯[כן שב]ע֯ן א֯סרי . א[לפי . ר](7)כב . ואלפי פרש .

> 'Bar Hadad, my father, **went up** [against him when] he was fighting at A[..] [3]and my father **lay down** (and) **went** to [his ancestors.] The king of Israel **entered** [4]formerly in my father's land, [but] **then** Hadad **made me king.** [5]**And** Hadad **went** before me; [and] **I departed** from seven[…] [6]of my kingdom. **And I slew** seve[nty ki]ngs harnessing thou[sands of cha][7]riots and thousands of horsemen.' (KAI[5] 310:2–6, my emphasis)

Following the discovery of this text, few scholars deny that *yqtl* in *w-yqtl* clauses was used as a narrative past tense in early Aramaic, and many maintain that the *yqtl* forms even without preceding *waw* can be analyzed as narrative pasts as well (Kottsieper 1999, 62; Rainey 2003a, 405).[96] Though the inscription is damaged, it seems that a perfective *yqtl* may be preceded by a subject noun (*ʾby* ***ysq*** 'my father went up'),[97] as is sometimes found in Amarna Canaanite, and it appears that an asyndetic *Ø-yqtl* (***yhk*** 'he went') can be attached to a foregoing past tense *w-yqtl* clause (***wyškb*** *ʾby* 'and my father lay down') as an elaboration (Muraoka 1995a, 19; Gzella 2015, 81 n. 225).[98] At least one form appears morphologically 'short': line 9 *wʾśm* 'and I laid' (Muraoka 1995b, 115; but against this, see Tropper 1996, 638f.). The conclusion is inevitable that the "altaramäische *w-yqtl*-Konstruktion ist nicht nur formal mit der hebr. *wayyiqtol*-Konstruktion vergleichbar, sie teilt mit dieser auch die gleiche Hauptfunktion, nämlich die Bezeichnung singularischer (pfv.), im Progreß verlaufender SVe der Vergangenheit" (Tropper 1998, 163f.).

An indicative past usage of the old *yaqtul* is attested also in the much disputed[99] Deir ʿAllā inscription from between 850 and 750 BCE, probably around 800 BCE,[100] painted by a professional scribe on a lime plaster wall in the mid-Jordan valley.[101] There are five clear examples of a realis perfective *yaqtul* in the inscription, all showing an initial *wa* conjunction (Smith 1991, 18).[102] A good example is (60):

(60) [זנה .] ס֯פ֯ר֯ [. ב]ל֯ע֯ם֯ [. בר בע]ר . אש֯ . חז֯ה֯ . אלהן֯ [.] ה֯א [.]
ויאתו . אלוה . אלהן . בליל֯ה֯ [. ויאמרו . ל]ה֯ (2) כמש֯א . אל . **ו֯יאמרו** .
ל֯[בלע]ם֯ . בר בער .

'[This is] the book of [Balaam, son of Beo]r. He was a seer of the gods. The gods **came** to him in the night, [and spoke to him] like an oracle of ʾEl. **And they said** to [Balaa]m, son of Beor'[103] (KAI^5 312:1–2, Combination I: lines 1–2)

The inscription starts with a headline: "[This is] the book of Balaam, son of Beor." After a verbless clause, a preamble with a presentation of Balaam as a seer of the gods, there follow at least two (possibly three) *w-yqtl* clauses that function as a historical elaboration of the preamble in the form of a narration of single events. In the narrative, details are given of Balaam's career as a seer. Instances of distinctively short jussive *yaqtul* are found in I:7 ואל תח̊ג̊י 'do not remove' (text quoted from KAI^5 312:7) and II:6 ירוי 'may he be satisfied' (Garr 1985, 138).[104]

The instances of at least two distinctively short jussive *yaqtul* (Lipiński 1994, 130, 163; Voigt 1987, 6), and especially the construction with the negation אל and a short 2fs form תחגי, point to the existence of a short prefix conjugation in Aramaic. Unfortunately, there are no clear cases of long imperfective *yaqtulu* with final *n* in this inscription, such as we expect to see in other Aramaic texts, "so it is impossible to know whether this dialect employed the long form of the 2 f. sg. imperfect" (Hackett 1984, 46).

After the earliest (inscriptional) state of Old Aramaic, represented by the Tel Dan, Zakkūr, and Deir ʿAllā inscriptions, the emerging perfective *qatal* came to replace the earlier perfective *yaqtul*, and only the jussive meaning of the old *yaqtul* was retained in Old and Imperial Aramaic (Gzella 2004, 305), as is in fact the case in all the classical languages except Biblical Hebrew (Huehnergard 2002, 126).[105] As a prohibitive, the jussive is negated by *ʾl*.[106] The morphological difference in the consonantal writing is slight: only in the plural of masculine forms can the characteristic final *-n* be a distinctive mark of the imperfective as against the ending *-w* of the short form (Degen 1969, 65, 113; Fales 2011, 568). In inscriptional Aramaic, this *-n* is an important retention of a distinguishing feature of the Central Semitic (or even Proto-Semitic; Kouwenberg 2010a, 95–103) imperfective *yaqtul-u, -ūna*:

(61) יהפכו אלהן אש̊(22)[א ה]א

‘**May** the Gods **destroy** that man!’ (jussive *yaqtul*, KAI[5] 222 1C: 21–22)

(62) והן יקרק מני קרק̊ חד פק̊די... ויהכן חלב

‘If a fugitive escapes from me... **and they go** to Aleppo...’ (imperfective *yaqtulu*, KAI[5] 224: 4–5)[107]

Verbs IIwy in Old Aramaic have short *yaqtul* forms (Gzella 2011a, 443), as is shown in the opposition between לשם /laśim/ ‘may he erect’ and וישים /wa-yaśīm/ ‘and he will erect’ (KAI[5] 309: 11, 12).[108] In verbs III*wy*, the orthography has a distinction between a final radical *y* (= *ay*)[109] or *w* (= *aw*) in the short form, and a final mater lectionis *h* (= *ê*) in the long prefix conjugation (Degen 1969, §§6–7, 62; Voigt 1987, 6; Gzella 2011a, 444).[110] This is illustrated in (63) with initial position of the verb, and (64) with non-initial (internal) position:

(63) תהוי מלכתה כמלכת חל מלכת חלם זי ימלך אשר̊

‘**may** his kingdom **become** like a kingdom of sand, a dream kingdom that Assur rules!’ (short *yqtl*, KAI[5] 222 I A: 25)

(64) והן֯ יאת֯ה֯ חד מלכן ויסב֯ני

‘if some king **comes** and surrounds me…’ (long *yqtl*, KAI^{5} 222 I B: 28)

Word order is one of the features that help distinguish the old *yaqtul* from the long imperfective *yaqtulu*. If a subject is preposed before a prefix conjugation verb, the latter is always long in Old Aramaic (Degen 1969, 108).[111] A jussive *yaqtul* is always negated by *ʾl* (*ʾal*), while *yaqtulu* is negated by *l* (*lā*; Degen 1969, 113f., 110f.; §§84, 86b).[112] In Imperial Aramaic, the initial position of the jussive is a tendency, and there are many exceptions to this rule (Muraoka and Porten 2003, 199).[113]

The distinction between a short jussive and a long imperfective is generally maintained in Imperial Aramaic, “but not all forms can be clearly distinguished on morphological grounds” (Gzella 2011b, 580), and there are groups of texts, such as the Aḥiqar proverbs, that seem to indicate a less consistent spelling (Muraoka and Porten 2003, 137, 198, 200; Gzella 2011b, 580).[114] The examples of jussives that are graphically long (with final *h* instead of *y*) are usually found in otherwise unambiguous syntagms, such as clauses negated by *ʾl*, used only before the short jussive (Segert 1975a, §§6.5.4.7, 6.6.6.3.2; Muraoka and Porten 2003, 138):

(65) לבבך אל יחדה

‘Let not your heart rejoice!’ (TAD3, p. 36: C1.1, 90)

In Biblical Aramaic verbs III*wy*, the morphological opposition between a short jussive and a long imperfective has disappeared and the long form is used for both purposes (Folmer 2012, 156).

Early Aramaic developed a distinctive morphological feature that compensated for the partial collapse of the short and long prefix conjugations. The short prefix conjugation always takes suffixes without 'energic' *n*, and the long imperfective shows a *tendency* to take suffixes preceded by the inherited 'energic' ending: in Old Aramaic, the 3ms suffix, and in Imperial Aramaic, all suffixes attached to the long form are 'energic' (Degen 1969, 80; Hug 1993, 87f.):[115]

(66) Old Aramaic

long form + 3mp suffix without energic clitic

רקה תרקהם ותהשבהם לי

'Rather you shall convince them and you shall bring them back to me' (KAI[5] 224, 6)

(67) Imperial Aramaic

long form + 3ms suffix with energic clitic

אתננהי לך

'I give him to you' (TAD2, p. 12: B1.1, 11)

(68) Imperial Aramaic

short form + 2ms suffix without energic clitic

יכטלוך

'May they kill you' (KAI[5] 225:11)

In summary: the earliest inscriptional stage of Aramaic exhibits a morphological distinction between a short *yqtl* and a long (imperfective) *yqtl*. The short *yqtl* has two meanings: jussive, and a perfective past used in narrative and report in the clause-type *w-yqtl*. In later inscriptions and in Official Aramaic, a perfective *qatal* has replaced perfective past *yqtl*, while a jussive short *yqtl* is retained.

3.2. The Short *Yiqṭol* in the Archaic Hebrew Poetry

The reflex of the old Semitic *yaqtul* is fully attested in the archaic poetry, both with indicative meaning and as a jussive.[116] The main divergences in comparison to the CBH corpus are syntactic: the indicative short *yiqṭol* occurs in some contexts without the proclitic conjunction *wa* (Finley 1981, 246; Hasselbach and Huehnergard 2008, 416; Baranowski 2016b, 11), and in at least one instance short *yiqṭol* is used in non-initial position. So the word order of the short *yiqṭol* is somewhat more free in the Archaic Hebrew poetry than in CBH, a situation that is even more prevalent in the Canaanite of the Amarna letters (Baranowski 2016b, 11).

The anterior meaning is one of the steps on the grammaticalisation path of a perfective gram. In distinction to simple pasts, an anterior may, as a generalisation of its meaning, describe a present state, even with a dynamic lexeme, which results in a general, or gnomic, present (Bybee et al. 1994, 69). An example is (69):

(69) *Ø-yiqṭol(Ø)! + «DEF-qoṭel + wa(y)-yiqṭol»*

יְהִי־דָן נָחָשׁ עֲלֵי־דֶרֶךְ שְׁפִיפֹן עֲלֵי־אֹרַח הַנֹּשֵׁךְ עִקְּבֵי־סוּס **וַיִּפֹּל** רֹכְבוֹ אָחוֹר׃

'Dan is a snake by the roadside, a viper along the path, that bites the horse's heels **and** its rider **falls** backward.' (Gen. 49.17)

In (69), the *wa(y)-yiqṭol* clause belongs to the *qoṭel*-clause, which with its definite article functions as a relative clause that characterises the viper (Dan).[117] Within this relative sentence, *wa(y)-yiqṭol* (וַיִּפֹּל) codes an action that is temporally sequential in relation to the previous clause (*qoṭel*). Both *qoṭel* and *wa(y)-yiqṭol* are gnomic and characterising, but they describe actions that are not simultaneous (Ges-K §111r–w; J-M §118o).[118]

The past perfective meaning of the short *yiqṭol* is mostly found in the narrative fragments. An example of short *yiqṭol* (*yiqṭol(Ø)*) without initial *wa* in narrative main line is (70):[119]

(70) *Ø-XØ + Ø-XØ +* ***Ø-yiqṭol(Ø)!***[120] *+ [9]kī-XØ + Ø-XØ + [10]**Ø-yiqṭol(Ø)** + Ø-yiqṭol(u)-N + Ø-yiqṭol(u)-N + Ø-yiqṭol(u)-N + [11]kə-S.noun-yiqṭol(u)! + Ø-PrP-yiqṭol(u) +* ***Ø-yiqṭol(Ø) + Ø-yiqṭol(Ø) + Ø-yiqṭol(Ø)***

בְּהַנְחֵל עֶלְיוֹן גּוֹיִם בְּהַפְרִידוֹ בְּנֵי אָדָם **יַצֵּב** גְּבֻלֹת עַמִּים לְמִסְפַּר בְּנֵי יִשְׂרָאֵל׃
9 כִּי חֵלֶק יְהוָה עַמּוֹ יַעֲקֹב חֶבֶל נַחֲלָתוֹ׃ 10 **יִמְצָאֵהוּ** בְּאֶרֶץ מִדְבָּר וּבְתֹהוּ יְלֵל
יְשִׁמֹן יְסֹבְבֶנְהוּ יְבוֹנְנֵהוּ יִצְּרֶנְהוּ כְּאִישׁוֹן עֵינוֹ׃ 11 כְּנֶשֶׁר יָעִיר קִנּוֹ עַל־גּוֹזָלָיו
יְרַחֵף **יִפְרֹשׂ** כְּנָפָיו **יִקָּחֵהוּ יִשָּׂאֵהוּ** עַל־אֶבְרָתוֹ׃

'When the Most High apportioned the nations, when he divided humankind, **he fixed** the boundaries of the peoples according to the number of the gods.[121] [9]The LORD's own portion was his people, Jacob his allotted share. [10]**He found him** in a desert land, in a howling wilderness waste:

> he shielded him, cared for him, guarded him as the apple of his eye. [11]As an eagle stirs up its nest, and hovers over its young, **he spread** his wings, **took them** up, and **bore them** aloft on his pinions.' (Deut. 32.8–11, Notarius 2013, 307, my verse numbers and emphasis)

Example (70) shows a narrative detached from speech time. The main line is coded by *yiqṭol(Ø)* clauses with the verb in clause-initial position. The main function of a switch to a *yiqṭol(u)* clause is to express simultaneous habitual or iterative meaning. But the *yiqṭol(u)* verbs are also mainly clause-initial, so word order is not decisive in distinguishing the perfective short *yiqṭol* from the imperfective *yiqṭol(u)*.[122] And the conjunction *wa* is not used as a connective of clauses in this section of the poetic narration. The same poem also exhibits linkings with *wa*, as can be seen in (71):

(71) *Ø-yiqṭol(Ø) + wa(y)-yiqṭol + wa(y)-yiqṭol*

> **יַרְכִּבֵ֙הוּ֙** עַל־בָּ֣מוֹתֵי אָ֔רֶץ **וַיֹּאכַ֖ל** תְּנוּבֹ֣ת שָׂדָ֑י **וַיֵּנִקֵ֤הוּ** דְבַשׁ֙ מִסֶּ֔לַע וְשֶׁ֖מֶן מֵחַלְמִ֥ישׁ צֽוּר׃
>
> '**He set him** atop the heights of the land, **and fed him**[123] with produce of the field; **he nursed him** with honey from the crags, with oil from flinty rock.' (Deut. 32.13, Notarius 2013, 307, my emphasis)

This syntax, with an initial asyndetically attached past perfective *Ø-yiqṭol(Ø)* and two following *wa(y)-yiqṭol*, is archaic.[124] It is found also in Amarna Canaanite (Bloch 2013; Baranowski 2016b, 11), but not in CBH. The two *wa(y)-yiqṭol* clauses connect semantically with the initial *yiqṭol(Ø)* clause, and have meanings that might be temporally sequential, but not necessarily so. In CBH, such a narrative chain might have been introduced by a *qaṭal* clause with past perfective meaning (see §§7.7–8). The typical CBH narrative/reportive sequence *qaṭal* + *wa(y)-yiqṭol* is attested in the relatively more innovative Blessing of Moses (Notarius 2013, 290):[125]

(72) Ø-O.noun-*qaṭal* + ⁵*wa(y)-yiqṭol*!

תּוֹרָ֥ה **צִוָּה**־לָ֖נוּ מֹשֶׁ֑ה מוֹרָשָׁ֖ה קְהִלַּ֥ת יַעֲקֹֽב׃ **וַיְהִ֥י** בִישֻׁר֖וּן מֶ֑לֶךְ בְּהִתְאַסֵּ֣ף רָ֣אשֵׁי עָ֔ם יַ֖חַד שִׁבְטֵ֥י יִשְׂרָאֵֽל׃

'Moses **charged** us with the law, as a possession for the assembly of Jacob. ⁵**There arose** a king in Jeshurun, when the leaders of the people assembled—the united tribes of Israel.' (Deut. 33.4–5, Notarius 2013, 239f., my emphasis)

The *qaṭal* form (צִוָּה) in (72) expresses a past perfective meaning and codes the foreground in a retrospective report. The *wa(y)-yiqṭol* is temporally sequential to the event in the *qaṭal* clause.[126]

But the archaic realis short *yiqṭol* may also have a future meaning, as is the case when it follows a so-called 'prophetic perfect' *qaṭal*.[127] This future meaning is achieved with a metaphorical transposition to a future-time reference in prophetic prospective report, as in (73):

(73) *kī-S.noun-qaṭal* + *wa(y)-yiqṭol* + *wa(y)-yiqṭol* + *wa(y)-yiqṭol*

כִּי־אֵשׁ֙ קָדְחָ֣ה בְאַפִּ֔י **וַתִּיקַ֖ד** עַד־שְׁא֣וֹל תַּחְתִּ֑ית **וַתֹּ֤אכַל** אֶ֙רֶץ֙ וִֽיבֻלָ֔הּ **וַתְּלַהֵ֖ט** מוֹסְדֵ֥י הָרִֽים׃

'For a fire will kindle by my anger, **and it will burn** to the depths of Sheol; **it will devour** the earth and its increase, **and will set on fire** the foundations of the mountains.' (Deut. 32.22, Notarius 2013, 87, 282, my emphasis)

In (73), the *qaṭal* form expresses a resultative aspect which is "metaphorically relocated to the future;" it is "an expression of the speaker's illocutionary intention to warn about the coming punishment" (Notarius 2013, 91, 88, 268 n. 6, 282).[128] It seems that the new perfective *qaṭal* has taken over (from short *yiqṭol*) the role of starting a chain of prospective report events viewed as finished in the future (Bybee and Dahl 1989, 74), while the discourse-continuous *wa(y)-yiqṭol* clause-type is retained for the expression of the sequential future actions in the sequence.

The short *yiqṭol* can also be used after a *qaṭal* clause to express a past action the effects of which are present in speech time (anterior). In this case also, *yiqṭol(Ø)* occurs in a clause expressing discourse continuity:

(74) *INT-PrP-yiqṭol(u)* + *INT-lō-XØ-«qaṭal»* + *Ø-S.pron-qaṭal* + ***wa(y)-yiqṭol***

הַ־לַיהוָה֙ תִּגְמְלוּ־זֹ֔את עַ֥ם נָבָ֖ל וְלֹ֣א חָכָ֑ם הֲלוֹא־הוּא֙ אָבִ֣יךָ קָּנֶ֔ךָ ה֥וּא עָֽשְׂךָ֖
וַֽיְכֹנְנֶֽךָ׃

'Do you thus repay the LORD, O foolish and senseless people? Is not he your father, who created you, who made you **and established you**?' (Deut. 32.6, Notarius 2013, 86, 282, my emphasis)

In (74), the speaker "contributes to the argument which develops within this conversational framework" (Notarius 2013, 87). The meaning of *wa(y)-yiqṭol* is present anterior rather than a remote perfective.[129] An anterior meaning of short *yiqṭol* is not frequent in the archaic poetry. It seems that the new perfective *qaṭal* has taken over this function in the verbal system too. The discourse-continuous *wa(y)-yiqṭol* (וַֽיְכֹנְנֶֽךָ) hardly attests to a (temporally) sequential meaning; it can possibly be defined as an elaboration (cf. Notarius 2013, 87).

The jussive meaning of the short *yiqṭol* is found in many types of modal domains, such as prayer, blessing, warning, or praise. This makes a confusion with indicative meanings impossible in the archaic poetry. The jussive *yiqṭol(Ø)* in affirmative clauses is practically always clause-initial. An example is (75):

(75) *Ø-yiqṭol(Ø)! + wa-yiqṭol(Ø)!*

תָּמֹ֤ת נַפְשִׁי֙ מ֣וֹת יְשָׁרִ֔ים **וּתְהִ֥י** אַחֲרִיתִ֖י כָּמֹֽהוּ׃

'**Let me die** the death of righteous ones, **and let** my end **be** like this!' (Num. 23.10b, Notarius 2013, 225, my emphasis)[130]

In at least one case, a perfective past *yiqṭol(Ø)* is non-initial. The syntax is complicated, with an asyndetic relative clause and a chiastic linking with the indicative short *yiqṭol* in final position in the first clause,[131] and an initial verb in the second clause (Isaksson 2017, 232f.):

(76) *Ø-O.noun-«Ø-qaṭal»-**yiqṭol(Ø)**! + wa(y)-yiqṭol*

צ֥וּר יְלָדְךָ֖ **תֶּ֑שִׁי** וַתִּשְׁכַּ֖ח אֵ֥ל מְחֹלְלֶֽךָ׃

'**You were unmindful** of the Rock that bore you; you forgot the God who gave you birth.' (Deut. 32.18, Notarius 2013, 307, my emphasis)

Joosten (2012, 417f.) describes this language as "a system where the preterite is free with regard to word order, and free of the *waw*." The statistics suggest, however, that it is a freedom bound by relatively consistent conventions. There is only one example of a non-initial affirmative jussive *yiqṭol(Ø)* in an archaic text, also in a case with a chiastic word order (Notarius 2013, 78, 146f., 281, 294, 307; 2015, 240):

(77) *Ø-yiqṭol(Ø)* + *Ø-PrP-**yiqṭol(Ø)***

תְּבֹרַךְ֙ מִנָּשִׁ֔ים יָעֵ֕ל אֵ֖שֶׁת חֶ֣בֶר הַקֵּינִ֑י מִנָּשִׁ֥ים בָּאֹ֖הֶל **תְּבֹרָֽךְ׃**

'Most blessed of women be Jael, the wife of Heber the Kenite, of tent dwelling women **most blessed**' (Judg. 5.24, Notarius 2013, 146f., 294, my emphasis)

Deviations from the word order rule are common when the verb is negated (always with *ʾal*), as in (78):

(78) *Ø-PrP-ʾal-yiqṭol(Ø)* + *Ø-S.noun-PrP-ʾal-yiqṭol(Ø)*...

בְּסֹדָם֙ **אַל־תָּבֹ֣א** נַפְשִׁ֔י בִּקְהָלָ֖ם **אַל־תֵּחַ֣ד** כְּבֹדִ֑י כִּ֤י בְאַפָּם֙ הָ֣רְגוּ אִ֔ישׁ וּבִרְצֹנָ֖ם עִקְּרוּ־שֽׁוֹר׃

'**May I never come** into their council; **may I not be joined** to their company—for in their anger they killed men, and at their whim they hamstrung oxen' (Gen. 49.6, Notarius 2013, 191, my emphasis)

Negative jussive clauses seem to have been employed with a free word order, in contrast to the word order in affirmative clauses.[132] Since the word order is relatively free also in the case of imperative and ventive/cohortative clauses,[133] I conclude that the more restricted word order applies primarily to affirmative *yiqṭol(Ø)* clauses in the archaic poetry. And this concerns both indicative and jussive clauses. It is not true that volitive forms in general are clause-initial. The word order restriction pertains specifically to the old *yaqtul* verb form in affirmative clauses and without the paragogic *heh*.

The jussive *yiqṭol(Ø)* is regularly employed in a specific type of subordinate clause, the syntagm *wa-yiqṭol(Ø)*, predominantly with the meaning of purpose in a modal domain, as in (79):

(79) *Ø-IMP + Ø-IMP + Ø-IMP +* ***wa-yiqṭol(Ø)****! + (IMP) +* ***wa-yiqṭol(Ø)***

זְכֹר֙ יְמ֣וֹת עוֹלָ֔ם בִּ֖ינוּ שְׁנ֣וֹת דּוֹר־וָד֑וֹר שְׁאַ֤ל אָבִ֙יךָ֙ **וְיַגֵּ֔דְךָ** זְקֵנֶ֖יךָ **וְיֹ֥אמְרוּ** לָֽךְ׃

'Remember the days of old, consider the years long past; ask your father, **and he will inform you**; your elders, **and they will tell you**.' (Deut. 32.7, Notarius 2013, 80, my emphasis)[134]

The example exhibits an unusual distinctively short *yiqṭol* with object suffix (וְיַגֵּ֔דְךָ; Notarius 2013, 101 n. 90). The semantic meaning of the *wa-yiqṭol* after the imperative is clearly the purpose of the action. The second imperative is left out by ellipsis.

The *wa-yiqṭol(Ø)* clause-type with purposive meaning seems to have attained a certain independence (as a non-main clause), and is not confined to modal series, an example of which is shown in (80):

(80) *Ø-lō-XØ +* ***wa-yiqṭol(Ø)*** *+ wa-(lō)-XØ +* ***wa-yiqṭol(Ø)***

לֹ֣א אִ֥ישׁ אֵל֙ **וִיכַזֵּ֔ב** וּבֶן־אָדָ֖ם **וְיִתְנֶחָ֑ם**

'El is not a human being, **that he should lie**, or a mortal, **that he should change his mind**.' (Num. 23.19a, Notarius 2013, 226, my emphasis)

The same syntagm as in the purpose clauses already described now expresses a subordination that is slightly more general than 'purpose'. Notarius (2013, 226) calls this "the subjunctive mood in a purpose clause," but it could just as well be regarded as a consequence clause.[135]

It has been argued that the jussive can also introduce a protasis in a conditional clause linking.[136] This idea is based on the Classical Arabic syntax of conditional sentences,[137] where both short jussives and perfects may occur (seemingly indiscriminately) in both protasis and apodosis. The prime alleged example of a jussive introducing protasis in Archaic Hebrew is (81).

(81) *Ø-yiqṭol(u)-N* + *wa-lō-ADV* + *Ø-yiqṭol(u)-N* + *wa-lō-ADJ* + *Ø-qaṭal* + *wa-qaṭal* + *wa-qaṭal* + *wa-qaṭal* + [18]*wa-qaṭal* + *wa-qaṭal* + *wa-S.noun-qoṭel* + [19]***wa-yiqṭol(Ø)!*** + *wa-qaṭal*

אֶרְאֶ֙נּוּ֙ וְלֹ֣א עַתָּ֔ה אֲשׁוּרֶ֖נּוּ וְלֹ֣א קָר֑וֹב דָּרַ֨ךְ כּוֹכָ֜ב מִֽיַּעֲקֹ֗ב וְקָ֥ם שֵׁ֙בֶט֙ מִיִּשְׂרָאֵ֔ל
וּמָחַץ֙ פַּאֲתֵ֣י מוֹאָ֔ב וְקַרְקַ֖ר כָּל־בְּנֵי־שֵֽׁת׃ 18 וְהָיָ֨ה אֱד֜וֹם יְרֵשָׁ֗ה וְהָיָ֧ה יְרֵשָׁ֛ה
שֵׂעִ֖יר אֹיְבָ֑יו וְיִשְׂרָאֵ֖ל עֹ֥שֶׂה חָֽיִל׃ 19 **וְיֵ֖רְדְּ** מִֽיַּעֲקֹ֑ב וְהֶֽאֱבִ֥יד שָׂרִ֖יד מֵעִֽיר׃

'I see him, but not now; I behold him, but not near—a star shall come out of Jacob, and a scepter shall rise out of Israel; it shall crush the borderlands of Moab, and ruin all the Shethites. [18]Edom will become a possession, Seir will become a possession of its enemies, while Israel does valiantly. [19]**So let** one out of Jacob **rule**! He shall destroy the survivors of Ir.' (Num. 24.17–19, verses 17–18 from Notarius 2013, 220, verse 19 my translation)

The interpretation of *wa-yiqṭol(Ø)!* (וְיֵרְדְּ) in verse 19 as a protasis[138] is dubious in several respects. First, it is not a conditional linking at all. There is no condition, not even a temporal clause. Second, there is no other example of a jussive introducing a protasis in CBH. The reference to Gesenius and Kautzsch's grammar

(Ges-K §109h) is pointless: this grammar bases the idea of a jussive as protasis on Arabic grammar. The interpretations of the adduced examples in Biblical Hebrew are strained (none represents mainstream exegesis), or refer to uses in LBH (in which the distinction between short and long *yiqṭol* was gradually lost).[139] In CBH, there is no example of a short *yiqṭol* being a predicate in the first clause of a protasis.

In summary: the short *yiqṭol* in the Archaic Hebrew poetry is an authentic remnant of the Proto-Semitic **yaqtul* and is marked by a shorter form where appropriate. This short *yiqṭol* is used both as past perfective and as jussive. With very few exceptions, it occurs in clause-initial position. This statement concerns affirmative propositions.

There is no example of a negated past perfective short *yiqṭol* in the archaic poetry, and it seems that a *qaṭal* clause was used in the corresponding cases, negated by *lō*. The jussive short *yiqṭol*, on the other hand, could be negated (by *ʾal*). The negated jussive seems to be unrestricted as to word order.

Since the imperfective *yiqṭol(u)* may sometimes occur in clause-initial position in the archaic poetry, this means, according to Notarius (2013, 79, 281, 293), that

> the morphosyntactic distinction between the preterite and the imperfective form of the prefix conjugation is not sufficient to distinguish between the two... one needs to take into consideration semantic, pragmatic, and discursive data in order to provide a more solid foundation for the postulated distinction.

The independent use of the past perfective *yiqṭol(Ø)* (without proclitic *wa*) is archaic.[140] With or without *wa*, it is typical of narrative discourse and tends to build chains of main clauses. In this unrestricted usage, it was gradually substituted by the new perfective *qaṭal* (Notarius 2013, 281), as was the case also in Ugaritic (Fenton 1973, 34f.).

The indicative *wa(y)-yiqṭol* clause-type is occasionally attested with future time reference after a 'prophetic perfect' (*qaṭal*) in prospective report (Notarius 2013, 282:1c). This shows that the perfective meaning of *wa(y)-yiqṭol* could be used metaphorically, describing a series of future events (cf. Fenton 1973, 37).

3.3. The Short *Yiqṭol* in the Pre-exilic Hebrew Inscriptions

Sáenz-Badillos (1993, 62) writes:

> With the earliest inscriptions dating as far back as the close of the second millennium BCE, the inscriptional material as a whole is contemporary with a substantial portion of the Bible, with the advantage of not having undergone revision over the centuries.

The grammar of the pre-exilic Hebrew inscriptions is practically identical to that of Classical Hebrew (Hackett 2002, 141; Hasselbach and Huehnergard 2008, 408; Hutton 2013; Sanders 2020, 283). The growing number of inscriptions, though reflecting several strata of society, shows that the verbal system of CBH "was part of everyday speech" (Pardee 2012, 285). A methodological advantage is that the "epigraphic texts were not subject to the exigencies of textual transmission" (Hutton 2013). As concerns *yiqṭol(Ø)*, the predominantly defective spelling in the pre-exilic

Hebrew inscriptions allows for only slight and sometimes disputable evidence for a morphologically distinctive *yiqṭol(Ø)*.[141] Only in the case of verbs III*wy* can a distinction be established (Gogel 1998, 95).[142] In the inscriptions, the 'long' imperfective *yiqṭol(u)* of verbs III*wy* consistently exhibits a final vowel letter *-h* in the non-affixed forms (Gogel 1998, 96). The *yiqṭol(Ø)* verb form, on the other hand, whether jussive or past perfective in meaning, lacks any final *mater lectionis*.

There are a few morphologically distinctive *yiqṭol(Ø)* forms with jussive meaning, as is shown in (82):

(82) *PrP + "Ø-yiqṭol(Ø)!"*

אל אדני יאוש . **ירא** . יהוה א(2)ת . אדני את העת הזה . שלם

'To my lord Ya'ush. **May** YHWH **cause** my lord **to see** this season in peace.' (HI Lachish 6:1–2, Gogel 1998, 418, my emphasis)[143]

In this typical letter formula, the *hifʿil* short jussive (ירא) occupies the initial position in the clause, after the address (Gogel 1998, 95 n. 51, 141, 256 n. 19, 287). An example of a morphologically distinctive jussive *yiqṭol(Ø)* with proclitic *wa* is found in (83):

(83) *Ø-yiqṭol(Ø) + wa-yiqṭol(Ø) + wa-yiqṭol(Ø)!*

יב(8)רך **וישמרך** (9) **ויהי** עם . אד[נ](10)י.

'May he bless **and keep you, and may he be** with my lo[rd…]' (HI KAjr 19A:7–10, my emphasis)

The passage in (83) contains three jussive clauses, of which two are linked by *wa*. All jussives occupy an initial position in their respective clauses.[144] The *yiqṭol(Ø)* in the last clause has a morphologically distinctive 'short' form (יהי) without the *h* vowel letter (Gogel 1998, 95 n. 51, 256 n. 19, 287).

In all other cases, the distinction between *yiqṭol(Ø)* (jussive or past perfective) and *yiqṭol(u)* must be worked out by considerations of word order, semantic context, and, when negated, the type of negation employed (Gogel 1998, 93, 258; Renz and Röllig 1995–2003, II/2:43). A semantically clear example is (84), from the late seventh or early sixth century:

(84) *wa-qaṭal + Ø-ʾal-yiqṭol(Ø)*

והֿ(6)סבת מחר . אל תאחר

'and you shall deliver (it) tomorrow. Do not be late!' (HI Arad 2:5–6, my translation)[145]

In (84), the jussive form is morphologically indistinctive and could formally be parsed as an imperfective *yiqṭol(u)*. But the clearly deontic preceding *wa-qaṭal* clause (obligation), and the modal negation אל, indicate that תאחר is a jussive form.

A disputed example of a past perfective IIIwy *yiqṭol(Ø)* form is found in (85):

(85) *Ø-qaṭal + wa(y)-yiqṭol + wa(y)-yiqṭol! + wa-qaṭal*

. עבדך (3) קצ̊ר . היה . עבדך . בח(4)צ̊ר אסם . ויקצר עבדך (5) **ויכל**
ואס̊ם כימם . לפני שב(6)ת כאשר כל[. ע]ב̊דך את קצר וא(7)סם כימם

'As for your servant, [3]your servant was harvesting at Ḥaṣar [4]Asam. And your servant harvested [5]**and measured** and stored, according to schedule, before quitting. [6]When your servant measured the harvest and stored, [7]according to schedule…' (HI Meṣad Ḥashavyahu 1:2–7, line numbers in translation inserted by me)[146]

The passage starts with a *qaṭal* clause and continues with two *wa(y)-yiqṭol* clauses, of which the second (ויכל) is analysed by Gogel (1998, 95, 131) as a *qal* or *pi‘‘el* form of the III*wy* root *klh*.[147] If this is correct, the verb would be morphologically distinctive, since a 'long' *yiqṭol(u)* form of a verb IIIwy would exhibit a final *h*. Such long *yiqṭol(u)* forms are attested in *yqrh* 'It will happen' (Arad 24:16),[148] *ymḥh* 'He will efface' (En Gedi 2:1),[149] *ymnh* 'He shall count out' (Samaria 109:3).[150] However, this interpretation does not withstand an examination of the immediate context. The temporal clause on line 6 contains a *qaṭal* verb (כל) which cannot be a *qal* or *pi‘‘el* of a verb III*wy*, since 3ms *qaṭal* forms of such verbs always have a final vowel letter *h*, indicating the long -*ā*. Gogel (1998, 129) concedes that such a *qaṭal* (כל) "simply has to be looked upon as anomalous." The reasonable solution must be that the hypothesis of a III*wy* root is wrong and that a II*w* verb (*kyl*) 'to measure' is being used, attested at three locations in the letter: line 5: ויכל 'and he measured', line 6: כל 'he measured', line 8: כלת 'I measured'.[151] The conclusion is inevitable that, though ויכל is evidently a past perfective *wa(y)-yiqṭol*, and the form itself is not morphologically distinctive, the text as a whole contains cases of narrative past perfective *wa(y)-yiqṭol* (Renz 2016, 634f.).[152]

A clear and commonly recognised example of a past perfective *wa(y)-yiqṭol* clause following a *qaṭal* clause is found in the Siloam inscription, dated to the end of the eighth century BCE (HI, 500; Smith 1991, 17):

(86) *wa-PrP-S.noun-qaṭal* + ***wa(y)-yiqṭol***

ובים . ה(4)נקבה . הכו . החצבם . אש . לקרת . רעו . גרזן . על . [ג]רזן
. **וילכו** (5) המים . מן . המוצא . אל . הברכה . במאתים̊ . ואלף . אמה .

'And on the day of the breakthrough, the hewers struck, each to meet his fellow, pick against [p]ick; **and then** the waters **flowed** from the spring to the pool for twelve hundred cubits.' (HI Silm 1:3–5, my emphasis and translation)

The Siloam inscription is divided in two parts, the second of which forms a paragraph telling "the climax of the story, the moment of the actual breakthrough" (HI, 499). This paragraph starts with a *qaṭal* clause (הכו) and is followed by a *wa(y)-yiqṭol* clause (וילכו) which has a clear notion of temporal succession (Schüle 2000, 178; Renz 2016, 633f.). Both clauses express a narrative past perfective.

3.4. The Short *Yiqṭol* in CBH

3.4.1. The Morphological Contrast *Yiqṭol(Ø)/Yiqṭol(u)* in CBH

Since short final vowels fell out of use at the end of the second millennium BCE,[153] the *yiqṭol(u)* singular forms of the strong verb came to coalesce with the *yiqṭol(Ø)* forms, which resulted in an extensive but incomplete grammatical homonymy (Garr 1998, xlvii; Gentry 1998, 12; J-M §§46a, 114g n. 3; Hasselbach and Huehnergard 2008, 416; Blau 2010, 145, 150f.; Gzella 2011a, 442).[154] In a levelling process, this morphological merger came to apply also to 2fs, 3mp, and 2mp *yiqṭol(u)* forms with the suffix

-na added (Gzella 2018, 27; 2021, 72; Huehnergard and Pat-El 2019, 9); see Table 6.[155]

Table 6: The morphology of short and long *yiqṭol* in Central Semitic and CBH

	Central Semitic		CBH
qal	***yaqtul***	***yaqtulu***	**levelled form**
3ms	*yaqtul*	*yaqtul-u*	*yiqṭol*
3fs	*taqtul*	*taqtul-u*	*tiqṭol*
2ms	*taqtul*	*taqtul-u*	*tiqṭol*
2fs	*taqtulī*	*taqtulī-na*	*tiqṭəlī*
1cs	*ʾaqtul*	*ʾaqtul-u*	*ʾɛqṭol*
3mp	*yaqtulū*	*yaqtulū-na*	*yiqṭəlū*
3fp	*yaqtulna*[156]	*yaqtulna*	*tiqṭolnā*[157]
2mp	*taqtulū*	*taqtulū-na*	*tiqṭəlū*
2fp	*taqtulna*	*taqtulna*	*tiqṭolnā*
1cp	*naqtul*	*naqtul-u*	*niqṭol*

When short final vowels fell out of use at the end of the second millennium BCE, only three forms in the regular paradigm remained explicitly 'long': those with an ending *na* after long vowel: 2fs, 3mp, 2mp (Bauer and Leander 1922, 300o). This was not enough for the speakers of Hebrew to uphold the morphological distinction in the strong verb, and they levelled the old 'short' form across both meanings, except in the *hifʿil* (Bauer and Leander 1922, 300r; Hasselbach and Huehnergard 2008, 416; Gzella 2011a, 442). In spite of this, "the functional… oppositions underlying the NWS-Can *yaqtul* and *yaqtulu* paradigms remain operative in BH, and need to be heeded" (Korchin 2008, 341 n. 24; see also Tropper 1998, 165f.). The distinction was made clear by syntactic and semantic signals. One such signal is the distinctive distribution of the negation: jussive *yiqṭol(Ø)* was negated by אַל and *yiqṭol(u)* was negated by לֹא. The indicative *yiqṭol(Ø)* was not negated at all, since *lō qaṭal* had replaced negated indicative *yiqṭol(Ø)* in BH.[158] Another signal is the נָא clitic after a prefix verb, which indicates that the verb is a jussive *yiqṭol(Ø)*. Thirdly, jussive *yiqṭol(Ø)* in affirmative clauses is practically always clause-initial (Kummerow 2008, 73–75).

There are about 300 cases of 2fs, 3mp, or 2mp prefix-conjugation forms in Biblical Hebrew with final *īn* or *ūn*, seemingly with the same meaning as 'normal' *yiqṭol(u)* forms (Hasselbach and Huehnergard 2008, 416). It is reasonable to suppose that verbal forms with a so-called paragogic *nun* represent a partial retention (for unclear reasons) of the Central Semitic imperfective suffix *na*, which continued to appear as a biform and stylistic variant in 2fs, 3mp, and 2mp, possibly reflecting a higher register.[159] Apart from the special cases of forms with *nun paragogicum*, Biblical Hebrew has lost this distinctive imperfective feature. It is, however, preserved in Amarna Canaanite (see §3.1.8; also Baranowski 2016a, 83), Ugaritic (§3.1.7), early Aramaic (§3.1.11), Phoenician (§3.1.9), and Classical Arabic (§3.1.5).

The marking of the imperfective (*yaqtulu*) in Central Semitic consisted of a special distribution of two suffixes, *-u* and *-na*, which, according to most scholars, were added to the old *yaqtul* (Kouwenberg 2010a, 97f.; Blau 2010, 205; Kogan 2015, 131, 159).[160]

3.4.1.1. The Short *Yiqṭol* in the Morphology of the Strong Verb: *Hifʿil*

In the strong verb, *yiqṭol(Ø)* presents distinctively short forms only in the *hifʿil* (Kummerow 2008, 71f.). When short final vowels were dropped in the early Iron Age, we would expect both **yaqtil* (the *hifʿil* of the old *yiqṭol(Ø)*) and **yaqtilu* (the *hifʿil* of the imperfective *yiqṭol(u)*) to coalesce in one form **yaqtil* (> *yaqtél*). This form was retained only as the old *yiqṭol(Ø)*, whereas **yaqtilu* was transformed by analogy with weak verbs II*wy* (i.e., *hifʿil* type *yāqīm*, as against *yāqém* for the short *yiqṭol*). Thus, the short final vowel dropped, but the distinction between the old *yiqṭol(Ø)* and the imperfective *yiqṭol(u)* was upheld by a secondary lengthening of the stem vowel: *yiqṭol(Ø) hifʿil* became *yaqtél* and *yiqṭol(u) hifʿil* became *yaqtīl* (Bauer and Leander 1922, 329 a–b; Blau 2010, 235).

3.4.1.2. The Short *Yiqṭol* in the Morphology of Verbs II*wy*

The old *yiqṭol(Ø)* of verbs II*w* developed from a form **yáqūm*, in which the stem vowel was shortened to **yáqum* in the closed syllable. This change had occurred already in Proto-Semitic (Bauer and Leander 1922, 231b, 388i; Kummerow 2008, 73; Huehnergard 2019, 66, word stress 53).[161] In Hebrew, the stem vowel *ú* was stressed and developed to *ó*. In the reading tradition, the prefix vowel was lengthened: *yāqóm* (יָקֹם; Hasselbach and Huehnergard 2008, 416). This is the form of the short *yiqṭol* with both jussive and indicative meanings in Biblical Hebrew, if not preceded by the proclitic *wa*.[162] When the short *yiqṭol* is preceded by *wa*, a differentiation has occurred in the reading tradition. When *wa* precedes the indicative form (*wa(y)-yiqṭol*), it has developed a different stress pattern in the Tiberian tradition so that *wa-yāqóm* is changed to *wayyāqǻm* (וַיָּקָם), with the stress on the prefix syllable (Bauer and Leander 1922, 389l).[163] In pause (but in the Babylonian reading tradition also in context), stress remained on the stem vowel (Bauer and Leander 1922, 390o). The *qal yiqṭol(u)* of verbs II*w* developed a form with retained long stem vowel in the open syllable, *yāqū́m* < **yaqū́mu* (Bauer and Leander 1922, 388i; Hasselbach and Huehnergard 2008, 416; Huehnergard and Pat-El 2019, 10).

In a similar way, a morphological distinction was retained in verbs II*y*: *yiqṭol(Ø) yāśém* (יָשֵׂם < **yaśim* < **yaśīm*) in contrast to *yiqṭol(u) yāśī́m* (יָשִׂים < **yaśīmu*).[164]

In the *hifʿil*, there was a similar shortening of the stem vowel in *yaqtul*, *yāqém* (יָקֵם), whereas the imperfective *yiqṭol(u)* in the *hifʿil* retained the long vowel, *yāqī́m* (יָקִים) < **yaqī́mu* (Bauer and Leander 1922, 395p).

The distinctive morphology of the *yiqṭol(Ø)* forms of verbs II*wy* is upheld only in the endingless forms, that is, in forms 3ms, 3fs, 2ms, 1cs, and 1cp. There is no formal distinction in verbs with object suffixes.

Morphologically 'long' forms of realis or irrealis *yiqṭol(Ø)* of verbs II*wy* are rare in CBH. One such example is (87):

(87) *wa-lō-qaṭal* + *wa(y)-yiqṭol* + ***wa(y)-yiqṭol*** + *wa(y)-yiqṭol* + *wa(y)-yiqṭol*

וְלֹא־שָׁמְעוּ אֶל־מֹשֶׁה וַיּוֹתִרוּ אֲנָשִׁים מִמֶּנּוּ עַד־בֹּקֶר **וַיָּרֻם** תּוֹלָעִים וַיִּבְאַשׁ
וַיִּקְצֹף עֲלֵהֶם מֹשֶׁה׃

'But they did not listen to Moses; some kept part of it until morning, and **it was full of worms** and began to stink, and Moses got angry with them.' (Exod. 16.20)

As the example illustrates, when morphologically 'long' *yiqṭol(Ø)* forms occur in the Pentateuch and the Book of Judges, they are most often defectively written.[165]

3.4.1.3. The Short *Yiqṭol* in the Morphology of Verbs III*wy*

In verbs III*wy* also, shorter *yiqṭol(Ø)* forms contrast with longer *yiqṭol(u)* forms (Kummerow 2008, 72). This holds in all stems except *puʿʿal* and *hofʿal*. In *yiqṭol(Ø)* forms, we would expect residues of the Proto-Semitic stem-final diphthongs *aw*, *ay*, *iy* in some verbs (**yáštay*, **yarḏ̣aw*, **yabniy*).[166] But system constraints led to a shortening of all *yiqṭol(Ø)* forms irrespective of stem vowel and word-final consonant (Bauer and Leander 1922, 408; Birkeland 1940, 44f.; Blau 2010, 249): **yašt* > **yišt* > *yešt* (with final plosive, וַיֵּ֫שְׁתְּ, Gen. 9.21), **yarḏ̣* > **yarṣ* > *yirṣ* (וְתִ֫רֶץ, Lev. 26.43), **yabni(y)* > **yabn* > **yibn* (וַיִּ֫בֶן, Gen. 12.7; Birkeland 1940, 44; Hasselbach and Huehnergard 2008, 416; Gzella 2013c, 861).[167]

The corresponding *yiqṭol(u)* forms all present a long ending *-ɛ̄* in the forms without another affix. This *ɛ̄* is practically always written with the vowel letter *h* in the textual tradition: *yištɛ̄* (יִשְׁתֶּה), *yirṣɛ̄* (יִרְצֶה) < **yirṣayu*, *yiḇnɛ̄* (יִבְנֶה) < **yabniyu* (Blau 1993, 27f.; Hasselbach and Huehnergard 2008, 416). Such forms are homophonous with short *yiqṭol* having a ventive/cohortative suffix.[168]

The morphological difference between short *yiqṭol(Ø)* and long *yiqṭol(u)* is upheld only in the forms without affixes. A form like יִשְׁתּוּ, with plural suffix, may formally be either jussive *yiqṭol(Ø)* or imperfective *yiqṭol(u)*. The same holds for verb forms with pronominal object suffixes.

The distinctive morphology described above is realised most consistently in the Pentateuch and the books of Joshua and Judges (Stipp 1987, 120). The examples of long forms (with *ɛ̄* ending, written with the vowel letter *h*) intended to represent a jussive or a past perfective *yiqṭol(Ø)* are relatively few.[169] One example is (88):

(88) *Ø-yiqṭol(Ø) + wa-yiqṭol(Ø)-V*

יִקָּו֨וּ הַמַּ֜יִם מִתַּ֤חַת הַשָּׁמַ֙יִם֙ אֶל־מָק֣וֹם אֶחָ֔ד וְתֵרָאֶ֖ה הַיַּבָּשָׁ֑ה

'Let the water under the sky be gathered to one place so that dry ground appears (for me).' (Gen. 1.9)

The clause that begins with וְתֵרָאֶה is obviously intended as jussive, here with a ventive suffix. What can be discussed regarding this example is whether the discourse-continuous jussive should be interpreted as a purpose clause or just a coordinated jussive (J-M §116).[170] *Wa(y)-yiqṭol* clauses with past perfective meaning may also contain verbs III*wy* with 'long' forms. Most such instances are in the first person singular and may hide a ventive/cohortative clitic, as in (89):

(89) *wa(y)-yiqṭol* ('long')

וָאֲצַוֶּ֥ה אֶתְכֶ֖ם בָּעֵ֣ת הַהִ֑וא אֵ֥ת כָּל־הַדְּבָרִ֖ים אֲשֶׁ֥ר תַּעֲשֽׂוּן׃

'So I instructed you at that time regarding everything you should do.' (Deut. 1.18)

It is conspicuous that deviations from the short form pattern are found most prominently in the first person (Stipp 1987, 120; Revell 1988, 423–25).[171] The first-person forms with the ending -ɛ̄ can, however, be intended as forms with 'hidden' ventive-cohortative clitic, in which case the -ɛ̄ in both alternatives would be regular, since the ventive/cohortative clitic -ā is unattested on verbs III*wy* (Tropper 1997b, 402f.; Fassberg 2013b; Stein 2016; Sjörs 2023, §6.2; cf. J-M §79m n. 2, based on Stipp 1987, 110; see §§1.2.2, 3.4.2.3).

3.4.2. The Meanings of the Short *Yiqṭol* in CBH

The short *yiqṭol* displays the same double semantics in CBH as in many other Semitic languages. It is able to express a realis (mostly past perfective) and an irrealis (jussive; Bybee and Dahl 1989, 84; Palmer 2001, ch. 8).[172] The two basic meanings are distributed evenly in the corpus (I have covered 871 short *yiqṭol* in the database).

3.4.2.1. The Realis/Indicative *Yiqṭol(Ø)* in CBH

Table 7: The meanings of the indicative short *yiqṭol* in CBH

Resultative	2
Stativic verb present	3
Stativic verb past	23
Anterior	45
Pluperfect	17
Counterfactual	1
Perfective past	355
Habitual past	23
Total	**469**

The grammaticalisation path of a perfective verbal morpheme usually starts in a resultative construction. Prototypical resultative meanings of *yiqṭol(Ø)* are rare in CBH, which indicates that it is a residual grammatical morpheme (Dahl 2000, 10). One of the few examples with present resultative meaning in the corpus is (86). It is retained in a relatively complex linking, in this case within a relative clause:

(90) *ʾal-nā-yiqṭol(Ø)! + «REL-PREP-VN +* ***wa(y)-yiqṭol****»*

אַל־נָ֥א תְהִ֖י כַּמֵּ֑ת «אֲשֶׁ֤ר בְּצֵאתוֹ֙ מֵרֶ֣חֶם אִמּ֔וֹ **וַיֵּאָכֵ֖ל** חֲצִ֥י בְשָׂרֽוֹ»:

‘Do not let her be like a baby born dead, «which, when it comes out of its mother’s womb, then half of its flesh **is consumed**!»’ (Num. 12.12)

The relative sentence begins with the relative pronoun and an infinite subordinate clause stating the relative time of the following *wa(y)-yiqṭol* clause. In this context, the *nifʿal qaṭal* of the dynamic verb אכל expresses a resultative with focus on the state of being consumed, created by a previous action (‘consuming’), the prototypical case of a resultative meaning.[173]

Another resultative *wa(y)-yiqṭol* is found in (91), also in a relative construction:

(91) *Ø-hinnē-S.noun-DEF-qoṭel +* ***wa(y)-yiqṭol!***

הִנֵּ֤ה הָעָם֙ הַיֹּצֵ֣א מִמִּצְרַ֔יִם **וַיְכַ֖ס** אֶת־עֵ֣ין הָאָ֑רֶץ

‘Behold, a people has come out of Egypt, **and it covers** the face of the earth.’ (Num. 22.11, Budd 1984, 249)

The participle with initial article functions as a descriptive relative clause. The *wa(y)-yiqṭol* clause is a constituent in this relative construction and continues the action described by the *qoṭel*. It is "a situation initiated in the past but continuing until the present" (Joosten 2012, 185). Focus is on the present state.[174]

Perfective grams usually used in past narration may retain early non-past meanings. Such grams can be used in future contexts, for example as future anterior or immediate future. With stative verbs, a perfective can signal a present state, while simple pasts have past meanings also with stative verbs. This is a proof that the indicative *yiqṭol(Ø)* in CBH is not just a past tense (Bybee et al. 1994, 95; Cook 2012b, 87). An example with a stativic verb and present time reference is (92) below:

(92) *gam-O.noun-«REL-qaṭal»-yiqṭol(u)* + *kī-qaṭal* + ***wa(y)-yiqṭol***

גַּ֣ם אֶת־הַדָּבָ֥ר הַזֶּ֛ה אֲשֶׁ֥ר דִּבַּ֖רְתָּ אֶֽעֱשֶׂ֑ה כִּֽי־מָצָ֤אתָ חֵן֙ בְּעֵינַ֔י **וָאֵדָעֲךָ֖** בְּשֵֽׁם׃

'Indeed the very thing you have spoken, I will do: because you really have found favor in my estimation, **and I know you** by name.' (Exod. 33.17, Durham 1987, 444)

Within the context of a complex cause/reason sentence (Dixon 2009, 6) introduced by the conjunction *kī*, a *qaṭal* clause (מָצָ֤אתָ) has resultative or anterior meaning focusing on a state which is the result of a previous event (Bybee et al. 1994, 63, 65). This state persists in speech time. The following *wa(y)-yiqṭol* clause also belongs to the cause/reason sentence and can be interpreted as also having resultative meaning 'I have known you and still do', but the stativic verb ידע in *wa(y)-yiqṭol* motivates a stativic present translation.

Another example is found in (93):

(93) *wa(y)-yiqṭol "Ø-XØ + wa-S.noun-qaṭal +* ***wa(y)-yiqṭol*** *+ wa-S.noun-qaṭal"*

וַנֹּאמֶר֙ אֶל־אֲדֹנִ֔י יֶשׁ־לָ֙נוּ֙ אָ֣ב זָקֵ֔ן וְיֶ֥לֶד זְקֻנִ֖ים קָטָ֑ן וְאָחִ֣יו מֵ֠ת **וַיִּוָּתֵ֨ר** ה֧וּא לְבַדּ֛וֹ לְאִמּ֖וֹ וְאָבִ֥יו אֲהֵבֽוֹ׃

'We said to my lord, We have an aged father, and there is a young boy who was born when our father was old. The boy's brother is dead. **He is** the only one of his mother's sons **left**, and his father loves him.' (Gen. 44.20)

In direct speech, in a report of previous events, a stativic *qaṭal* clause (מֵ֠ת) is followed by a *wa(y)-yiqṭol* clause. The most natural interpretation of this *nifʿal* of the root יתר is as a stativic verb with present time reference (Westermann 1982, 140; Wenham 1994, 422).[175]

But indicative *yiqṭol(Ø)* with stativic verbs may, of course, and more frequently, according to context, have past time reference, as in (94):

(94) *wayhī + kī-qaṭal +* ***wa(y)-yiqṭol*** *+ wa(y)-yiqṭol*

וַֽיְהִי֙ כִּֽי־זָקֵ֣ן יִצְחָ֔ק **וַתִּכְהֶ֥יןָ** עֵינָ֖יו מֵרְאֹ֑ת וַיִּקְרָ֞א אֶת־עֵשָׂ֣ו ׀ בְּנ֣וֹ הַגָּדֹ֗ל

'When Isaac was old **and** his eyes **were dim** so that he could not see, he called Esau his older son' (Gen. 27.1)

In (94), within a complex temporal sentence, a *wa(y)-yiqṭol* clause with stativic verb follows a *qaṭal* clause with stativic verb.[176] Both clauses have past time reference and refer to the same past state. The *wa(y)-yiqṭol* clause (וַתִּכְהֶ֥יןָ) functions as an elaboration, supplying additional information ('his eyes were dim') about the state described by the *qaṭal* clause (Dixon 2009, 27; Ges-K §111q; Joosten 2012, 178).[177]

In the anterior meaning, focus has shifted from a state to the action that caused the state (Bybee and Dahl 1989, 70; Bybee et al. 1994, 51–105). Such meanings of *wa(y)-yiqṭol* are frequent in the corpus. They differ, however, with regard to the remoteness of the state referred to. In some cases, the action described by *wa(y)-yiqṭol* is indicated to be close to speech time ('present anterior'), while other cases display actions whose temporal reference is more diffuse. In the major part of the anterior examples, a *wa(y)-yiqṭol* clause follows a *qaṭal* clause with anterior meaning. This indicates that the *qaṭal* morpheme has to a large extent taken over the function of expressing anterior meaning in CBH. There are, however, not a few cases when a *wa(y)-yiqṭol* clause describes a shift to anterior without support from preceding *qaṭal* clauses. In such cases, the anterior meaning must be inferred from the semantic context or is indicated by adverbs within the *wa(y)-yiqṭol* clause. A case where the shift to an anterior meaning must be inferred is (95):

(95) *wayhī* + *kī-qaṭal* + *wa(y)-yiqṭol-A*[178] + *wa-hinnē-XØ* + ***wa(y)-yiqṭol!***

וַֽיְהִ֗י כִּי־בָ֙אנוּ֙ אֶל־הַמָּל֔וֹן וַֽנִּפְתְּחָה֙ אֶת־אַמְתְּחֹתֵ֔ינוּ וְהִנֵּ֤ה כֶֽסֶף־אִישׁ֙ בְּפִ֣י אַמְתַּחְתּ֔וֹ כַּסְפֵּ֖נוּ בְּמִשְׁקָל֑וֹ **וַנָּ֥שֶׁב** אֹת֖וֹ בְּיָדֵֽנוּ׃

'When we reached camp and opened our sacks, there was each man's money in the mouth of his sack, to the full! **So we have brought it back** with us.' (Gen. 43.21)

The passage is a report in the mouth of Joseph's brothers in front of the one in charge of his household.[179] The particle *kī* introduces a complex temporal sentence (*kī-qaṭal* + *wa(y)-yiqṭol*). The two clauses in the temporal sentence have the same TAM value, namely, past perfective (an event that is remote from speech time). After the temporal sentence, the core of the report is coded by an initial verbless clause (with the deictic particle *hinnē*), followed by a second *wa(y)-yiqṭol* describing an action that is fulfilled in speech time in front of the man in charge. This latter *wa(y)-yiqṭol* (וַנֵּשֶׁב) expresses an understood 'here and now', and this shift to another TAM value is only inferred pragmatically (not specifically coded by a syntactic marker).[180] The example shows that the *wa(y)-yiqṭol* clause by itself may introduce a shift to an anterior meaning, although this is a rare phenomenon.

In some cases, a switch from a *qaṭal* clause to a *wa(y)-yiqṭol* clause in report also signals a shift from past perfective to anterior meaning with clear reference to an action close to speech time, as in (96):

(96) *wa-O.noun-lō-qaṭal* + ***wa(y)-yiqṭol!***

וְאֶת־הַיְבוּסִי יֹשֵׁב יְרוּשָׁלַםִ לֹא הוֹרִישׁוּ בְּנֵי בִנְיָמִן **וַיֵּשֶׁב** הַיְבוּסִי אֶת־בְּנֵי בִנְיָמִן בִּירוּשָׁלַםִ עַד הַיּוֹם הַזֶּה׃

'But the people of Benjamin did not drive out the Jebusites who lived in Jerusalem, **so** the Jebusites **have lived** with the people of Benjamin in Jerusalem to this day.' (Judg. 1.21)

In this retrospective report, the *qaṭal* clause has perfective past meaning, but a temporal prepositional phrase (עַד הַיּוֹם הַזֶּה) indicates that the *wa(y)-yiqṭol* should be interpreted as anterior with relevance in the present.

In some cases, a past time reference and anterior meaning of *wa(y)-yiqṭol* cannot be inferred from the surrounding clauses at all, as in (97):

(97) *wa-qaṭal* + *kī-XØ* + ***wa(y)-yiqṭol***

וִהְיִיתֶם לִי קְדֹשִׁים כִּי קָדוֹשׁ אֲנִי יְהוָה **וָאַבְדִּל** אֶתְכֶם מִן־הָעַמִּים לִהְיוֹת לִי׃

‘You shall be holy to me, for I YHWH am holy; **therefore I have set** you **apart** from other peoples to be mine.’ (Lev. 20.26, Milgrom 2000, 1301, my emphasis)[181]

In this part of a long utterance of YHWH, a *wa-qaṭal* clause expresses obligation. After that, a verbless clause states the reason for Israel to be holy. The verbless clause is then followed by a *wa(y)-yiqṭol* clause with anterior meaning. It is not clear if the temporal reference of the action (‘I have set you apart’) is a remote or recent action. The *wa(y)-yiqṭol* must be interpreted as anterior, because it describes an action that has resulted in a state that is valid and relevant in speech time.

In the most frequent case of an anterior *yiqṭol(Ø)*, a present anterior *qaṭal* precedes the *wa(y)-yiqṭol* clause. This is a sign that *qaṭal* is on its way to taking over as the prime anterior verbal morpheme, resulting in a diminishing use of *wa(y)-yiqṭol* with this meaning. In other words, indicative *yiqṭol(Ø)* is used with anterior meaning mainly in discourse-continuity clauses after an anterior *qaṭal* clause. A clear example is (98):

(98) *wa(y)-yiqṭol: “Ø-ADV-qaṭal* + ***wa(y)-yiqṭol*** + *Ø-IMP”*

וַתֹּאמֶר דְּלִילָה אֶל־שִׁמְשׁוֹן עַד־הֵנָּה הֵתַלְתָּ בִּי **וַתְּדַבֵּר** אֵלַי כְּזָבִים הַגִּידָה לִּי בַּמֶּה תֵּאָסֵר

‘Delilah said to Samson, “Up to now you have deceived me **and told** me lies. Tell me how you can be subdued.”’ (Judg. 16.13)

The adverb (עַד־הֵ֫נָּה) signals repeated actions and a state of deception at speech time. Focus is not on the state but on the actions that have caused this state.[182]

In some cases, the anterior meaning of *wa(y)-yiqṭol* has a more general temporal reference, and its relation to speech time is vague, as in (99):

(99) *kī-O.noun-qaṭal* + ***wa(y)-yiqṭol***

כִּי֩ אֶת־חֲזֵ֨ה הַתְּנוּפָ֜ה וְאֵ֣ת ׀ שׁ֣וֹק הַתְּרוּמָ֗ה לָקַ֙חְתִּי֙ מֵאֵ֣ת בְּנֵֽי־יִשְׂרָאֵ֔ל מִזִּבְחֵ֖י
שַׁלְמֵיהֶ֑ם **וָאֶתֵּ֣ן** אֹ֠תָם לְאַהֲרֹ֨ן הַכֹּהֵ֜ן וּלְבָנָיו֙ לְחָק־עוֹלָ֔ם מֵאֵ֖ת בְּנֵ֥י יִשְׂרָאֵֽל׃

'For the breast of the wave offering and the thigh of the contribution offering I have taken from the Israelites out of their peace offering sacrifices **and I have given** them to Aaron the priest and to his sons from the people of Israel as a perpetual allotted portion.' (Lev. 7.34)

The actions referred to in (99) have a more general character, since they describe decisions made by God. They have a relevance for a state in speech time but their temporal references are vague.[183]

A *wa(y)-yiqṭol* clause may also express an action that is anterior in relation to another past event (pluperfect), as in (100) (see also Pardee 2012, 291).

(100) *wa(y)-yiqṭol* + *wa-lō-qaṭal* + *wa(y)-yiqṭol* + *wa(y)-yiqṭol* + [34]*wa-S.noun-qaṭal* + ***wa(y)-yiqṭol*** + ***wa(y)-yiqṭol*** + *wa(y)-yiqṭol* + *wa-lō-qaṭal*

וַיָּבֹ֨א לָבָ֜ן בְּאֹ֧הֶל יַעֲקֹ֣ב ׀ וּבְאֹ֣הֶל לֵאָ֗ה וּבְאֹ֛הֶל שְׁתֵּ֥י הָאֲמָהֹ֖ת וְלֹ֣א מָצָ֑א וַיֵּצֵא֙
מֵאֹ֣הֶל לֵאָ֔ה וַיָּבֹ֖א בְּאֹ֥הֶל רָחֵֽל׃ וְרָחֵ֞ל לָקְחָ֣ה אֶת־הַתְּרָפִ֗ים **וַתְּשִׂמֵ֛ם** בְּכַ֥ר הַגָּמָ֖ל
וַתֵּ֣שֶׁב עֲלֵיהֶ֑ם וַיְמַשֵּׁ֥שׁ לָבָ֛ן אֶת־כָּל־הָאֹ֖הֶל וְלֹ֥א מָצָֽא׃

> 'So Laban entered Jacob's tent, and Leah's tent, and the tent of the two female servants, but he did not find the idols. Then he left Leah's tent and entered Rachel's. [34](Now Rachel had taken the idols **and put them** inside her camel's saddle **and sat** on them.) Laban searched the whole tent, but did not find them.' (Gen. 31.33–34)

Within a complex background sentence, a *qaṭal* clause with initial subject noun (רָחֵ֫ל) signals a pluperfect temporal reference, and this pluperfect meaning is continued by two *wa(y)-yiqṭol* clauses. The storyline is resumed by a new *wa(y)-yiqṭol* clause with change of subject (וַיְמַשֵּׁ֥שׁ לָבָ֛ן; Ges-K §111q; Wenham 1994, 262).[184] This type of temporal 'dependence' on a previous pluperfect *qaṭal* clause is the most common case of linking with a pluperfect *wa(y)-yiqṭol*.

The characteristic perfective past meaning of *yiqṭol(Ø)* in CBH represents a generalisation (Cook 2012a, 264). Such meanings indicate a view of a situation as a single whole (bounded viewpoint: Comrie 1976, 16). While the anterior indicates a past action "with current relevance" (Bybee et al. 1994, 61), a perfective meaning has lost the connection to speech time and expresses only the action itself. This is usually a past action (Bybee et al. 1994, 86). The perfective meaning represents a later stage in the developmental path of an anterior-perfective grammatical morpheme. Later meanings "overwhelmingly show inflectional expression" (Bybee et al. 1994, 52), which is certainly the case with the *yiqṭol(Ø)* gram. The perfective meaning, especially with past time reference, is a dominant meaning of realis *yiqṭol(Ø)* in CBH. While anterior expressions are not normally marked on several verbs in succession, perfectivity is "the aspect used for narrating sequences of discrete events" (Bybee et al. 1994, 54). This is the typical usage of the realis *wa(y)-yiqṭol* clause-type exemplified in all grammars for the expression of discourse continuity in narrative. One example is enough to show this:

(101) *wa(y)-yiqṭol + wa(y)-yiqṭol! + wa(y)-yiqṭol + wa(y)-yiqṭol! + wa(y)-yiqṭol*

וַיֵּ֤דַע קַ֙יִן֙ אֶת־אִשְׁתֹּ֔ו **וַתַּ֖הַר וַתֵּ֣לֶד** אֶת־חֲנֹ֑וךְ **וַֽיְהִי֙** בֹּ֣נֶה עִ֔יר **וַיִּקְרָא֙** שֵׁ֣ם הָעִ֔יר כְּשֵׁ֖ם בְּנֹ֥ו חֲנֹֽוךְ׃

'Cain **had intercourse** with his wife, **and she conceived and gave birth** to Enoch. **He became** the founder of a city **and gave** the city the name of his son Enoch.' (Gen. 4.17)

"Perfectivity involves lack of explicit reference to the internal temporal constituency of a situation" (Comrie 1976, 21). A perfective grammatical morpheme may be used for situations that are internally complex, for example, lasting for a period of time, or including "a number of distinct internal phases, provided only that the whole of the situation is subsumed as a single whole" (Comrie 1976, 21). This type of perfectivity, which can involve a habitual action during a long space of time, is illustrated in (102):

(102) *Ø-XØ + Ø-qaṭul +* ***wa(y)-yiqṭol***

זֶה־לִּ֞י עֶשְׂרִ֣ים שָׁנָה֮ בְּבֵיתֶ֒ךָ֒ עֲבַדְתִּ֜יךָ אַרְבַּֽע־עֶשְׂרֵ֤ה שָׁנָה֙ בִּשְׁתֵּ֣י בְנֹתֶ֔יךָ וְשֵׁ֥שׁ שָׁנִ֖ים בְּצֹאנֶ֑ךָ **וַתַּחֲלֵ֥ף** אֶת־מַשְׂכֻּרְתִּ֖י עֲשֶׂ֥רֶת מֹנִֽים׃

'This was my lot for twenty years in your house: I worked like a slave for you– fourteen years for your two daughters and six years for your flocks, **but you changed** my wages ten times!' (Gen. 31.41)

In (102), an elaboration initiated by an asyndetic *qaṭal* clause (עֲבַדְתִּיךָ) is continued by a perfective past *wa(y)-yiqṭol* (וַתַּחֲלֵף) which explicitly describes an iterative/habitual action ('ten times'; Notarius 2010a, 260 n. 55; cf. J-M §118n).[185]

We have already noticed the invasive nature of the new perfective gram *qaṭal* (Cook 2012a, 264). In the synchronic state of CBH, a realis *yiqṭol(Ø)* is attested exclusively in discourse-continuity clauses (*wa(y)-yiqṭol*).[186] In all other positions, the new *qaṭal* has replaced the (free-standing) realis *yiqṭol(Ø)*: in the beginning of new narrative units, in negative clauses, in clause-initial position in relative clauses, in clause-initial position in protases (see further §6.7.2). The realis *yiqṭol(Ø)* is not even found in clauses with an initial subordinating conjunction. There is only one possible example in CBH of a short *yiqṭol(Ø)* following a subordinating conjunction, and even this must be doubted. This example is (103), which exhibits a protasis with initial *kī* (as conditional conjunction) and a prefix verb form:

(103) *(kī-**yiqṭol** + wa-qaṭal + wa-qaṭal) + Ø-O.noun-yiqṭol(u)*

(כִּ֤י **יַבְעֶר**־אִישׁ֙ שָׂדֶ֣ה אוֹ־כֶ֔רֶם וְשִׁלַּח֙ אֶת־בְּעִירֹ֔ה וּבִעֵ֖ר בִּשְׂדֵ֣ה אַחֵ֑ר) מֵיטַ֥ב שָׂדֵ֛הוּ וּמֵיטַ֥ב כַּרְמ֖וֹ יְשַׁלֵּֽם׃

'(If a man **causes** a field or vineyard **to be grazed over**, and he lets the livestock loose and they graze in the field of another man), he must make restitution from the best of his own field and the best of his own vineyard.' (Exod. 22.4)

If יַבְעֶר־ in (103) is a *hifʿil* jussive, it would be the only jussive after *kī* or *ʾim* in the whole CBH corpus, and the only example of a jussive clause starting a protasis.[187] The philologists have not given enough attention to the phonetic unity of *yab̲ʿɛr-ʾīš*, in which the first word is unstressed: *yaḇʿɛr- < *yaḇʿir- < *yaḇʿīr-*. The form ־יַבְעֶר is read with short stem vowel, but it is intended as a long *yiqṭol* (*yiqṭol(u)*). Its position after the conjunction *kī* was a sufficient syntactic signal for it to be identified as a *yiqṭol(u)* form.

3.4.2.2. The Short *Yiqṭol* as Irrealis in CBH

The irrealis/jussive *yiqṭol(Ø)* clause expresses deontic modality in main clauses. Such meanings of *yiqṭol(Ø)* are commonplace in Hebrew grammars (J-M §46; Hornkohl 2019, 549). A typical example is a clause-initial affirmative jussive clause, as in (104):

(104) *Ø-yiqṭol(Ø)!*

> **תּוֹצֵ֨א** הָאָ֜רֶץ נֶ֤פֶשׁ חַיָּה֙ לְמִינָ֔הּ בְּהֵמָ֥ה וָרֶ֛מֶשׂ וְחַֽיְתוֹ־אֶ֖רֶץ לְמִינָ֑הּ
>
> ‘**Let** the earth **bring forth** living creatures according to their kinds—livestock and creeping things and beasts of the earth according to their kinds.’ (Gen. 1.24)

It is also well known that a discourse-continuity jussive clause, type *wa-yiqṭol(Ø)*, often expresses purpose meaning after a preceding volitive clause (J-M §116d):

(105) *Ø-IMP* + ***wa-yiqṭol(Ø)!*** + ***wa-yiqṭol(Ø)***

> נְטֵ֨ה יָדְךָ֜ עַל־אֶ֤רֶץ מִצְרַ֙יִם֙ בָּֽאַרְבֶּ֔ה **וְיַ֖עַל** עַל־אֶ֣רֶץ מִצְרָ֑יִם **וְיֹאכַל֙** אֶת־כָּל־עֵ֣שֶׂב הָאָ֔רֶץ אֵ֛ת כָּל־אֲשֶׁ֥ר הִשְׁאִ֖יר הַבָּרָֽד׃
>
> ‘Stretch out your hand over the land of Egypt for the locusts, **so that they may come** upon the land of Egypt **and eat** every plant in the land, all that the hail has left.’ (Exod. 10.12)

It is less well known that a *yiqṭol(Ø)* clause may code a complement in relation to a previous manipulation verb. Complement clauses in CBH are often introduced by *kī* (plus a predicate other than *yiqṭol(Ø)*), but after manipulation verbs, a *yiqṭol(Ø)* clause may form a complement without particle marking (Givón 2001, I:152). Such clauses may be asyndetic, but are more often syndetic (the latter with the conjunction *wa-*), and they can be negated by *ʾal*. An example with an asyndetic *yiqṭol(Ø)* forming a complement clause is found in (106):

(106) *Ø-IMP + Ø-IMP +* ***Ø-ʾal-yiqṭol(Ø)****!*

לֵ֣ךְ מֵעָלָ֑י הִשָּׁ֣מֶר לְךָ֗ **אַל־תֹּ֙סֶף֙** רְא֣וֹת פָּנַ֔י

‘Get away from me! Take care **that you do not see** my face again!’ (Exod. 10.28)[188]

This type of complementation, without marking other than a switch from an imperative predicate to a jussive predicate, is important to recognise when the prefix verb is morphologically indistinctive. In such a case, the initial position of the *yiqṭol(Ø)* is the decisive syntactic signal, as in (107):

(107) *Ø-XØ-«REL-qaṭal +* ***Ø-yiqṭol(Ø)****» + wa-yiqṭol!*

זֶ֧ה הַדָּבָ֛ר אֲשֶׁר־צִוָּ֥ה יְהוָ֖ה **תַּעֲשׂ֑וּ** וְיֵרָ֥א אֲלֵיכֶ֖ם כְּב֥וֹד יְהוָֽה׃

‘This is what YHWH has commanded you **to do** so that the glory of YHWH may appear to you.’ (Lev. 9.6)

In this utterance of Moses, a complex relative sentence is built up by a manipulation verb with a *qaṭal* verb form (צִוָּ֥ה), followed by a complement coded by an asyndetic irrealis *yiqṭol(Ø)* (תַּעֲשׂ֑וּ) in the second person. This תַּעֲשׂ֑וּ is not morphologically distinctive, but the initial position of the verb and examples such as Exodus

10.28 above are helpful in the analysis. The next irrealis *wa-yiqṭol!* clause (וְיֵרָ֔א) is not part of the relative complex and expresses a purpose meaning (J-M §116d).[189]

Complement clauses with *yiqṭol(Ø)* may also be syndetic, as in (108):

(108) *Ø-IMP* + ***wa-yiqṭol(Ø)!*** + *wa-O.noun-IMP* + *kī-qaṭal*

אֱמֹ֨ר אֶל־אֶלְעָזָ֜ר בֶּן־אַהֲרֹ֣ן הַכֹּהֵ֗ן **וְיָרֵ֤ם** אֶת־הַמַּחְתֹּת֙ מִבֵּ֣ין הַשְּׂרֵפָ֔ה וְאֶת־הָאֵ֖שׁ זְרֵה־הָ֑לְאָה כִּ֖י קָדֵֽשׁוּ׃

‘Order Eleazar son of Aaron the priest **to remove** the fire-pans from the remains of the fire blaze and to scatter the incense away, for they have [both] become holy—’ (Num. 17.2, Levine 1993, 409, my emphasis)

After an initial imperative with a manipulation verb (אֱמֹ֨ר), a clause-initial syndetic irrealis *yiqṭol(Ø)* (וְיָרֵ֤ם) expresses a complement to the previous clause.[190]

3.4.2.3. The Short *Yiqṭol* with Ventive/Cohortative Clitic *-ā*

It is a well-known phenomenon in CBH that a so-called cohortative form can be unlengthened, at least in the archaic poetry (Notarius 2010b, 398, 401). The paragogic *heh* is facultative. The historical origin of the cohortative *-ā* clitic is the West Semitic ventive/energic morpheme added to the jussive *yaqtul* (Notarius 2010b, 407f.; Sjörs 2019, 4; 2023, ch. 6). The cohortative in CBH is not a separate ‘tense’; it is not a ‘mood’. It is just a jussive short *yiqṭol* in the first grammatical person with an extra ventive/energic clitic having a meaning of interest and involvement of the sender (Notarius 2010b, 412). The remnants of the old ventive clitic in CBH also take the form of an energic morpheme before an object suffix. For this reason, the clitic will be called 'ventive/energic', following the terminology of Notarius (2010b, 394). In the volitive system of CBH, I thus count one modal prefix conjugation, the jussive short *yiqṭol*, used with or without a ventive/energic morpheme. The ventive/energic clitic was not used in plural forms. Before object suffixes, the reflex of the West Semitic ventive/energic morpheme emerges in CBH as the 'energic' verb forms (Notarius 2010b, 408, 411).

In first-person forms in CBH, the ventive/energic clitic (*-ā*) came to be added to all forms of the jussive. First-person jussives without this clitic were suppressed (Sjörs 2019, 19; 2021a, 20). This was possible because of the semantic nature of the first grammatical person (Notarius 2010b, 413f.). The clitic *-ā*, when applicable, became a marker of the first person in CBH.[191]

The West Semitic ventive/energic morpheme could also be added to imperfective *yaqtulu* forms (in the form of *-na*, the allomorph after a vowel). So *-a(n)* was the allomorph used after jussive *yaqtul*, and *-na* the allomorph after *yaqtulu* (Notarius 2010b, 409).

In some III*wy* verbs, the ventive/energic clitic came to be 'hidden' in a 'full' prefix form, though intended as a short jussive with ventive/energic clitic. This is the case with verbs III-ʾ, and especially verbs III*wy* (Sjörs 2019, 14; 2021b, 276). An illuminating example is (109):

(109) *(ʾim-yiqṭol(u))* + ***Ø-yiqṭol-A*** + ***Ø-yiqṭol-V***

אִם־תַּֽעֲשֶׂה־לִּי֙ הַדָּבָ֣ר הַזֶּ֔ה **אָשׁ֛וּבָה אֶרְעֶ֥ה** צֹאנְךָ֖ אֶשְׁמֹֽר׃

'If you will do this for me, **I will again pasture** your flock and keep it!' (Gen. 30.31)

In (109), the apodosis is asyndetic and consists of two jussives with ventive/energic suffix. The jussives are serial verbs, of which the first supplies the adverbial meaning 'again'. As serial verbs, they are syntactically equal: a short *yiqṭol* with ventive clitic. In the first verb (אָשׁוּבָה), the ventive/cohortative suffix takes the form of a lengthening with *-ā*. In the second verb (אֶרְעֶה), the ventive/energic morpheme is hidden in the final long *-ɛ̄*. The example shows that a formally 'full' *yiqṭol* of a verb III*wy* must in some instances be analysed as a jussive (short *yiqṭol*) with ventive/energic clitic.

In other instances, a jussive verb III*wy* with 'hidden' ventive/cohortative morpheme is syntactically equal to a verb with 'energic' suffix. Both verb forms must be analysed as jussives having a ventive/energic morpheme. An example is (110):

(110) *Ø-IMP + wa-yiqṭol-V + wa-yiqṭol-N(= V)*

גּוּר בָּאָרֶץ הַזֹּאת [וְאֶהְיֶה עִמְּךָ] [וַאֲבָרְכֶךָּ]

'Sojourn in this land, and I will be with you and will bless you!' (Gen. 26.3a)

This example illustrates how a first-person 'full' form (וְאֶהְיֶה) must be parsed as a short jussive *yiqṭol* with ventive/energic ending. The following first-person jussive with energic suffix (וַאֲבָרְכֶךָּ) has the same volitive meaning. The energic verb form must also be parsed as a jussive with ventive/energic ending plus following object pronoun. The two prefix forms in (106) cannot be 'long' *yiqṭols*, considering the extremely frequent pattern *IMP + wa-*

yiqṭol(Ø) in a modal sequence. The example shows that a verb with 'energic' object suffix may have a ventive meaning expressing involvement of the speaker.[192]

3.4.3. The Distinct Identity of *Yiqṭol(Ø)* in Contrast to *Yiqṭol(u)*: The Role of Word Order

Despite the partial loss of morphological distinctiveness, the later Canaanite languages still preserved a regular semantic distinction between the imperfective and jussive forms (Wilson-Wright 2019, 520). In CBH also, the identity of *yiqṭol(Ø)* was retained when many forms of the two prefix conjugations became identical. We have already discussed the consequent retention of morphologically short prefix forms wherever possible, as well as the distinguishing function of the negations אַל and לֹא in nearly complementary distribution (see §3.4.1).[193]

In affirmative clauses, other signals helped to uphold the distinction between a perfective/jussive short *yiqṭol* and an imperfective long *yiqṭol*. The grammatical problem that had to be resolved was the morphological ambiguity, or more precisely the partial homonymy, between *yiqṭol(Ø)* and *yiqṭol(u)*.[194] In most instances, these forms coalesced.[195] The grammatical development that could answer this problem was a refinement of word order. This refinement, or restriction, was incomplete in the archaic poetry and finished in CBH.[196] In the Archaic Hebrew poetry, word order is a tendency: *yiqṭol(Ø)* forms tend to be clause-initial,[197] and *yiqṭol(u)* forms are often non-initial. This is the case also in the Amarna texts (Baranowski 2016a, 202). In CBH, word order became a distinguishing feature: affirmative *yiqṭol(u)* was placed within a clause, while affirmative *yiqṭol(Ø)* was used in initial position (Gentry 1998, 12).[198] The short *yiqṭol*, irrespective of its having realis or irrealis meaning, was put in initial position, and the *yiqṭol(u)* morpheme had to be internal (Isaksson 2015d; Driver 1892, 245; Finley 1981, 246; Revell 1988, 422; 1989, 2; Gzella 2011a, 442; 2013c, 859).[199] Word order became the basic signal for distinguishing *yiqṭol(Ø)* from *yiqṭol(u)* in affirmative clauses (Revell 1989, 21; Joosten 2011b, 214; Notarius 2013, 17 n. 53).[200] "[T]his formal/syntactic distinction must be held to reflect a distinction in function" (Revell 1988, 422).[201] There are few exceptions in the corpus to this rule: an imperfective *yiqṭol(u)* must have internal position in the clause (Rabin 1984, 392; Revell 1989, 1).

There was a drawback: the long *yiqṭol(u)* could no longer be used in discourse-continuity clauses (type *wa-VX*), and had to be replaced. The substitute became the *wa-qaṭal* clause-type, an early CBH innovation (see §6).[202]

This word order rule was helpful for affirmative clauses.[203] In negated clauses, there was no need for extra clarity because of the complementary distribution of the two negations. In negated jussive clauses, word order remained relatively free (see §3.4.4).

The linguistic instinct did not count the proclitic *wa-* as a (first) constituent, so in a *wa(y)-yiqṭol* clause, the verb form (*yiqṭol*) was perceived as clause-initial. All other conjunctions, however, were felt to occupy the first position in the clause, and therefore a **kī-yiqṭol(Ø)* clause would have been unacceptable:

In וּתְחִי (Gen. 19.20), the verb is clause-initial (short jussive *yiqṭol*).

In וַתֵּ֫לֶד (Gen. 4.1), the verb is clause-initial (short perfective *yiqṭol*).

In כִּֽי־יָשִׁ֫ית (Gen. 48.17), the verb is perceived as internal (long *yiqṭol*).

3.4.4. When the Word Order Rule Did Not Apply in CBH

There are exceptions to the word order rule described in §3.4.3. They can be divided into cases when the word order restriction was uncalled for (negated clauses, §3.4.4.1); constructions that only appear to break the rule (§§3.4.4.2–3); an archaic use of *Ø-yiqṭol(u)* as asyndetic relative clause, rare in prose (§3.4.4.4); and a late use of *Ø-yiqṭol(u)* in Deuteronomy (§3.4.4.5). Finally, I analyse Baden's (2008) ten cases of (long) *wəyiqtol* in a volitive sequence, which illustrate many apparent violations of the word order rule, and demonstrate why in most cases a distinctively long *wa-yiqṭol* or *Ø-yiqṭol* should be analysed as jussive (§3.4.4.6).

3.4.4.1. Negated Clauses

The negated clauses constitute an obvious case when word order restriction remained unneeded. Since the negations אַל and לֹא are in complementary distribution (Kummerow 2008, 73),[204] a word order restriction is unnecessary in order to distinguish between short and long *yiqṭol*. In negated jussive clauses, the initial position of the negated verb is just a tendency, not a rule (as it is also in Amarna Canaanite and the Archaic Hebrew poetry). This is illustrated in (111):

(111) *wa-S.noun-lō-yiqṭol(u)! + wa-gam-S.noun-***ʾal-yiqṭol(Ø)***! +*
*Ø-gam-S.noun-***ʾal-yiqṭol(Ø)**

וְאִישׁ֙ לֹא־יַעֲלֶ֣ה עִמָּ֔ךְ וְגַם־אִ֥ישׁ **אַל־יֵרָ֖א** בְּכָל־הָהָ֑ר גַּם־הַצֹּ֤אן וְהַבָּקָר֙ **אַל־יִרְע֔וּ**
אֶל־מ֖וּל הָהָ֥ר הַהֽוּא׃

'No one is to come up with you; **do not let anyone be seen** anywhere on the mountain; **not** even the flocks or the herds **may graze** in front of that mountain.' (Exod. 34.3, Revell 1988, 422)

In (111), first a command is issued by means of a negated *yiqṭol(u)* clause, which seems to express a categorical prohibition.[205] It is followed by two more specific commands in negated jussive clauses. In both of the jussive clauses, the *ʾal-yiqṭol(Ø)* syntagm is clause-internal.[206]

3.4.4.2. Apparent Violations of the Rule for *Yiqṭol(Ø)*

The second category concerns cases where there only appears to be a violation of the rule. In such instances, the constituent before the jussive morpheme is perceived as not belonging to the clause. Some such constructions are left dislocations (extra-position constructions; for a discussion, see Khan 1988, 78–86; Gross 2013), vocatives (Hasselbach 2013b, 299), an honorary phrase, an exclamatory particle,[207] or an introductory *(wa)-ʿattā*. This interpretation is usually supported by the Masoretic accents: there is a distinctive accent before the jussive form. An example of both a left dislocation and an *ʿattā* before jussive forms is (112) (the left dislocation is marked by square brackets):

(112) *wa-ʿattā, Ø-yiqṭol(Ø)! + wa-[S.noun]-yiqṭol(Ø)!*

וְעַתָּ֗ה יֵֽשֶׁב־נָ֤א עַבְדְּךָ֙ תַּ֣חַת הַנַּ֔עַר עֶ֖בֶד לַֽאדֹנִ֑י וְהַנַּ֖עַר יַ֥עַל עִם־אֶחָֽיו׃

‘So now, please let your servant remain as my lord’s slave instead of the boy. As for the boy, let him go back with his brothers.’ (Gen. 44.33)

In (112), an introductory *wa-ʿattā* is perceived as a particle signalling the start of the main message.[208] It has the function of a colon and does not belong to the following clause. The *yiqṭol(Ø)* form that follows the *wa-ʿattā* is distinctively short, and the particle *nā* is a further signal that the verb is jussive. In the next clause, the *han-naʿar* has a distinctive accent and must be regarded as a left dislocation, not part of the main sentence.[209]

Vocatives constitute a typical preposed element that does not violate the word order rule, since there is a natural pause after a vocative. An example is:[210]

(113) *Ø-ADV-VOC, yiqṭol(Ø)-nā*

בִּ֣י אֲדֹנִ֗י יְדַבֶּר־נָ֨א עַבְדְּךָ֤ דָבָר֙ בְּאָזְנֵ֣י אֲדֹנִ֔י

‘Oh, my lord, please let your servant speak a word in my lord’s ears’ (Gen. 44.18)

3.4.4.3. Apparent Violations of the Rule for *Yiqṭol(u)*

A corresponding violation of the word order rule for *yiqṭol(u)* clauses may be caused by ellipsis: an element is understood to be placed before the verb. The long *yiqṭol(u)* is only apparently clause-initial, and linguistic competence perceives the *yiqṭol(u)* to be non-initial because of the understood element. An example of ellipsis with *yiqṭol(u)* is (114):

(114) *Ø-mī-yiqṭol(u)! + wa-yiqṭol(Ø) + wa-[mī]-yiqṭol(u) + wa-yiqṭol(Ø)-N*

מִ֣י יַעֲלֶה־לָּ֤נוּ הַשָּׁמַ֨יְמָה֙ וְיִקָּחֶ֣הָ לָּ֔נוּ וְיַשְׁמִעֵ֥נוּ אֹתָ֖הּ וְנַעֲשֶֽׂנָּה׃

'Who will go up for us to heaven to get it for us, and [who] will make us listen to it so that we may obey it?' (Deut. 30.12)

(114) contains an evident ellipsis: the understood interrogative pronoun (מִ֣י) in the third clause (וְיַשְׁמִעֵ֥נוּ). The first clause has a long *yiqṭol* (יַעֲלֶה) with futural meaning, and so we can expect that the *yiqṭol* in the third clause is also long.[211] The second and fourth clauses are jussive *wa-yiqṭol(Ø)* expressing purpose, of which the last (in the first person) has a ventive/energic morpheme (*pace* Zewi 1999, 85).[212]

3.4.4.4. The Archaic Use of *Ø-yiqṭol(u)* as Asyndetic Relative Clause

Asyndetic relative clauses with a *yiqṭol(u)* predicate may break the word order rule. In such examples, the *yiqṭol(u)* usually follows a head noun in the construct state (Zewi 2020). It is reasonable to suppose that such constructions are archaic, since most examples are from poetry. A rare example in prose is (115):[213]

(115) *wa(y)-yiqṭol: VOC-IMP-nā bə-yaḏ-«**Ø-yiqṭol(u)**»*

וַיֹּ֖אמֶר בִּ֣י אֲדֹנָ֑י שְֽׁלַֽח־נָ֖א בְּיַד־**תִּשְׁלָֽח**׃

'But he said, O, my Lord, please send by the hand of anyone else **whom you wish to send**!' (Exod. 4.13)

In (115), the *yiqṭol(u)* verb form is nominalised ('of anyone else whom you wish to send') in annexation to the noun (יַד־) in the construct state (Ges-K §130d; Zewi 2020, 94, 102). Some further examples are found in prose, but they are more frequent in poetry.[214]

3.4.4.5. A Late Use of *Ø-yiqṭol(u)* in Deuteronomy

One of very few clause-initial *yiqṭol(u)* is found in Deut. 19.3. It represents a clear break with the word order rule found in the rest of my corpus:

(116) *Ø-O.noun-yiqṭol(u)!* + [3]***Ø-yiqṭol(u)!*** + *wa-qaṭal* + *wa-qaṭal*

> שָׁל֥וֹשׁ עָרִ֖ים תַּבְדִּ֣יל לָ֑ךְ בְּת֣וֹךְ אַרְצְךָ֔ אֲשֶׁר֙ יְהוָ֣ה אֱלֹהֶ֔יךָ נֹתֵ֥ן לְךָ֖ לְרִשְׁתָּֽהּ׃ **תָּכִ֣ין**
> לְךָ֮ הַדֶּרֶךְ֒ וְשִׁלַּשְׁתָּ֙ אֶת־גְּב֣וּל אַרְצְךָ֔ אֲשֶׁ֥ר יַנְחִֽילְךָ֖ יְהוָ֣ה אֱלֹהֶ֑יךָ וְהָיָ֕ה לָנ֥וּס שָׁ֖מָּה
> כָּל־רֹצֵֽחַ׃
>
> ‘you must set apart for yourselves three cities in the middle of your land that the LORD your God is giving you as a possession. [3]**You shall build** a roadway and divide into thirds the whole extent of your land that the LORD your God is providing as your inheritance; anyone who kills another person should flee to the closest of these cities.’

The distinctively long *Ø-yiqṭol(u)* clause in (116) supplies a further detail in the same action, about how to allocate and organise the three cities (elaboration). The asyndetic *yiqṭol(u)* functions as an elaboration of the preceding *yiqṭol(u)* clause in the context of an instruction.

3.4.4.6. Baden's Supposed Cases of *Wa-yiqṭol(u)* Expressing Result

Baden (2008) has identified ten unambiguous examples of *wa-yiqṭol(u)* in the corpus from Genesis to 2 Kings. The examples are worth examining, because the forms are morphologically distinguishable as 'imperfects' and seem to violate the word order rule discussed above. Baden (2008, 158) argues that such clauses have a distinct purpose or result meaning, in contradistinction to the more general meaning of a jussive *wa-yiqṭol(Ø)*. This conclusion is unconvincing, and I agree with Joosten (2009, 497), who maintains that the cases discussed by Baden "appear to belong with the volitives," except in one case, which will be evident below.

(1) Genesis 1.9 (Baden 2008, 152)

Baden's parade example of "*wəyiqtol* in a volitive sequence" is (117) below.

(117) *Ø-yiqṭol(Ø)* + ***wa-yiqṭol(Ø)-V***

יִקָּו֨וּ הַמַּ֜יִם מִתַּ֤חַת הַשָּׁמַ֙יִם֙ אֶל־מָק֣וֹם אֶחָ֔ד **וְתֵרָאֶ֖ה** הַיַּבָּשָׁ֑ה

'Let the water below the sky be gathered into one area, **so that** the dry land **appears (for me/us)**.' (Gen. 1.9)

The long *yiqṭol* in the second clause (וְתֵרָאֶה) can be analysed as a jussive with ventive ending. The ventive of verbs III*wy* coincides with the long *yiqṭol* in the third person (Sjörs 2023, 105). At some point in the development of the Canaanite languages, the paragogic *heh* became nearly exclusively restricted to the first person

(Kogan 2015, 135 n. 369). However, this type of ventive morpheme is sometimes also added to third-person forms (Sjörs 2023, 113f.).[215] In (117), the verb in the second clause marks the speaker (God the creator) as beneficiary of the action, so the 'long' *yiqṭol* (וְתֵרָאֶה) should be analysed as short with a ventive morpheme.[216]

(2) Exodus 2.7 (Baden 2008, 152)

(118) *Ø-INT-yiqṭol(u)* + *wa-qaṭal* + ***wa-yiqṭol(Ø)-V***

הַאֵלֵךְ וְקָרָאתִי לָךְ אִשָּׁה מֵינֶקֶת מִן הָעִבְרִיֹּת **וְתֵינִק** לָךְ אֶת־הַיָּלֶד׃

'Shall I go and call you a nursing woman for you from the Hebrews, **so that she may nurse** the child **for you**?'

In Baden's second example, a clearly long volitive *yiqṭol* in the third person has a volitive, seemingly subordinate, meaning. This is the typical syntax of a subordinate jussive expressing purpose. The problem is the unexpected morphologically long form in the third person singular feminine (וְתֵינִק). This is not a verb III*wy*, as in Baden's first example (117), but my thesis is that this form is also a jussive with ventive marking. I will start by discussing similar first-person forms, then continue with third-person forms, as in (118).

In the archaic language type, there are examples of the ventive-cohortative without the suffix -*ā* (paragogic *heh*). In such cases, the long form that is used before the paragogic *heh* is retained even without the *heh*; the forms used in the first person are either the full form *with* paragogic *heh* or the full form *without* this morpheme (Notarius 2010b, 401, 413):

(119) *Ø-yiqṭol(Ø)* + ***Ø-yiqṭol(Ø)*** + *Ø-yiqṭol(Ø)* + *Ø-yiqṭol(Ø)* + ***Ø-yiqṭol(Ø)*** + *Ø-yiqṭol(Ø)*

אָמַ֥ר אוֹיֵ֛ב אֶרְדֹּ֥ף **אַשִּׂ֖יג** אֲחַלֵּ֣ק שָׁלָ֑ל תִּמְלָאֵ֣מוֹ נַפְשִׁ֔י **אָרִ֣יק** חַרְבִּ֔י תּוֹרִישֵׁ֖מוֹ יָדִֽי׃

'The enemy said, "Let me pursue, **overtake**, divide the spoil, so that my desire shall have its fill of them. **Let me draw** my sword, so that my hand shall destroy them."' (Exod. 15.9, Notarius 2013, 122, my emphasis in text and translation)

In this archaic series of volitives, four forms are in the first person and of them two are long. Semantically, the first-person forms are ventive-cohortative in meaning, but none exhibits a paragogic *heh*. If the verb forms are to be analysed as cohortatives, it seems that the ventive-cohortative suffix can be left out, and when it is left out, the resulting verb form remains long, as is shown in אַשִּׂ֖יג and אָרִ֣יק. The principle indicated in this example is that a long first-person *yiqṭol* without paragogic *heh* can sometimes, in a proper modal setting, be identified as a cohortative with the paragogic *heh* left out.[217] That this syntax is retained in CBH is confirmed in (120):

(120) *Ø-IMP-A-nā* + *wa-yiqṭol(Ø)-A* + ***wa-yiqṭol(Ø)-V***

לְכָה־נָּ֛א וְנָס֥וּרָה אֶל־עִיר־הַיְבוּסִ֥י הַזֹּ֖את **וְנָלִ֥ין** בָּֽהּ׃

'Come please, and let's turn to this Jebusite city, **that we may spend the night** there.' (Judg. 19.11)

In this modal sequence, the first two volitives are marked by ventive-cohortative endings (paragogic *heh*). But in the third volitive (וְנָלֶ֑ין), the paragogic *heh* is left out. Revell (1989, 18) expected a paragogic *heh* here and concluded that the paragogic *heh* is facultative. With paragogic *heh*, the form would have been וְנָלִ֫ינָה; without paragogic *heh*, וְנָלִ֫ין. The remaining ventive marking is a 'long' form of the *yiqṭol*, which should be analysed as a volitive (jussive) with ventive marking.

The following are my examples of 'long' first-person *yiqṭol* forms that are to be analysed as jussives with ventive marking and meaning, some of them mentioned by Revell (1989) as cohortatives with paragogic *heh* left out (R):[218] Judg. 19.11 (וְנָלֶ֑ין); 1 Sam. 12.3 (וְאַעְלִ֥ים and וְאָשִׁ֥יב; R 18); 12.19 (וְאַל־נָמ֑וּת; R 18); 2 Sam. 19.38 (וְאָמֻ֣ת; R 18); 1 Kgs 12.9 (וְנָשִׁ֣יב; R 18); 2 Kgs 4.10 (וְנָשִׂ֨ים; R 18); Zech. 1.3 (וְאָשׁ֣וּב); Ps. 12.6 (אָשִׁ֣ית); 46.11 (אָר֣וּם); 55.3 (אָרִ֥יד); 55.8 (אַרְחִ֣יק and אָלִ֣ין); 59.17 (אָשִׁ֣יר); 71.16 (אַזְכִּ֣יר); 95.2 (נְקַדְּמָ֣ה... נָרִ֥יעַ); 142.3 (אַגִּ֑יד).

In Ancient Canaanite, the jussive with ventive was used in the first and third persons, and less frequently in the second person because the imperative was used uniquely in that person. In CBH, the ventive-cohortative is mostly, but not always, used in the first person. One example has already been treated (Baden's first example: Gen. 1.9). Another is:

(121) *Ø-yiqṭol(Ø)-V*

וַתֹּ֙אמֶר֙ אֶל־אָבִ֔יהָ יֵעָ֥שֶׂה לִּ֖י הַדָּבָ֣ר הַזֶּ֑ה

'She then said to her father, "Please grant me this one wish!..."' (Judg. 11.37)

The jussive in (121) is 'long', but obviously volitive and speaker-benefactive, and the same must be said of (122) below:

(122) *Ø-yiqṭol(Ø)-V + wa-yiqṭol(Ø) + CONJ-yiqṭol(u)-N*

יָקֻם אָבִי וְיֹאכַל מִצֵּיד בְּנוֹ בַּעֲבוּר תְּבָרֲכַנִּי נַפְשֶׁךָ׃

'Let my father sit up and eat of his son's game, so that you may give me your blessing!' (Gen. 27.31)

The initial volitive in (122) has a long form (*yāqūm*), which can be analysed as a jussive with ventive marking to express that the father is the beneficiary of the action of sitting up.[219]

Even second-person long jussives are sometimes to be analysed as having ventive marking. An example is (123):

(123) *Ø-IMP + **Ø-ʾal-yiqṭol(Ø)-V** + wa-ʾal-yiqṭol(Ø) + Ø-ADV-IMP + pɛn-yiqṭol(u)!*

הִמָּלֵט עַל־נַפְשֶׁךָ **אַל־תַּבִּיט** אַחֲרֶיךָ וְאַל־תַּעֲמֹד בְּכָל־הַכִּכָּר הָהָרָה הִמָּלֵט פֶּן־תִּסָּפֶה׃

'Run for your lives! **Don't look** behind you or stop anywhere in the valley! Escape to the mountains or you will be destroyed!' (Gen. 19.17)

The action expressed by the negated jussive with ventive marking is obviously beneficial for the receivers of the message, Lot and his family. So the long *yiqṭol* form is not a mistake. It is a proper expression of a volitive, the obedience of which is beneficial for Lot.[220]

The following are my examples of 'long' second- and third-person jussives that should be analysed as jussives with ventive marking and meaning:[221] Gen. 1.9 (וְתֵרָאֶה, 3fs); 19.17 (אַל־תַּבִּיט, 2ms); 27.31 (יָקֻם, 3ms); 41.34 (יַעֲשֶׂה, 3ms); Exod. 2.7 (וְתֵינִק, 3fs); Josh. 1.7 (אַל־תָּסוּר, 2ms); Judg. 6.18 (אַל־נָא תָמֻשׁ, 2ms); 11.37 (יֵעָשֶׂה, 3ms);[222] 1 Sam. 25.25 (אַל־נָא יָשִׂים, 3ms); 2 Sam. 13.12 (אַל־

תַּעֲשֶׂה, 2ms); 14.17 (יְהִיֶה־נָּא, 3ms); 1 Kgs 15.19 (וְיַעֲלֶה, 3ms); 2 Kgs 6.17 (וְיִרְאֶה, 3ms); 18.29 (אַל־יַשִּׁיא, 3ms); Zech. 9.5 (וְתָחִיל, 3fs); Ps. 51.20 (תִּבְנֶה, 2ms); 68.2 (יָקוּם, 3ms); 90.16 (יֵרָאֶה, 3ms); 121.3 (אַל־יָנוּם, 3ms).

(3) Deut. 13.12 (Baden 2008, 153)

(124) *wa-S.noun-yiqṭol(u) + wa-[]-yiqṭol(u)-Npar*

וְכָל־יִשְׂרָאֵל יִשְׁמְעוּ וְיִרָאוּן

'Thus all Israel will hear and be afraid.'

The paragogic *nun* in the second clause clearly indicates a long *yiqṭol*. The two long *yiqṭol* in the example are indicative with future meaning and the same subject. It is a matter of ellipsis: the subject in the first clause is understood in the second. This means that the word order rule for long *yiqṭol* is not violated. For the same reason, the word order rule is not violated in Baden's (2008, 153) added parallels, Deut. 17.13; 19.20; 21.21. In all of them, the two *yiqṭol* are long with future time reference, and the subject is understood in the second clause.[223]

(4) Judg. 19.11 (Baden 2008, 153)

This example involves a ventive marking in the first person, as has already been explained above after (120).

(5) 1 Sam. 12.3 (Baden 2008, 153f.)

This example contains two jussives with ventive marking in the first person, as explained and enumerated after (120).

(6) 2 Sam. 19.38 (Baden 2008, 154)

This example involves a ventive marking in the first person, as explained and enumerated after (120).

(7) 1 Kgs 12.9 (Baden 2008, 154)

This example involves a ventive marking in the first person, as explained and enumerated after (120).

(8) 1 Kgs 15.19 (Baden 2008, 154)

This example involves a ventive marking in the third person, as explained and enumerated after (123).

(9) 2 Kgs 4.10 (Baden 2008, 154)

This example contains two forms with ventive marking in the first person, as explained and enumerated after (120).

(10) 2 Kgs 6.17 (Baden 2008, 154)

This example involves ventive marking in the third person, as explained and enumerated after (123).

My conclusion is that, in one of Baden's examples, the *yiqṭol* is actually long and indicative (ellipsis in Deut. 13.12 with three added parallels in Deut.), and in nine examples, the *yiqṭol* is a jussive with ventive marking.

3.4.5. How the Two Meanings of *Wa-yiqṭol(Ø)* Were Distinguished in CBH

In Amarna Canaanite and Archaic Hebrew, the two meanings of a free-standing *yiqṭol(Ø)* were distinguished by the domain type: in a narrative or reportive domain, a *yiqṭol(Ø)* was automatically identified as a perfective (usually past) verb form; in a modal domain, the linguistic instinct identified *yiqṭol(Ø)* as jussive.

In the synchronic state of CBH, however, the free-standing indicative *yiqṭol(Ø)*, in all its various uses, had been replaced by *qaṭal*. This means that a *yiqṭol(Ø)* without proclitic *wa-* must be jussive in CBH. With this change, one potential obscurity was remedied, but another remained. Since the gemination of the prefix consonant (*way-yiqṭol*) is a later, probably Second Temple, innovation in the reading tradition (see §1.2.5), the syntagm *wa-yiqṭol(Ø)* could still have both realis and irrealis meaning in the actual classical language (homonymy), and had to be identified with the help of the domain. A *wa-yiqṭol(Ø)* in narrative was perfective, a *wa-yiqṭol(Ø)* in a modal domain was identified as jussive. This was facilitated by the discourse function of the *wa-yiqṭol(Ø)* clause-type, which signalled pragmatic continuity: *wa-yiqṭol(Ø)* always followed after another clause that determined the temporal reference and the modality of the clause. Traditionally, the *wa-* in a jussive *wa-yiqṭol(Ø)* clause is called 'copulative', whereas the *wa-* in an indicative (perfective) *wa-yiqṭol(Ø)* has been termed 'consecutive'. But both signal discourse continuity. A jussive *wa-yiqṭol(Ø)* practically always comes as part of a modal series, an example of which is (125):

(125) *Ø-PP + wa-yiqṭol(Ø)! + Ø-yiqṭol(Ø)! + wa-yiqṭol(Ø) + wa-yiqṭol(Ø)!*

בָּר֥וּךְ יְהוָ֖ה אֱלֹ֣הֵי שֵׁ֑ם וִיהִ֥י כְנַ֖עַן עֶ֥בֶד לָֽמוֹ׃ יַ֤פְתְּ אֱלֹהִים֙ לְיֶ֔פֶת וְיִשְׁכֹּ֖ן בְּאָֽהֳלֵי־
שֵׁ֑ם וִיהִ֥י כְנַ֖עַן עֶ֥בֶד לָֽמוֹ׃

'Blessed be the LORD, the God of Shem; and let Canaan be his servant. May God enlarge Japheth's territory, and let him dwell in the tents of Shem, and let Canaan be his servant!' (Gen. 9.26–27)

The example shows two separate modal series (two modal domains), the first of which begins with a passive participle clause (PP), and the second with an asyndetic jussive *yiqṭol(Ø)* (יַ֤פְתְּ). In both domains, the initial volitive clause is continued by *wa-yiqṭol(Ø)* clauses, the identification of which poses no problem to the listener. In one of the *wa-yiqṭol(Ø)* clauses, the verb is non-distinctive (וְיִשְׁכֹּ֖ן) but its jussive meaning is evident semantically and syntactically (clause-initial).[224] All *wa-yiqṭol(Ø)* clauses in the example signal discourse continuity (*wa-VX*) in relation to the preceding clause (see §1.2.6).[225]

In a narrative domain, a discourse-continuous *wa-yiqṭol(Ø)*, that is, *wa(y)-yiqṭol*, is easily identified as an indicative perfective. But the beginning and end of a narrative domain are often more complicated to identify than those of a modal series, because the historical setting and temporal reference is presupposed and the narration just continues with new *wa(y)-yiqṭol* clauses. An example of an easily identifiable beginning of a narrative domain is (126).

(126) *wa-S.noun-lō-qaṭal* + *wa-XØ* + [2]*wa(y)-yiqṭol* + "…" + *wa(y)-yiqṭol* + [3]*wa(y)-yiqṭol* + *wa(y)-yiqṭol* + [4]*wa(y)-yiqṭol* + *wa(y)-yiqṭol* + *wa(y)-yiqṭol*

וְשָׂרַי֙ אֵ֣שֶׁת אַבְרָ֔ם לֹ֥א יָלְדָ֖ה ל֑וֹ וְלָ֛הּ שִׁפְחָ֥ה מִצְרִ֖ית וּשְׁמָ֥הּ הָגָֽר׃ 2 וַתֹּ֨אמֶר
שָׂרַ֜י אֶל־אַבְרָ֗ם הִנֵּה־נָ֞א עֲצָרַ֤נִי יְהוָה֙ מִלֶּ֔דֶת בֹּא־נָא֙ אֶל־שִׁפְחָתִ֔י אוּלַ֥י אִבָּנֶ֖ה
מִמֶּ֑נָּה וַיִּשְׁמַ֥ע אַבְרָ֖ם לְק֥וֹל שָׂרָֽי׃ 3 וַתִּקַּ֞ח שָׂרַ֣י אֵֽשֶׁת־אַבְרָ֗ם אֶת־הָגָ֤ר
הַמִּצְרִית֙ שִׁפְחָתָ֔הּ מִקֵּץ֙ עֶ֣שֶׂר שָׁנִ֔ים לְשֶׁ֥בֶת אַבְרָ֖ם בְּאֶ֣רֶץ כְּנָ֑עַן וַתִּתֵּ֥ן אֹתָ֛הּ
לְאַבְרָ֥ם אִישָׁ֖הּ ל֥וֹ לְאִשָּֽׁה׃ 4 וַיָּבֹ֥א אֶל־הָגָ֖ר וַתַּ֑הַר וַתֵּ֙רֶא֙ כִּ֣י הָרָ֔תָה וַתֵּקַ֥ל
גְּבִרְתָּ֖הּ בְּעֵינֶֽיהָ׃

'Now Sarai, Abram's wife, had not given birth to any children, but she had an Egyptian servant named Hagar. [2]So Sarai said to Abram, "Since the LORD has prevented me from having children, have sexual relations with my servant. Perhaps I can have a family by her." Abram did what Sarai told him. [3]So after Abram had lived in Canaan for ten years, Sarai, Abram's wife, gave Hagar, her Egyptian servant, to her husband to be his wife. [4]He had sexual relations with Hagar, and she became pregnant. Once Hagar realised she was pregnant, she despised Sarai.' (Gen. 16.1–4)

The domain starts with a background section involving a *qaṭal* clause and a verbless clause. This states the historical setting and the temporal reference. Narration continues with *wa-yiqṭol* clauses. The point here is that perfective *wa-yiqṭol* clauses are easily identifiable in a narrative domain, even though the *wa-yiqṭol* syntagm is homophonous with a jussive *wa-yiqṭol(Ø)* syntagm.

3.5. Summary: The Independent Status of the Short *Yiqṭol*

In this chapter, I have shown that the short *yiqṭol* is inherited from Proto-Semitic. It has a dual character as both past perfective and jussive. This is a property that the short *yiqṭol* shares with its cognate *yaqtul* in other ancient Semitic languages, like Akkadian (*iprus*), Amorite, Ugaritic, Amarna Canaanite, and the most ancient inscriptions of Aramaic. Even in the Archaic Hebrew poetry, the short *yiqṭol* could function as a 'free' narrative verb form without being restricted to the *wa-yiqṭol* (short) clause-type.

The indicative short *yiqṭol* in CBH is used only in the clause-type *wa-yiqṭol*, with normal *wa-* and short *yiqṭol*. This clause-type is mainly used in narration. In the present book, it is written *wa(y)-yiqṭol*, because the Second Temple reading tradition after the CBH era introduced a gemination of the prefix consonant in order to make a distinction in the reading between the indicative (perfective past) *wa-yiqṭol(Ø)* and the jussive *wa-yiqṭol(Ø)*.

The jussive short *yiqṭol* in CBH was less restricted. It could be used with or without a preceding *wa-*. With a preceding *wa-*, that is, as the clause-type *wa-yiqṭol*, it often expresses purpose.

Both the indicative short *yiqṭol* and the jussive short *yiqṭol* are restricted as to word order; they are used in initial position of the clause: the indicative short *yiqṭol* in the clause-type *wa(y)-yiqṭol*, and the jussive short *yiqṭol* with a restriction to initial position in affirmative clauses. The reason for the more restricted syntax of the indicative short *wa-yiqṭol* in CBH was the ongoing intrusion of the new powerful anterior/perfective formation *qaṭal* (see §5). The new *qaṭal* took over more and more functions from the indicative short *yiqṭol*, also in narrative. In CBH, only the discourse-continuous past perfective *wa-yiqṭol* (here written *wa(y)-yiqṭol*) was left to the indicative short *yiqṭol*. The rest of the uses had been taken over by *qaṭal*.

The restricted word order of the non-negated jussive is of great help when distinguishing jussive forms from the (partly) homophonous imperfective long *yiqṭol* forms (see §4), which are used in internal position.

Word order is of paramount importance in the syntax of the two *yiqṭol*, the short and the long. Word order makes it easy to distinguish the two.

The impression given by the theory of consecutive tenses that there is only one *yiqṭol* is false. It is typologically false and it is false in the synchronic state of CBH.

Past perfective *wa-yiqṭol(Ø)*, written *wa(y)-yiqṭol* in this book, and jussive *wa-yiqṭol(Ø)* were homophonous in CBH, seemingly without causing any problems. Other Semitic languages solved this potential problem of homophony by using a proclitic precative particle (PS **la-*) before the jussive *yaqtul*. But Hebrew never came to use this particle.

---

[1] Huehnergard (1983, 575): "**yaqtul* in PS was both injunctive (jussive) and preterite."

[2] Similar conclusions are expressed by Bloch (2013) and Baranowski (2016b, 1).

[3] Unfortunately "the data do not allow a confident etymological reconstruction" (Cook 2012a, 220, 263). A resultative signals that "a state exists as a result of a past action;" completive means "to do something thoroughly and to completion" (Bybee et al. 1994, 54). Past tenses do not arise directly, but have a long history (Givón 1991, 305; Bybee et

al. 1994, 51–105). Huehnergard and his followers reject the idea of grammaticalisation paths (and thus the empirical results of the investigations of Joan Bybee and Östen Dahl). Without this theoretical foundation, it is impossible to make any statement about the origin of *yaqtul*. Huehnergard instead supposes that it was "unmarked for TAM categories" (Huehnergard 2019, 62).

4 For the term prototypical, see §1.2.1.

5 This is true of Aramaic except for the earliest inscriptions, where a narrative *yaqtul* is retained, as in the Tel Dan inscription. Muraoka (1995b, 114): "all that can be claimed with certainty is that both idioms attest to an ancient preterital prefix conjugation."

6 In West Semitic, the extended use of the new perfective *qatal* gradually reduced the application field of *yaqtul*, which came to be limited to special text-types or specific syntactic contexts (Tropper 1998, 162). But the volitive use of *yaqtul* ('jussive') was not affected by the intrusion of *qatal*, which only took over the indicative functions of *yaqtul*.

7 For discussion, see Bergsträsser (1918–29, II, §3b); Kuryłowicz (1949, 48f.); Rainey (1986, 5); Tropper (1998, 161, 167); Gzella (2011a, 441); Cook (2012a, 96 n. 26); Kossmann and Suchard (2018, 47). For the concepts of realis and irrealis, see Bybee et al. (1994, 236–240). *Yaqtul* "was a single morpheme, perfective in meaning, that occurred both in statements and in injunctions" (Huehnergard 1988, 22; see also Blau 2010, 195). A short survey (without attempt at an explanation) of the perfective with both past and jussive meanings in the classical Semitic languages is found in Gai (2000). Kuryłowicz (1972a, 64) compares the Semitic 'preterite' *yaqtul* with the modern European languages, in which the indicative preterite is used to express an irrealis: English *if he wrote*, French *s'il écrivait*, Russian *esli by (na)pisal*. Fleischman (1989, 2–3) adds to this discussion the notion of temporal distance from the speaker: the past tense expresses a distance from the speaker that may be used to express irrealis nuances. The past, with its high degree of remoteness, is used as a "metaphorical vehicle for the expression of other linguistic notions" such as non-reality and non-actuality (Fleischman 1989, 3).

[8] See also Diakonoff (1988, 103): "the Jussive was originally a special application of the Old Perfective;" also Palmer (2001, ch. 8); Gzella (2012b, 229; 2018, 23).

[9] Some scholars maintain that *yaqtul* was originally two conjugations with different stress, the preterite with stress on the prefix (*yáqtul*) and the jussive with stress on the verbal stem (*yaqtúl*): see Hetzron (1969); Lipiński (1997, §§25.8, 38.2); Muraoka (1998, 77). But Hetzron is wrong (thus Goerwitz 1992; Garr 1998, lxxvii n. 240). Word stress seems to have been non-phonemic in Proto-Semitic: it was "assigned automatically (i) to the rightmost nonfinal heavy syllable (*CV:* or *CVC*), or (ii) in words having only nonfinal light syllables, to the initial syllable" (Huehnergard 2008, 232; also 1983, 587 n. 165; 2019, 53). In Proto-Hebrew as well, stress was not phonemic, "rather, it was automatic" (Blau 2010, 145, 150). At Blau's (2010, 150) stage iii, when final short vowels had dropped, stress became phonemic, but it did not distinguish irrealis *yiqṭol* from realis *yiqṭol*. According to Blau (2010, 150–51), stress created a distinction between the short *yiqṭol* form **yíšmor* and the long *yiqṭol* form **yišmór* (example forms from Blau); later, however, stress shifted to the ultima also in the short prefix form, so that both *yiqṭol* and *yiqṭol(u)* converged. In Blau's (2010, 151) view, the penultimate stress was retained in some occurrences of realis *wa(y)-yiqṭol* where the penultimate syllable was open, as in *wayyāšåḇ*. Rainey (1996, II:221) separates an indicative 'preterite' *yaqtul* from an injunctive 'jussive' *yaqtul* in Amarna Canaanite, so that "a certain symmetry may be observed" between three conjugations in each mood: the indicative has three, *yaqtul*, *yaqtulu*, and *yaqtulun(n)a*; and the injunctive has three, *yaqtul*, *yaqtula*, and *yaqtulan(n)a*. But symmetry is not something that must be expected in a verbal system; such an idea can instead be deceptive (Cook 2012a, 104; similarly also Dallaire 2014, 169). Similarly Korchin (2008, 325): Rainey is "influenced by a desire for symmetry."

[10] A first step is to use the past tense to mark a low certainty in conditional clauses (a phenomenon attested also in Semitic 'if'-clauses): "If you **told** them the real story, they **would** understand." Second, there is a historical shift of using past forms in non-past (present) volitive use:

"I **should** return soon." Such subjunctives of lower certainty may develop to deontic modals, as in the English "You **should** go" (Givón 2001, I:363).

[11] Bybee (1995, 514): "it is not the past tense alone that is contributing the hypothetical meaning, but rather the past in combination with a modal verb, a subjunctive mood, a hypothetical marker (such as *if*), or, in some cases, the imperfective aspect."

[12] This form shows a reflex of the asseverative PS proclitic particle **la-*; see Huehnergard (1983, 592; 2019, 68).

[13] "The distribution of the precative *lamedh* between East and West Semitic indicates that it was common to the entire Semitic language group" (Garr 1985, 118). For the development of the clitic *l-* to mark the modal meaning of the perfective in Akkadian, see Kouwenberg (2010a, 130ff.). The particle *lu* (< **law*) is obligatory in Old Assyrian as a proclitic particle before *iprus* (Kouwenberg 2017, 633f.). In first-millennium Northwest Semitic, the particle is attested only in Samalian and Fekheriyeh, i.e., in the eastern Aramaic area. "In later times, this feature became characteristic of eastern Aramaic as a dialect group" (Garr 1985, 119).

[14] The particle *li-* is usually not omitted in Classical Arabic prose, but in poetry its use is free (Wright 1896–98, II:35D; Huehnergard 1983, 578).

[15] Such durative examples of *iprus* are found also in Old Assyrian (Kouwenberg 2017, 616).

[16] Lexicostatistics unambiguously points to a rather close genealogical relationship between the dialects of Ethiopian Semitic (Kogan 2015, 449, 465).

[17] This is a disputed position. For a survey of research, see Kogan (2012, 314f.). Many scholars regard the optative *yəngər/yəlbas* as a residue of both the Proto-Semitic perfective *yaqtul* and an (possibly Proto-Semitic) imperfective *yaqtulu,* while the imperfective *yənaggər* is analysed as an inner Ethiopic development, diachronically unrelated to Akkadian *iparras* (thus Rundgren 1959, 50, 54; also Knudsen 1998; Stempel 1999, 133). Avanzini (2009, 209 n. 11) remarks: "maybe Marrassini is right

that 'one has got rid too hastly [*sic*] of the Rundgren hypothesis on the *réemploi de l'instensif* (Rundgren 1959).'" In Rundgren's (1959, 44f.) own words: "Es kann daher wirklich keinem Zweifel unterliegen, dass das akk. Präsens *iparras* eine urakkadische Neuerung darstellt, die als ein Fall vom *réemploi de l'intensif* zu beurteilen ist." Kouwenberg (2010a, 95–123), with many references to Rundgren, even regards the Akkadian imperfective *iparras* as an innovation from a Proto-Semitic 'pluractional' conjugation. In a review of Kouwenberg's position, Kogan (2012, 315) remains "sceptical about the possibility of a peaceful coexistence of *yaqtulu* and *iparras* in PS," and maintains that "the fundamental structural parameters of the PS verbal system should be broadly identical to what we observe in its most archaic daughter tongues" (that is, the *iparras* should be regarded as Proto-Semitic), the more so since corresponding imperfective formations are found in Berber and Beja (Kogan 2012, 316). Kogan's scepticism seems to be well-founded, and if so, an enigma remains to be explained: the complete morphological correspondence between the Akkadian subjunctive *iprusu* and the Central Semitic imperfective *yaqtulu*.

[18] There is a restricted usage of realis *yaqtul* after *ʾem-qedma* 'before' and *(za)ʾenbala* 'before' (Nebes 1994b, 67; cf. Smith 1991, 12f., who refers to private communication from J. Huehnergard). Schramm (1957–58, 5) and Hetzron (1969, 6–8; 1974, 189) identify the irregular past tense form *yəbē* 'he spoke' (of the root **bhl*) as a survival of realis *yaqtul* (see also Tropper 1997a, 39).

[19] In eastern Gurage, the short "jussive template" is used with negated perfective verbs (Meyer 2011b, 1245).

[20] Kogan (2012, 320): "I am confident that 'South Semitic' is a mythic concept which has to be abandoned as soon as possible." Similarly Huehnergard and Rubin (2011, 262f.), but cf. Blau (2010, 17).

[21] This is the term used by Simeone-Senelle (2011, 1092). The imperfective formation with a bisyllabic stem is often regarded as a retention from Proto-Semitic *yVqattVl* (Huehnergard 2005, 157f.). Other scholars regard the MSA *yəsɔ́fər* and the Ethiopic *yənággər* as internal innovations

(*réemploi de l'intensif*), independent from the Akkadian *iparras* (Cohen 1984, 67; Avanzini 2015, 7).

[22] The dialectal distribution of this *l* clitic is complicated. It is not found at all in Harsusi, while in Soqotri and the Mehri of Qishn it is used also in the third-person masculine forms, where the initial *y* is realised as vocalic [i] (Simeone-Senelle 2011, 1093, 1095).

[23] Avanzini (2009, 216; 2015), on the other hand, suggests that there is a closer genealogical affinity between Ancient South Arabian and MSA than generally thought. The Modern South Arabian dialects have not developed directly from Sabaic, but "these languages could derive from the archaic linguistic substratum of Yemen" (Avanzini 2015, 7). At the heart of the matter lies the question as to why the geographically remote Ancient South Arabian exhibits prototypical features that correspond to the Central Semitic languages in the northern part of the Semitic linguistic area. The answer of a majority of scholars has been a supposed migration of groups of speakers of Central Semitic, at least of speakers of Proto-Sabaic, from the southern Levant to the southernmost area of the Arabian Peninsula in the early first millennium BC (thus Nebes 2001; Kottsieper and Stein 2014, 85). Avanzini on this point argues that there are no archaeological or textual traces of such a migration, and that it is more probable that the Ancient South Arabian languages developed within Southern Arabia. According to Avanzini (2015, 4, 6), recent archaeological research provides an overall picture of an "endogenous formation process of settlements on the plateau."

[24] Avanzini (2015, 9, 33) maintains that this is just a hypothesis because of the defective writing system, and that an imperfective *yVqattVl* in Ancient South Arabian is still another possible working hypothesis, since there are a few possible traces of a geminated second radical in verbs IIy: the *y* is written plene in the imperfective example *ḏt* s^2*ym w-ys*^{2}*ymn wfy*... 'that He has set up and will set up the well-being of...' (München VM 91–315, 336, quoted from Stein 2011, 1061), which could possibly indicate a geminated consonant *y*, but defectively in the jussive example *l-ys*^{2}*mn wfy*... 'may He set up the well-being of...' (Ja 611, 16–17, quoted from Stein 2011, 1061). In Avanzini's (2015, 33)

opinion, the arguments that Ethiopian *yənaggər* represents an innovation independent from Akkadian *iparras* (= Rundgren's hypothesis) are convincing (and so also the corresponding formations in MSA).

[25] The distinction between short and long prefix conjugations does not refer to the endings with *-n* in Ancient South Arabian, for which earlier research used the 'short/long' terminology (*yfʿln* = 'long' form, *yfʿl* = 'short' form). It is to be presumed that the *-n* endings in Ancient South Arabian are reflexes of the 'energic' endings attested in Central Semitic. The *yfʿln* form seems to occur in all syntactical uses, except that the past tense narrative *w-yfʿl* tends to be used without *n* (Stein 2013, 77, 80). It must be pointed out that Stein's terminology presupposes only one prefix conjugation ("Die Präfixkonjugation (PK)", Stein 2013, 79). This does not prevent him from talking about "eine morphologische Kurzform" in the case of the jussive, while rejecting the idea that the *w-yfʿl* in past narrative contexts might be derived from the Proto-Semitic realis **yaqtul* that corresponds to the Akkadian *iprus*. According to Stein (2013, 132f.), the general meaning of the PK in Sabaic is to express "Sachverhalte, die gleich- oder nachzeitig zum jeweiligen Relationswert liegen," and therefore it can also "Fortschreiten der Verbalhandlung (Progreß)," and "[d]iese Verwendung entspricht ganz und gar dem sogenannten Konsekutiv-Imperfekt oder ‚Narrativ' (*way-yiqtol*) im Hebräischen." The idea of a Biblical Hebrew 'imperfect' *yiqṭol* that is somehow turned into a narrative tense is nowadays generally discarded by Biblical Hebrew scholarship (which derives it from the old Semitic 'preterite'). Only the unhappy terminology ('imperfect consecutive') is retained, and this unfortunate terminology becomes an argument in the discussion about the prefix conjugation(s) in Ancient South Arabian. Avanzini (2009, 212–216; see also Tropper 1997a) identifies the Ancient South Arabian prefix form in past narrative with the Proto-Semitic 'preterite' (Akkadian *iprus*), but this standpoint is cautiously rejected by Stein (2013, 165), since it "durchaus im Sinne eines Progresses (und damit nachzeitig) erklärt werden kann."

[26] Huehnergard refers to Voigt (1987) and Nebes (1994b), but neither of these authors argues for a reflex of *yaqtulu* in Ancient South Arabian.

[27] According to Multhoff (2019, 332, also 334), "a morphological differentiation between indicative (IND) and jussive (JUSS) forms can be deduced from some roots II *w/y*." Tropper (1997a, 36, 43f.) detects the following meanings for the 'Ø-Form' (without *n*-suffix) in main clauses: (a) "Gegenwart und Zukunft," (b) "Vergangenheit im Sinne des 'Progresses' in der Vergangenheit," (c) "Modale Aussagen." Such meanings of the 'Ø-Form' and comparative reflections on the existence of two prefix conjugations lead Tropper (1997a, 39) to conclude that it is "nicht nur möglich, sondern geradezu zwingend, daß Reste des Präteritums auch im Sabäischen, insbesondere in dessen älteren Sprachschichten, nachweisbar sind."

[28] Example quoted from Stein (2011, 1064, my emphasis on presumably short perfective *yaqtul* forms), cf. Avanzini (2006, 259). Avanzini (2006) maintains that the verbal forms in such examples must be regarded as reflexes of the old Semitic past tense *yaqtul* (thus also Nebes 1994b, 68; Kottsieper 1999, 71).

[29] A corresponding Arabic negated (with *lam*) clause is: *fa-lam-yaqtul.*

[30] Thus Qatabanic has achieved a morphological distinction between three prefix forms: past tense *yfˁl/yfˁlw*, jussive *l-yfˁl/l-yfˁlwn*, and imperfective *b-yfˁl/b-yfˁlwn*. It seems that the distinguishing clitic *l* in Qatabanic caused a morphological merger in the (originally short) jussive: in the jussive, the speakers could dispense with the morphological opposition between a short plural form (exhibited in *yfˁlw*) and a long plural form (*yfˁlwn*).

[31] Avanzini (2009, 215) goes so far as to describe the Proto-Ancient South Arabian verb system as "a protowestern not only a proto-northwestern verb system."

[32] The differentiation is easier to work out in Qatabanic and Minaic, where the expression of the imperfective has been renewed by a *b*-prefix, as in the modern Syro-Palestinian Arabic dialects (Avanzini 2009, 212f.). This *b*-prefix is not found in Sabaic.

[33] It is strange that this indicative use of the perfective *yaqtul* is called 'jussive' in Arabic grammars (thus Fischer 2002, §194). From a scientific standpoint, this represents a 'dead end' terminology, blocking further thoughts.

[34] *lm yfʿl* is also a feature of the North Arabian dialect Safaitic (Huehnergard 2017, 25).

[35] It is Marmorstein's emphasis in the transcription but mine in the translation.

[36] The stem vowel of the *iprus* of verbs II*wy* was conspicuously long in Old Assyrian *imūt*, 2ms *tamūt* (Kouwenberg 2017, 562), and Old Babylonian *imūt, iqīp* (Soden 1969, §104f.; Kouwenberg 2010a, 476). It is strange that Kouwenberg (2010a, 476) maintains that the Akkadian perfective *imūt* agrees "perfectly… with the Arabic Pfv (usually jussive) *yamūt, -ū*," without noticing that the Arabic jussive/perfective has a short(ened) form *yamut* (Wright 1896–98, I:82C).

[37] Brockelmann (1908, 620, 627f.) regards this shortening of a final vowel, in Classical Arabic as well as in Biblical Hebrew, as a secondary phenomenon that developed by analogy with verbs II*wy* (*yaqum* as against *yaqūmu*). But such a shortening is found also in Akkadian, preterite *ibni* 'he built' instead of *ibnī*; and Amarna Canaanite, optative *ia-aq-bi* 'may he speak' (Lipiński 1997, §39.14).

[38] The verb is to be analysed as *elʾakunn-annī* < **yilʾakun-*, a *yaqtul* 'preterite' with ventive/energic clitic; the verb has the same root as *malʾakum* 'messenger'.

[39] DIĜIR is the only logogram used in the left-hand column and should probably be identified with the proper name of the senior deity, El (George and Krebernik 2022, 15).

[40] The verb is a 3ms *yaqtul* with precative particle from the root *ḥwy* in the causative stem.

[41] The verb is a 2ms jussive *yaqtul* without precative *la* from the root *ʾmr*.

[42] For another view, see Knudsen (1982, 9).

[43] Another Northwest Semitic group is Aramaeo-Canaanite (Huehnergard and Pat-El 2019, 5). Huehnergard (1991, 284, 292) posits Northwest Semitic as a subbranch of Central Semitic, the innovative feature of which is the specific distribution of the *a*-insertion in the plural stem of *qatl* (example of plural marking: **malak-**ūma*** 'kings', **malak-**ātu*** 'queens'), *qitl*, and *qutl* forms, together with the external plural marker (thus having a double marking of the plural), and to this short list Kogan (2015, 228) adds the shift of word-initial **w* into *y*, and the pattern **qatt**i**l-* (instead of **qatt**a**l-*) in the D-stem suffix conjugation. According to Huehnergard (1991, 285f.), common Northwest Semitic shared the following features: (1) lack of a (graphically explicit) definite article; (2) "the relic consecutive prefix conjugation for past tense;" (3) preservation of final *-t* in the 3fs form of the suffix conjugation; (4) the N-stem; (5) the 2fs suffix pronoun *kī̆*; (6) the infinitive *daʕt* 'to know'; (7) the imperative *likū* 'go!'. Kogan (2015, 240f., 601), however, finds little evidence, if any, for a Northwest Semitic speech community as a historical reality. If such a community existed, it must have been "a very short-lived and amorphous one," since they might not have shared grammatical or lexical innovations that would justify the supposition of a Northwest Semitic genealogical unity (Kogan 2015, 240, 600f.). Kogan concludes that the subdivision of Northwest Semitic (within Central Semitic), comprising Canaanite and Aramaic, is hard to maintain; and thus also Blau (2010, 22): "Perhaps there existed no period in which the speakers of the languages that we call Northwest Semitic lived together."

[44] Thus also, in the main, Sivan (1997, 99, 103; 2001, 96–102), who follows the scheme of Rainey (1996, II:221–64). Some Ugaritologists regard the past tense use of *yqtl* in the poetic corpus to be a usage of the imperfective *yaqtulu*; for this view, see especially Greenstein (1988, 13; 2006), who has been followed by Bordreuil and Pardee (2009, 46). They see in the use of past *yqtl* in poetry a "free variation with the /YQTLu/ forms," and Greenstein (1988, 17) extends this scepticism to Canaanite in general: "It may well be that in earlier Canaanite, in dif-

ferent stages and/or dialects, prefixed verb forms indicated both narrated past and present-future;" but cf. the critique by Smith (1991, 66f.), and Bloch (2009, 39 n. 20); see also Greenstein's (2006, 81) step back on this point. Against this view, Huehnergard refers to the counter-evidence by Hackett (2012). It is clear that Greenstein (2006) managed to show that *yaqtulu* is extensively used as a historical present in the epic poetry. His corpus is this poetry (Baal, Aqhat, Kirta), but his claim concerning the Ugaritic language at large that it has no *yaqtul* preterite is unproven and remains unconvincing. Greenstein's (2006, 81) view of linguistic change seems to be one of a sudden innovation and substitution of verbal forms (a view criticised also by Hackett 2012, 112): "Nevertheless, one does not expect to find an extensive use of *yaqtul* preterite in Ugaritic, or in any other Semitic language, in which suffixed *qatala* regularly expresses past (or completed) action." But Greenstein (2006, 81) also adds, "[t]he development of the *qatala* as past tense (or perfect) eventually supplants that function of the *yaqtul* form," thus it is a step-by-step process. The period of Greenstein's "eventually" may represent more than a thousand years. In the meantime, there were two competing forms with past time reference (*yaqtul* and *qatal*), as can be seen in Amarna and CBH. Greenstein's most important contribution in his 2006 article is a clarification of the lack of certainty about the identification of many past perfective *yaqtul* in Ugaritic epic (Hackett 2012, 111). But he has not shown that there is no '*yaqtul* preterite' in Ugaritic at all (Renz, 2016, 440; Andrason and Vita 2017; also Gzella 2018, 23 n. 7).

[45] Tropper (1998, 162). The short form was pronounced *wa-yaʿni* (Huehnergard 2012, 57). The corresponding 'long' imperfective *yaqtulu* would have been written **yʿny*.

[46] The form *tdʿ* (3mp, perhaps **tadaʿū*) is distinctive, since the subject is the plural *šmm* (Tropper 2012, 634, 701).

[47] Non-negated jussive *yaqtul* is more frequently attested in the third person than in the second person. In the letter corpus, the imperative is practically always used instead of the second-person *yaqtul*. The second-person *yaqtul* is used in connection with a vocative, after the affirmative

particle *l*, and after an imperative in a modal sequence (Tropper 2012, 722, 810).

48 Huehnergard (2012, 56): /ʾilūma taġġurū-kă tvšallimū-kă/.

49 This usage is not disputed (Hackett 2012, 112).

50 As for verbs II*wy*, Tropper (2012, 643f.) alleges a short vowel in the endingless forms—as Gzella (2011a, 443) also suggests—but unfortunately the orthography is not distinctive on this point, which Gzella (2011a, 444) admits: "The situation in Ugaritic and other epigraphic languages is unknown." Thus *tud* (KTU^3 2.26:19, √ʾwd): Tropper *taʾud* < **taʾûd* (2ms); *yʿn* (KTU^3 1.3:I:23, etc., √ʿyn): Tropper *yaʿin* < **yaʿîn* (3ms). It is possible, even probable, that verbs III*wy* exhibited a secondary shortening of the endingless forms, as is attested in Akkadian (*ibni* < **ibniy*), Hebrew (*yigɛl* < **yigl* < **yigli* < **yigliy*), and Arabic (*yarmi* < **yarmiy*), but this cannot be substantiated in the Ugaritic orthography (Tropper 2012, 656).

51 It is disputed whether there were two homographic particles *l* in Ugaritic (*la* and *lŭ̄*), or only one (thus Tropper 2012, 810). Huehnergard (2012, 78) supposes only one "asseverative or topicalizing particle" *l*, which he transcribes *la* (with question mark).

52 This is a misprint for KTU^3 *ḥṭṭ* (ḥiṭṭata); the same misprint for ḥiṭṭata is found in example (35) (KTU^3 1.14.iv.10); the word is *ḥiṭṭatu* 'wheat'.

53 KTU^3 1.14.iv.12: m[ġ]*d* 'food'.

54 Huehnergard (1991, 285f., 291): "By about 1400 we may also isolate a sub-group we will call Canaanite, which has likewise separated itself from the rest of Northwest Semitic." Proto-Canaanite shared a number of linguistic innovations that distinguished Canaanite from the rest of Central Semitic (and also from the rest of Northwest Semitic): (1) the D and C stem suffix conjugation forms **qittila* and **hiqtila* (thus in at least one Amarna dialect but not in Ugaritic) in contrast to Proto-Northwest Semitic **qattila* and **haqtila*; (2) 1cs pronoun *ʾanōkī̆* (dissimilation from **ʾanōkū̆*), and the concomitant change of 1cs suffix conjugation ending **tū̆* > *-tī̆*; (3) generalisation of the 1cp suffix to *-nū̆* in all positions (levelling).

[55] On the methodological problems of drawing comparative linguistic data from the texts in the Amarna letters, see Baranowski (2016b, 2–3).

[56] Knudtzon (1915, 543) translates this as jussive: "daß sie verbrennen die Länder [mi]t Feuer."

[57] There is no evidence of the West Semitic *wa* in the Amarna letters, which must have been the form of the conjunction in the native language of the scribes (Rainey 1996, III:97). The conjunction is practically always written as the Akkadian *ù*. The conjunction *u* is not necessary before a realis *yaqtul*, which shows "daß die Progreßmarkierung durch die Konjunktion *ū* und nicht durch die verbale Kategorie selbst bezeichnet wird" (Tropper 1998, 163).

[58] Baranowski (2016a, 139), translates: 'Ṣumur is now raided up to its city gate. **They have been able** to raid it, but **they have** not **been able** to capture it.'

[59] Baranowski (2016a, 161), translates: 'Send me a large archer host so that it may drive out the king's enemies from his land and so that all lands **be joined** to the king.'

[60] This is also noted by Rainey (2007, 77) with an example from EA 245:16–18.

[61] The translation follows EA, but *ia-dì-na* is third person: 'so that he will give me'.

[62] As for verbs II*wy*, it is not possible to discern whether the perfective *yaqtul* has a short vowel or a long one: *ti-din* (EA 73:4) and *ti-di-in*$_4$ (EA 108:4); cf. Baranowski (2016a, 74). In verbs III*wy*, the final root vowel seems to be preserved: *ia-aq-bi* (EA 83:34) and *yi-iq-bi* (EA 85:32), as against the imperfective *yi-iq-bu* (EA 129:84; Rainey 1996 II:245).

[63] Baranowski (2016b, 10) translates 'and (it was) Zurata (who) took Labʾayu', which seems to assume a cleft sentence.

[64] See also Amadasi Guzzo (1997, 318). As for the verbal system, Röllig (2011, 474, 477) states that Biblical Hebrew "bore a close resemblance to the language spoken in Tyre," and in spite of the highly official style of the inscriptions and the limited text corpus, he thinks it is possible to

distinguish two prefix conjugations, corresponding to the short Proto-Semitic *yaqtul* and the Central Semitic long *yaqtulu*. Greenstein (1988, 14) denies any trace of a "preterite in Phoenician."

65 The 2fs long *yqtl* form is not attested.

66 Friedrich and Röllig (1999, §§135a, 264); Krahmalkov (2001, 183); Gzella (2012a, 66); Chatonnet (2020, 312); *pace* Segert (1976, §64.522). Hackett (2008, 96) adduces *yaqtul* jussive *tntn* /tantinī/ 'may you (fs) give!' (KAI 50:3), in contrast to *yaqtulu yqṣn* 'they (mp) will cut off' (KAI^5 14:22, root *qṣy*). However, this reading of a distinctively short fs jussive *tntn*, though supported in Hoftijzer and Jongeling (1995, 479), is no longer maintained in KAI^5 50:3, which reads *tntw*.

67 Friedrich and Röllig (1999, §177a) give some examples of a 'Kurz-imperfekt' that should be morphologically distinctive in verbs III*wy* of the type 3ms **yábnī* > **yabni* > *yabn* in old Byblian. This is shown by the example *yḥ* = *yáḥū* < **yaḥw* in the name *yḥmlk* 'Milk has shown himself living' (KAI^5 4:1, Friedrich and Röllig 1999, §§174bis, 264); the corresponding long form should have been written *yḥw* = *yaḥwī*. The *ygl* in KAI^5 1:2 should accordingly be read *yagl* (but this is disputed; see Smith 1991, 18). Unfortunately, there are no corresponding distinctive long forms (such as *yḥw*) in the Byblian inscriptional material.

68 Segert (1976, §§64.444, 77.63) calls the *w-yqtl* a "consecutive imperfect following a perfect" and translates both *qtl* and *w-yqtl* with present tense: "and if a king… goes up (perf.) against Byblos and uncovers (consecutive imperfect, cf. 64.444) this sarcophagus." But Friedrich and Röllig (1999, 229) call it "wohl Kurzimpf."

69 Num. 5.27 אִם־נִטְמְאָה וַתִּמְעֹל מַעַל בְּאִישָׁהּ 'if she has defiled herself and behaved unfaithfully toward her husband'; Num. 35.16 וְאִם־בִּכְלִי בַרְזֶל ׀ הִכָּהוּ וַיָּמֹת 'But if he has struck him down with an iron object, and he died'; Num. 35.17 וְאִם בְּאֶבֶן יָד אֲשֶׁר־יָמוּת בָּהּ הִכָּהוּ וַיָּמֹת 'And if he struck him down with a stone tool that could cause death, and he died'. Gzella (2009, 64 n. 5) adduces "eine paar wenige Belege" for the construction (Num. 5.27; Job 9.16), and calls the *w-yqtl* forms "einfache 'w-Imperfekta' (*imperfecta copulativa*), die erst sekundär als *imperfecta consecutiva*

vokalisiert worden sind, nachdem der eigentliche Gebrauch dieser Form längst in Vergessenheit geraten war?" Referring to Gibson (1982, 15–16), Gzella (2009, 65 n. 5) expresses scepticism "an der tiberischen Lesung." As can be seen, the examples are not so few as Gzella asserts and his doubts about the textual tradition appear unfounded.

[70] Instead of this simple solution, Gzella (2009, 65f.), interprets *ʿly gbl* as a background clause and *wygl* as 'Langimperfekt' (against Friedrich and Röllig 1999, §177a), and translates: 'if someone, having conquered (*ʿly*) Byblos, uncovers (*wygl*) this sarcophagus: the sceptre of his kingship may wither away' (same in Gzella 2013b, 179).

[71] "[B]oth these verbal forms are projected into the future" (Segert 1976, §64.444). Bron (1973–79, 608) concludes concerning this passage: "Là non plus, on ne peut guère parler purement et simplement de temps converti." He is right.

[72] "Das (Kurz-)Imperfekt mit Waw consecutivum, das der Erzählung vergangener Tatsachen im Hebräischen ein charakteristischen Gepräge gibt, kommt in den phönizischen und punischen Texten, wenn überhaupt, dann nur selten vor" (Friedrich and Röllig 1999, §266). Similarly Amadasi Guzzo (1997, 321). According to Smith (1991, 18), "Phoenician generally replaced the converted imperfect with the infinitive."

[73] This text is dated to 800 BCE based on the palaeography. The reading accords with the interpretation of Dupont-Sommer (1972, 292–94). In an earlier publication (Amadasi Guzzo and Karageorghis 1977, III D 21:1, pp. 149–55), the reading of the first line is "]kr mlš ʿr z p̊lb wypg̊/d̊[ʿš]trt wʿ [" and the translation is "En souvenir. Voici un pétrissage de genévrier et un gâteau; et (l') a offert[. . . ʿŠ] TRT et [."

[74] Krahmalkov (2001, 7, 11, 13, 180) maintains that some *wyqtl* examples "express past perfective action" and adduces three Phoenician texts to prove this. The first text is an inscription from Cyprus (ninth century BCE) and I presume Krahmalkov has line 3 in view, which exhibits the verbal clause ויאבד (KAI[5] 30:3). This verb is interpreted by Donner and Röllig (1971–76 II, 48) as a *yifil* imperfective 'and he destroys', but by Friedrich and Röllig (1999, §146) as possibly jussive, "sie mögen

zugrunderichten." Krahmalkov takes the verb as past perfective short *yaqtul*. The text is extremely fragmented and the context does not confirm that a narration is intended. Krahmalkov's second example is from Sakkāra (sixth century BCE), a letter with many imperatives. Nothing invites an interpretation of a prefix verb as past tense. There is a *Ø-yqtl* form יפעל̊ך שלם 'May they give you peace!' (KAI[5] 50:3). In the same text, there is a possible (jussive) *wyqtl* clause, ותנתו לי מש[ק]ל 'and you must give me the weight' (KAI[5] 50:3–4). But ויתת (KAI[5] 50:5) must be interpreted as a suffix conjugation 1cs **yatattī* < **yatantī* 'I gave' (Friedrich and Röllig 1999, §§155, 158; Donner and Röllig 1971–76 II, 67). Krahmalkov's third example is CIS I 5510. In this case, the context is narrative or reportive and the only *w-yqtl* clause is *w-ylk* on line 9: וילך רבם אדנבעל בן גרסכן הרב וחמלכת בן חנא הרב עלש 'Et venerunt rabim Adoniba'al filius Gersaconis, ὁ rab, [10] et Ḥimilco filius Ḥannonis, ὁ rab isti…' (text and translation CIS I 5510, 9–10); '**And** the *rbm* Adnibaal son of Gescon the *rb* and Himilco son of Hanno the *rb* **went to** (*H*)*alaisa*' (English translation Schmitz 1994, 11, my emphasis). This interpretation of *wylk* is adduced also by Février (1971, 193) and Korchin (2008, 339 n. 23), but the other narrative forms in the passage, before and after *ylk*, are past time *wqtl* (suffix conjugation: *wṭnt, wtmk, wšt*), so it is reasonable to expect *wylk* to be a form of the suffix conjugation (*yifʿil*) as well, and that the suffix conjugation was conjugated as the root *ylk* (thus Garbini 1967, 10; Bron 1973–79, 609; Friedrich and Röllig 1999, §§158, 163). Since the root is *hlk*, we would expect a 3mp suffix form to be *hlk*, but cf. the 3ms suffix form *ytn* 'he gave' in KAI[5] 24:8. Friedrich and Röllig (1999, §§158, 163) regard **hlk* in Phoenician as forming the suffix conjugation from a root **ylk*. Krahmalkov (2001, 11, 187), however, vocalises *weyelekū* ('they proceeded') and regards it as a sentence-initial past perfective *yqtl*. In sum, the example from the historiographic text CIS I 5510 seems to be Krahmalkov's prime example of a past perfective *wyqtl* clause; all the others are jussives or imperfectives. This is not enough to prove the existence of a past perfective *wyqtl* in a separate Punic dialect, even if it "showed divergences from standard Tyro-Sidonian" (Krahmalkov 2001, 10). According to many scholars, there is no evidence in

Phoenician or Punic that a *w-yqtl* was used as a realis past perfective clause-type in narrative (Schmitz 1994, 11). Olmo Lete (1986, 44) says that "un imperfecto narrativo… no se comprueba en fenicio," and perhaps the cautious position of Friedrich and Röllig (1999) is the most reasonable to adopt in the present state of research.

[75] Thus also Segert (1976, §64.533); Kienast (2001, 266). Krahmalkov and Segert quote the example from Berthier and Charlier (1952–55, 32:3). The example *lypth̩* from KAI[3] 27:22–24 (Arslan Taş, seventh century BCE) quoted by Segert (1976, §57.4, with hesitation; see also KAI[3] II:42) is dubious and should probably be read *lptḥy* (thus KAI[5]). Segert (1976, §§64.533, 57.4) seems to identify the "desiderative particle" *l* with *lū*.

[76] The only longer text is the Mēšaʿ inscription (KAI[5] 181), of which 34 lines are preserved.

[77] It is quite possible that we are "dealing with a dialect continuum rather than with three 'national languages'" (Hasselbach 2013a; also Parker 2002, 44). All three appear to be closely similar to the Standard Hebrew we know from the Bible. There are some attested dialectal isoglosses that separate the Trans-Jordanian languages from CBH, but these differences do not seem to concern the usage of the verb forms.

[78] One is from Ḥorvat ʿUzza, dated to the beginning of the sixth century, and the other from Tell el-Kheleifeh, dated to the seventh or sixth century (Aḥituv 2008, 351–56).

[79] The most interesting verb form in the corpus is *w-hbrktk* 'Now I have blessed you' (clause-type *wa-qatal*), an example of an epistolary blessing formula (Aḥituv 2008, 351f.).

[80] Lemaire (2004, 368) dates it to about 810 BCE. An up-to-date collection of all Moabite texts is found in Aḥituv (2008, 387–431; cf. Fassberg 2013a).

[81] For the syntax, see Schüle (2000, 164–72).

[82] It is obvious that the vertical strokes mark off meaningful small sections in the text. They "indicate the end of a syntactic and/or semantic unit" (Niccacci 1994, 234); *pace* Andersen (1966, 88), who calls this

"parallelism," and Segert (1961, 235) who proposes, "dass diese Satztrenner die Ausbildung von zu grossen Sätzen verhüten sollten."

83 The Mēšaʿ inscription, with its first-person narrative clauses, is not a genuine narrative, in which we would expect a third-person account of the events and an absent narrator. The genre is close to Phoenician and Old Aramaic 'dedicatory inscriptions', in which five elements are usually found: (1) object dedicated (line 3, 'I have made this high place for Kemosh in Qerihoh'), (2) name of official dedicating, (3) position of official, (4) patronym, (5) deity to whom the object is dedicated, 'dedicatory inscription'. It has also an element that belongs to the genre of 'memorial': "[m]ajor events, especially military victories, and building projects" (Drinkard 1989, 135, 140).

84 Thus also Schniedewind in the Accordance translation (Schniedewind and Abegg 2005–2007).

85 Muraoka (2001, 391). Other graphically short perfective forms in the Mēšaʿ inscription are: *w-ʾrʾ* (l. 7), *w-ʾbn* (l. 9 twice), *w-ʾʿś* (l. 9), *w-ybn* (l. 10). A special problem concerns verbs III*w* which seem to retain the third radical in the short prefix form (Donner and Röllig 1971–76, II:172): *w-yʿnw* 'he oppressed' (l. 5), and the first-person jussive *ʾʿnw* 'I want to oppress', which means that Moabite has retained the distinction between verbs III*w* and III*y*, a difference that is not upheld in Phoenician (Friedrich and Röllig 1999, §175a). Segert (1961, 214, 227), instead, without convincing arguments, reads the *-w* as *-ū*.

86 The *qatal* can also be translated with the English perfect: 'But Israel has been utterly destroyed for ever:…'.

87 But Segert (1961, 223): "Imperfectum consecutivum 33mal."

88 Also semantically evident but morphologically inconclusive is the Ammonite *ygl wyśmḥ bywmt rbm wbšnt rḥqt* (KAI[5] 308:6–8), with clear jussive meaning and syntax (verb in clause-initial position)—'May he rejoice and be happy for many days and in years far off'—reminiscent of CBH (Aḥituv 2008, 363; cf. Jackson 1983, 36).

89 Features of Proto-Aramaic that constitute innovations shared by all Aramaic dialects are (Huehnergard 1991, 289): (1) change of **ṇ* to *r* in

the words for 'son', 'daughter', and 'two'; (2) levelling of the 1cp ending **-nā̆* in all environments (as against the Proto-Canaanite levelling to **-nū̆*); (3) a new Ct-stem **hittaqtal*; (4) loss of the N-stem. Later Aramaic shared innovations are (Huehnergard 1991, 288): the 3fp form *yiqtəlān* (also 2fp *tiqtəlān*), the feminine noun plural ending in *-ān*, the G-stem infinitive *miqtal*, and the definite article **-aʾ*.

[90] There was most probably a regional diversity already in Old Aramaic. I follow Fales (2011, 555, 558; see also Folmer 2012, 130; Gzella 2015, 53) concerning the chronology of Old Aramaic down to the beginning of the Assyrian imperial system of provinces in the last half of the eighth century BCE. An overview of the diversity in early Aramaic is found in Gzella (2015, ch. 2; 2017). Two Aramaic texts from a transition period between Old and Imperial Aramaic are the Nērab inscriptions (KAI[5] 225–26) from about 700 BCE (seven kilometres south-east of Aleppo). For an analysis of these texts and a discussion of the transition from Old to Imperial Aramaic, see Yun (2006, 40).

[91] Bron (1973–79, 607) quotes Cohen (1976) and maintains concerning this verbal usage that "il s'agit d'inaccompli convertis. D'après D. Cohen, l'accompli converti serait une forme plus récente." This is an unfortunate conclusion, since the past verbal usage of *yaqtul* is a retention from PS. There is no necessity of a conversion.

[92] Degen (1969, 114) identifies this *w-yqtl* as a 'Kurzimpf.' in the function of the 'Erzählform', always at the beginning of the clause. The dominant opinion about the *w-yqtl* forms in the Zakkūr inscription, before the appearance of the Tel Dan inscription, was that they represented very special cases, solemn expressions, Canaanite dialectal influence, or a deviant Aramic dialect. For an overview of the previous scholarly opinions, see Degen (1969, 114f. n. 21). Degen's conclusion in his footnote is: "Es gibt m.E. keine schwerwiegenden Gründe gegen die Annahme, daß die *wayiqtol*-Konstruktionen auch im Aa. geläufig war. Die bisher geringe Zahl an Belegen ist bloß durch die Text-Gattung der uns bekannten Denkmäler bestimmt; in weiteren erzählenden Texten können jederzeit neue Belege auftreten." Emerton (1994, 258) evaluates the *wyqtl* examples in the Zakkūr text in the light of the Tel Dan and

Deir ʿAllā inscriptions, and concludes that "the presence of *waw* consecutive with the imperfect does not tell against its identification with a form of Aramaic."

[93] For example, Segert (1975a, §§5.6.4.1.6; 6.6.3.3.2): "Man darf in diesem »imperfectum consecutivum« einen Hebraismus bzw. Kanaanismus sehen."

[94] Thus Lipiński (1994, 87); Kottsieper (1999, 55f.); Gzella (2004, 322); Renz (2016, 631f.). For a discussion of dating, see Fales (2011, 558f.), who follows Athas (2003). Lemaire's (2004, 369) dating is the second half of the ninth century BCE. For a survey of research on the Tel Dan inscription, see Hagelia (2006).

[95] Gzella (2015, 81) admits that this is "a consensus view," although he argues against it.

[96] The alternative interpretations—for example, as a circumstantial Ø-*yqtlu* like in Arabic or a purpose clause or "consecutive imperfects" (thus Athas 2003, 202, 205, 213; 2006, 251, but he analyses *yhk* as jussive: 2003, 207)—are all less convincing (see Muraoka 1995a, 20 n. 4; 2001, 389).

[97] This interpretation rests on an identification of the clausal boundaries, which cannot be established with certainty because of the damaged text. In Rainey's (2003a, 405) interpretation, the two *yaqtul* without preceding *waw* are clause-initial ([...]*ʾby ysq* '[...] my father, went up'; *wyškb ʾby* 'and my father passed away, he went ...'). Lipiński (1994, 89) restores the text before *yhk* and arrives at '[he went] out agai[nst] my father, so as to go up [to .....]', which means that *ysq* is analysed as clause-initial, introducing a purpose clause.

[98] The asyndesis in *wyškb ʾby* ***yhk*** is certainly noticeable. If the two clauses are both main line, we would expect syndesis in both. The reason could be that the '(and) **went** to [his ancestors]' is an elaboration, being a more explicit expression of the same event. Tropper (1996, 641) argues that the lack of *wa* before *yhk* must mean that there is no temporal succession between the two events, and that one of the possibilities is that the two clauses are paratactically connected, "wobei *yhk*

logisch gleichbedeutend ist mit *(w)yskb*." Hagelia (2006, 154) suggests that *yhk* could be "an epexegetic explanation" (thus close to an elaboration). The other possibility for Tropper (1996, 641) is that *yhk* is a subordinate clause expressing "eine Begleit- oder Folgehandlung zu *wyškb*." Muraoka (1995a, 20) is decidedly for an interpretation of both *yhk* and *ysq* as "preterit prefix conjugations," and thus also Halpern (1994, 64), Müller (1995), and Kottsieper (1998, 61). In all these interpretations, the *yhk* is supposed to be the old perfective *yaqtul*. Lipiński (1994, 91; see also Gzella 2004, 323 n. 65) has argued in favour of a 'long' imperfective (*yaqtulu*) interpretation of *yhk* (also of *ysq*): "It is an imperfect that expresses the finality or the consequence of the action signified by the preceding verb, without the use of any coordinating conjunction" (but cf. J-M §116h-i and Ps. 13.6).

[99] It is quite possible that this inscription—as well as the Samalian (KAI[5] 214–15; cf. Gianto 2008, 12)—should not be classified as Aramaic, since it does not contain enough of the features that are commonly regarded as constitutive of the Aramaic language group. Huehnergard (1995, 281f.) suggests the term 'Proto-Aramaoid' (without being happy with it), and this is a type of classification that Kogan (2015, 600) arrives at in his conclusions: the 'Aramaoid' branch of Central Semitic comprises, according to him, the three groups Deir ʿAllā, Samalian, and Aramaic. Lemaire (1991, 49; 2004, 371) classifies it as "araméen archaïque" (also Pardee 1991, 105). For the purpose of the present book, it is not of decisive importance whether to classify the Deir ʿAllā text as Aramaoid or Aramaic or even Canaanite. Huehnergard and Pat-El (2019, 5), whom I as a rule follow, classify Deir ʿAllā as Canaanite of the Aramaeo-Canaanite branch of Northwest Semitic. However, the proposal that the past narrative usage of *yaqtul* might be a southern (or southwestern) early Aramaic dialectal feature cannot be easily dismissed (Tropper 1993a, 404f.; Schniedewind 1996; Kottsieper 1998, 73; Rainey 2007, 81). Rainey (2007, 81) speaks of "Transjordanian languages," among which he includes the language(s) of the Zakkūr, Tel Dan, and Deir ʿAllā inscriptions as well as Moabite and Biblical Hebrew; and Kaufman (2002, 303) regrets the rigidness of the classification models and says,

"[t]he language of Deir ʿAlla is what it is; it is what it should be, something in between Hebrew, Aramaic, and Ammonite. What it is not is an example of linguistic interference." The position of Rainey and Kaufman is close to the opinion of Parker (2002, 46), who prefers to name the language after the geographical location of Deir ʿAllā: "It is not a priori necessary that the Deir ʿAllā plaster texts should have been written in any other than the local dialect... we should be content simply to classify them as written in a Deir ʿAllā dialect." But the problem with only a geographical designation is the giving up of a genetic classification.

[100] The dating of the Deir ʿAllā inscription is based on ^{14}C samplings and concerns the physical painting on the wall, which means that the (probably papyrus) original text may be from an earlier date (Fales 2011, 559, who refers to Lemaire 1991, 45). The inscription was initially classified as Aramaic (thus the *editio princeps*: Hoftijzer and Kooij 1976, 183), but later on, many scholars, with Hackett (1984), have argued that the language is South-Canaanite with an Ammonite type of script. Against this, Lipiński (1994, 109) maintains that the script "is typologically Aramaic, with no peculiar features that might be termed 'Ammonite'." Folmer (2012, 131), on the other hand, argues that the inscription is "difficult to classify as Aramaic at all." Gzella (2013a) expresses extreme scepticism as to the Aramaic nature of the inscription and puts forward the suggestion that it constitutes "the transformation and expansion of a Canaanite original by speakers of Aramaic." Moreover, in Gzella (2017, 23), he suggests "that the text goes back to a local, and perhaps oral, tradition in a Trans-Jordanian language that was then recorded in a basically Aramaic grammatical code or literally translated into Aramaic after the shift from a Canaanite to an Aramaic literary culture as a result of political developments."

[101] Thus Lipiński (1994, 105f.). Lemaire (1991, 44; 2004, 371) maintains that the plaster writing was copied from an older scroll (quoting Millard 1978, 25). The arguments of Lemaire and Millard are based on palaeographic data, and these data are confirmed by the linguistic arguments of McCarter and Pardee, who maintain that the language of

the Deir ʿAllā inscription, with its numerous Northwest Semitic retentions, is "typologically a very archaic form of Aramaic" (Pardee 1991, 105), and "much older than the particular copy of the text that was made at Deir ʿAlla" (McCarter 1991, 95, who is hesitant as to the purely Aramaic affiliation). Schniedewind (1996, 82) writes concerning the *yqtl* preterites: "this new evidence suggests that in the earliest period a *yaqtul* preterite survived in southern Aramaic dialects." And he argues that "[i]t is no longer possible to posit a sharp break between Canaanite and Aramaic until a later period." According to Rainey (2007, 81), "we now have enough evidence (three inscriptions) in Southern Old Aramaic to show that the prefix preterite narrative sequences were common to that dialect just as in Hebrew and Moabite." The natural conclusion is that the *w-yqtl* sequences in narrative represented a survival from Proto-Northwest Semitic (McCarter 1991, 93, referring to Garr 1985, 186). McCarter's (1991, 93) conclusion is that 'consecutive imperfect' is not an appropriate term from a comparative Semitic perspective. More appropriate is Pardee's (1991, 101) term "*w* + *yaqtul* preterite... [a] proto-Northwest Semitic retention attested in both Canaanite and Aramaic."

[102] Pardee (1991, 101f.) on the '*w* + *yaqtul* preterite': "it remains indisputable that this feature is present in one Old Aramaic inscription, the Zakkur inscription (KAI[5] 202), and this fact makes the appearance of the feature in another dialect of Aramaic plausible" (see also Emerton 1994). The attested cases are: Combination I: *wyʾtw* (line 1), *wyʾmrw* (line 2), *wyqm* (line 3), *wyʿl* (line 4), and *wyʾmr* (line 4–5). A probable additional instance is *wy[ ]h blʿm brbʿr* 'and [they said to] him: Balaam, son of Beor' (line 4 in the text by Hackett 1984, 25, which differs somewhat from Aḥituv 2008, 435). Lipiński (1994, 162, 166) counts as many as "seven or eight" instances and describes them as "the ancient Semitic preterit *yiqtul/iprus*."

[103] Huehnergard (1991, 289) maintains that the words *brBʿr* 'son of Beor' belong to the name and therefore the construction (with the typical Aramaic word *bar* 'son') "is external to the dialect in which the text was written." For this reason, he reckons that the word *br* 'son' is unattested

in the dialect and that the text therefore lacks any typical Aramaic feature. For the opposite view, see McCarter (1991, 89). In this connection, it should be observed that the name in the corresponding Biblical narrative (Num. 22–24) is given as *Bilʿām bɛn-Bəʿōr* (Num. 22.5), with the Hebrew word for 'son' (Pardee 1991, 103 n. 7).

104 There is no certain example of a distinctively short realis *yaqtul* (Garr 1985, 138).

105 A jussive with the prefix *l* is attested in Mesopotamian Old Aramaic (Folmer 2012, 146), for example, Tell Fekheriyeh *lhynqn* 'may they suckle', but this is probably an Akkadianism (Fales 2011, 568; against him, Garr 1985, 118f.).

106 According to Gzella (2004, 272), the syntagm *ʾal yaqtul* is a retention from Proto-Semitic.

107 The imperfective form *w-yhkn* depends on the conditional particle *hn* in line 4, and is part of a complex protasis construction.

108 These examples are from the Tell Fekheriyeh inscription (KAI[5] 309) with optative particle *l* before *yaqtul* (the example is adduced by Folmer 2012, 146). As for Imperial Aramaic, Muraoka and Porten (2003, 129f.) suppose that there was a shortening of the jussive in verbs II*wy*: II*w* *táqom* and II*y* *táśim*. Concerning the accent in Aramaic, Beyer (1984, 142) proposes that from the tenth century there was a shift to stress on the final syllable of endingless forms of the long prefix conjugation, as against stress on the initial syllable in the short *yaqtul* forms: thus KAI[5] 309 has in line 11 a jussive short *yaqtul* /láśem/ 'er setze!', but in line 12 a long imperfective /yaśím/ 'er setzt'. According to Beyer, this difference in stress prevailed in Aramaic until the seventh century BCE. Segert (1975a, §6.6.6.3.1) suggests that it is "nicht ausgeschlossen" that a verb II*w* with defective spelling, as in Dan. 4.11 תְּנֻד 'let her (the animals) flee', reveals a distinctive spelling of the short jussive; however, as the reduced prefix vowel shows, the accent lies on the stem in the Masoretic text. There are some seeming counterexamples in the Aḥiqar proverbs, such as *[ʿl] ʾnpy m[l]k ʾl tqwm* 'Before the king you should not stand up!' (TAD1 A1.1:85), possibly because of "occasional failure of

the author (or redactor) of the Proverbs of Ahiqar to keep the indicative and jussive apart” (Muraoka and Porten 2003, 130).

[109] Segert (1975a, §§5.6.5.2.3, 5.7.8.3.1) says instead that *y* = *ī* < **-iy* in the jussive; and *h* = *ē* < **ay* in the long form, as in Dan. 6.8 *ybnh* = *yiḇnē* < **yibnay*.

[110] There are very few examples of this distinction in Biblical Aramaic: Dan. 5.10 וְזִיוָ֖יךְ אַל־יִשְׁתַּנּ֑וֹ ‘and do not let your face be so pale!’ (Rosenthal 1995, §152).

[111] [ב]רֿ[ה]דֿדֿ . אבי . יסקֿ ‘Barhadad my father went up’ (KAI[5] 310:2) might be a counter-example, but it is difficult to determine the beginning of the clause.

[112] This is also the case in Imperial Aramaic (Muraoka and Porten 2003, 104, 322; Rosenthal 1995, §108).

[113] Muraoka and Porten (2003, 199) give the following distinctive example (3mp short form and not initial): אלהיא כל ישאלו שלמכי בכל עדן ‘May all gods seek after your welfare at all times!’ (TAD1, p. 40: A3.7, 1).

[114] The distinction was upheld in Egyptian Aramaic and Biblical Aramaic, and in some inscriptions from the fifth century BCE, but, since most of the paradigmatic forms were identical, the morphological distinction was lost in later Aramaic dialects (Bauer and Leander 1927, §30n; Segert 1975a, §§5.6.5.2.3, 5.7.8.4.4).

[115] ‘Energicus’ is the usual designation of this morpheme in Semitic linguistics, but *n* in Aramaic seems unlikely to possess such a connotation (Degen 1969, 80).

[116] For a discussion of the concept of Archaic Biblical Hebrew, see Pat-El and Wilson-Wright (2013); Gianto (2016). My intention is to give a contrasting survey of *yiqṭol(Ø)* in the archaic texts on points that are of interest in relation to its use in CBH. I follow mainly the results presented in Notarius (2013; 2015), and my examples will be taken from the poems that are most archaic: the Song of Moses (Deut. 32), the Song of Deborah (Judg. 5), the Song of the Sea (Exod. 15.1–18), and the epic

poetry in the Song of David (2 Sam. 22/Ps. 18. 5–20, 33–46); cf. Notarius (2013, 296; 2015, 238).

[117] The initial distinctively short *yiqṭol(Ø)!* of the copula verb (יְהִי) is problematic and possibly diachronically innovative, with a semantic merging between volitive and non-volitive (thus Notarius 2013, 205, 299f. and §§13.1.10, 13.3.2). According to Joosten (2012, 187), it is jussive; according to Tropper (1998, 174), future. Westermann (1982, 267) designates יְהִי "eine Jussivform mit indikativer Bedeutung… keinesfalls kann es den Spruch als einen Wunsch bestimmen oder als futurisch."

[118] According to Joosten (2012, 187), the *wa(y)-yiqṭol* continues a relative participle. Notarius (2013, 197): "The whole passage is generally held to have habitual semantics and there is no way to interpret v. 17b as a retrospective report." The *wa(y)-yiqṭol* "comes in clear syntactic and semantic connection to the preceding circumstantial participial phrase" (Notarius 2013, 197); it is "a sequential form that does not have any past tense reference" (Notarius 2013, 197). It "rather represents a generalizing sentence" (Notarius 2013, 60, 195). Examples of generalising present-time *wa(y)-yiqṭol* are sometimes found in texts that are usually regarded as CBH, and often in linkings with a preceding *qoṭel*-clause. Some such cases are:

1 Sam. 2.6 (*Ø-qoṭel* + *wa(y)-yiqṭol*!)—thus Ges-K (§111u); Gross (1976, 111); J-M (§118r); Notarius (2010a, 260), who calls this "generic;" Joosten (2012, 187). This passage is commonly regarded as archaic, but, considering the use of *qoṭel* in predicative position and the following general present *wa(y)-yiqṭol* "used in the same syntactic slot as the participle with waw… namely without any past-time reference," the syntax is probably late; *qoṭel* and *yiqṭol(u)* are interchangeable with *wa(y)-yiqṭol* (Notarius 2013, 256 n. 15, 259).

1 Kgs 19.14 (*wa(y)-yiqṭol* + *wa(y)-yiqṭol*).

Isa. 3.16 (*Ø-CONJ-qaṭal* + *wa(y)-yiqṭol*)—according to J-M (§118p), "After a stative qatal with a present meaning." See also Driver (1892, 40 §36); Gross (1976, 126).

Isa. 24.6 (*Ø-ADV-S.noun-qaṭal + wa(y)-yiqṭol*)—according to Watts (2007a), present: "Therefore a curse devours the land, and inhabitants in her are held guilty;" *pace* Wildberger (1978, 912), who considers it anterior: "mußten es büßen, die auf ihr wohnten."

The Book of Amos has several passages with a *qoṭel* and following gnomic *wa(y)-yiqṭol*: 5.8 (Ges-K §111u; Gross 1976, 99; J-M §118r; Joosten 2012, 187); 6.3 (Hoftijzer 1985, 4; Notarius 2007, 266; Joosten 2012, 187); 9.5 (Ges-K §111u, Gross 1976, 102; J-M §118r; Joosten 2012, 187); 9.6 (Gross 1976, 89).

[119] Bergsträsser (1918-29, II, §34h); Gross (1976, 144); Rainey (1986, 15); Waltke and O'Connnor (1990, 498); Sáenz-Badillos (1993, 58); Tropper (1998, 170); Notarius (2007, 23; 2013, 280, 307; 2015, 239); Joosten (2012, 417).

[120] It is a special problem if this morphologically short *yiqṭol* should be analysed as clause-initial, or not. It is preceded by two infinitive clauses, and infinitive construct morphemes are normally perceived as constituents in another verbal clause. But in forming a separate hemistich, the VN clauses have a more independent status, marked by the *atnāḥ*; it is possible they are to be interpreted as verbless clauses, in which case the *yiqṭol(Ø)* form is clause-initial. This is indicated by Ø- before the form in the pattern. If the infinitives are analysed as constituents in the *yiqṭol(Ø)* clause, the pattern for verse 8 is: *Ø-PREP-VN-PREP-VN-yiqṭol(Ø)!*; in this case, the short *yiqṭol* is one of very few past perfective *yiqṭol(Ø)* that are clause-internal.

[121] For this interpretation, see Isaksson (2017, 244 n. 25).

[122] In this instance, the presence of 'energic' suffixes indicates that the verbs are imperfectives (long *yiqṭol*).

[123] This translation by Notarius is semantically attractive, but presupposes an emendation to a *hifʿil* form. An interpretation that retains the text with its change of subject, e.g., 'and he ate of the produce of the fields' (NET), does not affect the presentation of the short *yiqṭol*.

[124] All three are 'preterites' according to Rainey (1986, 16); Notarius (2015, 240).

[125] For a relative diachronic evaluation of the archaic poems, see Notarius (2013, 296f.).

[126] וַיְהִי is "consistent with classical usage," and so are five more *wa(y)-yiqṭol* in the Blessing of Moses (Notarius 2013, 240f.).

[127] Bybee and Dahl (1989, 74) give the example "*Morgen bin ich schon abgefahren*, 'Tomorrow I will already have gone'." See also Ges-K (§106n); J-M (§§112h, 118s). According to Notarius (2013, 88 n. 49), "the prophetic perfect and historical present are cognate pragmatic phenomena, but opposite semantic categories. The historical present is based on a metaphorical transmission of ST into the narrative past, while the events are simultaneous with this metaphorically transmitted ST. The prophetic perfect demands that ST be metaphorically transmitted into the future, while the events occurred before this metaphorically transmitted ST." Cf. Cook (2012a, 216).

[128] The temporal interpretation of the passage is disputed. See the discussion of alternatives in Notarius (2013, 87–89).

[129] On this point, I slightly disagree with Notarius (2013, 87), though she is open to an anterior interpretation in n. 42 ("anteriority/simple past").

[130] Notarius (2013, 225 n. 43), against tradition, interprets כָּמֹהוּ as referring to 'the death of righteous ones'. Other examples of clause-initial jussive *yiqṭol(Ø)* in affirmative clauses: Gen. 49.8b; 49.26; Exod. 15.9; Num. 24.7; Deut. 32.1 (Ø-IMP + *wa-yiqṭol(Ø)-A* + *wa-yiqṭol*, probably not purposive, *pace* Notarius 2013, 101); 32.2; 32.38; 33.6 (*Ø-yiqṭol(Ø)!* + *wa-ʾal-yiqṭol(Ø)!* + *wa-yiqṭol!*); 33.10 (*Ø-yiqṭol(Ø)* + *Ø-yiqṭol(Ø)*, jussives; Notarius 2013, 248); 33.24; Judg. 5.21b (*Ø-yiqṭol(Ø)*, archaic second-person jussive; Notarius 2013, 140, 147, 292; Ges-K §118m).

[131] The verb form תֶּשִׁי is regarded as a (distinctive) short *yiqṭol* by most scholars. See further Finley (1981, 246); Waltke and O'Connor (1990, 558); Tropper (1998, 170); Notarius (2013, 78, 240, 286; 2015, 240).

[132] Another example is Gen. 49.4 (*Ø-VN-ʾal-yiqṭol(Ø)!* + *kī-qaṭal* + *ʾāz-qaṭal*), where VN is adverbial (Notarius 2013, 191: 'Unstable as water').

[133] According to Notarius (2013, 293f.), "volitive forms are commonly non-initial in the clause." Examples: Judg. 5.2 (*bə-VN-bə-VN-IMP*); 5.3b (*Ø-S.pron-PrP-S.pron-yiqṭol(Ø)-A* + *Ø-yiqṭol(Ø)*; Notarius 2013, 140, 145f. n. 86, 292); 5.9 (*Ø-XØ* + *Ø-VOC-IMP*); 5.10 (*Ø-VOC-VOC-VOC-IMP*); Ps. 18.50 (*Ø-ADV-yiqṭol(Ø)* + *wa-PrP-yiqṭol(Ø)-A*); but 2 Sam. 22.50 (*Ø-ADV-yiqṭol(Ø)* + *wa-PrP-yiqṭol(Ø)*)—*pace* Notarius (2013, 153, 169), who analyses the two prefix forms as "present progressive for immediate future use," in spite of the ventive/cohortative clitic (with *-ā*) in Ps. 18.50.

[134] Notarius' (2013) translations generally conform to the NRSV, and this is the case here.

[135] Gibson (1994, §129) writes: "Consequence may be expressed by simple *Vav* with jussive." See also J-M (§§116e, 169b). Other *wa-yiqṭol* clauses expressing various shades of purpose or consequence in archaic poetry: Deut. 32.1 (*Ø-IMP* + *wa-yiqṭol(Ø)-A* + *wa-yiqṭol(Ø)*, possibly with purpose meaning; Notarius 2013, 101); 32.38 (*Ø-yiqṭol(Ø)* + *wa-yiqṭol(Ø)* + *Ø-yiqṭol(Ø)!*); 32.41 (*Ø-ʾim-qaṭal* + *wa-yiqṭol(Ø)*, jussive with future purposive force; Notarius 2013, 293).

[136] It is to be regretted that Notarius uses imprecise terminology on this point. She employs the term "conditional mood" (Notarius 2013, 220), disregarding the fact that the syntaxes of protasis and apodosis are different and must be held distinct from one another, since they constitute separate domains (see §1.2.4).

[137] I use the imprecise term 'sentence' (with hesitation) when it is obvious that it involves several clauses. The term 'conditional clause' referring to the linking of protasis and apodosis (thus Notarius 2013, 99, 116) is not appropriate, since the term clause should be confined to a syntagm with one predication.

[138] Notarius (2008, 83) says this is a jussive used in "conditional or rather subjunctive mood." Her translation (Notarius 2013, 220) is neither conditional nor subjunctive: 'The one who will rule out of Jacob will destroy the survivors of Ar'.

[139] Unfortunately, Ges-K (§§109h–k) makes no attempt to classify the examples diachronically. The adduced passages are (in order):

(1) Ps. 45.11–12 has the pattern [11]*Ø-IMP + wa-IMP + wa-IMP +* [12]*wa-yiqṭol(Ø)! + kī-XØ + wa-IMP*. The *wa-yiqṭol(Ø)* clause expresses a logical consequence or purpose after the IMP clauses in verse 11. The *wa-yiqṭol(Ø)* concludes the first hemistich in verse 12, and there then follows a *kī*-clause, so this cannot be a protasis. NET takes the *wa-yiqṭol* as a volitive consequence: 'Listen, O princess! Observe and pay attention! Forget your homeland and your family! **Then** the king **will be attracted** by your beauty. After all, he is your master! Submit to him!'. Kraus (1978, 486) takes וְיִתְאָו as a *wa(y)-yiqṭol* clause, 'Und er begehre deine Schönheit'.

(2) Ps. 104.20 is as dubious as Ps. 45.12. The pattern *Ø-yiqṭol(Ø)*! + *wa-yiqṭol(Ø)*! represents a late usage of the short prefix form to express a general present, in the same way as in Gen. 49.17 (Notarius 2013, 197, 205f., 299f.; thus also Westermann 1982, 267), a stage with a semantic merging between volitive and non-volitive moods of the prefix conjugation, in such a way that clause-initial forms are represented as morphologically short and non-initial forms are written long.

(3) Exod. 22.4; see §3.4.2, example (103).

(4) Lev. 15.24 has the pattern (*wa-ʾim-VNabs-yiqṭol(u)* + *wa-yiqṭol(Ø)*!) + *wa-qaṭal*, where the protasis is set within parentheses. It is introduced by a *ʾim… yiqṭol(u)* construction and the internal *wa-yiqṭol(Ø)*! constitutes a result clause *within* the protasis. This is a possibility that Milgrom (1991, 940) is open to, but Driver (1892, §172) argues that in this case an infinitive *lihyōt* "might be substituted for the jussive," which semantically means a consequence clause within the protasis. Milgrom (1991, 941) falsely concludes that, since "MT's *ûtĕtî* rather indicates a consequence," it must belong with the apodosis. If the *wa-yiqṭol(Ø)*! in Lev. 15.24 belongs to the protasis, it is certainly not a good example of a short *yiqṭol(Ø)* expressing a condition.

(5) Isa. 41.28 (with preceding verse) shows the pattern [27]*Ø-ADV-PrP-wa-PrP-O.noun-yiqṭol(u)* + [28]***wa-yiqṭol(Ø)***! + *wa-XØ* + *wa-XØ* + *wa-yiqṭol(Ø)* + *wa-yiqṭol(Ø)*, and the distinctively short *wa-yiqṭol* (וְאֵ֫רֶא) is best interpreted as a purpose clause, as are also the two concluding *wa-yiqṭol* in the verse (וְאֶשְׁאָלֵ֖ם וְיָשִׁ֥יבוּ דָבָֽר׃), as Elliger (1978, 171) translates: "daß ich sie fragte und sie Antwort gäben." My translation: '[27]I first sent a message to Zion, and a herald to Jerusalem, [28] **to look**, but there was no one, among them there was no one who could serve as an adviser, so that I might ask questions and they give me answers'; the introductory *wə-ʾērɛ̄* is never interpreted as a condition, but sometimes, without support in the text, as a temporal clause, as in Watts (2007b, 645), 'When I looked, there was no one'. Elliger (1978, 175f.), on the other hand, emendates the text, deleting the initial *wa-yiqṭol(Ø)*! clause.

(6) Ezek. 14.7 is LBH and the pattern is conditional linking: (*kī-S.noun-REL-yiqṭol(u)* + *wa-yiqṭol(u)* + *wa-yiqṭol(Ø)*! + *wa-O.noun-yiqṭol(u)*! + *wa-qaṭal*) + *Ø-S.pron-yiqṭol(u)*!. The short *wa-yiqṭol(Ø)*! (*wə-yaʿal*) is an internal part of the complex protasis, but does not initiate the protasis. It has the same meaning as the preceding *wa-yiqṭol(u)* and shows that the writer's linguistic competence did not correctly perceive the difference between short and long *yiqṭol*.

(7) Job 34.29 is late, probably from the Persian period (Horst 1974, xii). The verse is constructed by two conditional linkings, in which the first protasis has the structure *wa-S.pron-yiqṭol(u)!*, and the second protasis, apparently parallel, has the pattern *wa-yiqṭol(Ø)!* In this stage of the language, the semantic distinction between the two prefix forms has been lost. What remains of the old distinction is that clause-initial forms are short and, in non-clause-initial position, long forms are used (Joosten 2015, 33f.).

(8) 2 Kgs 6.27: this is not CBH proper, and belongs to a linguistic state later than the Pentateuch. The adduced form is not morphologically distinctive, but the classification as short *yiqṭol(Ø)* is seemingly se-

cured by the preceding negation (אַל־יוֹשִׁעֲךָ יְהוָה). Ges-K (§109h) interprets the utterance erroneously as a negative protasis, possibly presupposing an emendation to אִם לֹא (thus also HALOT). But, according to HALOT, the particle *ʾal* may also be an emphatic negation 'no!', which yields the plausible translation 'No, let the LORD help you!' (thus NET, NRSV). If the text is emended (אִם לֹא יוֹשִׁעֲךָ יְהוָה), the verb must be interpreted as *yiqṭol(u)* and is no longer a proof of a *yiqṭol(Ø)* starting a protasis.

[140] On this point, it reflects the usage of the equivalent form in Ugaritic poetry: "Ugaritic *yʿn*, for example, means 'he replied', whether preceded by *w*, *wyʿn* 'and he replied', or used alone" (Fenton 1973, 32).

[141] There are few, if any, traces in the Hebrew inscriptions of the so-called *nun paragogicum*, which in other Northwest Semitic languages may distinguish a long imperfective form *yaqtulūn* (3mp, similarly 2fs and 2mp) from a short perfective (usually jussive) *yaqtulū*. A possible but unclear example of *nun* paragogicum is Kuntillet ʿAğrūd 15:2 [1]]*wbzrḥ* . *ʾl* . *br*[[2]]*wymsn hrm*['[1]] and when God shone forth ... [[2]] and the mountains melted', where *wymsn* is seemingly a *nifʿal wa(y)-yiqṭol* clause with *nun paragogicum*, a combination that occurs now and then also in CBH (Deut. 1.22; 4.11; 5.23; Judg. 8.1; 11.18; see also Amos 6.3). This example from the early eighth century is quoted from Dobbs-Allsopp et al. (2005, 287); cf. Renz and Röllig (1995–2003, I:59 n. 3)

[142] *Pace* Gogel's (1998, 95 n. 51) estimation of the IIwy *hifʿil* jussive form, *yʾr* 'may he cause to shine' (root *ʾwr*), which he puts on a par with the morphologically distinctive 'short' III*wy* forms that will be quoted below (*yhy*, *yrʾ*, *ykl*). It does not help that Gogel quotes parallel uses of *yʾr* in BH. He is right that the *yʾr* in Ketef Hinnom 2:8 is a jussive, but it must be stated emphatically that *yʾr* is not morphologically distinctive. It is also strange that Gogel (1998, 95) calls *ykl* a "jussive" in *wykl* 'and he finished' (Meṣad Ḥashavyahu 1:5). For a critique of Gogel's morphosyntactic analyses, see Rainey (2001).

[143] The text of the Hebrew inscriptions in this section follows Dobbs-Allsopp et al. (2005 = HI).

[144] The example יהוה ישאל לשלמכ (Arad 18:2), which Gogel (1998, 288) translates as jussive, is probably an expression of assurance with long *yiqṭol*: 'YHWH will concern himself with your well-being'.

[145] I follow HI's (14) interpretation of the 2ms *hifʿil* והסבת as 'hand over', but I prefer not to translate it with an imperative.

[146] This example is datable to the late seventh/second half of the seventh century BCE (Gogel 1998, 24). My translation follows in the main that of HI (p. 359).

[147] This hypothesis is attractive because of the frequency of the verb in BH. See, for the scholarly discussion, Renz and Röllig (1995, I:325 n. 1), Gogel (1998, 95 n. 52), and Schade (2006, 272).

[148] The translation is Gogel's (1998, 92). The context is **פנ·יקרה** את ה 17 עיר·דבר· 'lest something happens to the [17] city'.

[149] The translation is Gogel's (1998, 92). The (rather fragmentary) context is: ארר·אשר·**ימחה** 'Cursed be the one who effaces…'.

[150] The context is fragmentary and we do not know what precedes the verb: 3 שערמ **ימנה** 3 [---], but it is reasonable to translate as an obligation 'he shall count out three (seah-measures) of barley'.

[151] Thus convincingly Schüle (2000, 173f.), HI (360f.), and Aḥituv (2008, 161).

[152] The syntagm ואסמ is commonly analysed as a *wa-qaṭal* clause with the same meaning as the preceding *wa(y)-yiqṭol* clauses. Renz and Röllig (1995, I:325 n. 2) suggest instead that it serves "zur Kennzeichnung der Umstände der mit Impf. consec. bezeichneten Haupthandlung," but prefer to interpret ואסמ as "Inf. absol. als Fortführung der beiden vorangehenden Impf. consec." The syntagm ואסמ could theoretically also be analysed as a 1cs *wa(y)-yiqṭol* form with weak pronunciation of the first root consonant (J-M §§73a, g), if a switch to first person would be acceptable in this type of context (cf. Schade 2006, 272). However, at the time of this 'letter' (the genre is disputed by Dobbs-Allsopp 1994), we may expect *wa-qaṭal* to regain the temporal value of a *qaṭal* in some positions, for example after a *qaṭal* clause, as can be seen in Isa. 40.12

(*qaṭal* + *wa-O.noun-qaṭal* + *wa-qaṭal* + *wa-qaṭal*), which is an example of transitional Hebrew syntax (Hornkohl 2016a).

[153] This loss of final short vowels occurred both in Canaanite and in Aramaic (Hasselbach and Huehnergard 2008, 412, 414; Baranowski 2016b, 11).

[154] An early résumé of the main arguments for a separate origin of the *yiqṭol* part in *wa(y)-yiqṭol* as opposed to the long *yiqṭol* is found in Finley (1981, 242). The dropping of final vowels is Blau's stage iii. According to Blau (2010, 150f.), long and short prefix forms were first distinguished by stress, short form **yíqtol*, long form *yiqtól* < **yiqtólu*. Later, stress shifted to the ultima also in the short prefix form, *yiqtól*, so that the two converged in most paradigmatic positions.

[155] Hans Bauer was the first to argue that *yaqtul* was the more ancient form; see Cook (2012a, 102). Contra my false position in Isaksson (1986), Bauer's *arguments* for the priority of *yaqtul* (the "Kurz-Aorist") were weak, but his position was correct.

[156] On this point, I follow Brockelmann (1908–13, I, §260g); see also Huehnergard and Pat-El (2019, 7). Bauer and Leander (1922, 297c) propose 3fp **yaqtulā* and 2fp **tVqtVlā*.

[157] The prefix *t-* developed by analogy with the singular feminine form.

[158] The *lā yaqtul* clause-type is attested at Amarna, but is not found in Biblical Hebrew, not even in the archaic language. In Biblical Hebrew, **lō yiqṭol(Ø)* has been replaced by *lō qaṭal*.

[159] Bauer and Leander (1922, 300o); Voigt (1987, 8); Garr (1998, xlviif.); Hasselbach and Huehnergard (2008, 416); Kummerow (2008, 76); Bloch (2009, 41 n. 31); Blau (2010, 152, 205); Gzella (2011a, 442; 2013c, 859; 2018, 27); Kogan (2015, 162f.). Sjörs (2023, 114 n. 51) also concludes that paragogic *nun* may reflect the imperfective morpheme **-nV*, since "[t]he "function of paragogic *nun* of the imperfective has proven difficult to determine." There are also some rare cases where the *nun paragogicum* is added to a *wa(y)-yiqṭol* syntagm (Deut. 1.22; 4.11 twice; 5.23; Judg. 8.1; 11.18; Isa. 41.5; Ezek. 44.8; Amos 6.3), or to a *qaṭal* form (Deut. 8.3; 8.16).

[160] The problem with this hypothesis (an imperfective built on the old *yaqtul*) is that "there is no attested grammaticalization path between the resultative-perfect-perfective path with which **yaqtul* is associated (based on its *iprus* Akkadian reflex) and the progressive-imperfective path with which **yaqtulu* is usually associated" (Cook 2012a, 220). The alternative that offers itself is to recognise the apparent morphological affinity between the infinitive, the imperative, the short *yiqṭol*, and the long *yiqṭol*, and to consider the infinitive to have been an original building block of both short and long *yiqṭol* (and the imperative). As for the long *yiqṭol*, its origin is then "fully in keeping with a common lexical source of progressives: locative constructions involving infinitives" (Cook 2012a, 220, 263 n. 98, referencing Bybee et al. 1994, 128; Heine and Kuteva 2002, 202).

[161] I follow Bauer and Leander (1922, 231b, 388i), who regard this shortening of the long stem vowel in closed syllables to be Proto-Semitic, but this is not certain. The shortening seems to be supported, however, by the data in Central Semitic.

[162] The free-standing indicative short *yiqṭol* is attested in the archaic poetry (see §3.2).

[163] Blau (2010, 151) instead regards the stress pattern in וַיָּ֫קָם as a retention of the general penultimate stress of the short prefix form in stage iii.

[164] The latter form in Proto-Hebrew according to Blau (2010, 196).

[165] Other examples of 'long' *yiqṭol(Ø)* forms in the Pentateuch and Judges: Gen. 19.17 (2ms irrealis, unusual plene writing); 27.31 (3ms irrealis, defective writing); Exod. 2.7 (3fs irrealis purpose, defective); 19.4 (1cs realis, defective); Lev. 20.23 (1cs realis, defective); 20.26 (1cs realis, defective); Judg. 6.18 (*Ø-ʾal-nā-yiqṭol(Ø)* 'long', 2ms irrealis, defective).

[166] Third radicals *w/y* were preserved in Proto-Semitic. They were elided in the individual Semitic languages (Blau 2010, 249).

[167] It seems that the shortening of the *yaqtul* forms of verbs III*wy* was a development after the Proto-Semitic stage, and for this class of verbs

the term 'apocopation' is appropriate. Historically, it is a false conclusion to regard this as an apocopation of the *yiqṭol(u)* form. The *yiqṭol(u)* form is not involved at all. The shortening concerns the expected result of the original endings *aw, ay, iw, iy, uw, uy* in the short *yiqṭol.* In some lexical cases, the root may also have been biradical (Blau 2010, 249, 251).

[168] For the short *yiqṭol* with the ventive/cohortative clitic *-ā*, see §1.2.2 and §3.4.2.3.

[169] According to J-M (§79m n. 2), "In the OT there are altogether 1,300 properly apocopated forms of Lamed-He verbs as against 110 non-apocopated ones, of which only three occur in the Pentateuch, all 1 sg. (see Stipp 1987). The non-apocopated 56 cases of 1sg. may be interpreted as cohortative in form." See also Ges-K (§49e); Stipp (1987); Tropper (1998, 164f.).

[170] Ges-K (§75t); Gross (1976, 41: "wohl… koordinierter Injunktiv"); Stipp (1987, 138); Waltke and O'Connor (1990, 566); J-M (§79m, and p. 376, n. 1); Diehl (2007, 36). Robar (2014, 80) regards it as a long *yiqṭol* with jussive meaning. I prefer the reading as purpose clause, as in Westermann (1976, 107, 167): "daß das Trockene sichtbar werde."

[171] Tropper (1998, 165) suggests that this is due to a slackening of awareness of the distinction betwwen the short and long prefix form and that "das Wissen um die unterschiedliche Herkunft und Funktion von PK^{L} und PK^{K} im Laufe der hebr. Sprachgeschichte offenbar bereits früh im Schwinden begriffen war." The data given by Stipp concern primarily indicative, not jussive, long *wa(y)-yiqṭol* forms. The other instances of indicative *yiqṭol* (mostly *wa(y)-yiqṭol*) forms in the Pentateuch, Joshua, and Judges are: Gen. 24.48 (*wa(y)-yiqṭol* + *wa(y)-yiqṭol*, long 1cs); Deut. 1.16 (*wa(y)-yiqṭol*, long 1cs); Josh. 9.24 (*wa(y)-yiqṭol* + *wa(y)-yiqṭol*, long 1cp); 10.40 (*wa(y)-yiqṭol* (long) + *Ø-lō-qaṭal*, 3ms); 19.50 (*wa(y)-yiqṭol* (long) + *wa(y)-yiqṭol*, 3ms); Judg. 2.1 (*Ø-yiqṭol(Ø)* (long) + *wa(y)-yiqṭol* (long), 1cs)—this is a disputed past perfective without proclitic *wa*, thus Tropper (1998, 16), but Joosten (1999, 24; 2012, 117), regards it as *yiqṭol(u)*, and J-M (§113g) alleges

"Durative action," while, according to Bloch (2009, 46 n. 49), it is a scribal mistake due to the following 'long' form *wā-ʾāḇī*; 12.3 (*wa(y)-yiqṭol* (long), 1cs); 19.2 (*wa(y)-yiqṭol* (long) + *wa(y)-yiqṭol*, 3fs).

[172] For realis, I also use the term indicative.

[173] Joosten (2012, 184) translates: 'whose flesh is half consumed when it comes out of its mother's womb'.

[174] Ges-K (§111u) describes this as a present action.

[175] Of the six attested examples of *nifʿal wa(y)-yiqṭol* clauses of this root in the Hebrew Bible, three are part of a narrative chain and have stativic past reference ('was/were left over': Gen. 32.25; Josh. 18.2; Judg. 9.5), but three are in direct speech report and best interpreted as stativic presents: Gen. 44.20; 1 Kgs 19.10; 19.14 (De Vries 2003, 232, 233, 236). Only one additional example of a stativic *wa(y)-yiqṭol* with present meaning is found in my corpus: Deut. 22.16, best interpreted as a stativic verb with present meaning, as in Christensen (2002, 513) 'and he hates her'. Outside my corpus, there are only a few cases in probable CBH texts: 1 Sam. 2.29 (Ges-K §111r; J-M §118q; Waltke and O'Connor 1990, §33.3.3c); 14.28 (Driver 1913, 114); 2 Sam. 1.27, in poetry, translated by Anderson (1989, 11) as 'How are the warriors fallen! Lost are the weapons of war!'.

[176] It must be admitted that זָקֵן is ambiguous and can be an adjective. This does not affect the analysis of the following *wa(y)-yiqṭol*.

[177] Wenham (1994, 197) translates, 'When Isaac was old and his eyesight was too poor for him to see'. Westermann (1981, 525) translates, 'und seine Augen erloschen waren'. Other examples of *wa(y)-yiqṭol* clauses with stativic verbs and past reference: Gen. 2.25; 6.6, 11 (Joosten 2012, 168); 25.28, 34; 27.1 (Wenham 1994, 197); 29.18; 34.7; 35.16 (Joosten 2012, 169 n. 24); 39.2; 46.12; Exod. 20.11; 38.24; Num. 3.17; 11.26 (within a series of *wa(y)-yiqṭol* clauses: 'and the spirit rested upon them'; Budd 1984, 123); Judg. 3.11, 30; 4.21—the accents support Sasson (2014, 251, 269), that PP and the first *wa(y)-yiqṭol* belong together in the description of a state; 5.31; 8.28; 18.31; 19.2; 20.46.

[178] For the ventive meaning of this paragogic *heh*, see Sjörs (2023, ch. 6).

[179] I am aware that the particle *kī* can be interpreted as a general deictic subordinator 'that', as in Brockelmann's (1956, §159a) translation: 'und es geschah, daß wir in das Nachtquartier kamen'. This does not alter the interpretation of the last *wa(y)-yiqṭol* clause.

[180] LXX translates with aorist and *νῦν*. Westermann (1982, 125) translates with present tense, 'Dies bringen wir hiermit zurück'. Wenham (1994, 414) translates, 'so we have brought it with us'.

[181] According to Milgrom (2000, 1762), "Whereas holiness is God's *nature* and is apprehensible solely from his selfrevelation, separation is the result of his *act*."

[182] Other examples of anterior *wa(y)-yiqṭol* clause(s) after anterior *qaṭal* clause(s): Gen. 19.9 (Gross 1976, 125; Joosten 2012, 191; Bergström 2014, 127); 19.19 (Bergström 2014, 127); 24.35 (Joosten 2012, 182; Bergström 2014, 128); 27.36; 27.36; 30.6; 32.5b–6 (Joosten 2012, 185); 32.29; 32.31; 33.10 (Westermann 1981, 636, but close to stativic present); 45.8; Exod. 1.18 (Joosten 2012, 180, 182); 3.8a (preceded by both present anterior *qaṭal* and present stativic *qaṭal*); 31.3; 32.8; 35.31 (*rəʾū Ø-qaṭal* + [31]*wa(y)-yiqṭol*); Num. 14.24a; 23.4; Judg. 6.13c; 10.10b (Butler 2009, 253); 16.10 (Boling 1975a, 246; Joosten 2012, 182).

[183] Thus Milgrom (1991, 381, 432). Other examples of a more general anterior expressed by *wa(y)-yiqṭol* clauses: Gen. 30.27; Num. 11.20; Deut. 4.33 (with 'double-duty', elliptic, interrogative particle; Joosten 2012, 191 n. 70).

[184] I disagree with Moshavi (2010, 113), who assumes that the two *wa(y)-yiqṭol* clauses that follow וְרָחֵ֖ל לָקְחָ֑ה do not share its pluperfect meaning. Other *wa(y)-yiqṭol* clauses with pluperfect meaning: Gen. 26.18 (within a relative clause: «*REL-qaṭal* + *wa(y)-yiqṭol*»; Ges-K §111q); 28.6, 7 (both Ges-K §111q); 31.19 (Ges-K §111q); 39.13 (Wenham 1994, 371); Exod. 2.11 'Moses had grown up'; 12.35; Num. 14.36 (within a complex relative sentence; Ges-K §111q); 21.26; 26.19; Judg.

1.16; 3.26; 4.11 (*nip̄rāḏ* is a *nifʿal* participle, so this pluperfect *wa(y)-yiqṭol* does not succeed a pluperfect *qaṭal*); 18.22 (part of background).

[185] Other examples of perfective *wa(y)-yiqṭol* with a meaning that includes iterative action or extends over a period of time: Gen. 30.30 (extended period); 30.39 (iterative; Joosten 2012, 174); 31.40 (iterative; Joosten 2012, 182); 33.3 (iterative; Joosten 2012, 174f.); 35.3 (*DEF-qoṭel* + *wa(y)-yiqṭol*, habitual past in discourse; Joosten 2012, 185); 37.2 (iterative and part of background; Joosten 2012, 174, 178); 50.3 (parade example of extended period); Exod. 16.21 (iterative; Joosten 2012, 174); Num. 14.22 (iterative; Joosten 2012, 185); Deut. 2.12—iterative, with an unusual switch from past habitual *yiqṭol(u)* to perfective *wa(y)-yiqṭol*: in this case, Joosten (1999, 24) regards *yiqṭol(u)* *yīrāšūm* as "anomalous;" Judg. 4.5 (with a switch from *qoṭel* to perfective and implicitly iterative *wa(y)-yiqṭol*; Joosten 2012, 174); 6.4 (with a switch from habitual *wa-qaṭal* to perfective *wa(y)-yiqṭol* and back to habitual *wa-lō-yiqṭol(u)*; Joosten 2012, 177); 9.25, iterative (Joosten 2012, 174); 16.16.

[186] Realis uses of 'waw-less' *yiqṭol(Ø)* verbs are attested in the Archaic Hebrew poetry; see §3.2. Unfortunately, Tropper (1998, 169f.) does not distinguish diachronic layers in BH. His examples of "PK^{K} (allein)" are mostly archaic poetry (Exod. 15.5; Judg. 5.26; Ps. 18.4–20; Deut. 32) or other poetic texts that are usually notoriously difficult to evaluate diachronically (Ps. 47; 68; 90; 107; Job). His analysis of the long form *ʾaʿălɛ̄* in Judg. 2.1 as narrative *yiqṭol(Ø)* is possible, but difficult to prove (Gzella 2021, 75, 81), though it might involve a ventive clitic. And *yaʿăśɛ̄* in 1 Kgs 7.8 is probably a relative clause with *yiqṭol(u)*. His example from Isa. 12.1 might be CBH, but the adduced short forms (יָשֹׁב and וּתְנַחֲמֵנִי) are jussives (Wildberger 1972, 477: 'so wende sich dein Zorn, daß du mich tröstest'; Watts 2007a, 218: 'May your anger turn that you may comfort me'). Finally, Tropper's Isa. 42.6; Hos. 6.1; 11.4; and Dan. 8.12 do not represent CBH syntax (for Hosea, see Notarius 2007, 201–211). The examples of *waw*-less *yiqṭol(Ø)* forms with past meaning mentioned by Bloch (2009) are either archaic poetry or late texts with an archaising style (Isa. 41.1–5; Ps. 44).

[187] This example is mentioned as jussive in Ges-K (§§53n, 109h); Bauer and Leander (1922, 333z); Bergsträsser (1918–1929 II, §19i*). According to Tropper (1998, 174), short prefix conjugation forms in a protasis should be interpreted as indicative (not jussive). His examples are from Akkadian and Arabic. The only Hebrew example he adduces is quoted from Ges-K (§109h), Ps. 104.20a, and he admits that J-M (§167a) has another interpretation of the two jussives ('Make darkness and let the night come'). Driver (1892, §171) regards the form in Exod. 22.4 as a problematic jussive. There are lots of examples of morphologically distinctive initial *kī-yiqṭol(u)!* in protases in CBH, but no *kī-yiqṭol(Ø)!*: Exod. 12.48; 21.14; 21.20; 21.33; 23.05; Lev. 1.2; 2.1; 2.4; 11.39; 12.2; 13.16; 13.31; 15.25; 19.33; 25.25; 25.35; 25.39; 25.47; 27.2; Num. 5.12; 6.2; 6.9; 9.10; 9.14; 19.14; 27.8; Deut. 4.25; 13.2; 19.16; 21.22. Similarly, there is no *ʾim-yiqṭol(Ø)!* in CBH. Examples of distinctively long *ʾim-yiqṭol(u)!* introducing a protasis in CBH: Gen. 4.7 (2 ×); Exod. 18.23; 21.11 (*wa-ʾim-O.noun-lō-yiqṭol(u)*!); 21.19; 21.23; 21.27; 40.37; Lev. 2.14; 4.32; 5.1; 5.7; 5.11; 13.7; 13.22; 13.27; 13.35; 13.53; 13.57; 14.44; 27.10; 27.16; 27.17; 27.18; 27.22; Num. 12.6; 20.19; 30.7; 30.9; 30.15; 36.4; Deut. 20.12; 30.4; 30.17; Judg. 11.10; 13.16. See also 1 Sam. 1.11; Amos 3.6.

[188] Codex Leningradensis reads אֱל־, but most other MT MSS read the expected אַל־ (Propp 1999, 307).

[189] Another possible example of asyndetic complement clauses, albeit in archaic poetry, is Deut. 32:29 (*lū-qaṭal* + *Ø-yiqṭol(Ø)* + *Ø-yiqṭol(Ø)*): 'Would that they were wise, **that they understood** this, **that they would discern** their future!'.

[190] Other examples of syndetic irrealis *yiqṭol(Ø)* complement clauses: Gen. 41.34 (*Ø-yiqṭol(Ø)* + *wa-yiqṭol(Ø)*!) 'Let Pharaoh proceed to appoint' (NRS)—but Westermann (1982, 95) has only coordination with the same subject; Exod. 8.4 (Ø-IMP + *wa-yiqṭol(Ø)*!)—*pace* Qimron (1986–87, 152), who regards it a purpose clause; Lev. 10.17 (Ø-IMP + *wa*-IMP + *wa-yiqṭol(Ø)*!); 16.2 (IMP + *wa-ʾal-yiqṭol(Ø)*); Judg. 13.4 (*wa-ʿattā-IMP-nāʾ* + *wa-ʾal-yiqṭol(Ø)* + *wa-ʾal-yiqṭol(Ø)*); 14.15 (Ø-IMP + *wa-yiqṭol(Ø)*!; Stipp 1987, 137).

[191] It is not easy to find first-person jussive forms without the clitic in CBH: Gen. 24.57 (*Ø-yiqṭol*), 58; 30.32; 33.15; 38.16 (but possibly a long *yiqṭol*; Joosten 2012, 319 n. 22); Exod. 15.9 (3×, but archaic); Deut. 10.2; Judg. 16.20 (2×).

[192] Examples in the corpus of 'full' III*wy* forms that represent jussives with 'hidden' ventive/energic morpheme: Gen. 1.26 (Sjörs 2019); 2.18; 6.7; 11.4 (2×; Sjörs 2019, 14); 16.26 (*wa-yiqṭol-(ā = V) + wa-yiqṭol-(L = V)*); 18.21; 19.32 (2×); 19.34; 24.14, 49; 26.3 (above); 27.9; 30.3 (ventive in the first-person form); 30.31 (above); 31.3; 35.3 (2×); 37.10; 42.2; 43.8 (*wa-yiqṭol-(ā = V) + wa-yiqṭol-(ā = V) + wa-yiqṭol-(L = V)*); 46.31; 47.19 (2×); 50.5; Exod. 3.3; 4.18; 17.2; 32.10 'from you I will make <me> a great nation'; 32.13; Num. 11.15 וְאַל־אֶרְאֶה (Dallaire 2014, 116); 14.12; 16.21; 17.10; Deut. 3.25; 9.14; 12.30 (Joosten 2012, 146); Judg. 6.39 (Zewi 1999, 155); 11.37a (third-person passive with preposition *lī*: יֵעָשֶׂה לִּי); 11.37b; 18.9.

[193] This holds also for Old Aramaic, where the negation *ʾal* became a signal of a short *yaqtul* (Kottsieper 1999, 68 n. 57). Morphologically 'short' *yiqṭol(u)* forms are rare in CBH: Gen. 24.8 לֹא תָשֵׁב (Ø-ADV-*O.noun-lō-yiqṭol(u)* [short])—thus Ges-K (§109k), but Tropper (1998, 177) regards it a jussive with negation *lō*; and Deut. 7.16 לֹא־תָחֹס (*lō-yiqṭol(u)* [short])—a variant *yiqṭol(u)* form, according to Bauer and Leander (1922, 399h); Bergsträsser (1929, 2, §28d).

[194] In Old Aramaic also, the loss of final vowels and the subsequent coalescence of most *yaqtul* and *yaqtulu* forms was the driving force behind the transformation of the verbal system (Kottsieper 1999, 73). But developments in Aramaic took another direction. Instead of a retention of the different prefix conjugations, as in CBH, the *qatal* morpheme took over completely as the narrative form, except in the most ancient inscriptions (see §3.1.11).

[195] Many scholars have concluded that "*yaqtulu* and *yaqtul* have *merged* in Hebrew to form a (nearly) common conjugation" (Waltke and O'Connor 1990, 469; this seems to be the position also of the authors themselves). The problem with such a position is the impreciseness of the

term 'Hebrew'. Waltke and O'Connor indicate that this merger occurred in Proto-Hebrew, not in the extant biblical texts. The position held in the present book is that the distinction is still upheld in Archaic Biblical Hebrew and CBH (the classical language corresponding to my corpus; see §1.2.3). The steps to a merger can be observed in LBH.

[196] For the cases of irregular word order in CBH, see §3.4.4.

[197] This tendency is found also in Old Aramaic (Kottsieper 1999, 68).

[198] For the (relatively late) history of this idea in Hebrew research, see Joosten (2011b, 213).

[199] Gzella (2012c, 101): "so word-order constraints to some extent restore the functional differentiation." A similar position is taken by Gentry (1998, 12): "The earlier framework was preserved and problems occasioned by loss of final vowels were offset by reworking the system through sequencing and word order." Some scholars consider the rule to concern all volitive forms, including the imperative (Joosten 2011a, 500 n. 30). I am at variance with many scholars who argue that *wə-yiqṭol* is a long *yiqṭol* (for example, Robar 2013, 33 n. 17) and that the significance of the *wə/wa* difference is one between a short *yiqṭol* and long *yiqṭol* (an alleged indicative *wə-yiqṭol(u)* in CBH). Robar (2013, 40) also suggests that, at some point in the history of early Hebrew, *wa(y)-yiqṭol* came to contain a long *yiqṭol*.

[200] This holds until a later diachronic stage when the distinction between short and long *yiqṭol* was no longer part of the linguistic instinct of Hebrew speakers (Qimron 1986–87, 151; Smith 1991). None of Qimron's purported realis (indicative) *wə-yiqṭol* forms (with long *yiqṭol*) are found in my corpus, and most are from texts commonly accepted as LBH.

[201] This view "has become part of scholarly consensus" (Notarius 2013, 17 n. 54).

[202] The other side of the coin is that a perfective *wa-qaṭal* did not replace narrative *wa(y)-yiqṭol* for the expression of perfective continuity, as was the case in other Northwest Semitic languages like Aramaic. The realis

wa(y)-yiqṭol clause-type was retained in CBH and became the only realis usage of *yiqṭol(Ø)*.

[203] In the long run, this resulted in a reanalysis of the correct classical language and a new orthographic rule: a form of the (only existing) prefix conjugation is to be (written) shortened in clause-initial position, and long otherwise. In this way, the syntax of CBH was imitated in some LBH texts at the same time as a new linguistic instinct was incorporated in the written language (Joosten 2015, 33).

[204] I have no explanation for the short prefix form in Gen. 24.8 (לֹא תָשֵׁב), which should be interpreted semantically as a long *yiqṭol*; for various solutions, see Ges-K (§109k); Tropper (1998, 177); Dallaire (2014, 134).

[205] Thus Dallaire (2014, 99), who regards the negated jussive as describing "a specific command for a specific occasion."

[206] Other examples of clause-internal negated jussives in the corpus: Gen. 37.22 (*wa-O.noun-ʾal-yiqṭol(Ø)*); 37.27 (*wa-S.noun-ʾal-yiqṭol(Ø)!*; Joosten 2012, 316); 45.20 (*wa-S.noun-ʾal-yiqṭol(Ø)!*); Exod. 8.25 (*Ø-ADV-ʾal-yiqṭol(Ø)*); 16.19 (*Ø-S.noun-ʾal-yiqṭol(Ø)!*); 23.7 (*wa-O.noun-ʾal-yiqṭol(Ø)*); 36.6 (*Ø-S.noun-ʾal-yiqṭol(Ø)*); Lev. 10.6 (*Ø-O.noun-ʾal-yiqṭol(Ø)*); 10.9 (*Ø-O.noun-ʾal-yiqṭol(Ø)!*); Num. 14.9 (*Ø-ʾaḵ-PrP-ʾal-yiqṭol(Ø)*); Judg. 13.14 (*wa-O.noun-ʾal-yiqṭol(Ø)!*); 19.20 (*Ø-ADV-PrP-ʾal-yiqṭol(Ø)!*). Some instances have the entreating particle *nā* attached to the negation, which causes the verb to occupy the third position in the clause: Gen. 13.8; 18.3 (apodosis); 18.30; 19.7; 47.29. Cf. also the Archaic Hebrew example Gen. 49.4 (Notarius 2013, 202).

[207] An example is Gen. 30.34 הֵן לוּ יְהִי כִדְבָרֶךָ׃ 'Good! Let it be as you have said' (ESV; Joosten 2012, 336). *Pace* Gentry (1998, 36), who regards the word order as problematic, and J-M (§163c), which says "לוּ is doubtful."

[208] Other instances of *wa-ʿattā* with jussive: Gen. 41.33; 47.4; 50.5 (with 'hidden' ventive morpheme); Num. 14.17.

[209] Other examples of left dislocations before jussive clauses: Gen. 1.22; 43.14 (with *rəḇīᵃʿ*)—Westermann (1982, 131) calls this a "Wunsch" and translates 'Gott möge ihnen sein Erbarmen zuwenden'; Deut. 1.11—but

this is an uncertain case: see Nyberg (1972, §51j), who regards the *yōsēp̄* as a long *yiqṭol*; 15.3 (the relative clause is a left dislocation; Steuernagel 1900, 55–56; Christensen 2001); Judg. 13.8 (first a polite vocative and then a left dislocation).

[210] Gen. 44.18 and Judg. 13.8 are the only examples of a vocative followed by jussive in the corpus. Outside the corpus, there is also, for example, 1 Kgs 17.21 and Ps. 40.18.

[211] Other examples of *(wa)-[]-yiqṭol(u)* clauses with an understood elliptic element extant in the preceding clause (the ellipsis is indicated by '[]'): Gen. 15.15 (poetic ellipsis; Joosten 2005, 330; 2011a, 215, 217; 2012, 266, 315 n. 19, 429); Exod. 19.3 (Ø-ADV-*yiqṭol(u)* + *wa*-[]-*yiqṭol(u)*!)—according to Joosten (2005, 330; 2012, 309, 429), poetic ellipsis, and according to Blum (2008, 112), ellipsis, *pace* Gropp (1991, 48), who calls it *yiqṭol(u)* without ellipsis, and Blau (2010, 194), who calls it jussive; 23.8 (poetic ellipsis; Joosten 2011a, 215, 217; 2012, 309, 429), *pace* Gropp (1991, 48 n. 9), and Diehl (2007, 40), who calls it futural 'Leerlauffunktion'; 23.12 (ellipsis of *ləmaʿan*; Joosten 2012, 429); 24.7—*pace* Waltke and O'Connor (1990, 653), who identify this as an instance of 'epexegetical' *waw*; and Joosten (2012, 311), who calls it one of "only two undoubted cases of non-volitive wᵊ + YIQTOL;" 26.24 וְיִהְי֣וּ (obligation with ellipsis); Deut. 13.12 (with *nun* paragogicum)—Baden (2008, 153) takes it as a long *yiqṭol* and result, not as ellipsis, *pace* Gropp (1991, 48); 16.19 (ellipsis of *S.noun*, *pace* Gropp 1991, 48); 17.13—according to Baden (2008, 153), long *yiqṭol* as result, not ellipsis, and according to Joosten (2015, 31), a possible *wa-qaṭal*; 19.20—again, according to Baden (2008, 153), long *yiqṭol* as result, not ellipsis, and according to Joosten (2015, 31), a possible *wa-qaṭal*; 21.21 (Baden 2008, 153)—according to Joosten (2015, 31), a possible *wa-qaṭal*; 30.13 (see the analysis of Deut. 30.12 above, *pace* Zewi 1999, 85); Judg. 6.5—the analysis depends on the interpretation of *kī*: I prefer to take *kī* as emphatic adverb, in which case *Ø-[hēm]-yiqṭol(u)* (thus *kethiv*) is elliptic, but if *kī* is a temporal conjunction, it is not ellipsis, as in ZUR: 'Wenn sie mit ihren Herden und Zelten heranzogen, kamen sie so zahlreich wie Heuschrecken'.

[212] The four clauses in Deut. 30.13 may be interpreted in the same way: *Ø-mī-yiqṭol(u) + wa-yiqṭol(Ø) + wa-[mī]-yiqṭol(u) + wa-yiqṭol(Ø)-N.*

[213] Possible but uncertain examples in prose: Gen. 22.14 בְּהַ֥ר יְהוָ֖ה יֵרָאֶֽה: (cf. ZUR ‘Auf dem Berg, wo der HERR sich sehen lässt’; thus also, with some hesitation, Ges-K §130d n. 2); Lev. 25.10.

[214] In prose, we find also Lev. 25.11, where the head noun is not in the construct state. Examples in archaic poetry: Gen. 49.27 (Notarius 2013, 198)—this example is not mentioned by Zewi (2020); Deut. 32.35 לְעֵ֖ת תָּמ֣וּט רַגְלָ֑ם (with distinctive morphology; Notarius 2013, 97; Isaksson 2017, 257; Zewi 2020, 96); 33.22 (Notarius 2013, 244); Ps. 18.3 (Notarius 2013, 168f.). Some other poetic examples: Ps. 12.6 יָפִ֥יחַ לֽוֹ; 61.3 יָר֖וּם מִמֶּ֣נִּי; 91.5 יָע֥וּף יוֹמָֽם.

[215] Sjörs (2023, 114) refers to the two third-person jussives with ventive clitic in the CBH text of Isa. 5.19: יְמַהֵ֣ר ׀ **יָחִ֧ישָׁה** מַעֲשֵׂ֛הוּ [לְמַ֣עַן נִרְאֶ֑ה] וְתִקְרַ֣ב **וְתָבֹ֗ואָה** עֲצַ֛ת קְד֥וֹשׁ יִשְׂרָאֵ֖ל [וְנֵדָֽעָה]: ‘May his (sc. the Lord’s) work hurry up, may it hasten hither, so that we can see it. May the plan of Israel’s Holy approach, may it come hither, so that we may know (it)’. Stein (2016, 159 n. 11) sees no reason to question the third-person forms in CBH with paragogic *heh*, including Isa. 5.19.

[216] Most scholars analyse וְתֵרָאֶה as jussive, in spite of the long form: Stipp (1987, 138); Waltke and O’Connor (1990, 566); J-M (376 n. 1); Diehl (2007, 36).

[217] Notarius (2010b, 414) has a morphological discussion of this long form of the cohortative without ending: “Two variants have been formed in the first person for the volitive—*ʾaqtúl* (with *malraʿ* accent after the fall of final vowel) and *ʾaqtúlāh* (with secondary lengthening of the final vowel)” (my translation). Sjörs (2023, 106) restricts the discussion to verbs IIIʾ, which recur relatively frequently in the examples (cf. Revell 1989, 13, 17f.).

[218] I leave out the many ‘long’ ventive forms of verbs III*wy*, which are less controversial in the first person (see Sjörs 2023, 105f.); for example, Gen. 11.4 (נִבְנֶה and וְנַעֲשֶׂה).

[219] Joosten (2012, 434) analyses this as a long *yiqṭol* in clause-initial position with volitive meaning.

[220] Kuriakos (1973, 181) and Stipp (1987, 135f.) analyse this as a jussive with long form.

[221] Many of the examples are recognised as jussives with long form, for example by Kuriakos (1973, 181) and Stipp (1987, 135f.). I am aware that there are more examples, especially in LBH texts.

[222] The beneficiary is the daughter. Revell (1989, 18) expected a short form.

[223] Other cases when *wa-yiqṭol(u)* is to be analysed as ellipsis in my corpus are: Exod. 19.3 (poetic ellipsis; Joosten 2005, 330; 2012, 309, 429)—but according to Blau (2010, 194), jussive 2ms; 23.8, 12 (ellipsis of *ləmaʿan*; Joosten 2012, 429); Deut. 16.19; 30.12 וְיַשְׁמִעֵ֥נוּ; 30.13.

[224] This is the 'consecutive tense' that the theory of 'consecutive tenses' forgot to recognise. The clause-type *wə-yiqṭol* disturbed the symmetry, and the *wə-* did not 'convert' anything.

[225] This is not the place to elaborate on modal sequences. For further studies on this topic, see Dallaire (2014) and Baranowski (2016a, 153–173).

4. THE IMPERFECTIVE LONG *YIQṬOL(U)* IN CBH

The purpose of this chapter is to establish the independent status of the long *yiqṭol* as an imperfective formation in CBH. Its place in the system of 'consecutive tenses' is peculiar: it is one of four primary constituents in the consecutive tenses, but it is used only in internal positions in a clause. This means that a long *yiqṭol* does not normally occur with *wa-VX* word order in CBH.

The status of the long *yiqṭol* as an imperfective gram in CBH is nowadays uncontroversial (Huehnergard 2017, 10; Gzella 2021, 71). The distinguishing features of the long prefix conjugation (type *yaqtulu*) seem to have been (see further §4.1):

1) Meanings typical of a gram on the grammaticalisation path of an imperfective;
2) Ability to express concomitant habitual action with past time reference;
3) Being a long form, in opposition to a short prefix conjugation.

4.1. The Semitic Background of the CBH Long *Yiqṭol*

4.1.1. Introduction

The emergence of a new imperfective formation *yaqtulu* is commonly held to be the prime isogloss separating the Central Semitic language family from Akkadian, Ethiopic, and Modern

 https://doi.org/10.11647/OBP.0414.04

South Arabian (Huehnergard 2005, 157–65; Kogan 2015, 130f., 158–66). The morphology of this new imperfective is usually presented in two forms, *yaqtul-u/yaqtulū-na*. The basic idea behind this presentation is that the old perfective *yaqtul* became imperfective by the addition of a subordinating suffix *-u* on singular forms and *-na* on plural forms (Huehnergard 1991, 283; Huehnergard and Pat-El 2019, 9).[1] Typologically, this is unexpected, because the usual grammaticalisation path of imperfective grams starts in a locative construction (Bybee and Dahl 1989, 77; Cook 2012a, 220). It is also problematic because, cross-linguistically, verbal usages in subordinate clauses do not develop into main clause formations (Kouwenberg 2010a, 98; Kogan 2015, 159–61). A third problem is the supposed shift in temporal value from perfective/past (*yaqtul*) to imperfective/present-future (*yaqtul-u*) (Kouwenberg 2010a, 231; Kogan 2015, 160).[2]

Nearly all progressives derive from locative constructions, and progressives in turn constitute the most frequent origin of imperfective formations.[3] It would be reasonable to expect that Semitic imperfectives also have a locative origin (cf. Diakonoff 1988, 103).[4] Another source of progressives is reduplications, which would indicate a locative origin also for the Proto-Semitic imperfective *yVqattVl* (Bybee et al. 1994, 125, 129, 131). It is therefore tempting to identify the *-u* in the Central Semitic *yaqtulu* as a locative clitic, the more so since there existed a locative marker *-u* in Proto-Semitic (Kienast 2001, 172; Hasselbach 2013b, 20; Retsö 2014, 68; Huehnergard 2019, 61).[5] In spite of such typological observations, it is widely assumed that the pair

-u/na in CS is identical to the subordination markers *-u/ni* in Assyrian Akkadian (Huehnergard 2019, 72). The two functionally identical allomorphs are assumed to have been added to the perfective *yaqtul* to create a new imperfective in CS, 3ms **yaḏkur-u*, 3mp **yaḏkurū-na*.[6] The distribution of *-u* in Babylonian conforms to that in Central Semitic: it cannot co-occur with other verbal suffixes such as gender-number markers or the ventive. It can be followed, though, by object suffixes, type **yaqtul-u-ka*.

The CS *yaqtulu*, as well as the CBH long *yiqṭol*, behaves like a gram on the imperfective grammaticalisation path. The imperfective aspect views a situation as unbounded from within "with explicit reference to its internal structure" (Bybee et al. 1994, 125). Imperfective verbal morphemes are typically used for setting up background situations in clauses that are simultaneous with the main line (cf. Cohen 2015, 398). An imperfective gram is "applicable to either past, present or future time" (Bybee et al. 1994, 126). The specific progressive meaning of a gram occurs early in the process of grammaticalisation. The imperfective meaning represents a generalisation, with a gradual loss of the strict progressive meaning. An imperfective gram can express ongoing progressive action, but also habitual occurrence as well as gnomic situations. It is common that the meaning of an imperfective gram includes habituality, and in such uses especially with past time reference. The situation in Kui is particularly relevant for some Northwest Semitic languages: an old present (cf. *yiqṭol(u)* in CBH) was used for habitual, progressive, and future. When a new periphrastic progressive arose, comprising the active participle and a verb 'to live, exist' (cf. *qoṭel* in CBH), the older form came to signal just habitual and future actions (Bybee et al. 1994, 125–127, 133, 137, 141, 147, 151, 156, 158–160).

In order to understand the diachronic path of the CS verbal gram *yaqtulu*, it is necessary to review the repository of finite verb forms in Proto CS: an old perfective/past *yaqtul*, an old imperfective *yVqattVl* (Kuryłowicz 1949, 52; Huehnergard 2019, 62),[7] a new emerging perfective *qatal(a)* (the characteristic innovation of West Semitic), and a new potentially imperfective formation *yaqtulu*. The old perfective *yaqtul* is step by step replaced by *qatal(a)*, and the old imperfective *yVqattVl* is gradually replaced by *yaqtulu*. The linguistic instinct for the nature of *yaqtul* as a full-blown perfective/past is weakening, except in specific functions, such as narration.[8] There is a growing tendency to avoid *yVqattVl* because of its homonymy with the prefix conjugations in the D stem: both jussive D and imperfective D were problematic (Blau 2010, 196f.).

It is often pointed out that the Akkadian relative construction *ša iprus-u* and the Central Semitic *yaqtul-u* are cognate formations (Kuryłowicz 1949, 52; Rubin 2005, 147). The term 'relative' for the Akkadian *iprus-u* does not sufficiently cover the gamut of subordinate clauses with *iprus-u*. Other subordinated clauses may have the same marker, as in *aššum uštamaḫḫar-u ittīka* 'because he will rival you' (OB Gilgameš, example quoted from Rubin 2005, 147). Rubin (2005, 147) assumes on the basis of Akkadian that there must have been a Proto-Semitic linking of the type **mutam iqabbi āmur* 'I saw a man speaking' (ungrammatical in Akkadian), which uses the regular imperfective *yVqattVl* to code the subordinate clause. The word order in the example is

Akkadian, so with PS word order, the example would amount to **āmur mutam iqabbi* 'I saw a man speaking'. This is the word order to be expected in the linguistic milieu in which the CS imperfective formation *yaqtul-u* developed, replacing the old *yVqattVl*. Rubin (2005, 147) suggests that the CS imperfective *yaqtulu* developed via an analogy between two types of subordinate clauses, in (A) and (C) below:

Type (A): *O.noun yVqattVl yaqtul* (Akkadian word order)
**mutam iqabbi āmur*
'I saw a man speaking' (Proto-Semitic but ungrammatical in Akkadian);

Type (B): *O.noun REL-yaqtul-u yaqtul* (Akkadian word order)
mutam ša iqbû āmur
'I saw a man who spoke'.

In type (A), the old imperfective *yVqattVl* is embedded in the main clause, whose object noun is placed first and the main verb (*āmur*) in final position. The asyndetic *yVqattVl* (*iqabbi*) has no external marker, but the Akkadian word order illustrates its status as an embedded clause. It is asyndetic, but the imperfective morphology of *yVqattVl* is itself a marker. The clause *yVqattVl* must be interpreted as a verbal description of the preceding object noun. Rubin (2005, 147) and Hamori (1973, 321) assume that the type (A) subordinate clause, though ungrammatical in Akkadian, existed in Proto-Semitic with VO word order in the main clause. In type (B), the subordinate state of the embedded clause is explicitly marked by a relative particle *ša* and the subordinating morpheme *-u*. The verb in the subordinate clause is a perfective *yaqtul* with subordinating marker (*iqbû* < **iqbi-u*).

Both types of subordinated clauses (A and B) describe an action that is concomitant with that in the main clause. Rubin and Hamori assume that a relative particle was facultative in Proto Semitic.[9] The final subordinating marker (*-u*) was itself a sufficient signal of subordination. If this is correct, we may assume a Proto Semitic linking of type (C):

> Type (C) *O.noun yaqtul-u yaqtul* (Akkadian word order)
> **mutam iqbû āmur*
> 'I saw a man who spoke'.

The difference in meaning between type (A) and type (C) is slight. In both cases, the verb in the subordinate clause is indicative. It is not correct to call *yVqattVl* or *yaqtul-u* 'subjunctive' verb forms. In a clause such as *bītum ša īmur-u* 'the house that he saw', the verb is indicative. It is the clause, not the verb form, that is marked for subordination (Huehnergard and Rubin 2011, 270). An imperfective such as *yVqattVl* in (A) is the typical choice in background or circumstantial clauses, where it carries over the temporal reference of the main clause. Simultaneity with a past action was an important secondary function of an imperfective in Proto-Semitic (Kuryłowicz 1962, 60; Hamori 1973, 319f.; Kouwenberg 2010a, 229). With past time reference in the main clause, the *yVqattVl* is likewise past time, often with continuative or habitual meaning. In the subordinate clause (*iqbû*) of type (C), the perfective aspect is neutralised. It is not marked for habitual or continuative action, but the perfective *iqbû* 'who spoke' may allow for meanings such as 'was speaking'. Thus, while in type (A) the continuative action of the *yVqattVl* is made explicit by the imperfectivity of the verb form, in type (C) a continuative meaning is inferred in many contexts.[10]

In West Semitic, the new perfective gram *qatal* step by step replaced the old perfective *yaqtul.*[11] When a verb was to express past time or anteriority, the linguistic instinct tended to choose *qatal.* The new perfective gram widened its semantic domain. In a sentence of type (C), *qatal* was the natural choice for expressing anteriority. The feeling for *yaqtul-u* as a past perfective was gradually lost. Instead, *yaqtul-u* could replace the old imperfective *yVqattVl.* The *yaqtulu* in a sentence like *qatal-O.noun* + *Ø-yaqtul-u* began to be reanalysed as an imperfective.

Summary:

1. In Proto-Semitic, the imperfective *yVqattVl* could express simultaneity with past action, even in an asyndetic clause, and the perfective *yaqtul* could express simultaneity in a subordinate (relative) clause (*yaqtul-u*) (Hamori 1973, 321f.).
2. In West Semitic, *qatal* replaced the perfective *yaqtul* in different degrees depending on the individual language (Kuryłowicz 1972c, 54; 1973, 119; Tropper 1998, 161).
3. *yaqtul-u* in a subordinate clause was reanalysed as a clause primarily expressing circumstantial action. If anteriority had to be expressed in relation to the main clause, *qaṭal* was used (Hamori 1973, 322).
4. *yaqtul-u* was generalised to express concomitance also with present time reference (extension of usage).
5. *yaqtulu* began to be used as an imperfective in main clauses.

6. *yaqtulu* heavily replaced the old imperfective *yVqattVl* in Proto Central Semitic.[12]

This is, by and large, the essence of Rubin's (2005, 146–48) hypothesis (partly based on Hamori 1973; see also Kuryłowicz 1949; 1962).

In the individual Central Semitic languages, the reflex of the old **yaqtulu* is usually not controversial, so the comparative sections in the present chapter can be kept relatively short.

4.1.1.1. Excursus: A Parallel Imperfective Formation (*Qoṭel*)

The hypothesis of a subordinate construction developing into a full-blown progressive verb form in main clauses is supported by the parallel development of the active participle (*qoṭel*) in Biblical Hebrew.[13] It is an example of the renewal of the progressive, the 'old progressive' in this case being the CS *yaqtulu* formation (Rundgren 1963; Kuryłowicz 1975, 104). A semantic split is inevitable in this process, so that the old present *yaqtulu* gradually expressed a more general (not actual) present and future. The beginning of this grammaticalisation was the use of the participle as an attribute after a head noun, in the same position as an asyndetic relative clause. In such a construction, the *qoṭel* refers back to a preceding nominal head. The participle is still not predicative, but may have circumstantial meaning. This is the syntax of *qoṭel* we encounter in the Archaic Hebrew poetry, in which *qoṭel* in predicative position is consistently lacking (Notarius 2010a, 262; 2013, 285, 304).[14]

An example from CBH is:

(1) *wa(y)-yiqṭol-O.noun-**qoṭel***

וַיַּרְא אִישׁ מִצְרִי **מַכֶּה** אִישׁ־עִבְרִי מֵאֶחָיו׃

'and he saw an Egyptian man **attacking** a Hebrew man, one of his own people' (Exod. 2.11)

The *qoṭel* (מַכֶּה) in example (1) fills the slot of an attribute. The verbal character of the participle allows a construction where it is an attribute of an object noun. This is the "prototypical context for the process of reanalysis that resulted in the predicative use of the participle" (Notarius 2013, 286). *Ø-qoṭel* in attributive position and the semiverbal character of the morpheme invite a reanalysis of it as an asyndetic relative clause. The *qoṭel* refers back to the immediately preceding head noun phrase (אִישׁ מִצְרִי), and has the same syntactic function as its adjective (מִצְרִי).[15]

A further generalisation of the attributive function of *qoṭel* is its use after an object suffix:

(2) *wa(y)-yiqṭol-O.pron + **Ø-qoṭel***

וַיַּקְרִיבוּ אֹתוֹ הַמֹּצְאִים אֹתוֹ **מְקֹשֵׁשׁ** עֵצִים אֶל־מֹשֶׁה וְאֶל־אַהֲרֹן וְאֶל כָּל־הָעֵדָה׃

'Those who found him **gathering wood** brought him to Moses and Aaron and to the whole community.' (Num. 15.33)

In (2), the *qoṭel* (מְקֹשֵׁשׁ) refers back to and describes the object suffix in אֹתוֹ.[16]

A further generalisation is exhibited when only a first *qoṭel* takes an attributive position (here after a possessive suffix), and a second (and third) *qoṭel* refers back to another head in the main clause, as in (3):

(3) *wa(y)-yiqtol-O.noun* + *REL-PrP* + **Ø-*qoṭel*** + **Ø-*qoṭel*** + **wa-*qoṭel***

וַיִּרְא֣וּ אֶת־הָעָ֣ם אֲשֶׁר־בְּקִרְבָּ֡הּ יוֹשֶֽׁבֶת־לָבֶטַח֩ כְּמִשְׁפַּ֨ט צִדֹנִ֜ים שֹׁקֵ֣ט ׀ וּבֹטֵ֗חַ

'They observed the people in it **dwelling carefree**, after the manner of the Sidonians, (a people) **tranquil and unsuspecting**.' (Judg. 18.7)

The first *qoṭel* (יוֹשֶׁבֶת) in (3) is feminine and describes the immediately preceding feminine possessive pronoun (in בְּקִרְבָּהּ). The feminine pronoun refers to the city (fem.) in which the people lives. The second and third *qoṭel* describe the people (הָעָם, masc.). The linguistic instinct to think of *qoṭel* as an attribute of a head noun is loosening.

A further step in the development towards a descriptive, more general subordinate clause is taken when there is no immediately preceding head noun (or head pronominal suffix). The *qoṭel* is free to refer back to any constituent in the main clause:[17]

(4) *wa-S.noun-qaṭal* + **Ø-*qoṭel***

וְדָתָ֨ן וַאֲבִירָ֜ם יָצְא֣וּ **נִצָּבִ֗ים** פֶּ֚תַח אָהֳלֵיהֶ֔ם וּנְשֵׁיהֶ֥ם וּבְנֵיהֶ֖ם וְטַפָּֽם׃

'Dathan and Abiram came out **stationing themselves** with their wives, children and little ones at the entrances to their tents.' (Num. 16.27)

In such a construction, the *qoṭel* is felt as a description of the action (יָצְאוּ) in the main clause, not a description of a head noun. The *qoṭel* has developed into a circumstantial clause. It is a subordinate clause: it is concomitant, but it cannot be analysed as just an attribute or as a relative clause. The *qoṭel* is predicative.[18]

A further step towards an independent clause is the introduction of a pronominal subject that clarifies the reference to a constituent in the main clause (and also the predicative function of *qoṭel* itself):

(5) *wa(y)-yiqṭol-S.noun-ADV* + ***Ø-qoṭel-S.pron***

וַיָּבֹ֥א גִדְע֖וֹן הַיַּרְדֵּ֑נָה **עֹבֵ֣ר ה֗וּא** וּשְׁלֹשׁ־מֵא֤וֹת הָאִישׁ֙ אֲשֶׁ֣ר אִתּ֔וֹ עֲיֵפִ֖ים וְרֹדְפִֽים׃

'And Gideon came to the Jordan **crossing over**, **he** and the 300 men who were with him, exhausted yet pursuing.' (Judg. 8.4)

In (5), the *qoṭel* is positioned asyndetically and first in the circumstantial clause.[19]

A further step towards independence is represented by syntactic variants where the *qoṭel* is no longer clause-initial. Such an example is (6):

(6) *wa(y)-yiqṭol* + *wa(y)-yiqṭol* + *wa-hinnē-S.noun-**qoṭel***

וַיִּקְח֤וּ אֶת־הַמַּפְתֵּ֙חַ֙ וַיִּפְתָּ֔חוּ וְהִנֵּה֙ אֲדֹנֵיהֶ֔ם **נֹפֵ֥ל** אַ֖רְצָה מֵֽת׃

'they took the key and opened, **and there lay** their lord dead on the floor.' (Judg. 3.25)

In (6), the *qoṭel* clause can still be analysed as circumstantial and with the same temporal reference as the preceding main clauses. It functions semantically as a complement (to an understood 'and they saw') but possesses a greater degree of independence than in the previous examples.[20]

From constructions such as (6) above, it is just a little step to use *qoṭel* in an independent clause in direct speech with speech time reference:

(7) *Ø-**qoṭel**-S.pron*

רֹאֶה אָנֹכִי אֶת־פְּנֵי אֲבִיכֶן כִּי־אֵינֶנּוּ אֵלַי כִּתְמֹל שִׁלְשֹׁם

'**I see** that your father's manner toward me is not as it has been in the past.' (Gen. 31.5)

As in most of the subordinate clauses illustrated above, the *qoṭel* is clause-initial and the subject pronoun follows, but the clause is now independent with progressive meaning.[21] This independence is easy to infer from *qoṭel* clauses that function as full utterances in direct speech, where the independence of the sentence is clear (8):

(8) *wa(y)-yiqṭol: "Ø-**qoṭel**-S.noun ..."*

וַיֹּאמְרוּ אֶל־מֹשֶׁה לֵּאמֹר **מַרְבִּים** הָעָם לְהָבִיא מִדֵּי הָעֲבֹדָה לַמְּלָאכָה אֲשֶׁר־צִוָּה יְהוָה לַעֲשֹׂת אֹתָהּ׃

'and they told Moses, "The people **are bringing much more** than is needed for the completion of the work which the LORD commanded us to do!"' (Exod. 36.5)

In (8), the *qoṭel* clause can be analysed as a complement clause, marked by a quotational frame particle (לֵּאמֹר). As such, it is subordinate, but within the direct speech quotation, it is perceived as an independent clause.

This digression about the Biblical Hebrew active participle is intended to illustrate that a subordinate construction may develop into a progressive/imperfective gram in main clauses in a Semitic language—as the *yaqtulu* construction possibly did.

4.1.2. Ancient South Arabian

The two prefix conjugations in Ancient South Arabian are not graphically distinguished in writing (see §3.1.4). The reflex of the Central Semitic *yaqtulu* has the same stem /qtVl/ as the short prefix conjugation (Avanzini 2015, 15).[22] The reflexes of *yaqtul* and *yaqtulu* can be distinguished only on the basis of their uses for perfective and imperfective meanings. A general present meaning is found in (9):

(9) *kl / ʾsdn / w-ʾnṯn / ʾ¦lw /* ***ystmynn*** */ ʾslm / w-mlkm w-whbm w-…*

‘all men and women who **are called** ʾSLM, MLKM, WHBM, and…’ (F 76/2–3, Stein 2011, 1064; 2013, §6.3.8)

(10) *w-kl ʾs²ʿbm* ***ymlk*** *Ydʿʾb*

‘All the tribes on which Ydʿʾb **is (and will be) reigning**’ (RES 3878, 3, Avanzini 2015, 19)

The contrast between a past *qatal* and future *yqtl(u)* is illustrated in (11):

(11) *b-kl ʾmlʾ stmlʾw* ***w-ystmlʾnn*** *b-ʿm-hw*

‘in all oracular fulfilments they have sought (in the past) **and they will seek** (in future) with him’ (NNAG 6 = J 627/13–14, Stein 2011, 1064)

4.1.3. Arabic

The Arabic imperfective *yaqtulu* is inherited from common Central Semitic (Huehnergard 2017, 14). In the grammars, it is called ‘imperfect’. It indicates a continuing or habitual action independent of temporal reference. “If the context does not refer to the past, the imperfect indicates the present or future" (Fischer 2002, §184). The Arabic *yaqtulu* can also express the prototypical progressive meaning: *māḏā tafʿalu* 'What are you doing?' (Fischer 2002, 104). One of the typical uses of an imperfective, that of a circumstantial action in the past, is frequently found in Classical Arabic (Kuryłowicz 1949, 53; 1973, 120):

(12) *qatala* + *Ø-yaqtulu*

baʿaṯa ʾilā muʿāwiyata yaṭlubu ṣ-ṣulḥa

'He sent (a message) to Muʿāwiya and asked for peace.'

(13) *qatala* + *Ø-yaqtulu*

ǧalasa n-nāsu yašrabūna l-ḫamra

'The people were seated and drank wine.'

The *yaqtulu* clauses in (12) and (13) are subordinate, and concomitant with the action in the *qatala* clause, but they cannot be analysed as relative clauses. In (12), there is no head noun to which such a clause would refer. The clauses refer back to the subject in the main clauses, and must be analysed as circumstantial with past time reference (Arabic *ḥāl*). The switch to the imperfective *yaqtulu* clause indicates simultaneity and subordination in relation to the preceding *qaṭal* clause.[23]

4.1.4. Amorite

Research on the proper names of Amorite origin has previously not been able to prove the existence of the Central Semitic imperfective formation *yaqtulu* in Amorite. Its existence has just been a plausible hypothesis (thus Baranowski 2017, 87). Recently, however, this gap in our knowledge has come to an end with the publication of two southern Old Babylonian tablets from the very beginning of the second millennium BCE (George and Krebernik 2022). The left column contains phrases in an Amorite language, including instances of a *yaqtulu* conjugation, and the forms are translated in the right-hand column by Akkadian present tense forms (*iparras*). This can be regarded as decisive proof of the existence of *yaqtulu* in the Amorite verbal system. It "expresses incomplete and future actions" (George and Krebernik 2022, 29). It can express a progressive present, as in (14):

(14) *an-ni-a-ki-an* ⸢***ta***⸣***-li-ku***

‘Where **are you going**?’ (1:10, George and Krebernik 2022, 5, 19, my emphasis)[24]

(15) *ra-ḫa-a-a* ***a-li-***⸢***ku*** *el*⸣*-kum la ta[aḫ-ni-ši]-*⸢*ia*⸣

‘My friends, **I am going off** to my woman.’ (2:16, George and Krebernik 2022, 5, 22, my emphasis)[25]

Two *yaqtulu* clauses may be connected with *wa*; in (16), they have future time reference:

(16) ***a-li-ku-na*** *wa pa-aḫ-ma-{x}-a ma-li-kum* ***am-si-qu***

‘**I shall come** and **kiss** the king’s feet.’ (2:24–25, George and Krebernik 2022, 6, 24, my emphasis)[26]

4.1.5. Ugaritic

As in Arabic, *yaqtulu* in Ugaritic is an imperfective form, the temporal reference of which must be inferred from context. It can refer to the present or future or be past habitual (Huehnergard 2012, 55; Tropper 2012, 685–689). It is also used to express obligation.

(17) is an example of a present progressive meaning in a question:

(17) *O.pron-yaqtulu*

mh . ***taršn*** */ l btlt . ʿnt*

‘Was **wünschst du**, Jungfrau ‘Anatu?’ (KTU^3 1.3:V:28f., Tropper 2012, 685, §76.322, my emphasis)

A circumstantial use of *yaqtulu* with past reference is illustrated in (18):

(18) *PrP-yaqtul +* ***Ø-yaqtulu! + wa-yaqtulu***

ʿl / abh . yʿrṣ[27] *.* ***ybky / w yšnn***

‘Er trat vor seinen Vater, **wobei er weinte und mit den Zähnen knirschte**’ (KTU^3 1.16:I:11–13, Tropper 2012, 906, §97.71, my emphasis)

In (18), the two coordinated *yaqtulu* clauses form a subordinated complex describing two circumstantial actions concomitant with the action in the main clause.

An example with obligational meaning is (19):

(19) *wa-**yaqtulu***

w ***tṣu*** *. lpn . ql . ṯʿy*

‘und **du mußt hinausgehen** vor/bei der Stimme des Beschwörers’ (KTU^3 1.169:2, Tropper 2012, 734, §77.51, my emphasis)

4.1.6. Amarna Canaanite

Yaqtulu in Amarna Canaanite describes actions that are "ongoing at the moment of speaking" (Baranowski 2016a, 140), or habitual, continuative, frequentative, and future. A habitual or frequentative *yaqtulu* with past reference "includes the reference time given by another verb that refers to a past, temporally contained event, or by the time of an adverbial" (Baranowski 2016a, 153; also Moran 2003, 214).

An example of present progressive, not expressed in a question, is (20), quoted by Baranowski (2016a, 140, his emphasis):

(20) *ADV-yaqtul + REL-yaqtul + S.pron-ADV-**yaqtulu***

a-nu-ma iš-te$_9$*-me* [22]*gáb-bi a-wa-te*^{MEŠ} [23]*ša yi-iq-bi* [24] ^{I}*Ma-ia* LÚ.‹MÁ›ŠKIM LUG[AL] [25]*a-na ia-ši a-nu-ma* [26]***i-pu-šu** gáb-ba*

'now I have heard all the words that Maya, the ‹com›missioner of the ki[ng] said to me. Now **I am carrying out** everything.' (EA 328:21–26)

The *yaqtulu* in Amarna could also express a habitual action in the past. In the following example, the past temporal reference is established by adverbs (Baranowski 2016a, 145):

(21) *ADV-yaqtulu + wa-ul-yaqtulu + … lā-yaqtulu*

pa-na-nu aš-pu-ru a-na LUGAL *ú-ul yi-iš-mu* [95] *a-wa-ti a-nu-ma i-na-na a-na* URU A.PÚ.‹MEŠ› [96]*aš-ba-ti ki-i*$_{15}$ UR.GI$_5$ *la-a tu-uš-mu* [97]*a-wa-ti* […]

'Formerly, I wrote to the king; he did not listen to my word. Right now, I am dwelling in Beirut like a dog (and) my word is not heeded.' (EA 138:94–97)[28]

An example of *yaqtulu* expressing an obligatory action is:

(22) *yaqtul*[29] + *wa-**lā-yaqtulu***

[…] *ti-de i-*[*nu*]*-*⌜*ma*⌝ *gáb-bu* [26]*ša-ru ù* ⌜***la***⌝*-*⌜***mi***⌝(?) ⌜***ti***⌝***-ša-lu-ni*** [27]*a-na* LÚ *ʾa_4-ia-*⌜*bi*⌝*-*⌜*ia*⌝

'Know that all of them are traitors, so **don't ask me** about my enemies!' (EA 102:25–27)[30]

4.1.7. Phoenician

In Phoenician, the long form of the prefix conjugation is morphologically distinguished in the second- and third-person masculine plural, where the verb forms have a final *-n*. Each type of prefix conjugation "has its own functional range and should be treated separately" (Gzella 2012, 67). The reflex of *yaqtulu* is used for present-future and progressive aspect, and, in addition, nuances of obligation. The difference between future and obligation is sometimes difficult to define (Gzella 2012, 67). The 2fs long form is not attested (Friedrich and Röllig 1999, 82). A 3mp form is attested in (23) and (24):

(23) אף אם אדמם **ידברנך**

'Even if people **persuade you**.' (KAI[5] 14:6)

In (23), the verb is used in a type of protasis, with present tense meaning projected into a future case. An example with future time reference is (24):

(24) **ויסגרנם** האלנם הקדשם את ממלכ<ת> אדר

'The holy gods **will deliver** them to a mighty king.' (KAI[5] 14:9)[31]

The word order in (24) is *w-yqtl(u)*, with clause-initial verb.

4.1.8. Aramaic

As has been observed above (§3.1.11), there was an imperfective *yaqtulu* in Old Aramaic and Imperial Aramaic. It could be used for present and future actions (Degen 1969, §75; 'long imperfect', Muraoka 2003, 195–98). Some of its forms are morphologically distinctive (Degen 1969, §§49–50; Voigt 1987, 6; Kogan 2015, 162). The prototypical progressive meaning is found in questions, such as (25) (KAI[5] 312 I:4):[32]

(25) *ADV-yaqtulu + [ ] yaqtulu!*

לם . תצם̊ [. ול]ם̊ . תב̊כה .

'Why do you fast [and why] do you weep?'

There are also examples of a long prefix conjugation with past reference describing a circumstantial action in relation to a narrative main line (KAI[5] 312 I:3–4):

(26) *wa-yaqtul*[33] + *wa-lā-qaṭal-VN* + *wa-yaqtul* + *wa-VN-* ***yaqtulu!***[34]

ויקם̊ . ב̊ל̊ע̊ם̊ . מן . מח̊ר̊[..]---[...]ל . י̊מן . -[........]-ה . ול̊ י̊כ̊[ל . אכל
. ויצ[ם [.] ו̊ב̊כ̊(4)ה . **יבכה̊** .

'And Balaam arose the next day[35] […] but he was not ab[le to eat and he fasted] **weeping** grievously.'

In (26), the circumstantial clause is syndetic with initial *wa*, as is often the case in Classical Arabic, and emphasis is achieved by means of a preceding ('absolute') infinitive.

4.2. The Long *Yiqṭol* in the Archaic Hebrew Poetry

The imperfective *yiqṭol(u)* in the archaic poetry attests to the typical functions of an imperfective formation: present progressive, historical present, past progressive, past simultaneous, and immediate future, meanings that are rare in CBH (Notarius 2013, 150, 282f.). Some of these uses were taken over step by step by the active participle (*qoṭel*) in CBH, but in the archaic poetry, the meanings of *yiqṭol(u)* suggest a broader imperfective usage. The archaic present progressive *yiqṭol(u)* (Notarius 2013, 150) is illustrated in (27), which exhibits a clause-initial *yiqṭol(u)*, an archaic syntactic feature:[36]

(27) *Ø-ADV-yiqṭol(u) + Ø-yiqṭol(u)*

הֲלֹא **יִמְצְאוּ יְחַלְּקוּ** שָׁלָל רַחַם רַחֲמָתַיִם לְרֹאשׁ גֶּבֶר שְׁלַל צְבָעִים לְסִיסְרָא
שְׁלַל צְבָעִים רִקְמָה צֶבַע רִקְמָתַיִם לְצַוְּארֵי שָׁלָל׃

‘Surely **they are finding and dividing** the spoil: a girl or two for every man; spoil of dyed stuffs for Sisera, spoil of dyed stuffs embroidered, two pieces of dyed work embroidered for the neck as spoil’ (Judg. 5.30, Notarius 2013, 282)

The two yiqṭol*(u)* in (27) are used in a main clause in direct speech. It is not a question, as is often the case when present progressive meanings of *yiqṭol(u)* are found in CBH.

The historical present in the archaic poetry is attested in intensive passages, as in (28).

(28) *Ø-O.noun-PrP-**yiqtol(u)**-N + wa-qaṭal + Ø-qaṭal + wa-qaṭal + wa-qaṭal*

יָדָהּ לַיָּתֵד **תִּשְׁלַ֫חְנָה** וִימִינָהּ לְהַלְמ֣וּת עֲמֵלִ֑ים וְהָלְמָ֤ה סִֽיסְרָא֙ מָחֲקָ֣ה רֹאשׁ֔וֹ וּמָחֲצָ֥ה וְחָלְפָ֖ה רַקָּתֽוֹ׃

'**She puts** her hand to the tent peg and her right hand to the workmen's mallet; she struck Sisera a blow, she crushed his head, she shattered and pierced his temple' (Judg. 5.26, Notarius 2013, 142, 283)

The *yiqtol(u)* form (תִּשְׁלַ֫חְנָה) is one of the very few *yiqtol(u)* forms with a ventive/energic ending and no suffix pronoun (J-M §119z n. 4; Notarius 2013, 284).[37] This energic ending, together with the word order, is a strong indication that the verb is a long prefix form (Notarius 2013, 136, 142). The intense narrative clause in (28) is continued by past perfective *qaṭal* forms (with or without proclitic *wa*).[38]

The past progressive meaning is found when the temporal reference of the imperfective *yiqtol(u)* is located in the past, for example in retrospective report:

(29) *Ø-PrP-yiqtol(u) + wa-PrP-yiqtol(u) + wa(y)-yiqtol(Ø)*

בַּצַּר־לִ֤י **אֶקְרָ֣א** יְהוָה֙ וְאֶל־אֱלֹהַ֣י **אֶקְרָ֑א** וַיִּשְׁמַ֤ע מֵהֵֽיכָלוֹ֙ קוֹלִ֔י וְשַׁוְעָתִ֖י בְּאָזְנָֽיו׃

'In my distress **I was calling upon** the LORD; to my God **I was calling**. From his temple he heard my voice, and my cry (came) to his ears.' (2 Sam. 22.7, my emphasis; concerning v. 7a, see Notarius 2013, 169, 283)

In (29), the verb form switch is marked in the reading tradition by a *wa(y)-yiqṭol* form with gemination of the prefix consonant. In Ps. 18.7, the corresponding verb lacks the proclitic *wa*.[39] The past progressive meaning of *yiqṭol(u)* is lost in CBH.

The archaic poetry also attests to semantically similar functions of *yiqṭol(u)* that are typical in CBH, "iterative and habitual aspect" (Notarius 2013, 283). The past simultaneous meaning involves a linking with another clause. In relation to this clause, it is often circumstantial. A good example is:

(30) *Ø-qaṭal* + ***Ø-yiqṭol(u)****-Npar* + [15]*ʾāz-qaṭal* + *Ø-(O.noun)-* ***yiqṭol(u)*** + *Ø-qaṭal-S.noun*

שָׁמְע֥וּ עַמִּ֖ים **יִרְגָּז֑וּן** חִ֣יל אָחַ֔ז יֹשְׁבֵ֖י פְּלָֽשֶׁת׃ 15 אָ֤ז נִבְהֲלוּ֙ אַלּוּפֵ֣י אֱד֔וֹם אֵילֵ֣י מוֹאָ֔ב **יֹֽאחֲזֵ֖מוֹ** רָ֑עַד נָמֹ֕גוּ כֹּ֖ל יֹשְׁבֵ֥י כְנָֽעַן׃

'The peoples heard, **they trembled**; pangs seized the inhabitants of Philistia. [15]Then the chiefs of Edom were dismayed; trembling **seized** the leaders of Moab; all the inhabitants of Canaan melted away' (Exod. 15.14–15, Notarius 2013, 283, my emphasis)

The יִרְגָּז֑וּן and יֹֽאחֲזֵ֖מוֹ in (30) are examples of the past circumstantial function of the imperfective *yiqṭol(u)*, a function that is relatively frequent in the archaic poetry, but rare in CBH texts, where it is substituted by the *qoṭel*. The first *yiqṭol(u)* is clause-initial, in contradiction to the rule in CBH. The second *yiqṭol(u)*, in verse 15, is also clause-initial, since there precedes it a left dislocation not properly belonging to the clause ('the leaders of Moab, trembling seized them'). Both *yiqṭol(u)* clauses code actions that are simultaneous with the action of the preceding *qaṭal* clause. In both cases, the switch to a *yiqṭol(u)* clause signals an action that is circumstantial in relation to the previous *qaṭal* clause.[40]

The *yiqṭol(u)* expressing the immediate future in the archaic poetry is illustrated by (31):

(31) *kī-lō-XØ* + *wa-lō-XØ* + *Ø-ADV-**yiqṭol(u)**:* *"O.pron-qaṭal"*

כִּ֤י לֹא־נַ֙חַשׁ֙ בְּיַֽעֲקֹ֔ב וְלֹא־קֶ֖סֶם בְּיִשְׂרָאֵ֑ל כָּעֵ֗ת **יֵאָמֵ֤ר** לְיַֽעֲקֹב֙ וּלְיִשְׂרָאֵ֔ל מַה־פָּ֖עַל אֵֽל׃

'Surely there is no enchantment against Jacob, no divination against Israel; now **it shall be said** of Jacob and Israel, "See what God has done!"' (Num. 23.23, Notarius 2013, 283)

There is no enchantment or divination in Israel. "The deictic כָּעֵת creates ST reference" (Notarius 2013, 222). The idea is that, after Balaam's blessing, Israel will immediately be spoken of with astonishment about what God has done with them (Notarius 2013, 222).[41] The *yiqṭol(u)* is amply used with a more general future time reference in the archaic poetry, as it is also in CBH (Notarius 2013, 283).

The imperfective *yiqṭol(u)* in the archaic poetry tends to be non-initial in the clause, but there are many cases when *yiqṭol(u)* is clause-initial (Notarius 2013, 283).[42] It has a wide range of functions and meanings, wider than in CBH. In CBH, the active participle has taken over the meanings of "present progressive, past progressive, and immediate future, and perfect קטל is used for past simultaneous and circumstantial acts/events/states, particularly in narrative" (Notarius 2013, 284 n. 16).

4.3. The Long *Yiqṭol* in the Pre-exilic Hebrew Inscriptions

For the distinction between *yiqṭol(u)* and *yiqṭol(Ø)* in the inscriptions, see §3.3. Only a few morphologically distinctive long *yiqṭol* are attested (III*wy* verbs, Gogel 1998, 95), and no *yiqṭol(u)* with progressive meaning. Since most of the inscriptions are letters, future and obligatory meanings are common. Sometimes a general present may have the nuance of ability:

(32) *wa-yiqṭol(Ø) + kī-PrP-S.pron-qoṭel + REL-qaṭal + kī-**lō-yiqṭol(u)!***

וידע כי אל . משאת לכש . נח(3)נו שמרם ככל . האתת אשר נתן (4) אדני . כי **לא נראה** את עז(5)קה

'And let him know that for the fire-signal of Lachish we are keeping watch according to all the signals which my lord gave, because **we cannot see** Azekah.' (HI Lachish 4:2–5 reverse)

For the writer of this Lachish letter, it was natural to express a habitual present with the active participle in a main clause (נחנו שמרם). The *yiqṭol(u)* verb is used for ('we do not see' =) 'we cannot see' in a general present subordinate clause introduced by *kī* (reason; Gogel 1998, 96).

A general present *yiqṭol(u)* can also be found in a relative clause, as in (33):

(33) *PP + REL-**yiqṭol(u)!***

ארר . אשר . **ימחה̊**

'Cursed be whoever **wipes out**…' (HI EnGd 2:1)

An obligation can be expressed by *yiqṭol(u)*, as in a relative clause in a Lachish ostracon (34):

(34) *IMP* + *REL*-***yiqṭol(u)!***

השׁ[ב] (5) [אל] ע֯ב֯ד֯ך֯ ד֯(6)בר ב(1)יד֯ שׁל֯מ֯יהו . א(2)שר **נעשה** . מ(3)ח֯ר֯

'Answer your servant a word through Shelemiah what **we are to do** tomorrow.' (HI Lachish 9:4–6 obverse, 1–3 reverse, my translation)

4.4. The Meanings of the Long *Yiqṭol* in CBH

Table 8: The meanings of long *yiqṭol* in CBH

Past progressive	20
Habitual past	56
Present progressive	14
Progressive in future	4
General present	26
Habitual present	19
Future	436
Future in protasis	325
Future in apodosis	22
Obligation	563
Obligation in apodosis	95
Past obligation	1
Future intention	12
Permissive	36
Ability	26
Diegetic present (?)[43]	1
Future past	7
Volitive	4
Total	**1790**

As was stated in §4.1.1, simultaneity with a past action is an important secondary function of an imperfective (Kuryłowicz 1962, 60; Hamori 1973, 319f.; Kouwenberg 2010a, 229). In the supposed Proto-Semitic example with Akkadian vocables **āmur mutam iqabbi* 'I saw a man speaking' (Rubin 2005, 147), the imperfective *iqabbi* (*yVqattVl*) functions as a subordinate clause that describes the object noun (*mutam*) and has the same past reference as the main clause. Such functions of the Hebrew *yiqṭol(u)* are archaic (Notarius 2010a, 248; 2013, 300), as in (35):

(35) *Ø-qaṭal-S.noun* + ***Ø-yiqṭol(u)****-Npar*

שָׁמְעוּ עַמִּים **יִרְגָּזוּן**

'The peoples heard (while) **they trembled**.' (Exod. 15.14)

Compared to the Proto-Semitic example, in (35), *qaṭal* has replaced the past perfective short *yiqṭol(Ø)* (PS **yaqtul*) in the main clause. It is important to observe both the simultaneity of יִרְגָּזוּן and its progressive action. The *yiqṭol(u)* could be interpreted as a relative clause (of the type that in Akkadian is marked by an initial *ša* and an *-u* subordinative marker), but it is more natural to apply the terminology of Arabic grammar and classify the *yiqṭol(u)* as a circumstantial clause (*ḥāl*; Tropper 1998, 169 n. 59; Notarius 2010a, 248; 2013, 116, 118–120, 283). In CBH, such a clause would have been ungrammatical, because of the initial position of the *yiqṭol(u)*. A more likely choice in CBH is a *qoṭel* clause, as in (36):

(36) *Ø-hinnē-qaṭal-O.noun* + *Ø-**qoṭel***

הִנֵּה שָׁמַעְתִּי אֶת־אָבִיךָ [**מְדַבֵּר** אֶל־עֵשָׂו אָחִיךָ לֵאמֹר]:

‘Listen! I heard your father **telling** Esau your brother:...’ (Gen. 27.6)

So in CBH, *qoṭel* has taken over most circumstantial uses from *yiqṭol(u)*. A corresponding *yiqṭol(u)* clause in CBH must use another syntax to express a progressive meaning, for example with a subordinating conjunction, as in (37):

(37) *wa(y)-yiqṭol* + *kī-***yiqṭol(u)!** + *wa(y)-yiqṭol*

וַיַּ֣רְא יוֹסֵ֗ף כִּֽי־**יָשִׁ֨ית** אָבִ֧יו יַד־יְמִינ֛וֹ עַל־רֹ֥אשׁ אֶפְרַ֖יִם וַיֵּ֣רַע בְּעֵינָ֑יו

‘Joseph saw that his father **was placing** his right hand on Ephraim’s head, and this displeased him.’ (Gen. 48.17)

In (37), the *yiqṭol(u)* is non-initial and the clause is introduced by a subordinating conjunction (כִּי). The temporal reference is past, and the meaning is progressive. *Yiqṭol(u)* can no longer be placed in initial position (see §3.4.3).[44] Another example with past continuative meaning is (38):

(38) *wayhī: S.noun-qoṭel* + *wa-qoṭel* + *Ø-S.noun-***yiqṭol(u)** + *wa-S.noun-***yiqṭol(u)***-N*

וַיְהִי֙ ק֣וֹל הַשּׁוֹפָ֔ר הוֹלֵ֖ךְ וְחָזֵ֣ק מְאֹ֑ד מֹשֶׁ֣ה **יְדַבֵּ֔ר** וְהָאֱלֹהִ֖ים **יַעֲנֶ֥נּוּ** בְקֽוֹל׃

‘The blast of the shofar grew louder and louder, while Moses **was speaking** and God **was answering** with thunder.’ (Exod. 19.19)

It can be argued that the initial *yiqṭol(Ø)* וַיְהִי֙ in this example is a focus marker (cf. Khan 2019, 19), and that the real main clause is the active participle (הוֹלֵ֖ךְ). But with this analysis also, the two *yiqṭol(u)* verbs function as circumstantial clauses with progressive action and past reference.[45] They display the standard word order for long *yiqṭol* in CBH.

The typical imperfective function of *yiqṭol(u)* expressing a habitual past remained in living usage in CBH.[46] This is illustrated in (39):

(39) *wayhī-PrP + wa(y)-yiqṭol + wa(y)-yiqṭol + wa-S.pron-lō-qaṭal + wa(y)-yiqṭol +* [40]*Ø-ADV-**yiqṭol(u)***

וַיְהִ֞י מִקֵּ֣ץ ׀ שְׁנַ֣יִם חֳדָשִׁ֗ים וַתָּ֙שָׁב֙ אֶל־אָבִ֔יהָ וַיַּ֣עַשׂ לָ֔הּ אֶת־נִדְר֖וֹ אֲשֶׁ֣ר נָדָ֑ר וְהִיא֙ לֹא־יָדְעָ֣ה אִ֔ישׁ וַתְּהִי־חֹ֖ק בְּיִשְׂרָאֵֽל׃ מִיָּמִ֣ים ׀ יָמִ֗ימָה **תֵּלַ֙כְנָה֙** בְּנ֣וֹת יִשְׂרָאֵ֔ל לְתַנּ֕וֹת לְבַת־יִפְתָּ֖ח הַגִּלְעָדִ֑י אַרְבַּ֥עַת יָמִ֖ים בַּשָּׁנָֽה׃ ס

‘After two months she returned to her father, and he did to her as he had vowed. She had never known a man, and this became a custom in Israel. [40]Every year Israelite women **went** to lament the daughter of Jephthah the Gileadite for four days.’ (Judg. 11.39–40)

In (39), verse 40 is an asyndetic *yiqṭol(u)* clause that is linked to the last *wa(y)-yiqṭol* clause in verse 39. The linking is an elaboration: the details of what became a custom in Israel. It is clear that the meaning of the *yiqṭol(u)* clause is habitual past.

The prototypical present progressive meaning of *yiqṭol(u)* is relegated to questions and some subordinate clause-types in CBH, because of the competition with the new progressive (*qoṭel*). An example of a progressive *yiqṭol(u)* in a question is:[47]

(40) *Ø-ADV-**yiqṭol(u)**-Npar + Ø-ADV-**yiqṭol(u)**-Npar*

מַה־**תְּרִיבוּן֙** עִמָּדִ֔י מַה־**תְּנַסּ֖וּן** אֶת־יְהוָֽה׃

‘Why **do you quarrel** with me? Why **do you put** the LORD **to the test**?’ (Exod. 17.2)

An expression of the progressive is easily generalised to a general present (Haspelmath 1998, 55; Cook 2012a, 221f.). This usage of *yiqṭol(u)* seems to be productive in CBH.[48] An example is (41):

(41) *Ø-S.pron-qaṭal* + *ʾō S.pron-**yiqṭol(u)**!* + *Ø-INT-XØ*

מִ֣י שָׂ֣ם פֶּה֮ לָֽאָדָם֒ א֚וֹ מִֽי־**יָשׂ֣וּם** אִלֵּ֔ם א֣וֹ חֵרֵ֔שׁ א֥וֹ פִקֵּ֖חַ א֣וֹ עִוֵּ֑ר הֲלֹ֥א אָנֹכִ֖י יְהוָֽה׃

'Who has made man's mouth? Who **makes** him mute, or deaf, or seeing, or blind? Is it not I, the LORD?' (Exod. 4.11)

The imperfective *yiqṭol(u)* can also express a habitual present, where the habitual action includes the present moment, as in (42):[49]

(42) *Ø-ADV-**yiqṭol(u)*** + *wa-O.noun-**yiqṭol(u)**!*

פֶּ֣ה אֶל־פֶּ֞ה **אֲדַבֶּר**־בּ֗וֹ וּמַרְאֶה֙ וְלֹ֣א בְחִידֹ֔ת וּתְמֻנַ֥ת יְהוָ֖ה **יַבִּ֑יט**

'With him **I speak** mouth to mouth, clearly, and not in riddles, and **he beholds** the form of YHWH.' (Num. 12.8)

The long *yiqṭol* also often expresses future meaning: "a general present imperfective… can also be used for future time reference in a future context" (Bybee et al. 1994, 275–77). And because of the new competing progressive *qoṭel* (Cook 2012a, 230), future became the dominating meaning of *yiqṭol(u)* in CBH, together with obligation (Bybee et al. 1994, 277–79; Notarius 2010a, 243). The *yiqṭol(u)* gram can be called an 'old present' in the terminology of Haspelmath (1998, 35f.; Cook 2012a, 221, 233).[50] An example is:

(43) *wa(y)-yiqṭol + "Ø-INT-S.noun-yiqṭol(u) + Ø-ʿattā-* ***yiqṭol(u)!*** *+ Ø-INT-yiqṭol(u) + Ø-ʾim-lō"*

וַיֹּאמֶר יְהוָה אֶל־מֹשֶׁה הֲיַד יְהוָה תִּקְצָר עַתָּה **תִרְאֶה** הֲיִקְרְךָ דְבָרִי אִם־לֹא׃

'And the LORD said to Moses, "Is the LORD's hand shortened? **Now you will see** whether my word to you will come true or not!"' (Num. 11.23)

Obligation is a meaning close to and sometimes difficult to distinguish from future. Future grams tend to have modal uses, and some of them are obligation, ability, and permission (Bybee et al. 1991, 22–24).[51] Obligation reports the existence of external social conditions compelling an agent to complete the predicate action (Bybee et al. 1994, 177). Future and obligation are the dominant meanings of *yiqṭol(u)* in my corpus, partly because of the legal and instructional character of many texts. A futural *yiqṭol(u)* uttered by God or a high official tends to be perceived as an obligation.[52] An example is:

(44) *wa(y)-yiqṭol + "Ø-XØ +* ***Ø-lō-yiqṭol(u)*** *+ kī-ʾim-S.noun-* ***yiqṭol(u)!"*** *+ wa(y)-yiqṭol*

וַיֹּאמֶר־לוֹ אֱלֹהִים שִׁמְךָ יַעֲקֹב **לֹא־יִקָּרֵא** שִׁמְךָ עוֹד יַעֲקֹב כִּי אִם־יִשְׂרָאֵל **יִהְיֶה** שְׁמֶךָ וַיִּקְרָא אֶת־שְׁמוֹ יִשְׂרָאֵל׃

'God said to him, "Your name is Jacob, but your name **will no longer be called** Jacob; Israel **will be** your name." So God named him Israel.' (Gen. 35.10)

An example of *yiqṭol(u)* expressing obligation in instruction is (45):

(45) *wa-PrP-yiqṭol(u)! + wa-qaṭal + wa-O.noun-yiqṭol(u)!*

וְלִבְנֵ֨י אַהֲרֹ֜ן תַּעֲשֶׂ֣ה כֻתֳּנֹ֗ת וְעָשִׂ֤יתָ לָהֶם֙ אַבְנֵטִ֔ים וּמִגְבָּעוֹת֙ תַּעֲשֶׂ֣ה לָהֶ֔ם לְכָב֖וֹד וּלְתִפְאָֽרֶת׃

'And for Aaron's sons you shall make tunics, and make sashes for them; and you shall make turbans for them for dignity and beauty.' (Exod. 28.40)

(45) shows two obligational *yiqṭol(u)* clauses in instructional discourse. It also illustrates a typical alternation with a *wa-qaṭal* clause, also expressing obligation.[53] For the linking, see further §6.11 and §7.2.2.

In a few cases, usually in the first person, the future meaning of *yiqṭol(u)* has a nuance of intention, as in (46):[54]

(46) *Ø-lō-yiqṭol(u) + kī-ʾim-PrP-yiqṭol(u)*

לֹ֣א אֵלֵ֑ךְ כִּ֣י אִם־אֶל־אַרְצִ֥י וְאֶל־מוֹלַדְתִּ֖י אֵלֵֽךְ׃

'No, I will not go, but I will go instead to my own land and to my kindred.' (Num. 10.30)

A future with reference point in the past can be expressed by a long *yiqṭol* (Brockelmann 1956, §42g). In such cases, the *yiqṭol(u)* has past time reference. An example is (47):

(47) *wa(y)-yiqṭol + kī-lō-PrP-yiqṭol(u)!*

וַיֵּ֣דַע אוֹנָ֔ן כִּ֛י לֹּ֥א ל֖וֹ יִהְיֶ֣ה הַזָּ֑רַע

'But Onan knew that the child would not be considered his.' (Gen. 38.9)

The long *yiqṭol* in (47) has past time reference, but refers to a point in time that is future in relation to the narrative reference point.[55]

In not a few cases, the long *yiqṭol* has a shade of permission, which means that the future action is permitted, but not obligatory, as in (48):[56]

(48) *Ø-PrP-VNabs-yiqṭol(u)*

מִכֹּ֥ל עֵֽץ־הַגָּ֖ן אָכֹ֥ל תֹּאכֵֽל׃

'You may eat from every tree of the orchard.' (Gen. 2.16)

The long *yiqṭol* may also express the ability of the actant to perform the action, as in (49):[57]

(49) *Ø-INT-lō-qaṭal + kī-VNabs-yiqṭol(u)*

הֲל֣וֹא יְדַעְתֶּ֔ם כִּֽי־נַחֵ֧שׁ יְנַחֵ֛שׁ אִ֖ישׁ אֲשֶׁ֥ר כָּמֹֽנִי׃

'Don't you know that a man like me can indeed practice divination?' (Gen. 44.15)

Finally, long *yiqṭol* can also, in special constructions, express a direct volitive; one of few examples is (50):[58]

(50) *Ø-lū-S.noun-yiqṭol(u)!*

ל֥וּ יִשְׁמָעֵ֖אל יִחְיֶ֥ה לְפָנֶֽיךָ׃

'O that Ishmael might live before you!' (Gen. 17.18)

4.5. Summary: The Independent Status of the Long *Yiqṭol* (< **yaqtulu*)

This chapter has established the long *yiqṭol* as a separate verbal morpheme in CBH, distinct from the short *yiqṭol*. While the short *yiqṭol* is a verbal formation inherited from Proto-Semitic **yaqtul* with two basic meanings, past perfective and jussive (see §3.1), the long *yiqṭol* is a common innovation in Central Semitic. The long *yiqṭol* is an old imperfective formation in CBH, with the prototypical meanings, such as progressive and past circumstantial, retained in relatively rare cases. The majority meanings in CBH are obligation and future. Many of the earlier imperfective functions of the long *yiqṭol* have been taken over by the active participle (*qoṭel*) in CBH, in a process of renewal of the expression for the progressive and imperfective aspect (§4.1.1.1). This takeover by the *qoṭel* is relatively late: it is not attested in Archaic Hebrew. In spite of the new *qoṭel*, the early function of the imperfective *yiqṭol(u)* to express the habitual past remained in living usage in CBH (§4.4).

Early CBH (after the archaic stage) was able to cope with the partial homonymy between the short *yiqṭol* and the long *yiqṭol* by means of a restriction of word order (described in §3.4.3). A word order that was a tendency in Amarna Canaanite and the Archaic Hebrew poetry—the long *yiqṭol* usually being used in non-initial position—became stricter in CBH. In this way, the identity of the long *yiqṭol* as an old imperfective ('old present' < **yaqtulu*) was preserved, as also the identity of the short *yiqṭol* (< **yaqtul*) as a separate verbal morpheme.

In the theory of consecutive tenses, the long *yiqṭol* is described as alternating with another equivalent 'tense', *wa-qaṭal*. Something has changed in CBH compared to the archaic stage: the long *yiqṭol* can no longer form discourse-continuity clauses (type **wa-VX*), and the *wa-qaṭal* clause-type has entered onto the scene as its substitute (see §6).

---

[1] According to Kuryłowicz (1972c, 54 n. 3), "[i]t is misleading to call Akk. *iprusu* etc. a 'subjunctive'." There is a morpheme *-u* also in certain

Cushitic and Chadic languages, which was added to the verbal base to mark subordination. This *-u* could express an indicative in some Chadic languages (Bole, Kwami, and Tangale) "où *-u* est utilisé pour marquer l'indicatif et le subjonctif" (Jungraithmayr 2005, 80).

[2] As for the assumption that *-u* was a nominal marker, see Kouwenberg (2010a, 230 n. 65).

[3] Progressives view an action as ongoing in the here and now of reference time (often speech time). They give the location of an agent as in the midst of an activity. That is why a locative construction easily develops into an expression of a progressive meaning. "The locative notion may be expressed either in the verbal auxiliary employed or in the use of postpositions or prepositions indicating location—'at', 'in', or 'on'" (Bybee et al. 1994, 129f.). The meaning of the locative that gives rise to a progressive "is probably 'be in the place of verbing' or 'be at verbing'" (Bybee et al. 1994, 136). In the development of a progressive, its use in habitual contexts is earlier than its use with stativic verbs (Bybee et al. 1994, 148). In CBH, for example, *yiqṭol(u)* is often used with past habitual meaning, but when the stativic verb יָדַע is used to express present time, *qaṭal* is used, not *yiqṭol(u)*.

[4] The locative is, however, only one of thirteen possible sources of progressives, according to Kuteva et al. (2019, 486).

[5] If such was the case, the locative *-u* attached to the CS finite prefix formation (thus **yaqtul-u*) could possibly yield a meaning such as: 'he (is) in (that) he kills', which presupposes that the CS *yaqtul* would be an old present ('imperfect') in need of renewal (thus Retsö 2014, 68), which is problematic in view of the comparative Semitic evidence. Kienast (2001, 179) assumes that the nominative ending *-u* itself is an old "Agentiv/Lokativ." If the hypothesis of a locative *-u* in *yaqtul-u* is correct, the *-na* ending on the plural forms in CS must be regarded as diachronically later. An assumption put forward by Diem (1975, 242, 256) is that the *-n* ending on the plural forms was a nunation taken over from the plural endings of the noun at a stage when those endings had

still not changed to *-m*, as was later the case in Amarna and Proto-Hebrew. Compare the state in Amarna, with *-m* in the plural and dual nominal inflection but *-n* in *yaqtulū-na*, and the same holds for Ugaritic (Tropper and Vita 2010, 49, 59; Baranowski 2016a, 83; Tropper and Vita 2019b, 490, 495). It is difficult to explain the *-na* by influence from the nominal inflection; it must have been effective in a linguistic state where the masculine plural of the noun had nunation. If there was such an influence, it must have been operative close to the common Central Semitic stage, since such a development is absent in Akkadian and Amorite (Diem 1975, 251, 256).

[6] In Assyrian, suffixed forms typically take *-ni*, but this *-ni* is attached to the whole verbal phrase after verbal suffixes and the ventive. If there are no other suffixes, the *-ni* is attached directly to *-u*: *-u-ni*. It is also unclear why the two morphemes *-u* and *-na* should be regarded as identical, since *-ni* is absent in Eblaite and Babylonian Akkadian (see Bjøru and Pat-El 2020, 71). It is clear that, in Old Assyrian, the distribution of *-u* and *-ni* is not phonologically conditioned. The two morphemes do not belong to the same grammatical category and are diachronically unrelated: "*-u* is a verbal inflectional suffix, while *-ni* is a clause-domain clitic" (see Bjøru and Pat-El 2020, 75). The scope of *-ni* is the clause rather than the verb, because it is always positioned at the end of the clause (Bjøru and Pat-El 2020, 72, 75f., 78). The conclusion of Bjøru and Pat-El's study is that, in Assyrian, *-ni* is a clause-level clitic and *-u* a verbal suffix. This would indicate that *-u* lost its independent status during the history of Assyrian and represents an internal Assyrian development. If such is the case, we should not expect *-ni* to be reflected in the Central Semitic imperfective formation *yaqtul-u*, and the suffix *-na* in the CS plural verb form *yaqtul-ūna* remains unexplained.

[7] For the *-a-* vowel, see Kogan (2015, 164).

[8] Kuryłowicz (1973, 119): "There must have been a period when the functions β and γ were distributed between the two forms; β = *qatala* (*passé indéfini*), γ = *i̯aqtul* (*passé défini* or narrative tense)."

[9] For Babylonian Akkadian, see Pat-El (2020, 320).

[10] "The functions of *yaqattal* and *yaqtulu* show a clear overlap" (Hamori 1973, 322).

[11] Rubin (2005, 148) writes that "*yaqtul* had already been supplanted by the verbal adjective *qatala*" in West Semitic. This is an exaggeration. The substitution was gradual, "reached by stages" (Kuryłowicz 1973, 119). The perfective *yaqtul* was retained in many West Semitic languages, at least in their early stages (see §3.1).

[12] This replacement has left no attested traces of a *yVqattVl* formation in Central Semitic, and this is a potential counter-argument against the mainstream hypothesis (Fenton 1970, 41). On the absence of such traces, see Bloch (1963) and Fenton (1970). Kogan (2015, 166) calls the absence of *yVqattVl* in CS "a shared loss." For Ugaritic, see Tropper (2012, 460f.). Vernet's (2013) attempt to explain the absence is not convincing.

[13] Another example is the verbal prefix *ð*- + imperfect in Omani Mehri (Rubin 2018, 187f.). It is a relative clause construction that has been reinterpreted as a simple circumstantial clause "referring to either the subject or object of the main verb" (Rubin 2018, 188).

[14] The predicative *qoṭel* is not attested in Amarna Canaanite (Notarius 2010a, 262).

[15] There is a slight generalisation: the head noun can be definite without the *qoṭel* having the definite article. Other examples of attributive *qoṭel*: Gen. 3.5; 3.8 (definite head); 27.6 (definite head); 49.14 (archaic); Exod. 5.10 (definite head); 14.30 (probably definite head); Num. 11.10; 22.23; 24.2 (definite head); Deut. 4.33 (definite head).

[16] An archaic example is Deut. 33.12 (Notarius 2010a, 261; 2013, 238). There is a parallel in Omani Mehri: *mayt hámak* ***tī ð-ōmər*** 'when did you hear **me singing**?' (Rubin 2018, 188).

[17] An analogical example in Omani Mehri is: *aġáyg rədd təwōli sέkənəh ðə-yəḳtōməḥ wə-ðə-yəxtəyūb* 'the man returned to his settlement, despairing and disappointed' (Rubin 2018, 188).

[18] Other examples of circumstantial predicative *qoṭel*: Gen. 21.9; Exod. 26.15; 36.20; Deut. 31.20.

[19] Similar examples are: Exod. 26.5; 36.12.

[20] An analogical example in Omani Mehri is: *xəṭərāt ġayg ðə-yəghōm bə-ḥōrəm* 'once there was a man who was walking on the road' or 'once there was a man walking on the road' or 'once a man was walking on the road' (Rubin 2018, 188).

[21] Some other examples are: Exod. 36.5; Num. 10.29; Judg. 19.18. An analogical example in Omani Mehri is: *ənḥāh ðə-nhəwrūd* 'we are taking (our) animals to the water' (Rubin 2018, 188).

[22] Stein (2020, 339) supposes that *yaqtulu* must have existed in Sabaic.

[23] For more examples, see Isaksson (2009, 91f.).

[24] This example features a long 2ms prefix form *taliku* from the root *hlk*; cf. Hebrew *yēlēk*.

[25] This example features a long 1cs prefix form *ʾaliku*, which is progressive with a nuance of immediate future.

[26] This example features two *yaqtulu* with futural intentional meaning: *a-li-ku-na*, with ventive/energic clitic, from root *hlk*; and *am-si-qu* < **ʾanšiqu* from root *nšq*.

[27] To be read *yʿrb* (KTU³ 44f.).

[28] Baranowski (2016a, 145) translates: 'Previously, I would write to the king: he would not heed my word. Now I am living in Beirut like a dog, and my word is (still) unheeded.'

[29] This is a 2ms form of the jussive (Baranowski 2016a, 74).

[30] Baranowski (2016a, 151) translates: 'Know that all are traitors, and **[y]ou must no[t] inquire about me** from my enemies.'

[31] But a nuance of obligation is also possible: 'They shall deliver them' (Gzella 2012, 67).

[32] For the classification of the Deir ʿAllā inscription, see §3.1.11. Kogan (2015, 600) classes it as belonging to the 'Aramaoid' branch of Central Semitic.

[33] Hackett (1984, 36) identifies this as "*waw* consecutive."

[34] Hackett (1984, 37): “The obvious interpretation of this phrase is that it is an infinitive absolute plus a finite verb of the root *bkh*, coupled for emphasis.”

[35] Hackett (1984, 36): “There must have been some mention in the following words of Balaam’s refusal to eat.”

[36] While Deut. 32 (which is more archaic) exhibits clause-initial *yiqṭol(u)*, 2 Sam. 22 does not (a relative innovation); see Notarius (2013, 166). Other examples of present progressive in the archaic poetry, many of them showing a clause-initial *yiqṭol(u)*: Num. 23.9 (Notarius 2013, 221, 282); 24.17 (*Ø-yiqṭol(u)*; Notarius 2013, 221, 224 n. 42); Deut. 32.40 (Notarius 2013, 95, 96, 282); Ps. 18.2 (*Ø-yiqṭol(u)*-VOC)—but not in 2 Sam. 22.2; 18.47—Notarius (2013, 162) takes the וְיָרוּם as a modal form, possibly because it is written defectively in the presumably older 2 Sam. 22.47 (for this interpretation, cf. §3.4.1.2).

[37] According to Freedman (1960, 102), *tišlaḥnā* “is anomalous” and should be read *tišlaḥanna*, with an energic ending like Arabic *-anna*. The energic ending in Amarna Canaanite was, according to Rainey (1996, II:234), “*-una*, perhaps *-unna*.” For the connection between *yiqṭol(u)* and the ventive/energic endings, cf. Rainey (1996, II:234–36) and Zewi (1999).

[38] Other cases of diegetic present in the archaic poetry: Exod. 15.1 (*ʾāz-yiqṭol(u)!*; Brockelmann 1956, §42a; Rundgren 1961, 97, 99)—*pace* Joosten (2012, 108–11), who says “the syntagm is not explained;” 15.7 (*wa*-PrP-*yiqṭol(u)* + *Ø-yiqṭol(u)* + *Ø-yiqṭol(u)*; Notarius 2013, 116 n. 29, 118, 119, 120, 283); 15.17 (*Ø-yiqṭol(u)* + *wa-yiqṭol(u)*; Notarius 2013, 116, 118, 283; 2015, 243–44); Num. 23.7 (Notarius 2008, 79; 2013, 222); Judg. 5.29 (Notarius 2013, 135f., 142, 283)—Notarius (2013, 284) is open to the possibility that תַּעֲנֶינָּה has an energic ending, as also suggested by Zewi (1999, 108); Ps. 18.4/2 Sam. 22.4 (Notarius 2013, 181); 18.37/2 Sam. 22.37 (*Ø-yiqṭol(u)*! + *wa-lō-qaṭal*), clause-initial historical present according to Notarius (2011, 276; 2013, 174 n. 69, 283; 2015, 245), but Joosten (2012, 432) takes the long prefix form as “preterite YIQTOL;” 18.38 (*Ø-yiqṭol(u)* + *wa-yiqṭol(u)* + *wa-lō-*

yiqṭol(u)!; cf. Notarius 2011, 273; 2013, 172, 283 for 2 Sam. 22.38); 18.40/2 Sam. 22.40—the syntax in Ps. 18.33–46 is deviant and the old reading tradition seemingly had problems with the innovative differentiation between the *wa* and *wə* readings of the conjunction, a differentiation which required a exegetical analysis of the text (cf. Notarius 2013, 160, 175): according to Notarius (2011, 262, 276; 2013, 175f.), this is a historical present based on the imperfective *yiqṭol(u)*, but against the view of Notarius, see Bloch (2009, 47–54); 18.42/2 Sam. 22.42 (*Ø-yiqṭol(u)*, historical present or habitual present; Notarius 2013, 176, 283; 2015, 245); 18.43/2 Sam. 22.43 (*wa-yiqṭol(u)* + *Ø-PrP-yiqṭol(u)*; Notarius 2013, 175, 283).

[39] Examples of past progressive *yiqṭol(u)* in the archaic poetry: Exod. 15.6; Deut. 32.12 (Notarius 2013, 80, 83, 94, 307); 32.14 (Notarius 2013, 80, 83, 85, 307; 2015, 240); Ps. 18.7a (2 Sam. 22.7a has *wa(y)-yiqṭol* instead of *Ø-yiqṭol(Ø)*; Notarius 2013, 165, 169; 2015, 240).

[40] Notarius (2013, 116–120, 283) analyses the prefix forms as imperfective *yiqṭol(u)* and past simultaneous/circumstantial. According to Zewi (1999, 139), this is one of few examples of a prefix form with -Npar and past time reference. Other examples of past simultaneous *yiqṭol(u)* clauses:

Exod. 15.5 (*Ø-S.noun-yiqṭol(u)* + *Ø-qaṭal*; Notarius 2013, 118–20, 283; 2015, 243)—König (1897, III, §152) translates, '[indem] Fluthen sie bedeckten', Moomo (2003, 73) 'The deep was covering them', and Shreckhise 2008, 293 'The deeps were covering them, they went down into the depths like a stone'.

15.12 (*Ø-qaṭal* + *Ø-yiqṭol(u)*; Notarius 2013, 116, 118, 120, 283);

Deut. 32.10 (*Ø-yiqṭol(Ø)* + *Ø-yiqṭol(u)*-N + *Ø-yiqṭol(u)* + *Ø-yiqṭol(u)*-N; Notarius 2013, 307)—יִמְצָאֵהוּ is a 'preterite' according to Notarius (2013, 78, 280), but *pace* Moomo (2003, 76), who translates 'He usually/used to meet him'. Considering the function of יַצֵּב in verse 8, it is plausible that יִמְצָאֵהוּ is a realis past *yiqṭol(Ø)* and codes a main line. A main point in Notarius' (2013, 94 n. 67) discussion is the presence of energic suffixes on the three *yiqṭol(u)* clauses and that the energic *nun* in יְבוֹנְנֵהוּ is left out by haplography, "if one accepts Lambert's and Rainey's opinion that the energic nun is obligatory in this form" (cf. also Notarius 2013, 94–95, 283, 307; 2015, 239f.; similarly Rainey 1986, 16; Joosten 2012, 418);.

32.16 (*Ø-yiqṭol(Ø)* + Ø-PrP-*yiqṭol(u)*; Notarius 2013, 83, 283)—both verbs are *yiqṭol(u)*, but Notarius (2015, 239f.) analyses the first verb as *yiqṭol(Ø)* and the second as *yiqṭol(u)*, while, according to Joosten (2012, 417), both are *yiqṭol(Ø)*.

33.3 (*Ø-ʾap̄-VOC-XØ* + *wa-qaṭal* + *Ø-yiqṭol(u)*; Notarius 2013, 214 n. 47, 239, 242).

33.7 (*Ø-IMP* + *wa-PrP-yiqṭol(u)-N*; Notarius 2013, 242f., 294)—but Gzella (2004, 85–86) calls this a volitive *yiqṭol(u)*).

33.8 (*Ø-XØ* + *«REL-qaṭal* + *Ø-yiqṭol(u)»*; Notarius 2013, 240 n. 47, 241f. n. 53, 300)—but Bergsträsser (1918–1929 II, §34h) calls this a 'preterite'.

33.9 (*kī-qaṭal* + *wa-O.noun-yiqṭol(u)*; Notarius 2013, 242 n. 55, 300).

Judg. 5.6 (Ø-PrP-PrP-*qaṭal* + *wa-S.noun-yiqṭol(u)*)—past iterative according to Notarius (2013, 133, 135, 142), who says it is "at work in the background for past iterative and habitual action" (Notarius 2015, 242), *pace* Müller (1983, 54), who considers it a consequence-result and translates 'die Wege lagen still, so daß die Pfadwanderer krumme Wege gingen'.

Ps. 18.5/2 Sam. 22.5 (*qaṭal* + *wa-S.noun-yiqṭol(u)*; Notarius 2013, 163, 167, 283, 307)—"with circumstantial simultaneous force in reference to simple past קטל" (Notarius 2013, 165).

Ps. 18.7 (*Ø-yiqṭol(Ø)* + *wa-S.noun-PrP-yiqṭol(u)*).

Ps. 18.8a/2 Sam. 22.8a (*wa(y)-yiqṭol* + *wa(y)-yiqṭol* + *wa-S.noun-yiqṭol(u)*; Notarius 2013, 164f., 170, 283; 2015, 240).

Ps. 18.9/2 Sam. 22.9 (*Ø-qaṭal* + *wa-S.noun-PrP-yiqṭol(u)* + *Ø-S.noun-qaṭal*; Notarius 2013, 164, 165, 170, 283, 308; 2015, 240).

Ps. 18.14 (*wa(y)-yiqṭol* + *wa-S.noun-yiqṭol(u)*; Notarius 2013, 164, 165, 170, 283; 2015, 240)—but Notarius (2007, 24) analyses the *yiqṭol(u)*, יִתֵּן, in 2 Sam. 22.14 as 'preterite'.

Ps. 18.34/2 Sam. 22.34 (*Ø-qoṭel* + *wa-PrP-yiqṭol(u)*; Notarius 2013, 172, 175).

[41] Levine (2000, 186) argues that the *qaṭal* in the relative clause has future reference, which is improbable. There is no example of a *qaṭal* in a relative construction referring to the future. The natural interpretation is anterior. Levine's reference to the Deir ʿAllā inscription, *šbw wʾḥwkm mh šdyn [pʿlw]* (Combination I, line 5) is pointless, since there is a lacuna where the verb is expected. Num. 23.23 is probably the only example of *yiqṭol(u)* with immediate future reference in the archaic poetry.

[42] There are about 26 clause-initial *yiqṭol(u)* forms in the archaic poetry, including their use in asyndetic relative clauses, here marked by «Ø-*yiqṭol(u)*» (cf. §3.2). In the following list, I have excluded the much-discussed 'Ugaritic type' of poetry in Ps. 18.33–46/2 Sam. 22.33–46; cf. Notarius (2011; 2013, 171): "the verbal tenses here deserve separate investigation. The main challenge is the formal status of the prefix conjugation." Gen. 49.27 ("heads an asyndetic relative clause," Notarius 2013, 198; see also Nyberg 1972, §94m); Exod. 15.7 (possibly with ellipsis of the initial PrP; Notarius 2013, 116, 118, 119, 120, 283); 15.12 (*Ø-qaṭal* + *Ø-yiqṭol(u)*; Notarius 2013, 116, 118, 120, 283); 15.14a (*Ø-qaṭal* + *Ø-yiqṭol(u)*-Npar; Notarius 2013, 116, 118); 15.17 (*Ø-yiqṭol(u)* + *wa-yiqṭol(u)*; Notarius 2013, 116, 118, 283; 2015, 243–44); Num. 24.17 (Notarius 2008, 67; 2013, 221, 224 n. 42); Deut. 32.10 (*Ø-yiqṭol(Ø)* + *Ø-yiqṭol(u)*-N + *Ø-yiqṭol(u)* + *Ø-yiqṭol(u)*-N; Notarius 2013, 94 n. 67, 95, 280, 283, 307; 2015, 239; Rainey 1986, 16; Joosten 2012, 418); 32.23 (*Ø-yiqṭol(u)* + *Ø-O.noun-yiqṭol(u)*; Notarius 2013, 94f., 294); 32.39 (*Ø-S.pron-yiqṭol(u)*! + *wa-yiqṭol(u)*; Notarius 2013, 94, 97, 294); 32.41b–42a ([41]*Ø-yiqṭol(u)*! + *wa*-PrP-*yiqṭol(u)* + [42]*Ø-yiqṭol(u)*! + *wa-S.noun-yiqṭol(u)*; Notarius 2013, 95); 33.3 (Notarius 2013, 214 n. 47, 242)—the *qaṭal* is analysed as *wa-qaṭal* according to Notarius (2013, 236); 33.8 (*Ø-XØ* + «*REL-qaṭal* + *Ø-yiqṭol(u)*»); 33.22 (*XØ*-«*Ø-yiqṭol(u)*»; Notarius 2013, 244); Judg. 5.8 (*Ø-yiqṭol(u)* + *ʾāz-qaṭal*, possibly an initial temporal clause; Notarius 2013, 133, 135, 142f.; also Bergsträsser 1918–29 II, §7b; Gibson 1994, 74 §63a; Waltisberg 1999, 224)—but the form can be a past perfective *yiqṭol(Ø)*, and in such a case it is "the sole, more or less plausible case of waw-less

preterite *yqtl* in the text" [i.e. in the Song of Deborah] (Notarius 2013, 135; 2015, 241); 5.30 (Ø-ADV-*yiqṭol(u)* + *Ø-yiqṭol(u)*; Notarius 2012, 195; 2013, 141, 282); Ps. 18.2 (*Ø-yiqṭol(u)*); 18.3/2 Sam. 22.3 (*NP-«Ø-yiqṭol(u)!»*; Notarius 2013, 168f.); 18.47 (*Ø-XØ* + *wa-XØ* + *wa-yiqṭol(u)*!)—thus Joosten (2012, 434), but Notarius (2013, 162), seems to regard the *yārūm* as a modal passive participle, in accordance with Dahood (1965a, 118; 1965b, 323).

[43] Gen. 37.7 וְהִנֵּה תְסֻבֶּינָה אֲלֻמֹּתֵיכֶם 'and your sheaves surrounded my sheaf' (thus NET); it is a possible diegetic present in a dream report which also makes use of *qoṭel* clauses in main line.

[44] Other examples of past progressive meanings of *yiqṭol(u)* in CBH: Gen. 2.5 (background, complicated syntax); 2.10 (after *qoṭel*, both in background); 2.25 (*wa(y)-yiqṭol* + *wa-lō-yiqṭol(u)*; Brockelmann 1908–13, II, §321b; Nyberg 1972, §86t, *pace* Joosten 1999, 24); Exod. 8.20 (*wa(y)-yiqṭol* + *wa*-PrP-*yiqṭol(u)*); 36.29 (*wa-qaṭal* + *wa*-ADV-*yiqṭol(u)*, both in background with past reference); Num. 9.15 (*wa*-PREP-VN-*qaṭal* + *wa*-PrP-*yiqṭol(u)*!); 9.18. Outside the corpus, there is 1 Sam. 13.17 (*wa(y)-yiqṭol* + *Ø-S.noun-yiqṭol(u)*; Driver 1892, §163; Joosten 2012, 133).

[45] Zewi (1999, 108) calls this an energic form with continuous action in past tense, but Joosten (1999, 24) calls it "iterative."

[46] I have more than 50 examples of past habituality expressed by *yiqṭol(u)*: Gen. 2.19; 6.4; 29.2; 30.38, 42; 31.8 (in temporal clause); 31.39 (*Ø-O.noun-qaṭal* + *Ø-S.pron-yiqṭol(u)-N* + *Ø-PrP-yiqṭol(u)-N*); Exod. 1.12, in comparative linking (Dixon 2009, 35); 13.22; 17.11; 18.26 (*wa-qaṭal* + *Ø-O.noun-yiqṭol(u)* + *wa-O.noun-yiqṭol(u)*, asyndesis and elaboration)—Zewi (1999, 119, 139) calls it continuous past; 33.7, 8, 9; 34.34; 40.32, 36, 37 (in temporal clause); 40.38; Lev. 26.41; Num. 8.19; 9.16 (with ellipsis of *yiqṭol(u)* in the last clause); 9.17–23; 10.36; 11.5, 9; Deut. 2.12, 20; Judg. 2.18, 19; 6.4, 5; 11.40; 12.5 (in temporal clause); 12.6; 14.10; 17.6 (Isaksson 2009, 92); 21.25.

[47] Examples of present progressive *yiqṭol(u)* in questions: Gen. 32.18, 30; 37.15 (*pace* Joosten 2012, 62); 42.1; Exod. 2.13; 5.4; 16.7; 17.2;

Judg. 17.9; 19.17. Examples not in questions: Gen. 31.35; Exod. 9.30 (in complement); Deut. 3.28 (in relative clause); Judg. 17.3 (close to performative); 21.22 (stativic verb). The long *yiqṭol* can also express a progressive in the future, three of my cases being in temporal clauses (T): Gen. 45.28 (T); Exod. 8.5; 23.23 (T); Lev. 15.25 (T).

[48] Examples in my corpus: Gen. 18.14, 28b (both questions); 41.27; 50.3; Exod. 4.11; 11.7 (in complement); 23.7, 8 (*kī-S.noun-yiqṭol(u) + wa-yiqṭol(u)*, with ellipsis of *S.noun* before the second long *yiqṭol*; Joosten 2012, 309, 429)—identified as long *yiqṭol* also by Gropp (1991, 48); 33.11; 34.7; 36.29; Lev. 4.22 (relative clause); 17.11; Num. 11.14; 11.23; 18.7; 21.14; 22.38; Deut. 1.44; 16.19 (same as Exod. 23.8 with ellipsis); Judg. 10.4; 11.35; 20.16.

[49] Other examples of *yiqṭol(u)* with habitual present meaning: Gen. 2.24 (custom); 10.9; 22.14 (asyndetic relative clause); 32.33 (explanation of a custom; Childs 1963, 281, 283, 288; Westermann 1981, 634); 43.32; Exod. 1.19; 8.22; 18.15; Lev. 4.10; 21.10 (relative construction); Num. 11.13; 12.6 (in apodosis); 12.8; Deut. 2.11, 20; 3.9; 7.10; Judg. 7.5 (in comparative clause).

[50] I have 435 examples of clear future *yiqṭol(u)* in CBH, obligations not included. In addition, there are 325 in protasis and 22 in apodosis. Ten are listed here: Gen. 1.29; 3.4; 3.16; 3.19; 4.12; 8.21; 9.5; 16.10; 17.20; 17.21. In several cases, the distinction between future and obligation is unclear, as in Deut. 13.12 (*wa-lō-yiqṭol(u)*); 31.7 (*wa-S.pron-yiqṭol(u)-N*)—for the NN-form, see Zewi (1999, 101).

[51] The agent-oriented sense of an obligation marker like *yiqṭol(u)* can also be used for an imperative: *You will go to bed!*, *You must call your mother* (Bybee et al. 1991, 28; 1994, 211).

[52] About 250 *yiqṭol(u)* have obligatory meaning in the corpus, including commandments by God. Only a few need be given here: Gen. 44.2 (^{1}*Ø-IMP + wa-IMP +* ^{2}*wa-O.noun-yiqṭol(u)*!); Exod. 13.7 (*Ø-S.noun-yiqṭol(u) + wa-lō-yiqṭol(u)*! + *wa-lō-yiqṭol(u)*!); 20.3–9 (commandments); Lev. 1.3 (legal discourse).

[53] Obligation with past time reference expresses a conditional mood in Lev. 10.18 אָכ֥וֹל תֹּאכְל֛וּ אֹתָ֖הּ בַּקֹּ֥דֶשׁ 'You should certainly have eaten it in the sanctuary!'.

[54] Long *yiqṭol* expressing future intention is also found in: Gen. 19.9; 24.58 (2fs); 32.21 וְאַחֲרֵי־כֵן֙ אֶרְאֶ֣ה פָנָ֔יו (after a ventive-cohortative); 47.19; Lev. 22.29 (2mp, in protasis); Deut. 1.41; 15.16; 18.16—Khan (2021, 337) argues that it is a short jussive *hifʿil*, but morphologically it could be a *qal* long *yiqṭol* (Huehnergard 2005, 467–68); 20.8 (3ms); Judg. 11.23 (2ms); 12.1.

[55] Other examples of long *yiqṭol* expressing a future in the past (often with the conjunction *ṭɛrɛm*): Gen. 41.50 בְּטֶ֥רֶם; 43.25 (future of pluperfect); Exod. 10.14; Num. 15.34; Deut. 1.18 (relative clause); 2.12—Joosten (1999, 24) regards *yiqṭol(u)* here as "anomalous," while according to Cook (2012, 260 n. 94), it is a free-standing preterite *yiqṭol(Ø)*); Judg. 21.22.

[56] Long *yiqṭol* expressing permission is also found in: Gen. 3.2; 38.16; 42.37 (in apodosis; Ges-K §159r); 44.26; Exod. 10.24 (last clause); 12.44; 22.10, 12; 23.11; Lev. 6.11; 7.6, 16, 19, 24; 11.3, 9; 13.36 (in apodosis); 16.28; 22.7, 11 (apodosis); 22.13 (apodosis); 22.23; 25.10; 25.46 לְעֹלָ֖ם בָּהֶ֣ם תַּעֲבֹ֑דוּ; Num. 6.20; 8.15, 26; 12.14; 18.13; 19.7; 35.28; Deut. 12.15, 22; 23.12.

[57] Other examples of long *yiqṭol* expressing a shade of ability or potentiality: Gen. 15.2; 16.2, 10; 17.17; 19.22; 31.43; 43.5; 44.1 (verb *ykl*); 44.8, 16; Exod. 3.11; 4.14; 18.18 (verb *ykl*); 28.32; 33.20—Ges-K (§159gg) translates 'for a man doth not see me and live'; 39.23; Num. 23.13; 30.14; Deut. 4.28; 18.16 (Christensen 2001, 401); 30.12 מִ֣י יַעֲלֶה; 30.13; Judg. 6.15; 16.10, 13 (both as complements).

[58] Other examples of volitive long *yiqṭol*: Exod. 32.32 אִם־תִּשָּׂ֣א חַטָּאתָ֑ם 'Oh, that you would forgive'; Num. 11.4 מִ֥י יַאֲכִלֵ֖נוּ בָּשָֽׂר׃ 'If only we had meat to eat!' (NET); Judg. 9.29 וּמִ֨י יִתֵּ֜ן אֶת־הָעָ֤ם הַזֶּה֙ בְּיָדִ֔י 'If only these men were under my command' (NET). It seems that *mī-yiqṭol(u)*, from being a question about the future, in some contexts receives a volitive nuance.

5. THE PERFECTIVE FORMATION *QAṬAL* IN CBH

5.1. The Semitic Background of *Qaṭal*

It is nowadays commonly accepted that the West Semitic *qatVl(a)* conjugation developed from a resultative construction (Kuryłowicz 1975, 128; Cook 2012a, 203), and that the old WS languages exhibit a concurrence of the resultative and the anterior in one verb form (Nedjalkov and Jaxontov 1988, 40–42). The starting point of the formation was a Proto-Semitic predicative construction with a verbal adjective and a suffixed subject pronoun (Huehnergard and Pat-El 2019, 7; Huehnergard 2019, 63), as in **k'abir-ku* (buried-1sg) 'I am/was buried' (transitive root, passive meaning), **θabir-nu* (broken-1cpl) 'we are/were broken' (passive meaning), **k'arub-ti* (near-2fsg) 'you are/were near' (stative root, stative meaning), or **wašib-a* 'he is/was seated' (intransitive root, resultative meaning; examples from Huehnergard 1987, 225, 227).[1] All these Proto-Semitic predicative *qatVl*-constructions are either passive, resultative, or stative in meaning. Such a construction "predicates the **condition** or **state** that is the result of the action of the verb" (Huehnergard 2011, 221, his emphasis).

Already in Proto-Semitic, a first step towards grammaticalisation was taken: the predicative base *qatVl-* was invariable, and did not agree with the subject pronoun.[2]

Cross-linguistically, resultative constructions are usually lexically restricted and can only be used with dynamic verbs

 https://doi.org/10.11647/OBP.0414.05

involving a change of a state (Dahl 1985, 135; Bybee and Dahl 1989, 69). This restriction did not exist in Proto-Semitic. With dynamic lexemes, *qatVl* signified a state that was the result of the verbal action (resultative meaning). With stativic lexemes, such as **maliʾ* 'full', *qatVl* in the same predicative construction described a state. From this perspective, the Biblical Hebrew stative *zāqēn* 'he is old' is a vestige of a Proto-Semitic usage (Huehnergard 2006, 6; Kouwenberg 2010a, 181).

There is also a predicative *qatil-* with transitive meaning. It is attested in Akkadian for some transitive roots. Huehnergard (1987, 232) prefers to call such constructions 'pseudo-verbal predications', since they are formed as an imitation of a real finite verb of the same root.[3] It seems that "the crucial step in the resultative > perfect shift" was the inferential identification of the subject of the main verb with the agent of the predicative verbal adjective (Cook 2012a, 206, referring to Haug 2008, 294). After the pattern of preterite *imḫur* 'he received' = 'he came into receipt of', an analogical *maḫir* 'he is in receipt of' was formed. After *iṣbat* 'he seized' = 'he took possession of', an analogical transitive *ṣabit* 'he is in possession of', *ṣabtāku* 'I am in possession of' was formed. Predicative constructions of the type *qatil/qatlāku* imitate the real finite verb also in their capacity to govern direct objects. Compare the English *I am in receipt of your letter.* Such pseudo-verbal constructions describe a state/condition and take a direct object. In addition to the normal passive verbal adjective *qatil-* (which may occur also in predicative constructions), there is for some verbs another base *qatil-* that is transitive and is exclusively used in the predicative construction: *ṣabit/ṣabtāku* may be passive 'I am seized', but also transitive 'I am in possession of'. A semantically parallel English example is *I have written what was said* (with direct object), in which the word *written* is transitive, whereas in *I have what was said written*, the word *written* is passive and the predication lacks a direct object.

It is reasonable to assume that the analogical formations attested in Akkadian existed also in Proto-West Semitic, either as a parallel development, or as shared inheritance. In the latter case, we may assume that various types of pseudo-verbal predications had already developed in Proto-Semitic. In Proto-West Semitic, this construction developed into an active suffix conjugation **k'abar-ku* (bury.sc-1sg) 'I (have) buried', **ðakar-a* (invoke.sc-3msg) 'he (has) invoked',[4] which eventually replaced the inherited perfective *yaqtul* "as the basic unmarked perfective and past" (Kogan 2015, 50f. n. 127; Huehnergard and Pat-El 2019, 7; Huehnergard 2019, 63).

As was stated above, a resultative signals a state that is the result of some action in the past, and that this state persists at reference time (Bybee and Dahl 1989, 69). The adverb 'still' is always acceptable with resultative uses of a verbal morpheme.[5] The adverb 'already' is not compatible with a resultative. This adverb is a typical rendering of an anterior (Bybee et al. 1994, 54).[6] A resultative focuses on a state that persists until something happens to change the state. An anterior focuses on the action itself (Bybee and Dahl 1989, 70). In a narrative sequence, the anterior is typically "used for events that are out of sequence" (Bybee et al. 1994, 62, 65).

An anterior has a more general meaning than a resultative. It expresses that a past action is in a general way relevant to the point of reference (often speech time). It does not require that a state exists as a result of the past action. The semantic change from resultative to anterior can be seen as a semantic generalisation (Bybee et al. 1994, 69; Cook 2012a, 204). If the resultative is used in narrative to express an introduction or background to subsequent actions, then the anterior meaning goes further, since it tends to involve not only actions that produce states but "actions that precede other actions" (Bybee et al. 1994, 69). In specific contexts, an anterior can be used with non-past reference, e.g., *Tomorrow I will already have gone.* Such uses of the anterior can be regarded as a metaphorical transposition of the present moment to some point with future time reference, which is also a common interpretation of the so-called 'prophetic perfect' for retrospective future-orientated report in Biblical Hebrew (Bybee and Dahl 1989, 74; Notarius 2013, 88).

When an anterior gram changes to include also perfective meanings (cf. Kuteva et al. 2019, 484), this development constitutes a further generalisation of meaning: there is "a loss of a specific component of meaning" (Bybee et al. 1994, 86). On the semantic level, the anterior loses the *relevance* (in the current moment) of the past action and signals only a past action. "The specification of current relevance is lost" (Bybee et al. 1994, 86). The development of a resultative/anterior morpheme to express also perfective and past meanings is well documented among the languages of the world. Such formations with several uses are more developed, or older, than such that have only one use (Bybee et al. 1994, 80f.; Cook 2012a, 204f., figure 3.6).

Though perfectives usually describe bounded actions in the past, the typical perfective formation also has non-past uses. This fact distinguishes perfectives "from simple pasts, which tend not to have other uses. In particular, perfectives may be used in future contexts." Such perfectives may signal future anterior or immediate future. Simple pasts, on the other hand, are only used in past contexts (Bybee et al. 1994, 95).

The most frequent meanings of *qatal* in the attested West Semitic languages, anterior and perfective past, represent later stages. We have reasons to expect the earlier and prototypical uses of the *qatal* grammatical morpheme ('gram') to occur more frequently in the Archaic Hebrew texts than in CBH (cf. Dahl 2000, 10).

The *qatal* gram in Central Semitic has many meanings: gnomic present, future, irrealis wish, anterior, pluperfect, and simple past (cf. Kouwenberg 2010a, 181 n. 67).[7] This multiplicity should not force anyone to presuppose that there must be a common, or basic, meaning for *qatal*.[8] Cross-linguistically, the various meanings indicate a history, during which the verbal morpheme acquires new meanings, while the more ancient are often retained. We may "assume on the basis of our knowledge of documented cases that one use developed after, and probably out of, the other" (Bybee et al. 1994, 52f.). When we attempt to reconstruct the CBH *qaṭal* with the diachronic path of perfective verbs, "there is ample evidence for identifying the TAM of the *qatal* conjugation at each stage of its development" (Cook 2012a, 205f.).

In West Semitic, the usage of the new perfective developed in competition with the old perfective *yaqtul* (Baranowski 2017, 85). In varying degrees, depending on the individual language, *yaqtul* became syntactically restricted, and in many languages it lost the narrative role, while *qatal(a)* "gradually took over all its functions" (Notarius 2013, 86; also Kuryłowicz 1975, 106; Tropper 1998, 182; Cook 2012a, 264).

5.1.1. Gəʿəz

As usual in West Semitic, the *qatala* gram in Gəʿəz can have both past perfective and anterior meaning (Weninger 2011, 1135). An example of anterior is:

(1) ***samāʿkəmu*** *kama tabəhᵊla la-qaddamt*

'Ihr **habt gehört**, dass zu den Vätern gesagt worden ist' (Mt. 5.21, Tropper 2002, 182)

But *qatal* can also be used with present time reference. As in other West Semitic languages, *qatala* of verbs for emotions and beliefs expresses a general present:

(2) ***nassāḥku*** *ʾəsma ʾangaśkəwwo la-sāʾol*

'**Es reut mich**, dass ich Saul zum König gemacht habe' (1 Kgs 15.11, Tropper 2002, 183)

Qatala can also express a future time reference in prophetic speech.

(3) *ḥəzb za-yənabbər wəsta ṣəlmat* ***rəʾəyu*** *bərhāna ʿabiya*

'Das Volk, das im Dunkel lebt, **wird** ein großes Licht **schauen**' (Isa. 9.2, Tropper 2002, 185)

(4) *wa-nāhu* ***maṣʾa*** *ba-təʾəlfit qəddusān*

'Und siehe, **er wird kommen** mit zehn-tausend Heiligen' (Hen. 1.9, Tropper 2002, 185)

A future meaning is sometimes found also in non-prophetic speech:

(5) *wa-ba-ḫaba* ***motki*** *ʾəmawwət*

'Wo du stirbst/**sterben wirst**, will auch ich sterben!' (Ruth 1.17, Tropper 2002, 185)

Future wishes can be expressed by *qatala*, as in:

(6) *ʾəm-kämä* ***gäsäsku*** *ṣənfä ləbsu ʾaḥayyu*

'if **I** only **will touch** the fringe of his garment, I shall live' (Mt. 9.21, Weninger 2011, 1135)[9]

5.1.2. Modern South Arabian

The West Semitic *qatal* in Soqotri can be used with stative verbs. In this case, it may describe a situation in the present, as in:

(7) *ho náʕa* ***nékerk*** *díʔjho ʔembórje*

'**I miss** my children now' (Kogan and Bulakh 2019, 306)

With transitive verbs, the *qatal* expresses a perfective:

(8) ***lʸékodk*** *márdof di-bᵉʕer*

'**I made** a camel saddle.' (Kogan and Bulakh 2019, 305)

In Omani Mehri, the basic use of the West Semitic *qatal* is as a past perfective, as in (9):

(9) ***ḳə́ṣṣəm*** *ḥərōhs*

'**they cut off** her head' (Rubin 2018, 163)

The Omani Mehri *qatal* can also be used for an immediate future in the first person:

(10) *hōh* ***səyə́rk***

'I'm off!' (Rubin 2018, 164)

The *qatal* in Mehri can express irrealis wishes in certain types of oaths:

(11) ***xályək*** *tēṯi, əl (t)ṭaym mən hənīn śxōf*

'**may I divorce** my wife [= I swear], you won't taste any milk from us' (Rubin 2018, 164)

5.1.3. Ancient South Arabian

According to Stein (2011, 1063f., 1066) the basic function of the suffix conjugation is to express anteriority, as in (12):

(12) *w-sṭr* ***sṭrk*** *b-ʿm rḥbm f-****mḍʾ*** *w-****rḍy***

'The letter **you have sent** (lit.: written) with RḤBM **has arrived and pleased.**' (Mon.script.sab. 68/2–7, quoted from Stein 2011, 1066)

All three *qatal* in (12) have anterior meaning: the first (*sṭrk*) in an asyndetic relative clause and the second in a resumptive clause with conjunction *f*- after a left dislocation.

With a stativic verb, *qatal* may have present tense meaning, as in (13):

(13) *šnʾ|m / ḏ-bn-hw /* ***šʿrw*** */ w-ḏ-bn-hw / ʾl /* ***šʿr|w***

'ein Feind, von welchem **sie wissen** und von welchem **sie nicht wissen**' (YM 438/10–12, quoted from Stein 2013, 131)

But *qatal* may also, in a narrative context, express a perfective past, as in (14):

(14) *w-**ḫmr-hmw** / ʾlmqh / hbʿln / hyt / hgrn / tʿrmn / w-ylfyw / b-hw / mhrgtm / w-ẖysbyw / kl / ʾwld / w-ʾnṯ-hw / w-ymtlyw / kl / ʾbʿl-hw*

‘(Der Gott) ʾLMQH **gewährte ihnen**, sich jener Stadt TʿRMN zu bemächtigen. Und sie erlangten darin Tötungen, und sie nahmen alle ihre (sc. der Stadt) Kinder und Frauen gefangen, und sie erbeuteten all ihre Einwohner’ (J 576/6f., quoted from Stein 2013, 132)

The narrative in (14) starts with a *qatal* clause and continues with *w-yqtl* clauses, a pattern that is frequent also in CBH (see §§7.7–8).

5.1.4. Classical Arabic

The *qatal* gram in Classical Arabic always has an *-a* ending in the 3ms form (thus 3ms *qatal-a*), a feature that may be Proto-Semitic. The origin of *qatala* in a predicative verbal adjective can be perceived in stative roots, when the *qatal* may express a present state, and often a general truth (Bybee et al. 1994, 82). Such meanings are primarily pre-classical:

(15) *fa-qāla lahu Baḥīrā **ṣadaqta** qad kāna mā taqūlu*

‘Baḥīrā answered: **You are right**, what you say has happened’ (Isḥ. 115, 19)

(16) *iḫtalafat-i l-ʿulamāʾu*

‘scholars are of differing opinions’ (Fischer 2002, §181)[10]

(17) *ʾallaḏīna kafarū*

'those who are unbelievers' (Qur. 2:6, 26, 89; Fischer 2002, §181; see Ambros 2004, 239)

(18) *taʿālā ʿan ʾan yakūna lahu šarīkun fī sulṭānihi*

'He is elevated beyond having a companion in his sovereignty' (Ṭab. I.1:5)

(19) *ṯumma qāla ʾayyuhā n-nāsu ʾinnahā maʿḏiratun ʾilā llāhi* ***ʿazza wa-ǧalla***

'Then he said: People! It is an excuse to God—**he is mighty and exalted—**' (Ṭab. II.297:18)

There are also instances of a pure resultative meaning of *qatala* in Classical Arabic, as in:[11]

(20) *daḫalat*

'«sie ist eingetreten» = «steht da»' (Ḥam. 248, 7; Reckendorf 1895–98, 54)

(21) *ṭaribtu*

'ich bin erregt' (Ḥam. 423, 14; Reckendorf 1895–98, 54)

A perfective may also be used in future contexts, either as future anterior, or as immediate future (Bybee et al. 1994, 95). An immediate future is found in:

(22) *ṯumma ʾinna ʾAbā Ṭālibin ḫaraǧa fī rakbin tāǧiran ʾilā š-Šām*

'Then Abū Ṭālib was about to go out by caravan for trading to Syria' (Isḥ. 115, 4)[12]

The *qatala* is also used to express volitive meanings, as in (Wright 1896–98, II:2D):[13]

(23) *raḥimahu l-lāhu*

'May God have mercy on him!' (Fischer 2002, §182)

(24) *būrikta*

'May you be blessed!' (Isḥ. 1022, 15; Fischer 2002, §182; Reckendorf 1895–98, 55)

An example of a present anterior is (cf. Wright 1896–98, II:1A):

(25) *fa-qatala* + *ʾanna-S.noun-**qatal*** + *PrP-«REL-qatal»* + *wa-**qatala*** + *PrP-«REL-qatala»*

*fa-kataba ʾilayhi ʾArdašīru ʾanna l-lāha **ḥabānī** bi-t-tāǧi l-laḏī labistuhu wa-**mallakanī** l-bilāda l-latī ftataḥtuhā*

'Ardašīr wrote (back) to him: "God **has bestowed** on me the crown which I have assumed and **has given me** authority over the lands which I have conquered."' (Ṭab. I.818:2)

An example of both past perfective and pluperfect meaning of *qatala* is found in (26):

(26) *fa-**qatala*** + *wa-**qatala*** + *bi-mā-**qatala*** + *wa-**qatala***

*fa-**ʾaǧābahu** ʾilā ḏālika wa-**kataba** bimā **saʾalahu** min ḏālika siǧillan wa-**ṣāra** bihi ʾilā Tīrā*

'He **agreed** to this and **wrote** a document about what **he had requested** about this and **took** him along to Tīrā.' (Ṭab. I.815:5)

Example (26) also illustrates how Classical Arabic makes use of two coordinating proclitic conjunctions *fa-* and *wa-* in order to create a coherent passage, in which the introductory *fa-* signals temporal succession, and the *wa-qatala* clauses describe the details in the fulfilment of the agreement (*wa-qatala* is close to an elaboration).

5.1.5. Amorite

It is probably diachronically significant that a verbal formation *qatal* is attested in the extant names in Amorite only as a verbal adjective *qatal*, which "denotes conditions of the grammatical subject and has the same meaning as the Akkadian stative in the G-stem" (Golinets 2020, 193). This is illustrated in (27):

(27) *ʿAṯtar-kabar*

'Aštar is great' (Golinets 2020, 193, 195)

A finite verb form *qatal* is not attested in the names. And the corpus from the very early second millennium recently published by George and Krebernik contains only imperatives and various forms of prefix conjugations—not one finite *qatal* (George and Krebernik 2022, 29).

5.1.6. Ugaritic

In Ugaritic, *qatal* is gradually replacing the past perfective *yaqtul* (Fenton 1973, 35). In addition to past actions, the non-stative *qatal* can express present and future events. For verbs with stative meaning, *qatal* functionally corresponds to the Akkadian stative and has no specific temporal reference (Huehnergard 2012, 53; Tropper 2012, 717f.; Tropper and Vita 2019b, 493).

(28) ***rbt*** . *ilm* . *l* ***ḥkmt*** /rabbātă̆ ʾilu-mv la-ḥakamtă̆/

'**you are great**, O El; **you are** truly **wise**' (KTU[3] 1.4.v:3, vocalised and translated by Huehnergard 2012, 53)

Qatal is the normal form for past actions:

(29) *at̠t* . ***trḫ̮*** . *w* ***tbˁt*** /ʾat̠t̠ata tarvḫ̮a wa-tabaˁat/

'**he acquired** a wife but **she departed**' (KTU[3] 1.14.i:14, vocalised and translated by Huehnergard 2012, 53)[14]

(30) *mhy* . ***rgmt***

'Was **hat sie gesagt**?' (KTU[3] 2.14:9, Tropper 2012, 703)

The Ugaritic *qatal* can also express a gnomic present:[15]

(31) *r*ġb . yd . ***mt̠*kt** / *mẓma* . *yd* . ***mt̠kt***

'Dem Hungernden **reicht** sie die Hand, dem Dürstenden **reicht** sie die Hand' (KTU[3] 1.15:I:1f., Tropper 2012, 715, my emphasis)

There are also volitive uses of *qatal*, uses that belong to the older poetic corpus:

(32) *Ø-S.noun-ʾal-yaqtul* + *Ø-S.noun-**qatal***

*šrš*k . *b arṣ* . *a*l / *ypˁ* . *riš* . ***ġly*** . *bd* . *nsˁk*

'Deine Wurzel soll sich nicht aus dem Boden erheben! (Dein) Kopf **möge verwelken/herabfallen** in der/die Hand dessen, der dich herausreißt!' (KTU[3] 1.19:III:53f., Tropper 2012, 726)

(33) *l* ***yrt*** / *b npš* . *bn ilm* . *mt* .

'May you go down [*lū/la yarattă̄*] into the throat of the son of the gods, Môt' (KTU[3] 1.5:I:6–7, Sivan 2001, 98: root yrd 2ms form)

There are also examples of a futural usage of the *wa-qatal* clause-type. In (34), it follows a protasis:

(34) *wa-hm-S.noun-qatal* + ***wa-qatal***

w . *hm* . *ḫt* . / *ʿl* . **w** . ***likt*** / *ʿmk* .

'and if the Hittite has attacked, **then I will send** [*wa-laʾiktŭ̄*] (a letter) to you…' (KTU 2.30:16–18, Sivan 2001, 98)

In (35), *wa-qatal* follows as apodosis after a temporal conditional clause:

(35) [w . u]n*ṯ ʾinn* / *lhm ʿd ttṯbn* / *ksp* . *iwrkl* / **w** . ***ṯb*** . *l unṯhm*

'and they do not have feudal obligation; as soon as they return the money of Iwirkallu, **then they will return** to their feudal obligation' (KTU[3] 3.4:16–19)[16]

The *wa-qatal* clause continues the *yaqtulu* clause (with initial conjunction *ʿd*), and has future time reference.

5.1.7. Amarna Canaanite

In Amarna Canaanite, *qatal* is used to describe "past events without any syntactical restrictions" (Baranowski 2016a, 124).

(36) *wa-qatal*

ù ***uš-‹šì›-ir-⌜ti⌝*** 3 G[IŠ].M[Á].M[EŠ *a-na*] [15]*ma-ḫar* [I]*Ia-*[*an-ḫa-*]*mi*

'So **I sent** three ships [to] Ya[nḥa]mu' (EA 105:14–15)

(37) *ADV-qatal* + *wa-qatal* + *Ø-ADV-qatal*

an-nu-ú i-na-na ***du-bi-r***[***u***] [28]LÚ.MAŠKIM-*ka ù* ***la-qú*** [29]URU.MEŠ-*šu a-na ša-šu-nu* [30]*a-nu-ma* ***la-qú*** URU *Ul-la-sà*

'Behold, now **they have expelled** your commissioner and **they have taken** his towns for themselves. Now **they have taken** the city of Ullasa.' (EA 104:27–30)

Anterior[17] and pluperfect meanings of *qatal* are illustrated in the following example (Baranowski 2016a, 125):

(38) […] *am-mi-nim-mì* ^{12}⸢***na***⸣***-ad-na-ta*** URU *Gi-ti-*⸢*pa*⸣*-da-al-la* ^{13}*[i-n]a* ŠU *šàr-ri* EN-*ka* URU.KI ^{14}*ša* ***la-qí-mi*** ^{I}⸢*La*⸣*-ab-a-yu* ^{LÚ}*a-bu-nu*

‘Why did you give the city of Gath-padalla [in]to the hand of the king, your lord, the city which Labʾayu, our father had taken over?’ (EA 250:11–14)[18]

With stative verbs, *qatal* has a general temporal reference (“across temporal spans;” Baranowski 2016a, 127), which is often best translated in the present tense (Baranowski 2016a, 127f.):

(39) *Ø-yaqtul* + *CONJ-**qatal***

yi-de LUGAL *be-li* ^{10}*i-nu-ma* ***da-na-***⸢***at***⸣ ^{11}*nu-kúr-tu* UGU-*ia* ^{12}*ù* UGU ^{I}*Šu-wa-*⸢*ar*⸣*-*⸢*da*⸣*-*⸢*ta*⸣

‘May the king, my lord, be apprised that hostility **is strong** against me and against Shuwardata’ (EA 271:9–12)

(40) *Ø-qatal*

[…] ***ma-ri-iṣ*** *ma-gal* ^{8}*a-na ia-ši*

‘**It is** very **distressing** for me.’ (EA 103:7–8)

(41) *IMP*[19] + *XØ* + *wa-**qatal*** + *wa-lā-yaqtulu*

a-⸢*mur*⸣*!* LÚ.MEŠ *ḫa-za-nu-tu* URU.MEŠ ^{46}*a-na ša-šu-nu ù* ***pa-aš-ḫu*** ^{47}*ù la-a ti-ìš-pu-ru-na* ^{48}*a-na šàr-ri*

‘Look, the city rulers have cities and **they are at peace** and they don’t write to the king.’ (EA 118:45–48)

(42) […] ⸢***aš***⸣*-*⸢***ba***⸣***-ti*** *a-na* [URU A.PÚ.MEŠ]

‘while **I am dwelling** in [the city of Beirut]’ (EA 138:88)

(43) *i-na* LÚ.MÁŠKIM *šàr-ri* [20]*ša i-šu-ú i-na* ⸢URU⸣ *Ṣu-mu-ur* [21] ***ba-⸢al⸣-ṭá-at*** URU ⸢*Gub*⸣*-la*

‘It is through the commissioner of the king whom he has in the city of Ṣumur that the city of Byblos **is sustained**.’ (EA 68:19–21)

In a past context, a *qatal* of a stative verb refers to the past (Baranowski 2016a, 130), as in (44):

(44) *Ø-yaqtul* + *CONJ-**qatal***

ti-i-de pa-ar-ṣa-ia [40]⸢*i*⸣*-nu-ma* ***i-ba-ša-ta*** *i-na* [41]⸢URU⸣ ⸢*Ṣu*⸣*-mu-ra*

‘You know my conduct when **you were** in Ṣumur’ (EA 73:39–41)

Such a *qatal* of a stative verb may receive an ingressive meaning in a narrative or reportive context (Baranowski 2016a, 130):

(45) [...] *i-na* u_4*-m*[*i*] [48]*pa-ṭá-ar* ÉRIN.MEŠ KI.KAL.KASKAL.KUR! *be-li-*[*ia*] [49]***na-ak-ru*** *gáb-bu*

‘On the day that the expeditionary force of [my] lord withdrew, they all **became hostile.**’ (EA 106:47–49)

A stative *qatal* may also extend its temporal reference into the future, describing “a state that will last in the future until the point specified” (Baranowski 2016a, 191),[20] as in the following example (Baranowski 2016a, 132f.):

(46) *yaqtul* + *wa-yaqtulu* + ***“Ø-qatal”***

[*ú*]-⸢*ra*⸣-⸢*ad*⸣ *iš-tu* ^{21}⸢KUR⸣ *A-mur-ri ù yi-qa* \ *bu* ^{22}*a-na ia-ši* ^{23}***ma-a-di*** ⸢ŠE⸣.MEŠ-*mi* ^{24}*a*!(2)-*na* [KUR *A-mu*]*r-ri* ^{25}[*a-di ka*$_4$*-ša*]-*ad* ⸢LÚ⸣ GAL ^{26}[.............]⸢\⸣ EN-*ia*

‘[...is] seeking to go down from the land of Amurru and he commands me, “Much grain for Amurru [until the arri]val of the senior official (great king?), my lord [......]”’ (EA 178:20–26; in Baranowski’s translation, ‘**There will be plen**[**ty** of gr]ain...’)

5.1.8. Phoenician

As in most other West Semitic languages, *qatal* in Phoenician may express a true anterior, describing events “die in der Vergangenheit abgeschlossen sind und in ihrem Ergebnis in die Gegenwart hereinragen” (Friedrich and Röllig 1999, §262; the German translations below are from the same paragraph). An example is (47):

(47) ארן . ז פעל . [א]תבעל

‘Sarg, den Itbaal gemacht hat’ (KAI^{5} 1:1)

The *qatal* can also be utilised as a perfective past, as in:

(48) כ שתה̊ . בעלם

‘als er ihn in der “Ewigkeit” niederlegte’ (KAI^{5} 1:1)

(49) **פעלן** בעל לדננים לאב ולאם

‘Baʿal **made me** a father and a mother to the Danunians’ (KAI^{5} 26 A I:3, Schade 2005, 40)

(50) ושברת מלצם

‘And I broke the scorners’ (KAI^{5} 26 A I:8, Schade 2005, 41)

The conjunction *wa* plus *qatal* of the copula verb may introduce a description of a state in the past:

(51) **וכן** בימתי כל נעם לדנני(6)ם

‘**Now there was** in my days every pleasure for the Danunians’ (KAI^{5} 26 A I:5–6, Schade 2005, 40, 48)

Performatives are also expressed by *qatal*, as in:

(52) בר̊כתך | לב(3)על צפן

‘hiermit erkläre ich dich als von Baal-Ṣaphon gesegnet’ (KAI^{5} 50:2–3)

Qatal with future time reference is rare in Phoenician. The specific case of the *wa-qatal* clause-type is attested following a *yaqtulu* clause within a complex protasis, and also as the initial clause of an apodosis (53):[21]

(53) (*wa-ʾim-XØ* + *Ø-ʾim-XØ* + *REL-yaqtulu* + ***wa-qatal*** + *Ø-ʾim-ʾap-yaqtulu* + *wa-yaqtulu* + *REL-qatal* + *wa-yaqtulu* + ***wa-qatal*** + *Ø-ʾim-PrP-yaqtulu* + *wa-PrP-yaqtulu*) + ***wa-qatal***

ואם מלך במלכם ורזן ברזנם אם א(13)דם אש אדם שם אש ימח שם אזתו(14)ד בשער ז **ושת** שם אם אף יחמד אי(15)ת הקרת ז ויסע השער ז אש פעל א(16)זתוד ויפעל לשער זר **ושת שם** עלי (17) אם בחמדת יסע בשנאת וברע יסע (18) השער ז **ומח** בעל שמם ואל קן ארץ (19) ושמש עלם וכל דר בן אלם אית הממלכת הא ואית המלך הא ואית (1) אדם הא אש אדם שם

‘(And if there is a king among kings and a prince among princes, if there is a ma[13]n of fame who wipes out the name of Azitawadda [14]from this gate **and puts down his own name**, even if he loves [15]this city, or he tears down this gate that Azitawadda has made [16]and makes a different gate **and puts his name** upon it, [17]whether he tears it down by love, by hatred, or he tears down [18]this gate through malice), **then** Baalshamen and El-Creator-of-the-earth [19]and Eternal-Sun and the entire pantheon of children of the Gods **shall wipe out** that kingdom and that king and that person of fame.’ (KAI^{5} 26 A III:12–IV:1)

In (53), a *wa-qatal* clause within the protasis twice (in both cases ושת) follows a *yaqtulu* clause with future time reference, and then a *wa-qatal* clause (ומח) introduces the apodosis with future time reference.

5.1.9. Old and Imperial Aramaic

In the *Old Aramaic* inscriptions, *qatal* usually refers to a past event.[22]

(54) *wa-qatal*

. וקם . עמי .

‘Und er erhob sich mit mir.’ (KAI^{5} 202 A:3, Degen 1969, 106)[23]

(55) *[wa]-qatal*

[..... ו]שמת . קדם̊ . [.א(14)ור .] נצבא ז̊נה .

‘und ich habe vor ʾlwr diese Stele errichtet’ (KAI^{5} 202 B:13–14, Degen 1969, 107)

(56) *wa-CONJ-qatal*

וכזי חבזו אלהן בית [אבי

'als die Götter das Haus meines Vaters geschlagen hatten' (KAI[5] 224:24, Degen 1969, 108)[24]

A *wa-qatal* clause expresses continuity with past meaning, as is shown in (57) from Deir ʿAllā:[25]

(57) *S.noun-qatal + wa-qatal + wa-qatal*

א֯ל֯[ה]ן֯ . א֯ת֯י֯ח֯דו (6) ונצבו . שדין . מו֯עד . ו֯א֯מ֯ר֯ו֯ . לש[מש .]

'the gods assembled, and the Shaddayin took their places as the assembly. And they said to the s[un]:' (KAI[5] 312 I:5–6)

The Deir ʿAllā text also exhibits an example of gnomic *qatal*:

(58) *S.noun-qatal... + wa-S.noun-qatal*

. ארנ֯בן . אכ֯ל֯ו (10) [ע]שב ...... וקבען . ש֯מעו . מוסר [.]

'Hares eat herbs... and hyenas give heed to chastisement' (KAI[5] 312 I:9–10)[26]

A future meaning is found in the following example:[27]

(59) ... + *Ø-qatal*

שקרת לכל אלהי [ע]ד֯יא

'..., (so) **bist du vertragsbrüchig** gegenüber allen Vertragsgöttern' (KAI[5] 224:14, Degen 1969, 108)[28]

In the *Imperial Aramaic* texts from Elephantine, there is a usage of *qatal* as an anterior projected into the future ('future perfect'). In the following example, *qatal* is used in both protasis and apodosis:

(60) *wa-hn-qatal + wa-ADV-qatal + wa-qatal*

והן **מאתת** ולעד **שלמת ויהבת** לך כספא זילך

‘**should I die**, and (by then) **I have** not yet **paid and given** you your silver’ (TAD B3.13:8 [402 BCE], Muraoka and Porten 2003, 193)

A *qatal* with future anterior meaning can be found also in a relative clause:

(61) *NP-REL-S.pron-qatal*

עבידתא זי אנת **עבדת**

‘the work which **you will have undertaken**’ (TAD B2.4:10 [460–459 BCE], Muraoka and Porten 2003, 193)

With verbs of knowing and mental states, a *qatal* may express a present, or even future, as in (62):

(62) *wa-PrP-REL-qatal*

ולמן זי **צבית** למנתן

‘whoever **you desire** to give (it) to’ (TAD B3.4:15 [437 BCE], Muraoka and Porten 2003, 194)

There are also examples of a gnomic (proverbial) *qatal* in Imperial Aramaic:

(63) *S.noun-**qatal** + wa-S.pron-REL-PP-**qatal***

מאן טב **כס[י]** מלה בלבבה וה֯ו֯ ז֯[י]תביר **הנפקה** ברא

‘a good vessel **cover[s]** a word in its midst, but one whi[ch] is broken **lets it go out**’ (TAD C1.1:93 [Aḥiqar, fifth century BCE], Muraoka and Porten 2003, 194)[29]

5.2. *Qaṭal* in the Archaic Hebrew Poetry

In the earliest Hebrew poetry, the new (West Semitic) perfective *qaṭal* still exhibits signs of a relatively new verbal formation. Its use in plain narrative, when speech time and narrator have faded away, is fairly limited (Notarius 2013, 86, 286). The impressiveness of the new perfective morpheme appears to advantage in poetic report, when the presence of the narrator shows through in an intense involvement of the speaker in the recapitulation of the events:

(64) *Ø-O.noun-**qaṭal*** + *Ø-O.noun-**qaṭal*** + *Ø-PrP-**qaṭal*** + [26]*Ø-O.noun-yiqṭol(u)-N* + ***wa-qaṭal*** + ***Ø-qaṭal*** + ***wa-qaṭal*** + ***wa-qaṭal*** + [27]*Ø-PrP-**qaṭal*** + ***Ø-qaṭal*** + ***Ø-qaṭal*** + *Ø-PrP-**qaṭal*** + ***Ø-qaṭal*** + *Ø-bə-«REL-qaṭal»-ADV**qaṭal***

מַ֥יִם **שָׁאַ֖ל** חָלָ֣ב **נָתָ֑נָה** בְּסֵ֥פֶל אַדִּירִ֖ים **הִקְרִ֥יבָה** חֶמְאָֽה: 26 יָדָהּ֙ לַיָּתֵ֣ד
תִּשְׁלַ֔חְנָה וִֽימִינָ֖הּ לְהַלְמ֣וּת עֲמֵלִ֑ים **וְהָלְמָ֤ה** סִֽיסְרָא֙ **מָחֲקָ֣ה** רֹאשׁ֔וֹ **וּמָחֲצָ֥ה**
וְחָלְפָ֖ה רַקָּתֽוֹ: 27 בֵּ֣ין רַגְלֶ֔יהָ **כָּרַ֥ע נָפַ֖ל שָׁכָ֑ב** בֵּ֤ין רַגְלֶ֙יהָ֙ **כָּרַ֣ע נָפָ֔ל** בַּאֲשֶׁ֣ר כָּרַ֔ע
שָׁ֖ם **נָפַ֥ל** שָׁדֽוּד:

‘**He asked for** water and **she gave** him milk, **she brought** him curds in a lordly bowl. [26]She puts her hand to the tent peg and her right hand to the workmen’s mallet; **she struck** Sisera a blow, **she crushed** his head, **she shattered and pierced** his temple. [27]**He sank, he fell, he lay still** at her feet; at her feet **he sank, he fell**; on the place he sank, there **he fell** dead.’ (Judg. 5.25–27, Notarius 2013, 142, 290, my emphasis)

In this emotionally charged report, the new perfective *qaṭal* expresses a simple perfective past (Notarius 2013, 289). There is no difference in meaning between *Ø-qaṭal* and the forms with proclitic *wa* (*wa-qaṭal*; J-M §119z n. 4.),[30] except that the latter in a general sense continue the preceding clause(s). Some of the events coded by *qaṭal* are temporally sequential, others are not (verse 26).[31] The *yiqṭol(u)* clause with energic ending without suffix (תִּשְׁלַ֫חְנָה) expresses a historical present (Notarius 2013, 136, 142, 283f.), and a concomitant action (Müller 1983, 53).

The *qaṭal* morpheme in the Archaic Hebrew poetry may be used as resultative,[32] as stative (with stativic verb), as expressing the ability of the subject ('perfect of confidence'), as performative, as counterfactual irrealis ('would that'), as anterior, as expressing a new stage in storytelling, and for past simultaneous events in storytelling. The anterior meaning of *qaṭal* may also, when the temporal reference is clearly indicated, be transposed into a 'prophetic' future.

The stativic *qaṭal* is illustrated in (65), where three *qaṭal* interrupt the narrative main line.

(65) *wa(y)-yiqṭol* + *wa(y)-yiqṭol* + ***Ø-qaṭal*** + ***Ø-qaṭal*** + ***Ø-qaṭal*** + *wa(y)-yiqṭol-O.noun-«Ø-qaṭal»* + *wa(y)-yiqṭol*

וַיִּשְׁמַ֤ן יְשֻׁרוּן֙ וַיִּבְעָ֔ט **שָׁמַ֖נְתָּ עָבִ֣יתָ כָּשִׂ֑יתָ** וַיִּטֹּשׁ֙ אֱל֣וֹהַ עָשָׂ֔הוּ וַיְנַבֵּ֖ל צ֥וּר יְשֻׁעָתֽוֹ׃

'Jeshurun grew fat, and kicked. **You are fat**, **thick**, **gorged**! He abandoned God who made him, and scoffed at the Rock of his salvation.' (Deut. 32.15, Notarius 2013, 287, 307, my emphasis)

The shift to second-person *qaṭal* forms involves an appeal to the predicament of the audience at speech time, a sort of comment to the listeners (Joosten 2012, 418), "an interpolation of the hymnal conversational framework" (Notarius 2015, 240).[33]

In specific contexts, a *qaṭal* as a resulting state of a previous action signifies the ability of the subject to perform the action of the lexeme (Notarius 2013, 218, 288).[34] This is shown in (66).[35]

(66) *Ø-S.pron-qaṭal* + *wa-S.pron-qaṭal*[36]

מִ֤י **מָנָה֙** עֲפַ֣ר יַעֲקֹ֔ב **וּמִסְפָּ֖ר** אֶת־רֹ֣בַע יִשְׂרָאֵ֑ל

'Who **can count** the dust of Jacob, or **number** the dust-cloud of Israel?' (Num. 23.10a, Notarius 2013, 218, 288, my emphasis)

A performative meaning is likewise close to the resultative *qaṭal*. An example is (67):

(67) *kī-yiqṭol(u)* + *wa-**qaṭal*** + *"Ø-XØ"*

כִּֽי־אֶשָּׂ֥א אֶל־שָׁמַ֖יִם יָדִ֑י **וְאָמַ֕רְתִּי** חַ֥י אָנֹכִ֖י לְעֹלָֽם׃

'For I lift up my hand to heaven, **and swear**: As I live forever' (Deut. 32.40, Notarius 2013, 288, my emphasis)

In (67), *wa-qaṭal* is an archaic performative,[37] while the *yiqṭol(u)* is present progressive.[38]

Like many perfectives cross-linguistically, *qaṭal* can also be used as an irrealis expressing counterfactual wishes, but only with an initial irrealis particle, as in (68).

(68) *Ø-lū-**qaṭal*** + *Ø-yiqṭol(Ø)* + *Ø-yiqṭol(Ø)*

ל֥וּ **חָכְמ֖וּ** יַשְׂכִּ֣ילוּ זֹ֑את יָבִ֖ינוּ לְאַחֲרִיתָֽם׃

'Would that **they were wise** to understand this and to discern what their end will be!' (Deut. 32.29)

The clause linking in (68) is often understood as conditional (thus Notarius 2013, 92, 284, 288; Christensen 2002, 801). But to introduce a protasis is not the normal function of the particle *lū*, which signals a counterfactual wish, 'oh that', 'would that', 'if only!' (cf. HALOT).[39]

It is commonly held that *qaṭal* in an oath introduced by the particle *ʾim*, at least diachronically, was an irrealis usage of the verb in an imprecation (J-M §165d). An example is (69):

(69) *kī-yiqṭol(u)* + *wa-qaṭal* + *"Ø-XØ"* + *Ø-ʾim-**qaṭal*** + *wa-yiqṭol(Ø)* + *Ø-yiqṭol(u)!* + *wa-PrP-yiqṭol(u)*

כִּֽי־אֶשָּׂ֥א אֶל־שָׁמַ֖יִם יָדִ֑י וְאָמַ֕רְתִּי חַ֥י אָנֹכִ֖י לְעֹלָֽם׃ אִם־**שַׁנּוֹתִי֙** בְּרַ֣ק חַרְבִּ֔י וְתֹאחֵ֥ז
בְּמִשְׁפָּ֖ט יָדִ֑י אָשִׁ֤יב נָקָם֙ לְצָרָ֔י וְלִמְשַׂנְאַ֖י אֲשַׁלֵּֽם׃

'For I lift up my hand to heaven, and swear: As I live forever: **I will not whet** my flashing sword, in order that my hand take hold of judgment; but I will take vengeance on my adversaries, and will repay those who hate me' (Deut. 32.40–41, Notarius 2013, 92 n. 59, my emphasis)

Example (69) is an oath by YHWH,[40] with a promise not to lift his sword with judgment against his people, but only against his enemies. The performative *wa-qaṭal* (וְאָמַ֕רְתִּי) has already been treated above. The use of the syntagm *ʾim qaṭal* without the appropriate apodosis in (69) indicates that it was already a set phrase in the archaic poetry: a solemn negative oath with future time reference.

There is only one instance of a *qaṭal* verb forming a conditional clause in a commonly accepted archaic text. It is in the Oracles of Balaam, a relatively innovative text.

(70) *Ø-hinnē-VN-qaṭal* + *wa-**qaṭal*** + *wa-lō-yiqṭol(u)-N*

הִנֵּ֥ה בָרֵ֖ךְ לָקָ֑חְתִּי **וּבֵרֵ֖ךְ** וְלֹ֥א אֲשִׁיבֶֽנָּה׃

‘Therefore I (= El) have taken (him = Balaam) to bless; **if he blesses**, I will not retract it’ (Num. 23.20, Notarius 2013, 220, 289)

The function of the *wa-qaṭal* syntagm as protasis is clear in this passage, but the temporal reference of the protasis is unclear. It could be taken as a conditional anterior, ‘if he has blessed’, or as present tense, ‘if he blesses’. Since *wa-qaṭal* as protasis is attested only in this archaic instance, it is not possible to conclude that *wa-qaṭal* is a ‘category’ that “is used for the conditional mood” (thus Notarius 2013, 220).[41] If we compare with the syntax of CBH, this is not the usual type of conditional clause linking (see §6.7). Protases with an initial *wa-qaṭal* are rare in CBH, and apodoses with a *yiqṭol(u)* clause are commonly asyndetic (not introduced by *wa*). We should beware of equating the syntax in Num. 23.20 with CBH syntax, and it is more cautious to suppose that *wa-qaṭal* involves a *qaṭal* with anterior aspect transferred into a condition: ‘and has he blessed, then I will not retract it’.

The anterior meaning of *qaṭal* is relatively frequent in the archaic poetry. The examples exhibit two dominant uses: in main clauses with speech time included in the temporal reference, and in relative, often asyndetic, clauses. An example of an anterior with the present time of the speaker included in the meaning is (71).

(71) *kī-qaṭal* + *wa-lō-qaṭal*

כִּ֥י **שָׁמַ֖רְתִּי** דַּרְכֵ֣י יְהֹוָ֑ה וְלֹ֥א **רָשַׁ֖עְתִּי** מֵאֱלֹהָֽי׃

'For **I have kept** the ways of the LORD, and **have** not **wickedly departed** from my God' (2 Sam. 22.22/Ps. 18.22, Notarius 2013, 168, 291, my emphasis)

Such anteriors are close to the prototypical resultative meaning of *qaṭal*, and "easily interpreted as habitual past, denoting the behavior patterns of the speaker" (Notarius 2013, 168).[42] The use of the *qaṭal* form in relative clauses is conspicuously well established in the most archaic texts. In such constructions, the anterior is more remote from the speech time and the speaker. An example is (72).

(72) *Ø-yiqṭol(Ø)* + *O.noun-«Ø-lō-**qaṭal**»* + *O.noun-«PrP-**qaṭal**»* + *«lō-**qaṭal**»*

יִזְבְּח֗וּ לַשֵּׁדִים֙ לֹ֣א אֱלֹ֔הַ אֱלֹהִ֖ים לֹ֣א **יְדָע֑וּם** חֲדָשִׁים֙ מִקָּרֹ֣ב **בָּ֔אוּ** לֹ֥א **שְׂעָר֖וּם** אֲבֹתֵיכֶֽם׃

'They sacrificed to demons, not God, to deities **they had never known**, to new ones recently **arrived**, whom your ancestors **had not feared**' (Deut. 32.17, Notarius 2013, 287; 2015, 240, my emphasis)

The three *qaṭal* verbs with pluperfect meaning in (72) are all found in asyndetic relative clauses and there is no clear relation to speech time. The narrative main line in this retrospective report is coded by a clause-initial old perfective *yiqṭol(Ø)* (יִזְבְּחוּ; Notarius 2013, 79).[43]

In the possibly earliest stage of archaic narrative poetry, represented by the first part of the Song of Moses (Deut. 32.8–20), the new perfective *qaṭal* plays a minor role and is used only in relative clauses (anterior). For background and circumstantial clauses, the imperfective *yiqṭol(u)* is used (Notarius 2013, 308).

At a slightly later stage (Notarius (2013, 296f.), represented by the first part of the Song of David (2 Sam. 22.5–20), *qaṭal* plays a role in the narration, and may signal an introduction, a new stage in the narrative framework, a simultaneous non-sequential event, or a background (with or without an initial particle *kī*), as in (73).[44]

(73) ***kī-qaṭal*** + *Ø-S.noun-yiqṭol(u)* + [6]*Ø-S.noun-**qaṭal*** + *Ø-**qaṭal*** + [7]*Ø-PrP-yiqṭol(u)* + *wa-PrP-yiqṭol(u)* + *wa(y)-yiqṭol* + *wa-XØ* + [8]*wa(y)-yiqṭol* + *wa(y)-yiqṭol* + *Ø-S.noun-yiqṭol(u)* + *wa(y)-yiqṭol* + ***kī-qaṭal*** + [9]*Ø-**qaṭal*** + *wa-S.noun-PrP-yiqṭol(u)* + *Ø-S.noun-**qaṭal*** + [10]*wa(y)-yiqṭol* + *wa(y)-yiqṭol* + *wa-XØ* + [11]*wa(y)-yiqṭol* + *wa(y)-yiqṭol* + *wa(y)-yiqṭol* + [12]*wa(y)-yiqṭol* + [13]*Ø-PrP-**qaṭal*** + [14]*Ø-yiqṭol(Ø)* + *wa-S.noun-yiqṭol(u)* + [15]*wa(y)-yiqṭol* + *wa(y)-yiqṭol* + *Ø-O.noun*[45] + *wa(y)-yiqṭol* + [16]*wa(y)-yiqṭol* + *Ø-yiqṭol(Ø)* + [17]*Ø-yiqṭol(Ø)* + *Ø-yiqṭol(Ø)* + *Ø-yiqṭol(Ø)* + [18]*Ø-yiqṭol(Ø)* + ***kī-qaṭal*** + [19]*Ø-yiqṭol(Ø)* + *wa(y)-yiqṭol* + [20]*wa(y)-yiqṭol* + *Ø-yiqṭol(Ø)* + ***kī-qaṭal***

כִּֽי **אֲפָפֻ֖נִי** מִשְׁבְּרֵי־מָ֑וֶת נַחֲלֵ֥י בְלִיַּ֖עַל יְבַעֲתֻֽנִי׃ 6 חֶבְלֵ֥י שְׁא֖וֹל **סַבֻּ֑נִי קִדְּמֻ֖נִי** מֹ֥קְשֵׁי־מָֽוֶת׃ 7 בַּצַּר־לִ֤י אֶקְרָ֣א יְהוָ֔ה וְאֶל־אֱלֹהַ֖י אֶקְרָ֑א וַיִּשְׁמַ֤ע מֵהֵֽיכָלוֹ֙ קוֹלִ֔י וְשַׁוְעָתִ֖י בְּאָזְנָֽיו׃ 8 ⟨וַתִּגְעַשׁ⟩ וַיִּתְגָּעַ֣שׁ וַתִּרְעַשׁ֮ הָאָרֶץ֒ מוֹסְד֥וֹת הַשָּׁמַ֖יִם יִרְגָּ֑זוּ וַיִּֽתְגָּעֲשׁ֖וּ כִּֽי־**חָ֥רָה** לֽוֹ׃ 9 **עָלָ֤ה** עָשָׁן֙ בְּאַפּ֔וֹ וְאֵ֥שׁ מִפִּ֖יו תֹּאכֵ֑ל גֶּחָלִ֖ים **בָּעֲר֥וּ** מִמֶּֽנּוּ׃ 10 וַיֵּ֥ט שָׁמַ֖יִם וַיֵּרַ֑ד וַעֲרָפֶ֖ל תַּ֥חַת רַגְלָֽיו׃ 11 וַיִּרְכַּ֥ב עַל־כְּר֖וּב וַיָּעֹ֑ף וַיֵּרָ֖א עַל־כַּנְפֵי־רֽוּחַ׃ 12 וַיָּ֥שֶׁת חֹ֛שֶׁךְ סְבִיבֹתָ֖יו סֻכּ֑וֹת חַֽשְׁרַת־מַ֖יִם עָבֵ֥י שְׁחָקִֽים׃ 13 מִנֹּ֖גַהּ נֶגְדּ֑וֹ **בָּעֲר֖וּ** גַּחֲלֵי־אֵֽשׁ׃ 14 יַרְעֵ֥ם מִן־שָׁמַ֖יִם יְהוָ֑ה וְעֶלְי֖וֹן יִתֵּ֥ן קוֹלֽוֹ׃ 15 וַיִּשְׁלַ֥ח חִצִּ֖ים וַיְפִיצֵ֑ם בָּרָ֖ק ⟨וַיְהֻמֵּם⟩ וַיָּהֹֽם׃ 16 וַיֵּֽרָאוּ֙ אֲפִ֣קֵי יָ֔ם יִגָּל֖וּ מֹסְד֣וֹת תֵּבֵ֑ל בְּגַעֲרַ֣ת יְהוָ֔ה מִנִּשְׁמַ֖ת ר֥וּחַ אַפּֽוֹ׃ 17 יִשְׁלַ֤ח מִמָּרוֹם֙ יִקָּחֵ֔נִי יַמְשֵׁ֖נִי מִמַּ֥יִם רַבִּֽים׃ 18 יַצִּילֵ֕נִי מֵאֹיְבִ֖י עָ֑ז מִשֹּׂ֣נְאַ֔י כִּ֥י **אָמְצ֖וּ** מִמֶּֽנִּי׃ 19 יְקַדְּמֻ֖נִי בְּי֣וֹם אֵידִ֑י וַיְהִ֧י יְהוָ֛ה מִשְׁעָ֖ן לִֽי׃ 20 וַיֹּצֵ֥א לַמֶּרְחָ֖ב אֹתִ֑י יְחַלְּצֵ֖נִי כִּי־**חָ֥פֵץ** בִּֽי׃

> ‘For the waves of death **have encompassed me**, the torrents of perdition assailed me; [6]the cords of Sheol **entangled me**, the snares of death **confronted me**. [7]In my distress I was calling upon the LORD; to my God I was calling. From his temple he heard my voice, and my cry came to his ears. [8]Then the earth reeled and rocked; the foundations of the heavens trembled and they quaked, because **he had become angry**. [9]Smoke **went up** from his nostrils, and devouring fire from his mouth; glowing coals **flamed forth** from him. [10]He bowed the heavens, and came down; thick darkness was under his feet. [11]He rode on a cherub, and flew; he was seen upon the wings of the wind. [12]He made darkness around him a canopy, thick clouds, a gathering of water. [13]Out of the brightness before him coals of fire **flamed forth**. [14]The LORD thundered from heaven; the Most High uttered his voice. [15]He sent out arrows, and scattered them—lightning, and routed them. [16]Then the channels of the sea were seen, the foundations of the world were laid bare at the rebuke of the LORD, at the blast of the breath of his nostrils. [17]He reached from on high, he took me, he drew me out of mighty waters. [18]He delivered me from my strong enemy, from those who hated me; for **they were too mighty** for me. [19]They came upon me in the day of my calamity, but the LORD was my stay. [20]He brought me out into a broad place; he delivered me, because **he finds delight** in me’ (2 Sam. 22.5–20, Notarius 2013, 163f., my emphasis and added verse numbers)

The *qaṭal* clauses in vv. 5–6, together with the past iterative *yiqṭol(u)* clauses in v. 7,[46] shape an introduction or preamble to the narrative.[47] The *qaṭal* forms render “different sides of the same situation without sequential meaning" (Notarius 2013, 164; 2015, 240f.). The temporal reference is present anterior. The narrative main line is coded by the old perfective *yiqṭol(Ø)*, asyndetic or syndetic (with proclitic *wa*).[48] In this narrative frame, the two *qaṭal* clauses in v. 9 mark "a new stage in storytelling" (Notarius 2013, 167, 287).[49] This beginning of a new narrative, which must be regarded as part of the main line, is followed by twenty past perfective *yiqṭol(Ø)* clauses, the last one in v. 20. The main line is interrupted in v. 13 by a *qaṭal* clause (בָּעֲר֫וּ), denoting a "simultaneous non-sequential event within the past narrative framework" (Notarius 2013, 165).

At the stage of the archaic poetry represented by 2 Sam. 22.5–20, in which the scope of the new perfective *qaṭal* "is a bit broader than in Deut. 32.8–20," on a continuum between narrative and report (Notarius 2013, 307, 311), *qaṭal* clauses have entered the narrative framework to signal introductory clauses, to signal a new beginning, and to denote backgrounded events, the latter function side-by-side with past habitual or progressive *yiqṭol(u)* clauses.[50]

The relatively later stage of the archaic poetry represented by the oracles of Balaam exhibits a prophecy with *Ø-qaṭal* and *wa-qaṭal* clauses having future time reference:[51]

(74) *Ø-yiqṭol(u)-N* + *wa-lō-ADV* + *wa-lō-XØ* + ***Ø-qaṭal*** + *wa-**qaṭal*** + *wa-**qaṭal*** + *wa-**qaṭal***[52] + [18]*wa-**qaṭal*** + *wa-**qaṭal*** + *wa-S.noun-qoṭel* + [19]*wa(y)-yiqṭol!* + *wa-**qaṭal***

אֶרְאֶ֙נּוּ֙ וְלֹ֣א עַתָּ֔ה אֲשׁוּרֶ֖נּוּ וְלֹ֣א קָר֑וֹב **דָּרַ֨ךְ** כּוֹכָ֜ב מִֽיַּעֲקֹ֗ב **וְקָ֥ם** שֵׁ֙בֶט֙ מִיִּשְׂרָאֵ֔ל
וּמָחַץ֙ פַּאֲתֵ֣י מוֹאָ֔ב **וְקַרְקַ֖ר** כָּל־בְּנֵי־שֵֽׁת׃ 18 **וְהָיָ֨ה** אֱד֜וֹם יְרֵשָׁ֗ה **וְהָיָ֧ה** יְרֵשָׁ֛ה
שֵׂעִ֖יר אֹיְבָ֑יו וְיִשְׂרָאֵ֖ל עֹ֥שֶׂה חָֽיִל׃ 19 וְיֵ֖רְדְּ מִֽיַּעֲקֹ֑ב **וְהֶאֱבִ֥יד** שָׂרִ֖יד מֵעִֽיר׃

'I see him, but not now; I behold him, but not near—a star **shall come** out of Jacob, and a scepter **shall rise** out of Israel; **it shall crush** the borderlands of Moab, and **ruin** all the Shethites. [18]Edom **will become** a possession, Seir **will become** a possession of its enemies, while Israel does valiantly. [19]So let one out of Jacob rule! **He shall destroy** the survivors of Ir.' (Num. 24.17–19, vv. 17–18 translation by Notarius 2013, 220, v. 19 my translation)[53]

The temporal reference is indisputable because of the adverbs supplied in v. 17, 'I see him, but not now' (וְלֹ֣א עַתָּ֔ה). In relation to speech time, the events that are described by *qaṭal* clauses occur in the future. It is a prospective report and there is no difference in temporal reference between the initial asyndetic *Ø-qaṭal* verb (דָּרַ֨ךְ) and the *wa-qaṭal* clauses that follow.[54] In this prophecy, a "prophetic perfect is interpreted as a simple past that requires future interpretation due to the metaphorical relocation of ST to future" (Notarius 2013, 217, 219 n. 29, 220, 268 n. 6).[55]

5.3. *Qaṭal* in the Pre-exilic Hebrew Inscriptions

There is ample evidence of an anterior meaning of 'epistolary' *qaṭal* in the letters, but the interpretation is disputed.[56] One example is (75):

(75) *Ø-qaṭal*

השב . עבדך . הספר(7)ם . אל אדני .

'Your servant **has returned** the letters to my lord.' (HI Lachish 5: 6–7)[57]

A certain anterior meaning of *qaṭal* is found in (76):

(76) *wa-ʿattā-qaṭal*

ועת **הטה** [ע]ב̊ד̊ך [ל]ב̊ה (5) אל . אשר אמ̊[רת [

'And now, your [se]rvant **has inclined** his [h]eart to what [you have] sai[d]' (HI Arad 40:4–5)[58]

A straightforward narrative (past perfective) *qaṭal* that initiates a new paragraph (with following *wa(y)-yiqṭol*) is attested in (77) (Gogel 1998, 279, 282; Rainey 2001, 424):[59]

(77) *wa-PrP-**qaṭal*** + *wa(y)-yiqṭol*

ובים . ה(4)נקבה . **הכו** . החצבם . אש . לקרת . רעו . גרזן . על . [ג]רזן
. וילכו (5) המים . מן . המוצא . אל . הברכה . במאתים . ואלף . אמה .

'At the time of the breakthrough, the hewers **struck**, each to meet his fellow, pick against [p]ick. And then the waters flowed from the spring to the pool for twelve hundred cubits.' (HI Silm 1:3–5)

A performative *qaṭal* with *piʿʿel* of *brk* is attested in several inscriptions, as in (78):

(78) *Ø-S.noun-qaṭal* + ***Ø-qaṭal***

אחך . חנניהו . שלח לשל(2)ם . אלישב . ולשלם ביתך **בר̊**(3)**כתך̊** ליהוה

'Your brother Hananiah greets Eliashib and your house. **I bless you** by YHWH.' (HI Arad 16:1–3)

The blessing formula with *qaṭal* (בר̊כתך̊) has a performative meaning—the action is executed by uttering the words—and cannot be interpreted as a Hebrew epistolary convention.[60]

5.4. The Meanings of *Qaṭal* in CBH

With *qaṭal*, Classical Hebrew inherited from West Semitic a full-blown perfective formation. The only step not yet taken on its diachronic path is the change to a simple past, and that step can be seen completed in Postbiblical Hebrew (Cook 2012a, 208). In CBH, *qaṭal* still applies to stative predicates, often with the effect of signalling a present state. But *qaṭal* with stative verbs may in other instances signal the beginning of a state (cf. Bybee et al. 1994, 92).[61] The CBH *qaṭal* is a perfective gram, and exhibits the expected range of historical meanings.[62] The statistics from my corpus are given in Table 9.

Table 9: The meanings of *qaṭal* in CBH

Resultative present	1
Stativic	154
Anterior	308
Perfective past	584
Pluperfect	135
Habitual past	19
Performative	32
Modal, volitive (?)[63]	1
Counterfactual	23
Future	13
As wa-qaṭal	8
Total	**1278**

As can be seen from Table 9, the dominant meanings of *qaṭal* in CBH are perfective (past) and anterior, which can be expected of a relatively old perfective gram. The usage of *qaṭal* with stativic verbs, with present or past temporal reference, is also frequent.

A pure resultative is a rare phenomenon in CBH, with only one certain example in the corpus.

5.4.1. The Resultative Meaning of *Qaṭal*

Resultative is the prototypical meaning of *qaṭal* and describes, with dynamic verbs, a condition or state that is the result of the action. The focus is on the result of an action, not on the action itself. Such meanings are easily confused with an anterior aspect. I have been restrictive on this point and found only one secure instance:

(79) *Ø-PrP-yiqṭol(u)* + *kī-PrP-**qaṭal***

לְזֹאת֙ יִקָּרֵ֣א אִשָּׁ֔ה כִּ֥י מֵאִ֖ישׁ **לֻֽקֳחָה**־זֹּֽאת׃

‘This one will be called woman, for **she was taken** out of man.’ (Gen. 2.23)

In (79), the action of *qaṭal* (לֻֽקֳחָה) describes a state, the situation of the woman being taken out of man. Focus is not so much on the action but on the state that has resulted from the action.

5.4.2. *Qaṭal* with Stativic Verbs

The usage of *qaṭal* with stativic verbs is inherited in CBH from the earliest stage of its formation. In total, 154 stativic *qaṭal* are registered in my database. Past temporal reference is frequent (101 ×; J-M §112a), but so is reference to speech time (48 ×; J-M §112b); see Table 10.

Table 10: Stativic uses of *qaṭal*

Stativic *qaṭal*	
Stativic verb past	59
Stativic copula verb past	42
Stativic verb present	48
Stativic in protasis	4
Stativic in apodosis	1

Stativic verbs include mental states, an example of which is (80):

(80) *wayhī Ø-CONJ-**qaṭal** + wa(y)-yiqṭol*

וַיְהִ֗י כַּאֲשֶׁ֨ר **יָרֵ֜א** אֶת־בֵּ֣ית אָבִ֗יו וְאֶת־אַנְשֵׁ֥י הָעִ֛יר מֵעֲשׂ֥וֹת יוֹמָ֖ם וַיַּ֥עַשׂ לָֽיְלָה׃

'Because **he was afraid** of the men in his father's household and those from the city, so he did it at night.' (Judg. 6.27)

Copula verbs with *qaṭal* can be either stativic ('was') or perfective ('became'; see below). A stativic example is:

(81) *wa-S.noun-**qaṭal***

וְהָאָ֗רֶץ **הָיְתָ֥ה** תֹ֙הוּ֙ וָבֹ֔הוּ

'The earth **was** unformed and void' (Gen. 1.2)

But stativic verbs with *qaṭal* frequently have present time reference. This is illustrated in (82):

(82) *Ø-S.noun-qoṭel + kī-**qaṭal***

קֵ֤ץ כָּל־בָּשָׂר֙ בָּ֣א לְפָנַ֔י כִּֽי־**מָלְאָ֥ה** הָאָ֛רֶץ חָמָ֖ס מִפְּנֵיהֶ֑ם

'The end of all living beings is coming before me, for the earth **is filled** with violence because of them.' (Gen. 6.13)

In the direct speech in (82), the *qaṭal* (מָלְאָה) has speech time reference.

Qaṭal can also be used with the same stativic meanings in protases and apodoses. In a conditional linking, the temporal reference becomes future, as in (83).

(83) *(wa-S.pron-CONJ-**qaṭal**)* + *Ø-**qaṭal***

וַאֲנִ֕י כַּאֲשֶׁ֥ר שָׁכֹ֖לְתִּי שָׁכָֽלְתִּי׃

'As for me, if **I am bereaved** (of children), **I am bereaved**.' (Gen. 43.14)

In (83), *qaṭal* clauses constitute both the protasis and the apodosis. The asyndetic *qaṭal* in the apodosis has a future time reference (Gropp 1991, 47; Cook 2012, 207 n. 46).[64] The meaning of both *qaṭal* is close to a prototypical resultative.

5.4.3. *Qaṭal* as Anterior

In the anterior meaning, focus has shifted to the action itself, and this action is still relevant for the situation at reference time. The most frequent case is when reference time coincides with speech time. The statistics are displayed in Table 11.

Table 11: *Qaṭal* as anterior in CBH (registered cases in the database)

Anterior *qaṭal*	
Present	228
Present, copula verb	10
Present in protasis	9
Present in apodosis	1
Future	9
Future in protasis	42
Future in apodosis	9
Pluperfect	135

A present anterior *qaṭal* describes an action in the past that is relevant at speech time (‘recent past’; J-M §112c). An example is:

(84) *Ø-kī-**qaṭal** + Ø-XØ*

כִּ֣י **עָשִׂ֣יתָ** זֹּאת֒ אָר֤וּר אַתָּה֙ מִכָּל־הַבְּהֵמָ֔ה וּמִכֹּ֖ל חַיַּ֣ת הַשָּׂדֶ֑ה

‘Because **you have done** this, cursed are you above all the wild beasts and all the living creatures of the field!’ (Gen. 3.14)

The action, what the snake has done, is in focus, and this sin, which is highly relevant in speech time, is coded by a *qaṭal* verb.

A present anterior can also occur in a conditional linking, of which the use in protases seems to be more frequent. It can be noted that *qaṭal* in protases has the same range of meanings as in other domains, only that the reference time is future and the truth value is not settled. An example of a present anterior in a protasis is given in (85):[65]

(85) *(Ø-ʾim-lō-**qaṭal** + wa-ʾim-lō-**qaṭal**) + Ø-IMP*

(אִם־לֹ֨א **שָׁכַ֥ב** אִישׁ֙ אֹתָ֔ךְ וְאִם־לֹ֥א **שָׂטִ֛ית** טֻמְאָ֖ה תַּ֣חַת אִישֵׁ֑ךְ) הִנָּקִ֕י מִמֵּ֛י הַמָּרִ֥ים הַֽמְאָרְרִ֖ים הָאֵֽלֶּה׃

‘If no man **has gonc to bed** with you, if **you have not gone astray** to make yourself unclean while under your husband’s authority, then be free from this water of embitterment and cursing.’ (Num. 5.19)

A present anterior *qaṭal* may occur also in an apodosis. There is only one example in the database:

(86) *(wa-yēš-XØ) + wa-ADV-qaṭal*

(וְיֵ֤שׁ יְהוָה֙ עִמָּ֔נוּ) וְלָ֥מָּה מְצָאַ֖תְנוּ כָּל־זֹ֑את

'(But if the LORD is with us,) why has such disaster overtaken us?' (Judg. 6.13)

The action of the *qaṭal* (מְצָאַ֖תְנוּ) lies in the past, but its relevance is in speech time.

The anterior aspect may be transferred into the future in certain syntactical constructions, for example with a temporal conjunction. In such a case, the action described by *qaṭal* is already finished, but still relevant at reference time. An example is:

(87) *Ø-PrP-yiqṭol(u) + Ø-ʿad-ʾim-**qaṭal***

גַּ֤ם לִגְמַלֶּ֙יךָ֙ אֶשְׁאָ֔ב עַ֥ד אִם־**כִּלּ֖וּ** לִשְׁתֹּֽת׃

'I'll draw water for your camels too, until **they have drunk** as much as they want.' (Gen. 24.19)

In (87), *qaṭal* (כִּלּ֖וּ) is used in a temporal subordinate clause. The conjunction clearly indicates futural temporal reference, and the action has already occurred at reference time.[66]

A special case is the examples of the verb נָתַן with God as subject. In such cases, *qaṭal* expresses a decision already made by God, as his promise, which will be fulfilled in the future:

(88) *Ø-ʾal-yiqṭol + kī-PrP-**qaṭal***

אַל־תִּירָ֣א אֹת֔וֹ כִּ֣י בְיָדְךָ֞ **נָתַ֧תִּי** אֹת֛וֹ וְאֶת־כָּל־עַמּ֖וֹ וְאֶת־אַרְצ֑וֹ

'Do not fear him, for **I have given** him into your hand, and all his people, and his land.' (Num. 21.34)

In (88), God describes the giving, the handing over of the land, as already accomplished, though the fulfilment of the action lies in the future.[67]

An anterior *qaṭal* with (eventual) future time reference can be found also in a protasis domain, a fairly frequent case. An example is:

(89) *(Ø-ʾim-qaṭal) + Ø-XØ;*

(אִם־זָרְחָה הַשֶּׁמֶשׁ עָלָיו) דָּמִים לוֹ

'(If the sun has risen on him,) then there is blood guilt for him.' (Exod. 22.2)

The conditional *qaṭal* in (89) still has an anterior meaning—this is not something that its use in a protasis domain changes—but this anterior is transposed into the future and the eventuality of a protasis.[68]

A future anterior *qaṭal* may also occur as apodosis. An example is:

(90) *(wa-NP-REL-yiqṭol(u)) + Ø-O.noun-**qaṭal** + Ø-VNabs-yiqṭol(u) + Ø-XØ*

(וְאִישׁ אֲשֶׁר יִשְׁכַּב אֶת־זָכָר מִשְׁכְּבֵי אִשָּׁה) תּוֹעֵבָה **עָשׂוּ** שְׁנֵיהֶם מוֹת יוּמָתוּ [דְּמֵיהֶם בָּם]׃

'If a man has sexual intercourse with a male as one has sexual intercourse with a woman, the two of them **have committed** an abomination. They must be put to death; their blood guilt is on themselves.' (Lev. 20.13)

The action expressed by *qaṭal* in (90) is something that has already happened when the condition is fulfilled. It is a past event with relevance in the reference time of the apodosis (future).[69]

The pluperfect *qaṭal* is a commonplace in CBH (see J-M §112c). It codes an action that is past in relation to another past action, and still relevant to this action. An example is:

(91) *wa(y)-yiqṭol* + *wa-hinnē-qaṭal* + *kī-**qaṭal***

וַיַּ֧רְא אֱלֹהִ֛ים אֶת־הָאָ֖רֶץ וְהִנֵּ֣ה נִשְׁחָ֑תָה כִּֽי־**הִשְׁחִ֧ית** כָּל־בָּשָׂ֛ר אֶת־דַּרְכּ֖וֹ עַל־הָאָֽרֶץ׃

‘And God saw the earth, and behold, it was corrupt, for all flesh **had corrupted** their way on the earth.’ (Gen. 6.12)

In (91), God looked at the earth. This action is past (perfective). The pluperfect *qaṭal* (הִשְׁחִית) is past in relation to God’s looking in the main clause (וַיַּרְא) and still relevant to it.

5.4.4. *Qaṭal* as Perfective

With perfective meanings, *qaṭal* loses its relevance in the current moment. A typical perfective describes bounded actions, usually in the past. A perfective past meaning of *qaṭal* is by far the most frequent in the corpus. An example is:

(92) *wa(y)-yiqṭol* + *wa-PrP-**qaṭal***

וַיִּקְרָ֨א אֱלֹהִ֤ים ׀ לָאוֹר֙ י֔וֹם וְלַחֹ֖שֶׁךְ **קָ֣רָא** לָ֑יְלָה

‘And God called the light Day, and the darkness **he called Night**.’ (Gen. 1.5)

In (92), the *qaṭal* clause is bounded as much as the *wa(y)-yiqṭol* is. The action has no relevance to a current moment. Both actions are remote; the difference is that, while the *wa(y)-yiqṭol* signals discourse continuity and a succession in relation to the preceding clause, the *qaṭal* clause describes an action that can be regarded as parallel or complementary in relation to the *wa(y)-yiqṭol*. No temporal succession is signalled by the *qaṭal* clause (type *wa-XV*; see §§1.2.6, 7.11–12). On the other hand, it is not natural to regard the *qaṭal* clause as background. Both clauses in (89) are main-line (foregrounded), but only the first signals discourse continuity (type *wa-VX*).

A bounded action can also have future time reference (so-called 'immediate future'; Bybee et al. 1994, 83; Isaksson 2009, 134). There are a few examples in my corpus. One is:

(93) *PrP* + *kī*-***qaṭal***

בְּאָשְׁרִ֔י [כִּ֥י **אִשְּׁר֖וּנִי** בָּנ֑וֹת]

'How happy I am, for women **will call me** happy!' (Gen. 30.13)

In (93), Leah expects the praise of the women to be imminent, which is expressed by a *qaṭal* clause (Ges-K §106n; Westermann 1981, 574).[70]

5.4.5. *Qaṭal* as Performative

As a perfective gram, *qaṭal* can also be used for performative meanings (J-M §112f.).[71] This is a fairly frequent usage of *qaṭal* in CBH.

(94) *Ø-VNabs*-***qaṭal***

הַקְדֵּ֣שׁ **הִקְדַּ֩שְׁתִּי֩** אֶת־הַכֶּ֨סֶף לַֽיהוָ֜ה מִיָּדִ֗י לִבְנִי֙ לַעֲשׂ֖וֹת פֶּ֣סֶל וּמַסֵּכָ֑ה

'**I solemnly dedicate** this silver to the LORD for my son to make a carved image overlaid with silver.' (Judg. 17.3)

In (94), the solemnity of the act is strengthened by an infinitive absolute placed before *qaṭal*.

In some cases, especially when first-person (referring to God) *qaṭal* of the lexeme נָתַן is used, a performative could also be interpreted as a present anterior, coding a decision already made within the Godhead.[72] Linguistic indications of a performative meaning are the adverbials *hinnē*, *rəʾē*, and *hay-yōm*. An example is:

(95) *Ø-rəʾē-qaṭal*

רְאֵה **נָתַ֤תִּי** לְפָנֶ֨יךָ֙ הַיּ֔וֹם אֶת־הַֽחַיִּ֖ים וְאֶת־הַטּ֑וֹב וְאֶת־הַמָּ֖וֶת וְאֶת־הָרָֽע׃

'See, **I set** before you (today) life and good, death and evil.' (Deut. 30.15)

In (95), the choice between life and good, death and evil, is set before the people of Israel in the moment it is uttered. The present time reference is emphasised by the adverbs *rəʾē* and *hay-yōm*.[73]

5.4.6. Virtually Habitual Perfective *Qaṭal*

Several past perfective uses of *qaṭal* describe actions that are habitual, repetitive, or continuative. Usually, this is indicated by adverbs in the clause. The action is seen as a whole, with a bounded aspect. An example is:

(96) *wa-S.noun-qaṭal + Ø-O.noun-qaṭal*

וּבְנֵ֣י יִשְׂרָאֵ֗ל **אָכְל֤וּ** אֶת־הַמָּן֙ אַרְבָּעִ֣ים שָׁנָ֔ה עַד־בֹּאָ֖ם אֶל־אֶ֣רֶץ נוֹשָׁ֑בֶת אֶת־הַמָּן֙ **אָכְל֔וּ** עַד־בֹּאָ֕ם אֶל־קְצֵ֖ה אֶ֥רֶץ כְּנָֽעַן׃

'Now the Israelites **ate** manna forty years, until they came to a land that was inhabited; **they ate** manna until they came to the border of the land of Canaan.' (Exod. 16.35)

In (96), the eating of the manna is seen from a distance, with perfective aspect. Both *qaṭal* clauses are perfective; they do not in themselves signal habituality. The habitual action is implied by the long temporal distance ('forty years').[74]

5.4.7. Irreal *Qaṭal*

Apart from the use of *qaṭal* in conditional linking, which is very similar to the realis meanings, *qaṭal* can be used to express irrealis meanings, commonly signalled by specific particles. I have found no directly volitive meaning of *qaṭal* in my corpus,[75] but there are counterfactual uses, relating to what has not happened, hypothetical assertions, wishes for the unexpected, and surprised questions (Waltke and O'Connor 1990, §30.5.4b; J-M §112j).

The counterfactual constructions are conditional in nature. A positive protasis contains a *lū-qaṭal* phrase, and a negative protasis, a *lūlē-qaṭal* phrase. A positive apodosis usually starts with *kī-ʿattā-qaṭal*, and the negated equivalent is phrased with *Ø-lō-qaṭal*. An example of a negative protasis with an affirmative apodosis is:

(97) *(kī-lūlē-**qaṭal**)* + *kī-ʿattā-**qaṭal***

(כִּ֖י לוּלֵ֣א הִתְמַהְמָ֑הְנוּ) כִּֽי־עַתָּ֥ה שַׁ֖בְנוּ זֶ֥ה פַעֲמָֽיִם׃

'If we had not delayed, we would now have returned twice.' (Gen. 43.10)

Both clauses contain a counterfactual *qaṭal*, but only the first is marked with the particle *lū* (negated *lūlē*; J-M §167f.). An example with negated apodosis is:[76]

(98) *(Ø-lū-qaṭal)* + *Ø-lō-**qaṭal***

(לוּ הַחֲיִתֶם אוֹתָם) לֹא **הָרַגְתִּי** אֶתְכֶם׃

'If you had saved them alive, **I would** not **kill** you.' (Judg. 8.19)

A hypothetical assertion is not formulated as a condition with result (Bybee et al. 1991, 20). An example with *qaṭal* and two *wa(y)-yiqṭol* clauses is the following:

(99) *kī-ʿattā-**qaṭal*** + *wa(y)-yiqṭol* + *wa(y)-yiqṭol*

כִּי עַתָּה **שָׁלַחְתִּי** אֶת־יָדִי וָאַךְ אוֹתְךָ וְאֶת־עַמְּךָ בַּדָּבֶר וַתִּכָּחֵד מִן־הָאָרֶץ׃

'For by now **I could have put out** my hand and struck you and your people with pestilence, and you would have been cut off from the earth.' (Exod. 9.15)

Example (99) shows that *wa(y)-yiqṭol* clauses may follow a hypothetical *qaṭal* without changing the hypothetical meaning.[77]

Wishes for something unexpected may also be expressed by *qaṭal*, as in (100):[78]

(100) *Ø-lū-**qaṭal*** + *ʾō-PrP-lū-**qaṭal***

לוּ־**מַתְנוּ** בְּאֶרֶץ מִצְרַיִם אוֹ בַּמִּדְבָּר הַזֶּה לוּ־**מָתְנוּ**׃

'Would that **we had died** in the land of Egypt! Or would that **we had died** in this wilderness!' (Num. 14.2)

Finally, a counterfactual intention can be formulated as a surprised question (J-M §112j):[79]

(101) *Ø-INT-**qaṭal*** + *wa-qaṭal*

הֶחֳדַלְתִּי אֶת־מָתְקִי וְאֶת־תְּנוּבָתִי הַטּוֹבָה וְהָלַכְתִּי לָנוּעַ עַל־הָעֵצִים׃

'**Should I give up** my fruit, so good and sweet, to hold sway over the trees?' (Judg. 9.11)

5.4.8. *Qaṭal* Functioning as *Wa-qaṭal*

In a few cases, *qaṭal* has the same meaning as the construction *wa-qaṭal* (see §6), that is, it functions as an imperfective formation. In most such cases, the *qaṭal* clause follows a *wa-qaṭal* clause, and is connected by the disjunctive conjunction *ʾō*. This is illustrated in (102):

(102) *(kī-yiqṭol(u) + wa-qaṭal +* ***ʾō-qaṭal****) + Ø-O.noun-yiqṭol(u)*

(כִּֽי יִגְנֹֽב־אִישׁ֙ שׁ֣וֹר אוֹ־שֶׂ֔ה וּטְבָח֖וֹ **א֣וֹ מְכָר֑וֹ**) חֲמִשָּׁ֣ה בָקָ֗ר יְשַׁלֵּם֙ תַּ֣חַת הַשּׁ֔וֹר וְאַרְבַּע־צֹ֖אן תַּ֥חַת הַשֶּֽׂה׃

‘(If someone steals an ox or a sheep and slaughters **or sells it**), he must pay five oxen for an ox and four sheep for a sheep.’ (Exod. 21.37)

There are only a few (8 ×) records in the database where *ʾō-qaṭal* has similar meanings to a *wa-qaṭal* clause. It is surprising that the disjunctive *ʾō-qaṭal* can express the same meanings as *wa-qaṭal*. The disjunctive clause-type *ʾō-qaṭal* is not a construction in Bybee’s (2010; 2015) sense. After an anterior *qaṭal*, the disjunction *ʾō-qaṭal* has anterior meaning (Lev. 15.3; Num. 30.11). The pattern that can be discerned is that the meaning of the preceding clause determines the meaning of *ʾō-qaṭal*:

qaṭal + *ʾō-qaṭal* = anterior;
wa-qaṭal + *ʾō-qaṭal* = imperfective;
yiqṭol(u) + *ʾō-qaṭal* = imperfective (Lev. 25.49).

It is possible that this extended functionality of *ʾō-qaṭal* as disjunctive clause to both *qaṭal* and *wa-qaṭal* is a heritage of the early developmental stage when *wa-qaṭal* emerged as a construction in Bybee’s sense (see §6).[80]

5.5. Why *Qaṭal* Came to Alternate with *Wa(y)-yiqṭol*: *Qaṭal* as Intruding Morpheme in CBH

The extant usage of *qaṭal* in CBH cannot be fully understood without its competition and interaction with the old perfective gram *yiqṭol(Ø)* (Isaksson 2014b). The coexistence of two perfective forms is attested already in Amarna Canaanite, a "coexistence of a newly emerged perfective (*qatal*) with the original perfective (*yaqtul*)" (Baranowski 2016a, 208). In CBH, the new perfective (*qaṭal*) has taken over all the earlier perfective functions of *yiqṭol(Ø)*, except its use in affirmative continuity clauses (clause-type *wa(y)-yiqṭol*). This development must be characterised as an invasive process, and a renewal of the expression of the perfective aspect (Smith 1991, 6; Joosten 2012, 75). As is commonly recognised, this process started at an early stage of West Semitic. Already in the Amarna letters from Canaan, "the original perfective *yaqtul* and the newly emerged perfective *qatal* were coexistent" (Baranowski 2016a, 215, also 188).

The replacement basically occurred in discontinuity clauses. In continuity clauses, an old clause-type for narrative action was retained during the whole CBH period: *wa(y)-yiqṭol*. It did a good job and was retained. In the storyline, a replacement was necessary only in negative continuity clauses, since the old *wa-lā-yaqtul*, in full use in Amarna Canaanite, was suppressed in Proto-Hebrew because of its word order and the risk of confusion with the old *wa-lā-yaqtulu* (Joosten 2012, 43). The expansion of the new perfective in the syntax of CBH resulted in a conspicuous alternation between short *yiqṭol* in affirmative continuity clauses (type *wa(y)-yiqṭol*) and *qaṭal* in other clause-types with perfective and anterior meanings. In this respect, CBH is a conservative West Semitic language: an old PS perfective **yaqtul* is retained side-by-side with a new perfective. In many of the other first-millennium WS languages, indicative *yaqtul* clauses are practically absent.

This is the reason why *qaṭal* came to interchange with *wa(y)-yiqṭol*. In all *X-verb* positions, including where *X* is just a negation, *qaṭal* became the verb form to be used instead of the old short *yiqṭol*. In Amarna, the realis sequence *u-yaqtul* may be broken by a negation, an adverb, or a subject (Baranowski 2016a, 207), but not in CBH. In Amarna and Archaic Hebrew, a realis *yaqtul* may occur at the beginning of a clause without the conjunction *wa*, in asyndesis, but not in CBH. "[T]he *yaqtul* in Canaanite was used as an unrestricted preterite, capable of both initiating and continuing a narrative" (Baranowski 2016a, 207). No longer so in CBH, which permits only the sequence *wa-yaqtul* (*wa(y)-yiqṭol*). Initiating a narrative, even in main line and not only in background, is done mainly by *qaṭal* clauses (for further details see §§7.7–8).

In affirmative discourse-continuity clauses in narration, the storyline, the *wa(y)-yiqṭol* clause-type has maintained its dominance. In my corpus of CBH, no affirmative *qaṭal* clause is attested in the same function as a narrative *wa(y)-yiqṭol*.

In negative continuity clauses in narration, in the storyline, *qaṭal* has crept in. The new negative discourse-continuity clause-type in CBH is *wa-lō-qaṭal*. Such a clause, with no other clausal constituent placed before the verb, signals discourse continuity, coded with the clausal pattern *wa-NEG-V* (see §7.12).

5.6. Summary: The Identity of *Qaṭal* as Perfective Gram in CBH

This chapter has established *qaṭal* as a perfective gram in CBH and its origin as a resultative construction in West Semitic.

In its relation to the perfective short *yiqṭol* of Proto-Semitic origin, it is new (see §3.1). But considered on its path of grammaticalisation from a resultative construction, it is old (§5.4). The traces of the prototypical resultative meanings exhibited in the corpus are rare. The anterior and past perfective uses dominate in the corpus.

Proto-Hebrew resultative uses of the *wa-qaṭal* clause-type—in modal sequences and as apodosis—probably became the basis for the new construction *wa-qaṭal*, a distinguishing feature of CBH (see §6). *Qaṭal* is also one of four basic constituents in the theory of consecutive tenses.

---

[1] This type of suffixed construction is an Afro-Asiatic inheritance and basically an "expression of state/result" (Kouwenberg 2010a, 189–91; Rubin 2010b, 49; Gragg 2019, 33; Huehnergard and Pat-El 2019, 18 n. 6).

[2] At the early stage of such a formation, grammatical agreement persists between the affix (the affected entity) and the adjective/passive participle in number and gender, and presumably also case. At a later stage of grammaticalisation, "the participle loses its adjectival nature and becomes part of the verb" (Bybee et al. 1994, 68). At this later stage, the participle constitutes the stem in a verbal formation and this "is reflected in the loss of agreement on the participle" (Bybee et al. 1994, 68).

[3] The description of pseudo-verbal predications in Akkadian is based on Huehnergard (1987).

[4] Development from a passive to an active construction is not unprecedented typologically (Huehnergard 2006, 6 n. 28); thus also Kouwenberg (2010a, 181, 186). For the short *-ă* in *qatal-a*, see Huehnergard (1987, 222 n. 14); Kouwenberg (2010a, 183, 187–189).

[5] A "resultative points to the state resulting from the action while the anterior points to the action itself" (Bybee et al. 1994, 63, 65; see also Dahl 1985, 134).

[6] 'He is still gone' is an acceptable sentence with resultative meaning, and 'He has gone already' would perfectly fit an anterior meaning (Dahl 1985, 134; Bybee and Dahl 1989, 69).

[7] For definitions of the terms, see §1.2.2. For 'anterior', many scholars use 'perfect' (cf. Bybee and Dahl 1989, 55). I prefer anterior in order to avoid a confusion between perfect (often used to refer to the verbal morpheme *qaṭal*) and perfective.

[8] The term 'verbal (grammatical) morpheme' is used in the sense of 'gram', discussed by Bybee and Dahl (1989, 51f.) as a term wider than 'inflectional category' and narrower than 'grammatical category'. The term 'gram' includes both bound and periphrastic expressions. It is understood that gram is a category which has both certain meaning(s) and a certain expression. Thus grams are language-specific. They belong to "a small set of cross-linguistic **gram-types**, identifiable by their semantic foci and associated with typical means of expression" (Bybee and Dahl 1989, 52). Grams such as the Hebrew *qaṭal* "develop out of lexical material by a gradual generalization of meaning which is paralleled by a gradual reduction in form" (Bybee and Dahl 1989, 56). An anterior gram "tends to develop into a past or perfective" (Bybee and Dahl 1989, 56). When I use a term such as 'the new perfective *qatal*', it is understood that the term involves a diachronic history along the usual path from resultative to anterior and further to perfective. This is one of three major paths of development of a verbal grammatical morpheme

('gram'). A universal theory of tense and aspect always includes a diachronic dimension, so that "the paths along which grams develop may be the same or similar across languages" (Bybee and Dahl 1989, 57). The evaluation of a verbal grammatical morpheme, such as the Hebrew *qaṭal*, should include an evaluation of the location this "particular gram occupies along one of these universal paths at a particular time" (Bybee and Dahl 1989, 57; see also 59). Its location on the universal path should not be expected to be the same in, say, the Archaic Hebrew poetry, and in CBH. See also Dahl (2000, 7). The first and oldest stage in the development of a gram can be called 'prototypical'. In the process of generalisation in several respects ('semantic bleaching'), the prototypical use of the gram may become less salient (Dahl 2000, 10). In the case of the *qaṭal* formation in CBH, the resultative uses have become less salient than the anterior and perfective meanings.

[9] The vowel of the first order is transcribed as *ä* by Weninger, but as *a* by Tropper. I have decided to quote the authors exactly on this point.

[10] See also Reckendorf (1895–98, 54), who translates *iḫtalafū* 'sie sind verschiedener Meinung'.

[11] In Reckendorf's (1895–98, 54) wording, "Sie bezeichnet so scheinbar eine noch immer in der Verwirklichung begriffene Dauer, ruft aber die Erinnerung an das Entstehung dieser Dauer wach."

[12] The action of *qatala* has not taken place at reference time and Abū Ṭālib is still in Mecca, but he is expected to go out in the immediate future (Isaksson 2009, 134).

[13] This volitive meaning of *qatal* is attested also in Taymanitic: ***rḍw*** *ṣlm* '**May** Ṣalm **be pleased**' (Esk 013; Kootstra 2016, 91).

[14] The last clause is interpreted as passive by Tropper (2012, 708): "aber sie wurde hinweggerafft."

[15] According to Tropper (1998, 183), the gnomic meaning of *qatal* is attested in practically all West Semitic languages.

[16] The translation follows Tropper (2012, 798). For the interpretation of *w ṯb* [*wa-ṯābū*] as apodosis, see also Sivan (2001, 98). The conditional construction has the pattern *ʿd-yaqtulu* + *wa-qatal* with initial temporal

conjunction *ʿd*, where *tṯṯbn* is *yaqtulu* 3mp ([*tuṯaṯîbūna*]; Tropper 2012, 651).

[17] Cook (2012a, 207) maintains that the anterior meaning of *qatal* is statistically dominant in Amarna Canaanite. According to Moran (1950, 30), the basic function of *qatal* is "a narrative preterite."

[18] Baranowski (2016a, 125) translates: 'Why **have you handed** Gittipadalla to the king, your lord, a city that Labʾayu, our father, **had taken**?'

[19] Knudtzon (1915, 514) has instead *a-na*.

[20] For a discussion of other interpretations of the passage, see Baranowski (2016a, 132f.).

[21] Karatepe, ca 720 BCE (Friedrich and Röllig 1999, §266). Krahmalkov (1986, 9) uses the terms 'anticipatory clause' and 'resumptive clause' and translates 'As for any king or any prince or a person who is a person of name…'. According to Krahmalkov (1986, 10) "the presence of the conjunction is purely stylistic, serving the sole function of co-ordinating the clauses. That is, there is no inherent syntactic force in W- that 'converts' a perfect (past) into an imperfect (future)."

[22] Fales, in addition, alleges an optative sense (2011, 568), *pace* Gzella (2004, 322).

[23] Gzella (2004, 322): "Die übliche Erzählform bildet, wie im Phönizischen, das 'Perfekt' mit und ohne *waw*."

[24] For an anterior meaning of *qatal* in Imperial Aramaic, see Gzella (2004, 162f.).

[25] See also Tel Dan (KAI[5] 310, 1, 8).

[26] Hackett (1984, 25, 29) reads ארנבן . אכלו . (10) [ ]אׄבׄ, and translates 'hares eat (10) [a wo]lf', which gives better sense.

[27] All futural examples adduced by Degen (1967, 108) are found in an apodosis. The apodoses in his examples are asyndetic. For a future meaning of *qatal* in Imperial Aramaic, see Gzella (2004, 232–37).

[28] The *qatal* (שקרת) in KAI[5] 224:14 can of course be regarded as an anterior projected into the future. Donner and Röllig (1971–76, II:265)

translate, 'Wenn (du) das jedoch nicht (tust), (dann) bist du vertragsbrüchig geworden gegenüber allen [Ve]rtragsgöttern'. In Imperial Aramaic, the use of *qatal* in apodosis seems to be a rare phenomenon (Muraoka and Porten 2003, 326).

29 TAD3 (Porten and Yardeni 1993, 37) translates with past tense ('A good vessel cover[ed] a word in its heart...'), which does not suit a proverbial saying.

30 In the traditional terminology, the *wa* in such syntagms is called '*waw* copulativum' (Ges-K §154a; Bergsträsser 1918–29 II, §9n).

31 "קטל marks temporal sequence, especially with the conjunction *waw*" (Notarius 2013, 134).

32 By this term I refer to the prototypical state that is the result of a previous action. With a stativic verb, it expresses a stative, and with a dynamic verb, it can often be translated with the English perfect. It seems to me that Notarius uses the term 'gnomic' for both, and with present tense translation.

33 Other examples of stativic and, rarely, resultative *qaṭal* (also called 'gnomic' by Notarius) in the archaic poetry: Gen. 49.7a (Notarius 2013, 193); 49.11 (*Ø-qaṭal*, resultative with dynamic verb, a present state of having washed his clothes; cf. Notarius 2013, 194, 268 n. 5); 49.15 (*wa(y)-yiqṭol* + *kī-qaṭal* + *wa-O.noun-kī-qaṭal*; Notarius 2013, 193)—though the *qaṭal* forms could be taken as adjectives; 49.26 (Notarius 2013, 193)—*qaṭal* is part of a relative clause, 'blessings of your father (that) are stronger than the blessings of the eternal mountains'; Num. 24.5 (Notarius 2013, 211, 217); 24.9 (dynamic verb)—"The characterization of the lion's behavior in its symbolic application is expressed by the resultant perfect, which under these discourse conditions acquires a certain generic nuance" (Notarius 2013, 218); Deut. 33.9 (Notarius 2013, 238; verbs of cognition with present and past temporal references); 33.12 (stativic verb; Notarius 2013, 238, 269); 33.20 (*Ø-PP* + *Ø-PrP-qaṭal* + *wa-qaṭal*, where *qaṭal* is stative, while *wa-qaṭal* has a dynamic verb and resultative meaning; Notarius 2013, 238); Judg. 5.17 (stativic verbs; Notarius 2013, 268 n. 5, 269); 1 Sam. 2.1 (*Ø-qaṭal* + *Ø*-

qaṭal + *Ø-qaṭal* + *kī-qaṭal*; Notarius 2013, 258); 2.4 (dynamic verb with resultative meaning); 2.5 (several dynamic verbs with resultative meaning; cf. Notarius 2013, 258, 268 n. 5); Ps. 18.20/2 Sam. 22.20 (*Ø-kī-qaṭal*, stativic verb)—Notarius (2013, 164 n. 49, 167) translates, 'because he finds delight in me'; Ps. 18.44/2 Sam. 22.44 (an asyndetic relative clause, «*Ø-lō-qaṭal*», cognitive lexeme).

34 According to Ges-K (§106n), this case involves "facts that are undoubtedly imminent." J-M (§112j) explains this meaning instead as a case of "future perfect."

35 I know of only one more *qaṭal* clause signifying ability in the archaic poetry: Num. 23.21 (*Ø-lō-qaṭal* + *wa-lō-qaṭal*, resultative *qaṭal* as perfect of confidence; Notarius 2013, 218, 288).

36 I accept, with Notarius (2013, 218 n. 23), the suggestion by BHS to read a *qaṭal* clause *mī sāp̄ar* instead of MT *mispār* in the second hemistich.

37 It is not a 'perfect consecutive'.

38 This *yiqṭol(u)* (אֶשָּׂא) is not performative, since it is not identical with the expressed action. Instead, it is present progressive (Notarius 2013, 95, 96, 282; *pace* Tropper 1998, 172). Other examples of performative *qaṭal* in the archaic poetry: Gen. 49.18 (Notarius 2013, 194); Deut. 32.26 (Notarius 2013, 102); 32.37 (Notarius 2013, 92).

39 Notarius (2013, 95) regards the *yiqṭol* clauses as long, and as imperfectives expressing simultaneous circumstantial actions.

40 Its nature as an oath is emphatically stated by Lehmann (1969, 83f.).

41 Notarius' terminology concerning conditional linkings is imprecise. A sharp distinction should be drawn between the syntaxes of protasis and apodosis. Notarius also exaggerates the frequency of the *wa-qaṭal* syntagm in conditional linkings, since her next example (with *wa-qaṭal* as apodosis) is not a conditional linking (Num. 24.19). See §3.2 on Num. 24.17–19 and my critique there.

42 Other examples of main-line *qaṭal* forms with present anterior meaning: Gen. 49.9 (Notarius 2013, 200); Num. 23.19—Notarius (2013, 217,

223f.) regards both *qaṭal* and *wa-qaṭal* as expressing anterior meaning, thus also Budd (1984, 252); 23.20 (a situation simultaneous with the speech moment; Notarius 2008, 72; 2013, 217); 23.23 (Notarius 2013, 222); Deut. 33.23—Notarius (2013, 236f.) regards יְרָשָׁה as an anterior *qaṭal* 3ms with anaphoric 3fs suffix pronoun written without *mappīq* (Ges-K §61i; J-M §58); Ps. 18.5/2 Sam. 22.5 (Notarius 2013, 164, 167; 2015, 240f.).

[43] Other examples of anterior *qaṭal* in relative clauses: Exod. 15.13a (Notarius 2013, 113, with the archaic *REL zū*); 15.16b, 17 (Notarius 2013, 113f.; 2015, 243f.); Num. 23.8 (Notarius 2013, 218); 24.6b (Notarius 2013, 218); Deut. 32.6b; 32.15b (Notarius 2015, 240); 32.18a; 33.8 (Notarius 2013, 237f., with *REL* אֲשֶׁר and *qaṭal* close to a simple past); 33.29a (Notarius 2013, 238). Anterior *qaṭal* is also sporadically found in other non-main clauses: a protasis construction (Deut. 32.30), a subordinate complement clause (with *kī*, Deut. 32.36b), and a cause/reason clause (with *kī*, Ps. 18.8b/2 Sam. 22.8b).

[44] It is sometimes difficult to distinguish the emphatic, adverbial, function of *kī* from its use as conjunction. In v. 5, the initial *kī* is analysed as adverbial, 'therefore', or emphatic, 'indeed'.

[45] The isolated object noun (בָּרָק) in v. 15 indicates an ellipsis of the initial *wa(y)-yiqṭol* (וַיִּשְׁלַח).

[46] The first-person *yiqṭol(u)* forms in v. 7 code a past progressive within the introductory part of the narrative (Notarius 2013, 163, 165, 169f., 283, 308; 2015, 240).

[47] In Ps. 18.5, the *kī* particle is dropped and the *qaṭal* (אֲפָפוּנִי) occupies an initial position.

[48] In Ps. 18.7b, the main line starts with asyndesis (יִשְׁמַע), while the form in 2 Sam. 22.7b has proclitic *wa* (וַיִּשְׁמַע).

[49] The *yiqṭol(u)* clause in v. 9 is circumstantial in relation to the first *qaṭal* clause (Notarius 2013, 164f., 170, 283, 308).

[50] The imperfective *yiqṭol(u)* codes simultaneous progressive or iterative action in v. 5 (יְבַעֲתֻנִי), v. 7 (אֶקְרָא twice), v. 8 (יִרְגָּזוּ), v. 9 (תֹּאכֵל), and v. 14 (יִתֵּן); cf. Notarius (2013, 163–65, 167, 169f., 283, 307f.; 2015, 240).

[51] There is an even more archaic attestation of future 'prophetic' *qaṭal*, in Deut. 32.22, but in that passage the prospective report is constructed as *kī-qaṭal* + *wa(y)-yiqṭol* + *wa(y)-yiqṭol* + *wa(y)-yiqṭol*, where the *wa(y)-yiqṭol* clauses also have future reference (Notarius 2013, 88 n. 49, 268 n. 6, 282).

[52] This is a *pilpel* form and thus a *wa-qaṭal* syntagm; see HALOT and Notarius (2013, 220): 'and ruin'.

[53] For the interpretation of the jussive *wa-yiqṭol!* in v. 19 (וְיֵרְדְּ), and my criticism of the common hypothesis that it constitutes a protasis (thus Notarius 2013, 220, 293), see §3.2, example (77).

[54] In the traditional terminology, the *waw* in all *wa-qaṭal* clauses in vv. 17–19 is 'conjunctive' or 'copulative' (Notarius 2013, 217). I propose that *wa-qaṭal* in v. 19 is also 'prophetic perfect' with future time reference, *pace* Notarius (2013, 220, 293), who regards the clause as an apodosis.

[55] See also Waltke and O'Connor (1990, 490, §30.5.1), who call this "a metaphorical use of the past tense," and Rogland (2001, 100). According to Notarius (2013, 220), the *wa-qaṭal* clauses express a "temporal text-progression." Other possible examples of *qaṭal* forms with future time reference in the archaic poetry: Num. 24.24 (*wa-S.noun* + *wa-qaṭal* + *wa-qaṭal*, with an initial left dislocation); Deut. 32.35—in this example, שִׁלֵּם is probably a noun, 'recompense' (Notarius 2013, 90), while the reading of וְחָשׁ as a future time *wa-qaṭal* is correct: the verse is a late addition (Isaksson 2017, 264); 32.43—also a late text, "[t]he clearest case of a *waw*-consecutive perfect" and "a very complex text-critical history" (Notarius 2013, 93): it is possible that the original verb form was instead ויכפר, attested in 4QDeut[q] (see Kooij 1994, 99).

[56] The 'epistolary perfect' is regarded by some scholars as a convention in ancient letters (Pardee 1983), by others as a case of performative usage of *qaṭal* (Gogel 1998, 278).

[57] But Gogel (1998, 278) translates 'Your servant (now) returns the letters' (the final prepositional phrase אל אדני is not translated by Gogel).

[58] Gogel (1998, 279): '… has applied himself…'.

[59] An evident anterior meaning is found also in HI Lachish 3:9 אם . נסה איש . לקרא לי . ספר ‘no one has tried to read a letter to me’.

[60] But Pardee (1983, 35) understands שלח (line 1) and ברׄכתׄך (lines 2–3) as ‘epistolary perfects’. The blessing formula occurs also in HI KAjr 18:1–2 (ברכת אתכם ליהוה) and HI KAjr 19:5–6 (ברכתך ל[י]הוה); see Schüle (2000, 141–42) and HI (33, 294).

[61] Since the new perfective *qaṭal* in CBH exhibits nearly all the expected meanings found on the grammaticalisation path of a perfective, it has a relatively high semantic age. If we call such a semantic age perfage, it can be estimated as perfage 4. For LBH, we should possibly assign ‘perfage 5’, which would include the change to a simple past (Bybee et al. 1994, 105). The data available to Bybee et al. (1994, 105) show only four “resultative grams that do not have other uses,” which means that there is not evidence enough to assign resultatives a perfage 1. The other perfages are: perfage 2: young anteriors, perfage 3: old anteriors, perfage 4: perfectives, perfage 5: simple pasts.

[62] Cook (2012a, 207ff. and 210ff.) gives an exposé of such meanings in CBH.

[63] *Qaṭal* in Gen. 40.14 is volitive and possibly counterfactual; see §5.4.7.

[64] For the transitivity of the stativic verb (‘of children’), see Ges-K (§117aa). But J-M (p. 610 n. 1) expected a *wa-qaṭal*: “the same form was preferred for the sake of assonance.” This is my only example of a stativic *qaṭal* in an apodosis. In protases, there are three more: Gen. 47.6; Lev. 5.3; 5.4, all with ידע.

[65] Other examples of present anterior *qaṭal* in protasis, of which many exhibit a variant of the politeness phrase אִם־נָא מָצָאתִי חֵן: Gen. 18.3; 47.29; 50.4 (Ges-K §159o); Exod. 33.13; 34.9; Num. 5.13 (not first clause in protasis); 5.19, 20 (Ges-K §159aa); Judg. 11.36 (*Ø-VOC-qaṭal*).

[66] More examples of futural anterior *qaṭal* in subordinate clauses: Gen. 24.33 עַד אִם; 28.15 עַד אֲשֶׁר אִם (Fenton 1973, 37; Cook 2012a, 207); Lev. 25.49 (within an apodosis domain); Num. 32.17 עַד אֲשֶׁר אִם (Cook 2012a, 207 n. 46); Deut. 15.6 כִּי (Steuernagel 1900, 56; Ges-K §106o).

[67] Similar examples with נתן: Gen. 24.17—but Schulz (1900, 32) regards the *qaṭal* as futural, and Westermann (1981, 304) translates as future; Deut. 8.10 (relative clause!); Judg. 1.2.

[68] Other examples of (future) anterior *qaṭal* in protases: Exod. 22.2, 7; Lev. 6.21; 13.3, 5, 6, 8, 13, 17, 25, 32, 34, 36, 51, 55, 56; 14.3, 39, 44, 48; 15.3, 29; 25.28; 27.20 (the second condition); Num. 5.13, 14, 27, 28; 30.6, 11, 12; 35.16, 17, 21, 22; Deut. 20.5f. (Ferguson 1882, 77). Gen. 43.9 is a special case. It is not legal code, but concerns one specific (eventual) action in the future. Most scholars take this *qaṭal* (הֲבִיאֹתִ֫יו) as a present: 'If I do not bring him to you' (thus Ges-K §159o; Garr 1998, lxxxiii; Rainey 2003b, 27), but the *qaṭal* is a (futural) anterior in protasis, 'If I have not brought him to you'; the following *wa-qaṭal* construction (see §6) is future, 'and (so that) I place him here before you'.

[69] Other examples of future anterior *qaṭal* in apodoses: Exod. 22.14; Lev. 13.37; 20.18, 20; Num. 16.29 'then the LORD has not sent me' (Ges-K §159p); 19.13; 32.23 (Ges-K §159p); Deut. 19.18.

[70] Other examples of *qaṭal* expressing immediate future: Gen. 4.14 'today'; 18.27, 31 (not performative); 35.18 (*kī-qaṭal*); 42.36 אֹתִ֫י שִׁכַּלְתֶּ֑ם; Exod. 10.7; Lev. 9.4 (*kī-ADV-S.noun-qaṭal*) 'for today the LORD is going to appear to you'; Num. 17.27 (J-M §112g).

[71] "[I]n languages where tense is grammaticalized, a present-tense form is used (e.g., English), but in languages where aspect is grammaticalized, perfective aspect grams are used" (Cook 2012a, 208, 213).

[72] E.g., Gen. 1.29; 17.5; 41.41 (with Pharaoh as subject); Exod. 7.1.

[73] The performative *qaṭal* clauses (not only *ntn*) registered in my database are: Gen. 1.29; 9.3, 13, 17; 14.22 (Brockelmann 1908–13, II: §76b; Cook 2012a, 207 n. 46); 15.18 (Dobbs-Allsopp 2004–2007, 47)—*pace* Brockelmann (1908–13, II: §76bs), who regards it as a future; 17.5 (Westermann 1981, 303, 314); 17.20 (Cook 2012a, 214); 19.21; 20.16; 22.16 (Cook 2012a, 207 n. 46); 23.11 (Cook 2012a, 214; Joosten 2012, 120); 23.13; 41.41; 45.19; 47.23; 48.22; Exod. 7.1; Num. 3.11; 14.20; 18.21; Deut. 2.31; 4.26 (as apodosis); 8.19 (as apodosis; Rainey 2003b,

11–12; Cook 2012a, 207 n. 46); 26.3 (Rainey 2003b, 11); 26.10; 30.15, 18 (as apodosis); 30.19; Judg. 2.3 (Ges-K §106n); 17.3.

[74] Other 'habitual' past perfective *qaṭal*: Gen. 7.19; 31.40; 38.9 (temporal clause, which is not a protasis, *pace* Ges-K §159o); Exod. 16.35 (2×); 36.3; Num. 2.34 (2×); 11.8 (*Ø-qaṭal*, elaboration of preceding *XØ* in 11.7)—but according to Joosten (2012, 218), the syntax is completely irregular; 14.22 (*wa(y)-yiqṭol* + *wa-lō-qaṭal*, both clauses perfective and repetitive); Deut. 2.20; 9.9 (*Ø-qaṭal* is an elaboration of *wa(y)-yiqṭol*); Judg. 2.18 (temporal clause, 'when', not a protasis); 6.2, 3 (temporal clause); 16.16 (*kī-qaṭal*).

[75] Joseph's volitive *qaṭal* in Gen. 40.14, expressing a (counterfactual?) wish in his prison (כִּ֤י אִם־זְכַרְתַּ֣נִי אִתְּךָ֗), is probably the second part of an exception, '(I desire nothing else) except that you remembered me', with future time reference (Ges-K §163d n. 1). According to Rainey (2003, 27), this is a phrase used instead of the imperative for politeness.

[76] Other counterfactual *qaṭal* in the corpus: Gen. 31.42 (negative–positive); Num. 22.29 (positive–positive); 22.33 (negative–positive); Judg. 13.23 (positive–negative); 14.18 (negative–negative).

[77] Other hypothetical *qaṭal*: Gen. 26.10 (Waltke and O'Connor 1990, 494); and possibly also Gen. 22.12—thus Givón (2001, I: 364), 'would not have spared'.

[78] There is also an example outside the corpus: Josh. 7.7.

[79] Other examples: Gen. 18.12; 21.7; Judg. 9.9, 13.

[80] The eight records showing one or more disjunctive *ʾō-qaṭal* having the same meaning as a *wa-qaṭal* clause are: Exod. 21.37, in protasis (Bergsträsser 1929, §9m); 22.9f., 13 (both in protasis); Lev. 4.23, 28 (both in protasis); 25.49 (in apodosis, after *yiqṭol(u)*); Num. 5.14 (in protasis); 11.8 (*Ø-qaṭal* + *wa-qaṭal* + *wa-qaṭal* + *ʾō-qaṭal*)—background with habitual past, where *Ø-qaṭal* introduces an elaboration, habitual seen with perfective aspect, and the following *wa-qaṭal* are habitual, as is also *ʾō-qaṭal*. The disjunctive *ʾō-qaṭal* with the same meaning as *wa-qaṭal* is discussed also by Kawashima (2010, 32).

6. THE CONSTRUCTION *WA-QAṬAL* IN CBH

This chapter investigates the much-discussed *wa-qaṭal* in CBH. *Wa-qaṭal* is a construction in the same sense as the English future construction *be going to*: the constituent parts are analysable, but the meanings of the construction cannot be deduced from its constituents.

6.1. The Construction Concept

The *wa-qaṭal* clause-type plays a major role in the system of consecutive tenses (see Notarius 2013, 22; Isaksson 2021, 201–4). While *wa(y)-yiqṭol* stands out in the most recent research as a relatively transparent clause-type from a Semitic typological perspective (see §3; Baranowski 2016b; Renz 2016, 439; Huehnergard and Pat-El 2019, 7, 9; Hornkohl 2019, 556; Khan 2020, I:534; Isaksson 2021, 209), *wa-qaṭal* and its alternation with the imperfective long *yiqṭol* is commonly regarded as inexplicable. How come *wa-qaṭal* is not an anterior and past perfective formation like *qaṭal*, but instead most often expresses future, obligation, and habituality (Renz 2016, 439)?

One answer is found in the theory of constructions, worked out by Joan Bybee (2010; 2015). This solution to the enigma has been offered by Geoffrey Khan (2021a).

All comparative evidence suggests that *wa-qaṭal* as an imperfective formation belongs to the diachronic level called Classical Hebrew (CBH). In Amarna Canaanite, an apodosis *wa-qatal*

 https://doi.org/10.11647/OBP.0414.06

is attested, but also, less frequently, an apodosis *Ø-qaṭal*, without initial *wa* and still with future time reference (Baranowski 2016a, 174). In the Archaic Hebrew poetry, there is no securely attested formation *wa-qaṭal* with future, obligational, or habitual meaning (Notarius 2013, 288f., 304). It is not attested in the earliest Aramaic inscriptions (Renz 2016, 656). *Wa-qaṭal* as a construction in Bybee's sense outside the apodosis domain must have developed at a diachronic stage close to, or early in, what we call CBH. If we seek examples of the successive extensions of the *wa-qaṭal* construction, we should preferably search for traces of such steps in the CBH texts. The construction *wa-qaṭal* is primarily a Classical Hebrew innovation (Renz 2016, 649).[1]

In Bybee's theory of constructions, high frequency is determinative. The more a sequence of morphemes or words is used together, the more strongly the sequence will be perceived as a unit and the less it will be associated with its component parts. The process leads to increasing autonomy of the construction (Bybee 2010, 36, 48). This is *chunking*: "When two or more words are often used together, they also develop a sequential relation" (Bybee 2010, 25, 33). And *constructions* are sequential chunks "that sometimes have special meanings and other properties" (Bybee 2010, 36).

It is the supposition of Geoffrey Khan that *wa-qaṭal* is a sequential chunk that has received increasing autonomy. *Wa-qaṭal* is not a morpheme (like English *gonna*), and absolutely not a 'tense'. But it is a construction, like the English futural phrase *be going to*. In *be going to*, the elements in the sequence are still analysable, but the futural/intentional meaning cannot be deduced from the parts of the construction, *be* + *going* + *to*. In a similar way, the meanings of *wa-qaṭal* cannot be deduced from its original components, *wa* + *qaṭal*. The constituents in *wa-qaṭal* are identifiable as the usual conjunction *wa* and the morpheme *qaṭal*, but the meanings of this specific sequence have developed in several diachronic steps, and in CBH they are in living usage. "Constructions often contain explicit lexical material" (Bybee 2010, 76f.), and such is the case with *wa-qaṭal*: we can identify the conjunction *wa* and the suffix conjugation *qaṭal*. The concept of construction explains why the meanings of *wa-qaṭal* cannot be deduced from its separate elements.

In this analysis of *wa-qaṭal*, *wa-* is the invariant part and *qaṭal* is schematic, with multiple forms: *wa-QAṬAL*. This invariant conjunction *wa-* is probably the reason why *wa-qaṭal* did not develop into a verbal morpheme like *gonna* (Khan 2021a, 342). In verbal morphemes, there is usually a degree of phonetic reduction, but *wa-qaṭal* is phonetically unreduced.

The comparative Northwest Semitic evidence indicates that *wa-qaṭal* began its development as a chunk in the function of apodosis (see §6.2.2) and probably also as constituent in modal sequences (see §6.2.1). The *wa-qatal(a)* clause-type achieved considerable frequency in apodosis (Smith 1991, 7–15). In Ugaritic, a futural *qatal(a)* in apodosis is as a rule syndetic with a proclitic *wa-* (Tropper 2012, 717; Renz 2016, 442), and in Amarna Canaanite, the connective *wa-* before *qaṭal* as apodosis is a much more frequent option (Baranowski 2016a, 173–178; Renz 2016, 448f., 451). This comparative evidence suggests that *wa-qaṭal* functioning as apodosis and result clause with future meaning had become a chunk already in early Northwest Semitic.[2] And there are indications of this chunk also in the later Iron Age Northwest Semitic (see §6.3).

On the other hand, *wa-qaṭal* as *construction* is absent in the contemporary Northwest Semitic languages of the Iron Age (Renz 2016, §2.2). And it is absent in the Archaic Hebrew poetry. This indicates that the *wa-qaṭal* construction is an internal CBH, or at least post-Archaic, development. This is the reason why we will search in the CBH texts for textual evidence of the first steps of this construction.

In the investigation of the development of the *wa-qaṭal* construction in CBH, targets of study must naturally be the conditional linkings (§6.7) and the result clauses (§§6.4–6) in CBH. The frequencies and semantic types of such sentences, especially the apodosis part, can be expected to reveal the semantic and syntactic milieu, and the initial steps, in which the construction *wa-qaṭal* developed (see §6.8).

The next natural step is an extension, a generalisation of what is permitted to precede *wa-qaṭal*: the clause preceding *wa-qaṭal* is allowed to be not only a protasis, but also a temporal or causal subordinate clause (see §§6.9–10). Thus Khan (2021a, 312): כִּֽי־יִרְא֤וּ אֹתָךְ֙ הַמִּצְרִ֔ים **וְאָמְר֖וּ** ‘When the Egyptians see you, **they will say**…’ (Gen. 12.12). This is not a conditional sentence, because there is no condition. Even with future time reference, the event in the temporal clause is presupposed to take place (Khan 2021a, 311).

A third natural extension of the preceding clause is to allow a shift of status of the preceding clause: from subordinate (protasis, temporal, or causal clause) to main clause (see §6.11). In such instances, *wa-qaṭal* has the same status as the preceding clause and is coordinated with it: וְק֥וֹץ וְדַרְדַּ֖ר תַּצְמִ֣יחַ לָ֑ךְ **וְאָכַלְתָּ֖** אֶת־עֵ֥שֶׂב הַשָּׂדֶֽה׃ 'It will yield you brambles and thistles, **and you will eat** the produce of the land.' (Gen. 3.18). In this step, if not before, the affinity between *yiqṭol(u)* and *wa-qaṭal* becomes evident. As in the example, *wa-qaṭal* takes over from *yiqṭol(u)* the role of coding discourse continuity. In a stage when an affirmative *yiqṭol(u)* clause can only express discontinuity (clause-type *X-yiqṭol(u)*), *wa-qaṭal* steps in as its continuity counterpart—which is the essence of half of the theory of consecutive tenses.

6.2. Precursors of the CBH Construction *Wa-qaṭal* in Northwest Semitic

The Classical Hebrew verbal system developed from a Canaanite language in the Late Bronze Age. The best-attested Northwest Semitic languages of this age are Ugaritic and the Canaanite in the Amarna letters. In such early texts, there are uses of the *wa-qatal* clause-type that in certain respects show similarities with the later construction *wa-qaṭal* in CBH.

The prototypical meaning of the *qatal* gram is resultative, that is, it expresses the resulting state of a previous action. It is certainly striking that many early functions of the *wa-qatal* clause-type, a clause-type used to code a linking with the preceding clause, so often describes a result of the action in that clause. Already in the earliest Northwest Semitic sources, *wa-qatal* has this type of 'modal' meaning (with a term taken from Baranowski

2016a) in addition to the 'normal' uses as anterior and past perfective. The modal *wa-qatal* is found in specific types of linkings, such as conditional sentences and modal series.

6.2.1. The Clause-type *Wa-qatal* in Modal Series

In Amarna, the *wa-qatal* clause-type is used as second or third clause in modal series. In this function, *wa-qatal* expresses purpose or result, never, as is often the case in CBH, a further instruction or command (Renz 2016, 456). An example is:

(1) *du-ku-mi* ^{26}⌜*eṭ*⌝*-la-ku-nu* ***ù i-ba-ša-tu-nu*** *ki-ma ia-ti-nu* ^{27}⌜***ù***⌝ ***pa-aš-ḫa-tu-nu***

'Kill your 'lad' **that you become** like us, **so that you will be** at rest.' (EA 74:25–27; translation according to Renz)

The linking pattern in the modal sequence is *IMP* + *wa-qatal* + *wa-qatal*, and the meaning of the two *wa-qatal* is a result of the action in the imperative. The sense of finality can also, as in CBH, be expressed by a jussive *wa-yaqtul* clause (Renz 2016, 456), as in:

(2) *ù uš-ši-ra* ÉRIN.MEŠ ^{30}*pí-ṭá-ti* ***ù ti-ìl-qé-šu*** ^{31}*ù ta-ap-šu-uḫ* KUR LUGAL

'So send the regular army **in order that it may capture** him so that the land of the king may be at peace.' (EA 107:29–31)

In (2), the linking pattern is *IMP* + *wa-yaqtul*, and the jussive clause has a meaning of purpose or result. A *wa-qatal* clause can express finality also after a jussive *yaqtul* with ventive clitic ('cohortative'), as in:

(3) *šu-te-ra a-wa-ta*$_5$ ^{24}*a-na ia-ši ù i-pu-ša a-na-ku* ^{25}*ki-ta it-ti* ^{I}ÌR-A-*ši-ir-ta* ^{26}⸢*ki*⸣-*ma* ^{I}*Ia-pa-*^{d}IŠKUR *ù* ^{I}*Zi-*⸢*im*⸣-*re-*⸢*da*⸣ ^{27}***ù*** ⸢***bal***⸣***-ṭá-ti***

'Just send me the word and I myself will make a treaty with ʿAbdi-Ashirta like Yapaʿ-Haddi and Zimredda, **and I will stay alive**.' (EA 83: 24–27; cf. Renz 2016, 456)

The linking pattern in (3) is *IMP + wa-yaqtul-a + wa-qatal*, where *wa-qatal* expresses the intended result of the preceding action. A *wa-qatal* can also be a result clause after a jussive *yaqtul* without ventive clitic (Renz 2016, 456):

(4) ⸢*ù*⸣ ⸢*ki*⸣-*tu ti-in‹-né-pu-uš›-ma* ^{37}*a-na ka-li* KUR.KUR.⸢KI⸣ ⸢***ù***⸣ ***pa-aš-ḫu*** DUMU.MEŠ ^{38}*ù* MUNUS.DUMU.MUNUS.MEŠ *a‹-na› da-ri-ti* UD.KAM.MEŠ

'and let an alliance be ‹made› for all the lands **so that** (our) sons and daughters **will be at peace** f[or]ever more.' (EA 74:36–38)

The linking pattern is *wa-X-yaqtul-ma + wa-qatal*, where the jussive *yaqtul* has been emphasised by an enclitic *-ma* (Rainey 1996, III:229).

If two semantically *separate* commands are to be given, volitive forms are used (Renz 2016, 457), as in (5):

(5) *du-ku-mi* EN-*ku-nu* ^{28}*ù in-né-ep-*⸢*šu*⸣ *a-na* ^{29}LÚ.MEŠ GAZ

'Slay your lord and join the *ʿapîru*.' (EA 73:27–29)

The pattern in (5) is *IMP + wa-IMP* (same verbs and pattern in EA 81:12f.).

6.2.2. The Clause-type *Wa-qatal* as First Clause after Some Types of Condition

6.2.2.1. Ugaritic

In Ugaritic, a *wa-qatal* clause can introduce an apodosis in a conditional linking.

(6) (*w . hm . ḫt . / ʿl*) . **w . likt** / *ʿmk* . (*w . hm / l . ʿl*) . *w . lakm / ilak*

'And if the Hittite comes up, **then I will send** to you. But if he does not come up, then surely I will send.' (KTU[3] 2.30:16–20, translation Smith 1991, 8; Tropper 2012, 717, 786, my parentheses enclosing the protases)[3]

The example illustrates that, in an apodosis, *wa-qatal* is replaced by *X-yaqtulu* if a constituent must be positioned before the verb (*w lakm ilak*, *waw* + infinitive + prefix verb; Tropper 2012, §76.542; Renz 2016, 441f.).[4]

The function of an apodosis, expressing the result of the truth of the preceding clause, is semantically close to being the main clause after a temporal or causal clause, or expressing the intended result of fulfilling certain rituals, examples of which are found in Ugaritic (Tropper 2012, 716f.; Renz 2016, 441):

(7) *w* **šmʿ** [. b]ʿl . *l* . ṣ*l*tk[m] / y*d*y . ʿz . *l* ṯǵrkm [. qrd] / *l* ḥmytkm

(After commanding certain ritual sacrifices in case of an attack of the city:) 'Then Baal **will hear** yo[ur] prayer. He will drive the strong one from your gates, [the warrior] from your walls.' (KTU[3] 1.119:34–36, my emphasis, translation Smith 1991, 10; Tropper 2012, 716)[5]

In case of danger, performing the correct rituals will result in the intervention of Baal. This result, which constitutes a promise about a future action, can be coded by a *wa-qatal* clause in Ugaritic. The condition, or instruction, starts with *k-* 'when' on line 26 (*k gr ʿz ṯġrkm…*; KTU^3 1.119:26). Similar future results of previous actions are expressed in the following examples:

(8) ***w prʿ*t** / *hy* . *ḫ̮lh*

'Und sie (sc. die Tamariske) **wird** seine Krankheit **lösen**' (KTU^3 1.124:9f., my emphasis, Tropper 2012, 716)[6]

(9) [w . u]nṯ *inn* / *lhm ʿd ṯṯṯbn* / *ksp* . *iwrkl* / ***w . ṯb*** . *l unṯhm*

'and they do not have a feudal obligation until they return the money of Iwirkallu, **then they return** to their feudal obligation' (KTU^3 3.4:16–19, my emphasis, Sivan 2001, 98; Tropper 2012, 716)

6.2.2.2. Amarna Canaanite

In conditional sentences, a relatively frequent case is *yaqtulu* in the protasis and *wa-qatal* in apodosis (Renz 2016, 449f.). An example is (Baranowski 2016a, 176):

(10) *(šumma-S.noun-yaqtulu)* + *wa-qatal*

šum-ma šàr-ru ***yi-ša-i-lu*** [16]***ù na-ad-na*** *pa-ni-nu a-na* [17]*a-ra-di-ka* […]

'If the king **will inquire, then ‹we› will devote ourselves** to serving you.' (EA 89:15–17)

But in Amarna it is not absolutely necessary that *qatal* in a futural apodosis is preceded by *wa* (Renz 2016, 451). In some cases, such an apodosis is asyndetic, as is illustrated in the following example (Baranowski 2016a, 174):

(11) *(šumma-qatal)* + ***Ø-qatal*** + *(šumma-XØ)* + ***Ø-qatal***

šum-ma i-ba-aš-ši LÚ ÉRIN.MEŠ *pi-ṭa-ti* [58]*i-na* MU *an-ni-ti* ***i-ba-aš-ši*** KUR.ḪI.A [59]LUGAL EN‹*-ia*› *ù šum-ma ia-a-nu-mi* LÚ ÉRIN *pi-*⸢*ṭa*⸣*-ti* [60]⸢***ḫal***⸣***-qa-at*** KUR.ḪI.A LUGAL EN-*ia*

'If there are regular troops in this year, **there will still be** lands of the king, ‹my› lord. But if there are no regular troops, the lands of the king, my lord, **are lost**.' (EA 286:57–60, my emphasis)

6.2.3. The Clause-type *Wa-qatal* as Second Clause in Apodosis

In Amarna Canaanite, a *wa-qatal* clause is sometimes used to continue the first clause of an apodosis with futural or volitive meaning (Renz 2016, 452). In some cases, a *wa-qatal* + *wa-qatal* linking even constitutes the whole apodosis, as in:

(12) [...] *šumma* [12]*ti-ìš-mu-na a-ṣí-mi* ÉRIN.MEŠ [13]*pí-ṭá-ti* ***ù i-zi-bu*** URU.MEŠ-*šu-nu* [14]***ù pa-aṭ-ru***

'If they hear of the coming forth of the regular troops **they will abandon** their towns **and desert**.' (EA 73:11–14)

In (12), the protasis has a *yaqtulu* predicate and the apodosis consists of two *wa-qatal* clauses, a type of linking that is very common in CBH.

In several cases, a *wa-qatal* clause expresses a direct result as a focal clause.[7] In such an apodosis, the *wa-qatal* often expresses finality in relation to the first clause (Renz 2016, 453). This is shown in the next example:

(13) *šá-ni-tam a-wa-[te]* [35]*la yu-šé-bi-la be-li a-na* ÌR!-⸢*šu*⸣ [36]*ki-ma ar-ḫi-iš a-na ṭup-pí ù na-‹ṣa›-⸢ri⸣-⸢šu⸣* [37]URU-KI *a-na ša-šu* ***ù er-ri-⸢iš⸣*** [38]⸢URU⸣.KI *iš-tu ša-šu* [39]*[a]-⸢na⸣ a-ša-bi-ia* ***ú bal-‹ṭá›-ti***

‘Furthermore, should my lord not have brought word[s], to his servant with all speed, by a tablet, and pro‹te›ct the city for himself, **then I will request** from him a city for me to dwell in **so that I may l‹iv›e.**’ (EA 88:34–39)

In (13), an apodosis begins with *wa* + Akkadian present (*iparras*) and continues with *wa-qatal* in a final sense. There are also examples of apodoses starting with a Central Semitic *yaqtulu* and continuing with a *wa-qatal* expressing the result of the preceding action (Renz 2016, 453):

(14) ⸢*šum*⸣-⸢*ma*⸣ ⸢ŠE⸣.⸢MEŠ⸣ ⸢*qè*⸣-*e-ṣí la-a yu-ši-r[u]* [16]LUGAL ⸢ÉRIN⸣.⸢MEŠ⸣ ⸢*pí*⸣-⸢*ṭá*⸣-⸢*ta*$_5$⸣ *a-na* URU.KI *Gub-l[a]* [17]*ù la-⸢qé⸣-⸢mi⸣ ti-ìl-qú-na-ši* [18]*ù ia-⸢a⸣-⸢ti⸣* [ÌR-*ka*] ⸢*ti*⸣-*du-ku-na* [19]***ù gu$_5$-⸢mi⸣-⸢ru⸣***

‘If by the time of the summer grain the king does not send regular troops to Byblos, then verily they will take it and me, [your servant] they will kill **so that they will have gained full control**.’ (EA 131:15–19)

In (14), the apodosis starts with a *wa-VNabs-yaqtulu* clause (*ù la-⸢qé⸣-⸢mi⸣ ti-ìl-qú-na-ši* ‘then verily they will take it’), and after that follows one more *yaqtulu* clause (*wa-O.pron-O.noun-yaqtulu*). The apodosis ends with a *wa-qatal* in a final sense.[8]

In many cases, the apodosis begins with a *yaqtul* in the first person (1cs) with futural meaning (expressing intention) and continues with *wa-qatal*. In such a case, *wa-qatal* may simply express a temporal succession with future time reference:

(15) *šum-ma* ^{42}2 ITU *ia-nu* ÉRIN.MEŠ *pí-ṭá-ti* ^{43}*ù i-te$_9$-zi-ib* URU.KI ^{44}***ù pa-aṭ-ra-ti ù*** ^{45}***bal-ṭá-at*** ZI-*ia a-*⸢*di*⸣ ^{46}*i-pé-šu i-pé-eš lìb-bi-i*⸢*a*⸣

'If in two months there are no regular troops, then I will leave the city **and I will go away so that I will stay alive** while I do as I please.' (EA 82:41–46)

In (15), the protasis is a verbless clause and the apodosis starts with *wa-yaqtul* in the first person and continues with two sequential *wa-qatal* clauses with future time reference. It can be noted that intention in a first-person jussive easily combines with a pure futural *wa-qatal* in the first person.[9]

A *wa-qatal* may also, within an apodosis, be continued by a *yaqtulu* clause in the simple sense of future and temporal succession, as in:

(16) *šu*[*m-ma la yi-iš-mu*] ^{30}⸢LUGAL⸣ BAD-*ia a-na a-wa-te* Ì[R-*šu*] ^{31}⸢***ù***⸣ ***in$_4$-né-ep-ša‹-at›*** URU *Gub*[-*la*] ^{32}*a-na ša-šu* ***ù*** *gáb-bi* KUR.KI.ḪI.A L[UGAL] ^{33}*a-di* KUR *Mi-iṣ-ri* ***ti-né-ep-šu*** ^{34}*a-na* LÚ.MEŠ SA.GAZ.MEŠ

'but i[f] the king, my lord, [does not heed] the words of [his] ser[vant], **then** the city of Byb[los] **will join** him (i.e. ʿAbdi-Ashrata) **and** all the cities of the k[ing] as far as the land of Egypt **will join** the *ʿapîru* men.' (EA 88:29–34)

The linking pattern in (16) is: *(šumma-la-yaqtulu)* + *wa-qatal* + *wa-X-yaqtulu*. The meaning of both *wa-qatal* and *yaqtulu* in the apodosis is simple future.

6.2.4. Observations Regarding the Use of *Wa-qatal* in Northwest Semitic Languages in the Late Bronze Age

It stands to reason that the *wa-qatal* clause-type, side-by-side with expected meanings of anterior and past perfective, was utilised with future and modal meanings in specific domains:[10] modal sequences and apodoses. The *wa-qatal* clause-type in such domains seems to exhibit a prototypical meaning of *qatal* as an originally resultative construction. In modal series, it follows an initial volitive and describes the (intended) result of the action in the command or wish. In second- or third-clause position of a modal sequence, discourse continuity was preferred, and thus *wa-qatal* (and not *Ø-qatal*) was favoured in relation to the preceding volitive clause(s). A *Ø-qatal* clause does not seem to have been tolerated in modal series.

As apodosis also, the *wa-qatal* clause-type expresses a result, a consequence. But as the first clause in the apodosis, it does not take part in a modal sequence (in which it signals discourse continuity with its initial *wa*). The first clause in an apodosis just describes a consequence of the truth-value of the protasis. In this position, the *wa-* in *wa-qatal* would not be absolutely necessary, because *qatal* in itself was able to express result. This is shown in some examples from Amarna where a *Ø-qatal* functions as futural apodosis. In a conditional linking, the clause that begins the apodosis is the first clause in a separate domain and the coding of continuity in relation to the preceding clause (the protasis) is unnecessary. Since an apodosis is often a complex of several clauses, the second and third clauses often signal continuity, but the first clause has no need of continuity marking (with initial *wa*).

My hypothesis is that the preponderance of *wa-qatal*, as against *Ø-qatal*, as the first clause in apodoses is due to influence from its use in modal sequences, where *wa-* before *qatal* is necessary.

The use of *wa-qatal* in both modal series and apodoses is an ancient Northwest Semitic syntactic practice. And its use as second clause in apodoses is similar to that in modal series.

Since the semantics of modal sequences is relatively limited and has few variations, I posit that the development of *wa-qaṭal* in CBH, what Bybee (2010; 2015) and Khan (2021a) call a construction process, had the conditional sentence, especially its apodosis, as its birthplace and first syntactic milieu (see further §6.8).

6.3. Parallels of the CBH Construction *Wa-qaṭal* in Iron Age Northwest Semitic

We have considered the traces of a resultative and modal *wa-qatal* in the Northwest Semitic languages of the Late Bronze Age. It is time to do the same for Northwest Semitic languages in the Iron Age, roughly contemporary with the CBH texts.

6.3.1. The Clause-type *Wa-qatal* in Modal Series

6.3.1.1. Pre-exilic Hebrew Inscriptions

The following example of a letter from the end of the sixth century displays modal series starting with an imperative:

(17) [2]*Ø-IMP* + [3]*wa-qaṭal* + [5]***wa-qaṭal*** + [7]*wa-IMP* + [8]***wa-qaṭal***

ועת (2) תן מן היין 1 1 1 ב\ ו(3)צוך חנניהו על ב(4)אר שבע עם משא
צ(5)מד חמרם **וצררת֯** (6) אתם בצק֯ ו(7)ספר החטם והל(8)ח֯ם֯ **ו֯לק֯ח֯ת**
(9)א֯לכ֯ם[ ]

‘And now, [2]give from the wine 3 *baths*. [3]Hananiah commands you to [4]Beersheba with the load of a [5]pair of donkeys, **and you shall pack** [6]them with dough. [7]Then count the wheat and the [8]bread **and take** [9]for yourself…’ (HI Arad 3:1–9)

Example (17) exhibits two modal series with at least two *wa-qaṭal* clauses that follow imperatives. The *wa-qaṭal* clauses express additional (obligatory) instructions in relation to the preceding imperative (Gogel 1998, 266; Renz 2016, 649).[11]

6.3.1.2. Edomite

An ostracon in Edomite script reveals a modal series of the type *IMP + wa-qatal*. It was found in Ḥorvat ʿUzza and dated to the beginning of the sixth century BCE:

(18) *IMP* + *REL-XØ* + ***wa-qatal***

ועת . תן . את . האכל (4) אשר . עמד . אחאמה . [ ] (5) **והרם** שאל
. על מז[בח קוס]

‘And now give the food (bread) which is with ʾ[A]ḥîʾimmô[h] […] **and** Šaʾul **shall offer** (it) on the al[tar of Qaws/Qōs]’ (Aḥituv 2008, 351–54)

The *wa-qatal* clause in (18) describes an additional instruction related to the preceding imperative.

6.3.2. The Clause-type *Wa-qatal* as First Clause in an Apodosis

6.3.2.1. Samalian

Samalian is nowadays classified as a separate Northwest Semitic language (Huehnergard and Pat-El 2019, 3). Tropper's study (1993b, §43.211.3) has one instance of a futural *qatal* in apodosis:

(19) *Ø-yaqtul(u) + wa-yaqtul(u) + wa-gam-qatal*

תשמ[ו(?)] (5) חרב בביתי ותהרגו חד בני ואג̊ם̊ הוית חרב בארק י̊אדי

'Shall you set [...] [5] the sword against my house, and slay one of my sons? Then also I will cause the sword to fall upon the land of Yaudi.' (KAI[5] 215:4–5)

If the interpretation is correct, then in Samalian a *qatal* morpheme in an apodosis may have future time reference even in clause-internal position (preceded by *wa-gam*).[12]

6.3.2.2. Phoenician

In the following example, the protasis starts with a quantifier instead of a conditional particle, a construction that is found also in CBH:[13]

(20) *kōl-S.noun-REL-qatal* + ***wa-qatal***

[כ]ל משאת אש איבל שת בפס ז **ונתן** לפי הכתבת אש [כתב

'was jede Abgabe angeht, die man nicht auf diese Tafel gesetzt hat, **so wird sie gegeben werden** gemäß den Aufzeichnungen, die...' (KAI[5] 69:18, Friedrich and Röllig 1999, §324.2)

In (20), a *wa-qatal* introduces the apodosis with future time reference. A similar example from the same text is:

(21) *kōl-S.noun-REL-qatal* + ***wa-qatal***

כל כהן אש יקח משאת בדץ לאש שת בספר ז **ונענ[ש**]

‘was jeden Priester angeht, der eine Abgabe nimmt entgegen dem, was in diesem Texte festgesetzt ist, **so wird er bestraft** [werden]’ (KAI[5] 69:20, Friedrich and Röllig 1999, §324.2)

6.3.2.3. Pre-exilic Hebrew Inscriptions

(22) *Ø-VNabs* + *wa-IMP* + *Ø-ʾal-yiqṭol(Ø)* + *wa-ʾim-XØ* + ***wa-qaṭal***

ועת . נתן ל(2)כתים . ב/ 1 1 יין . ל(3)ארבעת הימם [ ] ו(4) 300
לחם ו(5)מלא . החמר . יין וה(6)סבת מחר . אל תאחר . (7)ואם . עוד .
חמץ . **ונת**(8)**ת** . להם .

‘And now, give to the Kittim two *baths* of wine for the four days… and 300 (loaves of) bread. And fill with fermenting wine and turn (it) over tomorrow; do not be late. And if there is still sour wine, **you shall give** (it) to them.’ (Arad 2:1–8, HI 13)

Example (22) illustrates a simple conditional sentence with a verbless clause as protasis and *wa-qaṭal* as apodosis. The meaning of the *wa-qaṭal* is an obligation (instruction). The example also contains a modal sequence with initial infinitive absolute as imperative (נתן) and following *wa-qaṭal* (והסבת) expressing a further instruction, not a result (cf. Renz 2016, 650).

6.3.3. *Wa-qatal* as Second Clause in Protasis or Apodosis

6.3.3.1. Phoenician

A *wa-qatal* clause as the second within a protasis is attested in (23):

(23) [12]*(wa-ʾm-S.noun-REL-yaqtul(u)* + [14]***wa-qatal*** + *Ø-ʾm-ʾp-yaqtul(u)* + [15]*wa-yaqtul(u)* + [16]*wa-yaqtul(u)* + ***wa-qatal*** + [17]*Ø-ʾm-PrP-yaqtul(u)* + *Ø-ʾm-PrP* + *wa-PrP-yaqtul(u))* + [18]***wa-qatal***

ואם מלך במלכם ורזן ברזנם אם א(13)דם אש אדם שם אש ימח שם
אזתו(14)ד בשער ז **ושת** שם אם אף יחמד אי(15)ת הקרת ז ויסע השער
ז אש פעל א(16)זתוד ויפעל לשער זר **ושת** שם עלי (17) אם בחמדת יסע
אם בשנאת וברע יסע (18) השער ז **ומח** בעל שמם ואל קן ארץ (19)
ושמש עלם וכל דר בן אלם אית הממלכת הא ואית המלך הא ואית (1)
אדם הא אש אדם שם

‘And if any king or any prince or [13]a person who is a person of name who effaces the name of Azitawadda [14]from this gate **and places** his own name (upon it), if he even claims [15]this city, or tears out this gate which Azitawadda has made [16]and makes a different gate **and places** his own name upon it, [17]whether he tears it out through love or hatred or tears out this gate through malice, [18]**then** Baalsamem and El-Creator-of-the-Earth [19]and Eternal Samas and the entire pantheon **shall wipe out** that kingdom or that king or that [1]person who is a person of name!’ (KAI[5] 26A III:12–IV:1, translated according to Friedrich and Röllig 1999, §§266.2, 324.1b, and Renz 2016, 462; cf. also Krahmalkov 1986, 9f.)

Of the three *wa-qatal* clauses with future time reference in (23), two occur within the protasis and the third initiates the apodosis.

In the next example of a complicated conditional linking, the *wa-qatal* clause is used with future time reference after a *yaqtul(u)* clause in a text that appears to be an instruction with many subcases:

(24) *ʾm-XØ + wa-PrP-yaqtul(u) +* ***wa-qatal***

> (3) באלף כלל אם צועת אם שלם כלל לכהנם כסף עשרת 10 באחד
> וב̊כלל יכן לם עלת פן המשאת ז ש[אר משקל שלש מאת 300] (4)
> ובצועת קצרת ויצלת **וכן** הערת והשלבם והפעמם ואחרי השאר לבעל
> הזבח
>
> 'In case of a bull, an expiatory sacrifice: if (it is) a communal offering or a holocaust, the priests (shall get) ten silver pieces for one, and in case of holocaust belongs to them in addition to this payment [meat at a weight of 300 (sekel)]. [4]And in case of communal offering the neck and shoulder joint. But the hide and the entrails and the legs and the rest of the meat **will belong** to the sacrificer.' (KAI[5] 69:3f., referred to by Friedrich and Röllig 1999, §266.2)

The syntax in (24) is similar to a conditional linking in which the first clause of the apodosis has a *yaqtul(u)* predicate and the second is a *wa-qatal* clause (Renz 2016, 462).[14]

6.4. Survey of Modal Sequences with Internal *Wa-qaṭal* in CBH

As we have seen already in Amarna (§6.2.1), *wa-qatal* clauses in a modal sequence are utilised to express meanings of finality and intended result (Renz 2016, 456). And when *wa-qatal* is part of a modal series, there seems to have been no alternative: it must signal discourse continuity (type *wa-Verb*; Hornkohl 2019, 555). A *Ø-qatal* in this function seems to have been intolerable. The ancient *wa-qatal* in a modal sequence with (intended) result meaning and discourse-continuity syntax probably settled *wa-qatal* as a chunk in this type of domain. This function of *wa-qaṭal* is preserved, but also extended, in CBH modal sequences.

Renz (2016, 651–54, 659) perceives in the pre-exilic Hebrew inscriptions a semantic development from the old Canaanite function of *wa-qatal* to express finality, down to the the sixth-century BCE *wa-qaṭal* expressing an additional command. This range of meanings can be detected also in the CBH modal sequences.

Examples of a result meaning of *wa-qaṭal* often occur at the end of a modal sequence, as in (25):

(25) *Ø-IMP* + *wa-qaṭal* + ***wa-qaṭal***

הַקְרֵב֙ אֶת־מַטֵּ֣ה לֵוִ֔י וְהַעֲמַדְתָּ֣ אֹת֔וֹ לִפְנֵ֖י אַהֲרֹ֣ן הַכֹּהֵ֑ן **וְשֵׁרְת֖וּ** אֹתֽוֹ׃

‘Bring the tribe of Levi and station them in the presence of Aaron the priest, **so that they may serve** him.’ (Num. 3.6; Levine 1993, 152)

In (25), the first *wa-qaṭal* in the sequence is an additional instruction (obligation) of an intended action, while the second has a sense of finality.[15] Such meanings of finality are easily construed as expressing a complement in certain contexts, as in (26):

(26) *Ø-PREP-VN-IMP* + ***wa-qaṭal***

בְּלֶכְתְּךָ֙ לָשׁ֣וּב מִצְרַ֔יְמָה רְאֵ֗ה כָּל־הַמֹּֽפְתִים֙ אֲשֶׁר־שַׂ֣מְתִּי בְיָדֶ֔ךָ **וַעֲשִׂיתָ֖ם** לִפְנֵ֣י
פַרְעֹ֑ה

'When you go back to Egypt, see **that you do** before Pharaoh all the wonders I have put under your control.' (Exod. 4.21)

In (26), the *IMP* + wa-*qaṭal* 'see… so that you do' must be translated as a complement.[16]

The probably later usage of *wa-qaṭal* as an additional instruction after the volitive in modal sequences is much more frequent in CBH. In such cases, it carries connotations different from the initial volitive (Revell 1989, 23). The *wa-qaṭal* clause is not perceived as subordinate, but there remains in many cases a sense of intention, expressing the goal of the action in the initial volitive(s). An example is (27):

(27) *Ø-O.noun-IMP* + ***wa-qaṭal*** + ***wa-qaṭal*** + ***wa-qaṭal***

כָּל־הַחַיָּה אֲשֶׁר־אִתְּךָ מִכָּל־בָּשָׂר בָּעוֹף וּבַבְּהֵמָה וּבְכָל־הָרֶמֶשׂ הָרֹמֵשׂ עַל־
הָאָרֶץ הוֹצֵא אִתָּךְ **וְשָׁרְצוּ** בָאָרֶץ **וּפָרוּ וְרָבוּ** עַל־הָאָרֶץ׃

'Bring out with you every living thing that is with you of all flesh—birds and animals and every creeping thing that creeps on the earth—**they shall swarm** on the earth, **and be fruitful and multiply** on the earth.' (Gen. 8.17)

In (27), the *wa-qaṭal* clauses follow after a pausal stop and express the intended result of the command in the imperative. However, they can also be analysed as additional instructions.[17]

Baranowski (2016a, 160) observes a relative rarity of *wa-qatal* in modal sequences in Amarna. This is not the case in CBH. *Wa-qaṭal* is frequent. And while the choice of *wa-qatal* in a modal sequence in Amarna may be due to the lexically stative meaning of the verbs (Baranowski 2016a, 162), in CBH all lexical types are represented. In this respect, the frequency of *wa-qaṭal* in modal sequences, together with its wide semantic range, represents an extension compared to Ancient Canaanite, and traces of the same development can be detected in the pre-exilic Hebrew inscriptions (Renz 2016, 649).

My data indicate that a very frequent function of *wa-qaṭal* in modal series is to express instructions that are additional but still semantically related to the initial volitive (see also Renz, 2016, 639).[18] The first command in the series is most often an imperative, and the second might be a jussive (if in the first person, usually with a ventive/cohortative clitic). This is shown in (28):

(28) *Ø-IMP* + *wa-IMP* + *wa-yiqṭol(Ø)-V* + [10]***wa-qaṭal*** + *wa-qaṭal*

לֶךְ־נָא אֶל־הַצֹּאן וְקַח־לִי מִשָּׁם שְׁנֵי גְּדָיֵי עִזִּים טֹבִים וְאֶעֱשֶׂה אֹתָם מַטְעַמִּים לְאָבִיךָ כַּאֲשֶׁר אָהֵב׃ **וְהֵבֵאתָ** לְאָבִיךָ וְאָכָל

'Go to the flock and bring me two good young goats, so that I may prepare from them delicious food for your father, such as he loves. [10]**And you shall bring** it to your father to eat.' (Gen. 27.9–10a)

In (28), the modal series is fourfold: first two imperatives, then a jussive with ventive/cohortative clitic, and then two *wa-qaṭal* clauses. All clauses except the first signal discourse continuity (clause-type *wa-Verb*). The discourse-continuity jussive clause with ventive clitic (וְאֶעֱשֶׂה) expresses the personal purpose of the two imperatives ('so that I may prepare'), while the two *wa-qaṭal* clauses describe additional instructions.[19]

Another example of additional instructions expressed by *wa-qaṭal* is (29):

(29) *Ø-IMP* + *Ø-hinnē-qoṭel* + ***wa-qaṭal*** + *wa-O.noun-yiqṭol(u)* + [16]***wa-qaṭal***

לֵךְ אֶל־פַּרְעֹה בַּבֹּקֶר הִנֵּה יֹצֵא הַמַּיְמָה **וְנִצַּבְתָּ** לִקְרָאתוֹ עַל־שְׂפַת הַיְאֹר
וְהַמַּטֶּה אֲשֶׁר־נֶהְפַּךְ לְנָחָשׁ תִּקַּח בְּיָדֶךָ׃ **וְאָמַרְתָּ** אֵלָיו יְהוָה אֱלֹהֵי הָעִבְרִים
שְׁלָחַנִי אֵלֶיךָ לֵאמֹר

'Go to Pharaoh in the morning, as he is going out to the water. **You shall stand** on the bank of the Nile to meet him, and take in your hand the staff that turned into a serpent. [16]**And you shall say** to him The LORD, the God of the Hebrews, has sent me to you, saying…' (Exod. 7.15–16a)

In (29), the *qoṭel* clause is subordinated (circumstantial clause) and embedded in the imperative clause. The first *wa-qaṭal* (וְנִצַּבְתָּ) after the imperative expresses an added instruction about how to perform the task. Interestingly, the next instruction has a focused element (הַמַּטֶּה אֲשֶׁר־נֶהְפַּךְ לְנָחָשׁ) in clause-initial position, in which case the verb form to be used is a long *yiqṭol* (תִּקַּח). A further added instruction in the form of a *wa-qaṭal* clause (וְאָמַרְתָּ) then follows at the beginning of verse 16.[20]

The extended meaning of additional instruction, and not only finality, gives *wa-qaṭal* a sense of future obligation, which is a meaning close to that of the imperfective gram long *yiqṭol*. A long *yiqṭol* is a relatively infrequent phenomenon in modal series, but when it occurs in CBH, it replaces a *wa-qaṭal* with a focal element (*wa-X-yiqṭol(u)*) or as negated clause (*wa-lō-yiqṭol(u)*).[21]

A *wa-qaṭal* in a modal series can also, but less frequently, express added information *about* the commanded action, as in (30):

(30) *Ø-IMP-nā* + *Ø-IMP* + *wa-yiqṭol(Ø)* + ***wa-qaṭal*** + ***wa-qaṭal***

לִֽינוּ־נָ֞א הִנֵּ֨ה חֲנ֤וֹת הַיּוֹם֙ לִ֥ין פֹּה֙ וְיִיטַ֣ב לְבָבֶ֔ךָ **וְהִשְׁכַּמְתֶּ֥ם** מָחָר֙ לְדַרְכְּכֶ֔ם **וְהָלַכְתָּ֖** לְאֹהָלֶֽךָ׃

‘Please, spend the night, because the day draws to its close. Lodge here and enjoy yourself! **Then you can get up early** tomorrow for your journey **and go** home.’ (Judg. 19.9)

In (30), the two *wa-qaṭal* clauses do not constitute additional instructions, but a reminder of suitable times to return home.[22]

My conclusion is that *wa-qaṭal* clauses in modal sequences seem to be more frequent in CBH than in Amarna. As an extension in CBH, such clauses frequently express additional instructions related to the initial volitives (IMP and/or jussives). The sense of obligation and sometimes future pushes *wa-qaṭal* semantically closer to the imperfective formation *yiqṭol(u)*.

6.5. Result Functions of *Wa-qaṭal* in Other Domains in CBH

In the previous sections, we have identified some early Northwest Semitic functions of *wa-qatal*, and we have identified these early meanings of *wa-qaṭal* in modal sequences in CBH, that is, the sense of finality or result in modal sequences. It is therefore feasible to search for traces of early functions in other domains. Early functions of *wa-qaṭal* are important because they formed part of the initial linguistic context in which the construction *wa-qaṭal* started to extend its semantics and functional range. In this section, we shall investigate other domains in search of the early construction *wa-qaṭal*.

6.5.1. The Instructional Domain and *Wa-qaṭal*

In instructional domains, the dominating clause-types are long *X-yiqṭol* and *wa-qaṭal.* The meanings expressed are modal, but there is no immediate connection with initial volitives. If volitives can be identified in preceding textual units, they have no direct relation with the clauses in the instructional domain.

The dominant meaning expressed in instruction is obligation, but future is also frequent. The two meanings are closely related. Obligation always concerns a future action, and a statement about the future is easily perceived as obligatory.

In the text-types extant in my corpus, instruction dominates side-by-side with narration. It is plausible that the instructional domain types in CBH have developed from modal series. As we have seen, in modal series, additional instructions are expressed by *wa-qaṭal* and *yiqṭol(u)* clauses. In complicated instructions, it is easy to imagine that the connection with a preceding volitive fades away and *wa-qaṭal* and *X-yiqṭol(u)* take over as the backbone of the instruction. It is also reasonable that this is the linguistic milieu where *wa-qaṭal* became the discourse-continuity alternative to *yiqṭol(u)* when *wa-yiqṭol(u)* clauses had become intolerable in the Iron Age (see §3.4.3). If this supposition is true, this constitutes one of the beginnings of the 'alternation' between *yiqṭol(u)* and *wa-qaṭal.*

In this type of domain also, the old final function of *wa-qaṭal* can be detected. Frequently it occurs at the end of a sequence of instructional *yiqṭol(u)* and *wa-qaṭal* clauses, as in (31):

(31) *wa-ʾaḥar yiqṭol(u)* + [20]*wa-qaṭal* + *wa-qaṭal* + ***wa-qaṭal***

וְאַחַר יִשְׁחַט אֶת־הָעֹלָה׃ וְהֶעֱלָה הַכֹּהֵן אֶת־הָעֹלָה וְאֶת־הַמִּנְחָה הַמִּזְבֵּחָה
וְכִפֶּר עָלָיו הַכֹּהֵן **וְטָהֵר**׃

‘After that he is to slaughter the burnt offering, [20]and the priest is to offer the burnt offering and the grain offering on the altar. Thus the priest is to make atonement for him, **so that he will be clean**.’ (Lev. 14.19b–20)

In (31), a *wa-qaṭal* clause appears at the end of a sequence of instructions. The meaning is most easily interpreted as a result, the result of the priest’s fulfilling the proper ritual of atonement. As (31) exemplifies, the function of *wa-qaṭal* to express a result occurs at the end of a clausal sequence, in which other *wa-qaṭal* clauses may have other meanings, usually obligation.[23] A clear example in direct speech is (32):

(32) *Ø-X-yiqṭol(u)* + ***wa-qaṭal*** + *wa-X-yiqṭol(u)* + ***wa-qaṭal*** + *Ø-raq, yiqṭol(Ø)-A*[24]

אֹכֶל בַּכֶּסֶף תַּשְׁבִּרֵנִי וְאָכַלְתִּי וּמַיִם בַּכֶּסֶף תִּתֶּן־לִי וְשָׁתִיתִי רַק אֶעְבְּרָה בְרַגְלָי׃

‘You shall sell me food for cash **so that I can eat** and give me water **to drink**. Just allow me to go through on foot!’ (Deut. 2.28)

The meaning of *wa-qaṭal* in such positions is a semantic subordination, a usage probably inherited from earlier stages when *wa-qaṭal* was a subordinate clause in modal series.

6.5.2. Future Time Reference and *Wa-qaṭal*

The early sense of finality also occurs in linkings with futural *yiqṭol(u)* clauses. An example in direct speech is (33):

(33) *Ø-S.pron-yiqṭol(u)* + ***wa-qaṭal***

אָנֹכִ֞י אֲשַׁלַּ֣ח אֶתְכֶם֒ **וּזְבַחְתֶּ֞ם** לַיהוָ֤ה אֱלֹֽהֵיכֶם֙ בַּמִּדְבָּ֔ר

'I will let you go, **so that you can sacrifice** to the Lord your God in the desert.' (Exod. 8.24)

In (33), a *wa-qaṭal* clause expresses a result, but in this example the result meaning does not appear in a modal sequence. The preceding *yiqṭol(u)* has future time reference.[25]

A future-time clause can easily express the ability to perform the action. In this case also, a *wa-qaṭal* clause can follow to express a result:

(34) *Ø-INT-S.noun-yiqṭol(u)* + ***wa-qaṭal*** + *Ø-ʾim-O.noun-yiqṭol(u)* + ***wa-qaṭal***

הֲצֹ֧אן וּבָקָ֛ר יִשָּׁחֵ֥ט לָהֶ֖ם **וּמָצָ֣א** לָהֶ֑ם אִ֣ם אֶֽת־כָּל־דְּגֵ֥י הַיָּ֛ם יֵאָסֵ֥ף לָהֶ֖ם **וּמָצָ֥א** לָהֶֽם׃

'Could enough flocks and herds be slaughtered **to suffice** them? Or could even all the fish of the sea be caught for them **to suffice** them? (Num. 11.22)

In (34), both *yiqṭol(u)* clauses express ability, while the *wa-qaṭal* clauses express result.[26]

6.5.3. Result *Wa-qaṭal* within a Protasis

The result meaning of *wa-qaṭal* also often occurs within complex protases, as in (35):

(35) *(kī-yiqṭol(u)* + *wa-qaṭal* + ***wa-qaṭal*** + *wa-lō-yiqṭol(u))* + *Ø-VNabs-yiqṭol(u)* + *wa-qaṭal*

(וְכִֽי־יִנָּצ֣וּ אֲנָשִׁ֗ים וְנָ֨גְפ֜וּ אִשָּׁ֤ה הָרָה֙ **וְיָצְא֣וּ** יְלָדֶ֔יהָ וְלֹ֥א יִהְיֶ֖ה אָס֑וֹן) עָנ֣וֹשׁ יֵעָנֵ֗שׁ כַּאֲשֶׁ֨ר יָשִׁ֤ית עָלָיו֙ בַּ֣עַל הָֽאִשָּׁ֔ה וְנָתַ֖ן בִּפְלִלִֽים׃

‘(If men strive together and hit a pregnant woman, **so that** her children **come out**, but there is no harm), the one who hit her shall surely be fined, as the woman’s husband shall impose on him, and he shall pay as the judges determine.’ (Exod. 21.22)

In (35), in the domain of a complex protasis, *wa-qaṭal* as the third clause has result meaning.[27]

6.5.4. Result *Wa-qaṭal* within an Apodosis

Within the domain of an apodosis also, a *wa-qaṭal* often has result meaning as the second or third clause.

(36) *(wa-ʾim-O.noun-qaṭal + Ø-lō-qaṭal) + [21]wa-qaṭal + wa-qaṭal +* ***wa-qaṭal*** *+ kī-qaṭal + wa-qaṭal*

(וְאִם־אֱמֶת הָיָה הַדָּבָר הַזֶּה לֹא־נִמְצְאוּ בְתוּלִים לַנַּעֲרָ): וְהוֹצִיאוּ אֶת־הַנַּעֲרָ אֶל־פֶּתַח בֵּית־אָבִיהָ וּסְקָלוּהָ אַנְשֵׁי עִירָהּ בָּאֲבָנִים **וָמֵתָה** כִּי־עָשְׂתָה נְבָלָה בְּיִשְׂרָאֵל לִזְנוֹת בֵּית אָבִיהָ וּבִעַרְתָּ הָרָע מִקִּרְבֶּךָ׃

‘(But if the accusation has turned true, the young woman was not a virgin), [21]the men of her city must bring the young woman to the door of her father’s house and stone her **to death**, for she has done a disgraceful thing in Israel by behaving like a prostitute while living in her father’s house. In this way you will purge the evil from among you.’ (Deut. 22.20f.)

In this relatively long apodosis, the third *wa-qaṭal* ‘so that she dies’ is so frequent that the meaning is practically adverbial. It has the old subordinate result sense. In such cases, the accent before *wa-qaṭal* is usually not a pause. In (36), the *wa-qaṭal* after the pause (וּבִעַרְתָּ֥) is a focal clause presupposing the preceding actions: ‘in this way you will purge the evil’ (see §2.3.8).[28]

6.5.5. Result *Wa-qaṭal* in a *Pɛn*-domain

Complexes of clauses with an initial conjunction *pɛn* constitute well demarcated domains that often end with a *wa-qaṭal* clause with result meaning. An example is:

(37) *kī-lō-yiqṭol(u)!* + *kī-XØ* + *Ø-XØ* + [15]*pɛn-yiqṭol(u)* + *wa-qaṭal* + *wa-qaṭal* + *wa-qaṭal* + ***wa-qaṭal*** + [16]*wa-qaṭal* + *wa-qaṭal* + ***wa-qaṭal***

כִּ֛י לֹ֥א תִֽשְׁתַּחֲוֶ֖ה לְאֵ֣ל אַחֵ֑ר כִּ֤י יְהוָה֙ קַנָּ֣א שְׁמ֔וֹ אֵ֥ל קַנָּ֖א ה֑וּא׃ 15 פֶּן־תִּכְרֹ֥ת בְּרִ֖ית לְיוֹשֵׁ֣ב הָאָ֑רֶץ וְזָנ֣וּ ׀ אַחֲרֵ֣י אֱלֹֽהֵיהֶ֗ם וְזָבְחוּ֙ לֵאלֹ֣הֵיהֶ֔ם וְקָרָ֣א לְךָ֔ **וְאָכַלְתָּ֖** מִזִּבְחֽוֹ׃ 16 וְלָקַחְתָּ֥ מִבְּנֹתָ֖יו לְבָנֶ֑יךָ וְזָנ֣וּ בְנֹתָ֗יו אַחֲרֵי֙ אֱלֹ֣הֵיהֶ֔ן וְהִזְנוּ֙ אֶת־בָּנֶ֔יךָ אַחֲרֵ֖י אֱלֹהֵיהֶֽן׃

‘You shall not worship any other god, for the LORD, Jealous is his name, is a jealous God—[15]lest you make a covenant with the inhabitants of the land and they play the harlot with their gods, and sacrifice to their gods, and someone invite you **to eat** of his sacrifice; [16]and you take some of his daughters for your sons, and his daughters play the harlot with their gods, **so that they cause** your sons also to play the harlot with their gods.’ (Exod. 34.14–16)

In (37), the *pɛn* domain follows after a *yiqṭol(u)* clause with obligational meaning. The *pɛn* complex of clauses consists of an initial *yiqṭol(u)* clause and seven following *wa-qaṭal* clauses, which describe two scenarios, one concerning making a covenant with the inhabitants and one concerning the sons playing the harlot with their gods. Both scenarios end with a *wa-qaṭal* having a result meaning.[29]

6.5.6. Result *Wa-qaṭal* in Counterfactual Domains

The result meaning of *wa-qaṭal* can be detected also in some counterfactual sequences. Counterfactual meanings of *wa-qatal* are attested in Amarna.[30] It is reasonable to suppose that such uses are inherited in CBH.

(38) *INT-qaṭal* + ***wa-qaṭal***

הֶחֳדַ֙לְתִּי֙ אֶת־דִּשְׁנִ֔י אֲשֶׁר־בִּ֛י יְכַבְּד֥וּ אֱלֹהִ֖ים וַאֲנָשִׁ֑ים **וְהָ֣לַכְתִּ֔י** לָנ֖וּעַ עַל־הָעֵצִֽים׃

'Have I ceased making my oil, whereby gods and men are honored, **that I should go** to sway of the trees?' (Judg. 9.9, Boling 1975, 166)

In (38), the agent looks with contempt on the proposal. "The picture is that of the king who nods, sitting above his subjects" (Boling 1975, 173).[31]

6.6. The Significance of the Result Meaning in the Development of *Wa-qaṭal* in CBH

My hypothesis is that the result meaning of *wa-qaṭal* in CBH is inherited from Northwest Semitic. Since the result *wa-qaṭal* was very often used together with the imperfective gram *yiqṭol(u)* in modal series, as well as in instruction and in prediction, the semantic range of *wa-qaṭal* was gradually extended to future and obligation. The result meaning of *wa-qaṭal* was retained occasionally in CBH, especially at the end of sequences, but the dominant meanings of *wa-qaṭal* became future and obligation, meanings which the long *yiqṭol* could also express.

This process went hand-in-hand with the need to replace the no longer tolerable **wa-yiqṭol(u)* (see §3.4.3). The *wa-qaṭal* clause-type signalled discourse continuity and could easily be used instead of **wa-yiqṭol(u)*. The latter clause-type is attested in Amarna, but became intolerable in most positions in CBH because of its (partial) homonymy with *wa-yiqṭol(Ø)*, jussive or preterite.[32]

It remains to explain the habitual meaning of *wa-qaṭal*. I have found few early examples of the result meaning in sequences expressing habituality. The few examples may support, but cannot prove, the hypothesis that the meanings of habituality developed in sequences where, in earlier Northwest Semitic, *wa-qatal* had result meaning. If I am right, the meanings of habituality in CBH developed in sequences within which *wa-qaṭal* was originally used to express result. The habituality became an extension of the semantics of *wa-qaṭal*. In this case too, the old meaning of finality was retained in some positions. One example is:

(39) *Ø-ADV-yiqṭol(u)* + *wa-qaṭal* + ***wa-qaṭal***

עַל־כֵּן֙ יַֽעֲזָב־אִ֔ישׁ אֶת־אָבִ֖יו וְאֶת־אִמּ֑וֹ וְדָבַ֣ק בְּאִשְׁתּ֔וֹ **וְהָי֖וּ** לְבָשָׂ֥ר אֶחָֽד׃

'That is why a man leaves his father and mother and is united to his wife, **so that they become** one flesh.' (Gen. 2.24)

This editorial aetiological comment (Westermann 1976, 317) explains a custom, and the meaning of both *yiqṭol(u)* and *wa-qaṭal* is a present habituality, practised at the time of writing. The becoming one flesh is the result of the preceding actions (Garr 1998, lxxxiii). An example with past time reference is (40):

(40) *Ø-S.noun-qaṭal + CONJ-yiqṭol(u) +* **wa-qaṭal**

הַנְּפִלִ֞ים הָי֣וּ בָאָרֶץ֮ בַּיָּמִ֣ים הָהֵם֒ וְגַ֣ם אַֽחֲרֵי־כֵ֗ן אֲשֶׁ֨ר יָבֹ֜אוּ בְּנֵ֤י הָֽאֱלֹהִים֙ אֶל־בְּנ֣וֹת הָֽאָדָ֔ם **וְיָלְד֖וּ** לָהֶ֑ם

'The Nephilim were on the earth in those days, and also afterward, when the sons of God came in to the daughters of man **so that they bore children** to them.' (Gen. 6.4)

In (40), a complex subordinate sentence starts with a *yiqṭol(u)* clause describing a habitual sequence of events in the past. The most natural interpretation of *wa-qaṭal* (וְיָלְדוּ) is as a result of the habitual action. The example illustrates that a result clause after a habitual clause is easily interpreted as being itself habitual.

In (39) and (40), an initial imperfective *yiqṭol(u)* clause determines the intended habitual action.

In Northwest Semitic, the result meaning of *wa-qaṭal* could also be used as the first clause in an apodosis. Very early *wa-qaṭal* was used to code the expected result when the condition (the protasis) was fulfilled. As such, *qaṭal* itself was able to express this result, as the Amarna examples with *Ø-qaṭal* apodoses with future time reference show. But the dominance of the continuity clause-type *wa-qaṭal* was so overwhelming in modal series and other types of sequences that *wa-qaṭal* became a more natural choice than *Ø-qaṭal* for apodosis.

As apodosis, *wa-qaṭal* had its own unique development in CBH. The extensive use of *wa-qaṭal* in modal sequences and other types of sequences, together with its use as apodosis, settled *wa-*

qaṭal as construction in CBH, in the sense described by Bybee (2010)—a construction that had completely different semantics compared to the original gram *qatal*. This will be the theme for the following sections.

6.7. Survey of Conditional Sentences with *Wa-qaṭal* as Apodosis in CBH

6.7.1. The Types of Apodoses in CBH

In an assessment of the role of *wa-qaṭal* as apodosis, it is pertinent to investigate all types of apodoses in CBH. The result is displayed in Table 12.

Table 12: Statistics of apodosis types in CBH[33]

Ø-X-yiqṭol(u)	117	25.3%
Ø-yiqṭol(u)[34]	3	0.6%
Ø-(X)-qaṭal	17	3.7%
Ø-(ʾal)-yiqṭol(Ø)[35]	13	2.8%
Ø-yiqṭol(Ø)-A	4	0.9%
Ø-(X)-IMP	18	3.9%
Ø-(X)-qoṭel[36]	9	1.9%
Ø-VN (Gen. 4.7)	1	0.2%
Ø-XØ	32	6.9%
wa-X-yiqṭol(u)[37]	2	0.4%
wa-X-qaṭal (Judg. 6.13)	1	0.2%
wa-yiqṭol(Ø)[38]	4	0.9%
wa-yiqṭol(Ø)-A[39]	12	2.6%
kī-ʿattā-qaṭal[40]	4	0.9%
wa-haya[41]	4	0.9%
wa-qaṭal	221	47.8%
Total apodoses	**462**	**100%**

Table 12 shows that, apart from the *wa-qaṭal* type of apodoses, an initial *wa* is rare (in total 19×, or about 4% of all apodoses). In CBH, the rule is asyndesis for an apodosis, if we disregard the *wa-qaṭal* clause-type. As for the second most frequent apodosis type, that with a *yiqṭol(u)* predicate, only two instances have a connective *wa*. The rest of the *yiqṭol(u)* (25% of all apodoses) are asyndetic. The table shows that there was no need of a '*waw* of apodosis' in CBH (cf. J-M §176), since such a *waw* would nearly exclusively be confined to one construction, *wa-qaṭal* (*pace* Khan 2021a, 315).

A typical example of an asyndetic apodosis is (41). It represents the second most frequent apodosis type, with a *yiqṭol(u)* predicate.

(41) *(Ø-ʾim-lō-yiqṭol(u)) + Ø-lō-yiqṭol(u)-Npar*

אִם־לֹ֛א יֵרֵ֛ד אֲחִיכֶ֥ם הַקָּטֹ֖ן אִתְּכֶ֑ם לֹ֥א תֹסִפ֖וּן לִרְא֥וֹת פָּנָֽי׃

'Unless your youngest brother comes down with you, you shall not see my face again.' (Gen. 44.23)

The apodosis in (41) has a future time reference, which is a very frequent meaning of an apodosis (more on this later on). The example is typical also in the respect that the protasis has a *yiqṭol(u)* predicate, which is the most common protasis type in CBH (see below).

Since the *wa-qaṭal* clause-type is constructed from the elements *wa* and *qaṭal*, it is pertinent to investigate also the use of the *qaṭal* morpheme in apodoses, apart from the *wa-qaṭal* construction. *Qaṭal* (apart from *wa-qaṭal*) occurs in about 4% of all apodoses. The statistics show that *qaṭal* apodoses mostly express an anterior aspect (projected into the future), an example of which is displayed in (42):

(42) *(wa-ʾim-PrP-qaṭal + wa-S.noun-qaṭal) + Ø-qaṭal*

(וְאִם־בְּעֵינָיו֙ עָמַ֤ד הַנֶּ֙תֶק֙ וְשֵׂעָ֥ר שָׁחֹ֛ר צָֽמַח־בּ֖וֹ) נִרְפָּ֥א הַנֶּ֖תֶק

'If, as far as the priest can see, the scall has stayed the same and black hair has sprouted in it, the scall has been healed' (Lev. 13.37)

As can be seen in (42), an asyndetic clause-initial *qaṭal* is fully productive as apodosis. The meaning in the example is anterior-future. Anterior-future seems to be the default interpretation of *qaṭal* when used as predicate in an apodosis, if the linguistic coding does not indicate otherwise.[42]

The meanings of the *qaṭal* morpheme in apodoses are displayed in Table 13.

Table 13: Frequencies of *qaṭal* meanings in apodoses in corpus

	qaṭal	*qaṭal* %
Anterior-future	9	41%
Anterior-present[43]	1	5%
Counterfactual	7	32%
Future	1	5%
Performative	3	14%
Stativic (future)	1	5%
Total	**22**	**100%**

As can be seen from Table 13, anterior projected into the future is the most frequent meaning of *qaṭal* in an apodosis. Also a common meaning is the counterfactual, usually signalled by specific particles. An example of this is (43):[44]

(43) *(lūlē-S.noun-qaṭal) + kī-ʿattā-ADV-qaṭal*

(לוּלֵי אֱלֹהֵי אָבִי אֱלֹהֵי אַבְרָהָם וּפַחַד יִצְחָק הָיָה לִי) כִּי עַתָּה רֵיקָם שִׁלַּחְתָּנִי

'(If the God of my father, the God of Abraham and the Fear of Isaac, had not been on my side,) surely now you would have sent me away empty-handed' (Gen. 31.42)

In (43), not only is the *qaṭal* in the apodosis counterfactual (marked by the phrase כִּי עַתָּה), but so is the *qaṭal* in the protasis (marked by the preposed particle לוּלֵי).

In elevated speech, *qaṭal* can be used with performative function in CBH, and this usage is found also in certain apodoses, as in (44):[45]

(44) *(wa-ʾim-yiqṭol(u) + wa-lō-yiqṭol(u) + wa-qaṭal + wa-qaṭal) + ¹⁸Ø-qaṭal*

(וְאִם־יִפְנֶה לְבָבְךָ וְלֹא תִשְׁמָע וְנִדַּחְתָּ וְהִשְׁתַּחֲוִיתָ לֵאלֹהִים אֲחֵרִים וַעֲבַדְתָּם):
הִגַּדְתִּי לָכֶם הַיּוֹם כִּי...

'(But if your heart turns away, and you will not hear, but are drawn away to worship other gods and serve them,) ¹⁸I declare to you today, that…' (Deut. 30.17–18)

Of special interest are the rare cases of futural *qaṭal* in an apodosis. An example is (45):

(45) *(Ø-ʾim-yiqṭol(u)-Npar) + kī ʾim-qaṭal*

(אִם־תַּעֲשׂוּן כָּזֹאת) כִּי אִם־נִקַּמְתִּי בָכֶם וְאַחַר אֶחְדָּל:

'If this is the sort of thing you do, I will certainly be vindicated against you! Only after that I will quit.' (Judg. 15.7; cf. Boling 1975, 234)

In this oath formula, the temporal reference of *qaṭal* is future.[46] It is probable that a solemn oath reveals an old usage of *qaṭal*, in which future is a tolerable meaning of a *qaṭal* apodosis, even *Ø-qaṭal*, a clause-type attested in Amarna (Baranowski 2016a, 174). In CBH, a possible future time reference is also found in the stativic *Ø-qaṭal* in (46):

(46) *(wa-S.pron-CONJ-qaṭal)* + *Ø-qaṭal*

(וַאֲנִ֕י כַּאֲשֶׁ֥ר שָׁכֹ֖לְתִּי) שָׁכָֽלְתִּי׃

'(As for me, if I am bereaved,) I am bereaved.' (Gen. 43.14)

The temporal reference of the stativic *qaṭal* is future, even if the natural English translation is in the present.[47]

My conclusion concerning *qaṭal* in apodoses is that, in a few cases of archaic syntax, a future (result) time reference is attested in CBH. This usage points to a stage when *qaṭal* could more freely refer to the future, especially, as in Amarna, in the case of stativic verbs (Baranowski 2016a, 173).

An important issue is the connection between *wa-qaṭal* and long *yiqṭol(u)*. The theory of consecutive tenses suggests that there is a special relationship between *yiqṭol(u)* clauses and *wa-qaṭal* clauses. This is confirmed by the frequencies of both *yiqṭol(u)* and *wa-qaṭal* in apodoses. They exhibit practically equivalent meanings, as is shown in Table 14.

Table 14: Meanings of *yiqṭol(u)* and *wa-qaṭal* apodoses in the corpus, a comparison

	***yiqṭol(u)* in apodosis**	***wa-qaṭal* as apodosis**
Obligation	78%	67%
Future	16%	31%
Permission	4%	1%
Habitual present	1%	0%
Ability	1%	0.5%
Hypothetical	0%	0.5%
Total number	**121**	**226**

In a discussion of the development of the *wa-qaṭal* construction from its use in an apodosis, the relative frequencies of meanings in CBH should be recognised. As can be seen in Table 14, there is a correspondence between the frequencies of future and obligation. As is well known, future and obligation are related meanings (Bybee et al. 1994, 279), and if we compare their combined frequencies for *yiqṭol(u)* and *wa-qaṭal*, the correspondence is stunning: future-obligation is found in 94% of all *yiqṭol(u)* and in 98% of all *wa-qaṭal* in apodoses. The other meanings also correspond fairly well. My conclusion is that there is a semantic connection between *yiqṭol(u)* and *wa-qaṭal* in the formation of apodoses in CBH. They are used with the same meaning in the coding of apodoses, and the question arises as to why there were two types at all.

As we have seen, *wa-qatal* was current, though not very frequent, as apodosis in early Northwest Semitic (§6.2.2). It was also used in modal series (§6.2.1). And *yaqtulu* was used in apodoses as well. When we compare *wa-qaṭal* in CBH with *wa-qatal* in Northwest Semitic, the difference is frequency, extension of domains, and extension of meaning. In early Northwest Semitic texts, *wa-qatal* expressed a result in modal series and as apodosis. But the later pre-exilic Hebrew inscriptions indicate that there must have been a semantic shift, or rather widening, of *wa-qaṭal* to meanings closer to the functions of *yiqṭol(u)*: future, obligation, and habituality. This shift, the emergence of *wa-qaṭal* as a construction in Bybee's sense, must have taken place in a stage during or after Archaic Hebrew.[48]

The apodosis was one of the domains in which *wa-qaṭal* developed as a construction, but we need to investigate also the protasis domain.

6.7.2. Types of Protases in CBH

For an understanding of *wa-qaṭal* as apodosis, it is important to recognise also the protases in CBH. In a survey of the clause-types in protases, it is clear that *yiqṭol(u)* dominates; see Table 15.

Table 15: Protasis types in CBH[49]

	Protases	**% of all protases**
yiqṭol(u)	291	61%
wa-qaṭal[50]	11	2,3%
ellipsis[51]	3	0,6%
IMP	25	5,2%
XØ	56	11,7%
qoṭel	27	5,7%
qaṭal[52]	64	13,4%
Total in corpus[53]	**477**	**100%**

The dominant predicate in protases is *yiqṭol(u)*, about 60%.[54] This means that, when an apodosis is *wa-qaṭal*, the protasis is most often a *yiqṭol(u)* clause.[55] So the typical conditional sentence is one with a *yiqṭol(u)* predicate in the protasis and *wa-qaṭal* as apodosis. And the typical apodosis expresses obligation, very frequently so in legal discourse. An example is (47):

(47) *(wa-ʾim-O.noun-lō-yiqṭol(u)!) + wa-qaṭal*

(וְאִם־שְׁלָשׁ־אֵלֶּה לֹא יַעֲשֶׂה לָהּ) וְיָצְאָה חִנָּם אֵין כָּסֶף׃

'(And if he does not do these three things for her,) she shall go out for nothing, without payment of money.' (Exod. 21.11)

As we have already seen, *yiqṭol(u)* is also very frequent in apodoses. A comparison between *yiqṭol(u)* and *wa-qaṭal* in both protases and apodoses is significant.

Table 16: Statistics of *yiqṭol(u)* and *wa-qaṭal* in protases and apodoses

	% of all protases	**% of all apodoses**
yiqṭol(u)	61%	26%
wa-qaṭal	2.3%	48%
Total in corpus	**477**	**462**

As can be seen in Table 16, the dominant predicate in protases is *yiqṭol(u)*. This means that, when an apodosis *wa-qaṭal* began to develop as a construction, protases with a *yiqṭol(u)* predicate had high frequency. In apodoses, the dominating clause-type is *wa-qaṭal*, with nearly 50% of all apodoses. The second most frequent apodosis type has a *yiqṭol(u)* predicate, a quarter of all instances (26%). The apodoses in CBH are dominated by *yiqṭol(u)* and *wa-qaṭal* clauses.

If we consider Tables 12–16 from a diachronic perspective—more precisely, from the perspective of the relatively new construction *wa-qaṭal*—we get the impression that the *wa-qaṭal* clause-type was not needed in the protases (in CBH only about 2%),[56] but increasingly productive in the apodoses. The numbers reveal an extension of the new *wa-qaṭal*, and this extension took place in the apodosis domain, not as first clause in protases.

6.8. Discussion about the Birthplace of the Construction *Wa-qaṭal*

In early Northwest Semitic, *wa-qatal* seems to have been a clause-type with result meaning. This result mostly had future time reference. The meaning was extended in CBH, and one of the new acquired meanings was a plain future, or obligation. These are meanings close to the meanings expressed by the imperfective gram *yaqtulu*. Since *yaqtulu* dominates in protases and is frequent also in apodoses, this means that, in early texts, *yaqtulu* is often followed by a *wa-qatal* clause with result meaning. When the result meaning was bleached and/or extended to future, *wa-qatal* became a clause that, in a few steps of extension, could express the same meanings as *yaqtulu*, only with the exception that *wa-qatal* always signalled continuity.

The quality of continuity and the result meaning are not typical for *yaqtulu* clauses. They are specific qualities of *wa-qatal*.

The 'consecutive' phenomenon, whereby *wa-qaṭal* came to continue specifically *yiqṭol(u)* clauses, belongs to a later stage, what we call CBH.

Something happened; *wa-qaṭal* was now no longer only used to signify result, but also future, and obligation—in the proper contexts.

With the future meaning, *wa-qaṭal* acquired semantics close to those of *yiqṭol(u)*. Khan (2021a) has not explained why *wa-*

qaṭal came to acquire semantics close to those of *yiqṭol(u)*. In the sections above, I have tried to attain an answer.

The old result meaning of *wa-qaṭal* can be demonstrated in certain domains: in protases, in apodoses, in modal sequences, and also in other types of sequences, such as instructions.

When the result meaning of *wa-qaṭal* was extended to future-obligation, it became a clause-type that had the same meaning as *yiqṭol(u)*, apart from a continuity signal.

6.9. Temporal or Causal Clause with *Wa-qaṭal*

Since one linguistic birthplace of the construction *wa-qaṭal* is a linking of the type *conditional clause + wa-qaṭal*, where the conditional clause is subordinate, a logical extension of the construction would be a linking with a similar type of subordinated clause: the temporal. This type of linking is amply attested in CBH. In the present section, the emphasis will be on temporal, but also causal, clauses that precede a *wa-qaṭal* clause.

In many languages, there is a close association between conditional and temporal linkings (Dixon 2009, 14). In CBH also, a semantic affinity can be perceived between conditional clauses and temporal clauses (both followed by main clauses). This can be illustrated by a number of borderline cases in which the classification is disputable. In a linking *temporal clause + main clause*, the event or state described in the temporal clause lies in the future or in the past; if in the future, the action in the temporal clause is expected to occur (Khan 2021a, 311). By contrast, the conditional clause describes an eventuality that is not presupposed. A borderline case with the conjunction *ʾim* is illustrated in (48):

(48) *wa-ʾim-PrP-yiqṭol(u) + wa-qaṭal*

וְאִם־בְּאַחַת יִתְקָעוּ וְנוֹעֲדוּ אֵלֶיךָ הַנְּשִׂיאִים רָאשֵׁי אַלְפֵי יִשְׂרָאֵל׃

'But if they blow only one, then the chiefs, the heads of the tribes of Israel, shall gather themselves to you.' (Num. 10.4)

In (48), the event in the temporal clause is expected to occur. On certain occasions, one silver trumpet is really blown.[57] But on other occasions, they will blow two trumpets. So in this respect the case is an eventuality. The syntax of the temporal clause is exactly the same as in the most frequent type of a protasis: the conjunction *ʾim* and the predicate *yiqṭol(u)*.

Another borderline case of temporal linking is the following example with the conjunction *kī*:[58]

(49) *Ø-kī-yiqṭol(u) + wa-qaṭal*

כִּי תִבְנֶה בַּיִת חָדָשׁ וְעָשִׂיתָ מַעֲקֶה לְגַגֶּךָ

'When you build a new house, you shall make a parapet for your roof.' (Deut. 22.8; Christensen 2002, 501)

In (49), the 'you' represents any Israelite, and for this collective entity, the action in the temporal clause is certainly expected to occur many times. On the other hand, not everyone will build a new house, and in this respect, from the point of view of the individual, the clause expresses an eventuality.[59]

A temporal clause may refer to the future. In the following example, the temporal conjunction is *'im* and nothing in the syntax indicates that a temporal and not a conditional clause is at hand:

(50) *wa-'im-yiqtol(u)! + wa-qatal*

וְאִם־יִהְיֶ֣ה הַיֹּבֵל֮ לִבְנֵ֣י יִשְׂרָאֵל֒ וְנֽוֹסְפָה֙ נַחֲלָתָ֔ן עַ֚ל נַחֲלַ֣ת הַמַּטֶּ֔ה אֲשֶׁ֥ר תִּהְיֶ֖ינָה לָהֶ֑ם

'And when the jubilee of the people of Israel comes, then their inheritance will be added to the inheritance of the tribe into which they marry.' (Num. 36.4a)

In (50), the temporal clause is expected to occur in the future: the jubilee. Since this is something to be repeated as a custom, the *wa-qatal* here has a sense of habituality.

When the temporal clause linking refers to events in the past, habituality is often implied:

(51) *wa-'im-ADV-yiqtol(u) + wa-qatal*

וְאִם־כֹּ֣ה יֹאמַ֗ר עֲקֻדִּים֙ יִהְיֶ֣ה שְׂכָרֶ֔ךָ וְיָלְד֥וּ כָל־הַצֹּ֖אן עֲקֻדִּֽים׃

'and if he said, The striped shall be your wages, then all the flock bore striped.' (Gen. 31.8b)

In the case of a temporal clause referring to the past, a conditional interpretation is not possible, since its truth value is settled. There is no eventuality. A *yiqtol(u)* predicate in the temporal clause usually indicates habituality in the past, and the same meaning must be given to the main clause (וְיָלְדוּ). The example illustrates how *wa-qatal* extends to past habitual semantics when the temporal clause has past time reference, and this is also the case when the temporal clause is coded with a *qaṭal* morpheme with implied habitual meaning, as in (52):

(52) *wa-haya: Ø-ʾim-qaṭal + wa-qaṭal + wa-qaṭal*

וְהָיָה אִם־זָרַע יִשְׂרָאֵל וְעָלָה מִדְיָן וַעֲמָלֵק וּבְנֵי־קֶדֶם וְעָלוּ עָלָיו׃

'For whenever the Israelites planted crops, the Midianites and the Amalekites and the people of the East would come up and attack them.' (Judg. 6.3)

The *wa-haya* in (52) is a macro-syntactic signal for background (Isaksson 1998). It does not belong to the temporal clause, which has a *qaṭal* predicate (זָרַע) with implied habituality. The *wa-qaṭal* main clauses (וְעָלָה and וְעָלוּ) in this example too express past habituality. This habitual meaning represents an extension of the construction *wa-qaṭal*, since a meaning of habituality is not attested for an apodosis *wa-qaṭal* in CBH.[60]

The most frequent temporal conjunction is *kī*. Many such examples exhibit a *wa-qaṭal* main clause with future or obligational meaning, meanings that are current also in apodoses of conditional sentences. In the present corpus, with its immense amount of legal material, obligation dominates, as in (53):

(53) *IMP + wa-qaṭal: kī-yiqṭol(u) +* ***wa-qaṭal***

דַּבֵּר אֶל־בְּנֵי יִשְׂרָאֵל וְאָמַרְתָּ אֲלֵהֶם כִּי תָבֹאוּ אֶל־הָאָרֶץ אֲשֶׁר אֲנִי נֹתֵן לָכֶם **וְשָׁבְתָה** הָאָרֶץ שַׁבָּת לַיהוָה׃

'Speak to the people of Israel and say to them: When you come into the land that I give you, **the land shall keep** a Sabbath to the LORD.' (Lev. 25.2)

In (53), the temporal clause refers to a point in the future and describes an event that is presupposed to take place. The following *wa-qaṭal* (וְשָׁבְתָה) has a meaning of obligation. No habituality is expressed by this *wa-qaṭal*. The example illustrates that a temporal clause with future time reference is often followed by a non-habitual *wa-qaṭal* clause.[61]

A comparison with a temporal *kī*-clause and a following main *yiqṭol(u)* clause is illuminating:

(54) *(kī-yiqṭol(u)) + wa-qaṭal + wa-PrP-yiqṭol(u)-N +* [13]*wa-kī-yiqṭol(u)-N +* **Ø-lō-yiqṭol(u)-N**

(כִּֽי־יִמָּכֵ֨ר לְךָ֜ אָחִ֣יךָ הָֽעִבְרִ֗י א֚וֹ הָֽעִבְרִיָּ֔ה וַעֲבָֽדְךָ֖ שֵׁ֣שׁ שָׁנִ֑ים וּבַשָּׁנָה֙ הַשְּׁבִיעִ֔ת תְּשַׁלְּחֶ֥נּוּ חָפְשִׁ֖י מֵעִמָּֽךְ׃ וְכִֽי־תְשַׁלְּחֶ֥נּוּ חָפְשִׁ֖י מֵֽעִמָּ֑ךְ **לֹ֥א תְשַׁלְּחֶ֖נּוּ** רֵיקָֽם׃)

'If your brother, a Hebrew man or a Hebrew woman, is sold to you, he shall serve you six years, and in the seventh year you shall let him go free from you. [13]And when you let him go free from you, **you shall not let him go** empty-handed.' (Deut. 15.12f.)

The first *kī-yiqṭol(u)* clause in (54) is a protasis, but the second (וְכִֽי־תְשַׁלְּחֶ֥נּוּ) is clearly a temporal clause, since the context takes for granted that the release will take place. Example (54) also illustrates that, when the main line that follows is a *yiqṭol(u)* clause (לֹ֥א תְשַׁלְּחֶ֖נּוּ), it follows the word order rule with non-initial position of the verb, and is nearly always asyndetic, as is the case also with apodoses (see §6.7.1).[62]

A futural temporal *kī*-clause with following main *wa-qaṭal* can be habitual if this is implied by the context, an example of which is found in (55).

(55) *kī-S.noun-qaṭal* + ***wa-qaṭal*** + *wa-S.pron-lō-yiqṭol(u)* + ***wa-qaṭal*** + *wa-PrP-lō-yiqṭol(u)*

כִּֽי־יְהוָ֤ה אֱלֹהֶ֙יךָ֙ בֵּֽרַכְךָ֔ כַּאֲשֶׁ֖ר דִּבֶּר־לָ֑ךְ **וְהַעֲבַטְתָּ֞** גּוֹיִ֣ם רַבִּ֗ים וְאַתָּה֙ לֹ֣א תַעֲבֹ֔ט **וּמָֽשַׁלְתָּ֙** בְּגוֹיִ֣ם רַבִּ֔ים וּבְךָ֖ לֹ֥א יִמְשֹֽׁלוּ׃

'When the LORD your God has blessed you as he promised you, **then you shall lend** to many nations, but you shall not borrow, **you shall rule** over many nations, but they shall not rule over you.' (Deut. 15.6)

The blessing in the temporal clause describes an anterior action projected into the future.[63] The main clauses refer to habitual actions in the future.[64]

But a temporal clause with *qaṭal* predicate can of course have past time reference. Such instances usually describe habitual actions, as in (56):

(56) *wa-kī-qaṭal* + *wa-qaṭal* + *wa-qaṭal*

וְכִֽי־הֵקִ֨ים יְהוָ֥ה ׀ לָהֶ֮ם שֹׁפְטִים֒ וְהָיָ֤ה יְהוָה֙ עִם־הַשֹּׁפֵ֔ט וְהוֹשִׁיעָם֙ מִיַּ֣ד אֹֽיְבֵיהֶ֔ם כֹּ֖ל יְמֵ֣י הַשּׁוֹפֵ֑ט

'Whenever the LORD raised up judges for them, the LORD was with the judge, and he saved them from the hand of their enemies all the days of the judge.' (Judg. 2.18a)

In (56), the perfective aspect of the *qaṭal* morpheme means that the actions of the Lord are viewed as a single whole, but a habitual interpretation is necessitated by the plural form 'judges' (שֹׁפְטִים). The main line of *wa-qaṭal* clauses expresses repeated actions in the past.

A *wa-qaṭal* clause following a temporal clause can also express habituality in speech time, as in (57):

(57) *kī-lō-XØ* + *bəṭɛrɛm-yiqṭol(u)* + ***wa-qaṭal***

כִּ֣י לֹ֧א כַנָּשִׁ֛ים הַמִּצְרִיֹּ֖ת הָֽעִבְרִיֹּ֑ת כִּֽי־חָי֣וֹת הֵ֔נָּה בְּטֶ֨רֶם תָּב֧וֹא אֲלֵהֶ֛ן הַמְיַלֶּ֖דֶת **וְיָלָֽדוּ׃**

'Because the Hebrew women are not like the Egyptian women, for they are vigorous: before the midwife comes to them **they give birth**.' (Exod. 1.19)

In (57), reference time is the same as speech time, and *wa-qaṭal* has a present habitual meaning.

As *wa-qaṭal* can function as a conditional clause in relatively rare cases (about 2% of all protases), so it can also function as a temporal clause in special instances. In all such instances, the *wa-qaṭal* temporal clause has a close semantic connection with the preceding clause(s), as in (58):[65]

(58) *IMP* + *wa-IMP* + 13***[wa-qaṭal]*** + *wa-qaṭal*

עֲלֵ֛ה אֶל־הַ֥ר הָעֲבָרִ֖ים הַזֶּ֑ה וּרְאֵה֙ אֶת־הָאָ֔רֶץ אֲשֶׁ֥ר נָתַ֖תִּי לִבְנֵ֥י יִשְׂרָאֵֽל׃
[**וְרָאִ֣יתָה אֹתָ֔הּ**] וְנֶאֱסַפְתָּ֥ אֶל־עַמֶּ֖יךָ גַּם־אָ֑תָּה

'Go up into this mountain of Abarim and see the land that I have given to the people of Israel. 13[**When you see it**,] you also shall be gathered to your people' (Num. 27.13)

There are also examples of temporal clauses with verbal noun predicates (infinitive construct). Since the infinitive is not attested as predicate in a protasis in my corpus, I conclude that this is an extension of the construction *wa-qaṭal*. What was not tolerable as protasis before an apodosis with *wa-qaṭal* became acceptable as temporal clause. An example is (59):

(59) *wa-bə-yōm-VN* + *wa-qaṭal*

וּבְי֣וֹם פָּקְדִ֔י וּפָקַדְתִּ֥י עֲלֵיהֶ֖ם חַטָּאתָֽם׃

‘But in the day when I visit, I will visit their sin upon them.’ (Exod. 32.34)

In *protases*, verbless clauses and active participles are tolerable, but not verbal nouns. Verbal nouns are usually perceived as adverbial expressions embedded in a clause, not as clauses involved in a temporal linking. Example (59) illustrates how a prepositional phrase in a construct relation (בְּיוֹם) with a verbal noun (פָּקְדִי) fills the slot of a temporal clause with a following *wa-qaṭal* as main clause. This is an extension of what is tolerable as a preceding subordinated clause before the *wa-qaṭal* construction.[66]

An example of a *yiqṭol(u)* morpheme with a preceding temporal VN clause illustrates well how a long *yiqṭol* is used in this case (60):

(60) *wa-bə-VN-yiqṭol(u)! (*not *wa-bə-VN + Ø-yiqṭol(u)!)*

וּבְבֹא מֹשֶׁה לִפְנֵי יְהוָה לְדַבֵּר אִתּוֹ יָסִיר אֶת־הַמַּסְוֶה עַד־צֵאתוֹ

‘Whenever Moses went in before the LORD to speak with him, he would remove the veil, until he came out.’ (Exod. 34.34a)

In (60), the VN-clause is perceived by linguistic competence to be embedded in the *yiqṭol(u)* clause. There is no linking between two clauses, as would have been the case with a *wa-qaṭal* clause. And a constituent (the *VN* phrase) precedes the *yiqṭol(u)* morpheme, so the word order rule is fulfilled.[67]

When a verbal noun clause is accepted as temporal clause before *wa-qaṭal*, even a prepositional phrase can serve the same purpose (being a temporal clause) before *wa-qaṭal*, as in (61).

(61) *wa-PrP-wa-PrP-wa-PrP* + ***wa-qaṭal***

וּבְי֨וֹם שִׂמְחַתְכֶ֣ם וּֽבְמוֹעֲדֵיכֶם֮ וּבְרָאשֵׁ֣י חָדְשֵׁיכֶם֒ **וּתְקַעְתֶּ֣ם** בַּחֲצֹֽצְרֹ֗ת עַ֚ל עֹלֹ֣תֵיכֶ֔ם וְעַ֖ל זִבְחֵ֣י שַׁלְמֵיכֶ֑ם

'On the day of your gladness also, and at your appointed feasts and at the beginnings of your months, **you shall blow** the trumpets over your burnt offerings and over the sacrifices of your peace offerings.' (Num. 10.10a)

From a prepositional phrase, the step is not long to using an adverbialised noun as temporal clause before *wa-qaṭal*, as in (62), which is a rare case:[68]

(62) *Ø-noun* + ***wa-qaṭal*** + [7]*wa-noun* + ***wa-qaṭal***

עֶ֕רֶב **וִֽידַעְתֶּ֕ם** כִּ֧י יְהוָ֛ה הוֹצִ֥יא אֶתְכֶ֖ם מֵאֶ֥רֶץ מִצְרָֽיִם׃ וּבֹ֗קֶר **וּרְאִיתֶם֙** אֶת־כְּב֣וֹד יְהוָ֔ה

'At evening **you shall know** that it was the LORD who brought you out of the land of Egypt, [7]and in the morning **you shall see** the glory of the LORD.' (Exod. 16.6f.)

As in the case of conditional and temporal clauses, a subordinated cause/reason clause is usually also marked with an initial specific conjunction in CBH. An example with following *wa-qaṭal* is (63):

(63) *wa-(S.noun)-CONJ-qaṭal* + *wa(y)-yiqṭol* + *wa-qaṭal* + *wa-S.noun-yiqṭol(u)-N*

וְעַבְדִּ֣י כָלֵ֗ב עֵ֣קֶב הָֽיְתָ֞ה ר֤וּחַ אַחֶ֙רֶת֙ עִמּ֔וֹ וַיְמַלֵּ֖א אַחֲרָ֑י וַהֲבִֽיאֹתִ֗יו אֶל־הָאָ֙רֶץ֙ אֲשֶׁר־בָּ֣א שָׁ֔מָּה וְזַרְע֖וֹ יוֹרִשֶֽׁנָּה׃

'But my servant Caleb, because he has a different spirit and has followed me fully, I will bring him into the land into which he went, and his descendants shall possess it.' (Num. 14.24)

The cause/reason clause is marked by an initial conjunction (עֵ֚קֶב) after a left dislocation (עַבְדִּ֣י כָלֵ֗ב). The subordination also involves the *wa(y)-yiqṭol* clause (וַיְמַלֵּ֖א) with anterior meaning. This is the reason (or cause), and there then follows the main clause *wa-qaṭal* (וַהֲבִֽיאֹתִ֗יו), which expresses what will happen because of the stated reason. This is a promise, and the last *yiqṭol(u)* clause elaborates that promise with a focused element (זַרְע֖וֹ).[69]

6.10. Topics and their *Wa-qaṭal* Comments

Haiman (1978, 585) writes:

> The topic represents an entity whose existence is agreed upon by the speaker and his audience. As such, it constitutes the framework which has been selected for the following discourse.

A topic is something agreed upon by speaker and listener, while a conditional clause describes a hypothetical case, an eventuality. Topics are givens, conditionals are not (Haiman 1978, 571, 583). This difference is reflected in the syntactic marking of clauses in CBH. Conditional clauses are overwhelmingly coded by an initial subordinating conjunction, most often *ʾim* but frequently also *kī*. Verbless conditional clauses also nearly always contain a marker.[70] Topics, on the other hand, are often coded as main verbless clauses, without initial conjunction. Since topics are coded by main clauses, it is pertinent to define the distinction between topic and comment by using a semantic terminology: the topic clause is a supporting clause and comment clauses are focal. A consequence of this terminology is that chained clauses linked in a relation of temporal succession cannot describe a topic–comment relation, since clauses involved in temporal succession linking are focal (Dixon 2009, 2f.).

The primary interest in the present section will be the use of *wa-qaṭal* clauses as focal clauses after a topic clause. I will not treat linkings of the type *XØ* + *wa(y)-yiqṭol.*[71]

For the development of the construction *wa-qaṭal*, the *topic* + *wa-qaṭal* linking is of great interest, because it represents an expansion of the clauses that are tolerable before *wa-qaṭal.* When we have analysed extensions of the *conditional clause* + *wa-qaṭal* linking, we have until now treated only subordinate clauses before *wa-qaṭal*: conditional, temporal, and causal clauses. In the present type of linking, the clause that precedes *wa-qaṭal* is allowed to be a main clause, though with a supportive meaning (the topic) in relation to the following focal *wa-qaṭal* (the comment).

Before we turn to the *wa-qaṭal* clause as comment, it is practical to consider the corresponding use of *yiqṭol(u)*. The comparison is instructive, because it reveals a complementary distribution:

(64) *Ø-XØ* + *Ø-PrP-yiqṭol(u)* + *kī-PrP-qaṭal*

זֹ֣את הַפַּ֗עַם עֶ֚צֶם מֵֽעֲצָמַ֔י וּבָשָׂ֖ר מִבְּשָׂרִ֑י לְזֹאת֙ יִקָּרֵ֣א אִשָּׁ֔ה כִּ֥י מֵאִ֖ישׁ לֻֽקֳחָה־זֹּֽאת׃

‘This at last is bone of my bones and flesh of my flesh; she shall be called Woman, because she was taken out of Man.’ (Gen. 2.23)

It is not reasonable to regard the verbless clause in (64) as subordinate. It is a plain statement of what is agreed upon. The *yiqṭol(u)* clause supplies the new information, with a notion of obligation.[72] The *yiqṭol(u)* clause lacks a connective *wa*, which is the more frequent option when a *yiqṭol(u)* clause functions as comment after a verbless clause. The example illustrates that when a focal clausal constituent (in this case לְזֹאת) is to be placed before the verb in the comment, a *yiqṭol(u)* clause is used. It also illustrates that, in topic–comment linking, the comment can often be accurately translated with an initial *therefore*: 'therefore she shall be called Woman'. The topic is the starting point, the motivation for the comment.[73]

When no initial constituent is needed before the verb in the comment, a *wa-qaṭal* clause can be used. With a *wa-qaṭal* comment also, the nuance is often an understood 'therefore', as in (65):

(65) *Ø-XØ + wa-qaṭal + wa-qaṭal*

בִּגְדֵי־קֹ֣דֶשׁ הֵ֔ם וְרָחַ֥ץ בַּמַּ֛יִם אֶת־בְּשָׂר֖וֹ וּלְבֵשָֽׁם׃

'They are holy garments, so he must bathe his body in water and put them on.' (Lev. 16.4)

The topic expressed by the verbless clause (בִּגְדֵי־קֹ֣דֶשׁ הֵ֔ם) constitutes the motivation for the obligations in the *wa-qaṭal* clauses. In this case, there was no need of a clausal constituent in focal position in the comment clauses, or of a negated comment. Both an initial constituent and a negation would have required comment clauses with a *yiqṭol(u)* predicate. In my database, *wa-qaṭal* comment clauses seem to be as frequent as *yiqṭol(u)* comments.[74]

At the end of this section, it is necessary to discuss also the role of left dislocations, since they are coded as topics, sentence-initially, with the only difference being that the starting phrase is not a clause but a certain non-verbal constituent. A left dislocation also expresses old information, something agreed upon (Haiman 1978, 572).[75] Left dislocations occur in seemingly all types of clauses, but for our purposes, *yiqṭol(u)* clauses with left dislocation supply the most pertinent comparison for *wa-qaṭal*. All *yiqṭol(u)* clauses after a left dislocation are asyndetic, an example of which is found in (66):

(66) ***wa-PrP*** + *Ø-lō-yiqṭol(u)*

וּמֵעֵץ הַדַּעַת טוֹב וָרָע לֹא תֹאכַל מִמֶּנּוּ

'**but of the tree of the knowledge of good and evil** you shall not eat (of it)' (Gen. 2.17)

The *yiqṭol(u)* clause has no connective, but the status of the preceding constituent (*PrP*) as left dislocation is revealed by the presence of an anaphoric pronoun in the last phrase (מִמֶּנּוּ). The left dislocation in this case is a prepositional phrase with some complication, involving a verbal noun (הַדַּעַת) and its following direct objects (טוֹב וָרָע).[76]

The left dislocations with *wa-qaṭal* are apparently often semantically similar to protases with quantifier, which implicitly code an eventuality:

(67) *(kōl-NP-REL-yiqṭol(u)* + *wa-lō-yiqṭol(u))* + *wa-qaṭal* + *wa-qaṭal*

(כָּל־הָאָדָם וְהַבְּהֵמָה אֲשֶׁר־יִמָּצֵא בַשָּׂדֶה וְלֹא יֵאָסֵף הַבַּיְתָה) וְיָרַד עֲלֵהֶם הַבָּרָד וָמֵתוּ׃

‘(Every man or animal that will be found in the field and will not have been gathered into the house)—then the hail will descend upon them and they will die.’ (Exod. 9.19, Propp 1999, 289)

The segment before the *wa-qaṭal* clauses is basically a quantifier (כָּל־) and a noun phrase with a relative clause attribute (*REL-yiqṭol(u) + wa-lō-yiqṭol(u)*). That this noun phrase is perceived as a left dislocation is corroborated by the anaphoric pronoun (עֲלֵהֶם) in the first *wa-qaṭal* clause. At the same time, the quantifier and the pragmatics of the situation signal an eventuality: some have been gathered into the house, and some have not. In this sense, the linking is close to a conditional sentence, and the extension of the construction *wa-qaṭal* to be used after a left-dislocated noun phrase is easy to imagine.[77] A conditional meaning may also be achieved with a simple relative clause construction, as in (68):

(68) *(Ø-REL-yiqṭol(u)! + wa-qaṭal) + wa-qaṭal*

(אֲשֶׁר־יַכֶּה אֶת־קִרְיַת־סֵפֶר וּלְכָדָהּ) וְנָתַתִּי לוֹ אֶת־עַכְסָה בִתִּי לְאִשָּׁה׃

‘(Whoever devastates Qiriath-sepher and captures it,) to him I’ll give my daughter Achsah as wife.’ (Judg. 1.12, Boling 1975, 50f.)

The relative clause complex is syntactically a noun phrase, but semantically, it involves the rare eventuality that someone would dare to attack, and manage to capture, Qiriath-sepher.[78]

There are also less frequent instances when *wa-qaṭal* has a preceding left dislocation without a sense of conditionality:

(69) *(wa-O.noun-REL-qaṭal) + wa-qaṭal + wa-qaṭal*

וְטַ֨פְּכֶ֔ם אֲשֶׁ֥ר אֲמַרְתֶּ֖ם לָבַ֣ז יִהְיֶ֑ה וְהֵבֵיאתִ֣י אֹתָ֔ם וְיָֽדְעוּ֙ אֶת־הָאָ֔רֶץ אֲשֶׁ֥ר מְאַסְתֶּ֖ם בָּֽהּ׃

‘But your little ones, who you said would become a prey, I will bring them in, and they shall know the land that you have rejected.’ (Num. 14.31)

The left dislocation in (69) is a noun phrase (with relative clause) which is resumed as object pronoun (אֹתָם) in the first *wa-qaṭal* clause.[79]

The use of *wa-qaṭal* clauses after non-conditional left dislocations represents an extension of the *wa-qaṭal* construction, from its corresponding use as apodosis.

6.11. First Clause and *Wa-qaṭal* Being of Equal Status[80]

We have already seen that *wa-qaṭal*, apart from its function as apodosis, can be used as a main clause after a temporal clause, as comment in a topic–comment linking, and with result meaning in modal series and instructional text-types.

Khan (2021a, 309, examples 9 and 12) refers also to another extensional step of the construction *wa-qaṭal*. In this extension, all clauses are of equal status and semantically focal. This extension is systematically treated in the present section (see §§6.11.1–4). We will discuss the use of *wa-qaṭal* after the following clause-types: *(wa)-X-yiqṭol(u)*, *wa-qaṭal*, *qoṭel*, and *qaṭal*. The reversed clausal order (with *wa-qaṭal* first) is treated in §§6.12–13.

As we have seen already, *wa-qaṭal* is by its nature a clause that follows what is usually another clause, and the extension of its meaning discussed in the present section concerns the preceding clause. It is time to consider *wa-qaṭal* in some basic types of main-line discourse—that is, its linking with clauses of equal status.

6.11.1. *Yiqṭol(u)* + *Wa-qaṭal*

There is already a close connection between *yiqṭol(u)* and *wa-qaṭal* in conditional sentences, and it is not surprising that, in an overwhelming number of cases, *wa-qaṭal* as continuity clause-type continues a main-line *yiqṭol(u)* clause, whatever the meaning of this *yiqṭol(u)* may be.[81]

The meanings of the linking *yiqṭol(u)* + *wa-qaṭal* attested in my database are displayed in Table 17.

Table 17: *Yiqṭol(u)* + *wa-qaṭal* in main structures

Obligation	119
Future	88
Ability	8
Habitual past	5
Modal volitive[82]	3
Modal permissive[83]	3
General present	1
Habitual present	1
Past progressive	1
Total	**229**

As can be seen in Table 17, the related meanings of future and obligation dominate when the linking is used in main structures. An example of a future meaning is (70).

(70) *wa-O.noun-yiqṭol(u)!* + ***wa-qaṭal***

וְק֥וֹץ וְדַרְדַּ֖ר תַּצְמִ֣יחַ לָ֑ךְ **וְאָכַלְתָּ֖** אֶת־עֵ֥שֶׂב הַשָּׂדֶֽה׃

'thorns and thistles it shall bring forth for you; **and you shall eat** the plants of the field.' (Gen. 3.18)

Apart from the future meaning of the two clauses, the semantics of the linking are interesting. As it is usually translated, as above, the sense of the linking is remarkably pointless. But the discourse-continuity clause *wa-qaṭal* (וְאָכַלְתָּ֖) presupposes the world of the thorns and thistles—the pain of labour described in the preceding clauses—'and (under such circumstances) you shall eat the plants of the field'.[84]

But of course, in the text-types we encounter in the Pentateuch, a meaning of obligation dominates in the corpus.

(71) *Ø-VNabs-yiqṭol(u)* + *wa-qaṭal*

הִמּ֧וֹל ׀ יִמּ֛וֹל יְלִ֥יד בֵּיתְךָ֖ וּמִקְנַ֣ת כַּסְפֶּ֑ךָ וְהָיְתָ֧ה בְרִיתִ֛י בִּבְשַׂרְכֶ֖ם לִבְרִ֥ית עוֹלָֽם׃

'They must indeed be circumcised, whether born in your house or bought with money. Thus shall My covenant be marked in your flesh as an everlasting pact.' (Gen. 17.13)

As is often the case, the discourse-continuity *wa-qaṭal* presupposes the procedure in the preceding clause, and implies a specific semantic connection: 'in this way My covenant shall be marked in your flesh'.[85]

It is very common that both clauses in *yiqṭol(u)* + *wa-qaṭal* have the same meaning, for example, either obligation or future, but this is not necessary. An example with different meanings is (72):

(72) *Ø-VNabs-yiqṭol(u) + wa-qaṭal*

פָּקֹד יִפְקֹד אֱלֹהִים אֶתְכֶם וְהַעֲלִתֶם אֶת־עַצְמֹתַי מִזֶּה׃

'God will surely take care of you, and then you must carry my bones up from here.' (Gen. 50.25)

In (72), the first clause expresses a conviction about a future act of God, while the second clause is an obligation upon the sons of Joseph. The discourse-continuity *wa-qaṭal* implicitly carries over the point of time expressed by the *yiqṭol(u)* clause, which motivates a translation 'and then', 'and at that time'.[86]

The meaning of ability is usually found in only one of the clauses in the linking *yiqṭol(u) + wa-qaṭal*, but there are exceptions, as in (73):[87]

(73) *wa-ADV-yiqṭol(u) + wa-qaṭal*

וְאֵיךְ אֶעֱשֶׂה הָרָעָה הַגְּדֹלָה הַזֹּאת וְחָטָאתִי לֵאלֹהִים׃

'How then can I do this great wickedness and (in this way) sin against God?' (Gen. 39.9)

Though the meanings of future and obligation dominate when *yiqṭol(u)* and *wa-qaṭal* are linked, various shades of habituality and progressivity are also possible, as in example (74):

(74) *wa-S.noun-qoṭel + wa-PrP-yiqṭol(u) + wa-qaṭal*

וְנָהָר יֹצֵא מֵעֵדֶן לְהַשְׁקוֹת אֶת־הַגָּן וּמִשָּׁם יִפָּרֵד וְהָיָה לְאַרְבָּעָה רָאשִׁים׃

'A river flowed out of Eden to water the garden, and there it divided and became four rivers.' (Gen. 2.10)

In (74), a *yiqṭol(u)* clause is followed by *wa-qaṭal*, both with past progressive meaning. The example also illustrates the diachronic intrusion of the relatively new predicative active participle with past progressive meaning as first clause (but not as second clause).

As Table 17 shows, a sense of habituality seems to be slightly more frequent than pure progressivity. An example is (75):

(75) *wa-S.noun-yiqtol(u) + wa-qaṭal + wa-qaṭal*

וּמֹשֶׁה֩ יִקַּ֨ח אֶת־הָאֹ֜הֶל וְנָֽטָה־ל֣וֹ ׀ מִח֣וּץ לַֽמַּחֲנֶ֗ה הַרְחֵק֙ מִן־הַֽמַּחֲנֶ֔ה וְקָ֥רָא ל֖וֹ אֹ֥הֶל מוֹעֵ֑ד

'Now Moses used to take the tent and pitch it outside the camp, far off from the camp, and he called it the tent of meeting.' (Exod. 33.7)

In (75), *yiqtol(u)* and *wa-qaṭal* have a meaning of past habituality; in other instances, the temporal reference is present or has a more general habituality.[88]

6.11.2. The Linking Type *Wa-qaṭal + Wa-qaṭal*

In this type of linking, two or more discourse-continuity clauses are linked in such a way that there is a connection with the preceding clauses. The linking often describes temporally successive events, as in (76):

(76) *wa-qaṭal + wa-qaṭal + wa-qaṭal + wa-qaṭal*

וְנֶאֶסְפוּ־שָׁ֣מָּה כָל־הָעֲדָרִ֗ים וְגָלֲל֤וּ אֶת־הָאֶ֙בֶן֙ מֵעַל֙ פִּ֣י הַבְּאֵ֔ר וְהִשְׁק֖וּ אֶת־הַצֹּ֑אן וְהֵשִׁ֧יבוּ אֶת־הָאֶ֛בֶן עַל־פִּ֥י הַבְּאֵ֖ר לִמְקֹמָֽהּ׃

'and all the flocks were gathered there, and the shepherds would roll the stone from the mouth of the well and water the sheep, and put the stone back in its place over the mouth of the well.' (Gen. 29.3)

This type of chaining of only discourse-continuity clauses of course receives its past habituality from the preceding clauses, where the background description starts with a construction *kī-PrP-yiqṭol(u)* (כִּ֚י מִן־הַבְּאֵ֣ר הַהִ֔וא יַשְׁק֖וּ) in the preceding verse. In (76), only the verbal actions are focal, not other constituents.[89]

A more frequent type of *wa-qaṭal* + *wa-qaṭal* linking has future time reference or, in instruction, expresses obligation. An example is (77):

(77) *wa-qaṭal* + *wa-qaṭal* + *wa-qaṭal*

וְהִקְרִ֨יב אַהֲרֹ֜ן אֶת־פַּ֤ר הַֽחַטָּאת֙ אֲשֶׁר־ל֔וֹ וְכִפֶּ֥ר בַּעֲד֖וֹ וּבְעַ֣ד בֵּית֑וֹ וְשָׁחַ֛ט אֶת־פַּ֥ר הַֽחַטָּ֖את אֲשֶׁר־לֽוֹ׃

'Aaron shall present the bull as a sin offering for himself, and shall make atonement for himself and for his house. He shall kill the bull as a sin offering for himself.' (Lev. 16.11)

In (77), the semantics of the *wa-qaṭal* clauses are of obligation, and the first two exhibit a sequential linking. The third, however, is a summary. This illustrates the variation of the discourse-continuity linkings. A discourse-continuity clause may express, among other things, also elaboration and summary. The latter is the case with the third *wa-qaṭal* in (77).[90]

6.11.3. The Linking Type *Qoṭel* + *Wa-qaṭal*

Since we can observe a renewal of the coding of (immediate) future meanings within CBH, with an intrusion of active participles in predicative position (Joosten 1989, 144–46; Notarius 2010a, 251, 254, 259),[91] it is not surprising that we encounter *qoṭel* + *wa-qaṭal* linkings with future meaning. An example is:

(78) *kī-PrP-ADV-S.pron-qoṭel + wa-qaṭal*

כִּי֩ לְיָמִ֨ים ע֜וֹד שִׁבְעָ֗ה אָנֹכִי֙ מַמְטִ֣יר עַל־הָאָ֔רֶץ אַרְבָּעִ֣ים י֔וֹם וְאַרְבָּעִ֖ים לָ֑יְלָה
וּמָחִ֗יתִי אֶֽת־כָּל־הַיְקוּם֙ «אֲשֶׁ֣ר עָשִׂ֔יתִי» מֵעַ֖ל פְּנֵ֥י הָאֲדָמָֽה׃

‘For in seven days I will send rain on the earth forty days and forty nights, and every living thing that I have made I will blot out from the face of the ground.’ (Gen. 7.4)

In (78), a *wa-qaṭal* clause is linked to a predicative active participle clause. Both have the same future meaning (‘in seven days’).[92]

There are, however, examples that indicate that *wa-qaṭal* in CBH may, as an extension, have a more independent function, as discourse-continuity counterpart to *yiqṭol(u)*. In a linking with *qoṭel*, it may express meanings that deviate from that of the preceding participle:

(79) *wa-hinnē-S.noun-qoṭel +* [13]*wa-qaṭal + wa-qaṭal + wa-qaṭal*

וְהִנֵּ֤ה עֵֽינֵיכֶם֙ רֹא֔וֹת וְעֵינֵ֖י אָחִ֣י בִנְיָמִ֑ין כִּי־פִ֖י הַֽמְדַבֵּ֥ר אֲלֵיכֶֽם׃ וְהִגַּדְתֶּ֣ם לְאָבִ֗י
אֶת־כָּל־כְּבוֹדִי֙ בְּמִצְרַ֔יִם וְאֵ֖ת כָּל־אֲשֶׁ֣ר רְאִיתֶ֑ם וּמִֽהַרְתֶּ֛ם וְהוֹרַדְתֶּ֥ם אֶת־אָבִ֖י
הֵֽנָּה׃

‘And now your eyes see, and the eyes of my brother Benjamin see, that it is my mouth that speaks to you. [13]You must tell my father of all my honor in Egypt, and of all that you have seen. Hurry and bring my father down here.’ (Gen. 45.12f.)

The active participles (רֹא֔וֹת and הַֽמְדַבֵּ֥ר) in (79) express a progressive present, while the *wa-qaṭal* clauses have obligational meaning (‘You must tell’).[93]

6.11.4. The Linking Type *Qaṭal* + *Wa-qaṭal*

The linking *qaṭal* + *wa-qaṭal* indicates that the *wa-qaṭal* construction has attained a level of syntactic and semantic independence as an expression of imperfective meanings, such as future, obligation, and habituality. The most frequent case of *qaṭal* + *wa-qaṭal* having deviating meaning is the anterior/future combination, as in (80):

(80) *kī-ʿattā-qaṭal* + *wa-qaṭal*

כִּֽי־עַתָּ֞ה הִרְחִ֧יב יְהוָ֛ה לָ֖נוּ וּפָרִ֥ינוּ בָאָֽרֶץ׃

'For now the LORD has made room for us, and we shall be fruitful in the land.' (Gen. 26.22)

In (80), the initial *kī* starts a direct speech and is an emphatic adverb. The meaning of the *qaṭal* clause is clearly anterior, and the *wa-qaṭal* has an independent meaning (future finality).[94]

With a performative meaning of *qaṭal*, we often find that a following *wa-qaṭal* has future meaning, as in (81):

(81) *Ø-O.noun-qaṭal* + *wa-qaṭal*

אֶת־קַשְׁתִּ֕י נָתַ֖תִּי בֶּֽעָנָ֑ן וְהָֽיְתָה֙ לְא֣וֹת בְּרִ֔ית בֵּינִ֖י וּבֵ֥ין הָאָֽרֶץ׃

'I now set my bow in the clouds, and it will be the sign of the covenant between me and the earth.' (Gen. 9.13)

In (81), the performative meaning of the first-person *qaṭal* is followed by a promise expressed by *wa-qaṭal* (וְהָֽיְתָה֙).[95]

6.12. The Linking *Wa-qaṭal* + *(Wa)-X-yiqṭol(u)*

After having treated the linking *yiqṭol(u)* + *wa-qaṭal*, it is logical to consider also the reversed linking *wa-qaṭal* + *X-yiqṭol(u)*, where X is not merely the negation *lō*. *Wa-qaṭal* + *yiqṭol(u)* is not just a reversed clausal order; it is a different type of linking. While *yiqṭol(u)* + *wa-qaṭal* is a discourse-continuity linking, *wa-qaṭal* + *X-yiqṭol(u)* signals discontinuity. It cannot express temporal succession, if not equipped with specific temporal adverbs.[96] The discontinuity may signal a focal constituent, a contrast, a complementary action, elaboration with focal element, and sometimes also a comment (explanation). An example of the preverbal element X describing a contrasting element is (82):

(82) *kī-yiqṭol(u)* + *wa-qaṭal* + *wa-qaṭal* + *wa-***O.pron**-*yiqṭol(u)*

וְהָיָה כִּי־יִרְאוּ אֹתָךְ֙ הַמִּצְרִ֔ים וְאָמְר֖וּ אִשְׁתּ֣וֹ זֹ֑את וְהָרְג֥וּ אֹתִ֖י **וְאֹתָ֥ךְ** יְחַיּֽוּ׃

'and when the Egyptians see you, they will say, "This is his wife." Then they will kill me, but they will let **you** live.' (Gen. 12.12)

In (82), the last two clauses form a contrast linking: "the information conveyed by the Focal clause contrasts with that provided in the Supporting clause, and may be surprising in view of it" (Dixon 2009, 28). The *wa-qaṭal* clause (וְהָרְגוּ אֹתִי) is the supporting clause, and *X-yiqṭol(u)* (וְאֹתָךְ יְחַיּוּ:) is focal. The preverbal element puts the object pronoun in focal position, and sets it in contrast with the final object pronoun (אֹתִי) in the preceding clause.[97]

Frequently, a *wa-qaṭal* + *X-yiqṭol(u)* linking describes two complementary actions which are performed on the same occasion, as in (83):

(83) *wa-qaṭal* + *wa-**O.noun**-yiqṭol(u)* + *wa-qaṭal* + *wa-qaṭal*

וְנָתַ֤נּוּ אֶת־בְּנֹתֵ֙ינוּ֙ לָכֶ֔ם וְ**אֶת־בְּנֹתֵיכֶ֖ם** נִֽקַּֽח־לָ֑נוּ וְיָשַׁ֣בְנוּ אִתְּכֶ֔ם וְהָיִ֖ינוּ לְעַ֥ם אֶחָֽד׃

> 'Then we will give our daughters to you, and we will take **your daughters** to ourselves, and we will dwell with you and become one people.' (Gen. 34.16)

The chiasm in the first two clauses in (83) creates a complementarity between the two groups of daughters. The actions described are not sequential, but supposed to be concurrent during a certain period of time.[98]

Frequently, a *wa-qaṭal* + *X-yiqṭol(u)* linking codes an elaboration with a preverbal focal element (*X*), as in (84):

(84) *wa-qaṭal* + *Ø-PrP-PrP-bə-VN-yiqṭol(u)-N*

וְהִקְטִ֥יר עָלָ֛יו אַהֲרֹ֖ן קְטֹ֣רֶת סַמִּ֑ים בַּבֹּ֣קֶר בַּבֹּ֗קֶר בְּהֵיטִיב֛וֹ אֶת־הַנֵּרֹ֖ת יַקְטִירֶֽנָּה׃

> 'And Aaron shall burn fragrant incense on it. Every morning when he dresses the lamps he shall burn it.' (Exod. 30.7)

In (84), "the second clause echoes the first, adding additional information about the event" (Dixon 2009, 27). In the *yiqṭol(u)* clause, more detailed instruction is given as to how Aaron must burn the incense, and the two preverbal prepositional phrases (בַּבֹּ֣קֶר בַּבֹּ֗קֶר) are in focal position for emphasis.[99] Clauses expressing elaboration are sometimes discourse-discontinuous, sometimes continuous (but in the latter case, there is no preverbal focal element; see §2.3.1).

Even when not elaborative, a frequent function of a *wa-qaṭal* + *X-yiqṭol(u)* linking is to mark an element (*X*) as focal, as in (85):

(85) *wa-qaṭal* + [19]*wa-**PrP-PrP-O.noun**-yiqṭol(u)!*

וּבָאתָ֙ אֶל־הַתֵּבָ֔ה אַתָּ֕ה וּבָנֶ֛יךָ וְאִשְׁתְּךָ֥ וּנְשֵֽׁי־בָנֶ֖יךָ אִתָּֽךְ׃ **וּמִכָּל־הָ֠חַי מִֽכָּל־בָּשָׂ֞ר שְׁנַ֧יִם מִכֹּ֛ל** תָּבִ֥יא אֶל־הַתֵּבָ֖ה לְהַחֲיֹ֣ת אִתָּ֑ךְ

'And you shall come into the ark, you, your sons, your wife, and your sons' wives with you. [19]And **of every living thing of all flesh**, you shall bring **two of every sort** into the ark to keep them alive with you.' (Gen. 6.18b–19a)

The linking in (85) does not describe an elaboration, because the two clauses represent two different actions. There is a special emphasis on the prepositional phrases (מִכָּל־הָ֠חַי מִֽכָּל־בָּשָׂ֞ר) and on the direct object (שְׁנַ֧יִם מִכֹּ֛ל), positioned before the verb. The two actions in the instruction are not marked for sequentiality.[100]

A further frequent function of the *wa-qaṭal* + *X-yiqṭol(u)* linking is to add a comment or explanation. An example is:

(86) *wa-qaṭal* + *Ø-O.noun-yiqṭol(u)!*

וְעָשִׂ֣יתָ אֹת֗וֹ שֶׁ֚מֶן מִשְׁחַת־קֹ֔דֶשׁ רֹ֥קַח מִרְקַ֖חַת מַעֲשֵׂ֣ה רֹקֵ֑חַ שֶׁ֥מֶן מִשְׁחַת־קֹ֖דֶשׁ יִהְיֶֽה׃

'And you shall make of these a sacred anointing oil blended as by the perfumer; it shall be a holy anointing oil.' (Exod. 30.25)

The *yiqṭol(u)* clause supplies an explanation of the purpose of the preceding action and the status of the special holy oil.[101]

6.13. The Linking *Wa-qaṭal* + *(Wa)-lō-yiqṭol(u)*

While the linking *wa-qaṭal* + *(wa)-X-yiqṭol(u)* signals discontinuity, *wa-qaṭal* + *wa-lō-yiqṭol(u)* does not. Tenet 1 (cf. §§7.2–6) holds for affirmative clauses, but when clauses are negated, a clause-type *wa-lō-yiqṭol(u)*, without further preverbal elements, signals discourse continuity. From a diachronic perspective, *wa-qaṭal* has taken over from *yiqṭol(u)* the function of discourse continuity in affirmative clauses, but in negative clauses, no takeover has taken place; *wa-lō-yiqṭol(u)* is retained (cf. §7.12). An example that shows this is (87):

(87) *wa-qaṭal* + *wa-lō-yiqṭol(u)* + *wa-lō-yiqṭol(u)!*

וַהֲקִמֹתִ֤י אֶת־בְּרִיתִי֙ אִתְּכֶ֔ם וְלֹא־יִכָּרֵ֥ת כָּל־בָּשָׂ֛ר ע֖וֹד מִמֵּ֣י הַמַּבּ֑וּל וְלֹא־יִהְיֶ֥ה
ע֛וֹד מַבּ֖וּל לְשַׁחֵ֥ת הָאָֽרֶץ׃

‘I will maintain my covenant with you, and never again will all living things be wiped out by the waters of a flood; and never again will a flood destroy the earth.’ (Gen. 9.11)

The promise to Noah in (87) starts with a discourse-continuity *wa-qaṭal* clause (וַהֲקִמֹתִ֤י) which connects to the declaration of the covenant with Noah and his sons in Genesis 9.9f. The two negated *wa lō-yiqṭol(u)* clauses have no focal elements and describe in two steps the promises that God will maintain in the covenant that is referred to in the initial *wa-qaṭal* clause.[102]

6.14. Summary: The Identity of *Wa-qaṭal* as Imperfective Construction in CBH

This chapter has given a plausible explanation of *wa-qaṭal* as a construction in the sense formulated in the theory of Joan Bybee

(2010; 2015). *Wa-qaṭal* is not a tense, but it is a construction for the expression of typical imperfective meanings in CBH. The application of Bybee's theory to the *wa-qaṭal* clause-type was first proposed by Geoffrey Khan (2021a). In his view, *wa-qaṭal* is a construction in the same sense as the English future construction *be going to*: the constituent parts are analysable, but the meanings of the construction cannot be deduced from its constituents. This explains why the *wa-qaṭal* clause-type has seemed inexplicable to Hebrew scholarship. Many of its meanings are imperfective, while *qaṭal* is an anterior and perfective verbal gram in CBH, with its origin in a resultative formation (see §5.1).

If *qatal* was originally a resultative formation, then we must assume the resultative meaning to be prototypical also for *wa-qatal*. The precursors of the *wa-qaṭal* construction with result meaning are attested in early Northwest Semitic. It is used as result clause in modal sequences (§6.2.1), as well as in the function of apodosis (§6.2.2). Such functions and meanings remained in use even when the *qatal* morpheme developed into a verbal morpheme with mainly anterior and past perfective meanings. And in Iron Age Northwest Semitic, the *wa-qatal* clause-type continued to be used as a result clause in modal sequences and as apodosis.

In CBH, the inherited use of *wa-qaṭal* in modal sequences and as apodosis was gradually *extended* to other types of environments, (1) with extended type of the preceding clause: subordinate clauses (temporal and causal), and gradually main clauses before *wa-qaṭal*, but also (2) with extended meanings of *wa-qaṭal* itself, from result to plain future and obligation. This is confirmed by a corresponding development in the pre-exilic inscriptions (Renz 2016).

The interaction of *wa-qaṭal* as result clause with the long *yiqṭol* in many domain types developed into an alternation between a discontinuous *X-yiqṭol(u)* and a continuous *wa-qaṭal*, both expressing future or obligation. This alternation was reinforced by the necessity to replace the continuity clause-type **wa-yiqṭol(u)*, which was increasingly intolerable in CBH (see §3.4.3). A *wa-qaṭal* alternating with the imperfective *yiqṭol(u)* is not attested in the Archaic Hebrew poetry, but in CBH, it prevails as the continuity counterpart of *(wa)-X-yiqṭol(u)*. In this sense, the construction *wa-qaṭal* also, among all other uses, represents a replacement.

---

[1] For corresponding innovative uses of *wa-qaṭal* in pre-exilic Hebrew inscriptions, see Gogel (1998, 77f.); Schüle (2000, 137–39); Renz (2016, §4.2.1). See also §§6.2–3.

[2] For *wa-qatal* as apodosis in the Northwest Semitic languages of the Iron Age, contemporary with CBH, see Renz (2016, §2.2).

[3] Tropper (2012, 717) suggests that *qatal* is used in the first apodosis (but not in the second) because it directly succeeds the *w* that introduces the apodosis (this is not so in the second apodosis).

[4] Another example of an apodosis with a constituent before a prefix verb is pointed out by Smith (1991, 9) from KTU[3] 2.41:16–18: *mnm . irštk / d* [.] *ḫsrt* . ***w . ank / aštn*** . {.} *l . iḫy* 'Whatever you desire that you lack, **I will send** it for my brother' (linking pattern: *O.pron*-prefix verb + *wa-S.pron*-prefix verb).

[5] *ydy* is probably also a futural *qatal* (Tropper 2012, 716).

[6] *prʿ* can alternatively be interpreted as an infinitive (Tropper 2012, 716).

[7] For the terms result clause and focal clause, see Dixon (2009, 6, 22).

[8] The full linking pattern for the conditional sentence is: *(šumma-la-yaqtulu)* + *wa-la-VNabs-yaqtulu* + *wa-X-yaqtulu* + *wa-qatal* (Rainey 2015, 1485).

[9] I am not convinced that the first-person *yaqtul* in this case must be called "abgeschwächt" (thus Renz 2016, 454).

[10] Such meanings of *wa-qatal* "beschränkt sich auf feste Konstruktionen" (Renz 2016, 458).

[11] According to Renz (2016), the meaning of additional command (or obligation) is a relatively late function of *wa-qaṭal* in the Hebrew inscriptional material. As for the first *wa-qaṭal* (וצוך) in (17), I dare not decide whether the meaning is past tense, performative (letter convention, 'declarativum'), or future. The authorities differ on this point; see Renz (2016, §4.1.2.1) for a discussion. Other examples of *wa-qaṭal* in modal sequences in epigraphic Hebrew: Arad 2:4–6 (*wa-IMP* + *wa-qaṭal*); Arad 17:1–4 (*IMP* + *wa-qaṭal*; HI 35; Gogel 1998, 265); Arad 24:13–15 (… *wa-qaṭal* + *wa-qaṭal*), as instruction, probably with an initial erased imperative (HI 51; Renz 2016, §4.2.1.2).

[12] Donner and Röllig (1971–76, II:223) interpret the *qatal* (הוית) as an anterior: 'so habe auch ich das Schwert im Lande Jaʾudi sein lassen'. But cf. a parallel of a future *wa-gam-qaṭal* in CBH: Gen. 17.16 (*wa-qaṭal* + *wa-gam-qaṭal* + *wa-qaṭal* + *wa-qaṭal*, all with future interpretation; Westermann 1981, 304; see also Schulz 1900, 32).

[13] Exod. 31.15; Lev. 7.25, 27; 17.15; 18.29; 23.29, 30; Num. 19.13.

[14] Another similar use of *wa-qatal* in Phoenician is quoted by Renz (2016, 460 n. 153): KAI[3] 79:6–11, with a relative clause having the same function as a protasis: אש יסר... ושפט פן בעל 'jeder, der entfernen will… (Ipf.), Tinnit, Angesicht des Baʿal wird/soll richten…' (but KAI[5] 79:7 reads אש לסר...).

[15] Other examples of *wa-qaṭal* expressing finality in modal sequences: Exod. 8.12 (*Ø-IMP* + *wa-IMP* + *wa-qaṭal*) 'so that it may become gnats'; 18.19 (*Ø-IMP* + *wa-qaṭal*) 'to lay their cases before God'; 19.23 (*Ø-IMP* + *wa-qaṭal*) 'Set limits around the mountain to make it sacred'; Num. 4.19 (*wa-O.pron-IMP* + *wa-qaṭal* + *wa-lō-yiqṭol(u)*)—according to Garr

(1998, lxxxiii), a result from a preceding situation, 'and [as a result] they will live'; 7.5 (*Ø-IMP* + ***wa-qaṭal*** + *wa-qaṭal*) 'that they may be used'; 8.7 (*Ø-IMP* + *wa-qaṭal* + *wa-qaṭal* + ***wa-qaṭal***) וְהִטֶּהָרוּ׃, a frequent phrase, 'so that they become pure'; Judg. 16.5 (*Ø-IMP* + *wa-IMP* + *wa-qaṭal*) 'that we may bind him'.

[16] Other examples of *wa-qaṭal* as complement in modal series: Num. 15.38 (*Ø-IMP* + *wa-qaṭal* + ***wa-qaṭal*** + ***wa-qaṭal***); 35.2 (*Ø-IMP* + *wa-qaṭal*); Deut. 12.28 (*Ø-IMP* + *wa-qaṭal*).

[17] Other examples of *wa-qaṭal* clauses that add expression of intention in modal series: Gen. 1.14 (*Ø-yiqṭol(Ø)!* + *wa-qaṭal* + *wa-qaṭal*)—according to Dallaire (2014, 147), purpose; 6.21 (*wa-S.pron-IMP* + *wa-qaṭal* + *wa-qaṭal*, pause before *wa-qaṭal*); 19.2 (*Ø-IMP* + *wa-IMP* + *wa-IMP* + *wa-qaṭal* + *wa-qaṭal*); 30.32 (*Ø-yiqṭol(Ø)* + *wa-qaṭal*); 31.44 (*Ø-IMP* + *Ø-yiqṭol(Ø)-A* + *wa-qaṭal*)—but according to Dallaire (2014, 147), purpose; 37.20 (*wa-ʿattā-IMP* + *wa-yiqṭol(Ø)* + *wa-yiqṭol(Ø)* + *wa-qaṭal* + *wa-yiqṭol(Ø)-A*); 43.14 (*wa-S.noun, yiqṭol(Ø)* + *wa-qaṭal*); 45.9b–10 (*Ø-IMP* + *Ø-ʾal-yiqṭol(Ø)* + *wa-qaṭal* +[10] *wa-qaṭal* + *wa-qaṭal*); 45.19 (*Ø-O.pron-IMP* + *Ø-IMP* + *wa-qaṭal* + *wa-qaṭal*); 47.29 (*IMP* + *wa-qaṭal* + *Ø-ʾal-nā-yiqṭol(Ø)*); 47.30 (*IMP* + … + *wa-qaṭal* + *wa-qaṭal* + *wa-qaṭal*); Exod. 3.16; 4.21; 8.12; 18.19, 22; 19.23 (intended result); 19.24; 30.34–35; Num. 3.6 (first *wa-qaṭal*), 41; Deut. 28.8 (*Ø-yiqṭol(Ø)!* + *wa-qaṭal*, jussive; Joosten 2012, 271 n. 33, 339)—*pace* Tropper (1998, 175), who calls it future; 28.22 (jussive in a curse; Joosten 2012, 271 n. 33); Judg. 11.37 (*Ø-IMP* + *wa-yiqṭol(Ø)-A* + *wa-qaṭal* + *wa-yiqṭol(Ø)-A*); 16.5; 19.13—according to Blau (2010, 192), optional use of *wa-qaṭal* as modal form, but according to Dallaire (2014, 147), purpose; 20.32 (*Ø-yiqṭol(Ø)-A* + *wa-qaṭal*).

[18] I do not claim that I have registered all occurrences of *wa-qaṭal* in modal series in the corpus, but of those registered, nine express finality–result, 23 intention, six additional information, and as many as 74 code additional instructions.

[19] Motion purpose (Dixon 2009, 45) is often expressed by simple coordination in CBH, as in the case of the last *wa-qaṭal* (וְאָכַל), '(in order for him) to eat'.

[20] Other examples of *wa-qaṭal* describing additional instruction in modal series: Gen. 6.14 (*Ø-IMP* + *Ø-ADV-yiqṭol(u)* + *wa-qaṭal*); 6.21 (*wa-S.pron-IMP* + *wa-qaṭal* + *wa-qaṭal*); 27.44 (*wa-ʿattā-VOC-IMP* + *wa-IMP* + *Ø-IMP* + *wa-qaṭal*); 41.33f. (*wa-ʿattā, yiqṭol(Ø)!* + *wa-yiqṭol(Ø)* + [34] *Ø-yiqṭol(Ø)-V* + *wa-yiqṭol(Ø)!* + *wa-qaṭal*)—the 'long' יַעֲשֶׂה is volitive (Westermann 1982, 95; J-M §79m; Joosten 2011b, 214; 2012, 434), and probably jussive with ventive clitic, 'Let Pharaoh on his own behalf proceed to appoint' (see §1.2.2 and §3.4.1.3); 44.4 (*Ø-IMP* + *Ø-IMP* + *wa-qaṭal* + *wa-qaṭal*); 45.9 (*Ø-IMP* + *wa-IMP* + *wa-qaṭal*); 47.25 (*Ø-yiqṭol(Ø)* + *wa-qaṭal*); Exod. 7.26; 8.16; 9.1, 8, 13; 12.21b–22, 32; 17.5; 19.10; 24.1–2; 28.42–43; 34.1–2; Lev. 1.2; 2.6 (*Vnabs* + *wa-qaṭal*; Dallaire 2014, 146); 10.12f.; 15.2; 17.2; 18.2; 19.2; 21.1; 23.2, 10; 24.14; 25.2; 27.2; Num. 3.45; 5.12, 21f. (*Ø-yiqṭol(Ø)* + *wa-qaṭal*); 6.2; 8.2, 6, 7; 11.16; 13.17–20; 15.18, 38; 16.5 (*wa-yiqṭol(Ø)!* + *wa-qaṭal* + *wa-O.noun-yiqṭol(u)!*); 19.2–3 (*Ø-IMP* + *wa-yiqṭol(Ø)* + [3]*wa-qaṭal* + *wa-qaṭal* + *wa-qaṭal*); 20.8, 26; 25.17 (*VNabs* + *wa-qaṭal*; Dallaire 2014, 146); 27.18–19; 28.2; 33.51; 34.2; 35.10; Deut. 1.16 (Dallaire 2014, 152f.); 10.1f.; 16.1 (Dallaire 2014, 153); 31.26 (Dallaire 2014, 153); Judg. 4.6, 20; 6.25f. (Dallaire 2014, 146); 9.2; 11.6 (*Ø-IMP* + *wa-qaṭal* + *wa-yiqṭol(Ø)-A*); 21.10, 20.

[21] As in Exod. 13.3; 24.1–2; Judg. 6.25.

[22] Other instances where I have perceived that *wa-qaṭal* clauses in modal series express information rather than added instruction: Exod. 14.2–4 (*IMP* + *wa-qaṭal* + *wa-qaṭal* + *wa-qaṭal*); 33.1–2 (*Ø-IMP* + *Ø-IMP* + *wa-qaṭal* + *wa-qaṭal*); Num. 10.2 (*Ø-IMP* + *Ø-O.noun-yiqṭol(u)* + *wa-qaṭal*, an explanation, not a command).

[23] Other examples of *wa-qaṭal* with result meaning in a sequence expressing obligation: Gen. 24.4; Exod. 26.6, 11; 28.7; 40.9; Lev. 22.9 וּמֵתוּ; Num. 4.15 'so that they won't die'; 4.20 'so that they die'; Deut. 5.27; 13.11; 17.5; 21.21 'to death'; 22.21, 24; 24.13.

[24] In a few cases, an initial adverb like *raq* or *ʿattā* with distinctive accent can precede a jussive in direct speech, as in Gen. 50.5; Exod. 3.18; Deut. 2.28; see further §3.4.4.2.

[25] Other examples of *wa-qaṭal* with result meaning after a futural *yiqṭol(u)* clause: Gen. 24.40 (last *wa-qaṭal*); 27.12 (both *wa-qaṭal*); Exod. 22.23 (last *wa-qaṭal*); 23.27 (both *wa-qaṭal*); 23.31; Num. 4.15; 11.21; 17.20; Deut. 2.25 (both *wa-qaṭal*); Judg. 15.18. For result *wa-qaṭal* in *pɛn* complexes, see §6.5.5.

[26] Another example of an ability *yiqṭol(u)* clause followed by result *wa-qaṭal* is Exod. 10.25.

[27] Other instances of result *wa-qaṭal* clauses within a protasis: Exod. 21.12 (Garr 1998: lxxxiii); 21.20, 26 'so that he destroys it'; 21.28 (with a very frequent result clause וָמֵת 'to death'); 21.33 'so that either dies'; 21.35 'to death' or 'so that it dies'; 22.1, 5; Lev. 4.13 'so they become guilty'; 13.12 'so that the disease covers'; 20.17 'so that he sees'; Deut. 19.11.

[28] Other instances of result *wa-qaṭal* clauses within an apodosis: Gen. 34.16 'and we will stay with you to make one nation'; Lev. 12.7–8 'so that she will be clean'; Lev. 25.28 (last *wa-qaṭal*) 'that he may return to his property'; 25.35 'so that he can continue living with you'; Num. 27.11 'that he may possess it'; Deut. 22.24 'to death'.

[29] Other examples of *pɛn* complexes with result *wa-qaṭal* clauses: Gen. 3.22; 19.19—Westermann (1981, 360) translates, 'daß ich sterben müßte'; Exod. 13.17; 19.21; 23.29; Deut. 11.16 'to serve and worship other gods!' (see also Dallaire 2014, 148); 25.3; Judg. 18.25.

[30] EA 104:43–52: *XØ* + *qatal* + *wa-lā-yaqtulu* + *wa-qatal* (Baranowski 2016a, 175).

[31] Counterfactual *wa-qaṭal* with result meaning is also found in Gen. 26.10 (Schüle 2000, 126); 40.14 (*kī-ʾim-qaṭal* + *wa-qaṭal-nāʾ* + *wa-qaṭal* + *wa-qaṭal*, the first and third *wa-qaṭal* with result meaning, as in 'so that he will release me from this prison'); 43.9 (within a protasis, counterfactual; Nyberg 1972, §86gg:2)—Garr (1998, lxxxiii) and Rainey

(2003b, 27) interpret *wa-qaṭal* as a result clause; Judg. 9.11, 13 (both *INT-qaṭal* + *wa-qaṭal*; Boling 1975, 173).

[32] See §3.4.1. The most precarious homonymy was of course with the jussive *wa-yiqṭol(Ø)*.

[33] Temporal clause linkings are not included. The numbers refer to the conditional sentences registered in my database, excerpted as records from the corpus. I do not pretend that they represent exactly all conditional sentences in the corpus, only that the numbers are fairly complete. This is the reason I supply percentages in conditional linking statistics. They are significant. The '*X*' in the table is allowed to be a simple negation.

[34] The three exceptional instances of clause-initial *yiqṭol(u)* are probably cases of an understood VNabs before the *yiqṭol(u)* (ellipsis); all examples are found in the same chapter: Exod. 22.6, 11, 12. The morphology is not distinctive, but compare the *VNabs-yiqṭol(u)* construction of apodoses in Exod. 21.12, 15, 16, 17, 20, 22, 28, 36 שַׁלֵּם יְשַׁלֵּם; 22.5 שַׁלֵּם יְשַׁלֵּם; 22.13 שַׁלֵּם יְשַׁלֵּם׃; 22.15; 23.4; 31.15; Lev. 20.2, 9; 12, 15, 27; 24.17; Num. 35.21. In two of the clause-initial cases, the protasis has a *Vnabs* + *yiqṭol(u)* construction: Exod. 22.11, 12.

[35] All asyndetic short *yiqṭol* apodoses are volitive, some negated (with *ʾal*; Ges-K §159n): Gen. 18.3; Exod. 33.15; 34.9; Lev. 25.14; Num. 23.27; 32.5; Deut. 20.5, 6, 7; Judg. 6.31; 7.3; 9.15, 20.

[36] Gen. 4.7; 24.43; 30.1; 42.16; Exod. 7.27; 8.17; 9.3; 10.4; Lev. 21.9.

[37] The few syndetic *yiqṭol(u)* apodoses are questions that implicitly cast doubt about something: Exod. 8.22; Num. 16.22.

[38] All four syndetic jussive apodoses come after a protasis with imperative predicate, with the meaning 'if you fulfil the command, then this will happen'. There is a condition and there is a result. Such jussive apodoses seemingly tend to be coded in the same way as jussive purpose clauses (*wa-yiqṭol(Ø)*): Gen. 12.1–2 ([1]*(Ø-IMP)* + [2]*wa-yiqṭol(Ø)* + *wa-yiqṭol(Ø)* + *wa-yiqṭol(Ø)-A* + *wa-IMP*)—here the two first jussives have pronominal suffixes, which means they cannot take a ventive/cohortative clitic: the third jussive has a such a clitic, so this is probably the

intended meaning for all jussives in the example; Exod. 3.10; Judg. 9.7, 19.

[39] The sixteen (4 + 12) jussive apodoses with ventive/cohortative clitic seem to have a certain preference for syndesis, as in: Gen. 13.9 (2×); 17.2; 26.3; 29.27; 30.28; 31.3; 32.10; 34.12; 47.16 (*Ø-IMP* + *wa-yiqṭol(Ø)-A*); 47.19; Exod. 9.28; 24.12. But four are asyndetic: Gen. 18.21; 30.31; 43.4; Num. 22.34.

[40] The *kī-ʿattā-qaṭal* apodoses are counterfactual: Gen. 31.42; 43.10; Num. 22.29, 33.

[41] Macro-syntactic *wa-haya* (Isaksson 1998) sometimes introduce an apodosis: Lev. 5.5; 27.10, 33; Num. 15.24. They are not classified as *wa-qaṭal* apodoses in this study.

[42] Other examples of *qaṭal* predicates with anterior meaning in apodoses: Exod. 22.14 (*Ø-qaṭal*)—but the interpretation is disputed (see Propp 2006, 105, 252); Lev. 20.13, 18, 20; Num. 16.29; 19.13; 32.23 (*Ø-hinnē-qaṭal*); Deut. 19.18. Anterior-future apodoses with *qaṭal* predicate are asyndetic in the corpus.

[43] Anterior-present means that *qaṭal* has anterior aspect when reference time is speech time, as in Judg. 6.13, (וְיֵ֤שׁ יְהוָה֙ עִמָּ֔נוּ) וְלָ֥מָּה מְצָאַ֖תְנוּ כָּל־זֹ֑את ‘If the LORD is with us, why then has all this happened to us?’. See Müller (1994, 164), who calls this “Weiterführung eines Gesprächsgangs.”

[44] Other examples of counterfactual *qaṭal* in apodoses: Gen. 43.10 (*kī ʿattā-qaṭal*); Num. 22.29, 33 (both *kī-ʿattā-qaṭal*); Judg. 8.19 (*Ø-lō-qaṭal*; see Li 2017, 7); 13.23 (*Ø-lō-qaṭal*; Cook 2012, 250); 14.18 (*Ø-lō-qaṭal*; Cook 2012, 250).

[45] Other examples of performative *qaṭal* in apodoses: Deut. 4.26 (*Ø-qaṭal*); 8.19 (*Ø-qaṭal*).

[46] Cf. the solemn apodosis introduced by *kī ʾim* in Exod. 22.22 (with *yiqṭol(u)* predicate).

[47] Gropp (1991, 47) and Cook (2012, 207 n. 46) also regard the passage as a possible example of *qaṭal* with future reference. But J-M (§176o, p.

610 n. 1) suggests the *Ø-qaṭal* to be a *wa-qaṭal* clause in nature: "the same form was preferred for the sake of assonance."

[48] For the assumption that the corpus of Archaic Biblical Hebrew is earlier than CBH, see Pat-El and Wilson-Wright (2013, 400).

[49] I do not count embedded non-finite temporal expressions like verbal noun phrases as protases. Some such temporal phrases do express eventualities, as in Gen. 2.17 כִּי בְּיוֹם אֲכָלְךָ מִמֶּנּוּ מוֹת תָּמוּת׃ (*kī-PrP-VN-VNabs-yiqṭol(u)!*), a case of man's free choice. Other examples: Lev. 24.16; Num. 35.19.

[50] The *wa-qaṭal* clause-type is rare (as is the case also in Amarna; Renz 2016, 451). It marks discourse continuity and is used when there is a close connection with a preceding clause or context: Gen. 33.13 (related to the preceding *qoṭel*-clause); 34.30 (an eventuality; Westermann 1981, 650); 42.38; 44.22 (Ferguson 1882, 79; Ges-K §159d); 44.29 (connection to preceding discussion; Ferguson 1882, 46; Ges-K §159g); Exod. 12.44 (connection to a legal case); Lev. 10.19 (connection to preceding *wa(y)-yiqṭol*; Ferguson 1882, 80; Ges-K §159g); Num. 14.13 (connection to previous context, 'And if…'; same in 14.14–15); 14.14, 15; 36.3 (connects to a preceding *qaṭal* clause). A similar conclusion was reached by Dallaire (2014, 152) concerning the choice of *wa-qaṭal* (and not *yiqṭol(u)*) after a deontic VNabs: "The *weqatal* appears in clauses expressing sequentiality while, in disjunctive clauses, the *yiqtol* is preceded by a *waw* + a nonverbal element."

[51] Elliptic protases may have only a noun phrase or an adverb; the verb form is understood, e.g., Gen. 13.9; 18.21; 42.16.

[52] Most *qaṭal* protases have anterior meaning projected into a future eventuality (45 ×). None expresses a pure futurity. The rest express pluperfect (1 ×, Num. 12.14, though possibly counterfactual), or are counterfactual (6 ×), past perfective (1 ×, Judg. 9.19), or stativic (7 ×).

[53] The number of registered protases is somewhat higher than that of apodoses, because of the sometimes complicated structure of conditional sentences in legal discourse. Examples of more than one protasis

in a conditional sentence: Exod. 22.6; Lev. 3.1; 4.3; 5.1, 2, 4; 27.20; Num. 14.13f.; 35.20f.

[54] This is the case also in Phoenician, in which a reflex of Central Semitic **yaqtulu* dominates as predicate (Renz 2016, 460).

[55] This often the case also in Amarna Canaanite (Renz 2016, 449).

[56] I refer to the first introductory clause in a protasis. In complex protases, *wa-qaṭal* is often used as a second, third, or fourth clause.

[57] Levine (1993, 303) translates, 'When only one is sounded, the chieftains, heads of the Israelite militias, shall assemble before you'.

[58] The conjunction *kī* is frequent also as conditional particle. In my database of 477 protases, about 18%, or 88 protases, are introduced by *kī*. The most frequent conditional particle, *ʾim*, is found in 50% of all conditional clauses.

[59] Some other borderline cases of temporal/conditional linkings: Num. 10.9 (*wa-kī-yiqṭol(u)* + *wa-qaṭal*); 21.9 (*wa-haya* + *ʾim-qaṭal* + *wa-qaṭal* + *wa-qaṭal*)—according to Ges-K (§159o), conditional; Deut. 4.30 (*Ø-XØ* + *wa-qaṭal* + *wa-qaṭal* + *wa-qaṭal*); 23.25 (*Ø-kī-yiqṭol(u)* + *wa-qaṭal*).

[60] Other examples of temporal clauses with conjunction *ʾim* (*wa-qaṭal* has habitual meaning in all): Gen. 31.8a (*Ø-ʾim-ADV-yiqṭol(u)* + *wa-qaṭal*; Ferguson 1882, 81)—according to Ges-K (§159r, s), conditional; 38.9 (*wa-haya: Ø-ʾim-qaṭal* + *wa-qaṭal*)—according to Ges-K (§159o), conditional; Num. 36.4 (*wa-ʾim-yiqṭol(u)* + *wa-qaṭal*).

[61] Other cases of futural temporal *kī*-clause with following non-habitual *wa-qaṭal*: Gen. 12.12 (*wa-haya: kī-yiqṭol(u)* + *wa-qaṭal* + *wa-qaṭal* + *wa-O.pron-yiqṭol(u)*); 32.18f. ([18]*[kī-yiqṭol(u)* + *wa-qaṭal]* + [19]*wa-qaṭal*)—according to Ges-K (§159bb), conditional; 46.33f.; Exod. 7.9 (*kī-yiqṭol(u)* + *wa-qaṭal*); 30.12 (*kī-yiqṭol(u)* + *wa-qaṭal* + *wa-lō-yiqṭol(u)*); Lev. 5.23 (*wa-haya* + *[kī-yiqṭol(u)* + *wa-qaṭal]* + *wa-qaṭal*); 14.34f. (*[kī-yiqṭol(u)* + *wa-qaṭal]* + [35]*wa-qaṭal* + *wa-qaṭal*); 19.23 (*[wa-kī-yiqṭol(u)* + *wa-qaṭal]* + *wa-qaṭal*); 23.10; Num. 33.51f. (*kī-S.pron-qoṭel* + *wa-qaṭal*); 35.10f. (*kī-S.pron-qoṭel* + [11]*wa-qaṭal*); Deut. 7.1; 11.29; 30.1–3.

[62] Some other examples of main-line *yiqṭol(u)* clauses after a temporal clause of the type *kī-yiqṭol(u)* or *ʾim-yiqṭol(u)* (all except one of which are asyndetic): Gen. 4.12 (*Ø-kī-yiqṭol(u) + Ø-lō-yiqṭol(u)*); Exod. 3.21 (*wa-haya + kī-yiqṭol(u)-Npar + Ø-lō-yiqṭol(u)*); 22.22 (*kī-ʾim-VNabs-yiqṭol(u) + Ø-VNabs-yiqṭol(u)*); 23.23f.; 40.37 (*wa-ʾim-lō-yiqṭol(u) + wa-lō-yiqṭol(u)*, exception, habitual past); Lev. 19.5 (*kī-yiqṭol(u) + Ø-PrP-yiqṭol(u)*); Deut. 19.1f.; 20.1.

[63] It does not correspond to CBH usage to translate *qaṭal* as a plain future.

[64] Other temporal *kī*-clauses with following main line coded by future habitual *wa-qaṭal* clauses: Exod. 1.10 (*wa-haya: kī-yiqṭol(u) + wa-qaṭal + wa-qaṭal + wa-qaṭal*); 13.4f. (obligation concerning a custom); Lev. 15.13 (this statute concerning a man with a discharge can be expected to have validity many times in a man's life, which means that habituality is implied; the *kī*-clause is expected to occur, so it is not conditional); Num. 18.26 (*kī-yiqṭol(u) + wa-qaṭal*, habitual obligation).

[65] The temporal clause is enclosed within brackets. Other instances of *[wa-qaṭal] + wa-qaṭal* in a temporal clause linking: Exod. 4.14 (Ges-K §159g); 12.13 'when I see the blood, I will pass over you' (Fergusson 1882, 71; Ges-K §159g); 16.21 'but when the sun grew hot, it melted' (Fergusson 1882, 72, 80, Ges-K §159g); Lev. 22.7; Num. 10.3, 5, 6; 15.39.

[66] Other examples of verbal noun clauses (PREP-VN) functioning as temporal clauses before main-line *wa-qaṭal*: Gen 27.45 (future); 44.30f. (future); Lev. 26.26 (habitual future); Num. 9.19 (habitual past); Deut. 29.18 (future); Judg. 8.7 (future intention).

[67] Other examples of temporal *VN* before *yiqṭol(u)*: Exod. 3.12 (*bə-VN-yiqṭol(u)-Npar*); 9.29; 30.20; 33.8; Lev. 13.14; 23.22; 24.16; Num. 8.2; 10.7, 36; 15.19; Deut. 23.12; 25.19; Judg. 2.19; 8.9; 18.10.

[68] Brockelmann (1956, §13a) argues that the adverbial nouns are "Eingliedrige Nominalsätze." Joosten (2012, 292) analyses the *noun + wa-qaṭal* construction as a case of extraposition (left dislocation).

[69] Other cause/reason clauses with following main clause *wa-qaṭal*: Gen. 29.15 (*INT-kī-XØ* + *wa-qaṭal*, rhetorical question, 'because you are my kinsman, should you serve me for nothing?'); Num. 10.31 (*CONJ-qaṭal* + *wa-qaṭal*, obligation).

[70] In my database, of a total of 57 *XØ* protases, prepositions occur with the following frequencies: *ʾim* 75%, *hinnē* 14%, *lū* 2%, *yēš* 2%, *biltī* 2% (reversed clausal order with main clause before *XØ*).

[71] Such linkings show that a *XØ* topic clause can both be topic *and* describe an initial background in narration, a double duty. Some examples: Gen. 41.12 (*wa-XØ* + *wa(y)-yiqṭol* + *wa(y)-yiqṭol*); 42.6 (*wa-XØ* + *Ø-XØ* + *wa(y)-yiqṭol* + *wa(y)-yiqṭol*); 47.13 (*wa-XØ* + *kī-XØ* + *wa(y)-yiqṭol*). See further §7.10.

[72] Adam was given authority to give names to all livestock, and this is his namegiving of woman.

[73] Other examples of *yiqṭol(u)* clauses as comments after a verbless topic: Gen. 3.14 (*Ø-PP* + *Ø-PrP-yiqṭol(u)*); 3.17 (*Ø-PP* + *Ø-PrP-yiqṭol(u)-N*); 3.19 (*kī-XØ* + *wa-PrP-yiqṭol(u)!*, the *kī* is emphatic adverbial); 25.23 (*Ø-XØ* + *wa-S.noun-PrP-yiqṭol(u)*); 35.10 (*Ø-XØ* + *Ø-lō-yiqṭol(u)*)—according to Khan (2019, 50), *XØ* with no copula; 40.13 (*Ø-XØ* + *Ø-PrP-yiqṭol(u)* + *wa-qaṭal* + *wa-qaṭal*); 40.18f. ([18]*Ø-XØ* + [19]*Ø-PrP-yiqṭol(u)* + *wa-qaṭal* + *wa-qaṭal*); 41.44 (*Ø-XØ* + *wa-PrP-lō-yiqṭol(u)!*, the given is 'I am Pharaoh'); 48.5 (*Ø-XØ* + *Ø-S.noun-yiqṭol(u)*); Exod. 20.10 (*wa-XØ* + *Ø-lō-yiqṭol(u)*); 30.8f. (*Ø-XØ* + [9]*Ø-lō-yiqṭol(u)*); Lev. 6.14 (*Ø-XØ* + *Ø-PrP-yiqṭol(u)*); 18.7, 15 (both *Ø-XØ* + *Ø-lō-yiqṭol(u)*); 21.21 (*Ø-XØ* + *Ø-O.noun-lō-yiqṭol(u)*); 23.8 (*Ø-XØ* + *Ø-O.noun-lō-yiqṭol(u)*); 23.27 (*Ø-ʾak̠-XØ* + *Ø-O.noun-yiqṭol(u)!*); 23.35, 36 (both *Ø-XØ* + *Ø-O.noun-lō-yiqṭol(u)*); 25.11 (*Ø-XØ* + *Ø-lō-yiqṭol(u)*); Num. 28.17 (*wa-XØ* + *Ø-ADV-S.noun-yiqṭol(u)*, the comment is 'at that time'); 28.18 (*Ø-XØ* + *Ø-O.noun-lō-yiqṭol(u)*) 'at that time'; Deut. 12.23 (*kī-S.noun-S.pron-XØ* + *wa-lō-yiqṭol(u)*)—*kī* is adverbial, the *XØ* has a copula before the definite predicate (Khan 2019, 49); 16.9 (*wa-XØ* + *Ø-lō-yiqṭol(u)*) 'at that time' or 'therefore'; Judg. 17.6 (*Ø-XØ* + *Ø-S.noun-O.noun-PrP-yiqṭol(u)!*, habitual past); 21.25 (*Ø-XØ* + *Ø-S.noun-O.noun-yiqṭol(u)*).

[74] Other examples of *wa-qaṭal* comment clauses after an *XØ* topic: Gen. 17.4; 20.11 (Khan 2021a, 309); 26.24 (*kī-XØ* + *wa-qaṭal* + *wa-qaṭal*, adverbial *kī*); 28.15; 34.30 (*wa-XØ* + *wa-qaṭal* + *wa-qaṭal* + *wa-qaṭal*, where the first *wa-qaṭal*, וְנֶאֶסְפ֣וּ עָלַ֔י, expresses an eventuality and thus something conditional, but at the same time it is the first clause in a comment after the *XØ*); Exod. 5.5 (irony and contrast); 6.6 'I am YHWH, and therefore…'; 33.21; Lev. 11.44 'For I am the LORD your God. Consecrate yourselves therefore, and be holy' (ESV); 13.3, 11, 25, 42f. (all in apodoses); 16.31; 18.5; 19.37; 20.17, 25; 21.7f.; 23.32; 25.10; Num. 4.24f.; 14.40 (but this is a unique idiom; see Levine 1993, 361); 14.43.

[75] For left dislocations with following *wa-qatal* in Phoenician, see Krahmalkov (1986).

[76] From the statistics in my database, it seems that *yiqṭol(u)* clauses are constructed with left dislocation more frequently than are *wa-qaṭal* clauses: 52 *yiqṭol(u)* as against 25 *wa-qaṭal*. Some of the *yiqṭol(u)* examples with left dislocation: Gen. 6.20; 9.6; 17.12f., 15; 21.13; 28.13, 22; 31.43; 50.5; Exod. 1.22; 12.16; 30.37; Lev. 2.11; 7.7, 14, 19, 32f.; 11.3, 9; 13.45; 18.9, 10, 11; 21.14; 22.23, 28; 27.26; Num. 6.7; 9.17; 17.20; 22.20, 38; 23.26; 30.14; Deut. 14.27; Judg. 7.4; 11.24 (2×). A special case is the many instances of a left dislocation before a conditional *kī-yiqṭol(u)* in protases describing legal cases, as in Lev. 1.2; 2.1; 15.19; 19.20; Num. 5.6.

[77] Some more examples of *wa-qaṭal* clauses after a left dislocation which is semantically close to a protasis with quantifier: Exod. 12.15 (*kī-kōl-qoṭel* + *wa-qaṭal*); 12.19 (Propp 1999, 356); 12.44 (Propp 1999, 357); 31.14 (Propp 2006, 319); Lev. 15.11, 17; Num. 21.8. Examples without quantifier: Gen. 17.14; Lev. 26.36 (a *nifʿal* participle left dislocation)—according to Khan (2021a, 309, 312), "the *weqaṭal* clause is a comment on a preceding topical entity;" Num. 23.3 (Ferguson 1882, 78).

[78] Another relative clause example is Deut. 17.12.

[79] Other non-conditional left dislocations with *wa-qaṭal* are found in: Lev. 4.11 (a rather complicated object noun construction); 13.58; Num.

3.46f. (complicated object noun phrase); 17.3 (object noun phrase resumed in *wa-qaṭal*); 34.6 (geographical description); Deut. 21.3.

[80] For the terminology 'be of equal status', see Halliday (2004, 374, 489).

[81] For the pre-exilic Hebrew Inscriptions, see §6.3 and Renz (2016, §4.2.2). The linking *yiqṭol(u)* + *wa-qaṭal* with future meaning (cf. Table 17) is a late step in the development of *wa-qaṭal* (as a construction), attested in the inscriptions at the end of the pre-exilic period (Renz 2016, 661). In this connection, focusing on main-line clauses, we shall discard cases of *yiqṭol(u)* + *wa-qaṭal* in substructures such as complex relative sentences, complex protases, complex temporal sentences, etc. Even if the linking in substructures behaves as expected, and within the same semantic range as in main-line linking, for the sake of clarity, they are not considered here. We will discuss *yiqṭol(u)* + *wa-qaṭal* in main structures, which will include background but not subordinate clause complexes.

[82] *yiqṭol(u)* + *wa-qaṭal* has in rare cases a volitive nuance: Exod. 8.23 (both volitive); Exod. 12.48 (*wa-qaṭal* within a temporal clause complex, thus a substructure); Deut. 1.41 (both volitive).

[83] Lev. 25.40f. (*wa-qaṭal* permissive); Deut. 19.4 (*wa-qaṭal* within relative sentence); 24.13 (*wa-qaṭal* permissive).

[84] Walsh (1977, 168) concludes in his analysis that "The pain of insufficiency and labour will burden man's eating." Since the number of futural instances of *yiqṭol(u)* + *wa-qaṭal* is so large, I supply only those registered from Genesis and Exodus here: Gen. 13.15f.; 15.13; 18.18; 22.17f. (*wa-VNabs-yiqṭol(u)* + *wa-yiqṭol(Ø)* + [18]*wa-qaṭal*); 24.40; 26.4; 27.12; 28.14; 32.13 (*Ø-VNabs-yiqṭol(u)* + *wa-qaṭal*); 40.13, 19; 50.24; Exod. 3.20f.; 4.12 (promise after imperative); 4.15f.; 7.2 (first clause obligation, then *yiqṭol(u)* + *wa-qaṭal* future); 7.3f.; 8.24; 11.7f.; 12.48 (permissive + future); 16.12; 20.24; 22.22f. (adverbial *kī*); 23.27, 30f., 31 (adverbial *kī*); 28.43; 32.13; 33.14, 19; 34.10.

[85] Westermann (1981, 304) translates, 'Das soll mein Bund an eurem Fleisch sein, ein ewiger Bund'. I supply here examples of *yiqṭol(u)* +

wa-qaṭal with obligational meaning in Genesis and Exodus: Gen. 4.14; 6.3 (ability + obligation); 17.5; 24.4 (adverbial *kī*); 24.38; 32.20f.; 50.25 (future + obligation); Exod. 2.7; 5.7; 10.25 (obligation + ability); 12.11, 17; 13.19 (future + obligation); 18.21f.; 20.9, 24; 23.10, 11; 25.36f.; 26.3f., 24f.; 28.3, 25; 29.4, 8, 15, 17, 31; 30.30; 31.13f.; 40.2f., 14.

[86] Westermann (1982, 234) translates, 'Wenn sich Gott euer annimmt, dann bringt meine Gebeine von hier "mit euch" hinauf!'.

[87] Other examples with the meaning of ability in *yiqṭol(u)* + *wa-qaṭal* linkings: Gen. 6.3 (ability + obligation); 24.7 (future + ability); Exod. 10.25 (both, depending on interpretation; Propp 1999, 341); 28.7 (obligation + ability); Num. 11.22 (both); 22.11 (both).

[88] Examples of habitual or progressive *yiqṭol(u)* + *wa-qaṭal* in main structures: Gen. 2.6 (progressive past?; Gzella 2021, 76f.); 2.10 (progressive past; Hornkohl 2014, 288); 2.24 (present or general habituality); 29.3 (habitual past; Khan 2021a, 309, 312); 33.7 (above); Lev. 26.41 'had to continue in opposition(?)' (Milgrom 2001, 2274, 2332).

[89] Other habitual past *wa-qaṭal* + *wa-qaṭal* linkings: Exod. 34.34f.; Num. 10.21.

[90] Other examples of future, obligational, etc., *wa-qaṭal* + *wa-qaṭal* linkings: Gen. 9.16 (future, but by inference a temporal linking; Ferguson 1882, 79); 17.16 (future); Exod. 28.29f. (obligation); Lev. 5.13 (future); 16.13, 18–20 (both obligation); 20.22 (obligation); 22.31 (obligation); 26.16, 20 (both future); Num. 8.10f. (obligation); 10.3 (obligation); 11.17 (future, ability); 13.20 (obligation); 20.8 (ability); Deut. 4.39 (obligation); 24.13 (obligation and future); Judg. 7.18 (future and obligation); 21.21 (obligation).

[91] For the typological connection between present progressive and immediate future, see Bybee et al. (1994, 275–78).

[92] Other examples of *qoṭel* + *wa-qaṭal* linking with future meaning: Gen. 6.17f.; 9.9f.; 41.29f.; Exod. 3.13; 7.17f., 27f.; 8.25; 9.3f.; 10.4f.; 11.4f.; 16.4; 17.6; Deut. 4.22; 11.31.

[93] Other examples of *qoṭel* + *wa-qaṭal* with deviating meanings: Exod. 4.14 (progressive present, future); 13.15f. (progressive present, obligation); 16.5 (future, obligation); Num. 15.30 (apodosis: general present, obligation); Deut. 30.16 (progressive present, future).

[94] Other anterior-future combinations of *qaṭal* + *wa-qaṭal* linking: Gen. 33.10; Num. 19.13 (anterior-obligation); Judg. 13.3 (contrastive *wa-qaṭal*; Schüle 2000, 125).

[95] On this interpretation of *qaṭal* in Gen. 9.13, I follow Westermann (1976, 616, 634). Another example is Gen. 17.20; thus Brockelmann (1956, §135b), *pace* Westermann (1981, 304), who translates 'Siehe, ich will ihn segnen'.

[96] Cf. the common linking *wa-qaṭal* + *wa-ʾaḥar-yiqṭol(u)* 'only after that...' in Lev. 14.19, 'The priest shall offer the sin offering and make atonement for the one to be cleansed from his uncleanness. **Then afterward**, he shall slaughter the burnt offering'. Other examples: Lev. 15.29b; 22.7; Num. 5.26; 6.20; 19.7; Judg. 7.11.

[97] Other examples of focal contrasting *X-yiqṭol(u)* after *wa-qaṭal*: Gen. 17.20b–21a 'but *my covenant* I will establish with Isaac'; Exod. 4.21 (*you* contrasting *I*); 18.26; 24.2 (Hornkohl 2018, 37); 25.21; 33.11, 23; 34.3; 36.29; Lev. 2.12; 7.32; 16.25; 25.46; 26.12; Num. 5.31; 33.54; Deut. 15.12 (in apodosis); 28.12.

[98] Other examples of *wa-qaṭal* + *X-yiqṭol(u)* expressing complementarity: Gen. 44.9 (in apodosis); 47.24; Exod. 29.12, 13f.; Lev. 4.7, 17f., 25, 30, 34; 5.9; 14.5f.; 26.5, 29 (flesh of yours sons, flesh of your daughters); 26.33; Num. 6.16f.; 35.2, 3; Deut. 10.16; 12.3; Judg. 6.25; 7.7.

[99] Other examples of *wa-qaṭal* + *(wa)-X-yiqṭol(u)* expressing elaboration: Exod. 23.5; 26.31, 35; 27.2, 3; 28.6f., 9–11, 15f., 20f., 37; 30.1, 10; 40.31f. (habitual past); Lev. 3.9 (Milgrom 1991, 203); 4.12; 10.13f.; 12.2; 18.26; 23.11, 15f., 32; 24.5; 25.9, 10, 52; 27.8, 12; Num. 3.47; 6.9; 19.5, 11f. ([11]*wa-qaṭal* + [12]*Ø-S.pron-yiqṭol(u)* + *Ø-yiqṭol*, the latter verb is a textual error); 29.7.

[100] Other examples of *wa-qaṭal* + *(wa)-X-yiqṭol(u)* with preverbal focal element: Gen. 17.6, 16, 20 (all future, increase); 28.21f.; Exod. 7.15,

17f., 28f.; 8.7, 19; 12.8 (or elaboration); 12.12, 14; 19.5f. (or contrast); 21.19, 35; 25.11 (or elaboration); 25.14f., 18 (or elaboration); 25.27, 29, 31 (or elaboration); 26.7; 28.13f., 32, 39; Lev. 6.4f.; 16.14; Judg. 13.5 (but *wa-qaṭal* is a mixed formation: וְיֹלַדְתְּ could be *wa-qoṭel*).

[101] Other examples of *wa-qaṭal* + *(wa)-X-yiqṭol(u)* expressing a comment with further information: Exod. 28.4f.; 29.28, 37; 30.29, 36; Lev. 15.24; 23.20; 25.29; Num. 10.6; 35.5 (or summary).

[102] Similarly in Gen. 9.15, 'I will remember my covenant that is between me and you and every living creature of all flesh. And the waters shall never again become a flood to destroy all flesh'. Other examples: Gen. 17.4b–5; 41.30f., 36; Exod. 9.4; 10.5; 12.13, 23 'the LORD will pass over the door and will not allow the destroyer to enter your houses to strike you'; 22.10b; 30.12; Lev. 5.8; 11.44; 15.31; 17.6f.; 18.26 'But you shall keep my statutes and my rules and do none of these abominations'; 18.30; 20.22, 25; 22.9; 26.11 'I will make my dwelling among you, and my soul shall not abhor you'; 26.26b 'you shall eat and not be satisfied'; 26.31; Num. 9.19 (habitual past); 11.17; 18.5; 35.12.

7. THE LINGUISTIC REALITY BEHIND THE CONSECUTIVE TENSES

This chapter starts to make use of the main components of the verbal system established in the preceding chapters: the short *yiqṭol*, the long *yiqṭol*, *qaṭal*, and the relatively recently developed construction *wa-qaṭal*. It reinterprets the theory of consecutive tenses by performing a systematic investigation of clause linking in Classical Hebrew, with special emphasis on the discourse level. The chapter investigates the fundamental alternation between discourse continuity and discourse discontinuity and shows that this distinction has a signal: the switch from a *wa-Verb* clause-type, with the natural language connective *wa-*, to a discontinuity clause-type. The traditional hypothesis of a special 'consecutive' *wa-* is therefore unwarranted. This chapter is the centre of the book and represents a regeneration of Classical Hebrew text-linguistics. The emphasis lies on the continuity clause-types *wa(y)-yiqṭol* and *wa-qaṭal* (both *wa-Verb*), especially when they form chains of main-line clauses that are interrupted by discontinuity clauses.

7.1. A New Terminology

In §1.2.6, the essence of Biblical Hebrew text-linguistics was summarised as an alternation between two clause-types (where '*' indicates a preliminary formulation):

> Tenet 1*. A series of ***wa***-*VX* clauses is interrupted by a clause with (*wa*)-*XV* pattern (Isaksson 2021a, 212).

 https://doi.org/10.11647/OBP.0414.07

The boldface ***wa*** in the formula indicates the common assumption that the *wa-* before a consecutive clause has a special nature: it is a 'consecutive *waw*'. *V* in the formula is a finite verb and *X* is any non-verbal clausal constituent except negation. In the terminology of Buth (1995) and Hornkohl (2018, 48ff.), a discourse-continuity clause has a specific clause-type, ***wa****-VX*; a discontinuity clause is characterised by having a clausal constituent (*X*) before the verb. The parentheses enclosing the *wa* indicate that the *wa* is optional in the discontinuity clause.

Non-consecutive clauses more often than not start with a normal *wa*, but can also be asyndetic. Some oft-recognised alternatives in CBH text-linguistics are (Isaksson 2021, 212f.):

Tenet 1a*. A series of ***wa****-VX* is interrupted by a clause with *wa-XV* pattern.[1]

Tenet 1b*. A series of ***wa****-VX* is interrupted by a clause with *Ø-XV* pattern.[2]

Tenet 1c*. A series of ***wa****-VX* is interrupted by a verbless clause.[3]

The term adopted by most scholars for the boldface ***wa-*** is 'consecutive *waw*'. But some use 'conversive', 'inversive', 'energic', or another distinguishing term.

As is argued in the present book, the main arguments in favour of a special 'consecutive' *wa* must be refuted:

1. The differences in vocalisation and gemination represent an innovative and orthoepic feature of the Tiberian reading tradition (see §1.2.5).
2. The impression of a 'conversion' is just an impression, caused by a diachronic retention (*wa(y)-yiqṭol* with short indicative 'preterite' *yiqṭol*; Hasselbach and Huehnergard

2008, 416) and an internal Hebrew semantic innovation (*wa-qaṭal* as construction; see §3 and §6 respectively).[4]

3. The range of meanings exhibited by 'consecutive *waw*' has the same semantic complexity as that of 'copulative *waw*' (see §2). Both can express temporal succession, logical result, elaboration, simultaneity, etc. (Garr 1998, lxxxvi).[5] The impression of a special 'consecution' is due to its use in the discourse-continuity clause-types *wa(y)-yiqṭol* (often in narrative and report) and *wa-qaṭal* (often in instruction and legal discourse).[6] The Proto-Semitic conjunction **wa* has only one reflex (*wa*) in CBH (Isaksson 2021a, 214; see §2). It is a natural language connective in the sense described by Van Dijk (1977, 58).

So it is necessary to update the terminology in the traditional system of consecutive tenses. It is not so much a question of 'tenses', but of 'clauses'. And it is more apposite to regard the linkings with *wa(y)-yiqṭol* and *wa-qaṭal* as expressions of *pragmatic discourse continuity* (see §1.2.6).[7] A *wa-V(X)* clause signals pragmatic continuity, and may, according to context, express thematic continuity, action continuity, and topics/participants continuity.[8] *Wa(y)-yiqṭol* (see §3), with short *yiqṭol* and normal *wa*, and the construction *wa-qaṭal* (see §6), are typical clause-types that signal discourse continuity in CBH.

A typical discontinuous type of clause, (*wa*)-*XV*, may signal the beginning of a literary unit, topicalisation of *X* or focus thereon, anteriority, simultaneity, background,[9] or elaboration. Discontinuity is a suitable term by which to unite these under a single heading (Hornkohl 2018, 49).[10]

Accordingly, Tenet 1 of Classical Hebrew text-linguistics should be reformulated in terms of continuity and discontinuity and without the assumption of a special 'consecutive *waw*' (Isaksson 2021a, 217); see Table 18.

Table 18: Tenet 1 (updated): The signalling of discourse continuity and discontinuity in CBH prose texts

Tenet 1 (updated): Pragmatic discourse continuity // discontinuity in affirmative clauses (prose texts)[11]
Tenet 1a. *wa-VX // wa-XV*, where *X* is not a simple negation[12] (see §7.2)
Tenet 1b. *wa-VX // Ø-(X)V*. This includes *Ø-qaṭal* (see §7.3)
Tenet 1c. *wa-VX // (wa)-(X)-qoṭel*[13] (see §7.4)
Tenet 1d. *wa-VX // (wa)-XØ*. Linking with a verbless clause[14] (see §7.5)
Tenet 1e. The imperfective interruption[15] (see §7.6)

In the updated Tenet 1 formula (a–e), there is no boldface ***wa***. As is evident from Table 18, the traditional assumption of a special 'consecutive' *wa* would imply a *redundancy* in the signalling of pragmatic continuity (cf. Hornkohl 2018, 33). The fundamental alternation between discourse continuity and discourse discontinuity already *has* a signal, the switch from a *wa-VX* clause-type to a discontinuity clause-type. The hypothesis of a special 'consecutive' ***wa*** is unwarranted. A simple assumption of one natural language connective *wa* is enough to clarify the linguistic reality behind *wa* in the system of consecutive tenses (see §2.1; Isaksson 2021, 220f.).

Tenet 1 concerns various ways of coding interruptions (discontinuity) in a main line of continuity clauses, including interruption by way of aspectual contrast (1e). But a discontinuity clause of the type 1a–1d can also be the first in a main line which is then followed by continuity clauses. A second tenet must describe the many cases when a discontinuity clause starts a new literary unit, in which case it also signals a break with the preceding discourse unit.[16] The semantic functions of this type of macro-syntactic marking, a new literary unit or paragraph (often with a focused element), are pragmatically determined.[17]

This kind of discontinuity may either signal a semantic connection with the preceding context (2a: *wa-XV*, 2c: *wa-(X)-qoṭel*, or 2d: *wa-XØ*) or the absence of such a signal (2b: *Ø-(X)V*, 2c: *Ø-(X)-qoṭel*, or 2d: *Ø-XØ*).[18] See Table 19.

Table 19: Tenets 2a–d

Tenet 2
Tenet 2a. // *wa-XV* + (1a, 1b, 1c, or 1d) + *wa-VX*, where *X* is not a simple negation. Topic/focus and a new literary unit. With signal of backward connection (see §7.7)
Tenet 2b. // *Ø-(X)V* + (1a, 1b, 1c, or 1d) + *wa-VX*. Topic/focus and a new literary unit. Without signal of backward connection (see §7.8)
Tenet 2c. // *(wa)-(X)-qoṭel* + (1a, 1b, 1c, or 1d) + *wa-VX*. Topic/focus and a new literary unit with initial *qoṭel* clause. With or without signal of backward connection (see §7.9)
Tenet 2d. // *(wa)-XØ* + (1a, 1b, 1c, or 1d) + *wa-VX*. New literary unit with initial verbless clause. With or without signal of backward connection (see §7.10)

In Table 19, clause-types that may optionally be added as part of the discontinuous clause complex are put within parentheses. The initial // in 2a–d indicates that the discontinuity is signalled in relation to the clauses (if any) that precede the new literary unit. The clauses within parentheses (1a, 1b, 1c, or 1d) in 2a–d indicate that some of the typical discontinuity clauses (1a, 1b, 1c, 1d) can be inserted at the beginning of a new paragraph before the main line is resumed by a continuity clause (type *wa-VX*).[19]

The backward connection signal in Tenet 2a, and sometimes in 2c and 2d, means that the first *wa* (in *wa-XV*, *wa-(X)-qoṭel*, or *wa-XØ*) is a discourse marker (not a clausal connective), signalling a certain semantic contextual connection to the preceding clauses (Miller 1999, 168).

In Tenets 2a–b, the initial *wa-XV* or *Ø-XV* can be a mainline clause in spite of its discontinuity signal (§§7.7.1, 7.8.1). In other pragmatic contexts, the initial *(wa)-XV* is a background clause (§§7.7.2, 7.8.2). In some shorter paragraphs, especially in direct speech, there is no continuity clause (of the type *wa-VX*), which means that at least one discontinuity clause forms a mainline by itself and is foregrounded in that quotation.[20] *Qoṭel* clauses (§7.9) and *XØ* clauses (§7.10) may also be foregrounded when initiating a new paragraph, especially when introduced by the deictic particle *hinnē*.[21]

As Tenet 1 indicates, the normal *wa* with immediately following finite verb is the decisive signal of discourse continuity in affirmative clauses. This observation enables us to formulate another tenet.

> **Tenet 3 of CBH text-linguistics**: The clause-type *wa-V(X)* in CBH prose texts, where *V* is a finite verb, signals pragmatic discourse continuity in relation to corresponding clauses (see §7.11).[22]

In Tenet 3, *wa* is necessary[23] and *V* is necessary.[24] A *wa-V(X)* clause signals pragmatic continuity. No clausal element can be inserted between *wa* and *V*, because this would make the clause signal discontinuity. In this text-linguistic sense, it is pertinent to speak of an inseparable union between *wa* and the verb in discourse-continuity clauses. The 'inseparable union' in the syntagms *wa(y)-yiqṭol* and *wa-qaṭal* results from their functions as markers of discourse continuity and was a reality on the textual level in CBH (but not on the morphological level). Specifically, *wa(y)-yiqṭol* and *wa-qaṭal* are not 'tenses', they are clause-types (Petersson 2019, 250).

In Tenet 1a, it is stipulated that the initial *X* element in the finite discontinuity clauses is not a simple negation (in my corpus, *lō* or *ʾal*).[25] A simple negation between *wa* and the verb creates no break in the continuity.[26] This enables us to formulate a tenet of continuity for negated clauses.

> **Tenet 4 of CBH text-linguistics**: The negated clause-type *wa-NEG-V(X)* in CBH prose texts, where *V* is a finite verb, signals discourse continuity in relation to corresponding clauses. Here *NEG* may be *lō* or *ʾal* depending on the verbal morpheme that is negated (see §7.12).[27]

Tenets 1–3 are reformulations of observations that have been put forward now and then in the text-linguistic literature. Only the terminology is new, and with it the fundamental insight that there is only one *wa* in the verbal syntax, and no consecutive 'tenses', only clauses that are linked in continuity or discontinuity. This is the theme of this chapter. The remaining subsections will elaborate and exemplify and explain in detail the various cases of Tenets 1–4.

Since this book is mainly concerned with the linguistic reality behind the consecutive tenses, our emphasis lies on the continuity clause-types *wa(y)-yiqṭol* and *wa-qaṭal*. However, jussive *wa-yiqṭol(Ø)* with *wa-ʾal-yiqṭol(Ø)* and imperative *wa-IMP* with *wa-ʾal-yiqṭol(Ø)* probably also signal continuity and function according to Tenet 3 and Tenet 4, and deserve a full description (cf. §§7.11–12).[28] For an overview with emphasis on *wa-qaṭal*, see §6.4.

7.2. Tenet 1a: *Wa-VX // Wa-XV*

Tenet 1a refers to the case when a long or short sequence of continuity clauses (type *wa-VX*) is interrupted by a discontinuity clause with initial conjunction *wa*, where *X* is not merely a negation (see Table 18). Tenet 1a also presupposes Tenet 3: a continuity affirmative clause starts with *wa*, directly followed by the finite verb form, *wa-V(X)*, where the *X*, a clausal constituent, is optional. Finally, we presuppose also Tenet 4, which means that the *X* in the discontinuity clause *wa-XV* is not a simple negation (in which case the clause would signal continuity).[29]

7.2.1. Interruption Type *Wa(y)-yiqṭol // Wa-X-qaṭal*

A linking of the type *wa(y)-yiqṭol* + *wa-X-qaṭal* most often expresses contrast, complementary action(s), or background. It may describe a temporal succession only when *X* is an explicitly temporal adverb. The meanings of this linking that I have detected in the corpus are displayed in Table 20.

Table 20: The semantics of the *wa(y)-yiqṭol* + *wa-X-qaṭal* linking

Contrast	45
Complementary action	51
Background	48
Elaboration	11
Content of perception	12
Temporal succession	4
Focal result[30]	1
Temporal: relative time[31]	1
Enumeration of actions[32]	1
Unclear[33]	1
Total	**175**

Of the 175 registered cases in my database, about one quarter express a contrast, in which "the information conveyed by the Focal clause contrasts with that in the Supporting clause, and may be surprising in view of it" (Dixon 2009, 28). A simple example with *wa(y)-yiqṭol* clauses interrupted by focal *wa-X-qaṭal* expressing contrast is (1):

(1) *wa(y)-yiqṭol* + *wa(y)-yiqṭol* + [4]***wa-X-qaṭal*** + *wa(y)-yiqṭol* + [5]***wa-X-qaṭal*** + *wa(y)-yiqṭol* + *wa(y)-yiqṭol*

וַיְהִי מִקֵּץ יָמִים וַיָּבֵא קַיִן מִפְּרִי הָאֲדָמָה מִנְחָה לַיהוָה׃ 4 **וְהֶבֶל הֵבִיא** גַם־הוּא
מִבְּכֹרוֹת צֹאנוֹ וּמֵחֶלְבֵהֶן וַיִּשַׁע יְהוָה אֶל־הֶבֶל וְאֶל־מִנְחָתוֹ׃ 5 **וְאֶל־קַיִן וְאֶל־**
מִנְחָתוֹ לֹא שָׁעָה וַיִּחַר לְקַיִן מְאֹד וַיִּפְּלוּ פָּנָיו׃

'After some time Cain brought some of the fruit of the ground for an offering to the LORD. [4]**But Abel brought** some of the firstborn of his flock—even the fattest of them. And the LORD was pleased with Abel and his offering, [5]**but with Cain and his offering he was not pleased**. So Cain became very angry, and his expression was downcast.' (Gen. 4.3–5)

In (1), the core of the narration is expressed by *wa(y)-yiqṭol* clauses (Tenet 3). The first interrupting *wa-X-qaṭal* clause describes a *contrasting* action: the *X* (הֶ֥בֶל) is in focal position and the information conveyed by this focal clause contrasts with that provided in the preceding *wa(y)-yiqṭol* clauses describing Cain's offering. As is often the case, the contrasting action (of Abel) is surprising in view of what Cain does. There is no signal of sequentiality between the actions of Cain and Abel. They are foregrounded and possibly performed at the same time (Cook 2012, 296f.). But the offering of Abel is different, which surprises the listener. The second *wa-X-qaṭal* in (1) is also a contrast: the Lord was not pleased with Cain's offering, though the preceding *wa(y)-yiqṭol* (וַיִּ֣שַׁע) clause stated that he was pleased with Abel's—a new surprise. The last two *wa(y)-yiqṭol* are temporally sequential.[34]

Very often, *wa(y)-yiqṭol* + *wa-X-qaṭal* describe complementary actions. The events are expected rather than surprising. But there is a polarity in which the focused elements and/or their actions form a completed whole. An example is (2):

(2) *wa(y)-yiqṭol* + *wa(y)-yiqṭol!* + *wa-X-qaṭal*

וַיִּפֹּ֛ל עַל־צַוְּארֵ֥י בִנְיָמִֽן־אָחִ֖יו וַיֵּ֑בְךְּ וּבִנְיָמִ֔ן בָּכָ֖ה עַל־צַוָּארָֽיו׃

'Then he threw himself on the neck of his brother Benjamin and wept, and Benjamin wept on his neck.' (Gen. 45.14)

In (2), two simultaneous foregrounded events are described (Cook 2012, 296). There is a polarity between Joseph and Benjamin, but no surprise. The two actions instead form a completed whole, and the linking expresses mutuality.[35]

Another important function of a *wa(y)-yiqṭol* + *wa-X-qaṭal* linking is to code background. Background must be distinguished from circumstantial clauses, which are semantically embedded in the main clause and usually refer directly to a constituent in the main clause. A background description is a more independent section in the text and often consists of historical or geographical information (see §2.3.3). Sometimes *qaṭal* in the background clause expresses a pluperfect meaning, as in (3):

(3) *wa(y)-yiqṭol* + *"…"* + [8]*wa-X-qaṭal*

וַיֹּ֣אמֶר יְהוָ֗ה אֶמְחֶ֨ה אֶת־הָאָדָ֤ם «אֲשֶׁר־בָּרָ֨אתִי֙» מֵעַל֙ פְּנֵ֣י הָֽאֲדָמָ֔ה מֵֽאָדָם֙ עַד־
בְּהֵמָ֔ה עַד־רֶ֖מֶשׂ וְעַד־ע֣וֹף הַשָּׁמָ֑יִם כִּ֥י נִחַ֖מְתִּי כִּ֥י עֲשִׂיתִֽם׃ וְנֹ֕חַ מָ֥צָא חֵ֖ן בְּעֵינֵ֥י
יְהוָֽה׃ פ

'So the LORD said, "I will wipe humankind, whom I have created, from the face of the earth—everything from humankind to animals, including creatures that move on the ground and birds of the air, for I regret that I have made them." [8]But Noah had found favor in the sight of the LORD.' (Gen. 6.7f., 6.8 translated after Westermann 1976, 522)

In (3), at the end of a narrative unit, the listener receives an anticipating piece of information about one man amongst humankind, who will become the principal character in the following story. An example of background as topographical information is (4):

(4) *wa(y)-yiqṭol!* + *wa-X-qaṭal* + *wa-X-qaṭal*

וַיַּשֵּׂ֥ג לָבָ֖ן אֶֽת־יַעֲקֹ֑ב וְיַעֲקֹ֗ב תָּקַ֤ע אֶֽת־אָהֳלוֹ֙ בָּהָ֔ר וְלָבָ֛ן תָּקַ֥ע אֶת־אֶחָ֖יו בְּהַ֥ר
הַגִּלְעָֽד׃

'And Laban overtook Jacob. Now Jacob had pitched his tent in the hill country, and Laban with his kinsmen pitched tents in the hill country of Gilead.' (Gen. 31.25)

In (4), with two *wa-X-qaṭal* clauses, the reader is informed of the geographical situation when Laban overtakes Jacob. The first *qaṭal* has a pluperfect meaning (Hornkohl 2018, 45). The second *qaṭal* concerns the pitching of the arriving Laban and should probably be interpreted as past perfective (*pace* Westermann 1981, 594).[36]

But a *wa(y)-yiqṭol* + *wa-X-qaṭal* linking also often expresses an elaboration, where the second clause adds additional information about the event in the first clause (cf. Dixon 2009, 27). Elaborations can be coded by a discourse-continuity clause (see §2.3.1), but when *wa-X-qaṭal* is used, the constituent *X* is focal. An example is (5):

(5) *wa(y)-yiqṭol* + *wa-X-qaṭal*

וַיַּסֵּ֨ב אֱלֹהִ֧ים ׀ אֶת־הָעָ֛ם דֶּ֥רֶךְ הַמִּדְבָּ֖ר יַם־ס֑וּף וַחֲמֻשִׁ֛ים עָל֥וּ בְנֵֽי־יִשְׂרָאֵ֖ל מֵאֶ֥רֶץ מִצְרָֽיִם׃

'God led the people by a roundabout route, through the desert by the Sea of Suf. The people of Israel went up from the land of Egypt fully armed.' (Exod. 13.18)

The adverb 'fully armed' (חֲמֻשִׁים) is placed first in the second clause and is focal. This clause adds further information about the event in the first clause, Israel's going out from Egypt.[37]

The clause-type *wa-hinnē-qaṭal* is a special case. It expresses the content or result of a perception verb in the *wa(y)-yiqṭol* clause. It functions semantically as a complement clause, as in (6):

(6) *wa(y)-yiqṭol!* + *wa-hinnē-qaṭal*

וַיַּ֧רְא אֱלֹהִ֛ים אֶת־הָאָ֖רֶץ וְהִנֵּ֣ה נִשְׁחָ֑תָה

'God saw how corrupt the earth had become' (Gen. 6.12)

In (6), the *wa-hinnē-qaṭal* clause functions as the complement of a verb of seeing and observation. But sometimes the perception verb in the first clause is understood, as in (7):

(7) *wa(y)-yiqṭol!* + *wa(y)-yiqṭol* + *wa-hinnē-qaṭal*

וַיָּשֶׁב יָדוֹ אֶל־חֵיקוֹ וַיּוֹצִאָהּ מֵחֵיקוֹ וְהִנֵּה־שָׁבָה כִּבְשָׂרוֹ׃

‘So he put his hand back inside his cloak, and he took it out again, and it was restored like the rest of his flesh.’ (Exod. 4.7)

In (7), the perception verb is only understood, so that the *wa-hinnē-qaṭal* clause alone describes the content of the impression.[38]

If a *wa-X-qaṭal* is to express temporal succession, an explicit temporal adverb is used, as in (8):

(8) *wa(y)-yiqṭol* + *wa(y)-yiqṭol* + *wa(y)-yiqṭol* + *wa(y)-yiqṭol* + [22]***wa-ADV-qaṭal***

וַיִּתְחַטְּאוּ הַלְוִיִּם וַיְכַבְּסוּ בִּגְדֵיהֶם וַיָּנֶף אַהֲרֹן אֹתָם תְּנוּפָה לִפְנֵי יְהוָה וַיְכַפֵּר עֲלֵיהֶם אַהֲרֹן לְטַהֲרָם׃ **וְאַחֲרֵי־כֵן בָּאוּ** הַלְוִיִּם לַעֲבֹד אֶת־עֲבֹדָתָם בְּאֹהֶל מוֹעֵד לִפְנֵי אַהֲרֹן וְלִפְנֵי בָנָיו

‘The Levites purified themselves and washed their clothing; then Aaron presented them like a wave offering before the LORD, and Aaron made atonement for them to purify them. [22]**Only after this** the Levites **went in** to do their work in the tent of meeting before Aaron and before his sons.’ (Num. 8.21f.)

The temporal succession expressed by the *wa-ADV-qaṭal* (וְאַחֲרֵי־כֵן בָּאוּ) in (8) has special emphasis. It is not just the default temporal succession of a continuity clause (like *wa(y)-yiqṭol*); rather, the preceding actions described by *wa(y)-yiqṭol* clauses are a necessary condition for the next action described by the *wa-ADV-qaṭal* clause.[39]

7.2.2. Interruption Type *Wa-qaṭal // Wa-X-yiqṭol(u)*

See §6.12.

7.3. Tenet 1b: *Wa-VX // Ø-(X)V*

In a main line of continuity clauses, an asyndetic clause with a finite verbal predicate that is not a participle may signal a rich variety of discontinuities (see Tables 21–23). This is demonstrated in the present section.[40]

7.3.1. Interruption Type *Wa(y)-yiqṭol // Ø-X-qaṭal*

In this type of interruption, the discontinuity clause is asyndetic with a finite verbal predicate, *qaṭal*. *X* may be a simple negation (*lō*) or it may contain a focused clausal constituent *X* positioned before the verb. The meanings of the linking that are detected in my database are displayed in Table 21.

Table 21: The semantics of the *wa(y)-yiqṭol* + *Ø-X-qaṭal* linking

Elaboration	44
Summary	11
Same-event addition	6
Background	11
Editorial comment	14
Contrast	5
Peak	1
Complementary action[41]	1
Unclear[42]	2
Total	**95**

Out of the 95 registered examples in the corpus[43] of the linking *wa(y)-yiqṭol* + *Ø-X-qaṭal*, about half are cases of elaboration. An elaboration supplies more details with fuller information and has focus (a 'focal clause'; Dixon 2009, 6). Thus if *wa(y)-yiqṭol* is foregrounded as part of the main line, an elaboration must be analysed as foregrounded as well. One of the examples exhibits two elaborative *Ø-X-qaṭal* clauses:

(9) *wa(y)-yiqṭol* + *Ø-PrP-qaṭal* + *Ø-O.noun-qaṭal*

וַיִּבְרָ֨א אֱלֹהִ֤ים׀ אֶת־הָֽאָדָם֙ בְּצַלְמ֔וֹ בְּצֶ֥לֶם אֱלֹהִ֖ים בָּרָ֣א אֹת֑וֹ זָכָ֥ר וּנְקֵבָ֖ה בָּרָ֥א אֹתָֽם׃

'God created humankind in his own image, in the image of God he created them, male and female he created them.' (Gen. 1.27)

In (9), the two *qaṭal* clauses repeat with different word order the same action as in the initial *wa(y)-yiqṭol* clause and supply further details about this event: God created them male and female.[44]

There are also examples of *wa(y)-yiqṭol* + *Ø-X-qaṭal* expressing a summary. In this case, the *qaṭal* clause contains less detail than the main-line *wa(y)-yiqṭol*, which has focus. I consider a summary to be foregrounded also, as in (10):[45]

(10) *wa(y)-yiqṭol-kə-REL-qaṭal* + *Ø-ADV-qaṭal*

וַיַּ֖עַשׂ נֹ֑חַ כְּ֠כֹל אֲשֶׁ֨ר צִוָּ֥ה אֹת֛וֹ אֱלֹהִ֖ים כֵּ֥ן עָשָֽׂה׃

'And Noah did all that God commanded him. Thus he did.' (Gen. 6.22)

The case of same-event addition is more interesting than just a repetition with other or similar words (see §2.3.4). As an elaboration, it involves two clauses that "describe different aspects of a single event" (Dixon 2009, 27). A canonical English instance is *You are together with me; (and) as for me, I am together with you* (Dixon 2009, 27). I have identified six cases of same-event addition coded by the *wa(y)-yiqṭol* + *Ø-X-qaṭal* linking in my corpus, one of which is (11):

(11) *wa(y)-yiqṭol* + *Ø-S.noun-qaṭal*

וַיִּגְוַ֞ע כָּל־בָּשָׂ֣ר ׀ הָֽרֹמֵ֣שׂ עַל־הָאָ֗רֶץ בָּעֹוף֙ וּבַבְּהֵמָה֙ וּבַ֣חַיָּ֔ה וּבְכָל־הַשֶּׁ֖רֶץ הַשֹּׁרֵ֣ץ עַל־הָאָ֑רֶץ וְכֹ֖ל הָאָדָֽם׃ כֹּ֡ל אֲשֶׁר֩ נִשְׁמַת־ר֨וּחַ חַיִּ֜ים בְּאַפָּ֗יו מִכֹּ֛ל אֲשֶׁ֥ר בֶּחָֽרָבָ֖ה מֵֽתוּ׃

'And all living things that moved on the earth died, including the birds, domestic animals, wild animals, all the creatures that swarm over the earth, and all humankind. [22]Everything on dry land that had the breath of life in its nostrils died.' (Gen. 7.21f.)

In (11), the two clauses describe different aspects of the extinction of all living creatures on the earth. In English, the focal clause of a same-event addition is sometimes introduces by *moreover* (Dixon 2009, 43). This type of semantics is also found in CBH, as is exemplified in (12):

(12) *wa(y)-yiqṭol* + *wa(y)-yiqṭol* + *Ø-lō-qaṭal*

וַיִּשָּׂא֙ אֶת־הָ֣אַרְבֶּ֔ה וַיִּתְקָעֵ֖הוּ יָ֣מָּה סּ֑וּף לֹ֤א נִשְׁאַר֙ אַרְבֶּ֣ה אֶחָ֔ד בְּכֹ֖ל גְּב֥וּל מִצְרָֽיִם׃

'and it (the wind) picked up the locusts and blew them into the Red Sea. Not even one locust remained in all the territory of Egypt.' (Exod. 10.19)

In (12), the *qaṭal* clause is focal with an implicit *moreover*. It describes another aspect of the same event, blowing the locusts into the Red Sea.[46]

When *qaṭal* clauses are negated, the perfective aspect is neutralised, and they can be used to express circumstantial meanings, as in (13):

(13) *PREP-VN* + *wa(y)-yiqṭol* + ***Ø-O.noun-lō-qaṭal*** + ***wa-O.noun-lō-qaṭal***

בַּעֲלֹתִ֣י הָהָ֗רָה לָקַ֜חַת לוּחֹ֤ת הָאֲבָנִים֙ לוּחֹ֣ת הַבְּרִ֔ית אֲשֶׁר־כָּרַ֥ת יְהוָ֖ה עִמָּכֶ֑ם
וָאֵשֵׁ֣ב בָּהָ֗ר אַרְבָּעִ֥ים יוֹם֙ וְאַרְבָּעִ֣ים לַ֔יְלָה **לֶ֚חֶם לֹ֣א אָכַ֔לְתִּי וּמַ֖יִם לֹ֥א שָׁתִֽיתִי׃**

'When I went up the mountain to receive the stone tablets, the tablets of the covenant that the LORD made with you, I remained there forty days and nights, **eating and drinking nothing**.' (Deut. 9.9, NET, my emphasis)

The asyndetic *qaṭal* clauses are certainly simultaneous with the action in the *wa(y)-yiqṭol* clause, and their relational meaning (the semantics of the linking) comes close to that of circumstantial clauses, as can be seen in the New English Translation.[47]

A *wa(y)-yiqṭol* + *Ø-X-qaṭal* linking can also be used to express background, a comment by the narrator, or even a more specific comment by the editor. The distinction between these is not always possible to uphold and the borderline is diffuse. A piece of information supplied by the narrator is found in (14):

(14) *wa(y)-yiqṭol* + [10]*Ø-NP-REL-qaṭal* + *Ø-ADV-qaṭal*[48]

וַיִּקְבְּר֣וּ אֹת֗וֹ יִצְחָ֤ק וְיִשְׁמָעֵאל֙ בָּנָ֔יו אֶל־מְעָרַ֖ת הַמַּכְפֵּלָ֑ה אֶל־שְׂדֵ֞ה עֶפְרֹ֤ן בֶּן־
צֹ֙חַר֙ הַֽחִתִּ֔י אֲשֶׁ֖ר עַל־פְּנֵ֥י מַמְרֵֽא׃ הַשָּׂדֶ֛ה אֲשֶׁר־קָנָ֥ה אַבְרָהָ֖ם מֵאֵ֣ת בְּנֵי־חֵ֑ת
שָׁ֛מָּה קֻבַּ֥ר אַבְרָהָ֖ם וְשָׂרָ֥ה אִשְׁתּֽוֹ׃

‘His sons Isaac and Ishmael buried him in the cave of Machpelah near Mamre, in the field of Ephron the son of Zohar, the Hittite. [10]The field that Abraham had purchased from the sons of Heth, there Abraham was buried with his wife Sarah.’ (Gen. 25.9f.)

In (14), the *Ø-ADV-qaṭal* clause is the narrator’s reminder that this was the field that Abraham had already purchased (Westermann 1981, 486).[49]

An example of a comment by the editor(s) is (15):

(15) *wa(y)-yiqṭol + Ø-ADV-qaṭal*

וַיַּעֲלוּ וַיַּחֲנוּ בְּקִרְיַת יְעָרִים בִּיהוּדָה עַל־כֵּן קָרְאוּ לַמָּקוֹם הַהוּא מַחֲנֵה־דָן עַד הַיּוֹם הַזֶּה הִנֵּה אַחֲרֵי קִרְיַת יְעָרִים׃

‘They went up and camped in Kiriath Jearim in Judah. (That is why that place is called Camp of Dan to this very day. It is west of Kiriath Jearim.)’ (Judg. 18.12)

(15) supplies an example of a “late etiological and extranarrative note” (Boling 1975, 264).[50]

In a few examples, *wa(y)-yiqṭol + Ø-X-qaṭal* shows a contrastive addition, in which case the information conveyed by the second clause contrasts with that provided in the first clause (Dixon 2009, 28), as in (16):

(16) *wa(y)-yiqṭol + wa-O.noun-qaṭal + wa-O.noun-qaṭal +* [26]***Ø-raq-PrP-lō-qaṭal***

וַיַּךְ הַבָּרָד בְּכָל־אֶרֶץ מִצְרַיִם אֵת כָּל־אֲשֶׁר בַּשָּׂדֶה מֵאָדָם וְעַד־בְּהֵמָה וְאֵת כָּל־עֵשֶׂב הַשָּׂדֶה הִכָּה הַבָּרָד וְאֶת־כָּל־עֵץ הַשָּׂדֶה שִׁבֵּר׃ **רַק בְּאֶרֶץ גֹּשֶׁן** אֲשֶׁר־שָׁם בְּנֵי יִשְׂרָאֵל **לֹא הָיָה בָּרָד׃**

> 'The hail struck everything in the open fields, both people and animals, throughout all the land of Egypt. The hail struck everything that grows in the field, and it broke all the trees of the field to pieces. [26]**Only in the land of Goshen**, where the Israelites lived, **was there no hail**. (Exod. 9.25f.)

In (16), the *qaṭal* clause describes the surprising contrast that there was no hail in the land of Goshen, where the Israelites lived.[51]

An instance of a peak expressed by the linking *wa(y)-yiqṭol* + *Ø-X-qaṭal* is (17):

(17) *wa(y)-yiqṭol* + *wa-S.noun-qaṭal* + ***Ø-S.noun-qaṭal*** + ***wa-S.noun-qaṭal***

> וַיֵּ֨ט מֹשֶׁ֣ה אֶת־מַטֵּהוּ֮ עַל־אֶ֣רֶץ מִצְרַיִם֒ וַֽיהוָ֗ה נִהַ֤ג ר֙וּחַ קָדִים֙ בָּאָ֔רֶץ כָּל־הַיּ֥וֹם הַה֖וּא וְכָל־הַלָּ֑יְלָה **הַבֹּ֣קֶר הָיָ֔ה וְר֙וּחַ֙ הַקָּדִ֔ים נָשָׂ֖א אֶת־הָאַרְבֶּֽה׃**
>
> 'So Moses extended his staff over the land of Egypt, and the LORD brought an east wind on the land all that day and all night. **Morning was, and the east wind had already carried the locusts.**' (Exod. 10.13)

The *Ø-X-qaṭal* with copula verb is not an ordinary temporal expression. It cannot be translated by 'When there was morning', or 'In the morning'. As it stands, it has a dramatic effect on the reader, as if being there in the morning and seeing the locusts carried away (NET note).

7.3.2. Interruption Type *Wa-qaṭal // Ø-X-yiqṭol(u)*

In this type of linking, the dominant meanings are various types of elaborations. It seems that asyndesis is especially fitting for the expression of elaboration. See Table 22.

Table 22: The semantics of the *wa-qaṭal* + *Ø-X-yiqṭol* linking

Elaboration (no 'echo')	39
Elaboration ('echoing')	34
Same-event addition	3
Contrast	2
Explanation (comment)	1
Complement[52]	1
Apodosis[53]	2
Asyndetic relative clause[54]	2
Total	**84**

While one type of elaboration means that the second clause "echoes the first" with more details, another just describes more details about the action or state in the first clause (Dixon 2009). In practically all instances of *wa-qaṭal* + *Ø-X-yiqṭol(u)* linking, the second clause describes the same event (or state) as the first clause.

Since instructions and legal matter are prominent text-types in the corpus, the individual clauses in this type of linking express mainly various shades of obligation (70 out of 84 cases).[55]

An example of an elaboration where the second clause does not 'echo' the first, but just gives more details about the same event, is (18):

(18) *wa-qaṭal* + *Ø-lō-yiqṭol(u)!*

וְקַצֹּתָ֖ה אֶת־כַּפָּ֑הּ לֹ֥א תָח֖וֹס עֵינֶֽךָ׃

'then you must cut off her hand; your eye shall have no pity.' (Deut. 25.12)

In (18), the second clause describes in more detail how the action put forward as an obligation in the first clause is to be performed:

having no pity while cutting off her hand. The meaning of both clauses is obligation.[56]

Sometimes *Ø-X-yiqṭol(u)* clauses exhibit different semantics in relation to a preceding *wa-qaṭal*, as in (19):

(19) *wa-qaṭal + Ø-O.noun-yiqṭol(u) + Ø-S.noun-yiqṭol(u)*

וְעָשִׂיתָ מְנֹרַת זָהָב טָהוֹר מִקְשָׁה תֵּעָשֶׂה הַמְּנוֹרָה יְרֵכָהּ וְקָנָהּ גְּבִיעֶיהָ כַּפְתֹּרֶיהָ וּפְרָחֶיהָ מִמֶּנָּה יִהְיוּ׃

'You are to make a lampstand of pure gold. The lampstand is to be made of hammered metal; its base and its shaft, its cups, its buds, and its blossoms are to be from the same piece.' (Exod. 25.31)

In (19), the first *Ø-X-yiqṭol(u)* clause echoes the *wa-qaṭal*, adding a detail: hammered metal. The second *Ø-X-yiqṭol(u)* clause does not echo the *wa-qaṭal*, but describes a different aspect of the same action: when making the lampstand, its blossoms are to be from the same piece.

Another example of *wa-qaṭal + Ø-X-yiqṭol(u)* expressing elaboration with 'echoing' is (20):

(20) *wa-qaṭal + Ø-O.noun-yiqṭol(u)*

וְאָכְלוּ אֶת־הַבָּשָׂר בַּלַּיְלָה הַזֶּה צְלִי־אֵשׁ וּמַצּוֹת עַל־מְרֹרִים יֹאכְלֻהוּ׃

'They will eat the meat the same night; they will eat it roasted over the fire with bread made without yeast and with bitter herbs.' (Exod. 12.8)

In (20), the *yiqṭol(u)* clause echoes the first, and supplies more details about the event.[57]

A same-event addition with future meaning is exemplified in (21):

(21) *wa-qaṭal* + *wa-qaṭal* + *Ø-S.noun-yiqṭol(u)*

וְקִדַּשְׁתָּ֣ אֹתָ֔ם וְהָי֖וּ קֹ֣דֶשׁ קָֽדָשִׁ֑ים **כָּל־הַנֹּגֵ֥עַ בָּהֶ֖ם יִקְדָּֽשׁ׃**

‘You are to sanctify them, and they will be most holy; **anything that touches them will be holy**.’ (Exod. 30.29)

In (21), the meaning is future in the second and third clauses. The semantics of the linking *wa-qaṭal* + *Ø-S.noun-yiqṭol(u)* are same-event addition: the *yiqṭol(u)* clause describes another aspect of the same state (being most holy): anything that touches them will be holy.[58]

In a few instances, *wa-qaṭal* + *Ø-X-yiqṭol(u)* describes a contrast addition (Dixon 2009, 28). The registered instances are both signalled by an initial *raq* ‘only, but’. This is illustrated in (22):

(22) *wa-qaṭal* + *Ø-raq-PrP-yiqṭol(u)*

וְסָר֣וּ הַֽ֝צְפַרְדְּעִ֗ים מִמְּךָ֙ וּמִבָּ֣תֶּ֔יךָ וּמֵעֲבָדֶ֖יךָ וּמֵעַמֶּ֑ךָ רַ֥ק בַּיְאֹ֖ר תִּשָּׁאַֽרְנָה׃

‘The frogs will depart from you, your houses, your servants, and your people; they will be left only in the Nile.’ (Exod. 8.7)

In (22), the *Ø-X-yiqṭol(u)* describes an exceptional and possibly surprising contrast with the event in the *wa-qaṭal* clause: the frogs will not depart from the Nile. In both clauses, the temporal reference is future.[59]

A *wa-qaṭal* + *Ø-X-yiqṭol(u)* may also, but rarely, express an explanation of or comment on previous commands, as in (23):

(23) *wa-qaṭal* + ***Ø-O.noun-yiqṭol(u)!***

וְעָשִׂ֣יתָ אֹת֗וֹ שֶׁ֚מֶן מִשְׁחַת־קֹ֔דֶשׁ רֹ֥קַח מִרְקַ֖חַת מַעֲשֵׂ֣ה רֹקֵ֑חַ **שֶׁ֥מֶן מִשְׁחַת־קֹ֖דֶשׁ יִהְיֶֽה׃**

'You are to make this into a sacred anointing oil, a scented blend, the work of a perfumer. **It will be sacred anointing oil.**' (Exod. 30.25)

The *Ø-X-yiqṭol(u)* in (23) is probably not a command but an explanation of the purpose and intended use of the scented blend.

7.3.3. *Ø-qaṭal* as Discontinuity Clause

A *Ø-qaṭal* clause is a relatively infrequent phenomenon in CBH, represented by 62 instances (records) in my database; see Table 23. This clause-type will be examined in this section.

Table 23: The semantics of the *Ø-qaṭal*

Paragraph beginning	27
Elaboration ('echoing')	8
Elaboration (no echo)	4
Same-event addition	2
Complement	4
Parenthesis	1
Peak	2
Protasis	1
Apodosis	6
Topic–comment	4
Asyndetic relative clause	3
Total	**62**

Ø-qaṭal may be used as a main-line (foreground) clause; it can begin a new paragraph (§7.3.3.1), or it can be linked to a preceding main clause (§7.3.3.2). In addition, it may constitute an asyndetic relative clause (§7.3.3.4), express a peak in narration, code a parenthesis in speech, function as apodosis (§7.3.3.3) or (once) as protasis. What unites all these uses is that it is a discontinuity clause (Tenet 3) with the expected meanings of a *qaṭal* verbal morpheme (see §5).

I do not include in this section the five cases of virtual Ø-*qaṭal* in thetic cleft sentences (Khan 2019, 15–18), of which I quote only one example here:[60]

(24) *wayhī-PrP-PrP* + **Ø-qaṭal* (better: *FOCUS-PrP-PrP-qaṭal*)

וַֽיְהִי בְּאַחַת וְשֵׁשׁ־מֵאוֹת שָׁנָה בָּרִאשׁוֹן בְּאֶחָד לַחֹדֶשׁ חָרְבוּ הַמַּיִם מֵעַל הָאָרֶץ

'In the six hundred and first year, in the first day of the first month, the waters had dried up from the earth.' (Gen. 8.13)

In (24), *wayhī* is a focus marker, which has developed from the matrix verbal copula clause in CBH. The main informative element in the construction is the *qaṭal* morpheme (חָרְבוּ). As it is used in CBH, the construction exhibits a monoclausal syntax, which has developed from a biclausal cleft construction. Such constructions are excluded in this section because the *qaṭal* clause is only virtually of the Ø-*qaṭal* type.[61]

7.3.3.1. Ø-*qaṭal* as Paragraph Beginning (*// Ø-qaṭal*)

Ø-*qaṭal* is used relatively frequently at the beginning of direct speech (27 × in my database), either in report or other uses (for example, performative). The simplest type of report is the single informative utterance, as in (25):

(25) *wa-X-qaṭal:* ***"Ø-qaṭal"***

וְהַקֹּל נִשְׁמַע בֵּית פַּרְעֹה לֵאמֹר **בָּאוּ אֲחֵי יוֹסֵף**

'Now the report was heard in the household of Pharaoh, "**Joseph's brothers have arrived.**"' (Gen. 45.16)

Example (25) is a proof that a main line (foreground) may consist of only one non-continuity clause.

But a report in direct speech starting with *Ø-qaṭal* can of course be continued by *wa(y)-yiqṭol* clause(s), as in (26):[62]

(26) *Ø-qaṭal* + *wa(y)-yiqṭol*

דִּבֶּר הָאִישׁ אֲדֹנֵי הָאָרֶץ אִתָּנוּ קָשׁוֹת וַיִּתֵּן אֹתָנוּ כִּמְרַגְּלִים אֶת־הָאָרֶץ׃

'The man, the lord of the land, spoke harshly to us, and took us to be spies of the land.' (Gen. 42.30)

Another frequent meaning of *Ø-qaṭal* at the beginning of an utterance is the performative, as in (27):

(27) *Ø-qaṭal*

הֲרִימֹתִי יָדִי אֶל־יְהוָה אֵל עֶלְיוֹן קֹנֵה שָׁמַיִם וָאָרֶץ׃

'I raise my hand to the LORD, the Most High God, Creator of heaven and earth, (and vow):' (Gen. 14.22)

In (27), a performative *qaṭal* expresses Abraham's oath to the king of Sodom (Cook 2012, 207 n. 46). The oath clearly has present time reference (Brockelmann 1908–13, II, §76b).

But present time reference is not confined to performative utterances; it is found also with stativic *Ø-qaṭal* starting a new paragraph, as in (28):

(28) *wa(y)-yiqṭol* + *wa(y)-yiqṭol* + "*Ø-qaṭal* + *CONJ-lō-qaṭal*"

וַיַּכֵּר יְהוּדָה וַיֹּאמֶר צָדְקָה מִמֶּנִּי כִּי־עַל־כֵּן לֹא־נְתַתִּיהָ לְשֵׁלָה בְנִי

'Judah recognised them and said, "She is more upright than I, because I did not give her to Shelah my son."' Gen. 38.26)

I conclude that *Ø-qaṭal* clauses in direct speech are a normal way of initiating paragraphs in CBH.[63]

7.3.3.2. Main Clause // *Ø-qaṭal*

This section treats the cases (21 ×) when *Ø-qaṭal* as a discontinuity clause is linked to a preceding main-line clause. The range of meanings expressed by this discontinuity is considerable: elaboration, same-event addition, complement, parenthesis, and even peak; see Table 23. A relatively frequent relational meaning is elaboration, as in (29):

(29) *Ø-X-qaṭal* + [19]*Ø-qaṭal*

בַּיּוֹם֙ הַשֵּׁנִ֔י הִקְרִ֖יב נְתַנְאֵ֣ל בֶּן־צוּעָ֑ר נְשִׂ֖יא יִשָּׂשכָֽר׃ הִקְרִ֨ב אֶת־קָרְבָּנ֜וֹ קַֽעֲרַת־
כֶּ֣סֶף אַחַ֗ת שְׁלֹשִׁ֣ים וּמֵאָה֮ מִשְׁקָלָהּ֒ מִזְרָ֤ק אֶחָד֙ כֶּ֔סֶף שִׁבְעִ֥ים שֶׁ֖קֶל בְּשֶׁ֣קֶל
הַקֹּ֑דֶשׁ שְׁנֵיהֶ֣ם ׀ מְלֵאִ֗ים סֹ֛לֶת בְּלוּלָ֥ה בַשֶּׁ֖מֶן לְמִנְחָֽה׃

'On the second day Nethanel son of Zuar, leader of Issachar, presented an offering. [19]He offered for his offering one silver platter weighing 130 shekels and one silver sprinkling bowl weighing 70 shekels, both according to the sanctuary shekel, each of them full of fine flour mixed with olive oil as a grain offering.' (Num. 7.18f.)

In (29), the first clause is clearly foregrounded and main-line. In the elaboration, the second clause echoes the first, adding additional information about the event (Dixon 2009, 27). This is what is exemplified in (29). The second *qaṭal* clause concerns the same offering as described already by the first *qaṭal* clause, but it adds further details about it: the silver platter, the bowls, the flour, the olive oil. The passage is a piece of narration, and both *qaṭal* morphemes express a past perfective meaning.[64]

An elaboration can also describe the same event or state without echoing the first clause. The clause supplies some more details about the event or state (cf. Dixon 2009, 27, 50). In some cases, this is expressed by a *Ø-qaṭal* clause, as in (30):

(30) *wa-XØ + Ø-qaṭal*

וְאַבְרָהָם וְשָׂרָה זְקֵנִים בָּאִים בַּיָּמִים חָדַל לִהְיוֹת לְשָׂרָה אֹרַח כַּנָּשִׁים׃

'Abraham and Sarah were old and advancing in years; the way of women had ceased to be with Sarah.' (Gen. 18.11)

(30) is part of a background complex. Abraham and Sarah were old. Another detail in this situation was that Sarah had long since passed menopause. This is expressed by the *Ø-qaṭal* clause, which is semantically related to the preceding verbless clause. The *Ø-qaṭal* does not echo the fact expressed by *XØ*, but it supplies more detail about this state.

An example of same-event addition is (31):

(31) *Ø-ʾēn-XØ + Ø-qaṭal*

אֵין זֹאת בִּלְתִּי אִם־חֶרֶב גִּדְעוֹן בֶּן־יוֹאָשׁ אִישׁ יִשְׂרָאֵל נָתַן הָאֱלֹהִים בְּיָדוֹ אֶת־
מִדְיָן וְאֶת־כָּל־הַמַּחֲנֶה׃

'Without a doubt this symbolises the sword of Gideon son of Joash, the Israelite. God has handed Midian and all the army over to him.' (Judg. 7.14)

In his dream, a man identified the sword of Gideon, which is another aspect of saying that God had handed over Midian to Gideon. The second clause cannot be said to describe additional details of the state in the first clause, so the *Ø-qaṭal* is not an elaboration.[65]

In rare instances, *Ø-qaṭal* can express a complement in relation to the preceding clause. My examples have an anterior or counterfactual meaning, as in (32):

(32) *Ø-REL-qaṭal* + ***Ø-qaṭal*** + *Ø-IMP* + *Ø-IMP;*

מָֽה רְאִיתֶם֙ **עָשִׂ֔יתִי** מַהֲר֖וּ עֲשׂ֥וּ כָמֽוֹנִי׃

‘What you have seen me **do**, quickly copy me.’ (Judg. 9.48, Sasson 2014, 389)

Within a relative construction that constitutes the direct object of the following imperatives, the *Ø-qaṭal* clause forms a complement to the preceding perception verb (רְאִיתֶם֙).[66]

It is also possible to form a parenthesis with *Ø-qaṭal* in fluent direct speech, as is shown in (33):

(33) *Ø-X-(**Ø-qaṭal**)-yiqṭol(u)*

רַ֠ק נְשֵׁיכֶ֣ם וְטַפְּכֶם֮ וּמִקְנֵכֶם֒ (**יָדַ֕עְתִּי כִּֽי־מִקְנֶ֥ה רַ֖ב לָכֶ֑ם**) יֵשְׁבוּ֙ בְּעָ֣רֵיכֶ֔ם אֲשֶׁ֥ר נָתַ֖תִּי לָכֶֽם׃

‘But your wives, children, and livestock (—**I know you have much livestock**—) may remain in the cities I have given you.’ (Deut. 3.19)

In (33), within the main *yiqṭol(u)* clause, a *Ø-qaṭal* clause is inserted as a parenthesis, after the subject noun phrase but before the main verb.

The discontinuity signalling of a *Ø-qaṭal* clause may also, in specific but rare cases, be used to express a peak, an intensification of the events in a narration. This is attested in poetry (Gen. 49.9; Judg. 5.26f.) but sometimes also in prose, and especially with verbs of motion (Brockelmann 1956, §133a). By coding temporally successive events with discontinuity clauses, a ‘staccato’ motion is achieved with highly focused actions (J-M §177a; Isaksson 2017, 248). An example is (34):

(34) *wa(y)-yiqtol* + *Ø-qatal* + *Ø-qatal* + *wa-X-qotel* + *wa-XØ*

וַיַּעֲל֞וּ חֲמֵ֣שֶׁת הָאֲנָשִׁ֣ים הַהֹלְכִים֮ לְרַגֵּ֣ל אֶת־הָאָרֶץ֒ **בָּ֣אוּ** שָׁ֔מָּה **לָקְח֗וּ** אֶת־הַפֶּ֙סֶל֙ וְאֶת־הָאֵפ֜וֹד וְאֶת־הַתְּרָפִ֣ים וְאֶת־הַמַּסֵּכָ֗ה וְהַכֹּהֵן֙ נִצָּב֙ פֶּ֣תַח הַשַּׁ֔עַר וְשֵׁשׁ־מֵא֣וֹת הָאִ֔ישׁ הֶחָג֖וּר כְּלֵ֥י הַמִּלְחָמָֽה׃

'The five men who had gone spying out the land approached, **went in** there, **stole** the carved image, the ephod, the personal idols, and the metal image, while the priest was standing at the entrance to the gate with the 600 fully armed men.' (Judg. 18.17)

In (34), the two 'staccato' *Ø-qatal* clauses code temporally successive actions in the past. It is narration, the aspect is perfective, and the discontinuity *qatal* clauses produce a dramatic turning point in the narrative, in a fatal moment of the account that would not have been there with only *wa(y)-yiqtol* clauses.[67]

7.3.3.3. *Ø-qatal* in Conditional and Topic–comment Linkings

There are definite similarities between topics and conditions. Both can be said to formulate the framework for the following discourse. This is the reason why conditions and topics are treated in the same section here. But while a conditional clause describes a hypothetical case, an eventuality, a topic is something agreed upon by the speaker and his audience (see §6.10).

A condition is usually explicitly marked by a conjunction, usually *'im* or *kī*. But there are instances when this is not the case, and in one instance in my database, a *Ø-qatal* clause even introduces a protasis (35):

(35) *(Ø-qaṭal*[68] *+ ʾō-qaṭal) + Ø-XØ*

(רָר בְּשָׂרוֹ אֶת־זוֹבוֹ אוֹ־הֶחְתִּים בְּשָׂרוֹ מִזּוֹבוֹ) טֻמְאָתוֹ הִוא׃

'(whether his body has secreted his discharge or has blocked his discharge,) he is unclean.' (Lev. 15.3)

Usually, however, when a *Ø-qaṭal* clause is involved in a conditional linking, it is as apodosis, an example of which is displayed in (36):

(36) *(wa-ʾim-yiqṭol(u)! + wa-lō-yiqṭol(u) + wa-qaṭal + wa-qaṭal) +* [18]*Ø-qaṭal + kī-VNabs-yiqṭol(u)*

(וְאִם־יִפְנֶה לְבָבְךָ וְלֹא תִשְׁמָע וְנִדַּחְתָּ וְהִשְׁתַּחֲוִיתָ לֵאלֹהִים אֲחֵרִים וַעֲבַדְתָּם׃)
הִגַּדְתִּי לָכֶם הַיּוֹם כִּי אָבֹד תֹּאבֵדוּן

'(But if you turn aside and do not obey, but are lured away and worship other gods and serve them,) [18]I declare to you this very day that you will certainly perish!' (Deut. 30.17f.)

In the *Ø-qaṭal* apodosis in (36), the *qaṭal* morpheme has one of its expected meanings as a perfective gram: the performative. It illustrates that *qaṭal* retains its normal semantic characteristics in conditional linkings, in protases, and in apodoses (see §5).[69]

But a *Ø-qaṭal* clause can also express a comment on a preceding topic clause. As is the case also with apodoses, a comment is focal, while the topic is not. The topic just expresses an expected fact, a comment something that is not known or expected. An example of *Ø-qaṭal* as comment is (37):

(37) *Ø-XØ + Ø-qaṭal + wa(y)-yiqṭol*

זֶה־לִּי עֶשְׂרִים שָׁנָה בְּבֵיתֶךָ עֲבַדְתִּיךָ אַרְבַּע־עֶשְׂרֵה שָׁנָה בִּשְׁתֵּי בְנֹתֶיךָ וְשֵׁשׁ
שָׁנִים בְּצֹאנֶךָ וַתַּחֲלֵף אֶת־מַשְׂכֻּרְתִּי עֲשֶׂרֶת מֹנִים׃

'These twenty years I've been in your house—I worked like a slave for you—fourteen years for your two daughters and six years for your flocks—but you changed my wages ten times!' (Gen. 31.41)

The topic in (37) is the verbless clause, here with past time reference. This is the given, what is agreed upon by both Jacob and Laban. Then follows the comment coded by a Ø-qatal (עֲבַדְתִּ֫יךָ) followed by a wa(y)-yiqtol clause (וַתַּחֲלֵ֣ף). Both clauses in the comment express a perfective aspect with past time reference, but because of the adverbial expressions, they by implication involve habitual or repeated actions during the twenty years. We can expect that Jacob and Laban did not agree upon that.

Another example of a topic–comment construction with Ø-qatal is much disputed, which is the reason I quote it here (38):

(38) wa-XØ + wa-XØ + ⁸Ø-qatal + wa-qatal + wa-qatal + 'ō qatal + wa-qatal + wa-qatal + wa-qatal + ⁹wa-X-yiqtol(u)

וְהַמָּ֗ן כִּזְרַע־גַּ֣ד ה֔וּא וְעֵינ֖וֹ כְּעֵ֥ין הַבְּדֹֽלַח׃ 8 שָׁ֩טוּ֩ הָעָ֨ם וְלָֽקְט֜וּ וְטָחֲנ֣וּ בָרֵחַ֗יִם א֤וֹ דָכוּ֙ בַּמְּדֹכָ֔ה וּבִשְּׁלוּ֙ בַּפָּר֔וּר וְעָשׂ֥וּ אֹת֖וֹ עֻג֑וֹת וְהָיָ֣ה טַעְמ֔וֹ כְּטַ֖עַם לְשַׁ֥ד הַשָּֽׁמֶן׃ 9 וּבְרֶ֧דֶת הַטַּ֛ל עַל־הַֽמַּחֲנֶ֖ה לָ֑יְלָה יֵרֵ֥ד הַמָּ֖ן עָלָֽיו׃

'(Now the manna was like coriander seed, and its appearance was like that of bdellium. ⁸The people went about and gathered it, and ground it with mills or pounded it in mortars; they baked it in pans and made cakes of it. Its taste was like the taste of fresh olive oil. ⁹And when the dew came down on the camp in the night, the manna fell with it.)' (Num. 11.7–9)

The whole passage in (38) is a "parenthetical description of the manna that interrupts the continuing narrative" (Levine 1993,

322). It starts with two verbless clauses functioning as the topic. The comment is then introduced by a *Ø-qaṭal* clause, as we have seen already in the previous example (37). In this case also, the *Ø-qaṭal* has an implied past habitual meaning. It has been argued that the syntax is irregular (Joosten 2012, 218; but cf. Driver 1892, §114, who considers it regular).[70] The alternative syntax that is often argued for, with a *wa-qaṭal* introducing the comment with past (habitual) time reference, is found nowhere in my database. A *wa-qaṭal* as comment after a verbless clause topic always has future time reference or a meaning of obligation (see §6.10).

So the *Ø-qaṭal* in (38) introduces the comment and signals past time reference. The aspect is perfective, but the implied meaning is habitual. This habitual description proceeds with aspectually explicit *wa-qaṭal* clauses and a final *yiqṭol(u)*. The disjunctive *ʾō qaṭal* clauses alternating with *wa-qaṭal* and having the same past habitual meaning is a peculiarity of the development of the *wa-qaṭal* construction. A *wa-qaṭal* has no corresponding disjunctive clause. When *wa-qaṭal* developed in CBH, the *ʾō qaṭal* clause-type had to do double duty: serving as disjunctive clause for both *qaṭal* and *wa-qaṭal*. So a *ʾō qaṭal* clause may have the meaning of either *qaṭal* or the new *wa-qaṭal* (see §5.4.8).[71]

7.3.3.4. *Ø-qaṭal* as Relative Clause

In relatively few cases in prose, *Ø-qaṭal* constitutes an asyndetic relative clause. The *Ø-qaṭal* clause is then embedded in the main clause. This is a phenomenon more frequent in poetry.[72] An example in prose is (39):

(39) *wa(y)-yiqṭol* + *wa(y)-yiqṭol* + *wa-hinnē-XØ* + ***Ø-qaṭal*** + *wa(y)-yiqṭol* + *wa(y)-yiqṭol* + *wa(y)-yiqṭol*

וַיִּשָּׂא אַבְרָהָם אֶת־עֵינָיו וַיַּרְא וְהִנֵּה־אַיִל אַחַר **נֶאֱחַז בַּסְּבַךְ בְּקַרְנָיו** וַיֵּלֶךְ אַבְרָהָם וַיִּקַּח אֶת־הָאַיִל וַיַּעֲלֵהוּ לְעֹלָה תַּחַת בְּנוֹ׃

'Abraham looked up and saw behind him[73] a ram **caught in the bushes by its horns**. So Abraham went over and got the ram and offered it up as a burnt offering instead of his son.' (Gen. 22.13)

In (39), the asyndetic relative clause belongs to the verbless clause that constitutes the complement of the preceding perception verb (וַיַּרְא). The relative clause has the function of an enlarged attribute. It is detached somewhat from its head noun by an inserted adverbial *ʾaḥar*.[74]

7.4. Tenet 1c: *Wa-VX // (Wa)-(X)-qoṭel*

In a main line of continuity clauses, a *qoṭel* clause signals a specific range of discontinuities. This is what the present section demonstrates.

7.4.1. Interruption Type *Wa(y)-yiqṭol* + *Ø-(X)-qoṭel*

When a *qoṭel* clause interrupts a main line of *wa(y)-yiqṭol* clauses, it is usually circumstantial and directly related to the main clause. In such a case, the *qoṭel* morpheme qualifies a constituent in the main clause. The examples exhibit various degrees of dependence in relation to the constituent to be qualified in the main clause (Isaksson 2009, 57–59); see Table 24.

Table 24: The semantics of the *wa(y)-yiqṭol* + *(wa)-(X)-qoṭel* linking

	wa-(X)-qoṭel	*Ø-(X)-qoṭel*
Circumstantial	27	23
Focused progressive	8	0
Focused complement	13	0
Background	18	1
Total	**66**	**24**

The theme of the present section is *qoṭel* clauses qualifying a main line in asyndesis (see Table 24, right column). In such cases, the asyndetic *qoṭel* clauses generally lack a constituent *X* before the participle (thus *Ø-qoṭel*), and are closest to the status of an (adverbial) attribute, a qualifier, as in (40):

(40) *wa(y)-yiqṭol* + ***Ø-qoṭel*** + *wa(y)-yiqṭol*

וַיִּשְׁמְעוּ אֶת־קוֹל יְהוָה אֱלֹהִים **מִתְהַלֵּךְ בַּגָּן לְרוּחַ הַיּוֹם** וַיִּתְחַבֵּא הָאָדָם וְאִשְׁתּוֹ מִפְּנֵי יְהוָה אֱלֹהִים בְּתוֹךְ עֵץ הַגָּן׃

‘They heard the sound of the LORD God **moving about in the garden at the breezy time of the day**, and they hid from the LORD God among the trees of the orchard.’ (Gen. 3.8)

In (40), the *qoṭel* is positioned directly after the constituent (in the main clause) which it qualifies, in the same position as an attribute. But it is not determined, as an attribute would have been. Though its head noun (יְהוָה אֱלֹהִים) is a proper name, the participle has no definite article, a fact that reveals its adverbial nature. The *qoṭel* clause is dependent to a certain degree, which its position reveals, and it has no subject of its own, but it is a full clause (there is a predication, and the *qoṭel* has a verbal ‘force’).

A *Ø-qoṭel* clause can also refer back to a pronominal suffix, as in (41):

(41) *wa(y)-yiqṭol* + *wa(y)-yiqṭol* + ***Ø-qoṭel***

וַיִּרְדְּפ֨וּ מִצְרַ֜יִם אַחֲרֵיהֶ֗ם וַיַּשִּׂ֤יגוּ אוֹתָם֙ **חֹנִ֣ים עַל־הַיָּ֔ם**

‘The Egyptians chased after them and overtook them **camping by the sea**.’ (Exod. 14.9)

The *qoṭel* clause in (41) represents an extension of the use of the participle in the position of an attribute, since it now qualifies a pronominal suffix, but it is still positioned directly after the head (the suffix).

In several instances, the *Ø-qoṭel* clause is positioned with linguistic distance from its head noun in the main clause, as in (42):

(42) *wa(y)-yiqṭol* + *wa(y)-yiqṭol* + *wa(y)-yiqṭol* + ***Ø-qoṭel*** + ***Ø-qoṭel*** + ***wa-qoṭel***

וַיֵּלְכוּ֙ חֲמֵ֣שֶׁת הָאֲנָשִׁ֔ים וַיָּבֹ֖אוּ לָ֑יְשָׁה וַיִּרְא֣וּ אֶת־הָעָ֣ם אֲשֶׁר־בְּקִרְבָּ֣הּ **יוֹשֶֽׁבֶת־**
לָ֠בֶטַח כְּמִשְׁפַּ֨ט צִדֹנִ֜ים] **שֹׁקֵ֣ט ׀ וּבֹטֵ֗חַ**

‘So the five men journeyed on and arrived in Laish. They saw the people in the middle of the town **living securely** according to Sidonian custom, **undisturbed and unsuspecting**.’ (Judg. 18.7)

The participles in (42) have different referents in the main line, and they are positioned with a distance from their respective heads in the main line. The first *qoṭel* (יוֹשֶֽׁבֶת) is feminine and refers back to the preceding feminine pronominal suffix, referring to the city of Laish. In the translation, this is rendered ‘the town **living securely**’ (thus Butler 2009, 365). This *qoṭel* is positioned directly after its head (the feminine suffix in בְּקִרְבָּהּ), but the two last participles are masculine and refer back to, and qualify, the people (הָעָם). In the example, the verbal usage of the participle has developed far beyond the non-predicative attributive use of *qoṭel*, and it is remarkable that the two masculine participles (שֹׁקֵט | וּבֹטֵחַ) are positioned so remotely from their head noun. It is also noticeable that they can be coordinated with *wa*, so that a sequence of subordinated verbal *qoṭel* is formed (*Ø-qoṭel* + *wa-qoṭel*).

A preposed *X* constituent when *qoṭel* is asyndetically attached (thus *Ø-X-qoṭel*) is a rare phenomenon. I have found only one instance of *wa(y)-yiqṭol* + *Ø-X-qoṭel*:

(43) *wa(y)-yiqṭol* + ***Ø-X-qoṭel*** + ***wa-X-qoṭel***

וַיְדַבֵּר יְהוָה אֲלֵיכֶם מִתּוֹךְ הָאֵשׁ **קוֹל דְּבָרִים אַתֶּם שֹׁמְעִים וּתְמוּנָה אֵינְכֶם רֹאִים זוּלָתִי קוֹל׃**

'Then the LORD spoke to you from the middle of the fire; **you kept hearing the sound of the words, but didn't see a form—only a voice.**' (Deut. 4.12)

The *qoṭel* clauses in (43) describe events that are concomitant with that of the main clause. The participles also describe actions that are progressive with past time reference, a typical imperfective property of a verbal morpheme. And it is possible for the *X* be a complex of constituents, *O.noun-S.pron* and *O.noun-ʾēn-S.pron* respectively.

In one instance, an asyndetic *qoṭel* clause is not circumstantial, but is given a more independent relation to the main clause, in the function of background (44):

(44) *wa(y)-yiqṭol* + *wa-X-qaṭal* + [23]*Ø-ʾēn-X-qoṭel* + *CONJ-XØ* + *wa-X-qoṭel*

וַיִּתֵּ֞ן שַׂ֤ר בֵּית־הַסֹּ֙הַר֙ בְּיַד־יוֹסֵ֔ף אֵ֚ת כָּל־הָ֣אֲסִירִ֔ם אֲשֶׁ֖ר בְּבֵ֣ית הַסֹּ֑הַר וְאֵ֨ת כָּל־
אֲשֶׁ֤ר עֹשִׂים֙ שָׁ֔ם ה֖וּא הָיָ֥ה עֹשֶֽׂה׃ אֵ֣ין ׀ שַׂ֣ר בֵּית־הַסֹּ֗הַר רֹאֶ֤ה אֶֽת־כָּל־מְא֙וּמָה֙
בְּיָד֔וֹ בַּאֲשֶׁ֥ר יְהוָ֖ה אִתּ֑וֹ וַאֲשֶׁר־ה֥וּא עֹשֶׂ֖ה יְהוָ֥ה מַצְלִֽיחַ׃ ס

'The warden put all the prisoners under Joseph's care. He was in charge of whatever they were doing. [23]The warden did not concern himself with anything that was in Joseph's care because the LORD was with him and whatever he was doing the LORD was making successful.' (Gen. 39.22f.)

In (44), *wa(y)-yiqṭol* is the continuity clause, while the *qaṭal* describes a same-event addition to this clause (Dixon 2009, 27). The two *qoṭel* clauses have the character of a background description; they are not adverbial as circumstantial *qoṭel* clauses usually are.[75]

7.4.2. Interruption Type *Wa(y)-yiqṭol // Wa-(X)-qoṭel*

Since the verbal *qoṭel* stems from a semiverbal formation used as an adverbial clause in the position of an (adverbial) attribute, syndetic *qoṭel* clauses are generally more independent and have more diverse functions. They are also far more frequent than the asyndetic ones, by a ratio of 3:1; see Table 24, middle column. *Wa-(X)-qoṭel* is frequently used as background and, even when circumstantial, does not adapt to the syntax of an attribute, but begins with a subject noun or pronoun that refers back to an actant in the pragmatic world of the main clause, as in (45):

(45) *wa(y)-yiqṭol* + *wa(y)-yiqṭol* + ***wa-X-qoṭel***

וַיָּקֻמוּ מִשָּׁם הָאֲנָשִׁים וַיַּשְׁקִפוּ עַל־פְּנֵי סְדֹם **וְאַבְרָהָם הֹלֵךְ עִמָּם לְשַׁלְּחָם׃**

‘The men got up to leave and looked down toward Sodom, **Abraham walking with them to see them off**.’ (Gen. 18.16)

While an asyndetic circumstantial *qoṭel* clause is tightly connected to one preceding *wa(y)-yiqṭol*, the syndetic circumstantial *qoṭel* clause describes a more independent action. In (45), the subject noun (אַבְרָהָם) is not an actant in the preceding *wa(y)-yiqṭol*, but belongs to its pragmatic world.

If a constituent in the main clause is to be qualified by the *wa-X-qoṭel*, it can be repeated (in *X*), but is often referred to by an anaphoric personal pronoun instead, as in (46):

(46) *wa(y)-yiqṭol* + *wa(y)-yiqṭol* + ***wa-S.pron-qoṭel*** + *wa-XØ*

וַיִּשְׁמַע הָאֱלֹהִים בְּקוֹל מָנוֹחַ וַיָּבֹא מַלְאַךְ הָאֱלֹהִים עוֹד אֶל־הָאִשָּׁה **וְהִיא יוֹשֶׁבֶת בַּשָּׂדֶה** וּמָנוֹחַ אִישָׁהּ אֵין עִמָּהּ׃

‘God answered Manoah’s prayer. God’s angel came to the woman again **while she was sitting in the field**. But her husband Manoah was not with her.’ (Judg. 13.9)

In (46), the personal pronoun (הִיא) in the *qoṭel* clause refers back to the prepositional phrase (אֶל־הָאִשָּׁה) in the immediately preceding *wa(y)-yiqṭol* clause. It is reasonable to analyse *qoṭel* in this function as a finite imperfective formation.[76]

When *qoṭel* is introduced by the focus marker *hinnē* (thus *wa-hinnē-X-qoṭel*), the clause may function as a focused main-line clause. The meaning is progressive or stativic depending on the verb. An example is (47):

(47) *wa(y)-yiqṭol* + *wa-hinnē-S.noun-qoṭel*

וַיָּבֹא יִפְתָּח הַמִּצְפָּה אֶל־בֵּיתוֹ וְהִנֵּה בִתּוֹ יֹצֵאת לִקְרָאתוֹ בְּתֻפִּים וּבִמְחֹלוֹת

'Jephthah came home to Mizpah, and there was his daughter hurrying out to meet him, with tambourines and dancing.' (Judg. 11.34)

The *wa-hinnē-X-qoṭel* clause in (47) is a focused and foregrounded clause, in which the new and important information is described. It expresses a past progressive action.[77]

Very often, the focused *wa-hinnē-X-qoṭel* codes the content of a perception, in which case it functions as a complement clause with focus. The perception verb in itself is unimportant; the new and important information is what is perceived, as in (48):[78]

(48) *wa(y)-yiqṭol* + *wa-hinnē-S.noun-qoṭel*

וַיַּרְא וְהִנֵּה יִצְחָק מְצַחֵק אֵת רִבְקָה אִשְׁתּוֹ׃

'And he observed Isaac caressing his wife Rebekah.' (Gen. 26.8)

But *wa(y)-yiqṭol* + *wa-(X)-qoṭel* may also signal background descriptions, in which the *qoṭel* clause has an informative character, valuable to the receiver of thc text, as in (49):

(49) *wa(y)-yiqṭol* + [12]***wa-S.noun-qoṭel*** + *wa-XØ*

וַיֵּרֶד הוּא וּפֻרָה נַעֲרוֹ אֶל־קְצֵה הַחֲמֻשִׁים אֲשֶׁר בַּמַּחֲנֶה׃ **וּמִדְיָן וַעֲמָלֵק וְכָל־בְּנֵי־קֶדֶם נֹפְלִים בָּעֵמֶק** כָּאַרְבֶּה לָרֹב וְלִגְמַלֵּיהֶם אֵין מִסְפָּר כַּחוֹל שֶׁעַל־שְׂפַת הַיָּם לָרֹב׃

‘So he went down with Purah his servant to where the sentries were guarding the camp. [12]**Now the Midianites, Amalekites, and the people from the east covered the valley** as numerous as locusts. Their camels were too many to count; as innumerable as the sand on the seashore.’ (Judg. 7.11f.)

The *qoṭel* clause in (49) supplies a valuable description of the situation before the battle. It does not directly qualify anything in the main clause. This is typical of a background clause: it is a relatively independent description ‘behind the scene’ of the pragmatic world of the main clause(s). It is also typical that the background description is a complex of clauses: in this case, a verbless clause supplies additional facts.

This ‘behind the scene’ description can of course also be expressed by a *wa-S.pron-qoṭel* clause, as in (50):

(50) *wa(y)-yiqṭol* + ***wa-S.pron-qoṭel***

וַיָּקָם אַחֲרֵי אֲבִימֶלֶךְ לְהוֹשִׁיעַ אֶת־יִשְׂרָאֵל תּוֹלָע בֶּן־פּוּאָה בֶּן־דּוֹדוֹ אִישׁ יִשָּׂשכָר **וְהוּא־יֹשֵׁב בְּשָׁמִיר בְּהַר אֶפְרָיִם׃**

‘After Abimelech, in order to save Israel, arose Tola, “son” of Puah, “son” of Dodo, a man of Issachar. **He lived at Shamir in the Ephraimite hill country**.’ (Judg. 10.1, Boling 1975, 186, my emphasis)

In (50), the syntax of the *qoṭel* clause is exactly the same as many of the circumstantial clauses presented above, but it is obvious that is not a circumstantial qualifier in this sense. It is simply descriptive of a general fact: the place where Tola lived. This means that the syntax alone cannot always decide between a circumstantial clause and a more independent background description.

A canonical and instructive instance of a *wa-X-qotel* background description is (51):

(51) *wa(y)-yiqtol* + [10]***wa-X-qotel*** + *wa-X-yiqtol(u)* + *wa-qatal*

וַיַּצְמַ֞ח יְהוָ֤ה אֱלֹהִים֙ מִן־הָ֣אֲדָמָ֔ה כָּל־עֵ֛ץ נֶחְמָ֥ד לְמַרְאֶ֖ה וְט֣וֹב לְמַאֲכָ֑ל וְעֵ֤ץ הַֽחַיִּים֙ בְּת֣וֹךְ הַגָּ֔ן וְעֵ֕ץ הַדַּ֖עַת ט֥וֹב וָרָֽע׃ **וְנָהָר֙ יֹצֵ֣א מֵעֵ֔דֶן לְהַשְׁק֖וֹת אֶת־הַגָּ֑ן** וּמִשָּׁם֙ יִפָּרֵ֔ד וְהָיָ֖ה לְאַרְבָּעָ֥ה רָאשִֽׁים׃

'The LORD God made all kinds of trees grow from the soil, every tree that was pleasing to look at and good for food, and the tree of life in the middle of the garden, and the tree of the knowledge of good and evil. [10]**Now a river flows from Eden to water the garden**, and from there it divides and becomes four headstreams.' (Gen. 2.9f.)

The *qotel* clause in (51) constitutes a more independent description of the garden, the creation of which has been presented in the preceding clauses. The purpose of this background is to present geographical information still valid for the receivers of the text, and it is therefore to be translated by a general present: "es ist Wissenstradition in ursprünglich mündlicher Form" (Westermann 1976, 293). The background is a complex of clauses. It is introduced by a *qotel* clause, but 'continued' by *wa-X-yiqtol(u)*, where X is a focused prepositional phrase (מִשָּׁם), followed by a continuity clause *wa-qatal*. The participle is here fully verbal, and relatively young as an imperfective in the verbal system. Here it has the meaning of a general present. It has taken over the function of initiating clause-type in the background complex, but it was not natural to continue the description of the flowing river with coordinated *qotel* clauses. Instead, the old imperfective *yiqtol(u)* was used, together with its continuity counterpart *wa-qatal*.[79]

An exceptional case of background with prospective meaning expressed by a *wa-qoṭel* clause is found in (52):

(52) *wa(y)-yiqṭol* + *wa(y)-yiqṭol* + ***wa-qoṭel*** + *wa-X-qoṭel*

וַיִּקַּח מָנוֹחַ אֶת־גְּדִי הָעִזִּים וְאֶת־הַמִּנְחָה וַיַּעַל עַל־הַצּוּר לַיהוָה **וּמַפְלִא** לַעֲשׂוֹת וּמָנוֹחַ וְאִשְׁתּוֹ רֹאִים׃

'Manoah took a young goat and a grain offering and offered them on a rock to the LORD, **and he was about to do an amazing thing** while Manoah and his wife was watching.' (Judg. 13.19)

The *wa-qoṭel* in (52) is used immediately after the proper name of God, and it is reasonable to suppose that YHWH is the understood subject of the participle. The position of the clause after a pausal accent indicates that it has a certain independence. Normally, *qoṭel* clauses without explicit subject are asyndetic and circumstantial, as we have seen, so the syndesis indicates that the clause is not circumstantial. The *wa-qoṭel* (וּמַפְלִא לַעֲשׂוֹת) is probably not a concomitant action, but expresses what the Lord is going to do in the immediate future, a relatively frequent meaning of a verbal participle. The next *qoṭel* clause has an explicit subject (מָנוֹחַ וְאִשְׁתּוֹ) and is concomitant with what the Lord is going to do in the future: Manoah and his wife will be watching when YHWH does an amazing thing. It is a future action projected back to the past reference time of the narrative main line.

7.4.3. Interruption Type *Wa-qaṭal // (Wa)-(X)-qoṭel*

A *qoṭel* clause after a main line of *wa-qaṭal* is relatively infrequent. The reason is probably that a *qoṭel* clause does not easily express obligation. A second reason is that *wa-X-yiqṭol(u)* is still fully productive as discontinuity clause expressing obligation or future, the most frequent meanings of *wa-qaṭal*.

In the cases I have detected, the *qoṭel* clause is mostly circumstantial in relation to *wa-qaṭal*. See Table 25.[80]

Table 25: The semantics of the *wa-qaṭal* + *(wa)-(X)-qoṭel* linking

Temporal succession	1
Circumstantial	6
Total	**7**

In one example, a *qoṭel* clause is foregrounded with future time reference:

(53) *VNabs-yiqṭol(u)* + *kī-yiqṭol(u)!* + *wa-qaṭal* + *wa-qaṭal* + [14]***wa-gam-O.noun-qoṭel*** + *wa-X-yiqṭol(u)*

יָדֹ֨עַ תֵּדַ֜ע כִּי־גֵ֣ר ׀ יִהְיֶ֣ה זַרְעֲךָ֗ בְּאֶ֙רֶץ֙ לֹ֣א לָהֶ֔ם וַעֲבָד֖וּם וְעִנּ֣וּ אֹתָ֑ם אַרְבַּ֥ע מֵא֖וֹת
שָׁנָֽה׃ **וְגַ֧ם אֶת־הַגּ֛וֹי אֲשֶׁ֥ר יַעֲבֹ֖דוּ דָּ֣ן אָנֹ֑כִי** וְאַחֲרֵי־כֵ֥ן יֵצְא֖וּ בִּרְכֻ֥שׁ גָּדֽוֹל׃

'Know for certain that your descendants will be strangers in a foreign country. And they will be slaves there, and they will be oppressed for 400 years. [14]**But I will execute judgment on the nation** that they will serve. Afterward they will come out with many possessions.' (Gen. 15.13f.)

In (53), the *qoṭel* clause is foregrounded in a series of prospective clauses which starts with *kī-yiqṭol(u)* and continues with *wa-qaṭal*. It is possible that the futural *qoṭel* has a special nuance: that YHWH is already resolved to execute this judgement 400 years ahead in the future.[81]

In most cases, *wa-qaṭal* with a following *qoṭel* clause is a circumstantial linking, even with *qoṭel* in its prototypical attributive position, as in (54):

(54) *kī-qoṭel* + *kī-PrP-VN* + *wa-qaṭal* + *wa-qaṭal* + ***Ø-qoṭel***

כִּי יֹדֵעַ אֱלֹהִים כִּי בְּיוֹם אֲכָלְכֶם מִמֶּנּוּ וְנִפְקְחוּ עֵינֵיכֶם וִהְיִיתֶם כֵּאלֹהִים **יֹדְעֵי טוֹב וָרָע׃**

'for God knows that when you eat from it your eyes will open, and you will be like God, **knowing good and evil**.' (Gen. 3.5)

The *qoṭel* clause in (54) follows directly after its head noun (אלֹהִים), which is indefinite, and the *qoṭel* itself is a construct noun before its objects (טוֹב וָרָע). In such instances, it can be argued that the *qoṭel* is non-verbal. I have brought forward this example because of its prototypical nature. From this position, there developed the verbal *qoṭel* (see §4.1.1.1), and the borderline between verbal and non-verbal, finite and non-finite, in the case of *qoṭel*, is sometimes difficult to draw. An example of a verbal but infinite circumstantial use of *qoṭel* after *wa-qaṭal* is (55):

(55) *wa-qaṭal* + ***Ø-qoṭel*** + ***wa-qoṭel***

וְהִפְקַדְתִּי עֲלֵיכֶם בֶּהָלָה אֶת־הַשַּׁחֶפֶת וְאֶת־הַקַּדַּחַת **מְכַלּוֹת עֵינַיִם וּמְדִיבֹת נָפֶשׁ**

'I will inflict horror on you, consumption and fever, **diminishing eyesight and draining away the vitality of life**.' (Lev. 26.16)

In (55), the last two direct objects in the main clause (אֶת־הַשַּׁחֶפֶת וְאֶת־הַקַּדַּחַת) are determined by definite articles, but the following active participles are indefinite, and clearly adverbial. They form two circumstantial clauses qualifying the preceding objects (all are feminine plural). The *qoṭel* clauses are verbal (but infinite), each having one direct object.[82]

7.5. Tenet 1d: *Wa-VX // (Wa)-XØ*

In a main line of continuity clauses, a verbless clause signals a specific kind of discontinuity, since it always describes a state (see Tables 26–27). This is what the present section demonstrates.

7.5.1. Interruption Type *Wa(y)-yiqṭol // (Wa)-XØ*

In a verbless clause, there is no verb, and this determines the uses of *XØ* as an interruption in a narrative main line; see Table 26.

Table 26: The semantics of the *wa(y)-yiqṭol* + *(wa)-XØ* linking

Background	64
Editorial comment	24
Circumstantial	43
Complement	15
Contrast	1
Same-event addition	1
Temporal succession	2
Unclear[83]	2
Focus, no linking	(4)
Total	**156**

The semantics of the linking displayed in Table 26 are dominated by backgrounding and editorial information as well as circumstantial uses. In addition, some are (focal) complement clauses in the form of *wa-hinnē-XØ* constructions. The rest—contrast, same-event addition, temporal relative time, and temporal succession—are exceptional (for the terms, see Dixon 2009). I have found no semantic distinction between *wa-XØ* and *Ø-XØ* as interruptive clause after *wa(y)-yiqṭol*. In the following, syndetic and asyndetic verbless clauses are treated together.

In my classification in the database, background is defined as information beside the main line that was relevant or important to the contemporary receivers of the text. A large proportion of all *wa(y)-yiqṭol* + *(wa)-XØ* are background. A typical example of background is:

(56) *wa(y)-yiqṭol* + *wa(y)-yiqṭol* + *wa(y)-yiqṭol* + *Ø-XØ* + ***wa-XØ*** + ***wa-XØ***

וַיָּ֨קָם וַיֵּ֜לֶךְ וַיָּבֹ֗א עַד־נֹ֣כַח יְב֔וּס הִ֖יא יְרוּשָׁלִָ֑ם **וְעִמּ֗וֹ צֶ֤מֶד חֲמוֹרִים֙ חֲבוּשִׁ֔ים וּפִילַגְשׁ֖וֹ עִמּֽוֹ׃**

‘He got up, went away and traveled as far as Jebus (that is, Jerusalem). **He had with him a pair of saddled donkeys and his concubine.**’ (Judg. 19.10)

In (56), the first verbless clause is an editorial parenthesis, but the other *XØ* clauses belong to the narrative and constitute background information necessary for the receivers to understand the narration.

Information about the age of the protagonist probably also belongs to the world of the narrative and is background, as in (57):[84]

(57) *wa(y)-yiqṭol* + *wa(y)-yiqṭol* + ***wa-XØ***

וַיֵּ֣לֶךְ אַבְרָ֗ם כַּאֲשֶׁ֨ר דִּבֶּ֤ר אֵלָיו֙ יְהוָ֔ה וַיֵּ֥לֶךְ אִתּ֖וֹ ל֑וֹט **וְאַבְרָ֗ם בֶּן־חָמֵ֤שׁ שָׁנִים֙ וְשִׁבְעִ֣ים שָׁנָ֔ה בְּצֵאת֖וֹ מֵחָרָֽן׃**

‘So Abram left, just as the LORD had told him to do, and Lot went with him. **Now Abram was 75 years old when he departed from Haran.**’ (Gen. 12.4)

Editorial parentheses or comments are insertions meant to clarify the text for later readers, as in (58):[85]

(58) *wa(y)-yiqṭol* + ***(wa-XØ)*** + *wa(y)-yiqṭol*

וַיֵּ֣לֶךְ יְהוּדָ֗ה אֶל־הַֽכְּנַעֲנִי֙ הַיּוֹשֵׁ֣ב בְּחֶבְר֔וֹן (**וְשֵׁם־חֶבְר֥וֹן לְפָנִ֖ים קִרְיַ֣ת אַרְבַּ֑ע**)
וַיַּכּ֛וּ אֶת־שֵׁשַׁ֥י וְאֶת־אֲחִימַ֖ן וְאֶת־תַּלְמָֽי׃

'Judah moved against the Canaanites who lived in Hebron (**earlier, Hebron was called Qiryat-arba**) and they defeated Sheshay, Ahiman, and Talmay.' (Judg. 1.10, Sasson 2014, 136)

There is also a relatively frequent use of *wa(y)-yiqṭol* + *(wa)-XØ* to code a circumstantial state in relation to the mainline clause(s). In such cases, the verbless clause is *semantically* embedded in the main clause and corresponds to an attribute or prepositional phrase, a construction frequent also in Arabic (Isaksson 2009, 62f.). This is illustrated in (59):

(59) *wa(y)-yiqṭol-O.noun* + ***Ø-XØ*** + *O.noun* + ***Ø-XØ***

וַיִּקַּ֤ח הָאִישׁ֙ נֶ֣זֶם זָהָ֔ב **בֶּ֖קַע מִשְׁקָל֑וֹ** וּשְׁנֵ֤י צְמִידִים֙ עַל־יָדֶ֔יהָ **עֲשָׂרָ֥ה זָהָ֖ב מִשְׁקָלָֽם׃**

'The man took out a gold nose ring **weighing a beka** and two gold wrist bracelets **weighing ten shekels**, and gave them to her.' (Gen. 24.22)

Such circumstantial verbless clauses as in (59) are not syntactically embedded, and cannot be analysed, for example, as relative clauses, since the same semantic relation is achieved by syndetic verbless clauses, as is shown in (60):[86]

(60) *wa(y)-yiqṭol* + ***wa-XØ*** + ***wa-XØ***

וַיִּצֹ֣ק ל֗וֹ אַרְבַּע֙ טַבְּעֹ֣ת זָהָ֔ב עַ֖ל אַרְבַּ֣ע פַּעֲמֹתָ֑יו **וּשְׁתֵּ֣י טַבָּעֹ֗ת עַל־צַלְעוֹ֙ הָֽאֶחָ֔ת וּשְׁתֵּי֙ טַבָּעוֹ֔ת עַל־צַלְע֖וֹ הַשֵּׁנִֽית׃**

'He cast four gold rings for it at its four feet, **with two rings on one side and two rings on the other side**.' (Exod. 37.3)

Clauses of the type *wa-hinnē-XØ* after perception verbs constitute a special case. They have focus, and very often express a complement to a (sometimes implicit) sensory receptor verb in the main clause (Zewi 2011), as in (61):

(61) *wa(y)-yiqṭol* + *wa-hinnē-XØ*

וַתָּבֹ֨א אֵלָ֤יו הַיּוֹנָה֙ לְעֵ֣ת עֶ֔רֶב וְהִנֵּ֥ה עֲלֵה־זַ֖יִת טָרָ֣ף בְּפִ֑יהָ

'And the dove came back to him in the evening, and behold, in her mouth was a freshly plucked olive leaf.' (Gen. 8.11)

In instances such as (61), the perception verb is implicitly understood, which is indicated by the translation 'and behold'. When the perception verb is explicit in the main clause, the function of the *wa-hinnē-XØ* as (focused) complement is evident (62):

(62) *wa(y)-yiqṭol* + ***wa-hinnē-XØ*** + ***wa-hinnē-XØ*** + *Ø-qoṭel*[87]

וַיַּ֞רְא **וְהִנֵּ֧ה בְאֵ֣ר בַּשָּׂדֶ֗ה וְהִנֵּה־שָׁ֞ם שְׁלֹשָׁ֤ה עֶדְרֵי־צֹאן֙** רֹבְצִ֣ים עָלֶ֔יהָ

'He saw **a well in the field and three flocks of sheep** lying beside it.' (Gen. 29.2)

In (62), *wa(y)-yiqṭol* of a typical perception verb (וַיַּ֞רְא) is directly followed by two *wa-hinnē-XØ* clauses expressing the two complements of the perception. It is the detailed account of the perceived objects that is focal.[88]

In one instance, *wa(y)-yiqṭol* + *(wa)-XØ* expresses a contrast relation (63):

(63) *wa(y)-yiqṭol* + ***wa-XØ*** + *()-O.noun* + *Ø-qaṭal* + *kī-XØ*

וַיִּשְׁלַח יִשְׂרָאֵל אֶת־יְמִינוֹ וַיָּשֶׁת עַל־רֹאשׁ אֶפְרַיִם **וְהוּא הַצָּעִיר** וְאֶת־שְׂמֹאלוֹ
עַל־רֹאשׁ מְנַשֶּׁה שִׂכֵּל אֶת־יָדָיו כִּי מְנַשֶּׁה הַבְּכוֹר׃

'Israel stretched out his right hand and placed it on Ephraim's head, **although he was the younger**. (He put) his left hand on Manasseh's head, crossed his hands, even though Manasseh was the firstborn.' (Gen. 48.14)

In (63), the syndetic verbless clause has a contrast meaning, since the expected procedure would have been to place the right hand on the firstborn. Before the second direct object (אֶת־שְׂמֹאלוֹ), there is an ellipsis: a verb is understood ('placed'). The example also contains an unusual *Ø-qaṭal* expressing elaboration (see §7.3.3), and a concessive nuance of *kī* (HALOT meaning 12).

One instance of *wa(y)-yiqṭol* + *(wa)-XØ* expresses a same-event addition, describing a different aspect of the same event as in the main clause. A verbless clause in this type of clausal relation is not circumstantial. It is, however, semantically a supporting clause in Dixon's (2009, 6) sense, while the *wa(y)-yiqṭol* clause is focal.

(64) *wa(y)-yiqṭol!* + ***Ø-ʾēn-XØ***

וַתְּהִי שָׂרַי עֲקָרָה **אֵין לָהּ וָלָד׃**

'But Sarai was barren; **she had no child**.' (Gen. 11.30)

In (64), the verbless clause describes another aspect of the state described by the *wa(y)-yiqṭol* with stativic (copula) verb. The verbless clause is not circumstantial and absolutely not background. The two clauses express the same situation in different words.

Cases where *wa(y)-yiqṭol* + *(wa)-XØ* express temporal succession are extremely rare. In only two instances does *(wa)-XØ* describe such a sequentiality. The first is (65):

(65) *wa(y)-yiqṭol* + *"wa-hinnē-S.noun-qoṭel"* + [4]*wa-hinnē-XØ*

וַיֹּ֣אמֶר אַבְרָ֔ם הֵ֣ן לִ֔י לֹ֥א נָתַ֖תָּה זָ֑רַע וְהִנֵּ֥ה בֶן־בֵּיתִ֖י יוֹרֵ֥שׁ אֹתִֽי׃ **וְהִנֵּ֨ה דְבַר־יְהוָ֤ה אֵלָיו֙**

'Abram said, "After all, you have not given me an offspring, *so now,* a son > one born in my house will be my heir." [4]But *just then* the word of the Lord came to him.' (Gen. 15.3f., Van der Merwe 2007, 132)

In (65), the *wa-hinnē-XØ*, directly after *wa(y)-yiqṭol* with ensuing quotation, serves to express that the answer will contradict Abram's preceding expectation (Van der Merwe 2007, 132).

The second instance is the chronicle-type text where Enoch finishes his days on the earth:

(66) *wa(y)-yiqṭol* + ***wa-XØ*** + *kī-qaṭal*

וַיִּתְהַלֵּ֥ךְ חֲנ֖וֹךְ אֶת־הָֽאֱלֹהִ֑ים **וְאֵינֶ֕נּוּ** כִּֽי־לָקַ֥ח אֹת֖וֹ אֱלֹהִֽים׃

'Enoch walked with God, **and then he was no more**, because God had taken him.' (Gen. 5.24)

(66) is an anomaly in the genealogy of Genesis 5 (Westermann 1976, 484). Instead of this verse, we expected a simple וַיָּמֹת (in pause). A dynamic state persists (Enoch walked with God), and then suddenly Enoch is no more on the earth. A pluperfect is a reasonable translation of *kī-qaṭal* (thus Westermann 1976, 469).

In a few instances, *wa-hinnē-XØ* is a focused clause without describing the content of a perception, and with only a vague semantic relation to the preceding *wa(y)-yiqṭol*, as in (67):

(67) *wa(y)-yiqṭol* + *wa(y)-yiqṭol* + *wa(y)-yiqṭol* + ***wa-hinnē-XØ***

וַיִּשְׁמַ֤ע קֹלֵ֙נוּ֙ וַיִּשְׁלַ֣ח מַלְאָ֔ךְ וַיֹּצִאֵ֖נוּ מִמִּצְרָ֑יִם **וְהִנֵּה֙ אֲנַ֣חְנוּ בְקָדֵ֔שׁ** עִ֖יר קְצֵ֥ה גְבוּלֶֽךָ׃

'He heard our voice and sent a messenger, and has brought us up out of Egypt. **Now we are here in Kadesh**, a town on the edge of your border.' (Num. 20.16)

The verbless clause in (67) is focused and describes the present state of the speaker. Its semantic relation to preceding *wa(y)-yiqṭol* clauses is vague. The *wa-hinnē-XØ* must be analysed as a main clause in direct speech, and forms the starting point of Moses' appeal to the king of Edom in the following verses. From this perspective, the preceding *wa(y)-yiqṭol* just describe a historical background for the appeal, which now starts.[89]

7.5.2. Interruption Type *Wa-qaṭal // (Wa)-XØ*

Table 27: The semantics of the *wa-qaṭal* + *(wa)-XØ* linking

Explanatory note	29
Circumstantial	18
Addition: contrast	4
Reason	11
Complement	2
Unclear meaning[90]	1
Total	**65**

In the text-types where *wa-qaṭal* can be regarded as a main line in the corpus, interruption with a *(wa)-XØ* clause frequently expresses an explanatory note, to use a term taken from Milgrom (1991, 305); see Table 27. An example is (68):

(68) *wa-qaṭal* + ***Ø-XØ*** + ***Ø-XØ***

וְהִקְטִ֨יר אֹתֹ֤ו הַכֹּהֵן֙ הַמִּזְבֵּ֔חָה עַל־הָעֵצִ֖ים אֲשֶׁ֣ר עַל־הָאֵ֑שׁ **עֹלָ֣ה ה֗וּא אִשֵּׁ֛ה רֵ֥יחַ נִיחֹ֖חַ לַיהוָֽה׃**

‘Then the priest must offer it up in smoke on the altar on the wood which is in the fire—**it is a burnt offering, a gift of a soothing aroma to the Lord**.’ (Lev. 1.17)

Such an explanatory note is not circumstantial, but is to be regarded as a comment to the reader on the significance of the preceding instruction or procedure. It belongs to the text and corresponds to background information in narration.[91]

The second most frequent function of *wa-qaṭal* + *(wa)-XØ* is to code a circumstantial relation. Such clauses in some way refer back to the *wa-qaṭal* clause and are semantically part of it. An example is (69):

(69) *wa-qaṭal* + *Ø-XØ* + *wa-XØ* + *wa-XØ*

וְעָשׂ֥וּ אֲרֹ֖ון עֲצֵ֣י שִׁטִּ֑ים אַמָּתַ֨יִם וָחֵ֜צִי אָרְכֹּ֗ו וְאַמָּ֤ה וָחֵ֙צִי֙ רָחְבֹּ֔ו וְאַמָּ֥ה וָחֵ֖צִי קֹמָתֹֽו׃

‘They are to make an ark of acacia wood—its length being two cubits and a half, its width a cubit and a half, and its height a cubit and a half.’ (Exod. 25.10)

In (69), anaphoric pronouns refer back to the direct object in the main clause. But anaphoric pronouns are not necessary in a circumstantial clause, which may refer back to a phenomenon mentioned or not mentioned in the pragmatic world of the main clause, as in (70):

(70) *wa-qaṭal* + ***wa-ʾēn-XØ***

וְנָתַתִּ֤י שָׁלוֹם֙ בָּאָ֔רֶץ וּשְׁכַבְתֶּ֖ם **וְאֵ֣ין מַחֲרִ֑יד**

‘I will grant peace in the land, and you will lie down to sleep **without anyone terrifying you**.’ (Lev. 26.6)

The verbless clause in (70) mentions a phenomenon that belongs to the possible world of the *wa-qaṭal* clause. It does not refer to a constituent in the main clause, but nevertheless has circumstantial function.[92]

Some circumstantial verbless clauses take on a nuance of contrast, as in (71):

(71) *wa-qaṭal* + ***wa-XØ***

וְכָשְׁל֧וּ אִֽישׁ־בְּאָחִ֛יו כְּמִפְּנֵי־חֶ֖רֶב **וְרֹדֵ֣ף אָ֑יִן**

‘They will stumble over each other as those who flee before a sword, **though there is no pursuer**’ (Lev. 26.37)

In (71), the verbless clause has a nuance of contrast, and can be translated with an initial ‘though’ (thus Milgrom 2001, 2273). The verbless clause has an active participle which should be analysed as a noun.[93]

Some cases of *wa-qaṭal* + *(wa)-XØ* express a reason (Hartley 1992, 363). It is significant that many reason clauses are introduced by the particle *kī*, which is also used to express a temporal ‘when’, a cross-linguistic phenomenon (Dixon 2009, 20). An example is (72):

(72) *wa-qaṭal* + *wa-qaṭal* + *kī-XØ*

וְהִֽתְקַדִּשְׁתֶּ֔ם וִהְיִיתֶ֖ם קְדֹשִׁ֑ים כִּ֛י אֲנִ֥י יְהוָ֖ה אֱלֹהֵיכֶֽם׃

'You must sanctify yourselves and be holy, for I am YHWH your God.' (Lev. 20.7)

In (72), it is unclear whether *kī* is a conjunction or an emphatic adverb. But the function of the verbless clause is to remind the people that "[b]ecause of what Yahweh has done for them, they have every reason to keep his commandments" (Hartley 1992, 363). This seems to be the function of similar verbless clauses without *kī*, expressing that YHWH himself is the reason for obeying his commands, as in (73):[94]

(73) *wa-qaṭal* + *wa-qaṭal* + *Ø-XØ*

וּשְׁמַרְתֶּם֙ אֶת־חֻקֹּתַ֔י וַעֲשִׂיתֶ֖ם אֹתָ֑ם אֲנִ֥י יְהוָ֖ה מְקַדִּשְׁכֶֽם׃

'You must be sure to obey my statutes. I am YHWH who sanctifies you.' (Lev. 20.8)

Finally, in special cases, the interruption *wa-qaṭal* + *(wa)-XØ* may express a complement, as in (74):[95]

(74) *wa-qaṭal* + ***Ø-XØ*** + ***Ø-INT-XØ*** + ***Ø-INT-XØ***

וּרְאִיתֶ֥ם אֶת־הָאָ֖רֶץ **מַה־הִ֑וא** וְאֶת־הָעָם֙ הַיֹּשֵׁ֣ב עָלֶ֔יהָ **הֶחָזָ֥ק הוּא֙ הֲרָפֶ֔ה הַמְעַ֥ט ה֖וּא אִם־רָֽב׃**

'and you shall see the land, **what it is like**, and the people who lives in it, **whether it is strong or weak, few or many**' (Num. 13.18)

7.6. Tenet 1e: The Aspectual Interruption

Tenet 1e accounts for a different type of discourse interruption, what Fleischman (1985, 854) calls "narrative subordination," current in Classical Arabic and discussed in Isaksson (2009, 84–87). In this type of interruption, backgrounding and circumstantial clauses are not primarily coded by word order, but by a switch of tense–aspect. The signal is the shift from a narrative past perfective clause to a verbal morpheme expressing imperfective aspect. This type of interruption does not depend on the presence of an element *X* before the verb, but has a powerful tense–aspect switching effect, effective also in oral performance (Fleischman 1985, 865f.). The same phenomenon in Old French has puzzled investigators, because the temporal connections "often seem confused and the choice of tenses illogical," and the "consensus has been to view TS [tense switching] in older Romance as a stylistic LITERARY device" (Fleischman 1985, 866). Tense–aspect contrasts do "the discourse work of 'narrative subordination'" (Fleischman 1985, 868). This is a phenomenon predominantly found in narratives: "events in the foreground are expressed typically by perfective forms, while background information is expressed by imperfective forms" (Fleischman 1985, 869). This type of narrative subordination is typical of oral textuality in Old Romance, creating "an interruption in the temporal line for insertion of background material" (Fleischman 1985, 871).

This interruption is found also in Central Semitic languages, like Classical Arabic (Isaksson 2009, 84f.):

(75) *fa-qatala* + ***wa-yaqtulu***

fa-kāna rasūl-u llāh-i ṢLʿM maʿa ʾumm-i-hi ʾĀminat-a bint-i Wahb-in wa-ǧadd-i-hi ʿAbd-i l-Muṭṭalib-i bn-i Hāšim-in fī kilāʾat-i llāh-i wa-ḥifẓ-i-hi ***wa-yunbit-u-hu llāh-u nabāt-an ḥasan-an***

'The apostle of God lived with his mother Āmina d. Wahb and his grandfather ʿAbd al-Muṭṭalib b. Hāšim in God's care and keeping, **and God let him grow up like a fine plant**.' (Isḥ. 107:10-11)

In (75), the foregrounding *fa-qatala* clause is interrupted by a *wa-yaqtulu* clause expressing a background comment with past time reference. The background signal is exclusively coded by the tense–aspect switch from the perfective *qatala* to the imperfective *yaqtulu*. Word order is not crucial, only the aspectual contrast.

A similar background construction can be found in the Deir ʿAllā inscription, Combination I:

(76) *wa-yaqtul* + *wa-lā-qat[al* + *wa-yaq]tul* + ***wa-VN-yaqtulu***[96]

(3) ויק֯ם֯ . ב֯ל֯ע֯ם֯ . מן . מח֯ר֯[..] ... ול֯ י֯כ֯[ל . אכל . ויצ]ם [.] **ו֯ב֯כ֯(4)ה . יבכ֯ה֯** .

'And Balaam arose the next day […] and he was not able [to eat, and he fast]ed, **and thereby he wept grievously**.' (KAI⁵ 312:3–4)

In (76), a series of discourse-continuity clauses in narrative (including the *wa-lā-qatal* clause; cf. Tenet 4 below), is interrupted by a *yaqtulu* clause, expressing background with information about Balaam's simultaneous weeping.

In addition to the imperfective interruption of a narrative main line, it is important to recognise the slightly different semantics produced by the continuity clauses *wa-qaṭal* (Tenet 3, see §7.11) and *wa-lō-yiqṭol(u)* (Tenet 4, see §7.12). Such clauses have no focused constituent before the verb and display a closer semantic connection with the preceding main clause. There is an aspectual interruption, but the semantic relation is more intimate. In this type of clause combining, a main-line past perfective *wa(y)-yiqṭol* is linked with a following imperfective *wa-qaṭal* (see §7.6.3), or with the corresponding negated imperfective continuity *wa-lō-yiqṭol(u)* (see §7.6.2). Two continuity clauses are combined, but with an aspectual shift. In this way, a backgrounded event or state is coded with a special immediacy in relation to the preceding *wa(y)-yiqṭol*.

Aspectual interruption with continuity clause:
wa(y)-yiqṭol + *wa-qaṭal*
wa(y)-yiqṭol + *wa-lō-yiqṭol(u)*

In spite of the aspectual difference, the imperfective continuity clauses usually share the actants and the pragmatics of the preceding main clause. The interrupting *wa-lō-yiqṭol(u)* and *wa-qaṭal* are therefore treated separately in this section (in §7.6.2 and §7.6.3). The discontinuity clauses *(wa)-X-yiqṭol(u)*, where *X* is not a simple negation, are discussed first (§7.6.1).

To this must be added some imperfective uses of *qoṭel* (see §7.6.4).

7.6.1. Interruption Type *Wa(y)-yiqṭol* // *(Wa)-X-yiqṭol(u)*

It is conspicuous that this type of linking is so relatively infrequent. The imperfective use of the long *yiqṭol* in a switch from narrative main line is on the decrease in CBH and in the process of being replaced by the diachronically later *qoṭel* morpheme (see §7.4). Purely circumstantial uses of *yiqṭol(u)*—so frequently found in Arabic—are rare. See Table 28.[97]

Table 28: The semantics of the *wa(y)-yiqṭol* + *(wa)-X-yiqṭol(u)* linking

Circumstantial	1
Comment of redactor	6
Background	6
Reason[98]	2
Total	**15**

I have only one example of the circumstantial use of *X-yiqṭol(u)* (77):

(77) *wa(y)-yiqṭol* + *Ø-X-yiqṭol(u)* + *wa-X-yiqṭol(u)-N*

וַיְהִי֙ ק֣וֹל הַשּׁוֹפָ֔ר הוֹלֵ֖ךְ וְחָזֵ֣ק מְאֹ֑ד מֹשֶׁ֣ה יְדַבֵּ֔ר וְהָאֱלֹהִ֖ים יַעֲנֶ֥נּוּ בְקֽוֹל׃

‘The sound of the horn grew louder and louder, while Moses was speaking and God was answering him with a voice.’ (Exod. 19.19)

The two *yiqṭol(u)* clauses in (77) express continuous action with past time reference (Zewi 1999, 108).

A slightly more frequent use of *wa(y)-yiqṭol* + *(wa)-X-yiqṭol(u)* is as (editorial) comment with information that does not pertain to the actual pragmatic situation of the text, but to the time of the redactor. Indications of such a comment are phrases like עַל־כֵּן 'therefore' or עַד הַיּוֹם הַזֶּה 'to this very day' (Childs 1963, 281, 283, 288). An example is (78):

(78) *wa(y)-yiqṭol* + *CONJ-qaṭal* + *wa-X-qoṭel* + [33]***Ø-ʿal-kēn-lō-yiqṭol(u)*** + *REL-XØ* + *kī-qaṭal*

וַיִּזְרַח־לוֹ הַשֶּׁמֶשׁ כַּאֲשֶׁר עָבַר אֶת־פְּנוּאֵל וְהוּא צֹלֵעַ עַל־יְרֵכוֹ׃ **עַל־כֵּן לֹא־יֹאכְלוּ** בְנֵי־יִשְׂרָאֵל אֶת־גִּיד הַנָּשֶׁה אֲשֶׁר עַל־כַּף הַיָּרֵךְ עַד הַיּוֹם הַזֶּה כִּי נָגַע בְּכַף־יֶרֶךְ יַעֲקֹב בְּגִיד הַנָּשֶׁה׃

'The sun rose over him as he crossed over Penuel, but he was limping because of his hip. [33]**Therefore the Israelites do not eat** the sinew which is attached to the socket of the hip to this very day, because he struck the socket of Jacob's hip near the attached sinew.' (Gen. 32.32f.)

The *Ø-ʿal-kēn-lō-yiqṭol(u)* clause in (78) explains a custom, a frequent feature in comments. The custom, not otherwise mentioned in the Old Testament (Westermann 1981, 634), is not known to the supposed readers and the *yiqṭol(u)* must be interpreted as present habitual.[99]

The linking *wa(y)-yiqṭol* + *(wa)-X-yiqṭol(u)* is sometimes also used for background with information that is concomitant with or relevant to the event described by the *wa(y)-yiqṭol* clause. A *(wa)-X-yiqṭol(u)* clause describes background information in (79):

(79) *wa(y)-yiqṭol* + *wa(y)-yiqṭol* + *wa-X-yiqṭol(u)*

וַיַּעַשׂ יְהוָה כֵּן וַיָּבֹא עָרֹב כָּבֵד בֵּיתָה פַרְעֹה וּבֵית עֲבָדָיו וּבְכָל־אֶרֶץ מִצְרַיִם תִּשָּׁחֵת הָאָרֶץ מִפְּנֵי הֶעָרֹב׃

'And Yahweh did so, and heavy *ʿārōb* came to Pharaoh's house and his slaves' house. And in all the land of Egypt the land was being devastated from before the *ʿārob*.' (Exod. 8.20, Propp 1999, 288)

In (79), the imperfective *yiqṭol(u)* clause provides background information about similar concomitant events in the whole of Egypt. Temporal succession is not expressed here. The *wa-X-yiqṭol(u)* cannot be interpreted as one more *wa(y)-yiqṭol* clause, as is done in many translations (e.g., ESV; NIV). A contrast is expressed between the past perfectivity in the main line and the imperfectivity in the *yiqṭol(u)* clause. At the same time, *wa-X-yiqṭol(u)* is not a continuity clause in this linking, and should not be expected to express result.[100]

The same type of linking may be achieved from a main-line *qaṭal* clause to an imperfective *X-yiqṭol(u)*.[101]

7.6.2. Interruption Type *Wa(y)-yiqṭol // Wa-lō-yiqṭol(u)*

When the *yiqṭol(u)* clause is of the continuity type, there is still an aspectual contrast in the linking, but the semantic connection with the preceding main line is closer and can often, but not always, be translated with a focal result clause (§2.3.6), or as a clause carrying over the preceding manner (§2.3.8). I have registered five examples of this type of linking; one is (80):

(80) *wa(y)-yiqṭol-A* + ***wa-lō-yiqṭol(u)!***

וָאֶתְּנָה אֶת־הַלְוִיִּם נְתֻנִים ׀ לְאַהֲרֹן וּלְבָנָיו מִתּוֹךְ בְּנֵי יִשְׂרָאֵל לַעֲבֹד אֶת־עֲבֹדַת
בְּנֵי־יִשְׂרָאֵל בְּאֹהֶל מוֹעֵד וּלְכַפֵּר עַל־בְּנֵי יִשְׂרָאֵל **וְלֹא יִהְיֶה** בִּבְנֵי יִשְׂרָאֵל נֶגֶף
בְּגֶשֶׁת בְּנֵי־יִשְׂרָאֵל אֶל־הַקֹּדֶשׁ׃

'I have delegated the Levites to be assigned to Aaron and to his sons from among the Israelite people, to perform the tasks of the Tent of Meeting and to serve as redemption for the Israelite people, **so that no plague may afflict** the Israelite people as a result of Israelites' approaching the Sanctuary.' (Num. 8.19, Levine 1993, 270, my emphasis)

The continuity clause in (80) presupposes the pragmatic world of the events in the main clauses and the *wa-lō-yiqṭol(u)* easily takes a notion of 'in this way', referring to the previous actions or procedures. An alternative translation of the continuity clause in (80) is, 'in this way no plague may afflict the Israelite people'. If it is a result clause, it is a focal result clause.

A *wa-lō-yiqṭol(u)* in relation to a main-line *wa(y)-yiqṭol* is a continuity clause that depends semantically on the preceding main clause. Another example is (81):

(81) *wa(y)-yiqṭol* + ***wa-lō-yiqṭol(u)***

וַיִּרְכְּס֣וּ אֶת־הַחֹ֡שֶׁן מִטַּבְּעֹתָיו֩ אֶל־טַבְּעֹ֨ת הָאֵפֹ֜ד בִּפְתִ֣יל תְּכֵ֗לֶת לִֽהְיֹת֙ עַל־חֵ֣שֶׁב הָאֵפֹ֔ד **וְלֹֽא־יִזַּ֣ח הַחֹ֔שֶׁן** מֵעַ֖ל הָאֵפֹ֑ד כַּאֲשֶׁ֛ר צִוָּ֥ה יְהוָ֖ה אֶת־מֹשֶֽׁה׃

'They tied the breastpiece by its rings to the ephod's rings with blue cord, so that it was above the waistband of the ephod; **in this way the breastpiece did not come loose** from the ephod, just as the LORD had commanded Moses.' (Exod. 39.21)

In (81), the imperfective *wa-lō-yiqṭol(u)* clause expresses what is achieved by the precautions described in the main line: tying the breastpiece by its rings, placing it above the waistband. As a result of following these instructions, the breastpiece does not come loose. The breastpiece was expected to be used for a long time. The *yiqṭol(u)* has a nuance of habitual enduring, and, because of the main-line *wa(y)-yiqṭol*, past time reference.

The linking from a narrative main line to *wa-lō-yiqṭol(u)* should probably be classified as a special case of background.

But a *wa(y)-yiqṭol* + *wa-lō-yiqṭol(u)* may also express a circumstantial action, as in (82):

(82) *wa(y)-yiqṭol* + ***wa-lō-yiqṭol(u)***

וַיִּהְיוּ שְׁנֵיהֶם עֲרוּמִּים הָאָדָם וְאִשְׁתּוֹ **וְלֹא יִתְבֹּשָׁשׁוּ׃**

'The man and his woman were both naked, **and they felt no shame**.' (Gen. 2.25)

In the *yiqṭol(u)* clause, no new constituent is introduced; the actants are carried over from the main clause. The temporal reference is also carried over: it is past time, and the action or process is concomitant with the state described by the copula verb in the main clause. But the aspect is imperfectivity, describing an ongoing process. So the clause is circumstantial (thus Brockelmann 1908–13, II, §321b).[102]

A *wa-lō-yiqṭol(u)* clause may also, after a main-line *qaṭal* clause, express a nuance of 'in this way', referring to the precautions carried out in the main clause, as in (83):

(83) *wa-X-qaṭal* + [22]*wa-lō-yiqṭol(u)*

וְלִבְנֵי לֵוִי הִנֵּה נָתַתִּי כָּל־מַעֲשֵׂר בְּיִשְׂרָאֵל לְנַחֲלָה חֵלֶף עֲבֹדָתָם אֲשֶׁר־הֵם עֹבְדִים אֶת־עֲבֹדַת אֹהֶל מוֹעֵד׃ וְלֹא־יִקְרְבוּ עוֹד בְּנֵי יִשְׂרָאֵל אֶל־אֹהֶל מוֹעֵד לָשֵׂאת חֵטְא לָמוּת׃

'To the Levites I have given every tithe in Israel, in lieu of a land grant, as exchange for the tasks they will be performing by attending to the Tent of Meeting. [22]In this way Israelites will no longer encroach upon the Tent of Meeting, thereby incurring the penalty of death.' (Num. 18.21f.)

In (83), the *qaṭal* describes the precautions taken, to assign to the Levites the task of attending to the Tent of Meeting. In this way, the Israelites will be protected. "The careful attention of the Levites to their assigned tasks will prevent ordinary Israelites from encroaching on the area of the Sanctuary" (Levine 1993, 451). The meaning of the *yiqṭol(u)* morpheme is not obligation, but pure prospective future.

7.6.3. Interruption Type *Wa(y)-yiqṭol // Wa-qaṭal*

A *wa-qaṭal* clause signals imperfective aspect and continuity. Both these properties are important when *wa-qaṭal* is used in a narrative context. The imperfectivity of *wa-qaṭal* causes an interruption from the narrative main line, but the continuity signals a close semantic relation with the preceding main clause(s). "Its lack of temporal boundaries is exploited to disrupt the chain of perfective temporally bounded events" (Khan 2021a, 318). This is a controversial and relatively infrequent type of linking, which will be discussed in some detail below. See Table 29.

Table 29: The semantics of the *wa(y)-yiqṭol* + *wa-qaṭal* linking

Background	11
Subevent	5
Editorial comment	2
(Topic–comment obligation)	(1)
Total	**19**

The continuity of the *wa-qaṭal* clause-type gives the clause a nuance of immediacy in relation to the narrative main line, which can be used to express a direct response to a quoted speech—a response that is not expressed as a quoted rejoinder, but related in the background, as in (84):

(84) *wa(y)-yiqṭol* + *wa(y)-yiqṭol* + *wa(y)-yiqṭol* + "…" + ***wa-qaṭal*** + ***wa(y)-yiqṭol***

וַתֵּ֣רֶא דְלִילָ֗ה כִּֽי־הִגִּ֣יד לָהּ֮ אֶת־כָּל־לִבּוֹ֒ וַתִּשְׁלַ֡ח וַתִּקְרָא֩ לְסַרְנֵ֨י פְלִשְׁתִּ֤ים לֵאמֹר֙ עֲל֣וּ הַפַּ֔עַם כִּֽי־הִגִּ֥יד לָה [לִ֖י] אֶת־כָּל־לִבּ֑וֹ **וְעָל֤וּ אֵלֶ֙יהָ֙ סַרְנֵ֣י פְלִשְׁתִּ֔ים וַיַּעֲל֥וּ הַכֶּ֖סֶף בְּיָדָֽם׃**

'Delilah saw that he had told her his secret, and she sent and called the rulers of the Philistines, saying, "Come up here again, for he has told me his secret." **On which the rulers of the Philistines went up to her, and brought the silver in their hands**.' (Judg. 16.18)

The *wa-qaṭal* clause in (84) disrupts the chain of perfective, temporally-bounded events, with the effect that the event it describes is placed in the background. At the same time, the continuity signal of *wa-qaṭal* expresses an immediacy in the response of the Philistine rulers, possibly with a humorous nuance. The *wa-qaṭal* clause follows directly after the quoted message of Delilah, and its action is temporally sequential in relation to the preceding *wa(y)-yiqṭol*. In this context, it is not appropriate to regard *wa-qaṭal* as habitual, nor as frequentative (as Rubinstein 1963, 64). This *wa-qaṭal* is sequential and describes a single past event, but in the background.[103] The next action in the background is coded by a *wa(y)-yiqṭol* clause (cf. §2.3.3).

Another example of backgrounded *wa-qaṭal* after quotation is (85):

(85) *wa(y)-yiqṭol* + "*Ø-X-yiqṭol(u)*" + ***wa-qaṭal***

וַיֹּ֣אמֶר֙ אַבְרָהָ֔ם אָנֹכִ֖י אִשָּׁבֵֽעַ׃ **וְהוֹכִ֥חַ אַבְרָהָ֖ם** אֶת־אֲבִימֶ֑לֶךְ עַל־אֹדוֹת֙ בְּאֵ֣ר הַמַּ֔יִם אֲשֶׁ֥ר גָּזְל֖וּ עַבְדֵ֥י אֲבִימֶֽלֶךְ׃

'And Abraham said, "I will swear," **on which Abraham lodged a complaint** against Abimelech concerning a well that Abimelech's servants had seized.' (Gen. 21.24f.)

The direct speech rejoinder in (85) is coded by a *yiqṭol(u)* clause (אָנֹכִ֖י אִשָּׁבֵֽעַ׃), which is often translated as a performative, as if Abraham were swearing an oath. But the *yiqṭol(u)* morpheme is not regularly used as performative. The normal syntax of performative utterances uses *qaṭal*. It fits the pragmatics of the situation better to interpret the *yiqṭol(u)* as expressing a promise to swear, if only some conditions are fulfilled. These conditions are not expressed in a full quotation, but reviewed or summarised in a background clause introduced by *wa-qaṭal*. This *wa-qaṭal* follows directly after the quotation and is intended to substitute a longer continued quotation with a shorter summary. The *wa-qaṭal* is temporally sequential, but not part of the main-line narration. It is not frequentative. It continues the quoted direct speech with a review in the background of the rest of the speech.[104]

A similar background example of *wa-qaṭal* directly after a quotation is (86):

(86) *wa(y)-yiqṭol* + *wa(y)-yiqṭol* | "…" + *wa(y)-yiqṭol* + "…" + [6]***wa-qaṭal*** + ***wa(y)-yiqṭol***

וַיּוֹצֵ֨א אֹת֜וֹ הַח֗וּצָה וַיֹּ֙אמֶר֙ הַבֶּט־נָ֣א הַשָּׁמַ֔יְמָה וּסְפֹר֙ הַכּ֣וֹכָבִ֔ים אִם־תּוּכַ֖ל לִסְפֹּ֣ר אֹתָ֑ם וַיֹּ֣אמֶר ל֔וֹ כֹּ֥ה יִהְיֶ֖ה זַרְעֶֽךָ׃ **וְהֶאֱמִ֖ן בַּֽיהוָ֑ה וַיַּחְשְׁבֶ֥הָ לּ֖וֹ צְדָקָֽה׃**

'The LORD took him outside and said, "Gaze into the sky and count the stars—if you are able to count them!" Then he said to him, "So will your descendants be." [6] **On which Abram trusted the LORD**, and the LORD credited it to him as righteousness.' (Gen. 15.5f.)

Abram's response comes directly after the quoted utterance of God. What the LORD said inspired Abram's confidence (Rainey 2003b, 16), and his response is related as a single mental event in the background. The background also contains a discourse-continuity past perfective *wa(y)-yiqṭol* relating God's evaluation of Abram's trust, which seems to be a natural continuation if *wa-qaṭal* is past narrative, but not if it is habitual. Two mental responses, from Abram and from God, are described behind the scene. The imperfective *wa-qaṭal* clause disrupts "the flow of narrative by removing temporal boundaries in order to signal closure and climax" (Khan 2021a, 317f.). This simple background clause about Abram's response to God is a single event that, together with the ensuing *wa(y)-yiqṭol*, codes both closure and climax.[105]

In many cases, the background character of a *wa-qaṭal* clause after *wa(y)-yiqṭol* is obvious, for example, in the case of the copula verb in (87):

(87) *wa(y)-yiqṭol* + *wa(y)-yiqṭol* + *wa-haya*

וַתֹּ֤סֶף עוֹד֙ וַתֵּ֣לֶד בֵּ֔ן וַתִּקְרָ֥א אֶת־שְׁמ֖וֹ שֵׁלָ֑ה וְהָיָ֥ה בִכְזִ֖יב בְּלִדְתָּ֥הּ אֹתֽוֹ׃

'Then she had yet another son, and she named him Shelah. It was at Kezib that she gave birth to him.' (Gen. 38.5)

The *wa-haya* in (87) has a neutral subject.[106] It is a continuity clause and expresses "the immediate background of another action" (Hornkohl 2014, 288).[107]

As example (86) shows, a *wa-qaṭal* clause inserted into the backbone of the narrative does not necessarily play an unimportant role. It just plays a different role with its continuity signalling and imperfectivity. A *wa-qaṭal* in narration "can have the effect of marking an event as a subevent cohering with what precedes, embedded in the higher-level narrative chain” (Khan 2021a, 318). Such a subevent often also signals closure, as in (88):

(88) *wa-hinnē-X-qoṭel* + *wa(y)-yiqṭol* + *wa(y)-yiqṭol* + *wa(y)-yiqṭol* + *wa(y)-yiqṭol* + ***wa-qaṭal***

וְהִנֵּה צְלוּל [צְלִיל] לֶחֶם שְׂעֹרִים מִתְהַפֵּךְ בְּמַחֲנֵה מִדְיָן וַיָּבֹא עַד־הָאֹהֶל וַיַּכֵּהוּ וַיִּפֹּל וַיַּהַפְכֵהוּ לְמַעְלָה **וְנָפַל הָאֹהֶל׃**

‘There was a round loaf of barley tumbling into the Midianite camp. It reached the tent and struck it, so that it fell; it turned it upside down, **on which the tent collapsed**.’ (Judg. 7.13)[108]

The syntax of this dream report is the typical one. The scene starts with a *qoṭel* clause (with initial *hinnē*), and within the same scene the event line goes on with *wa(y)-yiqṭol* clauses. The closure of the report is coded by a *wa-qaṭal* clause that expresses the immediate final event, the collapse of the tent.[109]

Example (86) has a *wa-qaṭal* clause with an intransitive verb, which could give the impression that the duration of the action is important. But duration or repetition is not necessary for the *wa-qaṭal* clause to code a subevent after *wa(y)-yiqṭol*, as is shown in (89):

(89) *wa(y)-yiqṭol* + *wa(y)-yiqṭol* + *wa-qaṭal*

וַיֵּצֵא אֵהוּד הַמִּסְדְּרוֹנָה וַיִּסְגֹּר דַּלְתוֹת הָעֲלִיָּה בַּעֲדוֹ וְנָעָל׃

‘Ehud slipped out toward the colonnade, and shut the doors of the upper chamber behind him, on which he bolted them.’ (Judg. 3.23)[110]

The *wa-qaṭal* in (89) codes a subevent in the main chain of actions, a detail that is worth mentioning, a closure of a series of events that belong together:[111] the getting out, shutting the doors and, as a closure, the bolting.[112]

A special case is (90), where the subevent takes the form of a temporal clause with following *wa-qaṭal*:

(90) *wa(y)-yiqṭol* + *wa-qaṭal* + *wa-qaṭal*

וַיִּלְקְטוּ אֹתוֹ בַּבֹּקֶר בַּבֹּקֶר אִישׁ כְּפִי אָכְלוֹ וְחַם הַשֶּׁמֶשׁ וְנָמָס׃

'They picked it up morning after morning, each man according to what he needed to eat, and when the sun grew hot, it melted away.' (Exod. 16.21)

In the main-line *wa(y)-yiqṭol*, the aspect is bounded but has an inferred habitual meaning because of the adverbial expressions. This is the main event. The subevent is coded by two *wa-qaṭal* clauses, of which the first functions as a temporal clause, the second as the main clause in the temporal linking. The two *wa-qaṭal* clauses display a mutual linking that is sometimes encountered also in conditional sentences (see §2.3.10). Instead of a protasis marked with a conjunction, the conditional clause may take the form of a *wa-qaṭal* clause (see §6.7.2; Ges-K §159g). This syntax is used when there is a special semantic connection with the preceding clause, in this case the *wa(y)-yiqṭol*. So the two *wa-qaṭal* clauses should be analysed as one *wa-qaṭal* (וְנָמָס׃), with a preceding temporal clause coded by *wa-qaṭal* (וְחַם). By implication, the last *wa-qaṭal* clause is habitual. We know this from the context, but as the examples discussed above show, a *wa-qaṭal* clause may express a single subevent without habituality or repetition.[113]

There are also cases when one or more *wa-qaṭal* clauses code an independent background complex after a *wa(y)-yiqṭol* main line. In such instances, the *wa-qaṭal* can be an editorial comment, rather than a background that belongs to the pragmatic world of the main line. An example is (91):

(91) *wa(y)-yiqṭol* + *wa(y)-yiqṭol* + [26]*wa-qaṭal* + *Ø-X-yiqṭol(u)* + *Ø-X-yiqṭol(u)*

וַיִּבְחַ֨ר מֹשֶׁ֤ה אַנְשֵׁי־חַ֙יִל֙ מִכָּל־יִשְׂרָאֵ֔ל וַיִּתֵּ֥ן אֹתָ֛ם רָאשִׁ֖ים עַל־הָעָ֑ם שָׂרֵ֤י אֲלָפִים֙
שָׂרֵ֣י מֵא֔וֹת שָׂרֵ֥י חֲמִשִּׁ֖ים וְשָׂרֵ֥י עֲשָׂרֹֽת׃ וְשָֽׁפְט֥וּ אֶת־הָעָ֖ם בְּכָל־עֵ֑ת אֶת־הַדָּבָ֤ר
הַקָּשֶׁה֙ יְבִיא֣וּן אֶל־מֹשֶׁ֔ה וְכָל־הַדָּבָ֥ר הַקָּטֹ֖ן יִשְׁפּוּט֥וּ הֵֽם׃

'Moses selected men of ability from the whole of Israel, then set them in charge over the people, leaders over thousands, leaders over hundreds, leaders over fifties, and leaders over tens. [26]They decided cases for the people on a continuing basis: the difficult problem, they brought straight to Moses; every routine problem, they dealt with.' (Exod. 18.25f., Durham 1987, 247)

The *wa-qaṭal* clause in (91) belongs to a situation that is clearly subsequent to the one when Moses did the actual selection of the men of competence. The meaning is past habitual, and the following asyndetic *yiqṭol(u)* clauses, also habitual, express elaborations in relation to the *wa-qaṭal* clause (cf. §7.3.2).[114]

An editorial comment with *wa-qaṭal* after *wa(y)-yiqṭol* is also exemplified in (92):

(92) *wa(y)-yiqṭol* + *wa(y)-yiqṭol* + [31]*wa-qaṭal*

וַיָּ֫שֶׂם אֶת־הַכִּיֹּר בֵּֽין־אֹ֣הֶל מוֹעֵ֖ד וּבֵ֣ין הַמִּזְבֵּ֑חַ וַיִּתֵּ֥ן שָׁ֛מָּה מַ֖יִם לְרָחְצָֽה׃ וְרָחֲצ֣וּ
מִמֶּ֔נּוּ מֹשֶׁ֖ה וְאַהֲרֹ֣ן וּבָנָ֑יו אֶת־יְדֵיהֶ֖ם וְאֶת־רַגְלֵיהֶֽם׃

'And he put the large basin between the tent of meeting and the altar, and set there water for washing. [31]Moses and Aaron and his sons would wash their hands and their feet from it.' (Exod. 40.30f.)

The *wa-qaṭal* clause in (92) describes a later phase, when Moses and Aaron and his sons habitually washed their hands and feet in the large basin. In relation to the *wa(y)-yiqṭol* clauses, *wa-qaṭal* expresses future and iterated action (Propp 2006, 658).

Finally, a *wa-qaṭal* after a *wa(y)-yiqṭol* clause may also express an independent future/obligation meaning, as in (93):

(93) *Ø-X-qaṭal* + *wa(y)-yiqṭol* + [16]*wa-qaṭal* + *wa-X-yiqṭol(u)*

רַ֣ק בַּאֲבֹתֶ֗יךָ חָשַׁ֛ק יְהוָ֖ה לְאַהֲבָ֣ה אוֹתָ֑ם וַיִּבְחַ֞ר בְּזַרְעָ֤ם אַחֲרֵיהֶם֙ בָּכֶ֣ם מִכָּל־
הָֽעַמִּ֖ים כַּיּ֥וֹם הַזֶּֽה׃ וּמַלְתֶּ֕ם אֵ֖ת עָרְלַ֣ת לְבַבְכֶ֑ם וְעָ֨רְפְּכֶ֔ם לֹ֥א תַקְשׁ֖וּ עֽוֹד׃

'Only to your ancestors did he show his loving favour, and he chose you, their descendants, from all peoples—as is apparent today, [16]so you should circumcise the foreskin of your heart, and stiffen your necks no more!' (Deut. 10.15f.)

In (93), a report *qaṭal* + *wa(y)-yiqṭol* summarises the deeds of God in relation to Israel. It is not strictly narration, but the aspect is perfective (past) anyway. The first two clauses state something that is agreed upon by the receivers of the text and have the function of a topic. This topic constitutes the reason for the comment, coded by a *wa-qaṭal* clause with obligational meaning. This meaning is independent of the meaning of the *qaṭal* and *wa(y)-yiqṭol* clauses. The *wa(y)-yiqṭol* + *wa-qaṭal* is a topic–comment linking (see §6.10), and the aspectual contrast discussed in the present section is irrelevant here, which is the reason for the parentheses in Table 29.

7.6.4. Interruption Type *Wa(y)-yiqṭol // (Wa)-(X)-qoṭel*

The interruption type *wa(y)-yiqṭol // (wa)-(X)-qoṭel* is aspectual when *qoṭel* functions as a finite imperfective morpheme. The opposition is not so much a matter of word order, but of tense–aspect opposition (cf. Fleischman 1985). I have decided to treat all uses of *qoṭel* in relation to a *wa(y)-yiqṭol* clause in the same place, for which I refer to Tenet 1c (see §§7.4.1–2).

7.7. Tenet 2a: // *Wa-XV* + (1a, 1b, 1c, or 1d) + *Wa-VX*

This section concerns the instances when there is a break with the preceding main line and this break starts a new paragraph and a new continuity main line (*wa-VX*).[115] The new beginning may consist of clause(s) in the background (§7.7.2), or in the foreground (§7.7.1). It is often very simple (only *wa-XV*), but can be complicated by several types of discontinuity clauses (such as those within parentheses). I have found no *wa-X-yiqṭol(u)* beginning a new paragraph,[116] so in this section only *wa-X-qaṭal* clauses are discussed, foregrounded or backgrounded. The foregrounded *wa-X-qaṭal* are nearly always past perfective, while the backgrounded *wa-X-qaṭal* express a stativic or pluperfect meaning; see Table 30.

Table 30: The *wa-X-qaṭal* + *wa(y)-yiqṭol* beginning a new paragraph

Foregrounded (59)		
	Perfective past	57
	Anterior[117]	1
	Stativic[118]	1
Backgrounded (14)		
	Pluperfect	8
	Stativic	6
Total		**73**

7.7.1. *Wa-X-qaṭal* (foreground) + (1a, 1b, 1c, or 1d) + *Wa(y)-yiqṭol*

When *V* = *qaṭal* in the initial discontinuity clause, the most frequent case is that the *(wa)-X-qaṭal* is itself a main-line clause and also syndetic (with initial *wa*, thus foreground *wa-X-qaṭal*). The syndesis in such a case signals a semantic connection with the preceding context (Isaksson 2021, 219, 226). A canonical instance of Tenet 2a, without further complicating discontinuity clauses (Tenet 1a–d) before the continuity clause (*wa-VX*), is (94):

(94) *wa-VX* + *wa-VX* + *wa-VX* + *wa-V* + *wa-VX* + [2]***wa-XV*** + *wa-VX* + [3]*wa-VX* + *wa-VX* (= Tenet 2a)

wa(y)-yiqṭol + *wa(y)-yiqṭol* + *wa(y)-yiqṭol* + *wa(y)-yiqṭol* *wa(y)-yiqṭol* + [2]***wa-S.noun-qaṭal*** + *wa(y)-yiqṭol* + [3]*wa(y)-yiqṭol* + *wa(y)-yiqṭol*[119]

וַיַּשְׁכֵּם לָבָן בַּבֹּקֶר וַיְנַשֵּׁק לְבָנָיו וְלִבְנוֹתָיו וַיְבָרֶךְ אֶתְהֶם וַיֵּלֶךְ וַיָּשָׁב לָבָן
לִמְקֹמוֹ׃ 2 **וְיַעֲקֹב הָלַךְ לְדַרְכּוֹ** וַיִּפְגְּעוּ־בוֹ מַלְאֲכֵי אֱלֹהִים׃ 3 וַיֹּאמֶר יַעֲקֹב
כַּאֲשֶׁר רָאָם מַחֲנֵה אֱלֹהִים זֶה וַיִּקְרָא שֵׁם־הַמָּקוֹם הַהוּא מַחֲנָיִם׃ פ

'Laban got up early in the morning and kissed his grandchildren and his daughters goodbye and blessed them.

Then Laban left and returned home. [2]**So Jacob went on his way** and the angels of God met him. [3]Jacob exclaimed when he saw them, “This is the camp of God!” So he named that place Mahanaim.’ (Gen. 32.1–3)

The events described in (94) follow after Laban’s pursuit of Jacob, and their peace agreement. Laban leaves (= five *wa(y)-yiqṭol*), and then a new paragraph starts with Jacob alone as actant. This new paragraph is marked by a *wa-X-qaṭal* clause and ensuing continuity clauses (three *wa(y)-yiqṭol*). The initial *wa* in *wa-X-qaṭal* signals a semantic connection with the preceding context (Laban and Jacob).

Slightly more complicated is the example from Genesis 14 (95):

(95) ***wa-X-qaṭal*** + *wa-XØ* + [19]*wa(y)-yiqṭol* + *wa(y)-yiqṭol* + “…” + [20]*wa(y)-yiqṭol* (= Tenet 2a + 1d)

וּמַלְכִּי־צֶ֙דֶק֙ מֶ֣לֶךְ שָׁלֵ֔ם הוֹצִ֖יא לֶ֣חֶם וָיָ֑יִן וְה֥וּא כֹהֵ֖ן לְאֵ֥ל עֶלְיֽוֹן׃ וַֽיְבָרְכֵ֖הוּ וַיֹּאמַ֑ר
בָּר֤וּךְ אַבְרָם֙ לְאֵ֣ל עֶלְי֔וֹן קֹנֵ֖ה שָׁמַ֥יִם וָאָֽרֶץ׃ וּבָרוּךְ֙ אֵ֣ל עֶלְי֔וֹן אֲשֶׁר־מִגֵּ֥ן צָרֶ֖יךָ
בְּיָדֶ֑ךָ וַיִּתֶּן־ל֥וֹ מַעֲשֵׂ֖ר מִכֹּֽל׃

‘Melchizedek king of Salem brought out bread and wine. (Now he was the priest of the Most High God.) [19]He blessed Abram, saying,

“Blessed be Abram by the Most High God,
Creator of heaven and earth.
[20]Worthy of praise is the Most High God,
who delivered your enemies into your hand.”

Abram gave Melchizedek a tenth of everything.’ (Gen. 14.18–20, NET)

In (95), the new paragraph is signalled by a foregrounded *wa-X-qaṭal* clause marking discontinuity and, at the same time, a semantic connection with the preceding context (Abram's return after defeating Kedorlaomer). A new actant (Melchizedek) enters with a separate, and unexpected, series of events. After the *wa-XV* clause (*wa-S.noun-qaṭal*) comes another parenthetical discontinuity clause (*wa-XØ*), before the main line is resumed by *wa-VX* clauses (*wa(y)-yiqṭol*).

An example of an added participle clause after the initial discontinuity *wa-X-qaṭal* is the following:

(96) ***wa-X-qaṭal*** + ***wa-X-qoṭel*** + *wa(y)-yiqṭol* + *wa-XØ* (= Tenet 2a + 1c)

וְאַֽחֲרֵי־כֵ֞ן יָצָ֣א אָחִ֗יו וְיָד֤וֹ אֹחֶ֙זֶת֙ בַּעֲקֵ֣ב עֵשָׂ֔ו וַיִּקְרָ֥א שְׁמ֖וֹ יַעֲקֹ֑ב וְיִצְחָ֛ק בֶּן־שִׁשִּׁ֥ים שָׁנָ֖ה בְּלֶ֥דֶת אֹתָֽם׃

'After this, his brother came out, with his hand grasping Esau's heel; so he was named Jacob. Isaac was sixty years old when Rebekah gave birth to them.' (Gen. 25.26)

In (96), the discontinuous *wa-X-qaṭal* clause is foregrounded and starts a new paragraph. It is followed by a circumstantial participle clause before the main line is resumed by a continuous *wa-VX* clause (וַיִּקְרָ֥א שְׁמ֖וֹ יַעֲקֹ֑ב). The added verbless clause is backgrounded (see §7.5.1).[120]

7.7.2. *Wa-X-qaṭal* (background) + (1a, 1b, 1c, or 1d) + *Wa(y)-yiqṭol*

The typical backgrounded *wa-X-qaṭal* that begins a new paragraph is stativic (including copula verbs) or, alternatively, has pluperfect meaning. The initial *wa* signals a semantic connection with the preceding context. An example with pluperfect meaning is (97):

(97) *wa-X-qaṭal* + *wa-XØ* + *wa-XØ* + [2]*wa(y)-yiqṭol* + "…" + *wa(y)-yiqṭol* (= Tenet 2a with Tenet 1d)

וְשָׂרַי֙ אֵ֣שֶׁת אַבְרָ֔ם לֹ֥א יָלְדָ֖ה ל֑וֹ וְלָ֛הּ שִׁפְחָ֥ה מִצְרִ֖ית וּשְׁמָ֥הּ הָגָֽר׃ וַתֹּ֨אמֶר שָׂרַ֜י
אֶל־אַבְרָ֗ם הִנֵּה־נָ֞א עֲצָרַ֤נִי יְהוָה֙ מִלֶּ֔דֶת בֹּא־נָא֙ אֶל־שִׁפְחָתִ֔י אוּלַ֥י אִבָּנֶ֖ה מִמֶּ֑נָּה
וַיִּשְׁמַ֥ע אַבְרָ֖ם לְק֥וֹל שָׂרָֽי׃

'Now Sarai, Abram's wife, had not given birth to any children, but she had an Egyptian servant named Hagar. [2]So Sarai said to Abram, "The LORD has prevented me from having children. Please sleep with my maidservant. Perhaps I can build a family through her." And Abram listened to Sarai.' (Gen. 16.1f.)

In (97), the *qaṭal* clause is clearly pluperfect (Westermann 1981, 277). The background also includes the verbless clauses, and begins a new paragraph (Moshavi 2013), within which the continuity clauses (*wa-VX*) follow in the next verse.

An example with copula verb is (98):

(98) *wa-X-qaṭal* + *wa(y)-yiqṭol* + "…" (= Tenet 2a)

וְהַנָּחָשׁ֙ הָיָ֣ה עָר֔וּם מִכֹּל֙ חַיַּ֣ת הַשָּׂדֶ֔ה אֲשֶׁ֥ר עָשָׂ֖ה יְהוָ֣ה אֱלֹהִ֑ים וַיֹּ֨אמֶר֙ אֶל־
הָ֣אִשָּׁ֔ה אַ֚ף כִּֽי־אָמַ֣ר אֱלֹהִ֔ים לֹ֣א תֹֽאכְל֔וּ מִכֹּ֖ל עֵ֥ץ הַגָּֽן׃

'Now the serpent was shrewder than any of the wild animals that the LORD God had made. He said to the woman, "Has God really said, You must not eat from any tree of the garden?"' (Gen. 3.1)

In (98), *qaṭal* of the copula verb establishes the discontinuity clause as background, and "the fronting serves to mark both the serpent as a topic of the ensuring [*sic*] discourse and the start of an episode" (Hornkohl 2018, 52). Though the serpent is a new topic, there is a clear semantic connection with the preceding context.[121]

7.8. Tenet 2b: // *Ø-(X)V* + (1a, 1b, 1c, or 1d) + *Wa-VX*

Asyndetic finite discontinuity clauses that begin a new paragraph lack a signal of backward connection (to a previous context). When a *Ø-X-qaṭal* clause begins a new paragraph, it is usually foregrounded with past perfective meaning (§§7.8.1–2). In the rare case of *Ø-X-yiqṭol(u)* starting a literary unit in narration, it forms a temporal clause (§7.8.3), or, with a following main line of *wa-qaṭal* clauses, is prospective with future time reference (§7.8.4); see Table 31.

Table 31: The *Ø-XV* + *wa-VX* beginning a new paragraph

Ø-X-qaṭal + *wa(y)-yiqṭol*		
	Foregrounded	19
	Backgrounded	3
Ø-X-yiqṭol(u) + *wa(y)-yiqṭol*		
	Past temporal clause	1
Ø-X-yiqṭol(u) + *wa-qaṭal*		
	Prospective (future)	3
Total		**26**

7.8.1. *Ø-X-qaṭal* (foreground) + (1a, 1b, 1c, or 1d) + *Wa(y)-yiqṭol*

So far, we have treated syndetic *qaṭal* clauses (*wa-X-qaṭal*) beginning a new paragraph. But asyndetic *qaṭal* clauses (*Ø-X-qaṭal*) are also fairly frequent in this function.[122] The difference is the lack of backward signalling. In some cases, it is possible to detect a semantic connection with the preceding context, but this is not signalled in the linguistic code (Isaksson 2021, 226). A case without backward semantic connection is the start of a report in direct speech in (99):

(99) *Ø-XV* + [5]*wa-VX* + *wa-VX* (= Tenet 2b)

הַגִּבְעָ֙תָה֙ אֲשֶׁ֣ר לְבִנְיָמִ֔ן בָּ֛אתִי אֲנִ֥י וּפִֽילַגְשִׁ֖י לָלֽוּן׃ וַיָּקֻ֤מוּ עָלַי֙ בַּעֲלֵ֣י הַגִּבְעָ֔ה וַיָּסֹ֥בּוּ עָלַ֛י אֶת־הַבַּ֖יִת לָ֑יְלָה

"'I and my concubine came to Gibeah in the territory of Benjamin to spend the night. [5]The leaders of Gibeah attacked me, and surrounded the house where I was staying at night....'" (Judg. 20.4f.)

Since this is the start of a narration (report) in direct speech, there is nothing before this clause to connect to, and the quotation does not start with a *wa*. The Levite begins his report with an asyndetic *qaṭal* clause, with past perfective meaning (*Ø-ADV-qaṭal*). The report then continues with discourse-continuity clauses (*wa(y)-yiqṭol*), also with past perfective meaning. Since this is a quotation, it starts a new paragraph. And it is foreground.

A more complicated paragraph beginning, with both foreground and background before the main line, is (100):

(100) *Ø-XV* + [2]*wa-XV* + *wa-XØ* + *wa-X-qoṭel* + [3]*wa-VX* + "..." + *wa-VX* (= Tenet 2b with Tenet 1a + 1d + 1c)

בְּרֵאשִׁ֖ית בָּרָ֣א אֱלֹהִ֑ים אֵ֥ת הַשָּׁמַ֖יִם וְאֵ֥ת הָאָֽרֶץ׃ 2 וְהָאָ֗רֶץ הָיְתָ֥ה תֹ֙הוּ֙ וָבֹ֔הוּ וְחֹ֖שֶׁךְ עַל־פְּנֵ֣י תְה֑וֹם וְר֣וּחַ אֱלֹהִ֔ים מְרַחֶ֖פֶת עַל־פְּנֵ֥י הַמָּֽיִם׃ 3 וַיֹּ֥אמֶר אֱלֹהִ֖ים יְהִ֣י א֑וֹר וַֽיְהִי־אֽוֹר׃

> 'In the beginning God created the heavens and the earth. [2]Now the earth was formless and empty, and darkness was over the surface and the deep, and the Spirit of God was hovering over the waters. [3]Then God said, "Let there be light." And there was light.' (Gen. 1.1–3)

The passage starts with asyndesis, and there is nothing before this asyndetic clause to connect to (Isaksson 2021, 226f.). This first asyndetic *qaṭal* clause has a dynamic past perfective meaning and belongs to the foreground. Focus is on the first constituent, 'In the beginning' (בְּרֵאשִׁ֖ית). This first clause signals discourse discontinuity and marks a new literary unit (Tenet 2b). The next three clauses, in Genesis 1.2, are backgrounded. The *wa-XV* clause (וְהָאָ֗רֶץ הָיְתָ֥ה תֹ֙הוּ֙ וָבֹ֔הוּ) has a stativic (copula) predicate and describes the state of the earth (Tenet 1a); the *wa-XØ* clause (וְחֹ֖שֶׁךְ עַל־פְּנֵ֣י תְה֑וֹם) is descriptive of the darkness (Tenet 1d); and the *wa-X-qoṭel* clause concerns the ongoing activity of the Spirit of God (Tenet 1c). The foreground is resumed with continuity clauses in Genesis 1.3 (*wa-VX*). Example (100) illustrates Tenet 2b well, with an initial discontinuity *Ø-XV*, in this case foregrounded, and nearly all possible added discontinuity clauses expressing background, corresponding to Tenet 1a, d, c: a *wa-XV* clause (with *V* = *qaṭal*), a *wa-XØ* clause, and a *wa-X-qoṭel* clause.

Another example with several discontinuous *qaṭal* clauses with past perfective meaning is (101):

(101) *Ø-XV* + *wa-XV* + [24]*wa-XV* + [25]*wa-VX* (= Tenet 2b with Tenet 1a)

הַשֶּׁ֙מֶשׁ֙ יָצָ֣א עַל־הָאָ֔רֶץ וְל֖וֹט בָּ֥א צֹֽעֲרָה׃ 24 וַֽיהוָ֗ה הִמְטִ֧יר עַל־סְדֹ֛ם וְעַל־
עֲמֹרָ֖ה גָּפְרִ֣ית וָאֵ֑שׁ מֵאֵ֥ת יְהוָ֖ה מִן־הַשָּׁמָֽיִם׃ 25 וַֽיַּהֲפֹךְ֙ אֶת־הֶֽעָרִ֣ים הָאֵ֔ל וְאֵ֖ת
כָּל־הַכִּכָּ֑ר וְאֵת֙ כָּל־יֹשְׁבֵ֣י הֶֽעָרִ֔ים וְצֶ֖מַח הָאֲדָמָֽה׃

'As the sun rose over the land, Lot entered Zoar, [24]and the LORD rained brimstone and fire on Sodom and Gomorrah, from the LORD, from the sky, [25]so he overthrew these cities, the whole valley and their inhabitants and the vegetation of the soil.' (Gen. 19.23–25, after Wenham 1994, 34)

The three *X-qaṭal* clauses in (101) all signal discontinuity. The first is asyndetic, which marks a weak semantic connection with the preceding context. An interpretation where one of them expresses temporal succession would contradict the linguistic code. What they signal is simultaneity, and this is what a translation has to cope with.[123] At the same time, they express a dramatic highlighting (Hornkohl 2018, 48, 49 n. 64). Three past perfective *qaṭal* clauses begin a new paragraph (Brockelmann 1956, §122n; Blau 1959, 134 n. 2). Like many interpreters, I take the three *qaṭal* clauses as foreground, with past perfective meaning.[124] The continuity clauses start in Genesis 19.25 with *wa-VX* (וַֽיַּהֲפֹךְ֙).[125]

7.8.2. Ø-*X-qaṭal* (background) + (1a, 1b, 1c, or 1d) + *Wa(y)-yiqṭol*

The backgrounding asyndetic *qaṭal* clauses that introduce a new paragraph are few (in my database, only 3×). Here also we encounter *qaṭal* as a stativic verb, or with pluperfect meaning, or as the beginning of a report in speech. A beginning of a report is (102):

(102) *Ø-X-qaṭal* + *wa(y)-yiqṭol* + *wa-lō-qaṭal* (= Tenet 2b, Tenet 4)

אִ֣ישׁ רִ֗יב הָיִ֛יתִי אֲנִ֥י וְעַמִּ֖י וּבְנֵֽי־עַמּ֣וֹן מְאֹ֑ד וָאַזְעִ֣ק אֶתְכֶ֔ם וְלֹֽא־הוֹשַׁעְתֶּ֥ם אוֹתִ֖י מִיָּדָֽם׃

'My people and I were in a struggle and the Ammonites were oppressing me greatly. I asked for your help, but you did not deliver me from their power.' (Judg. 12.2)

The copula verb in the first clause is stativic and the clause describes a situation in the past. This is the background for the following continuity clauses in the foreground.[126]

7.8.3. *Ø-X-yiqṭol(u)* + (1a, 1b, 1c, or 1d) + *Wa(y)-yiqṭol*

The originally imperfective *yiqṭol(u)* is rare in background, and even more so as the beginning of a narrative. I have found one example, in the report uttered by Abraham's servant. It clearly starts a new paragraph; see (103):

(103) *Ø-X-yiqṭol(u)!* + *wa-hinnē-qoṭel* + *wa-XØ* + *wa(y)-yiqṭol* + *wa(y)-yiqṭol* (= Tenet 2b with Tenet 1d)

אֲנִי֩ טֶ֨רֶם אֲכַלֶּ֜ה לְדַבֵּ֣ר אֶל־לִבִּ֗י וְהִנֵּ֨ה רִבְקָ֤ה יֹצֵאת֙ וְכַדָּ֣הּ עַל־שִׁכְמָ֔הּ וַתֵּ֥רֶד הָעַ֖יְנָה וַתִּשְׁאָ֑ב וָאֹמַ֥ר אֵלֶ֖יהָ הַשְׁקִ֥ינִי נָֽא׃

'Before I finished praying in my heart, along came Rebekah with her water jug on her shoulder! She went down to the spring and drew water. So I said to her, "Please give me a drink."' (Gen. 24.45)

In the initial subordinate (temporal) clause, after the adverb *ṭɛrɛm*, *yiqṭol(u)* has retained its imperfectivity (with past time reference). The *wa-hinnē-qoṭel* clause is focal (foregrounded, see §7.4.2) and the verbless clause is circumstantial. After the three subordinate clauses, the main line begins with continuity clauses (*wa(y)-yiqṭol*).

7.8.4. *Ø-X-yiqṭol(u)* + (1a, 1b, 1c, or 1d) + *Wa-qaṭal*

Since *wa-qaṭal* as continuity clause is most frequent in instruction with initial *(wa)-X-yiqṭol(u)* in a modality of obligation, and is also very frequent in modal series with an initial volitive, the cases of *yiqṭol(u)* clauses starting a new paragraph with following continuous *wa-qaṭal* are relatively rare. This happens in prospective sentences with future time reference, and there is usually a sense of narration, though the series of events is transposed to the future. An example is (104):

(104) *Ø-X-yiqṭol(u)* + *wa-qaṭal* + *wa-qaṭal* (= Tenet 2b)

> יְהוָ֞ה אֲשֶׁר־הִתְהַלַּ֣כְתִּי לְפָנָ֗יו יִשְׁלַ֨ח מַלְאָכ֤וֹ אִתָּךְ֙ וְהִצְלִ֣יחַ דַּרְכֶּ֔ךָ וְלָקַחְתָּ֤ אִשָּׁה֙ לִבְנִ֔י מִמִּשְׁפַּחְתִּ֖י וּמִבֵּ֥ית אָבִֽי׃
>
> ‘The LORD, before whom I have walked, will send his angel with you. He will make your journey a success and you will find a wife for my son from among my relatives, from my father’s family.’ (Gen. 24.40)

In (104), Abraham’s servant quotes his master and relates Abraham’s conviction about the future success of the journey. It is clearly a new unit in the speech (Hornkohl 2018, 49 n. 64). The *X* before *yiqṭol(u)* in this case also includes a relative clause, which functions as an attribute to the subject YHWH.[127]

7.9. Tenet 2c: // *(Wa)-(X)-qoṭel* + (1a, 1b, 1c, or 1d) + *Wa-VX*

This section treats the cases when a *qoṭel* clause introduces a new paragraph in narration before continuous *wa(y)-yiqṭol* (§7.9.1), or, in direct speech and future time reference, before continuous *wa-qaṭal* (§7.9.2).

7.9.1. // *(Wa)-X-qoṭel* + (1a, 1b, 1c, or 1d) + *Wa(y)-yiqṭol*

A *qoṭel* clause beginning a new paragraph in narration may form a subordinated (temporal) clause, be backgrounded, or, with an initial *wa-hinnē*, be foregrounded, often in dream reports; see Table 32.

Table 32: The functions of *qoṭel* beginning a new paragraph in narration

Qoṭel is a temporal clause	3
Qoṭel is backgrounded	6
Qoṭel is foregrounded	4
Total	**13**

An example of an initial *qoṭel* clause with temporal meaning at the start of a new paragraph is (105):

(105) ***Ø-X-qoṭel*** + *wa-hinnē-X-qaṭal* + *wa(y)-yiqṭol* + "…" (= Tenet 2c + 1a)

הֵ֜מָּה מֵיטִיבִ֣ים אֶת־לִבָּ֗ם וְהִנֵּה֩ אַנְשֵׁ֨י הָעִ֜יר אַנְשֵׁ֣י בְנֵֽי־בְלִ֗יַּעַל נָֽסַבּוּ֙ אֶת־הַבַּ֔יִת מִֽתְדַּפְּקִ֖ים עַל־הַדָּ֑לֶת וַיֹּאמְר֗וּ אֶל־הָאִ֨ישׁ בַּ֤עַל הַבַּ֙יִת֙ הַזָּקֵ֣ן לֵאמֹ֔ר הוֹצֵ֗א אֶת־הָאִ֛ישׁ אֲשֶׁר־בָּ֥א אֶל־בֵּיתְךָ֖ וְנֵדָעֶֽנּוּ׃

'**While they were having a good time**, then suddenly some men of the city, some good-for-nothings, surrounded

> the house and kept beating on the door. They said to the old man who owned the house, “Send out the man who came to your house, so we can take carnal knowledge of him.”’ (Judg. 19.22)

The *qoṭel* clause is circumstantial in relation to the following foregrounded *qaṭal* clause. These two clauses form a break with the preceding narration and constitute, with the past perfectivity of *qaṭal*, the beginning of a new paragraph. The continuity clauses, in the form of *wa(y)-yiqṭol*, follow directly after the *qaṭal* clause. The directive particle *wa-hinnē* puts the action of the *qaṭal* clause in the foreground of the narration.[128]

Often, the initial *qoṭel* morpheme forms a background clause. A straightforward example, without further discontinuity clauses before *wa(y)-yiqṭol*, is (106):

(106) ***wa-X-qoṭel*** + *wa(y)-yiqṭol* (= Tenet 2c)

> **וְעֶפְרֹ֖ון יֹשֵׁ֣ב בְּת֣וֹךְ בְּנֵי־חֵ֑ת** וַיַּעַן֩ עֶפְרֹ֨ון הַחִתִּ֤י אֶת־אַבְרָהָם֙ בְּאָזְנֵ֣י בְנֵי־חֵ֔ת לְכֹ֛ל בָּאֵ֥י שַֽׁעַר־עִיר֖וֹ לֵאמֹֽר׃
>
> ‘(**Now Ephron was sitting among the sons of Heth.**) And Ephron the Hittite replied to Abraham in the presence of the sons of Heth—before all who entered the gate of his city—’ (Gen. 23.10)

In (106), the *qoṭel* clause gives background information about Ephron being present in the city gate. This introduces a new paragraph. There then directly follows the foregrounded and discourse-continuity *wa(y)-yiqṭol* (וַיַּעַן֩).[129]

A more complex background construction with initial *qoṭel* clauses is found in (107):

(107) *wa-(S.noun)-S.pron-qoṭel* + [5]*wa-X-qoṭel* + *wa(y)-yiqṭol* + [6]*wa(y)-yiqṭol* + *wa(y)-yiqṭol* (= Tenet 2c + 1c)

וּדְבוֹרָה֙ אִשָּׁ֣ה נְבִיאָ֔ה אֵ֖שֶׁת לַפִּיד֑וֹת הִ֛יא שֹׁפְטָ֥ה אֶת־יִשְׂרָאֵ֖ל בָּעֵ֥ת הַהִֽיא׃ 5
וְ֠הִיא יוֹשֶׁ֨בֶת תַּֽחַת־תֹּ֜מֶר דְּבוֹרָ֗ה בֵּ֧ין הָרָמָ֛ה וּבֵ֥ין בֵּֽית־אֵ֖ל בְּהַ֣ר אֶפְרָ֑יִם וַיַּעֲל֥וּ
אֵלֶ֛יהָ בְּנֵ֥י יִשְׂרָאֵ֖ל לַמִּשְׁפָּֽט׃ 6 וַתִּשְׁלַ֗ח וַתִּקְרָא֙ לְבָרָ֣ק בֶּן־אֲבִינֹ֔עַם מִקֶּ֖דֶשׁ
נַפְתָּלִ֑י

'Now Deborah, a prophetess, wife of Lappidoth, was leading Israel at that time. [5]She would sit under the Date Palm Tree of Deborah between Ramah and Bethel in the Ephraimite hill country. The Israelites came up to her to have their disputes settled. [6]She sent and summoned Baraq son of Abinoam from Kedesh in Naphtali.' (Judg. 4.4–6)

The first hemistich of Judges 4.4 is a left dislocation (וּדְבוֹרָה֙ אִשָּׁ֣ה נְבִיאָ֔ה אֵ֖שֶׁת לַפִּיד֑וֹת), and the *qoṭel* clause is resumed with a corresponding subject pronoun (הִ֛יא).[130] The background consists of two *qoṭel* clauses, of which the second is followed by a *wa(y)-yiqṭol* belonging to the background description (וַיַּעֲל֥וּ; see §2.3.3.3). The perfective aspect does not in itself signal habituality, but allows for the action to be repeated or customary. The background construction with *wa(y)-yiqṭol* (וַיַּעֲל֥וּ אֵלֶ֛יהָ בְּנֵ֥י יִשְׂרָאֵ֖ל לַמִּשְׁפָּֽט׃) after the habitual *qoṭel* clause has an implied habitual meaning, 'and the people of Israel would come up to her for judgment' (Sasson 2014, 250). The foreground and main line is resumed with the *wa(y)-yiqṭol* clauses in Genesis 4.6 (וַתִּשְׁלַ֗ח וַתִּקְרָא֙). The example illustrates that a discourse-continuity clause may be used in a background complex and thus be backgrounded, but in such cases, the background is introduced by at least one discontinuous clause.[131]

Wa-hinnē is a focus particle that puts *qoṭel* in the foreground at the beginning of a new paragraph. An example is (108):

(108) *wa-hinnē-S.noun-qoṭel* + *wa(y)-yiqṭol* + *wa(y)-yiqṭol* + "..." (= Tenet 2c)

וְהִנֵּ֣ה בָרָק֮ רֹדֵ֣ף אֶת־סִֽיסְרָא֒ וַתֵּ֤צֵא יָעֵל֙ לִקְרָאתוֹ֙ וַתֹּ֣אמֶר ל֔וֹ לֵ֣ךְ וְאַרְאֶ֔ךָּ אֶת־הָאִ֖ישׁ אֲשֶׁר־אַתָּ֣ה מְבַקֵּ֑שׁ

'Baraq just then was tracking Sisera. Jael went out to meet him, saying, "Come, I will show you the man you are seeking."' (Judg. 4.22, Sasson 2014, 103)

With Baraq entering the scene, a new paragraph begins, with the aftermath of the narrative. And this is done by means of a foregrounded *qoṭel* with progressive action visible to Jael (Sasson 2014, 270). The main line is continued by *wa(y)-yiqṭol* clauses.[132]

Dream reports display a special syntax when using the active participle. In the following example, the first *qoṭel* clause is backgrounded (109):

(109) *Ø-X-hinnē-X-qoṭel* + [18]*wa-hinnē-X-qoṭel* + *wa(y)-yiqṭol* (= Tenet 2c)

בַּחֲלֹמִ֕י הִנְנִ֥י עֹמֵ֖ד עַל־שְׂפַ֥ת הַיְאֹֽר׃ וְהִנֵּ֣ה מִן־הַיְאֹ֗ר עֹלֹת֙ שֶׁ֣בַע פָּר֔וֹת בְּרִיא֥וֹת בָּשָׂ֖ר וִיפֹ֣ת תֹּ֑אַר וַתִּרְעֶ֖ינָה בָּאָֽחוּ׃

'In my dream I was standing by the edge of the Nile, [18]and there came up out of the Nile seven cows, fat and sleek, and they grazed in the reeds.' (Gen. 41.17f.)

It is typical of the syntax of dream reports that scene reports are introduced by the deictic particle *wa-hinnē* before *qoṭel*. In (109), the first *hinnē-qoṭel* clause (asyndetic) is a background description of the initial situation in the dream. I interpret the following *wa-*

hinnē-X-qoṭel (וְהִנֵּה מִן־הַיְאֹר עֹלֹת) as a main line in this dream report syntax. It is notable that a *wa-hinnē-X-qoṭel* clause within the same scene can be continued by a *wa(y)-yiqṭol* that describes another successive event in the dream, both foregrounded.[133]

7.9.2. // Ø-X-qoṭel + Wa-qaṭal

The active participle may also introduce a new paragraph with following discourse-continuity *wa-qaṭal* clauses. The six instances in my database all start a quotation and are focused. Since there is nothing to connect to in preceding clauses, no conjunction *wa* introduces the speech. The temporal reference of the clauses is future or near future. Often, *qoṭel* is preceded by the deictic particle *hinnē*, as in (110):

(110) *wa(y)-yiqṭol* + *"Ø-hinnē-X-qoṭel* + *wa-qaṭal* + *wa-qaṭal* + *wa-qaṭal"* (= Tenet 2c)

וַיֹּ֣אמֶר אֵלַ֗י הִנְנִ֤י מַפְרְךָ֙ וְהִרְבִּיתִ֔ךָ וּנְתַתִּ֖יךָ לִקְהַ֣ל עַמִּ֑ים וְנָ֨תַתִּ֜י אֶת־הָאָ֧רֶץ הַזֹּ֛את לְזַרְעֲךָ֥ אַחֲרֶ֖יךָ אֲחֻזַּ֥ת עוֹלָֽם׃

'He said to me, "I am going to make you fruitful and will multiply you. I will make you into a community of peoples, and I will give this land to your descendants as an everlasting possession."' (Gen. 48.4)

The example shows that discourse-continuity clauses are not always temporally successive, even when they describe a series of promised events that will take place in the future. The *qoṭel* and the first *wa-qaṭal* are related as same-event additions, while the second *wa-qaṭal* is an elaboration (Dixon 2009, 27). And the promise given to Abraham and Isaac is repeated in the third *wa-qaṭal*. Joseph is reminded of the blessing and promise given to

Jacob in Lus: the multiplicity of descendants and the possession of the land (Westermann 1982, 207).[134]

7.10. Tenet 2d: // *(Wa)-XØ* + (1a, 1b, 1c, or 1d) + *Wa-VX*

7.10.1. // *(Wa)-XØ* + (1a, 1b, 1c, or 1d) + *Wa(y)-yiqṭol*

The thirteen instances of a verbless clause followed by *wa(y)-yiqṭol* introducing a new paragraph are found in narrative texts and, not surprisingly, in most of them the *XØ* is backgrounded. See Table 33.

Table 33: The linking *(wa)-XØ* + *wa(y)-yiqṭol* beginning a new paragraph

Backgrounded		
	wa-XØ	6
	Ø-XØ	5
Foregrounded		
	wa-XØ	2
Total		**13**

In some cases, a new paragraph or literary unit is introduced by just a verbless clause followed by main-line *wa(y)-yiqṭol* clauses. This verbless clause may be either syndetic or asyndetic. If it is syndetic, a semantic connection with the previous context is indicated. A backgrounded syndetic example is (111):

(111) *wa-XØ* + *wa(y)-yiqṭol* + *wa(y)-yiqṭol* + *wa(y)-yiqṭol* (= Tenet 2d)

וּלְכֹהֵ֥ן מִדְיָ֖ן שֶׁ֣בַע בָּנ֑וֹת וַתָּבֹ֣אנָה וַתִּדְלֶ֗נָה וַתְּמַלֶּ֙אנָה֙ אֶת־הָ֣רְהָטִ֔ים לְהַשְׁק֖וֹת
צֹ֥אן אֲבִיהֶֽן׃

> ‘Now, Midian’s priest had seven daughters; they came and drew and filled the troughs in order to water their father’s flock.’ (Exod. 2.16)

In the preceding clauses, Moses had fled from Pharaoh and settled by a certain well. The new paragraph in (111) signals a connection to these events with its initial conjunction *wa* (in וּלְכֹהֵ֥ן). The verbless clause expresses a background to the following main-line events coded by three discourse-continuity *wa(y)-yiqṭol* clauses.[135]

A more complex beginning of a new paragraph with asyndetic initial verbless clause is found in (112):

(112) *Ø-XØ* + *wa-X-qaṭal* + *wa(y)-yiqṭol* + “…” (= Tenet 2d with 1a)

> הֵ֣ם עִם־יְב֔וּס וְהַיּ֖וֹם רַ֣ד מְאֹ֑ד וַיֹּ֨אמֶר הַנַּ֜עַר אֶל־אֲדֹנָ֗יו לְכָה־נָּ֛א וְנָס֥וּרָה אֶל־עִיר־הַיְבוּסִ֥י הַזֹּ֖את וְנָלִ֥ין בָּֽהּ׃
>
> ‘When they were near Jebus, the day was almost gone. Therefore the servant said to his master, “Come on, let’s stop at this Jebusite city and spend the night in it.”’ (Judg. 19.11)

In (112), a background complex consists of a verbless clause and a *qaṭal* clause. It is reasonable to interpret the verbless clause as temporal in relation to the following *qaṭal* clause.[136] Both clauses are backgrounded (*qaṭal* has pluperfect meaning). The background complex expresses the reason for the following discourse-continuity *wa(y)-yiqṭol* (וַיֹּ֨אמֶר), and constitutes the start of a new scene in which the small group approaches a Jebusite city.[137]

But a verbless clause initiating a new paragraph can also be foregrounded. Both of my examples are from genealogies (Westermann 1981, 482). One is (113):

(113) *wa-S.pron-XØ-«REL-qaṭal»* + [8]*wa(y)-yiqṭol* + *wa(y)-yiqṭol* + *wa(y)-yiqṭol* (= Tenet 2d)

וְאֵ֗לֶּה יְמֵ֛י שְׁנֵֽי־חַיֵּ֥י אַבְרָהָ֖ם אֲשֶׁר־חָ֑י מְאַ֥ת שָׁנָ֛ה וְשִׁבְעִ֥ים שָׁנָ֖ה וְחָמֵ֥שׁ שָׁנִֽים׃
וַיִּגְוַ֨ע וַיָּ֧מָת אַבְרָהָ֛ם בְּשֵׂיבָ֥ה טוֹבָ֖ה זָקֵ֣ן וְשָׂבֵ֑עַ וַיֵּאָ֖סֶף אֶל־עַמָּֽיו׃

'These were the days of the years of Abraham's life, 175 years. [8]And Abraham breathed his last and died in a good old age, an old man and full of years; and he was gathered to his ancestors.' (Gen. 25.7f.)

The natural interpretation of the verbless clause is as a foregrounded clause, with focused information about the exact age of Abraham at the beginning of a short genealogical narrative (Westermann 1981, 481f.).[138]

7.10.2. // *(Wa)-XØ* + *Wa-qaṭal*

The instances of a verbless clause starting a new paragraph with following main-line *wa-qaṭal* are mainly found at the beginning of utterances. For this reason, the examples I have found are asyndetic (*Ø-XØ*); there is nothing to connect to backwards. An obvious use of this type of linking seems to be as topic, with the comments coded by the following *wa-qaṭal* clauses (see §6.10). Of the five examples in my database, four are topic–comment linkings. The fifth, in (114), exhibits an even closer semantic relation:

(114) ***Ø-hinnē-XØ*** + ***wa-qaṭal*** + *REL-qaṭal* + *kī-qaṭal* (= Tenet 2d)

הִנֶּ֗נּוּ וְעָלִ֛ינוּ אֶל־הַמָּק֥וֹם «אֲשֶׁר־אָמַ֥ר יְהוָ֖ה» כִּ֥י חָטָֽאנוּ׃

‘**We are ready to invade the place** designated by YHWH. We have been remiss!’ (Num. 14.40, Levine 1993, 361)

As Levine (1993, 371) points out, the idiom *hinnɛnnū wə-ʿālīnū* is unique. The deictic particle *hinnē* forms, with its pronominal suffix, a separate verbless clause, ‘We are ready’, which is followed by a *wa-qaṭal* clause that specifies what they are ready for. Semantically, this usage of *wa-qaṭal* comes close to a complement clause.

But many examples are topics with following comments.

(115) *Ø-S.pron-hinnē-XØ* + *wa-qaṭal* (= Tenet 2d)

אֲנִ֕י הִנֵּ֥ה בְרִיתִ֖י אִתָּ֑ךְ וְהָיִ֕יתָ לְאַ֖ב הֲמ֥וֹן גּוֹיִֽם׃

‘Siehe, das ist mein Bund mit dir: Du sollst zum Vater vieler Völker werden.’ (Gen. 17.4, Westermann 1981, 303)

After a first-person personal pronoun in extraposition (Khan 1988, 67), the verbless clause is given additional emphasis by the particle *hinnē*. This clause announces God’s part in the covenant. Abraham’s part is formulated later (Gen. 17.9). So the verbless clause describes the topic. The comment, the covenant promise, is specified in the *wa-qaṭal* clause with future time reference.

Another example of a topic–comment linking, but without the particle *hinnē* introducing the verbless clause, is (116):

(116) *Ø-XØ* + *wa-qaṭal* + *wa-qaṭal* + *wa-qaṭal* (= Tenet 2d)

אֲנִ֣י יְהוָ֗ה וְהוֹצֵאתִ֣י אֶתְכֶ֗ם מִתַּ֙חַת֙ סִבְלֹ֣ת מִצְרַ֔יִם וְהִצַּלְתִּ֥י אֶתְכֶ֖ם מֵעֲבֹדָתָ֑ם
וְגָאַלְתִּ֤י אֶתְכֶם֙ בִּזְר֣וֹעַ נְטוּיָ֔ה וּבִשְׁפָטִ֖ים גְּדֹלִֽים׃

'I am YHWH. I will bring you out from your enslavement to the Egyptians, and I will rescue you from the hard labour they impose, and I will redeem you with an outstretched arm and with great judgments.' (Exod. 6.6)

The one who speaks is YHWH. This is what is agreed upon. And because he is YHWH, he will bring the Israelites out from their slavery. The translation of the *wa-qaṭal* clauses could have started with 'And therefore I will bring you out…'. The temporal reference is future. The series of main-line *wa-qaṭal* clauses continues with five more (the whole prospective utterance is found in Exodus 6.6–8).

It is not necessary that the *wa-qaṭal* clauses express a plain prediction or promise. Obligation is also possible, as in (117):

(117) *wa(y)-yiqṭol* + *"Ø-hinnē-XØ* + *wa-qaṭal* + [22]*wa-haya-bə-VN* + *wa-qaṭal* + *wa-qaṭal"* (= Tenet 2d)

וַיֹּ֣אמֶר יְהוָ֔ה הִנֵּ֥ה מָק֖וֹם אִתִּ֑י וְנִצַּבְתָּ֖ עַל־הַצּֽוּר׃ וְהָיָה֙ בַּעֲבֹ֣ר כְּבֹדִ֔י וְשַׂמְתִּ֖יךָ
בְּנִקְרַ֣ת הַצּ֑וּר וְשַׂכֹּתִ֥י כַפִּ֛י עָלֶ֖יךָ עַד־עָבְרִֽי׃

'YHWH said, "Here is a place near me. You are to stand on the rock, [22]and when my glory passes by, I will put you in the crevice of the rock and cover you with my hand during my passing."' (Exod. 33.21f.)

In (117), the verbless clause describes what is agreed upon, the place near YHWH. The next *wa-qaṭal* is an instruction in the second person ('you are to stand'), and the first-person *wa-qaṭal* clauses provide information about the future actions of YHWH.[139]

7.11. Tenet 3: The Prototypical Discourse-continuity Clause-type *Wa-V(X)*

Tenet 3 is a statement about the pattern of discourse-continuity clauses in CBH. This book has shown in detail that it holds for the clause-types *wa(y)-yiqṭol* and *wa-qaṭal*. It probably holds also for volitives and modal sequences, but to show this is not part of our aim (see §1.1).

> **Tenet 3 of CBH text-linguistics**: The clause-type *wa-V(X)* in CBH prose texts, where *V* is a finite verb, signals discourse continuity in relation to corresponding clauses.

The characteristic feature of discourse-continuity clauses is that they can form an unbroken main-line sequence with corresponding clauses (see Table 34). This book is full of examples of Tenet 3, but it is of course falsifiable. One or two counterexamples are enough to disprove the assertion.

Tenet 3 states that a normal conjunction *wa*, with immediately following finite verbal morpheme, forms a main line of continuity clauses. As finite verbs (*V*), I have identified the following verbal morphemes: the short *yiqṭol* (indicative and jussive), the *qaṭal*, and the imperative. The long *yiqṭol* does not form affirmative continuity clauses in CBH (type *wa-yiqṭol(u)*), due to word order restrictions (see §3.4.3).

The continuity clause-type has special properties that concern its relation to preceding clause(s). There is an immediacy and a closeness in the semantic connection. A continuity clause easily carries over (understands) the previous pragmatic world, its actants and temporal reference.

Remark 1. The *wa-qaṭal* clause-type has developed into a construction with imperfective meanings similar to those of the long *yiqṭol* (see §6). Its meaning cannot be deduced from its components *wa* + *qaṭal*, but it still conforms to Tenet 3 and has a normal conjunction *wa*.

Remark 2. In modal series, *wa-qaṭal* after volitives (*IMP*; *yiqṭol(Ø)*) has certain continuity properties, but does not correspond to *wa-IMP* or *wa-yiqṭol(Ø)*. After a volitive, *wa-qaṭal* can express finality or instructional details that are semantically related to the initial volitive (see §6.4).

Remark 3. In narration, *wa-qaṭal* has certain continuity properties, but with aspectual interruption (see §7.6.3).

Remark 4. The *qoṭel* morpheme does not form a main line of continuity clauses (*wa-qoṭel* is attested in a few cases, but not as main line); see §4.1.1.1.

In the following, I will restrict myself to a few typical examples of *wa-V(X)* as continuity clause.

The prime example of a continuity clause in narration is *wa(y)-yiqṭol*, as in (118):

(118) *wa(y)-yiqṭol* + *wa(y)-yiqṭol* + [17]*wa(y)-yiqṭol* + *wa(y)-yiqṭol* + *wa(y)-yiqṭol* + *wa(y)-yiqṭol* + *wa(y)-yiqṭol*

וַיֵּצֵא קַיִן מִלִּפְנֵי יְהוָה וַיֵּשֶׁב בְּאֶרֶץ־נוֹד קִדְמַת־עֵדֶן׃ וַיֵּדַע קַיִן אֶת־אִשְׁתּוֹ וַתַּהַר
וַתֵּלֶד אֶת־חֲנוֹךְ וַיְהִי בֹּנֶה עִיר וַיִּקְרָא שֵׁם הָעִיר כְּשֵׁם בְּנוֹ חֲנוֹךְ׃

‘So Cain went out from the presence of the LORD and settled in the land of Nod, east of Eden. [17]And Cain was intimate with his wife, and she became pregnant and gave birth to Enoch. And he became the founder of a city,[140] and he named the city after his son Enoch.’ (Gen. 4.16f.)

The *wa(y)-yiqṭol* clauses in (118) have past perfective meaning and, in this example, each expresses temporal succession in relation to the preceding clause.

A good example of a series of continuous *wa-qaṭal* clauses is (119):

(119) *wa-qaṭal* + *wa-qaṭal* + [10]*wa-qaṭal* + [11]*wa-qaṭal* + *wa-qaṭal* + *wa-qaṭal* + *wa-qaṭal*

וְחִבַּרְתָּ֞ אֶת־חֲמֵ֤שׁ הַיְרִיעֹת֙ לְבָ֔ד וְאֶת־שֵׁ֥שׁ הַיְרִיעֹ֖ת לְבָ֑ד וְכָפַלְתָּ֙ אֶת־הַיְרִיעָ֣ה
הַשִּׁשִּׁ֔ית אֶל־מ֖וּל פְּנֵ֥י הָאֹֽהֶל: 10 וְעָשִׂ֜יתָ חֲמִשִּׁ֣ים לֻֽלָאֹ֗ת עַ֣ל שְׂפַ֤ת הַיְרִיעָה֙
הָֽאֶחָ֔ת הַקִּיצֹנָ֖ה בַּחֹבָ֑רֶת וַחֲמִשִּׁ֣ים לֻֽלָאֹ֗ת עַ֚ל שְׂפַ֣ת הַיְרִיעָ֔ה הַחֹבֶ֖רֶת הַשֵּׁנִֽית:
11 וְעָשִׂ֛יתָ קַרְסֵ֥י נְחֹ֖שֶׁת חֲמִשִּׁ֑ים וְהֵבֵאתָ֤ אֶת־הַקְּרָסִים֙ בַּלֻּ֣לָאֹ֔ת וְחִבַּרְתָּ֥ אֶת־
הָאֹ֖הֶל וְהָיָ֥ה אֶחָֽד:

‘And you shall fasten the five curtains separate and the six curtains separate. And you shall double the sixth curtain against the Tent’s front. [10]And you shall make fifty loops on the one curtain’s *lip*, the outermost on the *fastening*, and fifty loops on the *lip* of the curtain, the second *fastening*. [11]And you shall make bronze clasps, fifty, and bring the clasps into the loops and fasten the Tent, so that it shall be one.’ (Exod. 26.9–11, Propp 2006, 312)

In (119), a series of instructions is formulated by seven *wa-qaṭal* clauses, of which the last (וְהָיָה) has the old result meaning (see §6.5). All *wa-qaṭal* have the same subject ‘you’ and the meaning is obligation. If not otherwise stated, we can presume that the instructions are to be performed in the textual order.

Imperatives may also take part in (shorter) series of continuity clauses, as in (120):

(120) *Ø-IMP + wa-IMP + wa-IMP + wa-IMP + wa-IMP*

> פְּר֥וּ וּרְב֛וּ וּמִלְא֥וּ אֶת־הָאָ֖רֶץ וְכִבְשֻׁ֑הָ וּרְד֞וּ בִּדְגַ֤ת הַיָּם֙ וּבְע֣וֹף הַשָּׁמַ֔יִם וּבְכָל־חַיָּ֖ה הָֽרֹמֶ֥שֶׂת עַל־הָאָֽרֶץ׃
>
> ‘Be fruitful and multiply and fill the earth and subdue it, and rule over the fish of the sea and over the birds of the heavens and over every living thing that moves on the earth.’ (Gen. 1.28)

In (120), the first imperative starts without a conjunction. This is the beginning of the paragraph (start of utterance). So this first clause signals discontinuity (*Ø-IMP*), and is a corresponding initial clause (see Table 34). The rest of the imperatives signal continuity, adding one command to the other, directed to the created humankind.

The jussive *yiqṭol(Ø)* does not usually form long series of continuity clauses. It is normally combined with imperatives and sometimes also *wa-qaṭal* clauses in modal sequences. A short example is (121):

(121) *Ø-yiqṭol(Ø)! + wa-yiqṭol(Ø) + wa-yiqṭol(Ø)!*

> יַ֤פְתְּ אֱלֹהִים֙ לְיֶ֔פֶת וְיִשְׁכֹּ֖ן בְּאָֽהֳלֵי־שֵׁ֑ם וִיהִ֥י כְנַ֖עַן עֶ֥בֶד לָֽמוֹ׃
>
> ‘May God enlarge Japheth, and let him dwell in the tents of Shem, and let Canaan be his servant!” (Gen. 9.27)

As the beginning of a (poetic) utterance, the sequence starts with an initial discontinuity clause signalling the beginning of the unit. There then follow two jussive *wa-yiqṭol(Ø)* which add further volitive blessings to Japheth.

7.12. Tenet 4: The Prototypical Negated Discourse-continuity Clause-type *Wa-NEG-V(X)*

Tenet 4 is a statement about the pattern of negated discourse-continuity clauses in CBH. This book has shown that it holds for the clause-types *wa-lō-qaṭal* and *wa-lō-yiqṭol(u)*. It probably holds also for *wa-ʾal-yiqṭol(Ø)* in modal sequences, but it is not part of our aim to show this.

Tenet 4 of CBH text-linguistics: The clause-type *wa-NEG-V(X)* in CBH prose texts, where *V* is a finite verb, signals discourse continuity in relation to corresponding clauses.

The characteristic feature of negated continuity clauses is that they may alternate seamlessly with corresponding affirmative continuity clauses (see Table 34), forming an unbroken main-line sequence. *NEG* may be *lō* or *ʾal* depending on the verbal morpheme that is negated. This book has many examples of Tenet 4, but it is of course falsifiable. One or two counterexamples are enough to disprove the assertion.

Remark. In narration, *wa-lō-yiqṭol(u)* has certain continuity properties, but with aspectual interruption (see §7.6.2).

For each affirmative continuity clause, there is a corresponding negated continuity clause. For historical reasons, CBH does not usually form negated continuity clauses from the same verbal morpheme (*V*) as in the corresponding affirmative clause.

If the affirmative continuity clause is *wa-*V_1, the negated continuity clause is in several cases *wa-NEG-*V_2, where $V_2 \neq V_1$, and not the expected *wa-NEG-*V_1. The jussive *wa-ʾal-yiqṭol(Ø)* is exceptional; it is the negative counterpart of both *wa-yiqṭol(Ø)* and *wa-IMP*.[141]

Of course, a corresponding initial clause is usually discontinuous, but can be part of the main line (see §§7.7–8). A set of corresponding affirmative and negated continuity clauses is displayed in Table 34.

Table 34: Initial discontinuous clauses and corresponding affirmative and negated continuity clauses

Initial discont.	**Affirmative cont.**	**Negated cont.**
(wa)-X-qaṭal[142]	*wa(y)-yiqṭol*	*wa-lō-qaṭal*
(wa)-X-yiqṭol(u)	*wa-qaṭal*	*wa-lō-yiqṭol(u)*
Ø-yiqṭol(Ø)	*wa-yiqṭol(Ø)*	*wa-ʾal-yiqṭol(Ø)*
Ø-(X)-IMP	*wa-IMP*	*wa-ʾal-yiqṭol(Ø)*

The corresponding affirmative and negated continuity clauses are treated below.

7.12.1. *Wa(y)-yiqṭol* and Non-interruptive *Wa-lō-qaṭal*

This type of alternating with a negative clause without interruption of the main line has already been mentioned (see §5.5, and Isaksson 2015a, 256; cf. example in §7.8.2). The non-interruption of the main line is easiest to detect when the verbal semanteme is dynamic. An example is (122):

(122) *wa(y)-yiqṭol* + *wa(y)-yiqṭol* + *wa-lō-qaṭal* + *wa(y)-yiqṭol* + *wa(y)-yiqṭol* + "…"

וַיַּעְתֵּ֣ק מִשָּׁ֗ם וַיַּחְפֹּר֙ בְּאֵ֣ר אַחֶ֔רֶת וְלֹ֥א רָב֖וּ עָלֶ֑יהָ וַיִּקְרָ֤א שְׁמָהּ֙ רְחֹב֔וֹת וַיֹּ֕אמֶר
כִּֽי־עַתָּ֞ה הִרְחִ֧יב יְהוָ֛ה לָ֖נוּ וּפָרִ֥ינוּ בָאָֽרֶץ׃

'He went away from there and dug another well, and over that one they didn't quarrel. So he called it Rechovot, and he said: "Now at last the LORD has granted us ample space to increase in the land."' (Gen. 26.22)

The *wa-lō-qaṭal* clause expresses a temporal succession in relation to the preceding *wa(y)-yiqṭol* clauses, and the succeeding *wa(y)-yiqṭol* clauses are also temporally sequential relative to the negated clause.[143]

It must be stated that discourse continuity may signal a great variety of clausal relations; temporal succession is only one of them. For a survey of the semantics of *wa*-linking in CBH, including discourse-continuity linking, see §2.3.

7.12.2. *Wa-qaṭal* and *Wa-lō-yiqṭol(u)*

While *wa-qaṭal* has nearly completely replaced the clause-type **wa-yiqṭol(u)*, the negated counterpart *wa-lō-yiqṭol(u)* is retained from Central Semitic. It functions as the negated continuity counterpart of *wa-qaṭal*. An example is (123):

(123) *wa-qaṭal* + *wa-qaṭal* + *wa-qaṭal* + *wa-X-lō-yiqṭol(u)* + [23]*wa-qaṭal* + *wa-qaṭal* + *wa-qaṭal* + ***wa-lō-yiqṭol(u)***

וּלְקַחְתֶּ֞ם אֲגֻדַּ֣ת אֵז֗וֹב וּטְבַלְתֶּם֮ בַּדָּ֣ם אֲשֶׁר־בַּסַּף֒ וְהִגַּעְתֶּ֤ם אֶל־הַמַּשְׁקוֹף֙ וְאֶל־
שְׁתֵּ֣י הַמְּזוּזֹ֔ת מִן־הַדָּ֖ם אֲשֶׁ֣ר בַּסָּ֑ף וְאַתֶּ֗ם לֹ֥א תֵצְא֛וּ אִ֥ישׁ מִפֶּֽתַח־בֵּית֖וֹ עַד־בֹּֽקֶר׃
23 וְעָבַ֣ר יְהוָה֮ לִנְגֹּ֣ף אֶת־מִצְרַיִם֒ וְרָאָ֤ה אֶת־הַדָּם֙ עַל־הַמַּשְׁק֔וֹף וְעַ֖ל שְׁתֵּ֣י
הַמְּזוּזֹ֑ת וּפָסַ֤ח יְהוָה֙ עַל־הַפֶּ֔תַח **וְלֹ֤א יִתֵּן֙** הַמַּשְׁחִ֔ית לָבֹ֥א אֶל־בָּתֵּיכֶ֖ם לִנְגֹּֽף׃

> 'You shall take a branch of hyssop, and dip in the blood that is in the basin, and apply to the lintel and to the two doorposts some of the blood that is in the basin. And not one of you is to go out the door of his house until morning. 23The LORD will pass through to strike the Egyptians, and then he will see the blood on the lintel and the two doorposts, therefore the LORD will pass over the door, **and will not permit** the destroyer to enter your houses to strike you.' (Exod. 12.22f.)

(123) contains an instruction section, and a section that describes what will happen in the near future (in the night) when the instruction is obeyed. The instruction (obligation) starts with three *wa-qaṭal* clauses. They describe actions that are clearly temporally sequential. There then follows as the last clause in verse 22 a discontinuity clause with a focused subject pronoun (אַתֶּם). It is a general instruction that no one is to go out of the door until morning. The next verse is a description of what will happen during the night. The actions are temporally sequential and the meaning is future, not obligation. The last two clauses, *wa-qaṭal* + *wa-lō-yiqṭol(u)*, express what is achieved when the instruction is obeyed: the Lord will pass over and will not permit the destroyer. This is a relatively frequent meaning of continuity clauses: the focal result (see §2.3.6), which can often be translated with an initial 'therefore'. It is important to note that the two clauses together, as a clausal complex, express the focal result: it begins with *wa-qaṭal* (וּפָסַח) and ends with *wa-lō-yiqṭol(u)* (וְלֹא יִתֵּן), and both have the same meaning, except that the second is negated. In (114), the *wa-lō-yiqṭol(u)* is not a result clause in

relation to the immediately preceding *wa-qaṭal*; it is just the negated counterpart of *wa-qaṭal*.[144]

In the semantic linking of focal result illustrated above, the result is based on facts and circumstances that are presented in the preceding clause(s). The known facts motivate what is expressed by the continuity clauses (*wa-qaṭal* or *wa-lō-yiqṭol(u)*). But there is another type of result in CBH, also expressed by continuity clauses, which is based on obligational instructions. In this type of result, the linking with a continuity clause (*wa-qaṭal* or *wa-lō-yiqṭol(u)*) expresses what is achieved by following the instruction (see §2.3.8). This type of result cannot be translated with an initial 'therefore'. A better option in many cases is an initial 'in this way'. Such a result clause is not syntactically subordinate. We have already shown that *wa-qaṭal* may begin this type of supporting result clause (see §2.3.8), so it is reasonable to expect that its negated counterpart can too. An example of this is (124):

(124) *wa-qaṭal* + ***wa-lō-yiqṭol(u)*** + *wa-qaṭal*

> וְהָיוּ֩ עַל־אַהֲרֹ֨ן וְעַל־בָּנָ֜יו בְּבֹאָ֣ם ׀ אֶל־אֹ֣הֶל מוֹעֵ֗ד א֣וֹ בְגִשְׁתָּ֤ם אֶל־הַמִּזְבֵּ֙חַ֙ לְשָׁרֵ֣ת בַּקֹּ֔דֶשׁ **וְלֹא־יִשְׂא֥וּ** עָוֺ֖ן וָמֵ֑תוּ
>
> 'These must be on Aaron and his sons when they enter the tent of meeting, or when they approach the altar to minister in the Holy Place; **in this way they will not incur guilt** and die.' (Exod. 28.43)

A continuity clause carries over the pragmatic 'world' of the preceding clause(s). In this case, it carries over and presupposes the cultic instructions and procedures described in the previous clauses. This is what the negated *wa-lō-yiqṭol(u)* expresses. In the

CBH syntax, an explicit phrase ‘in this way’ would be redundant. In (124), it is followed by its affirmative continuity counterpart (וָמֵ֑תוּ) taking part in the same result complex. The clauses that describe the cultic regulations are focal, and the result, coded by *wa-lō-yiqṭol(u)* + *wa-qaṭal*, is supporting.[145]

But carrying over the preceding pragmatic ‘world’ may also imply carrying over the preceding temporal reference. This is a relatively frequent function of *wa-qaṭal* clauses.[146] An example with both *wa-qaṭal* and *wa-lō-yiqṭol(u)* is (125):

(125) *Ø-hinnē-X-qoṭel* + [4]*wa-qaṭal* + *wa-lō-yiqṭol(u)!*

הִנֵּ֨ה יַד־יְהוָ֜ה הוֹיָ֗ה בְּמִקְנְךָ֙ אֲשֶׁ֣ר בַּשָּׂדֶ֔ה בַּסּוּסִ֤ים בַּחֲמֹרִים֙ בַּגְּמַלִּ֔ים בַּבָּקָ֖ר
וּבַצֹּ֑אן דֶּ֖בֶר כָּבֵ֥ד מְאֹֽד׃ וְהִפְלָ֣ה יְהוָ֔ה בֵּ֚ין מִקְנֵ֣ה יִשְׂרָאֵ֔ל וּבֵ֖ין מִקְנֵ֣ה מִצְרָ֑יִם וְלֹ֥א
יָמ֛וּת מִכָּל־לִבְנֵ֥י יִשְׂרָאֵ֖ל דָּבָֽר׃

‘The hand of the LORD is about to be on your livestock in the field, on the horses, the donkeys, the camels, and the sheep and goats— a very heavy plague. [4]At that time the LORD will distinguish between the livestock of Israel and the livestock of Egypt, and nothing will die of all that the Israelites have.’ (Exod. 9.3f.)

In (125), the *wa-qaṭal* clause presupposes the temporal reference of the *qoṭel* clause, and its negated counterpart follows with the same temporal reference. It is of course not necessary to translate with an explicit phrase ‘at that time’, which can be left understood also in a translation.[147]

An example with *wa-lō-yiqṭol(u)* alone carrying over the preceding temporal reference is (126):

(126) *"wa-X-hinnē-qoṭel* + ¹¹*wa-qaṭal* + **wa-lō-yiqṭol(u)** + *wa-lō-yiqṭol(u)!"* + ¹²*wa(y)-yiqṭol* + *"Ø-XØ-REL-X-qoṭel* + ¹³*Ø-X-qaṭal* + *wa-qaṭal"*

וַאֲנִ֕י הִנְנִ֥י מֵקִ֛ים אֶת־בְּרִיתִ֖י אִתְּכֶ֑ם וְאֶֽת־זַרְעֲכֶ֖ם אַחֲרֵיכֶֽם׃ 10 וְאֵ֣ת כָּל־נֶ֤פֶשׁ הַֽחַיָּה֙ אֲשֶׁ֣ר אִתְּכֶ֔ם בָּע֧וֹף בַּבְּהֵמָ֛ה וּֽבְכָל־חַיַּ֥ת הָאָ֖רֶץ אִתְּכֶ֑ם מִכֹּל֙ יֹצְאֵ֣י הַתֵּבָ֔ה לְכֹ֖ל חַיַּ֥ת הָאָֽרֶץ׃ 11 וַהֲקִמֹתִ֤י אֶת־בְּרִיתִי֙ אִתְּכֶ֔ם **וְלֹֽא־יִכָּרֵ֧ת כָּל־בָּשָׂ֛ר ע֖וֹד** מִמֵּ֣י הַמַּבּ֑וּל וְלֹֽא־יִהְיֶ֥ה ע֛וֹד מַבּ֖וּל לְשַׁחֵ֥ת הָאָֽרֶץ׃ 12 וַיֹּ֣אמֶר אֱלֹהִ֗ים זֹ֤את אֽוֹת־הַבְּרִית֙ אֲשֶׁר־אֲנִ֣י נֹתֵ֗ן בֵּינִי֙ וּבֵ֣ינֵיכֶ֔ם וּבֵ֛ין כָּל־נֶ֥פֶשׁ חַיָּ֖ה אֲשֶׁ֣ר אִתְּכֶ֑ם לְדֹרֹ֖ת עוֹלָֽם׃ 13 אֶת־קַשְׁתִּ֕י נָתַ֖תִּי בֶּֽעָנָ֑ן וְהָֽיְתָה֙ לְא֣וֹת בְּרִ֔ית בֵּינִ֖י וּבֵ֥ין הָאָֽרֶץ׃

"'I am about to establish my covenant with you, with your descendants after you, ¹⁰and with every living creature that is with you: the birds, the livestock and every wild animal with you, all going out of the ark, every animal on earth. ¹¹I will establish my covenant with you, **and then never again will all living beings be destroyed** by the waters of a flood, and there will never again be a flood to destroy the earth." ¹²God added, "Here is the sign of the covenant that I am about to make between myself and you and every living creature with you, for all generations to come: ¹³I herewith put my rainbow in the cloud—it will be a sign of the covenant between myself and the earth."' (Gen. 9.9–13)

(126) is an aetiological narrative about the origin of the rainbow (Westermann 1976, 634). It tells of God establishing a covenant between himself and the descendants of Noah and the rest of all living creatures. The clause-types used for making this covenant are *X-qoṭel*, *wa-qaṭal*, *wa-lō-yiqṭol(u)*, and *Ø-X-qaṭal*. All of them are sometimes translated with English present tense, as if all could express a performative meaning. But the regular means of expressing a performative in CBH is by using the *qaṭal* morpheme

(see §5.4.5). The active participle in main clauses in such formulations describes an intention for the immediate future. And *wa-qaṭal* and *X-yiqṭol(u)* are regular expressions for future actions (see §§4.4, 6.11.1). It is therefore reasonable to interpret the *qaṭal* clause as the one with a performative meaning which establishes the covenant: "Meinen Bogen setze ich in die Wolken" (Westermann 1976, 616). The *wa-qaṭal* (וַהֲקִמֹתִ֤י) in verse eleven 'I will establish my covenant' is still describing an intention about a future action, and the following *wa-lō-yiqṭol(u)* (וְלֹא־יִכָּרֵ֧ת כָּל־בָּשָׂ֛ר ע֖וֹד) takes over this futural temporal reference point: at that time, when this is done, 'never again will all living beings be destroyed'.[148]

The function of *wa-lō-yiqṭol(u)* as the negative counterpart of *wa-qaṭal* is illustrated also in some complex protases in legal language, as in (127):

(127) *wa-kī-yiqṭol(u)* + *wa-qaṭal* + *wa-lō-yiqṭol(u)!* + *wa-qaṭal*

וְכִֽי־יְרִיבֻ֣ן אֲנָשִׁ֔ים וְהִכָּה־אִישׁ֙ אֶת־רֵעֵ֔הוּ בְּאֶ֖בֶן א֣וֹ בְאֶגְרֹ֑ף וְלֹ֥א יָמ֖וּת וְנָפַ֥ל לְמִשְׁכָּֽב׃

'If men fight, and one strikes his neighbor with a stone or with his fist and he does not die, but must remain in bed...' (Exod. 21.18)

(127) shows one complete protasis with a legal case that is formulated as a story about a man who strikes his neighbor. The events described in the story are temporally sequential and coded by *wa-qaṭal* and *wa-lō-yiqṭol(u)* clauses with the same meaning.[149]

The function of *wa-lō-yiqṭol(u)* as the negative counterpart of *wa-qaṭal* is also displayed in descriptions of future series of events, as in (128):

(128) *Ø-bə-VN* + *wa-qaṭal* + *wa-qaṭal* + *wa-qaṭal* + *wa-lō-yiqṭol(u)*

בְּשִׁבְרִ֣י לָכֶם֮ מַטֵּה־לֶחֶם֒ וְאָפוּ֩ עֶ֨שֶׂר נָשִׁ֤ים לַחְמְכֶם֙ בְּתַנּ֣וּר אֶחָ֔ד וְהֵשִׁ֥יבוּ
לַחְמְכֶ֖ם בַּמִּשְׁקָ֑ל וַאֲכַלְתֶּ֖ם וְלֹ֥א תִשְׂבָּֽעוּ׃ ס

'When I cut off your supply of bread, ten women will bake your bread in one oven; and they will ration your bread by weight, and you will eat and not be satisfied.' (Lev. 26.26)

As continuity clauses, both *wa-qaṭal* and *wa-lō-yiqṭol(u)* may in specific text-types express temporally successive actions, and this is the case in (128). In the example, *wa-lō-yiqṭol(u)* does not express a result. It is just the negated counterpart of affirmative *wa-qaṭal*.[150]

7.12.3. *Wa-yiqṭol(Ø)* and *Wa-ʾal-yiqṭol(Ø)*

Jussive *wa-yiqṭol(Ø)* and *wa-ʾal-yiqṭol(Ø)* do not form long sequences of continuity clauses. Modal sequences usually combine imperatives, jussives (including cohortatives), and additional instructions in the form of *wa-qaṭal* clauses (see §6.4). An example of a modal sequence with only jussives is (129):

(129) *Ø-yiqṭol(Ø)* + *wa-yiqṭol(Ø)* + *wa-ʾal-yiqṭol(Ø)*

תִּכְבַּ֧ד הָעֲבֹדָ֛ה עַל־הָאֲנָשִׁ֖ים וְיַעֲשׂוּ־בָ֑הּ וְאַל־יִשְׁע֖וּ בְּדִבְרֵי־שָֽׁקֶר׃

'Let the work be hard upon the men; so let them do it, and not look to words of deceit.' (Exod. 5.9, Propp 1999, 244)

In (129), the initial main-line jussive is asyndetic and discontinuous. It is followed by two continuity jussives with initial *wa*, of which the last is negated with *ʾal*. As is often, but not always, the case, the continuity jussives receive a nuance of purpose (see

§2.3.9). (129) illustrates that *wa-ʾal-yiqṭol(Ø)* may function as the negative continuity counterpart of *wa-yiqṭol(Ø)*.[151] Most other cases of *wa-ʾal-yiqṭol(Ø)* are to be analysed as negated imperative clauses (see §7.12.4).

7.12.4. *Wa-IMP* and *Wa-ʾal-yiqṭol(Ø)*

The main focus in this section is on the negated continuity volitive clause-type *wa-ʾal-yiqṭol(Ø)*. The exact sequence *wa-IMP* + *wa-ʾal-yiqṭol(Ø)*, with a discourse-continuity *wa-IMP* clause directly followed by a negated continuity clause *wa-ʾal-yiqṭol(Ø)*, is not attested in my database. An example of *wa-ʾal-yiqṭol(Ø)* functioning as a discourse-continuity negated imperative clause is (130):

(130) *Ø-IMP* + *Ø-ʾal-yiqṭol(Ø)*[152] + *wa-ʾal-yiqṭol(Ø)* + *Ø-IMP* + *pɛn-yiqṭol(u)!*

הִמָּלֵ֣ט עַל־נַפְשֶׁ֔ךָ אַל־תַּבִּ֣יט אַחֲרֶ֔יךָ וְאַל־תַּעֲמֹ֖ד בְּכָל־הַכִּכָּ֑ר הָהָ֥רָה הִמָּלֵ֖ט פֶּן־
תִּסָּפֶֽה׃

‘Flee for your lives! Don’t look back, and don’t stop anywhere in the plain! Flee to the mountains or you will be swept away!’ (Gen. 19.17)

The modal sequence in (130) consists of three syntactically independent imperative clauses, of which one is negated (*Ø-IMP*; *Ø-ʾal-yiqṭol(Ø)*; *Ø-IMP*). A discourse-continuity negated imperative (וְאַל־תַּעֲמֹד) follows the asyndetic negated clause (אַל־תַּבִּיט). The negated jussives are combined as if they form a semantic unit.

Continuity clauses after an initial imperative may create a semantically unified sequence of events, as in (131):

(131) *wa-ʿattā-IMP* + *wa-ʾal-yiqṭol(Ø)* + *wa-ʾal-yiqṭol(Ø)*

וְעַתָּה֙ הִשָּׁמְרִי֙ נָ֔א וְאַל־תִּשְׁתִּ֖י יַ֣יִן וְשֵׁכָ֑ר וְאַל־תֹּאכְלִ֖י כָּל־טָמֵֽא׃

'Now be careful! Do not drink wine or beer, and do not eat anything unclean.' (Judg. 13.4)

The modal sequence in (131) concerns what Manoah's wife should take care to do. Because of the semantics of the first verb (הִשָּׁמְרִי), the following negated continuity clauses with jussive morphemes are interpreted as complements, 'Now see to it that you do not drink wine and beer…' (see §2.3.9).[153]

---

[1] For *wayyiqṭol* and *wa-X-qaṭal*, this is formulated by Niccacci (1990, §§39, 40). Also, but more generally, Longacre and Hwang (1994, 345): "Discontinuities marked by departure from *wayyiqtol* clauses, introduce further information into the narrative."

[2] Niccacci (1990, 64, 71): "WAYYIQTOL → (WAW-)x-QATAL (note that the WAW can be omitted)."

[3] As Niccacci (1990, 65, 71, 112), for example, puts it: "simple nominal clause, usually preceded by WAW."

[4] Pardee (2012, 290) proposes the term "*w*-retentive forms" for both *wa(y)-yiqṭol* and *wa-qaṭal.* But *wa-qaṭal* has developed imperfective meanings which cannot be called retention of the original West Semitic perfective *qatal.* 'Symmetry' has also been adduced as a driving force behind the development of 'consecutive' *wa-qaṭal*, but symmetry is not a feature that must be expected in a living language (Cook 2012, 104).

[5] In a similar way, Müller (1991, 156) compares *wa* with the German *und.* Tropper (1996, 635) defines its meaning in Biblical Hebrew and Old Aramaic as "und (dann)."

[6] For a critical discussion of discourse types, see Notarius (2008, 57–59; 2013, 10f., 51–53).

[7] Givón (1983, 7): "The thematic paragraph is the most immediately relevant level of discourse within which one can begin to discuss the

complex process of *continuity in discourse*." See further Bailey and Levinsohn (1992, 193–205); Buth (1995); Hornkohl (2018, 48f.).

[8] The most concrete of these is the last one, 'topics/participants continuity'; cf. Givón (1977, 203; 1983, 7); Buth (1995, 97–99); Hornkohl (2018, 48). "Action continuity pertains primarily to *temporal sequentiality* within thematic paragraph, but also to temporal *adjacency* therein... In the grammar/syntax, which is primarily (though not exclusively) a clause-level coding instrument, action continuity receives its expression strongly and universally via the tense–aspect–modality sub-system most commonly attached to the verbal word" (Givón 1983, 8). According to the traditional terminology, it is "the converted forms" that express continued topicality and, in the case of *wa(y)-yiqṭol*, "controls the *flow* of the story" (Smith 1991, 14, quoting Givón 1977, 198). From a cross-linguistic perspective, common signals of continuity are "zero anaphora" and "unstressed/bound pronouns or grammatical agreement" (Givón 1983, 17). Among the grammatical signals of discontinuity, Givón (2001, II:225) enumerates "*Y-movement* or *contrastive topicalization*," which "often involves fronting of the contrasted topic—if it is normally in a non-initial position in the clause" (see also Fox 1983, 219).

[9] In the Ugaritic poetry, there are examples of discontinuity marked by **qatala* introducing background information, for example, KTU[3] 1.16:III: 13–15, where *kly* expresses that the food, wine and oil 'had been consumed' or 'used up' (Smith 1991, 69).

[10] Biblical Hebrew has, according to Givón (1983, 33), a "pragmatically-controlled word-order flexibility," and thus "the preverbal position of NP's covers a wide range of *discontinuity*;" the post-verbal position, on the other hand, includes both the neutral word order and right dislocation. Smith (1991, 14) also refers to Givón (1983). Cook (2012a, 297f.) argues that "deviations from *wayyiqṭol*" may indicate e.g. "focus fronting," avoidance of temporally successive interpretation, "marking of a new discourse section," and "signaling of background information," but he disregards the role of *wa* in the signalling of continuity. According to Fox (1983, 226), who works with the text of Genesis, "the OV word-

order for objects in EBH is always a contrastive, localized referential device," while the SV word order is often "used to re-introduce a topic back into the register over a much larger gap of absence." SV-ordered subjects are much more discontinuous than VS-ordered, and an OV word order has a definite discontinuous nature (Fox 1983, 236, 226, 247).

[11] Here '//' means 'is interrupted by'. Parentheses mark a variant: '(*wa*)' means that *wa* is an option, and the alternative is zero marking (asyndesis). Tenet 1 is revised compared to Isaksson (2021, 217–20), in order to account for the various discontinuity functions of *qoṭel* clauses (1c) and the aspectual contrast of *wa-qaṭal* in narrative discourse (1e).

[12] The *X* in a *wa-XV* discontinuous clause cannot be a simple negation such as *lō* (cf. Tenet 4). Tenet 1a should be read: a series of clauses of the type *wa-VX* is interrupted by a clause of the *wa-XV* type. The *wa*-introduced discontinuity is the most frequent type of discontinuous linking in my corpus, but asyndesis is also used (Tenet 1b). For example, after a *wa(y)-yiqṭol* main line, I have registered 101 discontinuity clauses of the *Ø-X-qaṭal* type and 267 of the *wa-X-qaṭal* type. Similarly, after a *wa-qaṭal* main line, I have 86 clauses of the type *Ø-X-yiqṭol(u)*, but 138 of the type *wa-X-yiqṭol(u)*.

[13] This includes all linkings with *qoṭel* clauses, finite and infinite. Some of them could have been discussed under Tenet 1e, because of some obvious imperfective meanings of *qoṭel* such as habitual action, but I have decided to treat all linkings with *qoṭel* clauses under 1c in order to achieve a unified description of the variety of *qoṭel* linkings.

[14] To achieve a consistent and intuitive notation, I designate verbless clauses as *XØ*, where *X* stands for any first constituent in the clause and *Ø* the absence of a verb. Tenets 1c and 1d indicate that participle clauses and verbless clauses, with or without initial *wa*, may also signal discourse discontinuity.

[15] This concerns the aspectual contrast perfective // imperfective, which from a comparative perspective is not dependent on word order, but is coded by a gram-switch from a perfective to an imperfective morpheme

(Isaksson 2009, 91f.). The originally imperfective *yiqṭol(u)* in CBH is sometimes used in imperfective contrast linking; see §7.6.1. *Wa-qaṭal* (§7.6.3) and *qoṭel* (§7.6.4) also express imperfective contrast in relation to a main-line *wa(y)-yiqṭol*.

[16] The case of *wa-X-qaṭal* + *wayyiqṭol* starting a "short independent narrative" is pointed out by Niccacci (1990, §89). He also mentions *wa-X-yiqṭol* + *wayyiqṭol* and *(wa)-XØ* + *wayyiqṭol* as comprising "the beginning of the narrative" (Niccacci 1990, §91).

[17] For a discussion of the concept of paragraph, see Longacre (1979, 115–17).

[18] This is what Givón (1983, 9) calls a chain initial topic: "(i) Characteristically a newly-introduced, newly-changed or newly-returned topic; thus (ii) Characteristically a *discontinuous* topic in terms of the preceding discourse context; but (iii) Potentially—if an important topic—a rather *persistent* topic in terms of the *succeeding* discourse context." There is a parallel in the chaining syntax of Ugaritic poetry: "While the Ugaritic prefix forms are used to present sequence of action in the main narrative poems, the Baal Cycle, Keret and Aqhat (so Fenton 1973, 32), Ugaritic **qatala* signals a disjunction in the narrative. Furthermore, those instances of Ugaritic **qatala* beginning a new narrative section which reverts to prefix verbal forms... correspond to the BH prose construction of initial **qātal* followed by converted imperfects" (Smith 1991, 67f. n. 3). By 'converted imperfects' Smith refers to *wa(y)-yiqṭol* clauses.

[19] I define 'main-line clause' as a foregrounded clause (see §1.2.8, and Hopper and Thompson 1980, 280, 283, 294; Cook 2012, 283–88). Such a clause often, but not always, signals discourse continuity.

[20] As in Sarah's reply to the Lord in a one-clause rejoinder: לֹא צָחַקְתִּי 'I did not laugh!' (Gen. 18.15).

[21] Examples of foregrounded *(wa)-hinnē-(X)-qoṭel* beginning a new paragraph: Gen. 38.13; 48.4, 21; Exod. 8.25; 16.4; Num. 25.6; 25.12; Judg. 4.22 (new scene with a new actant); 7.13 (dream report); 19.16. Foregrounded *(wa)-hinnē-XØ* is not found in the corpus, but cf. 1 Kgs 19.13.

[22] For the term 'corresponding', see §7.12 and Table 34. I exclude *V* = *qoṭel*, because *wa-qoṭel* as finite verb clause is an extremely rare phenomenon. Possible but doubtful examples with *V* = *qoṭel* are: Gen. 16.11 (but could be *wa-qaṭal*; according to HALOT, it is a mixed formation); 20.16; 28.12 (functions as an added attribute after another *qoṭel*, in dream report); 41.32 (future); Judg. 8.4 (but in attributive circumstantial position; see further §4.1.1.1 and §7.4); 13.19 (*wa-qoṭel* after pause expresses background: immediate future action in the past by an actant in the foregoing clause); 18.7 (but attributive). The *wa-hinnē-qoṭel* clause-type is not used as a discourse-continuity clause in dream reports. Every *wa-hinnē-qoṭel* introduces a new scene in the dream, and the discourse-continuity clause-type to be used within the scene is often *wa(y)-yiqṭol*, as many *wa-hinnē-qoṭel* + *wa(y)-yiqṭol* linkings show, for example Gen. 28.13; 41.2–4 (past time reference; Joosten 2012, 187); 41.6f., 18–20, 23f.; Judg. 7.13.

[23] Schüle (2000, 105): "Damit liegt nahe, daß sich in der festen Verbindung von *wa-* und *yáqtul* Progreß nicht auf die Verbalform, sondern auf das *wa* = bezieht." It must be added that *wa(y)-yiqṭol* is often used as continuity clause in background complexes, as in Judg. 4.4f.

[24] Joosten (2012, 38) maintains that "[i]n Hebrew texts, verb-initial clauses imply discursive continuity, while non-verb-initial clauses normally imply some type of discontinuity." This is necessary, but it is not sufficient. A discourse-continuity clause must also be preceded by the conjunction *wa*. It seems that Joosten recognises only two types of continuity clauses, *wa(y)-yiqṭol* and *wa-qaṭal*, leaving out the possibility that jussive *wa-yiqṭol* (short) can express discourse continuity in a modal domain (cf. Joosten 2012, 18 n. 26).

[25] For negation in CBH, see Sjörs (2018, ch. 5).

[26] For historical reasons, the *qaṭal* gram has replaced indicative *yiqṭol(Ø)* (< **yaqtul*) in negated narrative main-line clauses, so that the negative continuity counterpart of *wa(y)-yiqṭol* is not **wa-lō-yiqṭol(Ø)* but *wa-lō-qaṭal* (an innovation). Simple negated clauses of the types *wa-lō-qaṭal*

and *wa-lō-yiqṭol(u)* signal discourse continuity in spite of the clausal element (only the negation) between the conjunction and the verb. In Biblical Hebrew, the *qaṭal* morpheme has taken over the application field of negated realis short *yiqṭol*, whereas in Amarna Canaanite, *wa-lā-yaqtul* and *wa-lā-qatal* are used interchangeably (Baranowski 2016a, 188). So the negative clause-type *wa-lā-yaqtul* is attested in Amarna, but not in Biblical Hebrew. We do not find an indicative **wa-lō-yiqṭol(Ø)* anywhere in CBH. As for imperfective clauses, the negative counterpart of *wa-qaṭal* in CBH is *wa-lō-yiqṭol(u)* (the latter being a retention). The innovative imperfective clause-type *wa-qaṭal* never developed a corresponding negative clause, since *wa-lō-yiqṭol(u)* existed and was fully functional in all phases of CBH (it could not be confused with **wa-lō-yiqṭol(Ø)* since the latter had been discarded already in Proto-Hebrew).

[27] *Pace* Gentry (1998, 14), who assigns the "negated forms" to the non-sequential category.

[28] For an attempt, see Dallaire (2014).

[29] For *wa(y)-yiqṭol // (wa)-X-yiqṭol(u)*, the imperfective interruption, see §7.6.1.

[30] See §2.3.6. My example is Gen. 44.20 with a stativic *qaṭal*: וְאָבִ֥יו אֲהֵבֽוֹ׃ 'and (therefore) his father loves him', because he is the only one of his mother's sons left.

[31] I have one example of a stativic *wa-X-qaṭal* functioning as a temporal clause after *wa(y)-yiqṭol*: Judg. 4.1, 'The Israelites again did evil in the LORD's sight **after Ehud's death** (וְאֵה֖וּד מֵֽת׃)'.

[32] This is Exod. 6.3–5, where 6.4 *wa-gam-qaṭal* and 6.5 *wa-gam-S.pron-qaṭal* in a personal report and summary enumerate the actions of YHWH.

[33] "Some of the details of Jacob's methods are obscure" (Wenham 1994, 256), and so is the function of the discontinuity *wa-X-qaṭal* clause in Gen. 30.40 (וְהַכְּשָׂבִים֮ הִפְרִ֣יד יַעֲקֹב֒), preceded by *wa(y)-yiqṭol* in 30.39. It may perhaps signal a new paragraph.

[34] Examples of contrasting *wa(y)-yiqṭol* + *wa-X-qaṭal*: Gen. 1.5 (day/night; Rainey 2003, 13; Hornkohl 2018, 37); 1.10; 2.20; 4.2; 11.3;

12.15f.; 14.10, 16; 15.10; 18.33; 20.15f.; 25.6—Cook (2012, 297) calls this “focus fronting;” 31.47; 32.22 (but it could be a *wa-S.pron-qoṭel* and circumstantial clause); 35.18 (cf. Cook 2012, 298); 37.11; 40.21f.; 41.54; 42.3f., 8 (Hornkohl 2018, 37); Exod. 6.3; 9.6; 12.38; 14.28f.; 15.19; 16.13 (also temporal succession because of בַּבֹּקֶר); 20.21; Num. 11.10 (I interpret רַע as *qaṭal*, in accordance with HALOT); 12.15; 14.38; 16.27, 34—but according to Buth (1995, 96), this is background; Judg. 1.25 (simultaneous foregrounded event; Cook 2012, 296); 1.28 (*wa-VNabs-lō-qaṭal*, contrasting actions); 4.16; 6.40; 7.3, 6, 8 (2×), 25; 9.18; 20.32.

[35] Examples of complementary *wa(y)-yiqṭol* + *wa-X-qaṭal*: Gen. 18.6f.—Cook (2012, 297) calls this “focus fronting;” 19.6 (went out and shut the door); 19.9–11 (this is a case of polarity of actions, where four sequential *wa(y)-yiqṭol* and then two simultaneous *wa-X-qaṭal* make up a whole sequence of actions, and the last *wa(y)-yiqṭol*, וַיִּלְאוּ, is sequential to the preceding *qaṭal* clause, ‘therefore’); 24.46, 53; 27.15f.; 32.2; 33.16f. (Esau and Jacob), 17 (he built a house and shelters, expected complementary actions); 41.51f. (Manasseh and Ephraim); 43.15, 21f.; 45.14; 47.20f.; Exod. 9.23 (Moses and the Lord, a mutuality); 9.25, 33; 14.6 (his chariots and his army); 17.10; 24.6 (“reciprocity,” according to Propp 2006, 295); 36.10 (five curtains and five other curtains); 36.17, 23f., 24f.; 37.26f.; 39.17f.; 40.34 (the cloud and the glory of the Lord, a mutual action); Lev. 8.15 (the blood and the rest of the blood); 8.16f. (the bull and the rest of the bull); 8.19f. (the ram and the rest of the ram); 8.20f., 25f.; 9.9–11 (the blood, the rest of the blood, and the fat and the kidneys); Num. 13.30f. (Caleb and the men); 13.33 (mutuality); 24.25; 31.9; 32.34–37 (the Gadites and the Reubenites); 32.40f.; Judg. 1.8 (put the city to the sword and set it on fire); 3.6 (their daughters and their own daughters); 7.25; 8.12, 16f.; 9.45, 56f.; 11.17, 29; 18.27.

[36] Examples of *wa(y)-yiqṭol* + *wa-X-qaṭal* expressing background: Gen. 6.8; 8.5 (Hornkohl 2018, 49 n. 64); 8.13f.; 22.20–23 (anticipating information about who was the father of Isaac’s wife Rebekah); 31.25, 33f. (Moshavi 2013; Hornkohl 2018, 45, 49 n. 64); 34.4f. (inserted

background complex; *pace* Hornkohl 2018, 49 n. 64, 52); 34.7 (Joosten 2012, 169 n. 24; Hornkohl 2018, 49 n. 64); 37.35f.; 41.56f. (Hornkohl 2018, 49 n. 64); 42.22f.; 48.9f. (Cook 2012, 212); Exod. 9.30–32; 10.13; 11.9f.; 12.34–36; 16.34f. (narrator's comment); 17.12; 24.10f., 13f. (pluperfect; Propp 2006, 107); 36.3, 6f.; Lev. 24.23; Num. 13.22; 14.10, 44; 17.12, 15 (Buth 1995, 95); 26.9–11 (within a relative clause complex); Judg. 1.20f., 33; 2.16f.; 3.19; 4.3 (pluperfect); 6.21 (pluperfect); 7.1 (geographical information); 7.8; 8.11, 29f.; 9.51f.; 11.39; 14.3f.; 16.20, 31; 18.30; 20.34, 42; 21.8.

[37] Examples of *wa(y)-yiqṭol* + *wa-X-qaṭal* expressing elaboration, where I include also cases where there is no 'echoing' but only more details of the event (cf. Dixon 2009, 27): Gen. 7.15f. (with left dislocation and then focused elements); 19.3 (a detail is focused, מַצּוֹת); 39.4, 22; Exod. 12.29 (or the *wayhī* clause starts a thetic cleft; Khan 2019); 13.18; 35.21; 36.33f. (details in the production of the bars in the tabernacle); 38.27f.; Num. 31.7b–8; Judg. 12.9 (*wa(y)-yiqṭol* + *wa-X-qaṭal* + *wa-X-qaṭal*).

[38] Examples of *wa(y)-yiqṭol* + *wa-hinnē-qaṭal* expressing the content of a (sometimes understood) perception: Gen. 6.12; 8.13 'and he saw that the surface of the ground was dry'; 19.28; Exod. 4.7; 9.7; 16.10 (understood perception verb); 34.30; 39.43; Num. 17.7, 23; Judg. 6.28; 20.40. I count Num. 17.12 and Judg. 21.8 as background.

[39] JPS TANAKH 1985: 'Thereafter the Levites were qualified to perform their service in the Tent of Meeting'. Other examples of *wa(y)-yiqṭol* + *wa-ADV-qaṭal* describing an emphatic temporal succession: Gen. 23.17–19; 45.15 (see also §2.3.5); Exod. 34.32.

[40] For *wa(y)-yiqṭol* + *Ø-X-yiqṭol(u)*, see §7.6.1.

[41] Complementary actions are usually syndetic (*wa-X-qaṭal*), but Exod. 36.11 is an exception, describing the production of the first and second (complementary) sets of the end curtain.

[42] The semantics of the *Ø-X-qaṭal* linking in Gen. 7.8 are unclear. The asyndesis and the discontinuity are probably a case of literary style (Westermann 1976). Gen. 7.7f. constitutes the fulfilment of the God's

command in Gen. 7.1 and 7.2–3, where we also encounter asyndesis in 7.2 (see Wenham 1987, 179). The linking is also unclear in Gen. 8.18f., and for the same reason (fulfilment of command in Gen. 8.16f. with asyndetic syntax).

43 Since *Ø-lō-qaṭal* also signals discontinuity, such examples are included here (it does not fulfil Tenet 3).

44 Other examples of *wa(y)-yiqṭol* + *Ø-X-qaṭal* expressing elaboration: Gen. 7.19f.; 13.11f.; 27.36 (*wa(y)-yiqṭol* + *Ø-O.noun-qaṭal* + *wa-hinnē-ʿattā-qaṭal*); 34.27f.; 41.11, 12, 13 (the first *qaṭal* clause is elaborative in relation to the initial *wayhī*, and the two following *qaṭal* clauses with initial object pronouns form contrastive topics; Hornkohl 2018, 37); 41.48; 44.12; 45.21f. (a fulfilment of Pharaoh's instructions in vv. 16–20); 46.6f.; 49.28; 50.23; Exod. 8.13; 10.23 (*Ø-lō-qaṭal*); 34.28; 35.22; 36.8—Propp (2006, 625) translates, 'Griffins, webster's work he made them'; 36.11f., 14, 35; 37.7f. (*wa(y)-yiqṭol* + *Ø-O.noun-qaṭal* + *Ø-O.noun-qaṭal*); 37.9, 17, 25; 38.3, 7; 39.8f.; Num. 2.34; 3.49f.; 7.6–9; 8.3; 11.32; 33.3; Deut. 9.9, 18; 29.4; Judg. 6.2; 20.48.

45 Nearly all my summary examples have an initial *kēn*: Gen. 6.22; Exod. 7.6; 12.28; 37.23f. (but [23]*wa(y)-yiqṭol* + [24]*Ø-O.noun-qaṭal*); 39.32; 40.16; Num. 1.54; 5.4; 8.20; 9.5; 17.26.

46 Examples of same-event addition coded by the linking *wa(y)-yiqṭol* + *Ø-X-qaṭal* in CBH: Gen. 7.21f.; Exod. 8.27 'not even one was left'; 10.19; 14.28; Deut. 2.34; Judg. 4.16.

47 Similar negated clauses with circumstantial semantics in a *wa(y)-yiqṭol* + *Ø-X-qaṭal* linking: Exod. 10.22f.; 34.28; Deut. 9.18; 29.4.

48 The *Ø-NP-REL-qaṭal* is a left dislocation.

49 Possible examples of background information coded by *wa(y)-yiqṭol* + *Ø-X-qaṭal*: Gen. 25.9f., 18; 29.34 (with initial adverbial *ʿal-kēn*); 29.35 (*ʿal-kēn*); 30.6 (*ʿal-kēn*); Exod. 37.14 (with copula verb); Lev. 8.29; Num. 4.48f.; Judg. 6.19 (the clauses *Ø-O.noun-qaṭal* + *wa-O.noun-qaṭal* are both background); 7.19 'just after they had changed the guards'; 20.15.

[50] Examples of comments by the editor(s) coded by the linking *wa(y)-yiqṭol* + *Ø-X-qaṭal*: Gen. 6.4 (for a discussion, see Westermann 1976, 509f.); 11.8f. (*ʿal-kēn*); 16.13f. (*ʿal-kēn*); 19.22 (*ʿal-kēn*); 21.30f. (*ʿal-kēn*); 25.30 (*ʿal-kēn*); 31.48 (*ʿal-kēn*); 33.17 (*ʿal-kēn*); Exod. 4.25f. (*Ø-ʾāz-qaṭal*); Exod. 15.23 (*ʿal-kēn*); Num. 13.23f.; 31.52f. 'Each soldier had taken plunder for himself'; Judg. 15.19 (*ʿal-kēn*); 18.12. I have generally not taken examples from genealogies, but there is one in Gen. 4.20.

[51] Examples of contrast coded by the linking *wa(y)-yiqṭol* + *Ø-X-qaṭal*: Gen. 3.14–17 (*wa(y)-yiqṭol* + *Ø-PrP-qaṭal* + *wa-PrP-qaṭal*)—according to Hornkohl (2018, 36, 52), the non-subjectival frontings here serve as genuine topics highlighting the addressee of each curse; 47.20–22 (*raq*); 47.26 (*raq*); 50.8 (*raq*); Exod. 9.26.

[52] In one instance, Lev. 23.21 (וּקְרָאתֶ֞ם בְּעֶ֣צֶם ׀ הַיּ֣וֹם הַזֶּ֗ה מִֽקְרָא־קֹ֙דֶשׁ֙ יִהְיֶ֣ה לָכֶ֔ם כָּל־מְלֶ֥אכֶת עֲבֹדָ֖ה לֹ֣א תַעֲשׂ֑וּ), with linking pattern *wa-qaṭal* + *Ø-S.noun-yiqṭol(u)!* + *Ø-O.noun-lō-yiqṭol(u)*, the asyndetic *yiqṭol(u)* clauses describe the content of the proclamation in the *wa-qaṭal* clause. It is an account, a summary, not a quotation of the proclamation. On this point, I follow Milgrom (2001, 1933, 2009), who finds the syntax awkward; he translates 'On that very day, you shall proclaim: It shall be for you a sacred occasion, you must do no laborious work'. The linking can, however, be interpreted simply as an elaboration with more details.

[53] Two rare cases when *wa-qaṭal* forms a protasis and *Ø-X-yiqṭol(u)* is the apodosis: Exod. 12.44; Lev. 10.19. It is a linking, but the *wa-qaṭal* cannot be said to form a main line which is interrupted.

[54] In two instances, the *Ø-X-yiqṭol(u)* constitutes an asyndetic relative clause: Deut. 13.17 וְהָיְתָה֙ תֵּ֣ל עוֹלָ֔ם לֹ֥א תִבָּנֶ֖ה עֽוֹד׃; 27.5 וּבָנִ֤יתָ שָּׁם֙ מִזְבֵּ֔חַ לַיהוָ֖ה אֱלֹהֶ֑יךָ מִזְבַּ֣ח אֲבָנִ֔ים לֹא־תָנִ֥יף עֲלֵיהֶ֖ם בַּרְזֶֽל׃. In my estimation, the *Ø-X-yiqṭol(u)* are relative clauses, each closely related to a preceding constituent in the *wa-qaṭal*, but many translators take them as elaborations; thus NET Deut. 13.17 'It will be an abandoned ruin forever—it must never be rebuilt again'.

[55] There is future meaning in ten cases: Gen. 17.16, 20; Exod. 8.7, 19; 29.37; 30.25, 29; Lev. 10.19; Num. 11.18f.; Deut. 13.17. Habitual past

meaning: Exod. 18.26; 40.31f. Permissive meaning: Lev. 6.6; 25.46; Num. 6.20 (the *yiqṭol(u)* clause).

[56] Other examples of *wa-qaṭal* + *Ø-X-yiqṭol(u)* expressing elaboration without echoing the first clause: Gen. 17.16, 20; Exod. 8.19; 21.8 (the apodosis); 23.5 (*wa-qaṭal* + *Ø-VNabs-yiqṭol(u)*, in apodosis); 25.14f., 26f., 31; 27.2, 3; 28.6f., 20; 29.34; 30.36; Lev. 1.17; 3.9 (difficult; see Milgrom 1991, 203); 5.11; 13.11 (*wa-qaṭal* + *Ø-lō-yiqṭol(u)*); 23.15 (thus Milgrom 2001, 1933); 23.20, 32; 24.5; 25.29 (the apodosis); 25.30, 46, 52; 27.12, 33; Num. 5.15; 10.6; 11.19; 19.11f.; 28.19; 29.7; 35.5; Deut. 7.2 (two asyndetic *yiqṭol(u)* clauses); 12.7f.; 25.12.

[57] Other examples of *wa-qaṭal* + *Ø-X-yiqṭol(u)* expressing elaboration with 'echoing': Exod. 12.4, 8, 14; 18.26 (both *Ø-X-yiqṭol(u)* have past habitual meaning; Zewi 1999, 119, 139); 25.11, 18, 29, 31 (the first *Ø-X-yiqṭol(u)*); 26.7, 17, 31; 28.9–11, 13f., 15, 32, 37; 30.1, 7, 10; 40.31f.; Lev. 4.12; 7.12f.; 12.2; 14.5f.; 23.11, 15f., 41; 25.9; 27.8; Num. 3.47; 6.9; 19.5; 33.54.

[58] Examples of *wa-qaṭal* + *Ø-X-yiqṭol(u)* expressing same-event addition: Exod. 29.37; 30.29; Deut. 5.32 (not turning right or left is another aspect of doing what the LORD has commanded).

[59] The other contrast example in my corpus is Exod. 21.19 (*wa-qaṭal* + *Ø-raq-O.noun-yiqṭol(u)* + *wa-VNabs-yiqṭol(u)*), with obligational meaning in both clauses.

[60] I also exclude from the discussion the cases of *Ø-qaṭal* after a left dislocation, as in Gen. 34.8; 47.21; Exod. 9.30.

[61] Other examples of virtual **Ø-qaṭal* in monoclausal constructions with initial focus marker *wayhī*: Exod. 12.51; 16.27; 40.17; Deut. 1.3.

[62] Other examples of reports beginning with *Ø-qaṭal* (performatives not included): Gen. 27.35; 30.6 (anterior, with 'energic' suffix on *qaṭal*; Zewi 1999, 150); 30.18 (anterior); 37.17 (anterior, clause-initial *qaṭal*; Korchin 2008, 332); 38.24 (anterior); 39.14 (*rəʾū* with anterior *Ø-qaṭal* + *Ø-qaṭal*; Korchin 2008, 331 n. 15); 42.28 (anterior); 47.25 (anterior); Exod. 32.9 (anterior); 35.30 (anterior after *rəʾū*); Deut. 1.20, 41 (both anterior); Judg. 16.2, 23 (both anterior and single clause utterances).

[63] Non-reportive examples in my corpus: Gen. 14.22 (performative); 23.13 (performative, not beginning of speech, but new paragraph); 32.11 (stativic verb, preceded in 32.10 only by a vocative with quotation); 38.26 (stativic); Exod. 21.5 (stativic); 32.9 (anterior); Num. 11.5 (stativic; Brockelmann 1908–13, II, §76b—it is an independent clause in direct speech); 14.20 (performative or anterior); Deut. 1.20, 41 (both anterior); 26.3 (performative; Rainey 2003b, 11); 30.19 (performative); Judg. 15.3 (stativic).

[64] According to Joosten (2012, 218), *Ø-qaṭal* here is "text-critically or otherwise doubtful." Instances of *Ø-qaṭal* expressing elaboration (with echoing): Gen. 21.14—the *Ø-qaṭal* clause elaborates upon וַיִּתֵּן אֶל־הָגָר, but Joosten (2012, 218), regards it as completely irregular, while Driver (1892, §163), interprets it as circumstantial, 'having placed it and the boy on her shoulder': some scholars analyses *śām* as *qoṭel*, which is possible; 48.14—'he crossed his hands' is past perfective and elaborates upon the preceding *wa(y)-yiqṭol*: it is not circumstantial, as argued by Driver (1892, §163); Exod. 35.31–35; 32.7f.; Num. 7.18f.; 30.15 (*wa-qaṭal* + *Ø-qaṭal*, anterior); Deut. 9.16 (*wa-hinnē-qaṭal* + *Ø-qaṭal* + *Ø-qaṭal*); Judg. 20.42f. (*qoṭel* + *Ø-qaṭal* + *Ø-qaṭal* + *Ø-qaṭal*)—according to Boling (1975, 283), within background complex, and according to Joosten (2012, 218), text-critically doubtful.

[65] Examples of *Ø-qaṭal* expressing elaboration without echo or same-event addition (another aspect of the same event) in relation to the preceding clause: Exod. 14.3 (*Ø-XØ* + *Ø-qaṭal*, elaboration); Num. 17.11 (*kī-qaṭal* + *Ø-qaṭal* 'for wrath has gone out from the LORD—the plague has begun!', elaboration); Judg. 2.17 (elaboration); 7.14 (*Ø-ʾēn-XØ* + *Ø-qaṭal*, same-event); 20.31 (*wa(y)-yiqṭol* + *Ø-qaṭal*) 'The Benjaminites went out to attack the army, they left the city unguarded'—this is another aspect of the same event, but Driver (1892, §163) takes it as circumstantial.

[66] Other examples of *Ø-qaṭal* as complement: Gen. 21.7 (after utterance verb); Deut. 13.15 (*wa-hinnē-XØ* + *Ø-qaṭal*); 17.4 (same as 13.15).

[67] According to Joosten (2012, 218), the use of *Ø-qaṭal* here is completely irregular. Another possible example is Gen. 40.10, in a dream report (*wa-XØ* + *Ø-qaṭal* + *Ø-qaṭal*, where the second *Ø-qaṭal* is temporally sequential).

[68] The *rār* is admittedly a hapax, but it is *qaṭal* (Milgrom 1991, 908).

[69] Other examples of *Ø-qaṭal* as apodosis: Gen. 43.14 (stativic verb with implied future time reference; Gropp 1991, 47; Cook 2012, 207 n. 46)—J-M (§176o, p. 610 n. 1) argues that the asyndesis is caused by assonance and should be analysed as *wa-qaṭal*; Exod. 22.14 (*(Ø-ʾim-XØ)* + *Ø-qaṭal*, 'then he has already paid for it', but the interpretation of apodosis is disputed; see Propp 2006: 105, 252); Lev. 13.37 (anterior projected into a future case); Deut. 4.25f. (performative in an oath formula); 8.19 (performative; Rainey 2003b, 11f.; Cook 2012, 207 n. 46).

[70] Schulz (1900, 41) and Li (2017, 6) consider the *wa-qaṭal* to be simple past (same as *qaṭal*).

[71] Topic–comment examples with *Ø-qaṭal* as comment: Gen. 31.41; Num. 11.8; 14.4; Deut. 34.4 (present anterior: 'This is the land… I have let you see it').

[72] Some examples from archaic poetry: Deut. 32.6, 15, 18, 37 (Isaksson 2017, 242f., 248, 249f., 258f.).

[73] The אחר is often emendated to אחד (Westermann 1981, 432), but this is not necessary. *ʾaḥar* can be an adverb 'behind' (HALOT). Wenham (1994, 98) retains the text.

[74] Other instances of *Ø-qaṭal* functioning as relative clause in my prose corpus: Lev. 13.39 (in an apodosis, *Ø-XØ* + *Ø-qaṭal* + *Ø-XØ*); 14.46 (after a construct head noun; Zewi 2020, 94).

[75] Instances of *wa(y)-yiqṭol* + *Ø-(X)-qoṭel*: Gen. 3.8; 21.9 (Brockelmann 1956, §103a; Westermann 1981, 412); 21.14—*pace* Driver (1892, §163), who takes it as *Ø-qaṭal*, while Joosten (2012, 218 n. 40) calls it an anomalous *qaṭal*; 25.27 (close to nominal יֹשֵׁב); 39.23 (background, see above); Exod. 2.11; 5.20; 14.9, 30; 36.20; 37.9 (*wa(y)-yiqṭol* + *Ø-qoṭel* + *Ø-qoṭel* + *wa-XØ*); Num. 7.89; 11.10; 15.33; 22.23, 31; 24.2; Deut. 4.12 (*Ø-X-qoṭel*); 28.7; Judg. 1.24; 12.14; 18.7. I am unable to

explain Judg. 8.4 (*wa(y)-yiqṭol* + *Ø-qoṭel*); see Sasson (2014, 360) for a discussion.

[76] Examples of circumstantial *wa(y)-yiqṭol* + *wa-(X)-qoṭel*: Gen. 14.13 (X = *S.pron*); 18.1, 8 (both *S.pron*); 18.10 (*S.noun*, but possibly background); 18.16, 22 (both *S.noun*); 19.1 (*S.noun*); 24.30 (with focus marker *hinnē*); 37.15 (with *hinnē*); Exod. 2.5 (*S.noun*); 9.24; 14.8, 27 (both *S.noun*); Num. 22.22 (*S.pron*); 23.6, 17 (both with *hinnē*); 25.6 (*S.pron*); Deut. 4.11 (*S.noun*); 9.15 (*S.noun*); Judg. 3.25 (*hinnē*); 6.11; 8.4 (*wa-qoṭel*); 13.9 (*S.pron*); 13.20 (*S.noun*); 16.12 (*S.noun*); 19.28 (nominal, probably to be analysed as *XØ*); 20.33 (*S.noun*).

[77] 'Focused' means: "One clause refers to the central activity or state of the biclausal linking" (Dixon 2009, 3). Instances of focused *wa-hinnē-X-qoṭel* after *wa(y)-yiqṭol*: Exod. 2.13; Judg. 3.25 (stativic); 4.22 (stativic); 7.13; 11.34; 14.5; 19.18, 27.

[78] Examples of focused complement *wa-hinnē-X-qoṭel* after perception verb (*wa(y)-yiqṭol*): Gen. 18.2; 24.63; 26.8; 28.12; 33.1; 37.25 (three *qoṭel* clauses of which only the first is introduced by *wa-hinnē*; the second continues the perception content with *wa-S.noun-qoṭel* and the third with *Ø-qoṭel*); 39.3 (special case: perception introduced by *kī-XØ* and continued by *wa-X-qoṭel*); 40.6; 41.22 (dream); Exod. 3.2; 14.10; Judg. 9.43.

[79] Examples of backgrounding *wa(y)-yiqṭol* + *wa-X-qoṭel*: Gen. 2.9f.; 13.7; 14.12; 24.20f.; 25.28; 27.4f.; 30.36; Exod. 5.12f.; 13.20f.; Num. 10.33; 33.40; Judg. 7.11f.; 10.1; 13.19 (*wa-qoṭel*, see below); 14.3f.; 17.7; 18.15f.

[80] I have excluded Exod. 25.31f. ([31]*wa-qaṭal* + *Ø-O.noun-yiqṭol(u)* + *Ø-S.noun-yiqṭol(u)* + [32]***wa-S.noun-qoṭel*** + *Ø-XØ* + *wa-XØ*), although the *wa-S.noun-qoṭel* (וְשִׁשָּׁה קָנִים יֹצְאִים מִצִּדֶּיהָ) is often translated as a main clause in the instruction text with obligational meaning, e.g., 'Six branches are to extend from the sides of the lampstand' (NET). In view of the extreme rarity of *qoṭel* clauses with a meaning of obligation (I have no evident examples), it is more plausible that the verbal force of the preceding *wa-qaṭal* (וְעָשִׂיתָ) is understood also here (i.e., ellipsis), as in Propp (2006, 311), who translates, 'And six reeds going out from its

sides—', where 'six reeds' is the direct object of *wa-qaṭal* in verse 31 ('And (you shall make) six reeds going out from its sides'). In such a case, the *qoṭel* clause is circumstantial, an expected relational meaning. But the passage is disputed, and not included in the table.

[81] Wenham (1987, 324): 'But I am to judge the nation which they serve'.

[82] Examples of a linking *wa-qaṭal + (wa)-(X)-qoṭel*, where *qoṭel* is circumstantial: Gen. 3.5; 15.13f. ([14]*wa-gam-O.noun-qoṭel-S.pron*, where *O.noun* is a complex with a relative clause); Exod. 25.20; 26.15 (*wa-qaṭal + Ø-qoṭel*); 33.10; Lev. 26.16; Num. 10.25.

[83] Two cases of *wa(y)-yiqṭol + (wa)-XØ* with unclear semantic relations, both in genealogies: Gen. 4.19; 36.22.

[84] Gen. 12.4b belongs to *P* (Westermann 1981, 176f.). Further examples of *wa(y)-yiqṭol + (wa)-XØ* expressing background: Gen. 2.19 (*wa(y)-yiqṭol + wa-()-XØ*, with left dislocation coded by quantifier and relative clause); 9.18; 11.29; 12.4; 13.1f.; 16.15f.; 17.23–25; 25.26 (age of Isaac); 28.19; 29.31; 36.8, 32, 35, 39 (the first *XØ* is circumstantial, but the second is background); 37.24; 38.6; 39.11; Exod. 7.6f.; 12.39–42; 16.31; 17.1; 24.16f.; 32.15f.; 36.8f.; Lev. 8.21, 28; 24.11; Num. 10.33f.; 11.26; 12.2.f.; 13.3, 17–20, 22; 20.12f.; 22.4; 33.9, 38f.; Deut. 2.17–21 ([21]*Ø-XØ + wa(y)-yiqṭol + wa(y)-yiqṭol + wa(y)-yiqṭol*, where the three *wa(y)-yiqṭol* also belong to the background); 34.6f.; Judg. 1.22 'and the LORD was with them'; 1.35f.; 3.17; 4.2; 8.9f.; 11.34; 13.2, 9; 16.26f.; 17.5f., 7; 18.7, 28, 29; 19.3; 20.27; 21.24f.

[85] Further examples of *wa(y)-yiqṭol + (wa)-XØ* expressing editorial insertion: Gen. 10.12; 12.6; 14.7, 8, 17; 19.37, 38; 23.2; 26.33; 35.6, 19, 20, 27; 48.7; Num. 33.36; Judg. 1.11, 23, 26; 6.24; 7.1; 18.12 (*Ø-hinnē-XØ*); 19.10.

[86] Examples of *wa(y)-yiqṭol + (wa)-XØ* describing a circumstantial state relation: Gen. 9.23 (but possibly background); 12.8 (Brockelmann 1908–13, II §321a); 13.1; 24.10, 22; 25.1, 6, 25 (first an adverbial adjective and then *Ø-XØ*); 25.29; 36.39 (only the first *XØ* is circumstantial, the second is background); 38.1, 2; 41.8, 24; 44.14; Exod. 14.7, 22; 24.10; 32.15; 36.36; 37.1, 3, 6, 10, 25; 38.1; Lev. 24.10; Num. 10.14–

28; 22.7; 31.6; Deut. 9.15; 25.18 (but I take the last clause as *wa-lō-qaṭal* with stativic verb); Judg. 3.16 'Ehud made himself a sword with two edges and a length of 18 inches'; 3.27; 10.4; 13.2; 14.6; 16.4; 17.1; 18.7; 19.15 (the circumstantial *wa-XØ* implicitly expresses a reason; Boling 1975, 272); 20.35.

[87] For the adverbial *qoṭel* clause, see Isaksson (2009, 57–59).

[88] Other examples of *wa(y)-yiqṭol* + *wa-hinnē-XØ* expressing complementation, sometimes with only implicit perception verb: Gen. 1.31; 22.13; 31.2, 10; 37.29 (implicit); 41.7 (implicit); 42.27; 43.21 (implicit); Num. 12.10; 32.1; Judg. 3.24; 14.8; 21.9.

[89] Since the semantic relation with the preceding *wa(y)-yiqṭol* clause(s) is vague and the verbless clause is a main clause, we should not use the term linking here. The *wa(y)-yiqṭol* clauses just precede the verbless clause in the same verse. Other examples of focused verbless clauses functioning as main clauses (and with preceding *wa(y)-yiqṭol*): Gen. 25.24; Exod. 11.3 (not *wa-hinnē*, but *Ø-gam-XØ* 'moreover'); 16.14.

[90] The unclear case is Exod. 13.12; according to Propp (1999, 371), MT is suspiciously redundant.

[91] Other examples of *wa-qaṭal* + *(wa)-XØ* expressing an explanatory note: Exod. 12.11; 29.18 (*wa-qaṭal* + *Ø-XØ* + *Ø-XØ* + *Ø-XØ*); 29.25; 30.10; Lev. 1.13; 2.3, 9f., 15; 3.16 'all the fat belongs to the Lord'; 4.21, 24; 5.9 (*wa-qaṭal* + *wa-S.noun-yiqṭol(u)* + *Ø-XØ*; Milgrom 1991, 305); 5.12, 18f.; 6.8–10; 7.5; 12.7 ("subscript," according to Milgrom 1991, 761); 13.8 (in apodosis), 13, 15, 17 (in apodosis); 13.20 (with asyndetic relative clause; Milgrom 1991, 769); 13.22, 25, 27, 30; 27.16 (an algorithm for a homer of barley being priced in silver; Milgrom 2001, 2366).

[92] I regard the participle (מַחֲרִ֑יד) as being used as a noun here. Other instances of *wa-qaṭal* + *(wa)-XØ* coding a circumstantial relation are: Exod. 22.9 (in protasis); 22.13 (in protasis); 25.12, 17, 20, 23; 26.15–17, 37; 27.1; 36.30, 38; Num. 3.9; 10.18 (*wa-qaṭal* is habitual past; *pace* Pat-El 2021, 105 n. 47); 35.5, 27 (in apodosis); Deut. 28.26.

[93] Other instances of *wa-qaṭal* + *(wa)-XØ* expressing contrast (Dixon 2009, 28): Lev. 5.1 (within a protasis, *wa-qaṭal* + *wa-XØ ʾō qaṭal ʾō*

qaṭal)—Milgrom (1991, 292) translates, 'and although he was a witness'; 26.17, 36.

[94] Other reason clauses in linkings of the type *wa-qaṭal* + *(wa)-XØ*: Lev. 22.31, 32; Num. 5.13 (not about YHWH, but within a protasis, and can be taken as a circumstantial with nuance of reason). Reason linkings of the type *wa-qaṭal* + *kī-XØ*, where *kī* may be emphatic-adverbial: Exod. 22.26; 29.33; 31.14; Lev. 5.11; 20.7; 24.9; Deut. 14.29.

[95] In Deut. 13.15 (*wa-qaṭal* + *wa-hinnē-XØ* + *Ø-qaṭal*), both *XØ* and *Ø-qaṭal* function as complements.

[96] For the analysis, see Hackett (1984, 36f.). VN is an infinitive absolute. A parallel construction is found outside my corpus in 1 Sam. 1.10 וַתִּתְפַּלֵּ֥ל עַל־יְהוָ֖ה וּבָכֹ֥ה תִבְכֶּֽה׃ 'She prayed to the LORD and was weeping greatly' (*wa(y)-yiqṭol* + *wa-VNabs-yiqṭol(u)*). But Joosten (1999, 24) argues that the *yiqṭol(u)* here is "prospective."

[97] The clause-type *wa-lō-yiqṭol(u)* is treated separately and not included here; see §7.6.2.

[98] Two instances of reason clauses introduced by an adverbial (emphatic) *kī*: Gen. 50.3; Judg. 14.10 (both with the pattern *wa(y)-yiqṭol* + *kī-kēn-yiqṭol(u)*, and both habitual).

[99] Other examples of comments coded by *wa(y)-yiqṭol* + *Ø-X-yiqṭol(u)* (all are asyndetic): Num. 21.13f. (a historical written source); Deut. 2.17–20 (*Ø-X-yiqṭol(u)* + *Ø-X-qaṭal* + *wa-X-yiqṭol(u)*, historical information); 3.8f.; Judg. 10.4 עַד הַיּוֹם הַזֶּה (present habitual); 11.39f. 'year after year' (present habitual).

[100] There is no causal relationship between the ruin of the houses of Pharaoh and his officials and the ruin of the whole of Egypt; *pace* Gzella (2021, 83) 'so that it was corrupted'. Examples of backgrounding *wa-X-yiqṭol(u)* after main-line *wa(y)-yiqṭol*: Gen. 2.24; 29.2 (adverbial *kī*); 43.32 (adverbial *kī*); Exod. 8.20; 34.33f.; 40.34–36 (habitual past).

[101] Some main-line *qaṭal* clauses with imperfective *X-yiqṭol(u)*: Gen. 31.39 (*Ø-X-qaṭal* + *Ø-X-yiqṭol(u)-N* + *Ø-X-yiqṭol(u)-N*, habitual past); Num. 9.15 (*wa-X-qaṭal* + *wa-X-yiqṭol(u)!*, past progressive). In none of the examples is *X* merely a negation (*lō*).

[102] My only five examples of *wa(y)-yiqṭol* + *wa-lō-yiqṭol(u)* linking are: Gen. 2.25 (circumstantial); Exod. 39.21 'thus', 'in this way'; Num. 8.19 'in this way'; Judg. 6.4 'in this way' (habitual past; Isaksson 2009, 86); 12.6 'thus he could not pronounce the word correctly' (repeated action; Isaksson 2009, 86).

[103] Practically all authorities argue that this *wa-qaṭal* is anomalous. Despite *lectio difficilior*, BHS emends to *wa(y)-yiqṭol*, and thus also Ges-K (§112tt). Schulz (1900, 38) and Joosten (2012, 227), among many, regard it as '*wa* + *qaṭal*'.

[104] BHS emendates to *wa(y)-yiqṭol*. Ges-K (§112rr) considers the *wa-qaṭal* frequentative. J-M (§119z) says there is omission of "energic Waw" in the *wa-qaṭal*. Joosten (2012, 227) identifies the form as "wᵊ + QATAL."

[105] Hornkohl (2014, 261, 288) describes this *wa-qaṭal* as continual, imperfective, past, durative. Schulz (1900, 37), Gropp (1991, 48), and Joosten (2012, 226) identify it as *wa* + *qaṭal*. Gropp (1991, 48) prefers to read *wa(y)-yiqṭol*. J-M (§119z) calls it an anomalous occurrence of *w-qatálti*. Nyberg (1972, §86kk) states that *wa-qaṭal* here has the same function as *yiqṭol(u)* and codes a verbal circumstantial clause describing a subevent ("biomständighet") beside the main event. Ges-K (§112ss) says: "A longer or constant continuance in a past state is perhaps represented by the perfect with וְ (as a variety of the frequentative perfect with וְ)." Westermann (1981, 252) concludes that the *wa-qaṭal* clause "die Erzählung nicht weiterführt," that is, it does not belong to the narrative main line but to the background.

[106] It is possible to interpret *wa-haya* as having a personal subject: Judah, as Wenham (1994, 361) translates: 'He was in Chezib when she bore him'. It makes sense, but the problem is that Judah is not mentioned in the clause, nor in the immediately preceding clauses (he is explicitly mentioned in Gen. 38.2).

[107] Schulz (1900, 37), Ges-K (§112uu), and Westermann (1982, 42) emendate to a *XØ* clause. Joosten (2012, 227 n. 70) identifies this instance as "wᵊ + QATAL." I have registered the following eleven instances of *wa(y)-yiqṭol* + *wa-qaṭal* coding background: Gen. 15.5f.; 21.24f.;

38.5 (Wenham 1994, 361)—Hornkohl (2014, 288) regards *wa-qaṭal* here as the immediate background of another action; 38.9 (*wa-haya* with temporal clause and habitual past); Num. 10.14–17; 21.9 (*wa-haya* with temporal clause); Judg. 6.3 (*wa-haya* with temporal clause and habituality); 12.5 (*wa-haya* with temporal clause and habitual past); 16.18; 19.8 (Isaksson 2009, 77; after quotation); 19.30 (*wa-haya* with temporal clause and habitual past).

[108] For the hapax *ṣəlūl* (Ketiv) or *ṣəlīl* (Qere), see Sasson (2014, 109, 353). According to Sasson, 'the tent' is "presumably the one central to the military operation."

[109] Schulz (1900, 38) identifies this form as *wa* + *qaṭal*. König (1881–97, II 2 §367i) attributes it to the "beharrenden Charakter des Vorgangs," but cf. the next example (Judg. 3.23). Lambert (1893, 56) prefers to emendate to VNabs.

[110] Several words translated according to Sasson (2014, 101).

[111] Renz (2016, 644–47) adduces one example from the pre-exilic inscriptions of *wa-qaṭal* "am Abschluss einer Erzählkette:" HI MHsh 1.4–5 ויקצר עבדך ויכל **ואסם** כימם 'And your servant harvested and measured **and stored**, according to the schedule'; Renz translates the *wa-qaṭal* 'und häufte (währenddessen/Schließlich) in den Speicher'.

[112] Hornkohl (2014, 290) suggests the translation "'and he was locking' for the closing of a scene; cf. 2 Sam 13.18." Nyberg (1972, §86kk) calls this a single past event described in a verbal circumstantial clause as a subevent ("biomständighet vid sidan av huvudhandlingen"). Gentry (1998, 17f.) also argues that *wa-qaṭal* is circumstantial: 'was locking up'. But Ges-K (§112tt) suggests an error in the text, "[o]r does ונעל, as a frequentative, imply fastening with several bolts?" (n. 1). The *wa-qaṭal* (וְנָעָֽל:) has been questioned widely by Biblical Hebrew scholarship. BHS suggests emendation to *wayyinʿol*. Boling (1975, 87) prefers to "read as infinitive absolute, rather than the anomalous perfect of MT." J-M (§119z) calls this omission of energic Waw in *wa-qaṭal*. Schulz (1900, 38) and Joosten (2012, 227) identify it as *wa* + *qaṭal*.

[113] According to Joosten (2012, 174), *wa-qaṭal* is iterative. Examples of *wa-qaṭal* describing subevents after *wa(y)-yiqṭol* in the corpus: Exod. 36.37f.—Propp (2006, 649) expected *wa(y)-yiqṭol*, and his translation 'and he will plate' is problematic, while Joosten (2012, 228 n. 73) calls this a problematic use of *wa-qaṭal*; 39.3—according to Schulz (1900, 38), this is *wa* + *qaṭal*, but according to Propp (2006, 653), VNabs, while Joosten (2012, 228 n. 73) says it "may be regarded as iterative," and Hornkohl (2014, 288) calls it a multi-step process; Judg. 3.23; 7.13. Outside the corpus: 2 Sam. 12.31; 13.18; 1 Kgs 18.4—Joosten (2012, 227, 307) calls this "Single WEQATAL," but translates (p. 370) 'and provided them [continually] with bread and water'; 2 Kgs 23.4—according to Khan (2021a, 316f.), a subevent of the same overall event.

[114] Instead of *wa-qaṭal*, Propp (1999, 627) reads *wəyišpəṭū*, which in CBH must be analysed as *wa* + jussive.

[115] When estimating new paragraphs, one must bear in mind that paragraph units in CBH are shorter than what is acceptable in English printed texts.

[116] For *Ø-X-yiqṭol(u)*, see §§7.8.3–4.

[117] Gen. 24.35 'The LORD has richly blessed my master' (NET).

[118] Exod. 1.7 'The Israelites, however, were fruitful' (NET).

[119] Two subordinated clauses are disregarded in the pattern: the temporal clause (כַּאֲשֶׁר רָאָם) and the quotation (מַחֲנֵה אֱלֹהִים זֶה).

[120] Other examples of foregrounded *wa-X-qaṭal* clauses introducing a new paragraph: Gen. 4.1 (Cook 2012, 298; Hornkohl 2018, 49 n. 64; Isaksson 2021, 223f.); 13.14–18 (Westermann 1981, 209; Hornkohl 2018, 49); 19.4f., 38; 21.1 (Hornkohl 2018, 49 n. 64); 24.35 (anterior in report); 24.62f.; 25.26, 34 (new paragraph and foreground; *pace* Hornkohl 2018, 49 n. 64); 26.15, 26f. (Hornkohl 2018, 49 n. 64); 27.6–11 (Hornkohl 2018, 49 n. 64); 27.30f.; 33.3, 7, 17; 34.26; 38.30; 41.50; 45.16; Exod. 1.7; 7.21; 14.10; 19.3—Givón (2001, I:349) calls this "use of the perfect in topic switching;" 19.18; Lev. 10.16; Num. 1.18 (Levine 1993, 127); 11.4; 12.16; 16.35 (foreground; *pace* Buth 1995, 96); Deut. 4.21 (report); 9.20; 10.6; Judg. 1.9, 27 (*wa-lō-qaṭal*, וְלֹא־הוֹרִישׁ מְנַשֶּׁה פ: an

unusual beginning of a paragraph, but there is a connection with the previous actant, Joseph); 1.29; 3.5f., 31; 4.17; 6.19, 33—but Joosten (2012, 177) calls this background; 6.34, 35; 7.24; 9.44 (two paragraphs with parallel series of events); 16.23; 18.18, 27; 20.17, 33, 37, 40, 41, 48; 21.1f., 15 (*qaṭal*, not *qoṭel*). For Gen. 29.9 (with initial temporal *qoṭel* clause, *Ø-X-qoṭel* + *wa-X-qaṭal*, where *qaṭal* is foregrounded), and Gen. 38.25 (with initial subordinate *Ø-X-qoṭel*), see Tenet 2c (§7.9).

[121] Other examples of *wa-X-qaṭal* (background) + *(Tenet 1a–d)* + *wa(y)-yiqṭol*: Gen. 13.5–7 (copula verb); 19.15 (pluperfect; Hornkohl 2018, 49 n. 64); 31.19–21 (pluperfect; Hornkohl 2018, 45, 49 n. 64); 39.1 (pluperfect, new discourse section; Cook 2012, 298; Hornkohl 2018, 45, 52); 46.28 (pluperfect, resumes the narrative from 46.7); Exod. 3.1 (copula verb, not to be classified as *qoṭel*); Num. 1.47f. (pluperfect; Levine 1993, 3); 20.2f. (copula verb); 32.1 (copula verb); Deut. 34.9 (stativic verb); Judg. 1.16 (pluperfect; Boling 1975, 51); 3.26f. (pluperfect; Boling 1975, 85).

[122] For *Ø-qaṭal* beginning a new paragraph in direct speech, see §7.3.3.1.

[123] Wenham (1994, 58): “The syntax suggests that sunrise, Lot’s arrival in Zoar, and the fire from heaven coincide.”

[124] For an interpretation of the first two *qaṭal* clauses with pluperfect meaning, and thus as backgrounded, see Westermann (1981, 360, 373). The problem with this interpretation is that the third *qaṭal* (וַֽיהוָ֗ה הִמְטִ֧יר) must be taken as equivalent to a *wa(y)-yiqṭol*, expressing temporal succession.

[125] Other asyndetic foregrounded *qaṭal* clauses (thus *Ø-X-qaṭal*) introducing a new paragraph: Gen. 7.13 (beginning of the flood story of P; Westermann 1976, 586); 15.1—the formula אַחַ֣ר ׀ הַדְּבָרִ֣ים הָאֵ֗לֶּה “markiert nie die einfache Fortsetzung, sondern überbrückt immer einen Abstand zum Vorhergehenden” (Westermann 1981, 257); 25.19f. (start of genealogy); 41.10 (beginning of report in direct speech; אֶת־חֲטָאַ֕י אֲנִ֖י מַזְכִּ֥יר is just an introduction and not an event to connect to; see also Hornkohl 2018, 49 n. 64); 43.20 (beginning of report in direct speech); 44.19 (beginning of report in direct speech; Hornkohl 2018, 49 n. 64); Exod.

19.1f.—"it is an independent event, not logically consequent to what precedes" (Propp 2006, 154); Num. 11.35; 21.12f. (in a formulaic chronicle); Deut. 10.1–3 (new paragraph in report); 22.16 (start of a fictive direct speech in a legal case); Judg. 1.30, 31, 33 (I cannot explain why Manasseh 1.27, and Ephraim 1.29, the sons of Joseph, are syndetic, whereas Zebulon, Asher, Naphtali, are asyndetic; it is a sort of list from Zebulon 1.30); 6.8 (beginning of report in speech); 20.4f. (beginning of report).

[126] Other asyndetic backgrounded *qaṭal* clauses introducing a new paragraph (thus *Ø-X-qaṭal*): Gen. 6.9f. (copula verb, the *XØ* is a headline); Judg. 18.22f. (two *qaṭal* with pluperfect meaning, *Ø-X-qaṭal* + *wa-X-qatal*, but the clauses could be just background, not starting a new paragraph).

[127] Other examples of *Ø-X-yiqṭol(u)* + (Tenet 1a–d) + *wa-qaṭal* beginning a new paragraph: Lev. 26.34 (future, *Ø-ʾāz-yiqṭol(u)* + *wa-qaṭal*); Judg. 7.7 (*Ø-PrP-yiqṭol(u)!* + *wa-qaṭal*, future, beginning of speech).

[128] Other examples of a circumstantial *qoṭel* clause starting a new paragraph: Gen. 29.9f. (*Ø-ADV-S.pron-qoṭel* + *wa-X-qaṭal* + *kī-qoṭel* + [10]*wayhī-(CONJ-qaṭal)* + *wa(y)-yiqṭol*)—here *wa-X-qaṭal* is foregrounded, *pace* Lunn (2006, 46), who argues that Rachel "fades into the background;" 38.25 (*Ø-X-qoṭel* + *wa-X-qaṭal* + *wa(y)-yiqṭol*)—the participle is circumstantial with temporal meaning (Westermann 1982, 42), 'when she was about to be brought out', and as such, related to *qaṭal*, which is foregrounded, a dramatic turning point and a new scene.

[129] Other relatively uncomplicated instances of backgrounding *qoṭel* before a *wa(y)-yiqṭol* main line are: Exod. 20.18; Judg. 9.45—Butler (2009, 248) regards the paragraph as a summary.

[130] *Pace* Sasson (2014, 250), who takes the initial expression as a verbless clause, 'Deborah was a woman prophet' (see also Boling 1975, 92).

[131] All my registered backgrounded *qoṭel* clauses beginning a new paragraph in narration: Gen. 23.10; 41.17; Exod. 20.18; Judg. 4.4; 9.45; 15.14.

[132] Examples of foregrounded *qoṭel* beginning a new paragraph in narration: Num. 25.6; Judg. 4.22; 7.13; 19.16f. Some cases of *qoṭel* introducing a new paragraph are not morphologically distinctive (all concern the form בָּא); those with initial focus particle *wa-hinnē* are foregrounded, the others backgrounded: Num. 25.6 (*wa-hinnē-X-qoṭel* + *wa(y)-yiqṭol*); Judg. 15.14 (*Ø-X-qoṭel* + *wa-X-qaṭal* + *wa(y)-yiqṭol*)—although according to Driver (1892, 211), it is *qaṭal*; 19.16f. (*wa-hinnē-X-qoṭel* + *wa(y)-yiqṭol*).

[133] Another start of a dream report is found in Judg. 7.13 (*Ø-hinnē-O.noun-qaṭal* + *wa-hinnē-X-qoṭel* + *wa(y)-yiqṭol* + *wa(y)-yiqṭol* + *wa-qaṭal*), where the initial *qaṭal* does not belong to the dream but functions as background outside the dream discourse ('I had a dream'). There then follows the start of the dream report, with *wa-hinnē-X-qoṭel* and then two *wa(y)-yiqṭol*. For the last *wa-qaṭal*, see §7.6.3.

[134] Other examples of // *Ø-X-qoṭel* + *wa-qaṭal* as a paragraph beginning: Gen. 17.19; 48.21 (*Ø-hinnē-S.pron-qoṭel*); Exod. 8.25 (*Ø-hinnē-S.pron-qoṭel*); 11.4f.; 16.4f. (*Ø-hinnē-S.pron-qoṭel*).

[135] Other examples of backgrounded *wa-XØ* + *wa(y)-yiqṭol* beginning a new paragraph: Gen. 7.6f. ([6]*wa-XØ* + *wa-S.noun-qaṭal* + [7]*wa(y)-yiqṭol*, where *XØ* is a temporal clause); 24.1f. (*wa-S.noun-XØ* + *Ø-qaṭal* + *wa-S.noun-qaṭal* + *wa(y)-yiqṭol*)—Hornkohl (2018, 49 n. 64) calls this a new unit; 41.46f.; 43.1f.; 47.13.

[136] Boling (1975, 275) takes *rad* as a biform of *yrd* (*qaṭal*); HALOT instead emends the text to *yāraḏ*.

[137] Other examples of backgrounded *Ø-XØ* + *wa(y)-yiqṭol* beginning a new paragraph: Num. 11.33 (*Ø-XØ* + *Ø-ṭɛrɛm-yiqṭol(u)* + *wa-S.noun-qaṭal* + *wa(y)-yiqṭol*); 33.1f.; Deut. 26.5 (*Ø-XØ* + *wa(y)-yiqṭol* + *wa(y)-yiqṭol*, report); Judg. 18.1f.

[138] The next example, the beginning of Ishmael's genealogy, is similar: Gen. 25.17f. (*wa-XØ* + *wa(y)-yiqṭol* + *wa(y)-yiqṭol* + *wa(y)-yiqṭol* + *wa(y)-yiqṭol*; Westermann 1981, 482).

[139] Another instance of *Ø-XØ* + *wa-qaṭal* beginning a paragraph: Gen. 20.11 (cf. Khan 2021a, 309, 312).

[140] The clause is translated according to Westermann (1976, 437): 'und gebar den Henoch, der wurde Erbauer einer Stadt'.

[141] For the so-called cohortative, see §§1.2.2, 3.4.2.3.

[142] For *Ø-qaṭal*, see §7.3.3.

[143] Further examples of *wa(y)-yiqṭol* + *wa-lō-qaṭal*, with temporal succession if not otherwise stated: Gen. 8.8f. ([8]*wa(y)-yiqṭol* + [9]*wa-lō-qaṭal* + *wa(y)-yiqṭol* + *kī-XØ*); 8.12; 30.40 (same-event addition; see §2.3.4); 31.33–35 (3×); 34.18f.; 35.5 (implicit result meaning); 38.20, 26; 40.21–23; Exod. 1.17; 6.9; 7.13, 22, 23 (summary; see §2.3.1); 8.11, 15, 28; 9.7, 10f., 12; 10.15, 20, 27; 11.10; 14.20 (implicit result); 15.22, 23 (stativic verb, can be interpreted as temporal succession); 16.18, 19f., 24; 33.3 (possibly simultaneous with the immediately preceding *wa(y)-yiqṭol*, but not background; cf. the discussion in §2.3.3); 40.34f. (stativic verb and focal result; see §2.3.6); Num. 11.25 (*wa-lō-qaṭal* is temporally sequential in relation to *wa(y)-yiqṭol*, and both express repeated actions after *qoṭel*; Joosten 2012, 185); 21.21–23; 24.1 (focal result); 33.14; Deut. 1.45; 9.23 (*wa(y)-yiqṭol* + *wa-lō-qaṭal* + *wa-lō-qaṭal*, elaboration; see §2.3.1, §2.3.4); Judg. 2.2, 14 (stativic verb, focal result clause); 2.23 (summary); 3.28; 6.10; 8.20, 28, 33–35 (2×, focal result); 10.6 (same-event addition); 11.17, 18, 19f., 28; 12.2; 13.20f.; 14.6 (sequential), 9 (focal negative clause, no sequentiality); 15.1; 16.9; 19.23–25; 20.12f.; 21.14.

[144] Some instances when *wa-lō-yiqṭol(u)* alone expresses focal result: Gen. 9.15; 17.5 'Therefore your name will no longer be Abram'; 41.31 (less clear case); Exod. 10.5; 12.13; Lev. 11.44.

[145] Other supporting result clauses coded by *wa-lō-yiqṭol(u)* (can often be translated with an initial 'in this way'), many of the type וְלֹא יָמוּת: Gen. 41.36 (*wa-qaṭal* + *wa-lō-yiqṭol(u)*); Exod. 28.35; 30.12, 21; Lev. 8.35; 14.36; 15.31; 16.13; 18.28, 30; 20.22, 25; Num. 4.19 (second part of a result complex, *wa-X-IMP* + ***wa-qaṭal*** + ***wa-lō-yiqṭol(u)***); 11.17 (second part of the result complex, *wa-qaṭal* + *wa-lō-yiqṭol(u)*); 18.5; 35.12; Deut. 19.10; 22.8.

[146] Examples of a *wa-qaṭal* clause carrying over the preceding temporal reference: Gen. 50.25; Exod. 8.7; 13.19; 16.12; 17.6; Lev. 25.6; Num. 28.19; 28.27; 29.7, 12; 32.17.

[147] Another example of *wa-qaṭal* + *wa-lō-yiqṭol(u)* carrying over the temporal reference from the preceding clause is Exod. 12.23: instead of translating the preceding *wa-qaṭal* as 'and when he sees the blood' (thus NET), it can be translated with a simple 'and will see the blood' (thus Propp 1999, 356), and the following *wa-qaṭal* + *wa-lō-yiqṭol(u)* both carry over the temporal reference: 'at that moment the LORD will pass over the door, and he will not permit the destroyer'.

[148] Another example of *wa-lō-yiqṭol(u)* carrying over the preceding temporal reference point (outside the corpus): Amos 9.15 (*wa-qaṭal* + *wa-lō-yiqṭol(u)*).

[149] Similar examples of *wa-lō-yiqṭol(u)* alternating with *wa-qaṭal* as a substructure in protases: Exod. 21.22, 29; Deut. 21.18.

[150] An example of temporally successive *wa-qaṭal* and *wa-lō-yiqṭol(u)* in apodosis: Exod. 22.10.

[151] Another instance of discourse-continuity negated jussive clause: Gen. 44.18 (*Ø-ADV-VOC-yiqṭol(Ø)-nā* + *wa-ʾal-yiqṭol(Ø)* + *kī-XØ*). An example in archaic poetry: Deut. 33.6 (*Ø-yiqṭol(Ø)!* + *wa-ʾal-yiqṭol(Ø)!* + *wa-yiqṭol(Ø)!*; Notarius 2013, 248).

[152] For the 'long' form of the jussive, see §3.4.4.6 and cf. Sjörs (2023).

[153] More instances of *wa-ʾal-yiqṭol(Ø)* as negated continuous imperative: Gen. 22.12; 45.5; Exod. 20.19; Lev. 16.2 (semantic complement); Num. 11.15—purpose, with ventive clitic, but according to Dallaire (2014, 116), cohortative; Num. 16.26 (elaboration); Deut. 1.21; 2.9, 19; 21.8 (*Ø-IMP* + *wa-ʾal-yiqṭol(Ø)* + *wa-qaṭal*); 31.6; Judg. 13.7.

8. DID THIS BOOK ACHIEVE ITS AIM? A SUMMARY

The aim of this book was formulated in §1.1. The aim was to explain and clarify:

1. why *wa* has two formal variants (*wə*- and *way*-) in the Masoretic text;
2. the status of the short *yiqṭol* (with both past and jussive meanings) as a separate verbal morpheme distinct from long *yiqṭol*;
3. how long *yiqṭol* was distinguished from short *yiqṭol*;
4. why *qaṭal* came to alternate with the inherited *wayyiqṭol*;
5. why *wa-qaṭal* acquired imperfective meanings and came to alternate with the inherited long *yiqṭol* (< **yaqtulu*);
6. the linguistic reality behind *wa* in the 'consecutive tenses'.

(1) The origin of the two variants of *wa*, and the origin of the gemination of the prefix consonant in *wa(y)-yiqṭol*, was clarified already in Isaksson (2021a) and further treated in §1.2.5, §2, and §7.1 of this book. The distinction achieved by the gemination was introduced into the reading tradition probably as early as the Second Temple period. But in the living language of Classical Hebrew, the conjunction *wa* was pronounced *wa* in all positions, jussive *wa-yiqṭol* and indicative (perfective) *wa-yiqṭol* were homophonous, and *we-qaṭal* was pronounced *wa-qaṭal*.

 https://doi.org/10.11647/OBP.0414.08

(2) The status of the short *yiqṭol* in CBH was treated in Isaksson (2021a) and §3 of this book. The short *yiqṭol*, both the jussive and the perfective past, was inherited from Proto-Semitic.

(3) The distinct identity of the short *yiqṭol(Ø)* was upheld by restrictions of word order in affirmative clauses. An imperfective *yiqṭol(u)* must have internal position in the clause (§3.4.3). The morphological contrast between *yiqṭol(Ø)* and *yiqṭol(u)* was upheld in CBH when applicable (§3.4.1).

(4) The verbal morpheme *qaṭal* in CBH was inherited from West Semitic, and partly took over the anterior and perfective functions of the Proto-Semitic perfective *yaqtul*. The only indicative use of the short *yiqṭol* that was retained in CBH was in the extremely frequent continuity clause-type *wa(y)-yiqṭol*. This resulted in a type of syntax where discourse-discontinuity *qaṭal* clauses 'alternate' with continuity *wa(y)-yiqṭol* clauses (§5.5). The linking patterns of this alternation were further treated in §7.

(5) Why and how *wa-qaṭal* acquired imperfective meanings was discussed in §6, where Geoffrey Khan's proposal that *wa-qaṭal* is a construction in Bybee's (2010; 2015) sense was adopted and developed. The *wa-qaṭal* clause-type came to fill an empty syntactic slot in CBH: the absence of the continuity clause-type *wa-yiqṭol(u)*, which had become obsolete in CBH because of its partial homonymy with *wa-yiqṭol(Ø)* and ensuing word order restrictions (§3.4.3). This is the reason why the imperfective discourse continuity *wa-qaṭal* came to alternate with discontinuity *(wa)-X-yiqṭol(u)* clauses. The linking patterns were further treated in §7.

(6) Finally, the linguistic reality behind *wa* in the 'consecutive tenses' was investigated in §7. The old theory of consecutive tenses is essentially a theory of the linking of clauses in CBH on the textual level. Foreground alternates with background and this alternation is coded by an alternation between discourse-continuity clauses and discontinuity clauses in patterns that create an intricate textual web. For the details of this web, see §7. I have shown that there is no special 'consecutive *waw*'; rather, there is one natural language connective *wa* in CBH. I have also shown that *wa(y)-yiqṭol* and *wa-qaṭal* are not 'tenses', but clause-types. Finally, I have shown—and this is in part based on the old theory—that a discourse-continuity clause in CBH is of the type *wa-V(X)*, where *wa* is a normal natural language connective (cf. §2.1 and §7.1), and *V* is a finite verb (a following clausal constituent *X* is optional).

After all this, as a corollary, we can conclude that the term 'consecutive' is uncalled for in the grammatical description of Classical Biblical Hebrew.

REFERENCES

AbB = Kraus, Fritz Rudolf, ed. 1964. *Altbabylonische Briefe in Umschrift und Übersetzung.* Leiden: Brill.

Aḥituv, Shmuel. 2008. *Echoes from the Past: Hebrew and Cognate Inscriptions from the Biblical Period.* Jerusalem: Carta.

Amadasi Guzzo, Maria Giulia. 1997. 'Phoenician-Punic'. In *Oxford Encyclopedia of the Archaeology of the Near East*, edited by E. Meyers, vol. 4: 317–24. Oxford: Oxford University Press.

Amadasi Guzzo, Maria Giulia, and Vassos Karageorghis. 1977. *Excavations at Kition.* Vol. 3, *Inscriptions phéniciennes.* Nicosia: Department of Antiquities for the Republic of Cyprus.

Ambros, Arne Amadeus, and Stephan Procházka. 2004. *A Concise Dictionary of Koranic Arabic.* Wiesbaden: Reichert.

Andersen, Francis I. 1966. 'Moabite Syntax'. *Orientalia* 35: 81–120.

———. 1974. *The Sentence in Biblical Hebrew.* Janua Linguarum 231. Mouton: The Hague. Reprint, 1980.

Andersen, T. David. 2000. 'The Evolution of the Hebrew Verbal System'. *Zeitschrift für Althebraistik* 13 (1): 1–66.

Anderson, A. A. 1989. *Word Biblical Commentary.* Vol. 11, *2 Samuel.* Waco, Tex.: Word Books.

Andrason, Alexander, and Juan Pabloo Vita. 2014. 'The Present-future in Amorite'. *Journal for Semitics* 23: 21–36.

———. 2017. 'The YQTL-Ø "preterite" in Ugaritic Epic Poetry'. *Archiv Orientální* 85 (3): 345–87.

Athas, George. 2003. *The Tel Dan Inscription: A Reappraisal and a New Interpretation.* Journal for the Study of the Old Testament Supplement Series 360. London: Sheffield Academic Press.

———. 2006. 'Setting the Record Straight: What are We Making of the Tel Dan Inscription?'. *Journal of Semitic Studies* 51 (2): 241–55.

Aufrecht, Walter E. 1989. *A Corpus of Ammonite Inscriptions.* Ancient Near Eastern Texts and Studies 4. Lewiston, N.Y.: Edwin Mellen Press.

Avanzini, Alessandra. 2006. 'A Fresh Look at Sabaic'. Review of *Untersuchungen zur Phonologie und Morphologie des Sabäischen*, by Peter Stein (2003). *Journal of the American Oriental Society* 126 (2): 252–60.

———. 2009. 'Origin and Classification of the Ancient South Arabian Languages'. *Journal of Semitic Studies* 54 (1): 205–20.

———. 2015. *Ancient South Arabian within Semitic, and Sabaic within Ancient South Arabian.* Quaderni di Arabia Antica 2. Rome: L'Erma di Bretschneider.

Baden, Joel S. 2008. 'The *wəyiqtol* and the Volitive Sequence'. *Vetus Testamentum* 58: 147–58.

Bailey, N. A., and S. H. Levinsohn. 1992. 'The Function of Preverbal Elements in Independent Clauses in the Hebrew Narrative of Genesis'. *Journal of Translation and Textlinguistics* 5 (3): 179–207.

Baker, David W. 1980. 'Further Examples of the *waw Explicativum*'. *Vetus Testamentum* 30 (2): 129–36.

Baranowski, Krzysztof J. 2016a. *The Verb in the Amarna Letters from Canaan.* Winona Lake, Ind.: Eisenbrauns.

———. 2016b. 'The Biblical Hebrew *wayyiqtol* and the Evidence of the Amarna Letters from Canaan'. *Journal of Hebrew Scriptures* 16: 1–18.

———. 2017. 'The Present-Future in Amorite: A Rejoinder'. *Ancient Near Eastern Studies* 54: 81–89.

Bauer, Hans. 1910. 'Die Tempora im Semitischen, ihre Entstehung und ihre Ausgestaltung in den Einzelsprachen'. *Beiträge zur Assyriologie und semitischen Sprachwissenschaft* 8 (1): 1–53.

Bauer, Hans, and Pontus Leander. 1922. *Historische Grammatik der hebräischen Sprache des Alten Testamentes.* Vol. 1, *Einleitung, Schriftlehre, Laut- und Formenlehre.* Halle: Max Niemeyer. Reprint, Hildesheim: Georg Olms, 1965.

———. 1927. *Grammatik des Biblisch-Aramäischen.* Tübingen: Max Niemeyer. Reprint, Hildesheim: Georg Olms, 1969.

Beeston, Alfred Felix Landon. 1984. *Sabaic Grammar.* Journal of Semitic Studies Monograph Series 6. Manchester: University of Manchester.

Ben-Ḥayyim, Zeev. 2000. *A Grammar of Samaritan Hebrew: Based on the Recitation of the Law in Comparison with the Tiberian and Other Jewish Traditions.* Rev. English ed. Jerusalem; Winona Lake, Ind.: Hebrew University Magnes Press; Eisenbrauns.

Ben-Mordecai, C. A. 1939. 'Chezib'. *Journal of Biblical Literature* 58 (3): 283–86.

Bergsträsser, Gotthelf. 1929. *Hebräische Grammatik, mit Benutzung der von E. Kautzsch bearbeiteten 28. Auflage von Wilhelm Gesenius' hebräischer Grammatik.* Part 2, *Verbum.* Leipzig: Vogel. Reprint, Hildesheim: Georg Olms, 1962.

Bergström, Ulf. 2014. 'Time and the Semantics of the Biblical Hebrew Verbal System'. PhD diss., Uppsala University.

Berthier, André, and René Charlier. 1952–55. *Le sanctuaire punique d'El-Hofra à Constantine.* 2 vols. Paris: Arts et métiers graphiques.

Beyer, Klaus. 1984. *Die aramäischen Texte vom Toten Meer, samt den Inschriften aus Palästina, dem Testament Levis aus der Kairoer Genisa, der Fastenrolle und den alten talmudischen Zitaten.* Göttingen: Vandenhoeck & Ruprecht.

Biran, Avraham, and Joseph Naveh. 1993. 'An Aramaic Stele Fragment from Tel Dan'. *Israel Exploration Journal* 43 (2–3): 81–98.

———. 1995. 'The Tel Dan Inscription: A New Fragment'. *Israel Exploration Journal* 45 (1): 1–18.

Birkeland, Harris. 1940. *Akzent und Vokalismus im Althebräischen mit Beiträgen zur vergleichenden semitischen Sprachwissenschaft.* Skrifter utgitt av det norske videnskaps-akademie i Oslo, historisk-filosofisk klasse 3. Oslo: Jacob Dybwad.

Birnstiel, Daniel. 2019. 'Classical Arabic'. In *The Semitic Languages,* edited by John Huehnergard and Na'ama Pat-El, 367–402. Routledge Language Family Series. London: Routledge.

Bjøru, Øyvind, and Na'ama Pat-El. 2020. 'The Historical Syntax of the Subordinative Morphemes in Assyrian Akkadian'. *Zeitschrift für Assyriologie* 110 (1): 71–83.

Blake, Frank R. 1951. *A Resurvey of Hebrew Tenses: With an Appendix—Hebrew Influence on Biblical Aramaic*. Scripta Pontificii Instituti Biblici 103. Rome: Pontifical Biblical Institute.

Blau, Joseph L. 1959. 'Adverbia als psychologische und grammatische Subjekte/Praedikate im Bibelhebraeisch'. *Vetus Testamentum* 9 (2): 130–37.

———. 1993. *A Grammar of Biblical Hebrew*. 2nd amended ed. Porta Linguarum Orientalium, n.s., 12. Wiesbaden: Harrassowitz.

———. 2010. *Phonology and Morphology of Biblical Hebrew: An Introduction*. Linguistic Studies in Ancient West Semitic 2. Winona Lake, Ind.: Eisenbrauns.

Bloch, Ariel A. 1963. 'Zur Nachweisbarkeit einer hebräischen Entsprechung der akkadischen Verbalform *iparras*'. *Zeitschrift der Deutschen Morgenländischen Gesellschaft* 113 (1): 41–50.

Bloch, Yigal. 2007. 'From Linguistics to Text-criticism and Back: *wayyiqṭōl* Constructions with Long Prefixed Verbal Forms in Biblical Hebrew'. *Hebrew Studies* 48: 140–70.

———. 2009. 'The Prefixed Perfective and the Dating of Early Hebrew Poetry: A Re-evaluation'. *Vetus Testamentum* 58: 34–70.

———. 2013. 'Archaisms: Biblical Hebrew'. In *Encyclopedia of Hebrew Language and Linguistics*, online, edited by Geoffrey

Khan. Leiden: Brill. https://doi.org/10.1163/2212-4241_ehll_EHLL_COM_00000121

Blum, Erhard. 2008. 'Das althebräische Verbalsystem: Eine synchrone Analyse'. In *Sprachliche Tiefe–Theologische Weite*, edited by Oliver Dyma and Andreas Michel, 91–142. Neukirchen-Vluyn: Neukirchener.

Boer, P. A. H. de. 1974. 'The Perfect with Waw in 2 Samuel 6:16'. In *On Language, Culture, and Religion: In Honor of Eugene A. Nida*. 43–52. The Hague: Mouton.

Boling, Robert G. 1975. *Judges: Introduction, Translation, and Commentary*. The Anchor Bible 6A. Garden City, N.Y.: Doubleday.

Bordreuil, Pierre, and Dennis Pardee. 2009. *A Manual of Ugaritic*. English rev. ed. Linguistic Studies in Ancient West Semitic 3. Winona Lake, Ind.: Eisenbrauns.

Bril, Isabelle. 2010. 'The Syntax and Pragmatics of Clause Linkage and Clause Hierarchy: Some New Perspectives'. In *Clause Linking and Clause Hierarchy: Syntax and Pragmatics*, edited by Isabelle Bril, 1–21. Studies in Language Companion Series 121. Amsterdam: John Benjamins.

Brockelmann, Carl. 1908–13. *Grundriß der vergleichenden Grammatik der semitischen Sprachen*. 2 vols. Berlin: Reuther & Reichard. Reprint, Hildesheim: Georg Olms, 1982.

———. 1951. 'Die "Tempora" des Semitischen'. *Zeitschrift für Phonetik und allgemeine Sprachwissenschaft* 5: 133–54.

———. 1956. *Hebräische Syntax*. Neukirchen-Vluyn: Kreis Moers.

———. 1977. *Arabische Grammatik. Paradigmen, Literatur, Übungsstücke und Glossar.* 19th ed. Leipzig: VEB Verlag Enzyklopädie.

Bron, François. 1973–1979. '*Waw* conversif en phénico-punique?'. *Comptes rendus du Groupe Linguistique d'Études Chamito-Sémitiques* 18–23 (3): 607–10.

Brongers, H. A. 1978. 'Alternative Interpretationen des sogenannten Waw copulativum'. *Zeitschrift für die Alttestamentliche Wissenschaft* 90: 273–77.

Brünnow, Rudolf-Ernst, August Fischer, Lutz Edzard, and Amund Bjørsnøs, eds. 2008. *Chrestomathy of Classical Arabic Prose Literature.* 8th rev. ed. Porta Linguarum Orientalium, n.s., 17.2. Wiesbaden: Harrassowitz.

Budd, Philip J. 1984. *Word Biblical Commentary.* Vol. 5, *Numbers.* Waco, Tex.: Word Books.

Buth, Randall John. 1995. 'Functional Grammar, Hebrew and Aramaic: An Integrated Textlinguistic Approach to Syntax'. In *Discourse Analysis of Biblical Literature: What It Is and What It Offers*, edited by Walter Ray Bodine, 77–102. The Society of Biblical Literature: Semeia Studies. Atlanta, Ga.: Scholars Press.

Butler, Trent C. 2009. *Word Biblical Commentary.* Vol. 8, *Judges.* Nashville: Thomas Nelson.

Butts, Aaron Michael. 2019. 'Gəʕəz (Classical Ethiopic)'. In *The Semitic Languages*, edited by John Huehnergard and Na'ama Pat-El, 117–44. Routledge Language Family Series. London: Routledge.

Bybee, Joan L. 1985. *Morphology: A Study of the Relation Between Meaning and Form.* Typological Studies in Language 9. Amsterdam: John Benjamins.

———. 1995. 'The Semantic Development of Past Tense Modals in English'. In *Modality in Grammar and Discourse*, edited by Joan L. Bybee and Suzanne Fleischman, 503–17. Typological Studies in Language 32. Amsterdam: John Benjamins.

———. 2010. *Language, Usage and Cognition.* Cambridge: Cambridge University Press.

———. 2015. *Language Change.* Cambridge Textbooks in Linguistics. Cambridge: Cambridge University Press.

Bybee, Joan L., and Östen Dahl. 1989. 'The Creation of Tense and Aspect Systems in the Languages of the World'. *Studies in Language* 13 (1): 51–103.

Bybee, Joan L., William Pagliuca, and Revere D. Perkins. 1991. 'Back to the Future'. In *Approaches to Grammaticalization*, edited by Elizabeth Closs Traugott and Bernd Heine. Vol. 2, *Focus on Types of Grammatical Markers*, 17–58. Typological Studies in Language 19.2. Amsterdam: John Benjamins.

———. 1994. *The Evolution of Grammar: Tense, Aspect, and Modality in the Languages of the World.* Chicago: University of Chicago Press. Reprint, 2003.

Chatonnet, Françoise Briquel, and Robert Hawley. 2020. 'Phoenician and Punic'. In *A Companion to Ancient Near Eastern Languages*, edited by Rebecca Hasselbach-Andee, 297–318. Hoboken, N.J.: Wiley-Blackwell.

Childs, Brevard S. 1963. 'A Study of the Formula "Until this Day"'. *Journal of Biblical Literature* 82 (3): 279–92.

Chisholm, Raymond H. 1985. 'An Exegetical and Theological Study of Psalm 18, 2 Samuel 22'. PhD diss., Dallas Theological Seminary.

Christensen, Duane L. 2001. *Word Biblical Commentary*. Vol. 6a, *Deuteronomy 1:1–21:9*. Rev. 2nd ed. Nashville: Thomas Nelson.

———. 2002. *Word Biblical Commentary*. Vol. 6b, *Deuteronomy 21:10–34:12*. Nashville: Thomas Nelson.

CIS I = *Corpus Inscriptionum Semiticarum ab Academia Inscriptionum et Litterarum Humaniorum conditum atque digestum.* 1926. Part 1, *Inscriptiones Phoeniciae,* vol. 3. Paris: Klincksieck.

Cohen, David. 1976. 'Hébreu, araméen et sémitique comparé'. *École pratique des hautes études, 4e section, Sciences historiques et philologiques* 108: 241–47.

———. 1984. *La phrase nominale et l'évolution du système verbal en sémitique: Études de syntaxe historique.* Collection Linguistique publiée par la Société de Linguistique de Paris 72. Paris: Société de Linguistique de Paris.

Cohen, Eran. 2006. 'The Tense-Aspect System of the Old Babylonian Epic'. *Zeitschrift für Assyriologie* 96 (1): 31–68.

———. 2012. *Conditional Structures in Mesopotamian Old Babylonian.* Languages of the Ancient Near East 4. Winona Lake, Ind.: Eisenbrauns.

———. 2014. 'The Domain: A Formal Syntactic Unit above Sentence Level'. In *Strategies of Clause Linking in Semitic Languages: Proceedings of the International Symposium on Clause*

Linking in Semitic Languages, 5–7 August 2012 in Kivik, Sweden, edited by Bo Isaksson and Maria Persson, 233–52. Abhandlungen für die Kunde des Morgenlandes 93. Wiesbaden: Harrassowitz.

———. 2015. 'Circumstantial Clause Combining in Old Babylonian Akkadian'. In *Clause Combining in Semitic: The Circumstantial Clause and Beyond*, edited by Bo Isaksson and Maria Persson, 365–406. Abhandlungen für die Kunde des Morgenlandes 96. Wiesbaden: Harrassowitz.

Comrie, Bernard. 1976. *Aspect: An Introduction to the Study of Verbal Aspect and Related Problems.* Cambridge Textbooks in Linguistics. Cambridge: Cambridge University Press. Reprint, with corrections, 1981.

———. 1986. 'Tense and Time Reference: From Meaning to Interpretation in the Chronological Structure of a Text'. *Journal of Literary Semantics* 15: 12-22.

Cook, John A. 2004. 'The Semantics of Verbal Pragmatics: Clarifying the Roles of *wayyiqtol* and *weqatal* in Biblical Hebrew Prose'. *Journal of Semitic Studies* 49 (2): 247–73.

———. 2012a. *Time and the Biblical Hebrew Verb: The Expression of Tense, Aspect, and Modality in Biblical Hebrew.* Linguistic Studies in Ancient West Semitic 7. Winona Lake, Ind.: Eisenbrauns.

———. 2012b. 'Detecting Development in Biblical Hebrew Using Diachronic Typology'. In *Diachrony in Biblical Hebrew*, edited by Cynthia L. Miller-Naudé and Ziony Zevit, 83–95. Linguistic Studies in Ancient West Semitic 8. Winona Lake, Ind.: Eisenbrauns.

———. 2013. 'Verb'. In *Encyclopedia of Hebrew Language and Linguistics*, edited by Geoffrey Khan, vol. 3, 896–901. Leiden: Brill.

———. 2014. 'Putting Old Wine in New Wineskins: A New Synthesis of the Verbal System of Biblical Hebrew That is Neither New Nor a Coherent Synthesis'. Review of *The Verbal System of Biblical Hebrew: A New Synthesis Elaborated on the Basis of Classical Prose* by Jan Joosten. *Hebrew Studies* 55: 351–60.

Cotrozzi, Stefano. 2010. *Expect the Unexpected: Aspects of Pragmatic Foregrounding in Old Testament Narratives*. Library of Hebrew Bible/Old Testament Studies 510. New York: T&T Clark.

Croft, William. 2003. *Typology and Universals*. 2nd ed. Cambridge Textbooks in Linguistics. Cambridge: Cambridge University Press.

Cunchillos, Jesús-Luis, Juan-Pablo Vita, and José-Angel Zamora. 2003. *The Texts of the Ugaritic Data Bank*. Translated by A. Lacadena and A. Castro. 4 vols. Publications of the Ugaritic Data Bank. Piscataway, N.J.: Gorgias.

Dahl, Östen. 1985. *Tense and Aspect Systems*. Oxford: Blackwell.

———. 2000. 'The Tense-aspect Systems of European Languages in a Typological Perspective'. In *Tense and Aspect in the Languages of Europe*, edited by Östen Dahl, 3–25. Empirical Approaches to Language Typology (EUROTYP) 20.6. Berlin: Mouton de Gruyter.

Dahood, Mitchell. 1965a. *Psalms I, 1–50.* The Anchor Bible 16. Garden City, N.Y.: Doubleday. Reprint, New Haven: Yale University Press, 2011.

———. 1965b. 'Hebrew-Ugaritic Lexicography III'. *Biblica* 46: 311–32.

Dallaire, Hélène. 2014. *The Syntax of Volitives in Biblical Hebrew and Amarna Canaanite Prose.* Winona Lake, Ind.: Eisenbrauns.

DeCaen, Vincent J. J. 2001. 'The Morphosyntactic Argument for the *waw* Consecutive in Old Aramaic'. *Vetus Testamentum* 51 (3): 381–85.

Degen, Rainer. 1969. *Altaramäische Grammatik der Inschriften des 10.–8. Jh. v. Chr.* Abhandlungen für die Kunde des Morgenlandes 38.3. Wiesbaden: Franz Steiner.

Delitzsch, Friedrich. 1920. *Die Lese- und Schreibfehler im Alten Testament.* Berlin: Walter de Gruyter.

Diakonoff, Igor Michajlovic. 1988. *Afrasian Languages.* Translated by A. A. Korolev and V. Y. Porkhomovsky. Languages of Asia and Africa. Moscow: Nauka.

Diehl, Johannes Friedrich. 2007. 'Hebräisches Imperfekt mit *Waw* copulativum: Ein Arbeitsbericht'. In *"...der seine Lust hat am Wort des Herrn!" Festschrift für Ernst Jenni zum 80. Geburtstag*, edited by Jürg Luchsinger, Hans-Peter Mathys, and Markus Saur, 23–45. Alter Orient und Altes Testament 336. Münster: Ugarit-Verlag.

Diem, Werner. 1975. 'Gedanken zur Frage der Mimation und Nunation in den semitischen Sprachen'. *Zeitschrift der Deutschen Morgenländischen Gesellschaft* 125: 239–58.

Van Dijk, Teun Adrianus. 1977. *Text and Context: Explorations in the Semantics and Pragmatics of Discourse.* Longman Linguistics Library 21. London: Longman.

Dillmann, August. 1907. *Ethiopic Grammar: Orthography and Phonology, Morphology and Syntax of the Ethiopic Language, also in Comparison with Other Semitic Languages.* Translated by James A. Crichton. Edited by Carl Bezold. 2nd enlarged and improved ed. London: Williams & Norgate. Reprint, Amsterdam: Philo, 1974.

Dixon, Robert M. W. 2009. 'The Semantics of Clause Linking in Typological Perspective'. In *The Semantics of Clause Linking: A Cross-linguistic Typology*, edited by Robert M. W. Dixon and Alexandra Y. Aikhenvald, 1–55. Explorations in Linguistic Typology 5. Oxford: Oxford University Press. Reprint, 2011.

———. 2010. *Basic Linguistic Theory.* Vol. 1, *Methodology.* Oxford: Oxford University Press. Reprint, with corrections, 2012.

Dobbs-Allsopp, F. W. 1994. 'The Genre of the Meṣad Ḥashavyahu Ostracon'. *Bulletin of the American Schools of Oriental Research* 295: 49–55.

———. 2004–2007. '(More) on performatives in Semitic'. *Zeitschrift für Althebraistik* 17–20: 36–81.

Drinkard, Joel Flood. 1989. 'The Literary Genre of the Mesha Inscription'. In *Studies in the Mesha Inscription and Moab*, edited by J. Andrew Dearman, 131–54. The Society of Biblical Literature: Archaeology and Biblical Studies 2. Atlanta, Ga.: Scholars Press.

Driver, Samuel Rolles. 1892. *A Treatise on the Use of the Tenses in Hebrew and Some Other Syntactical Questions.* 3rd rev. and improved ed. Oxford: Clarendon. Reprint, 2004.

———. 1913. *Notes on the Hebrew Text and the Topography of the Books of Samuel with an Introduction on Hebrew Palaeography and the Ancient Versions and Facsimiles of Inscriptions and Maps.* 2nd rev. and enlarged ed. Oxford: Clarendon.

Dupont-Sommer, André. 1972. 'Une inscription phénicienne archaïque récemment trouvée à Kition (Chypre)'. *Mémoires présenteés par divers savants à l'Académie des Inscriptions et Belles-Lettres* 44 (2): 273–94.

Durham, John I. 1987. *Word Biblical Commentary.* Vol. 3, *Exodus.* Waco, Tex.: Word Books.

EA = Rainey, Anson F. 2015. *The El-Amarna Correspondence: A New Edition of the Cuneiform Letters from the Site of El-Amarna Based on Collations of All Extant Tablets.* Edited by William M. Schniedewind. Handbook of Oriental Studies 1.110. Leiden: Brill.

Ehrlich, Arnold B. 1909. *Randglossen zur hebräischen Bibel: Textkritisches, Sprachliches und Sachliches.* Vol. 2, *Leviticus, Numeri, Deuteronomium.* Leipzig: J. C. Hinrich.

Eissfeldt, Otto. 1922. *Hexateuch-Synopse: Die Erzählung der fünf Bücher Mose und des Buches Josua mit dem Anfange des Richtersbuches.* Leipzig: Hinrichs. Reprint, Darmstadt: Wissenschaftliche Buchgesellschaft, 1983.

Elitzur, Yoel. 2018. 'Diachrony in Standard Biblical Hebrew: The Pentateuch vis-à-vis the Prophets/Writings'. *Journal of Northwest Semitic Languages* 44 (2): 81–101.

Elliger, Kurt. 1978. *Deuterojesaja (Jesaja 40,1–45,7)*. Biblischer Kommentar: Altes Testament 11.6. Neukirchen-Vluyn: Neukirchener.

Emerton, John Adney. 1994. 'New Evidence for the Use of *waw* Consecutive in Aramaic'. *Vetus Testamentum* 44: 255–58.

———. 1997. 'Further Comments on the Use of Tenses in the Aramaic Inscription from Tel Dan'. *Vetus Testamentum* 47 (4): 429–40.

———. 2000. 'Two Issues in the Interpretation of the Tel Dan Inscription'. *Vetus Testamentum* 50 (1): 27–37.

Esk = Eskoubi, K. M. A. 1999. *Dirāsah Taḥliyyah Muqārinah li-Nuqūš min Minṭaqat (Ramm) Ǧanūb Ġarb Taymā'*. Riyadh: Wazārat al-Maʿārif.

Fales, Frederick Mario. 2011. 'Old Aramaic'. In *The Semitic Languages: An International Handbook*, edited by Stefan Weninger, Geoffrey Khan, Michael P. Streck, and Janet C. E. Watson, 555–73. Handbücher zur Sprach- und Kommunikationswissenschaft 36. Berlin: De Gruyter Mouton.

Fassberg, Steven Ellis. 2013a. 'Moabite and Hebrew'. In *Encyclopedia of Hebrew Language and Linguistics*, online, edited by Geoffrey Khan. Leiden: Brill. https://doi.org/10.1163/2212-4241_ehll_EHLL_COM_00000679

———. 2013b. 'Cohortative'. In *Encyclopedia of Hebrew Language and Linguistics*, online, edited by Geoffrey Khan. Leiden: Brill. https://doi.org/10.1163/2212-4241_ehll_EHLL_COM_00000270

Fenton, Terry L. 1970. 'The Absence of a Verbal Formation **ya-qattal* from Ugaritic and North-West Semitic'. *Journal of Semitic Studies* 15: 31–41.

———. 1973. 'The Hebrew "Tenses" in the Light of Ugaritic'. In *Proceedings of the Fifth World Congress of Jewish Studies 1969*. Vol. 4: 31–39. Jerusalem: World Union of Jewish Studies.

Ferguson, H. 1882. 'An Examination of the Use of the Tenses in Conditional Sentences in Hebrew'. *Journal of the Exegetical Society* 2: 40–94.

Fevrier, James. 1971. 'Le *waw* conversif en Punique'. In *Hommages à André Dupont-Sommer*, 191–94. Paris: Adrien-Maisonneuve.

Finley, Thomas J. 1981. 'The WAW-Consecutive with "Imperfect" in Biblical Hebrew: Theoretical Studies and its Use in Amos'. In *Tradition and Testament: Essays in Honor of Charles Lee Feinberg*, edited by John S. Feinberg and Paul D. Feinberg, 241–62. Chicago: Moody Press.

Fischer, Wolfdietrich. 2002. *A Grammar of Classical Arabic*. Translated by Jonathan Rodgers. 3rd rev. ed. New Haven: Yale University Press.

Fleischman, Suzanne. 1985. 'Discourse Functions of Tense-aspect Oppositions in Narrative: Toward a Theory of Grounding'. *Linguistics: An International Review* 23 (6): 851–82.

———. 1989. 'Temporal Distance: A Basic Linguistic Metaphor'. *Studies in Language* 13: 1–50.

———. 1990. *Tense and Narrativity: From Medieval Performance to Modern Fiction.* Croom Helm Romance Linguistics Series. London: Routledge. Reprint, 2002.

Florentin, Moshe. 2016. 'Samaritan Tradition'. In *A Handbook of Biblical Hebrew*, vol. 1, *Periods, Corpora, and Reading Traditions*, edited by W. Randall Garr and Steven Ellis Fassberg, 117–32. Winona Lake, Ind.: Eisenbrauns.

Folmer, Margaretha L. 1995. *The Aramaic Language in the Achaemenid Period: A Study in Linguistic Variation.* Orientalia Lovaniensia Analecta 68. Leuven: Peeters.

———. 2012. 'Old and Imperial Aramaic'. In *Languages from the World of the Bible*, edited by Holger Gzella, 128–59. Berlin: De Gruyter.

Fox, Andrew Jordan. 1983. 'Topic Continuity in Biblical Hebrew Narrative'. In *Topic Continuity in Discourse: A Quantitative Cross-language Study*, edited by Talmy Givón, 215–54. Typological Studies in Language 3. Amsterdam: John Benjamins.

Freedman, David Noel. 1960. 'Archaic Forms in early Hebrew Poetry'. *Zeitschrift für die Alttestamentliche Wissenschaft* 72 (2): 101–7.

Frayne, Douglas. 1993. *Sargonic and Gutian periods, 2334–2113 BC.* The Royal Inscriptions of Mesopotamia: Early Periods 2. Toronto: University of Toronto Press.

Friedrich, Johannes, and Wolfgang Röllig. 1970. *Phönizisch-punische Grammatik.* 2nd rev. ed. Analecta Orientalia 46. Rome: Pontifical Biblical Institute.

Friedrich, Johannes, Wolfgang Röllig, Maria Giulia Amadasi Guzzo, and Werner R. Mayer. 1999. *Phönizisch-punische Grammatik*. 3rd rev. ed. Analecta Orientalia 55. Rome: Pontifical Biblical Institute.

Gai, Amikam. 2000. 'The Connection Between Past and Optative in the Classical Semitic Languages'. *Zeitschrift der Deutschen Morgenländischen Gesellschaft* 150: 17–28.

Garbini, Giovanni. 1967. 'Note di epigrafia punica II'. *Rivista degli studi Orientali* 42: 8–13.

Garr, W. Randall. 1985. *Dialect Geography of Syria-Palestine, 1000–586 B.C.E.* Philadelphia: University of Pennsylvania Press. Reprint, Winona Lake, Ind.: Eisenbrauns, 2004.

———. 1998. 'Driver's *Treatise* and the Study of Hebrew: Then and Now'. In *A Treatise on the Use of the Tenses in Hebrew and Some other Syntactical Questions, by S. R. Driver*, xviii–lxxxvi. Biblical Resource Series. Grand Rapids: Eerdmans.

Garr, W. Randall, and Steven Ellis Fassberg, eds. 2016. *A Handbook of Biblical Hebrew*. Vol. 1, *Periods, Corpora, and Reading Traditions*. Winona Lake, Ind.: Eisenbrauns.

Geiger, Abraham. 1928. *Urschrift und Übersetzungen der Bibel in ihrer Abhängigkeit von der innern Entwicklung des Judentums*. 2nd ed. Frankfurt am Main: Madda.

Gelb, Ignace J., and Burkhart Kienast. 1990. *Die altakkadischen Königsinschriften des dritten Jahrtausends v. Chr.* Freiburger altorientalische Studien 17. Stuttgart: Franz Steiner.

Gentry, Peter J. 1998. 'The System of the Finite Verb in Classical Biblical Hebrew'. *Hebrew Studies* 39: 7–39.

George, Andrew, and Manfred Krebernik. 2022. 'Two Remarkable Vocabularies: Amorite–Akkadian Bilinguals!'. *Revue d'assyriologie et d'archéologie orientale* 116 (1): 113–66.

Ges-K = Gesenius, Wilhelm, and Emil Kautzsch. 1910. *Gesenius' Hebrew Grammar.* Translated by A. E. Cowley. Edited by Emil Kautzsch. 2nd revised English ed. Oxford: Clarendon. Reprint, 1976.

Gianto, Agustinus. 2008. 'Lost and Found in the Grammar of First-millennium Aramaic'. In *Aramaic in its Historical and Linguistic Setting*, edited by Holger Gzella and Margaretha L. Folmer, 11–25. Veröffentlichungen der Orientalischen Kommission 50. Wiesbaden: Harrassowitz.

———. 2016. 'Archaic Biblical Hebrew'. In *A Handbook of Biblical Hebrew*, vol. 1, *Periods, Corpora, and Reading Traditions*, edited by W. Randall Garr and Steven Ellis Fassberg, 19–29. Winona Lake, Ind.: Eisenbrauns.

Gibson, John C. L. 1982. *Textbook of Syrian Semitic Inscriptions.* Vol. 3, *Phoenician Inscriptions Including Inscriptions in the Mixed Dialect of Arslan Tash.* Oxford: Oxford University Press.

———. 1994. *Davidson's Introductory Hebrew Grammar: Syntax.* Edinburgh: T&T Clark.

Givón, Talmy. 1971. 'Historical Syntax and Synchronic Morphology: An Archaeologist's Field Trip'. *Chicago Linguistic Society* 7: 349–415.

———. 1977. 'The Drift from VSO to SVO in Biblical Hebrew: The Pragmatics of Tense-Aspect'. In *Mechanisms of Syntactic*

Change, edited by Charles N. Li, 181–254. Austin: University of Texas Press.

———. 1979. *On Understanding Grammar.* Perspectives in Neurolinguistics and Psycholinguistics. New York: Academic Press.

———. 1983. 'Topic Continuity in Discourse: An Introduction'. In *Topic Continuity in Discourse: A Quantitative Cross-language Study*, edited by Talmy Givón, 1–42. Typological Studies in Language 3. Amsterdam: John Benjamins.

———. 1991. 'The Evolution of Dependent Clause Morpho-syntax in Biblical Hebrew'. In *Approaches to Grammaticalization*, vol. 2, *Focus on Types of Grammatical Markers*, edited by Elizabeth Closs Traugott and Bernd Heine, 257–310. Typological Studies in Language 19.2. Amsterdam: John Benjamins.

———. 2001. *Syntax: An Introduction.* Rev. ed. 2 vols. Amsterdam: John Benjamins.

Goerwitz, Richard L. 1992. 'The Accentuation of the Hebrew Jussive and Preterite'. *Journal of the American Oriental Society* 112 (2): 198–203.

Gogel, Sandra Landis. 1998. *A Grammar of Epigraphic Hebrew.* Resources for Biblical Study 23. Atlanta, Ga.: Scholars Press.

Golinets, Viktor. 2010. 'Das amurritische Onomastikon der altbabylonischen Zeit, Band 2: Verbalmorphologie und Glossar der Verbalwurzeln'. PhD diss., Universität Leipzig.

———. 2020. 'Amorite'. In *A Companion to Ancient Near Eastern Languages*, edited by Rebecca Hasselbach-Andee, 185–202. Hoboken, N.J.: Wiley-Blackwell.

Gordon, Cyrus H. 1983. 'The "Waw Conversive": From Eblaite to Hebrew'. *Proceedings of the American Academy for Jewish Research* 50: 87–90.

Gragg, Gene B. 2019. 'Semitic and Afro-Asiatic'. In *The Semitic Languages*, edited by John Huehnergard and Na'ama Pat-El, 22–48. Routledge Language Family Series. London: Routledge.

Greenstein, Edward L. 1988. 'On the Prefixed Preterite in Biblical Hebrew'. *Hebrew Studies* 29: 7–17.

———. 2006. 'Forms and Functions of the Finite Verb in Ugaritic Narrative Verse'. In *Biblical Hebrew in its Northwest Semitic Setting: Typological and Historical Perspectives*, edited by Steven Ellis Fassberg and Avi Hurvitz, 75–102. Publication of the Institute for Advanced Studies 1. Jerusalem; Winona Lake, Ind.: Hebrew University Magnes Press; Eisenbrauns.

Gropp, Douglas Marvin. 1991. 'The Function of the Finite Verb in Classical Biblical Hebrew'. *Hebrew Annual Review* 13: 45–62.

Gross, Walter. 1976. *Verbform und Funktion: wayyiqṭol für die Gegenwart? Ein Beitrag zur Syntax poetischer althebräischer Texte*. Arbeiten zu Text und Sprache im Alten Testament 1. Sankt Ottilien: EOS.

———. 2013. 'Extraposition: Biblical Hebrew'. In *Encyclopedia of Hebrew Language and Linguistics*, online, edited by Geoffrey Khan. Leiden: Brill. https://doi.org/10.1163/2212-4241_ehll_EHLL_COM_00000331

Gzella, Holger. 2004. *Tempus, Aspekt und Modalität im Reichsaramäischen.* Veröffentlichungen der Orientalischen Kommission 48. Wiesbaden: Harrassowitz.

———. 2009. 'Ein auffälliger Konditionalsatz in der Aḥīrōm-Inschrift'. In *Philologisches und historisches zwischen Anatolien und Sokotra: Analecta Semitica in Memoriam Alexander Sima,* edited by Werner Arnold, Michael Jursa, Walter W. Müller, and Stephan Procházka, 63–71. Wiesbaden: Harrassowitz.

———. 2011a. 'Northwest Semitic in General'. In *The Semitic Languages: An International Handbook,* edited by Stefan Weninger, Geoffrey Khan, Michael P. Streck, and Janet C. E. Watson, 425–51. Handbücher zur Sprach- und Kommunikationswissenschaft 36. Berlin: De Gruyter Mouton.

———. 2011b. 'Imperial Aramaic'. In *The Semitic Languages: An International Handbook,* edited by Stefan Weninger, Geoffrey Khan, Michael P. Streck, and Janet C. E. Watson, 574–86. Handbücher zur Sprach- und Kommunikationswissenschaft 36. Berlin: De Gruyter Mouton.

———. 2012a. 'Phoenician'. In *Languages from the World of the Bible,* edited by Holger Gzella, 55–75. Berlin: De Gruyter.

———. 2012b. 'Some General Remarks on Interactions Between Aspect, Modality, and Evidentiality in Biblical Hebrew'. In *Studia Andreae Zaborski Dedicata,* edited by Jerzy Chmiel, Anna Krasnowolska, Tomasz Plański, Ewa Siemieniec-Gołaś, Lidia Sudyka, and Joachim Śliwa, 225–32. Folia Orientalia 49. Cracow: Polish Academy of Sciences.

———. 2012c. 'Ancient Hebrew'. In *Languages from the World of the Bible*, edited by Holger Gzella, 76–110. Berlin: De Gruyter.

———. 2013a. 'Deir ʿAllā'. In *Encyclopedia of Hebrew Language and Linguistics*, online, edited by Geoffrey Khan. Leiden: Brill. https://doi.org/10.1163/2212-4241_ehll_EHLL_COM_00000333

———. 2013b. 'The Linguistic Position of Old Byblian'. In *Linguistic Studies in Phoenician: In Memory of J. Brian Peckham*, edited by Robert D. Holmstedt and Aaron Schade, 170–98. Winona Lake, Ind.: Eisenbrauns.

———. 2013c. 'Northwest Semitic Languages and Hebrew'. In *Encyclopedia of Hebrew Language and Linguistics*, edited by Geoffrey Khan, vol. 2, 852–63. Leiden: Brill.

———. 2015. *A Cultural History of Aramaic: From the Beginnings to the Advent of Islam.* Handbook of Oriental Studies 1.111. Leiden: Brill.

———. 2017. 'New Light on Linguistic Diversity in Pre-Achaemenid Aramaic: Wandering Arameans or Language Spread?'. In *Wandering Arameans: Arameans outside Syria—Textual and Archaeological Perspectives*, edited by Aren M. Maeir, Andreas Schüle, and Angelika Berlejung, 19–37. Leipziger Altorientalische Studien 5. Wiesbaden: Harrassowitz.

———. 2018. 'Untypical *wayyiqṭol* Forms in Hebrew and Early Linguistic Diversity'. In *The Unfolding of Your Words Gives Light: Studies on Biblical Hebrew in Honor of George L. Klein,* edited by Ethan C. Jones, 21–37. University Park, Pa.: Eisenbrauns.

———. 2021. 'Non-Progressive and Non-Habitual Uses of Imperfective Aspect in Ancient Hebrew'. In *Tempus und Aspekt in den alten Sprachen*, edited by Markus Witte and Brinthanan Puvaneswaran, 71–92. KUSATU: Kleine Untersuchungen zur Sprache des Alten Testaments und seiner Umwelt 24. Kamen: Spenner.

Hackett, Jo Ann. 1984. *The Balaam Text from Deir ʿAllā*. Harvard Semitic Monographs 31. Chico, Cal.: Scholars Press.

———. 2002. 'Hebrew (Biblical and Epigraphic)'. In *Beyond Babel: A Handbook for Biblical Hebrew and Related Languages*, edited by Steven L. McKenzie and John Kaltner, 139–56. Leiden; Atlanta, Ga.: Brill; Society of Biblical Literature.

———. 2008. 'Phoenician and Punic'. In *The Ancient Languages of Syria-Palestine and Arabia*, edited by Roger D. Woodard, 82–102. Cambridge: Cambridge University Press.

———. 2012. '*Yaqtul* and a Ugaritic Incantation Text'. In *Language and Nature: Papers Presented to John Huehnergard on the occasion of His 60th Birthday*, edited by Rebecca Hasselbach and Na'ama Pat-El, 111–18. Studies in Ancient Oriental Civilization 67. Chicago: Oriental Institute of the University of Chicago.

Hagelia, Hallvard. 2006. *The Tel Dan Inscription: A Critical Investigation of Recent Research on Its Palaeography and Philology*. Studia Semitica Upsaliensia 22. Uppsala: Acta Universitatis Upsaliensis.

Haiman, John. 1978. 'Conditionals are Topics'. *Language* 54 (3): 564–89.

Haiman, John, and Sandra A. Thompson. 1988. 'Introduction'. In *Clause Combining in Grammar and Discourse*, edited by John Haiman and Sandra A. Thompson, ix–xiii. Amsterdam: John Benjamins.

Halliday, Michael A. K. 2004. *An Introduction to Functional Grammar.* Revised by Christian M. I. M. Matthiessen. 3rd rev. ed. London: Arnold.

HALOT = Koehler, Ludwig, and Walter Baumgartner. 2001. *The Hebrew and Aramaic Lexicon of the Old Testament.* Translated by M. E. J. Richardson. 2 vols. Leiden: E. J. Brill.

Halpern, Baruch. 1994. 'The Stela from Dan: Epigraphic and Historical Considerations'. *Bulletin of the American Schools of Oriental Research* 296: 63–80.

Ḥam = Freytag, G. W., ed. 1828. *Šarḫ Dīwān al-Ḥamāsa taʾlīf a. Zakarīyāʾ at-Tabrīzī.* Vol. 1, *Continens textum Arabicum et quator indices.* Bonn.

Hamori, Andras. 1973. 'A Note on *yaqtulu* in East and West Semitic'. *Archiv Orientální* 41: 319–24.

Hartley, John E. 1992. *Word Biblical Commentary.* Vol. 4, *Leviticus.* Waco, Tex.: Word Books.

Haspelmath, Martin. 1998. 'The Semantic Development of Old Presents: New Futures and Subjunctives Without Grammaticalization'. *Diachronica* 15 (1): 29–62.

———. 2007. 'Coordination'. In *Language Typology and Syntactic Description*, vol. 2, *Complex Constructions*, edited by Timothy Shopen, 1–51. Cambridge: Cambridge University Press.

Hasselbach, Rebecca. 2013a. 'Canaanite and Hebrew'. In *Encyclopedia of Hebrew Language and Linguistics*, online, edited by Geoffrey Khan. Leiden: Brill. https://doi.org/10.1163/2212-4241_ehll_EHLL_COM_00000351

———. 2013b. *Case in Semitic: Roles, Relations, and Reconstruction.* Oxford Studies in Diachronic and Historical Linguistics 3. Oxford: Oxford University Press.

Hasselbach, Rebecca, and John Huehnergard. 2008. 'Northwest Semitic Languages'. In *Encyclopedia of Arabic Language and Linguistics*, edited by Kees Versteegh, Mushira Eid, Alaa Elgibali, Manfred Woidich, and Andrzej Zaborski, vol. 3, 408–22. Leiden: Brill.

Hatav, Galia. 2004. 'Anchoring World and Time in Biblical Hebrew'. *Journal of Linguistics* 40 (3): 491–526.

Haug, Dag. 2008. 'From Resultatives to Anteriors in Ancient Greek: On the Role of Paradigmaticity in Semantic Change'. In *Grammatical Change and Linguistic Theory: The Rosendal Papers*, edited by Eythórsson Thórhallur, 285–305. Linguistik Aktuell. Amsterdam: John Benjamins.

Heimerdinger, Jean-Marc. 1999. *Topic, Focus and Foreground in Ancient Hebrew Narratives.* Journal for the Study of the Old Testament Supplement Series 295. Sheffield: Sheffield Academic Press.

Heine, Bernd, Ulrike Claudi, and Friederike Hünnemeyer. 1991. *Grammaticalization: A Conceptual Framework.* Chicago: University of Chicago Press.

Hetzron, Robert. 1969. 'The Evidence for Perfect **y'aqtul* and Jussive **yaqt'ul* in Proto-Semitic'. *Journal of Semitic Studies* 14 (1): 1–21.

———. 1974. 'La division des langues sémitiques'. In *Actes du premier congrès international de linguistique sémitique et chamito-sémitique, Paris 16–19 juillet 1969,* edited by André Caquot and David Cohen, 181–94. Janua Linguarum, Series Practica, 159. The Hague: Mouton.

HI = Dobbs-Allsopp, F. W., J. J. M. Roberts, Coon L. Seow, and R. E. Whitaker. 2005. *Hebrew Inscriptions: Texts from the Biblical Period of the Monarchy with Concordance.* New Haven: Yale University Press.

Hoftijzer, Jacob. 1985. *The Function and Use of the Imperfect Forms with Nun Paragogicum in Classical Hebrew.* Studia Semitica Neerlandica 21. Assen: Van Gorcum.

Hoftijzer, Jacob, and Gerrit van der Kooij, eds. 1976. *Aramaic Texts from Deir ʿAlla.* Documenta et Monumenta Orientis Antiqui 19. Leiden: Brill.

Hoftijzer, Jacob, and Karel Jongeling. 1995. *Dictionary of the North-West Semitic Inscriptions.* With appendices by Richard C. Steiner, Mosak A. Moshavi, and Bezalel Porten. 2nd ed. 2 vols. Handbook of Oriental Studies 1.21.1–2. Leiden: Brill.

Hopper, Paul J. 1979. 'Aspect and Foregrounding in Discourse'. In *Syntax and Semantics*, vol. 12, *Discourse and Syntax*, edited by Talmy Givón, 213–41. New York: Academic Press.

Hopper, Paul J., and Sandra A. Thompson. 1980. 'Transitivity in Grammar and Discourse'. *Language* 56: 251–99.

Hopper, Paul J., and Elizabeth Closs Traugott. 2003. *Grammaticalization*. 2nd ed. Cambridge Textbooks in Linguistics. Cambridge: Cambridge University Press.

Hornkohl, Aaron D. 2014. *Ancient Hebrew Periodization and the Language of the Book of Jeremiah: The Case for a Sixth-Century Date of Composition*. Studies in Semitic Languages and Linguistics 74. Leiden: Brill.

———. 2016a. 'Transitional Biblical Hebrew'. In *A Handbook of Biblical Hebrew,* vol. 1, *Periods, Corpora, and Reading Traditions*, edited by W. Randall Garr and Steven Ellis Fassberg, 31–42. Winona Lake, Ind.: Eisenbrauns.

———. 2016b. 'Hebrew Diachrony and the Linguistic Periodisation of Biblical Texts: Observations from the Perspective of Reworked Pentateuchal Material'. *Journal for Semitics* 25 (2): 1004–63.

———. 2017. 'All is not Lost: Linguistic Periodization in the Face of Textual and Literary Pluriformity'. In *Advances in Biblical Hebrew Linguistics: Data, Methods, and Analyses*, edited by Adina Moshavi and Tania Notarius, 53–80. Linguistic Studies in Ancient West Semitic 12. Winona Lake, Ind.: Eisenbrauns.

———. 2018. 'Biblical Hebrew Tense–Aspect–Mood, Word Order and Pragmatics: Some Observations on Recent Approaches'. In *Studies in Semitic Linguistics and Manuscripts: A Liber Discipulorum in Honour of Professor Geoffrey Khan*, edited by Nadia Vidro, Ronny Vollandt, Esther-Miriam Wagner, and Judith Olszowy-Schlanger, 27–56. Studia Semitica Upsaliensia 30. Uppsala: Acta Universitatis Upsaliensis.

———. 2019. 'Pre-modern Hebrew: Biblical Hebrew'. In *The Semitic Languages*, edited by John Huehnergard and Na'ama Pat-El, 533–70. Routledge Language Family Series. London: Routledge.

Horst, Friedrich. 1974. *Hiob*. Vol. 1. *Hiob 1–19*. 3rd ed. Biblischer Kommentar: Altes Testament 16.1. Neukirchen-Vluyn: Neukirchener.

Huehnergard, John. 1983. 'Asseverative **la* and hypothetical **lu/law* in Semitic'. *Journal of the American Oriental Society* 103 (3): 569–93.

———. 1987. '"Stative", Predicative Form, Pseudo-Verb'. *Journal of Near Eastern Studies* 46: 215–32.

———. 1988. 'The Early Hebrew Prefix-conjugations'. *Hebrew Studies* 29: 19–23.

———. 1991. 'Remarks on the Classification of the Northwest Semitic Languages'. In *The Balaam Text from Deir ʿAlla Re-evaluated: Proceedings of the International Symposium Held at Leiden, 21–24 August 1989*, edited by Jacob Hoftijzer and Gerrit van der Kooij, 281–93. Leiden: Brill.

———. 1995. 'What is Aramaic?'. *Aram* 7: 261–82.

———. 2002. 'Comparative Semitic Linguistics'. In *Semitic Linguistics: The State of the Art at the Turn of the Twenty-first Century*, edited by Shlomo Izre'el, 119–59. Israel Oriental Studies 20. Winona Lake, Ind.: Eisenbrauns.

———. 2005. 'Features of Central Semitic'. In *Biblical and Oriental Essays in Memory of William L. Moran*, edited by Agustinus Gianto, 155–203. Biblica et Orientalia 48. Rome: Pontifical Biblical Institute.

———. 2006. 'Proto-Semitic and Proto-Akkadian'. In *The Akkadian Language in its Semitic Context: Studies in the Akkadian of the Third and Second Millennium BC*, edited by Guy Deutscher and N. J. C. Kouwenberg, 1–18. Leiden: Nederlands Instituut voor het Nabije Oosten.

———. 2008. 'Afro-Asiatic'. In *The Ancient Languages of Syria-Palestine and Arabia*, edited by Roger D. Woodard, 225–46. Cambridge: Cambridge University Press.

———. 2011. *A Grammar of Akkadian.* 3rd ed. Harvard Semitic Studies 45. Winona Lake, Ind.: Eisenbrauns.

———. 2012. *An Introduction to Ugaritic.* Peabody, Mass.: Hendrickson.

———. 2017. 'Arabic in its Semitic Context'. In *Arabic in Context: Celebrating 400 Years of Arabic at Leiden University*, edited by Ahmad Al-Jallad, 3–34. Leiden: Brill.

———. 2019. 'Proto-Semitic'. In *The Semitic Languages*, edited by John Huehnergard and Na'ama Pat-El, 49–79. Routledge Language Family Series. London: Routledge.

Huehnergard, John, and Na'ama Pat-El. 2019. 'Introduction to the Semitic Languages and their History'. In *The Semitic Languages*, edited by John Huehnergard and Na'ama Pat-El, 1–21. Routledge Language Family Series. London: Routledge.

Huehnergard, John, and Aaron D. Rubin. 2011. 'Phyla and Waves: Models of Classification of the Semitic Languages'. In *The Semitic Languages: An International Handbook*, edited by Stefan Weninger, Geoffrey Khan, Michael P. Streck, and Janet C. E. Watson, 259–78. Handbücher zur Sprach- und

Kommunikationswissenschaft 36. Berlin: De Gruyter Mouton.

Hug, Volker. 1993. *Altaramäische Grammatik der Texte des 7. und 6. Jh.s v.Chr.* Heidelberger Studien zum Alten Orient 4. Heidelberg: Heidelberger Orientverlag.

Hutton, Jeremy M. 2013. 'Epigraphic Hebrew: Pre-Roman Period'. In *Encyclopedia of Hebrew Language and Linguistics*, online, edited by Geoffrey Khan. Leiden: Brill. https://doi.org/10.1163/2212-4241_ehll_EHLL_COM_00000401

Isaksson, Bo. 1986. 'Concerning Two Arguments of H. Bauer for a Priority of the So-called Imperfect (the "Aorist")'. In *On the Dignity of Man: Oriental and Classical Studies in Honour of Frithiof Rundgren*, edited by Tryggve Kronholm and Eva Riad, 181–87. Orientalia Suecana 33–35. Uppsala: Almqvist & Wiksell International.

———. 1998. '"Aberrant" Usages of Introductory *wəhāyā* in the Light of Text Linguistics'. In *"Lasset uns Brücken bauen..." Collected Communications to the XVth Congress of the International Organization for the Study of the Old Testament, Cambridge 1995*, edited by Klaus-Dietrich Schunck and Matthias Augustin, 9–25. Beiträge zur Erforschung des Alten Testaments und des Antiken Judentums 42. Frankfurt am Main: Peter Lang.

———. 2007. 'Semitic Circumstantial Qualifiers in the Book of Judges: A Pilot Study on the Infinitive'. *Orientalia Suecana* 56: 163–72.

———. 2009. 'Introduction' and 'An Outline of Comparative Arabic and Hebrew Textlinguistics'. In *Circumstantial Qualifiers in Semitic: The Case of Arabic and Hebrew*, edited by Bo Isaksson, 1–35, 36–150. Abhandlungen für die Kunde des Morgenlandes 70. Wiesbaden: Harrassowitz.

———. 2013. 'Subordination: Biblical Hebrew'. In *Encyclopedia of Hebrew Language and Linguistics*, online, edited by Geoffrey Khan, vol. 3, 657–64. Leiden: Brill. https://doi.org/10.1163/2212-4241_ehll_EHLL_COM_000541

———. 2014a. 'Archaic Biblical Hebrew Poetry: The Linking of Finite Clauses'. In *Strategies of Clause Linking in Semitic Languages: Proceedings of the International Symposium on Clause Linking in Semitic Languages, 5–7 August 2012 in Kivik, Sweden*, edited by Bo Isaksson and Maria Persson, 109–41. Abhandlungen für die Kunde des Morgenlandes 93. Wiesbaden: Harrassowitz.

———. 2014b. 'The Main Line of a Biblical Hebrew Narrative and What to Do with Two Perfective Grams'. In *Proceedings of the Oslo–Austin Workshop in Semitic Linguistics, Oslo, May 23 and 24, 2013*, edited by Lutz Edzard and John Huehnergard, 73–94. Abhandlungen für die Kunde des Morgenlandes 88. Wiesbaden: Harrassowitz.

———. 2015a. 'The Verbal System of Biblical Hebrew: A Clause Combining Approach'. In *Clause Combining in Semitic: The Circumstantial Clause and Beyond*, edited by Bo Isaksson and Maria Persson, 169–268. Abhandlungen für die Kunde des Morgenlandes 96. Wiesbaden: Harrassowitz.

———. 2015b. 'The So-called *we-qatal* Conjugation in Biblical Hebrew Once Again'. In *Papers Read at the 11 Mainz International Colloquium on Ancient Hebrew (MICAH), University of Mainz, 1–3 November 2013*, edited by Reinhard G. Lehmann and Kwang Cheol Park, 71–117. KUSATU: Kleine Untersuchungen zur Sprache des Alten Testaments und seiner Umwelt 19. Kamen: Hartmut Spenner.

———. 2015c. '"Subordination": Some Reflections on Matthiessen and Thompson's Article "The Structure of Discourse and 'Subordination'" and its Bearing on the Idea of Circumstantial Clause in Arabic and Hebrew'. In *Arabic and Semitic Linguistics Contextualized: A Festschrift for Jan Retsö*, edited by Lutz Edzard, 404–24. Wiesbaden: Harrassowitz.

———. 2015d. 'The Importance of Word Order for the Biblical Hebrew Verbal System'. Paper Read at the *SBL Annual Meeting Atlanta, November 21–24, 2015*.

———. 2017. 'Clause Combining in the Song of Moses (Deuteronomy 32:1–43): An Example of Archaic Biblical Hebrew Syntax'. In *Advances in Biblical Hebrew Linguistics: Data, Methods, and Analyses*, edited by Adina Moshavi and Tania Notarius, 233–69. Linguistic Studies in Ancient West Semitic 12. Winona Lake, Ind.: Eisenbrauns.

———. 2021. 'The Biblical Hebrew Short *yiqṭol* and the "Consecutive Tenses"'. In *New Perspectives in Biblical and Rabbinic Hebrew*, edited by Geoffrey Khan and Aaron D. Hornkohl, 197–240. Cambridge Semitic Languages and Cultures 7. Cambridge: Open Book Publishers.

———. Forthcoming. 'A Critical Examination of Khan's "The Coding of Discourse Dependency in Biblical Hebrew Consecutive *Weqaṭal* and *Wayyiqṭol*"'. In *Interconnected Traditions: Semitic Languages, Literatures, Cultures*, edited by J. C. E. Watson et al. Cambridge: Open Book Publishers.

Isaksson, Bo, and Maria Persson, eds. 2014. *Strategies of Clause Linking in Semitic Languages: Proceedings of the International Symposium on Clause Linking in Semitic Languages, 5–7 August 2012 in Kivik, Sweden*. Abhandlungen für die Kunde des Morgenlandes 93. Wiesbaden: Harrassowitz.

———, eds. 2015. *Clause Combining in Semitic: The Circumstantial Clause and Beyond*. Abhandlungen für die Kunde des Morgenlandes 96. Wiesbaden: Harrassowitz.

Isḥ = Wüstenfeld, Ferdinand, ed. 1859. *Kitâb sîrat rasûl Allâh: Das Leben Muhammed's nach Muhammed Ibn Ishâk bearbeitet von Abd el-Malik Ibn Hischâm*. Vol. 1, *Text*. Göttingen: Dieterichsche Universitäts-Buchhandlung.

Jackson, Kent P. 1983. *The Ammonite Language of the Iron Age*. Harvard Semitic Monographs 27. Chico, Cal.: Scholars Press.

J-M = Joüon, Paul, and Takamitsu Muraoka. 2006. *A Grammar of Biblical Hebrew*. 2nd rev. English ed. Subsidia Biblica 27. Rome: Gregorian & Biblical Press. Reprint, with corrections, 2009.

Joosten, Jan. 1989. 'The Predicative Participle in Biblical Hebrew'. *Zeitschrift für Althebraistik* 2 (2): 128–59.

———. 1999. 'The Long form of the Prefix Conjugation Referring to the Past in Biblical Hebrew Prose'. *Hebrew Studies* 40: 15–26.

———. 2005. 'The Distinction Between Classical and Late Biblical Hebrew as Reflected in Syntax'. *Hebrew Studies* 46: 327–39.

———. 2009. 'A Note on "weyiqtol" and Volitive Sequences'. *Vetus Testamentum* 59: 495–98.

———. 2011a. 'The Operation of a Syntactic Rule in Classical Biblical Hebrew and in Hebrew inscriptions of the Monarchic Period'. In *On Stone and Scroll: Essays in Honour of Graham Ivor Davies*, edited by J. K. Aitken, Katharine J. Dell, and Brian Arthur Mastin, 493–505. Beihefte zur Zeitschrift für die Alttestamentliche Wissenschaft 420. Berlin: De Gruyter.

———. 2011b. 'A Neglected Rule and its Exceptions: On Non-volitive *yiqtol* in Clause-Initial Position'. In *En pāsē grammatikē kai sophiā: Saggi di linguistica ebraica in onore di Alviero Niccacci, ofm*, edited by Gregor Geiger and Massimo Pazzini, 213–19. Collana Analecta: Studium Biblicum Franciscanum 78. Jerusalem; Milano: Franciscan Printing Press; Editioni Terra Santa.

———. 2012. *The Verbal System of Biblical Hebrew: A New Synthesis Elaborated on the Basis of Classical Prose.* Jerusalem Biblical Studies 10. Jerusalem: Simor.

———. 2015. 'The Tiberian Vocalization and the Hebrew of the Second Temple Period'. In *Hebrew of the Late Second Temple Period: Proceedings of a Sixth International Symposium on the*

Hebrew of the Dead Sea Scrolls and Ben Sira, edited by Eibert J. C. Tigchelaar and Pierre Van Hecke, 25–36. Leiden: Brill.

———. 2016. 'Diachronic Linguistics and the Date of the Pentateuch'. In *The Formation of the Pentateuch: Bridging the Academic Cultures of Europe, Israel, and North America*, edited by Jan Christian Gertz, Bernard M. Levinson, Dalit Rom-Shiloni, and Konrad Schmid, 327–44. Tübingen: Mohr Siebeck.

———. 2019. 'The Linguistic Dating and the Joseph Story'. *Hebrew Bible and Ancient Israel* 8: 24–43.

Joüon, Paul. 1923. *Grammaire de l'hébreu biblique.* Rome: Pontifical Biblical Institute. Reprint, 1965.

Jungraithmayr, Herrmann. 2005. 'Le paradigme verbal en *–U* dans les languages chamito-sémitiques'. In *Les langues chamito-sémitiques (afro-asiatiques)*, vol. 1, edited by Antoine Lonnet and Amina Mettouchi, 65–80. Paris: Ophrys.

KAI^3 = Donner, Herbert, and Wolfgang Röllig. 1971–1976. *Kanaanäische und aramäische Inschriften: Mit einem Beitrag von O. Rössler.* 3rd ed. 3 vols. Wiesbaden: Harrassowitz.

KAI^5 = Donner, Herbert, and Wolfgang Röllig. 2002. *Kanaanäische und aramäische Inschriften.* 5th enlarged and rev. ed. Vol. 1, *Texte.* Wiesbaden: Harrassowitz.

Kantor, Benjamin. 2020. 'The Development of the Hebrew *wayyiqṭol* Verbal Form ("*waw Consecutive*") in Light of Greek and Latin Transcriptions of Hebrew'. In *Studies in Semitic Vocalisation and Reading Traditions*, edited by Aaron D. Hornkohl and Geoffrey Khan, 55–132. Cambridge Semitic

Languages and Cultures 3. Cambridge: Open Book Publishers.

Kaufman, Stephen A. 2002. 'Languages in Contact: The Ancient Near East'. In *Semitic Linguistics: The State of the Art at the Turn of the Twenty-first Century*, edited by Shlomo Izre'el, 297–306. Israel Oriental Studies 20. Winona Lake, Ind.: Eisenbrauns.

Kawashima, Robert S. 2010. '"Orphaned" Converted Tense Forms in Classical Biblical Hebrew Prose'. *Journal of Semitic Studies* 55 (1): 11–35.

Khan, Geoffrey A. 1988. *Studies in Semitic Syntax.* London Oriental Series 38. Oxford: Oxford University Press.

———. 1991. 'Morphological Markers of Individuation in Semitic Languages and Their Function in the Semitic Tense System'. In *Proceedings of the Fifth International Hamito-Semitic Congress, 1989*, vol. 2, *Cushitic, Egyptian, Omotic, Semitic*, edited by Hans G. Mukarovsky, 235–44. Beiträge zur Afrikanistik 41. Vienna: Afro-Pub.

———. 2013a. *A Short Introduction to the Tiberian Masoretic Bible and Its Reading Tradition.* 2nd ed. Gorgias Handbooks. Piscataway, N.J.: Gorgias.

———. 2013b. 'Shewa: Pre-modern Hebrew'. In *Encyclopedia of Hebrew Language and Linguistics*, edited by Geoffrey Khan, vol. 3, 543–54. Leiden: Brill.

———. 2013c. 'The Languages of the Old Testament'. In *The New Cambridge History of the Bible*, vol. 1, *From the Beginnings to 600*, edited by James Carleton Paget and Joachim Schaper, 3–21. Cambridge: Cambridge University Press.

———. 2016. 'Karaite Transcriptions of Biblical Hebrew'. In *A Handbook of Biblical Hebrew*, vol. 1, *Periods, Corpora, and Reading Traditions*, edited by W. Randall Garr and Steven Ellis Fassberg, 147–60. Winona Lake, Ind.: Eisenbrauns.

———. 2018a. 'How Was the *Dageš* in Biblical Hebrew בתים Pronounced and Why Is It There?'. *Journal of Semitic Studies* 63 (2): 323–51.

———. 2018b. 'Orthoepy in the Tiberian Reading Tradition of the Hebrew Bible and its Historical Roots in the Second Temple Period'. *Vetus Testamentum* 68 (3): 378–401.

———. 2019. 'Copulas, Cleft Sentences and Focus Markers in Biblical Hebrew'. In *Ancient Texts and Modern Readers: Studies in Ancient Hebrew Linguistics and Bible Translation*, edited by Gideon R. Kotzé, Christian S. Locatell, and John A. Messarra, 14–62. Studia Semitica Neerlandica 71. Leiden: Brill.

———. 2020. *The Tiberian Pronunciation Tradition of Biblical Hebrew: Including a Critical Edition and English Translation of the Sections on Consonants and Vowels in the Masoretic Treatise Hidāyat al-Qāriʾ 'Guide for the Reader'*. 2 vols. Cambridge Semitic Languages and Cultures 1. Cambridge: Open Book Publishers.

———. 2021a. 'The Coding of Discourse Dependency in Biblical Hebrew Consecutive *Weqaṭal* and *Wayyiqṭol*'. In *New Perspectives in Biblical and Rabbinic Hebrew*, edited by Geoffrey Khan and Aaron D. Hornkohl, 299–354. Cambridge Semitic Languages and Cultures 7. Cambridge: Open Book Publishers.

———. 2021b. 'Verbal Forms Expressing Discourse Dependency in North-Eastern Neo-Aramaic'. In *Studies in the Grammar and Lexicon of Neo-Aramaic*, edited by Geoffrey Khan and Paul M. Noorlander, 143–93. Cambridge Semitic Languages and Cultures 5. Cambridge: Open Book Publishers.

Kienast, Burkhart. 2001. *Historische semitische Sprachwissenschaft: Mit Beitr. von Erhart Graefe (Altaegyptisch) und Gene B. Gragg (Kuschitisch)*. Wiesbaden: Harrassowitz.

Kilchör, Benjamin. 2019. 'Wellhausen's Five Pillars for the Priority of D over P/H: Can They Still Be Maintained?'. In *Paradigm Change in Pentateuchal Research*, edited by Matthias Armgardt, Benjamin Kilchör, and Markus Zehnder, 101–14. Beihefte zur Zeitschrift für Altorientalische und biblische Rechtsgeschichte 22. Wiesbaden: Harrassowitz.

Knudsen, Ebbe Egede. 1982. 'An Analysis of Amorite: A Review Article'. Review of *A Computer-Aided Analysis of Amorite* by I. J. Gelb. *Journal of Cuneiform Studies* 34: 1–18.

———. 1998. 'Central Semitic **yaqtulum* Reconsidered: A Rejoinder to J. Tropper'. *Journal of Semitic Studies* 43: 1–9.

Knudtzon, J. A. 1892. 'Zur assyrischen und allgemein semitischen Grammatik III'. *Zeitschrift für Assyriologie* 7: 33–63.

———. 1915. *Die El-Amarna-Tafeln: Mit Einleitung und Erläuterungen.* Vorderasiatische Bibliothek 2. Leipzig: Hinrichs. Reprint, Aalen: Otto Zeller, 1964.

Kogan, Leonid. 2012. Review of *The Akkadian Verb and its Semitic Background* by N. J. C. Kouwenberg. *Zeitschrift für Assyriologie* 102: 304–23.

———. 2014. ‘*Waw sargonicum*: On Parataxis in Sargonic Royal Inscriptions’. *Zeitschrift für Assyriologie* 104 (1): 42–55.

———. 2015. *Genealogical Classification of Semitic: The Lexical Isoglosses.* Berlin: De Gruyter.

Kogan, Leonid, and Maria Bulakh. 2019. ‘Soqotri’. In *The Semitic Languages*, edited by John Huehnergard and Na’ama Pat-El, 280–320. Routledge Language Family Series. London: Routledge.

König, F. Eduard. 1881–97. *Historisch-kritisches Lehrgebäude der hebräischen Sprache.* 3 vols. Leipzig: Hinrichs. Reprint, Hildesheim: Georg Olms 1979.

Kooij, Arie van der. 1994. ‘The Ending of the Song of Moses: On the Pre-masoretic Version of Deut 32: 43’. In *Studies in Deuteronomy: In Honour of C.J. Labuschagne on the Occasion of His 65th Birthday*, edited by Florentino García Martínez, A. Hilhorst, J. T. A. G. M. van Ruiten, and A. S. van der Woude, 93–100. Leiden: Brill.

Kootstra, Fokelien. 2016. ‘The Language of the Taymanitic Inscriptions and Its Classification’. *Arabian Epigraphic Notes* 2: 67–140.

Korchin, Paul D. 2008. *Markedness in Canaanite and Hebrew Verbs.* Harvard Semitic Studies 58. Winona Lake, Ind.: Eisenbrauns.

Kossmann, Maarten, and Benjamin D. Suchard. 2018. ‘A Reconstruction of the System of Verb Aspects in Proto-Berbero-Semitic’. *Bulletin of the School of Oriental and African Studies* 81 (1): 41–56.

Kottsieper, Ingo. 1998. 'Die Inschrift vom Tell Dan und die politischen Beziehungen zwischen Aram-Damaskus und Israel in der 1. Hälfte des 1. Jahrtausends vor Christus'. In *"Und Mose schrieb dieses Lied auf": Studien zum Alten Testament und zum Alten Orient—Festschrift für Oswald Loretz zur Vollendung seines 70. Lebensjahres mit Beiträgen von Freunden, Schülern und Kollegen*, edited by Manfried Dietrich, Ingo Kottsieper, and Hanspeter Schaudig, 475–500. Alter Orient und Altes Testament 250. Münster: Ugarit-Verlag.

———. 1999. '"...und mein Vater zog hinauf...": Aspekte des älteren aramäischen Verbalsystems und seiner Entwicklung'. In *Tempus und Aspekt in den semitischen Sprachen: Jenaer Kolloquium zur semitischen Sprachwissenschaft*, edited by Norbert Nebes, 55–76. Wiesbaden: Harrassowitz.

Kottsieper, Ingo, and Peter Stein. 2014. 'Sabaic and Aramaic—A Common Origin?'. In *Languages of Southern Arabia: Papers from the Special Session of the Seminar for Arabian Studies Held on 27 July 2014*, edited by Orhan Elmaz and Janet C. E. Watson, 81–87. Supplement to the Proceedings of the Seminar for Arabian Studies Volume 44. Oxford: Archaeopress.

Kouwenberg, N. J. C. 2010a. *The Akkadian Verb and its Semitic Background*. Languages of the Ancient Near East 2. Winona Lake, Ind.: Eisenbrauns.

———. 2010b. 'The Recycling of the *T*-infix in Prehistoric Akkadian: A Case of Exaptation'. In *Proceedings of the 53e Rencontre assyriologique internationale*, vol. 1, *Language in the Ancient Near East*, edited by Leonard Kogan, N. Koslova, S.

Loesov, and S. Tishchenko, 617–46. Winona Lake, Ind.: Eisenbrauns.

———. 2017. *A Grammar of Old Assyrian.* Handbook of Oriental Studies 1.118. Leiden: Brill.

Krahmalkov, Charles R. 1986. 'The *Qatal* with Future Tense Reference in Phoenician'. *Journal of Semitic Studies* 31: 5–10.

———. 2001. *A Phoenician-Punic Grammar.* Handbook of Oriental Studies 1.54. Leiden: Brill.

Kraus, Hans-Joachim. 1978. *Psalmen.* 5th rev. ed. 2 vols. Biblischer Kommentar: Altes Testament 15. Neukirchen-Vluyn: Neukirchener.

KTU³ = Dietrich, Manfried, Oswald Loretz, and Joaquín Sanmartín. 2013. *Die keilalphabetischen Texte aus Ugarit, Ras Ibn Hani und anderen Orten / The Cuneiform Alphabetic Texts from Ugarit, Ras Ibn Hani and Other Places.* 3rd enlarged ed. Alter Orient und Altes Testament 360.1. Münster: Ugarit-Verlag.

Kummerow, David. 2008. 'How Can the Form יִקְטֹל be a Preterite, Jussive, and a Future/Imperfective?: A Brief Elaboration of the Forms and Functions of the Biblical Hebrew Prefix Verbs'. *KUSATU: Kleine Untersuchungen zur Sprache des Alten Testaments und seiner Umwelt* 8–9: 63–95.

Kuriakos, Luke M. 1973. *Non-Paradigmatic Forms of Weak Verbs in Masoretic Hebrew.* Quilon: Assisi Press.

Kuryłowicz, Jerzy. 1949. 'Le système verbal du sémitique'. *Bulletin de la Société de Linguistique de Paris* 45: 47–56.

———. 1962. *L'apophonie en sémitique.* Komitet Jezykoznawstwa, Polskiej Akademii Nauk: Prace Jezykoznawcze 24. Warsaw: Zakład Narodowy Imienia Ossolinskich.

———. 1964. 'On the Methods of Internal Reconstruction'. In *Proceedings of the 9th International Congress of Linguistics*, edited by Horace G. Lunt, 9–36. The Hague: Mouton.

———. 1972a. *Studies in Semitic Grammar and Metrics.* Prace Językoznawcze 67. Wrocław: Polska Akademia Nauk.

———. 1972b. 'The Role of Deictic Elements in Linguistic Evolution'. *Semiotica* 5 (2): 174–83.

———. 1972c. *Studies in Semitic Grammar and Metrics.* Prace Językoznawcze 67. Wrocław: Polska Akademia Nauk.

———. 1973. 'Verbal Aspect in Semitic'. *Orientalia* 42 (1–2): 114–20.

———. 1975. *Esquisses linguistiques II.* Internationale Bibliothek für Allgemeine Linguistik 37. München: W. Finck.

Kuteva, Tania, Bernd Heine, Bo Hong, Haiping Long, Heiko Narrog, and Seongha Rhee, eds. 2019. *World Lexicon of Grammaticalization.* 2nd extensively rev. and updated ed. Cambridge: Cambridge University Press.

Lam, Joseph, and Dennis Pardee. 2016. 'Standard/Classical Biblical Hebrew'. In *A Handbook of Biblical Hebrew*, vol. 1, *Periods, Corpora, and Reading Traditions*, edited by W. Randall Garr and Steven Ellis Fassberg, 1–18. Winona Lake, Ind.: Eisenbrauns.

Lambdin, Thomas O. 1971a. 'The Junctural Origin of the West Semitic Definite Article'. In *Near Eastern Studies in Honor of*

William Foxwell Albright, edited by Hans Goedicke, 315–33. Baltimore: The Johns Hopkins Press.

———. 1971b. *Introduction to Biblical Hebrew*. London: Darton, Longman and Todd. Reprint, 1976.

———. 1978. *Introduction to Classical Ethiopic (Geʿez)*. Harvard Semitic Studies 24. Missoula: Scholars Press. Reprint, Winona Lake, Ind: Eisenbrauns, 2006.

Lambert, Mayer. 1893. 'Le vav conversif'. *Revue des études juives* 26: 47–62.

Lehmann, Christian. 1988. 'Towards a Typology of Clause Linkage'. In *Clause Combining in Grammar and Discourse*, edited by John Haiman and Sandra A. Thompson, 181–225. Amsterdam: John Benjamins.

Lehmann, Manfred R. 1969. 'Biblical Oaths'. *Zeitschrift für die Alttestamentliche Wissenschaft* 81: 74–92.

Lemaire, André. 1983. 'L'inscription phénicienne de Hassan Beyli reconsidérée'. *Rivista di studi fenici* 11: 9–19.

———. 1991. 'Les inscriptions sur plâtre de Deir ʿAlla et leur signification historique et culturelle'. In *The Balaam Text from Deir ʿAlla Re-evaluated: Proceedings of the International Symposium held at Leiden, 21–24 August 1989*, edited by Jacob Hoftijzer and Gerrit van der Kooij, 33–57. Leiden: Brill.

———. 2004. 'Hebrew and West Semitic Inscriptions and Pre-exilic Israel'. In *In Search of Pre-exilic Israel: Proceedings of the Oxford Old Testament Seminar*, edited by John Day, 366–85. London: T&T Clark International. Reprint, 2006.

———. 2013a. 'Ammonite and Hebrew'. In *Encyclopedia of Hebrew Language and Linguistics*, online, edited by Geoffrey

Khan. Leiden: Brill. https://doi.org/10.1163/2212-4241_ehll_EHLL_COM_00000500

———. 2013b. 'Edomite and Hebrew'. In *Encyclopedia of Hebrew Language and Linguistics*, online, edited by Geoffrey Khan. Leiden: Brill. https://doi.org/10.1163/2212-4241_ehll_EHLL_COM_00000499

Levine, Baruch A. 1993. *Numbers 1–20*. The Anchor Bible 4. New York: Doubleday. Reprint, New Haven: Yale University Press, 2008.

———. 2000. *Numbers 21–36*. The Anchor Bible 4A. New York: Doubleday. Reprint, New Haven: Yale Universty Press, 2009.

Li, Tarsee. 2017. 'The multifaceted *weqatal* in Biblical Hebrew'. Paper read at annual meeting of the Society of Biblical Literature, Boston, 18 November, 2017.

Lipiński, Edward. 1994. *Studies In Aramaic Inscriptions and Onomastics*. Vol. 2. Orientalia Lovaniensia Analecta 57. Leuven: Peeters.

———. 1997. *Semitic Languages: Outline of a Comparative Grammar*. Orientalia Lovaniensia Analecta 80. Leuven: Peeters.

Longacre, Robert E. 1979. 'The Paragraph as a Grammatical Unit'. In *Syntax and Semantics*, vol. 12, *Discourse and Syntax*, edited by Talmy Givón, 115–34. New York: Academic Press.

———. 1992. 'Discourse Perspective on the Hebrew Verb: Affirmation and Restatement'. In *Linguistics and Biblical Hebrew*, edited by Walter R. Bodine, 177–89. Winona Lake, Ind.: Eisenbrauns.

Longacre, Robert E., and Andrew C. Bowling. 2015. *Understanding Biblical Hebrew Verb Forms: Distribution and Function Across Genres*. Publications in Linguistics 151. Dallas, Tex.: SIL International, Global Publishing.

Longacre, Robert E., and Shin Ja Joo Hwang. 1994. 'A Textlinguistic Approach to the Biblical Hebrew Narrative of Jonah'. In *Biblical Hebrew and Discourse Linguistics*, edited by Robert D. Bergen, 336–58. Dallas: Summer Institute of Linguistics.

Loprieno, Antonio. 1980. 'The Sequential Forms in Late Egyptian and Biblical Hebrew: A Parallel Development of Verbal Systems'. *Afroasiatic Linguistics* 7 (5): 1–20.

Lunn, Nicholas P. 2006. *Word-order Variation in Biblical Hebrew Poetry: Differentiating Pragmatics and Poetics*. Paternoster Biblical Monographs. Carlisle: Paternoster Press.

Macdonald, Michael C. A. 2008. 'Ancient North Arabian'. In *The Ancient Languages of Syria-Palestine and Arabia*, edited by Roger D. Woodard, 179–224. Cambridge: Cambridge University Press.

Marmorstein, Michal. 2016. *Tense and Text in Classical Arabic: A Discourse-oriented Study of the Classical Arabic Tense System*. Studies in Semitic Languages and Linguistics 85. Leiden: Brill.

Matthiessen, Christian, and Sandra A. Thompson. 1988. 'The Structure of Discourse and "Subordination"'. In *Clause Combining in Grammar and Discourse*, edited by John Haiman and Sandra A. Thompson, 275–329. Amsterdam: John Benjamins.

McCarter, P. Kyle. 1991. 'The Dialect of the Deir ʿAlla Texts'. In *The Balaam Text from Deir ʿAlla Re-evaluated: Proceedings of the International Symposium Held at Leiden, 21–24 August 1989*, edited by Jacob Hoftijzer and Gerrit van der Kooij, 87–99. Leiden: Brill.

McFall, Leslie. 1982. *The Enigma of the Hebrew Verbal System: Solutions from Ewald to the Present Day.* Sheffield: Almond.

Meyer, Ronny. 2011a. 'Amharic'. In *The Semitic Languages: An International Handbook*, edited by Stefan Weninger, Geoffrey Khan, Michael P. Streck, and Janet C. E. Watson, 1178–1211. Handbücher zur Sprach- und Kommunikationswissenschaft 36. Berlin: De Gruyter Mouton.

———. 2011b. 'Gurage'. In *The Semitic Languages: An International Handbook*, edited by Stefan Weninger, Geoffrey Khan, Michael P. Streck, and Janet C. E. Watson, 1220–1257. Handbücher zur Sprach- und Kommunikationswissenschaft 36. Berlin: De Gruyter Mouton.

Milgrom, Jacob. 1991. *Leviticus 1–16: A New Translation with Introduction and Commentary.* The Anchor Bible 3. New York: Doubleday. Reprint, New Haven: Yale University Press, 2009.

———. 2000. *Leviticus 17–22: A New Translation with Introduction and Commentary.* The Anchor Bible 3A. New York: Doubleday. Reprint, New Haven: Yale University Press, 2008.

———. 2001. *Leviticus 23–27: A New Translation with Introduction and Commentary.* The Anchor Bible 3B. New York: Doubleday. Reprint, New Haven: Yale University Press, 2010.

Millard, Alan R. 1978. 'Epigraphic Notes, Aramaic and Hebrew'. *Palestine Exploration Quarterly* 110: 23–26.

Miller, Cynthia L. 1999. 'The Pragmatics of *waw* as a Discourse Marker in Biblical Hebrew Dialogue'. *Zeitschrift für Althebraistik* 12: 165–91.

Moomo, David O. 2003. 'Parameters of Tense, Aspect, and Mood, and Biblical Hebrew: A Model for Determining Tense, Aspectual and Mood Languages'. *Journal for Semitics* 12 (1): 58–80.

Moran, William L. 1950. 'A Syntactical Study of the Dialect of Byblos as Reflected in the Amarna Tablets'. PhD thesis, Johns Hopkins University.

———. 1960. 'Early Canaanite *yaqtula*'. *Orientalia* 29: 1–19.

———. 2003. *Amarna Studies: Collected Writings*. Edited by John Huehnergard and Shlomo Izre'el. Harvard Semitic Studies 54. Winona Lake, Ind.: Eisenbrauns.

Moshavi, Adina. 2010. *Word Order in the Biblical Hebrew Finite Clause: A Syntactic and Pragmatic Analysis of Preposing*. Linguistic Studies in Ancient West Semitic 4. Winona Lake, Ind.: Eisenbrauns.

———. 2013. 'Word Order: Biblical Hebrew'. In *Encyclopedia of Hebrew Language and Linguistics*, online, edited by Geoffrey Khan. Leiden: Brill. https://doi.org/10.1163/2212-4241_ehll_EHLL_COM_00000572

Müller, Hans-Peter. 1983. 'Zur Geschichte des hebräischen Verbs—Diachronie der Konjugationsthemen'. *Biblische Zeitschrift* 27: 34–57.

———. 1991. '*wa-*, *ha-* und das Imperfectum consecutivum'. *Zeitschrift für Althebraistik* 4: 144–60.

———. 1994. 'Nicht-junktiver Gebrauch von *w-* im Althebräischen'. *Zeitschrift für Althebraistik* 7 (2): 141–74.

———. 1995. 'Die aramäische Inschrift von Tel Dan'. *Zeitschrift für Althebraistik* 8 (2): 121–39.

Multhoff, Anne. 2019. 'Ancient South Arabian'. In *The Semitic Languages*, edited by John Huehnergard and Na'ama Pat-El, 321–41. Routledge Language Family Series. London: Routledge.

Muraoka, Takamitsu. 1995a. 'Linguistic Notes on the Aramaic Inscription from Tel Dan'. *Israel Exploration Journal* 45 (1): 19–21.

———. 1995b. 'The Tel Dan Inscription and Aramaic/Hebrew Tenses'. *Abr-Nahrain* 33: 113–15.

———. 1998. 'Again on the Tel Dan Inscription and the Northwest Semitic Verb Tenses'. *Zeitschrift für Althebraistik* 11: 74–81.

———. 2001. 'The Prefix Conjugation in Circumstantial Clauses in the Tel Dan Inscription?'. *Vetus Testamentum* 51 (3): 389–92.

Muraoka, Takamitsu, and Bezalel Porten. 2003. *A Grammar of Egyptian Aramaic*. 2nd rev. ed. Handbook of Oriental Studies 1.32. Leiden: Brill.

Muraoka, Takamitsu, and M. F. Rogland. 1998. 'The waw Consecutive in Old Aramaic? A Rejoinder to Victor Sasson'. *Vetus Testamentum* 48 (1): 99–104.

Naumkin, Vitaly, Leonid Kogan, 'Isa Gum'an al-Da'rhi, Ahmed 'Isa al-Da'rhi, Dmitry Cherkashin, Maria Bulakh, and Ekaterina Vizirova. 2014. *Corpus of Soqotri Oral Literature.* Vol. 1. Studies in Semitic Languages and Linguistics 76. Leiden: Brill.

Nebes, Norbert. 1994a. 'Verwendung und Funktion der Präfixkonjugation im Sabäischen'. In *Arabia Felix: Beiträge zur Sprache und Kultur des vorislamischen Arabien—Festschrift für Walter W. Müller zum 60. Geburtstag,* edited by Norbert Nebes, 191–211. Wiesbaden: Harrassowitz.

———. 1994b. 'Zur Form der Imperfektbasis des unvermehrten Grundstammes im Altsüdarabischen'. In *Festschrift Ewald Wagner zum 65. Geburtstag,* edited by Wolfhart Heinrichs and Gregor Schoeler, vol. 1, *Semitistische Studien unter besonderer Berücksichtigung der Südsemitistik,* 59–81. Beiruter Texte und Studien 54. Beirut: Franz Steiner.

———. 2001. 'Zur Genese der altsüdarabischen Kultur: Eine Arbeitshypothese'. In *Migration und Kulturtransfer: Der Wandel vorder- und zentralasiatischer Kulturen im Umbruch vom 2. zum 1. vorchristlichen Jahrtausend—Akten des Internationalen Kolloquiums, Berlin, 23. bis 26. November 1999,* edited by Ricardo Eichmann and Hermann Parzinger, 427–35. Bonn: Rudolf Habelt.

Nebes, Norbert, and Peter Stein. 2008. 'Ancient South Arabian'. In *The Ancient Languages of Syria-Palestine and Arabia,* edited by Roger D. Woodard, 145–78. Cambridge: Cambridge University Press.

Nedjalkov, Vladimir P., and Sergej J. Jaxontov. 1988. 'The Typology of Resultative Constructions'. In *Typology of Resultative Constructions*, edited by Vladimir Petrovic Nedjalkov and Bernard Comrie, 3–62. Typological Studies in Language 12. Amsterdam: John Benjamins.

Niccacci, Alviero. 1986. *Sintassi del verbo ebraico nella prosa biblica classica.* Studium Biblicum Franciscanum Analecta 23. Jerusalem: Franciscan Printing Press.

———. 1990. *The Syntax of the Verb in Classical Hebrew Prose.* Translated by Wilfred G. E. Watson. Journal for the Study of the Old Testament Supplement Series 86. Sheffield: JSOT Press.

———. 1994. 'The Stele of Mesha and the Bible: Verbal System and Narrativity'. *Orientalia* 63: 226–48.

Notarius, Tania. 2007. 'The System of Verbal Tenses in Archaic and Classical Biblical Hebrew Poetry'. PhD thesis, Hebrew University of Jerusalem. [Hebrew].

———. 2008. 'Poetic Discourse and the Problem of Verbal Tenses in the Oracles of Balaam'. *Hebrew Studies* 49: 55–86.

———. 2010a. 'The Active Predicative Participle in Archaic and Classical Biblical Poetry: A Typological and Historical Investigation'. *Ancient Near Eastern Studies* 47: 241–69.

———. 2010b. 'Modal Forms of Prefix Conjugation in Archaic Biblical Poetry and in Old Canaanite'. *Leshonenu* 72: 393–419. [Hebrew].

———. 2011. 'Text, Discourse and Tenses in the Victory Song in 2 Sam 22,33–46: In Search of the Underlying Literary Convention'. In *En pāsē grammatikē kai sophiā: Saggi di linguistica ebraica in onore di Alviero Niccacci, ofm*, edited by Gregor Geiger and Massimo Pazzini, 257–81. Collana Analecta: Studium Biblicum Franciscanum 78. Jerusalem; Milano: Franciscan Printing Press; Editioni Terra Santa.

———. 2012. 'The Archaic System of Verbal Tenses in "Archaic" Biblical Poetry'. In *Diachrony in Biblical Hebrew*, edited by Cynthia L. Miller-Naudé and Ziony Zevit, 193–207. Linguistic Studies in Ancient West Semitic 8. Winona Lake, Ind.: Eisenbrauns.

———. 2013. *The Verb in Archaic Biblical Poetry: A Discursive, Typological, and Historical Investigation of the Tense System.* Studies in Semitic Languages and Linguistics 68. Leiden: Brill.

———. 2015. 'Narrative Tenses in Archaic Hebrew in the North-West Semitic Linguistic Context'. In *Neue Beiträge zur Semitistik: Fünftes Treffen der Arbeitsgemeinschaft Semitistik in der Deutschen Morgenländischen Gesellschaft vom 15.–17. Februar 2012 an der Universität Basel*, edited by Viktor Golinets, Hanna Jenni, Hans-Peter Mathys, and Samuel Sarasin, 237–59. Münster: Ugarit-Verlag.

———. 2017. 'The Second-person Nonnegated Jussive in Biblical Hebrew and Ancient Northwest Semitic'. In *Advances in Biblical Hebrew Linguistics: Data, Methods, and Analyses*, edited by Adina Moshavi and Tania Notarius, 125–49. Linguistic Studies in Ancient West Semitic 12. Winona Lake, Ind.: Eisenbrauns.

Nyberg, Henrik Samuel. 1972. *Hebreisk grammatik*. 2nd ed. Stockholm: Almqvist & Wiksell.

Olmo Lete, Gregorio del. 1986. 'Fenicio y Ugarítico: Correlación lingüística'. *Aula Orientalis* 4: 31–49.

Palmer, Frank Robert. 2001. *Mood and Modality*. 2nd ed. Cambridge Textbooks in Linguistics. Cambridge: Cambridge University Press.

Pardee, Dennis. 1983. 'The "Epistolary Perfect" in Hebrew Letters'. *Biblische Notizen* 22: 34–40.

———. 1991. 'The Linguistic Classification of the Deir ʿAlla Text Written on Plaster'. In *The Balaam Text from Deir ʿAlla Re-evaluated: Proceedings of the International Symposium Held at Leiden, 21–24 August 1989*, edited by Jacob Hoftijzer and Gerrit van der Kooij, 100–5. Leiden: Brill.

———. 2012. 'The Biblical Hebrew Verbal System in a Nutshell'. In *Language and Nature: Papers Presented to John Huehnergard on the Occasion of His 60th Birthday*, edited by Rebecca Hasselbach and Na'ama Pat-El, 285–318. Studies in Ancient Oriental Civilization 67. Chicago: Oriental Institute of the University of Chicago.

Parker, Simon B. 2002. 'Ammonite, Edomite, and Moabite'. In *Beyond Babel: A Handbook for Biblical Hebrew and Related Languages*, edited by Steven L. McKenzie and John Kaltner, 43–60. Leiden; Atlanta, Ga.: Brill; Society of Biblical Literature.

Pat-El, Na'ama. 2019. 'The Semitic Language Family: A Typological Perspective'. In *The Semitic Languages*, edited by John Huehnergard and Na'ama Pat-El, 80–94. Routledge Language Family Series. London: Routledge.

———. 2020. 'On Shared Structural Innovations: The Diachrony of Adverbial Subordination in Semitic'. In *Reconstructing Syntax*, edited by Jóhanna Barðdal, Spike Gildea, and Eugenio R. Lujan, 314–35. Leiden: Brill.

———. 2021. 'The Linguistic Profile of V'. In *The Valediction of Moses: A Proto-Biblical Book*, edited by Idan Dershowitz, 96–130. Forschungen zum Alten Testament 145. Tübingen: Mohr Siebeck.

Pat-El, Na'ama, and Aren Wilson-Wright. 2013. 'Features of Archaic Biblical Hebrew and the Linguistic Dating Debate'. *Hebrew Studies* 54: 387–410.

Peckham, Brian. 1997. 'Tense and Mood in Biblical Hebrew'. *Zeitschrift für Althebraistik* 10 (2): 139–68.

Pedersen, Johannes. 1934. *Israel.* 2nd ed. 2 vols. Copenhagen: Povl Branner.

Petersson, Lina. 2019. 'The Linguistic Profile of the Priestly Narrative of the Pentateuch'. In *Paradigm Change in Pentateuchal Research*, edited by Matthias Armgardt, Benjamin Kilchör, and Markus Zehnder, 243–64. Beihefte zur Zeitschrift für Altorientalische und Biblische Rechtsgeschichte 22. Wiesbaden: Harrassowitz.

Polak, Frank. 2017. 'Syntactic-Stylistic Aspects of the So-Called "Priestly" Work in the Torah'. In *Le-maʿan Ziony: Essays in Honor of Ziony Zevit*, edited by Frederick E. Greenspahn and Gary A. Rendsburg, 345–82. Eugene, Ore.: Cascade Books.

———. 2021. 'The Identification of Preexilic Material in the Pentateuch'. In *The Oxford Handbook of the Pentateuch*, edited by Joel S. Baden and Jeffrey Stackert, 315–44. Oxford Handbooks. Oxford: Oxford University Press.

Posner, Roland. 1980. 'Semantics and Pragmatics of Sentence Connectives in Natural Language'. In *Speech Act Theory and Pragmatics,* edited by John R. Searle, Ferenc Kiefer, and Manfred Bierwisch, 169–203. Synthese Language Library 10. Dordrecht: Reidel.

Procksch, Otto. 1913. *Die Genesis übersetzt und erklärt.* Edited by Ernst Sellin. Kommentar zum Alten Testament 1. Leipzig: A. Deichert.

Propp, William Henry C. 1998. *Exodus 1–18.* The Anchor Bible 2. New York: Doubleday. Reprint, New Haven: Yale University Press, 2010.

———. 2006. *Exodus 19–40.* The Anchor Bible 2A. New York: Doubleday.

Qimron, Elisha. 1986–87. 'Consecutive and Conjunctive Imperfect: The Form of the Imperfect with WAW in Biblical Hebrew'. *Jewish Quarterly Review* 77 (2–3): 149–61.

Rabin, Chaim. 1984. 'The Genesis of the Semitic Tense System'. In *Current Progress in Afro-Asiatic Linguistics: Papers of the Third International Hamito-Semitic Congress,* edited by James Bynon, 391–97. Amsterdam Studies in the Theory and History of Linguistic Science, Series IV: Current Issues in Linguistic Theory 28. Amsterdam: John Benjamins.

Rainey, Anson F. 1986. 'The Ancient Hebrew Prefix Conjugation in the Light of Amarnah Canaanite'. *Hebrew Studies* 27: 4–19.

———. 1996. *Canaanite in the Amarna Tablets: A Linguistic Analysis of the Mixed Dialect Used by Scribes from Canaan.* 4 vols. Handbook of Oriental Studies 1.25. Leiden: Brill.

———. 2001. 'Grammar and Syntax of Epigraphic Hebrew'. Review of *A Grammar of Epigraphic Hebrew* by Sandra Landis Gogel. *Jewish Quarterly Review* 91: 419–27.

———. 2003a. 'The *yaqtul* Preterite in Northwest Semitic'. In *Hamlet on a Hill: Semitic and Greek Studies Presented to Professor T. Muraoka on the Occasion of His Sixty-fifth Birthday*, edited by M. F. J. Baasten and W. T. van Peursen, 395–407. Leuven: Peeters.

———. 2003b. 'The Suffix Conjugation Pattern in Ancient Hebrew: Tense and Modal Functions'. *Ancient Near Eastern Studies* 40: 3–42.

———. 2007. 'Redefining Hebrew—A Transjordanian Language'. *Maarav* 14 (2): 67–81.

———. 2015. *The El-Amarna Correspondence: A New Edition of the Cuneiform Letters from the Site of El-Amarna based on Collations of All Extant Tablets.* Edited by William M. Schniedewind and Zipora Cochavi-Rainey. Leiden: Brill.

Reckendorf, Hermann. 1895–98. *Die Syntaktischen Verhältnisse des Arabischen.* 2 vols. Leiden: Brill.

———. 1921. *Arabische Syntax.* Heidelberg: Carl Winter.

Renz, Johannes. 2016. 'Alt oder spät? Die Abfolge *wa*-Perfekt als Element der althebräischen Verbalsyntax im Kontext des nordwestsemitischen Verbalsystems: Eine Problemanzeige aus der Perspektive der nordwestsemitischen Epigraphik'.

Zeitschrift für die alttestamentliche Wissenschaft 128: 433–67; 626–67.

Renz, Johannes, and Wolfgang Röllig. 1995–2003. *Handbuch der Althebräischen Epigraphik*. Darmstadt: Wissenschaftliche Buchgesellschaft.

RES = *Répertoire d'Épigraphie Sémitique*. 1929–68. Paris: Imprimerie nationale.

Retsö, Jan. 2014. 'The *b*-imperfect once again: Typological and Diachronic Perspectives'. In *Proceedings of the Oslo–Austin Workshop in Semitic Linguistics, Oslo, May 23 and 24, 2013*, edited by Lutz Edzard and John Huehnergard, 64–72. Abhandlungen für die Kunde des Morgenlandes 88. Wiesbaden: Harrassowitz.

———. 2017. Review of *The Post-priestly Pentateuch: New Perspectives on its Redactional Development and Theological Profiles* by Federico Guintoli and Konrad Schmid, eds. *Svensk Exegetisk Årsbok* 82: 256–60.

Revell, E. J. 1984. 'Stress and the *waw* "consecutive" in Biblical Hebrew'. *Journal of the American Oriental Society* 104: 437–44.

———. 1988. 'First Person Imperfect Forms with *waw* Consecutive'. *Vetus Testamentum* 38 (4): 419–26.

———. 1989. 'The System of the Verb in Standard Biblical Prose'. *Hebrew Union College Annual* 60: 1–37.

Robar, Elizabeth. 2014. *The Verb and the Paragraph in Biblical Hebrew: A Cognitive-linguistic Approach.* Studies in Semitic Languages and Linguistics 78. Leiden: Brill.

Rosenthal, Franz. 1995. *A Grammar of Biblical Aramaic.* 6th rev. ed. Porta Linguarum Orientalium, n.s., 5. Wiesbaden: Harrassowitz.

Rubin, Aaron D. 2005. *Studies in Semitic Grammaticalization.* Harvard Semitic Studies 57. Winona Lake, Ind.: Eisenbrauns.

———. 2010a. *The Mehri Language of Oman.* Studies in Semitic Languages and Linguistics 58. Leiden: Brill.

———. 2010b. *A Brief Introduction to the Semitic Languages.* Gorgias Handbooks 19. Piscataway, N.J.: Gorgias.

———. 2014. *The Jibbali (Shaḥri) Language of Oman: Grammar and Texts.* Studies in Semitic Languages and Linguistics 72. Leiden: Brill.

———. 2015. 'The Classification of Hobyot'. In *Semitic Languages in Contact*, edited by Aaron Michael Butts, 311–32. Studies in Semitic Languages and Linguistics 82. Leiden: Brill.

———. 2018. *Omani Mehri: A New Grammar with Texts.* Studies in Semitic Languages and Linguistics 93. Leiden: Brill.

Rubinstein, Amnon. 1963. 'The Anomalous Perfect with *waw*-conjunctive in Biblical Hebrew'. *Biblica* 44 (1): 62–69.

Rudolph, Wilhelm. 1934. 'Zum Text des Buches Numeri'. *Zeitschrift für die Alttestamentliche Wissenschaft* 52: 113–20.

Rundgren, Frithiof. 1961. *Das Althebräische Verbum: Abriss der Aspektlehre.* Stockholm: Almqvist & Wiksell.

———. 1963. *Erneuerung des Verbalaspekts im Semitischen: Funktionell-diachronische Studien.* Acta Societatis Linguisticae Upsaliensis 1.3. Uppsala: Acta Universitatis Upsaliensis.

Röllig, Wolfgang. 2011. 'Phoenician and Punic'. In *The Semitic Languages: An International Handbook*, edited by Stefan Weninger, Geoffrey Khan, Michael P. Streck, and Janet C. E. Watson, 472–79. Handbücher zur Sprach- und Kommunikationswissenschaft 36. Berlin: De Gruyter Mouton.

Sáenz-Badillos, Angel. 1993. *A History of the Hebrew Language.* Translated by John F. Elwolde. Cambridge: Cambridge University Press. Reprint, 2002.

Sanders, Seth. 2020. 'Ancient Hebrew'. In *A Companion to Ancient Near Eastern Languages*, edited by Rebecca Hasselbach-Andee, 279–96. Hoboken, N.J.: Wiley-Blackwell.

Sasson, Jack M. 2014. *Judges 1–12: A New Translation with Introduction and Commentary.* The Anchor Yale Bible 6D. New Haven: Yale University Press.

Sasson, Victor. 1997. 'Some Observations on the Use and Original Purpose of the *waw* Consecutive in Old Aramaic and Biblical Hebrew'. *Vetus Testamentum* 47: 111–27.

———. 2001. 'The *waw* Consecutive/*waw* Contrastive and the Perfect: Verb Tense, Context, and Texture in Old Aramaic and Biblical Hebrew, with Comments on the Deir ʿAlla Dialect and Post-Biblical Hebrew'. *Zeitschrift für die Alttestamentliche Wissenschaft* 113: 602–17.

Schade, Aaron. 2005. 'A Text Linguistic Approach to the Syntax and Style of the Phoenician Inscription of Azitawada'. *Journal of Semitic Studies* 50 (1): 35–58.

———. 2006. *A Syntactic and Literary Analysis of Ancient Northwest Semitic Inscriptions.* Lewiston, N.Y.: Edwin Mellen Press.

Schiffrin, Deborah. 1986. 'Functions of "and" in Discourse'. *Journal of Pragmatics* 10 (1): 41–66.

Schmitz, Philip C. 1994. 'The Name "Agrigentum" in a Punic Inscription (CIS I 5510.10)'. *Journal of Near Eastern Studies* 53 (1): 1–13.

Schniedewind, William M. 1996. 'Tel Dan Stela: New Light on Aramaic and Jehu's Revolt'. *Bulletin of the American Schools of Oriental Research* 302: 75–90.

Schramm, Gene M. 1957–58. 'A Reconstruction of Biblical Hebrew *waw* Consecutive'. *General Linguistics* 3 (1): 1–8.

Schroeder, N. W. 1766. *Institutiones ad fundamenta linguae hebraicae in usum studiosae juventutis.* Groningen.

Schüle, Andreas. 2000. *Die Syntax der althebräischen Inschriften: Ein Beitrag zur historischen Grammatik des Hebräischen.* Alter Orient und Altes Testament 270. Münster: Ugarit-Verlag.

Schulz, Albert Oswald. 1900. *Über das Imperfekt und Perfekt mit* וַ (וְ) *im Hebräischen.* Kirchhain: Albertus-Universität zu Königsberg in Preussen.

Segert, Stanislav. 1961. 'Die Sprache der moabitischen Königinschrift'. *Archiv Orientální* 29: 197–268.

———. 1975a. *Altaramäische Grammatik mit Bibliographie, Chrestomatie und Glossar.* Leipzig: VEB Verlag Enzyklopädie.

———. 1975b. 'Verbal Categories of Some Northwest Semitic Languages: A Didactical Approach'. *Afroasiatic Linguistics* 2 (5): 83–94.

———. 1976. *A Grammar of Phoenician and Punic.* Munich: C. H. Beck.

Sheehan, John F. X. 1971. 'Egypto-Semitic Elucidation of the Waw Conversive'. *Biblica* 52: 39–43.

Schiffrin, Deborah. 1986. 'Functions of "and" in Discourse'. *Journal of Pragmatics* 10 (1): 41–66.

Schniedewind, William M., and Martin G. Abegg, eds. 2005–2007. *Hebrew Inscriptions: Text and Grammatical Tags*. Accordance Bible Software.

Shirtz, Shahar, and Doris L. Payne. 2015. 'Discourse Structuring and Typology: How Strong is the Link with Aspect?'. In *Beyond Aspect: The Expression of Discourse Functions in African Languages*, edited by Doris L. Payne and Shahar Shirtz, 1–22. Typological Studies in Language 109. Amsterdam: John Benjamins.

Shreckhise, Robert. 2008. 'The Problem of Finite Verb Translation in Exodus 15.1–18'. *Journal for the Study of the Old Testament* 32 (3): 287–310.

Simeone-Senelle, Marie-Claude. 2011. 'Modern South Arabian'. In *The Semitic Languages: An International Handbook*, edited by Stefan Weninger, Geoffrey Khan, Michael P. Streck, and Janet C. E. Watson, 1073–1113. Handbücher zur Sprach- und Kommunikationswissenschaft 36. Berlin: De Gruyter Mouton.

Sivan, Daniel. 1997. *A Grammar of the Ugaritic Language*. Handbook of Oriental Studies 1.28. Leiden: Brill.

———. 2001. *A Grammar of the Ugaritic Language*. 2nd ed. Handbook of Oriental Studies 1.28. Leiden: Brill. Second impression, with corrections, 2008.

Sjörs, Ambjörn. 2015. *The History of Standard Negation in Semitic.* PhD thesis, Uppsala University.

———. 2018. *Historical Aspects of Standard Negation in Semitic.* Studies in Semitic Languages and Linguistics 91. Leiden: Brill.

———. 2019. 'Aspects of the Ventive in Biblical Hebrew'. Paper read at The Semitic Seminar in Uppsala, 16 January 2019.

———. 2021a. 'Notes on the Lengthened Imperfect Consecutive in the Samaritan Pentateuch'. *Journal of Semitic Studies* 66: 17–26.

———. 2021b. 'Notes on the Lengthened Imperfect Consecutive in Late Biblical Hebrew'. In *New Perspectives in Biblical and Rabbinic Hebrew*, edited by Geoffrey Khan and Aaron D. Hornkohl, 275–98. Cambridge Semitic Languages and Cultures 7. Cambridge: Open Book Publishers.

———. 2023. *Motion, Voice, and Mood in the Semitic Verb.* Languages of the Ancient Near East 12. University Park, Pa.: Eisenbrauns.

Smith, Mark S. 1991. *The Origins and Development of the waw-consecutive: Northwest Semitic Evidence from Ugarit to Qumran.* Harvard Semitic Studies 39. Atlanta, Ga.: Scholars Press.

Soden, Wolfram von. 1969. *Grundriss der akkadischen Grammatik samt Ergänzungsheft zum Grundriss der akkadischen Grammatik.* 2nd unchanged ed. Analecta Orientalia 33/47. Rome: Pontifical Biblical Institute.

Song, Jae Jung. 2001. *Linguistic Typology: Morphology and Syntax.* Longman Linguistics Library. Harlow: Pearson Education.

Stadelmann, Luis I. J. 1970. *The Hebrew Conception of the World.* Analecta Biblica 39. Rome: Biblical Institute Press.

Stein, Peter. 2003. *Untersuchungen zur Phonologie und Morphologie des Sabäischen.* Epigraphische Forschungen auf der Arabischen Halbinsel 3. Rahden: Verlag Marie Leidorf.

———. 2011. 'Ancient South Arabian'. In *The Semitic Languages: An International Handbook*, edited by Stefan Weninger, Geoffrey Khan, Michael P. Streck, and Janet C. E. Watson, 1042–73. Handbücher zur Sprach- und Kommunikationswissenschaft 36. Berlin: De Gruyter Mouton.

———. 2013. *Lehrbuch der sabäischen Sprache.* Vol. 1, *Grammatik.* Subsidia et Instrumenta Linguarum Orientis 4.1. Wiesbaden: Harrassowitz.

———. 2015. 'Die altsüdarabischen Minuskelinschriften auf Holzstäbchen in der Sammlung des Oosters Institut in Leiden'. In *South Arabia and its Neighbours: Phenomena of Intercultural Contacts—14. Rencontres sabéennes*, edited by Iris Gerlach, 193–211. Wiesbaden: Deutsches Archäologisches Institut Ṣanʿāʾ/Reichert Verlag.

———. 2016. 'The Cohortative in Biblical Hebrew—Subjunctive or Energic? A New Approach from the Sabaic Perspective'. In *Babel und Bibel 9: Proceedings of the 6th Biennial Meeting of the International Association for Comparative Semitics and Other Studies*, edited by Leonid Kogan, N. Koslova, S. Loesov, and S. Tishchenko, 155–70. Winona Lake, Ind.: Eisenbrauns.

———. 2020. 'Ancient South Arabian'. In *A Companion to Ancient Near Eastern Languages*, edited by Rebecca Hasselbach-Andee, 337–54. Hoboken, N.J.: Wiley-Blackwell.

Steiner, Richard C. 2000. 'Does the Biblical Hebrew Conjunction -ו have Many Meanings, one Meaning, or no Meaning at all?'. *Journal of Biblical Literature* 119 (2): 249–67.

Stempel, Reinhard. 1999. *Abriß einer historischen Grammatik der semitischen Sprachen.* Nordostafrikanisch-westasiatische Studien 3. Frankfurt am Main: Peter Lang.

Steuernagel, Carl. 1900. *Übersetzung und Erklärung der Bücher Deuteronomium und Josua und Allgemeine Einleitung in den Hexateuch.* Handkommentar zum Alten Testament 1.3. Göttingen: Vandenhoeck & Ruprecht.

Stipp, H. J. 1987. 'Narrativ-Langformen 2. und 3. Person von zweiradikaligen Basen nach qalY im biblischen Hebräisch: Eine Untersuchung zu morphologischen Abweichungen in den Büchern Jeremia und Könige'. *Journal of Northwest Semitic Languages* 13: 109–49.

Strack, Hermann L. 1894. *Die Bücher Genesis, Exodus, Leviticus und Numeri.* Kurzgefasster Kommentar zu den heiligen Schriften Alten und Neuen Testamentes A.1. Munich: C. H. Beck.

Streck, Michael P. 2011. 'Amorite'. In *The Semitic Languages: An International Handbook*, edited by Stefan Weninger, Geoffrey Khan, Michael P. Streck, and Janet C. E. Watson, 452–59. Handbücher zur Sprach- und Kommunikationswissenschaft 36. Berlin: De Gruyter Mouton.

Swiggers, Pierre. 1982. 'The Moabite Inscription of el-Kerak'. *Annali dell'istituto universitario orientale di Napoli* 42: 521–25.

Ṭab = Barth, Jakob, Theodor Nöldeke, et al., eds. 1879–1901. *Annales Auctore Abu Djafar Mohammed ibn Djarir at-Tabari.* Leiden: E. J. Brill.

TAD = Porten, Bezalel, and Ada Yardeni. 1986–99. *Textbook of Aramaic Documents from Ancient Egypt: Newly Copied, Edited and Translated into Hebrew and English.* 4 vols. Texts and Studies for Students. Jerusalem: Hebrew University, Department of the History of the Jewish People.

Talstra, Eep. 2013. 'Text Linguistics: Biblical Hebrew'. In *Encyclopedia of Hebrew Language and Linguistics*, online, edited by Geoffrey Khan. Leiden: Brill. https://doi.org/10.1163/2212-4241_ehll_EHLL_COM_00000839

Tate, Marvin E. 1990. *Word Biblical Commentary*. Vol. 20, *Psalms 51–100.* Waco, Tex.: Word Books.

Thacker, T. W. 1954. *The Relationship of the Semitic and Egyptian Verbal Systems.* Oxford: Oxford University Press.

Traugott, Elizabeth Closs. 1986. 'On the Origins of "and" and "but" Connectives in English'. *Studies in Language* 10 (1): 137–50.

Tropper, Josef. 1993a. 'Eine altaramäische Steleninschrift aus Dan'. *Ugarit-Forschungen* 25: 395–406.

———. 1993b. *Die Inschriften von Zincirli: Neue Edition und vergleichende Grammatik des phönizischen, samʾalischen und aramäischen Textkorpus.* Abhandlungen zur Literatur Alt-Syrien-Palästinas 6. Münster: Ugarit-Verlag.

———. 1994. 'Paläographische und linguistische Anmerkungen zur Steleneinschrift aus Dan'. *Ugarit-Forschungen* 26: 487–92.

———. 1996. 'Aramäisches *wyqtl* und hebräisches *wayyiqtol*'. *Ugarit-Forschungen* 28: 633–45.

———. 1997a. 'Subvarianten und Funktionen der sabäischen Präfixkonjugation'. *Orientalia* 66: 34–57.

———. 1997b. 'Ventiv oder *yaqtula*-Volitiv in den Amarnabriefen aus Syrien-Palästina?'. In *Ana šadî Labnāni lū allik: Beiträge zu altorientalischen und mittelmeerischen Kulturen—Festschrift für Wolfgang Röllig*, edited by Beate Pongratz-Leisten, Hartmut Kühne, and Paolo Xella, 397–405. Alter Orient und Altes Testament 247. Kevelaer; Neukirchen-Vluyn: Butzon und Bercker; Neukirchener.

———. 1998. 'Althebräisches und semitisches Aspektsystem'. *Zeitschrift für Althebraistik* 11: 153–90.

———. 2002. *Altäthiopisch: Grammatik des Ge'ez mit Übungstexten und Glossar*. Elementa Linguarum Orientis 2. Münster: Ugarit-Verlag.

———. 2012. *Ugaritische Grammatik*. 2nd revised ed. Alter Orient und Altes Testament 273. Münster: Ugarit-Verlag.

Tropper, Josef, and Juan-Pablo Vita. 2019a. *Das Kanaano-akkadische der Amarnazeit*. Lehrbücher orientalischer Sprachen, Section I: Cuneiform Languages 1. Münster: Ugarit-Verlag.

———. 2019b. 'Ugaritic'. In *The Semitic Languages*, edited by John Huehnergard and Na'ama Pat-El, 482–508. Routledge Language Family Series. London: Routledge.

Van der Merwe, Christo H. J., Jacobus A. Naudé, and Jan H. Kroeze. 1999. *A Biblical Hebrew Reference Grammar*. Biblical Languages: Hebrew 3. Sheffield: Sheffield Academic Press. Reprint, 2004.

———. 2007. 'A Cognitive Linguistic Perspective on הִנֵּה in the Pentateuch, Joshua, Judges, and Ruth'. *Hebrew Studies* 48: 101–40.

———. 2017. *A Biblical Hebrew Reference Grammar*. 2nd ed. London: Bloomsbury T&T Clark.

Van de Sande, Axel. 2008. *Nouvelle perspective sur le système verbal de l'hébreu ancien: Les formes *qatala, *yaqtul et *yaqtulu.* Publications de l'Institut orientaliste de Louvain 57. Leuven; Louvain-la-Neuve: Peeters; Institut orientaliste de l'Université Catholique de Louvain.

Vennemann, Theo. 1973. 'Explanation in Syntax'. In *Syntax and Semantics.* Vol. 2, edited by John P. Kimball. New York: Academic Press.

Vernet, Eulalia. 2013. 'New Considerations on the Historical Existence of a West Semitic *yaqattal* Form'. In *Archaism and Innovation in the Semitic Languages: Selected Papers*, edited by Juan Pedro Monferrer-Sala and Wilfred G. E. Watson, 145–61. Semitica Antiqva 1. Cordoba: Oriens Academic; CNERU (University of Cordoba); DTR (Durham University).

Verstraete, Jean-Christophe. 2005. 'Two Types of Coordination in Clause Combining'. *Lingua* 115: 611–26.

Voigt, Rainer Maria. 1987. 'The Classification of Central Semitic'. *Journal of Semitic Studies* 32 (1): 1–21.

———. 2011. 'Tigrinya'. In *The Semitic Languages: An International Handbook*, edited by Stefan Weninger, Geoffrey Khan, Michael P. Streck, and Janet C. E. Watson, 1153–69. Handbücher zur Sprach- und Kommunikationswissenschaft 36. Berlin: De Gruyter Mouton.

von Ewald, G. Heinrich A. 1870. *Ausführliches Lehrbuch der hebräischen Sprache des Alten Bundes.* 8th ed. Leipzig: Hinrichs.

———. 1891. *Syntax of the Hebrew Language of the Old Testament.* Translated by James Kennedy. Edinburgh: T&T Clark. Reprint, Wipf & Stock: Eugene, Ore., 2004.

De Vries, Simon J. 2003. *Word Biblical Commentary.* Vol. 12, *1 Kings.* 2nd ed. Nashville: Thomas Nelson.

Wagner, Ewald. 2011. 'Harari'. In *The Semitic Languages: An International Handbook*, edited by Stefan Weninger, Geoffrey Khan, Michael P. Streck, and Janet C. E. Watson, 1257–65. Handbücher zur Sprach- und Kommunikationswissenschaft 36. Berlin: De Gruyter Mouton.

Walsh, J. T. 1977. 'Genesis 2:4b–3:24: A Synchronic Approach'. *Journal of Biblical Literature* 96: 161–77.

Waltisberg, Michael. 1999. 'Zum Alter der Sprache des Deboraliedes Ri 5'. *Zeitschrift für Althebraistik* 12: 218–32.

———. 2011. 'Syntactic Typology of Semitic'. In *The Semitic Languages: An International Handbook*, edited by Stefan Weninger, Geoffrey Khan, Michael P. Streck, and Janet C. E. Watson, 303–29. Handbücher zur Sprach- und Kommunikationswissenschaft 36. Berlin: De Gruyter Mouton.

Waltke, Bruce K., and Michael Patrick O'Connor. 1990. *An Introduction to Biblical Hebrew Syntax.* Winona Lake, Ind.: Eisenbrauns.

Watts, John D. W. 2007a. *Word Biblical Commentary.* Vol. 24, *Isaiah 1–33.* Rev. ed. Nashville: Thomas Nelson.

———. 2007b. *Word Biblical Commentary*. Vol. 25, *Isaiah 34–66*. Rev. ed. Nashville: Thomas Nelson.

Wenham, Gordon J. 1987. *Word Biblical Commentary*. Vol. 1, *Genesis 1–15*. Waco, Tex.: Word Books; Nelson Reference & Electronic.

———. 1994. *Word Biblical Commentary*. Vol. 2, *Genesis 16–50*. Waco, Tex.: Word Books.

Weninger, Stefan. 2011. 'Old Ethiopic'. In *The Semitic Languages: An International Handbook*, edited by Stefan Weninger, Geoffrey Khan, Michael P. Streck, and Janet C. E. Watson, 1124–41. Handbücher zur Sprach- und Kommunikationswissenschaft 36. Berlin: De Gruyter Mouton.

Westermann, Claus. 1976. *Genesis*. Vol. 1, *Genesis 1–11*. 2nd ed. Biblischer Kommentar: Altes Testament 1.1. Neukirchen-Vluyn: Neukirchener.

———. 1981. *Genesis*. Vol. 2, *Genesis 12–36*. Biblischer Kommentar: Altes Testament 1.2. Neukirchen-Vluyn: Neukirchener.

———. 1982. *Genesis*. Vol. 3, *Genesis 37–50*. Biblischer Kommentar: Altes Testament 1.3. Neukirchen-Vluyn: Neukirchener.

Wildberger, Hans. 1972. *Jesaja*. Vol. 1, *Jesaja 1–12*. Biblischer Kommentar: Altes Testament 10.1. Neukirchen-Vluyn: Neukirchener.

Wilson-Wright, Aren M. 2019. 'The Canaanite Languages'. In *The Semitic Languages*, edited by John Huehnergard and Na'ama Pat-El, 509–32. Routledge Language Family Series. London: Routledge.

Wright, William. 1896–98. *A Grammar of the Arabic Language: Translated from the German of Caspari and Edited with Numerous Additions and Corrections.* 3rd ed. Cambridge: Cambridge University Press. Reprint, 1975.

Yahalom, Joseph. 2016. 'Palestinian Tradition'. In *A Handbook of Biblical Hebrew*, vol. 1, *Periods, Corpora, and Reading Traditions*, edited by W. Randall Garr and Steven Ellis Fassberg, 161–73. Winona Lake, Ind.: Eisenbrauns.

Yeivin, Israel. 1980. *Introduction to the Tiberian Masorah.* Translated by E. J. Revell. Masoretic Studies 5. Missoula: Scholars Press.

Young, Gordon Douglas. 1953. 'The Origin of the *waw* Conversive'. *Journal of Near Eastern Studies* 12: 248–52.

Yuditsky, Alexey Eliyahu. 2016. 'Hebrew in Greek and Latin Transcriptions'. In *A Handbook of Biblical Hebrew*, vol. 1, *Periods, Corpora, and Reading Traditions*, edited by W. Randall Garr and Steven Ellis Fassberg, 99–116. Winona Lake, Ind.: Eisenbrauns.

———. 2017. *A Grammar of the Hebrew of Origen's Transcriptions.* Jerusalem: The Academy of the Hebrew Language. [Hebrew].

Yun, Ilsung Andrew. 2006. 'A Case of Linguistic Transition: The Nerab Inscriptions'. *Journal of Semitic Studies* 51 (1): 19–43.

Zewi, Tamar. 1999. *A Syntactical Study of Verbal Forms Affixed by -n(n) Endings in Classical Arabic, Biblical Hebrew, el-Amarna Akkadian and Ugaritic.* Alter Orient und Altes Testament 260. Münster: Ugarit-Verlag.

———. 2011. ‘On רָאָה כִּי and רָאָה וְהִנֵּה in Biblical Hebrew’. In *En pāsē grammatikē kai sophiā: Saggi di linguistica ebraica in onore di Alviero Niccacci, ofm*, edited by Gregor Geiger and Massimo Pazzini, 405–14. Collana Analecta: Studium Biblicum Franciscanum 78. Jerusalem; Milano: Franciscan Printing Press; Editioni Terra Santa.

———. 2020. ‘Nouns in the Construct State Followed by Relative Clauses in Biblical Hebrew’. *Journal of Northwest Semitic Languages* 46 (2): 87–109.

INDICES

Index of Scripture

Genesis

1.1–3: 124, 556
1.2: 142, 143, 149, 371
1.3: 149
1.5: 376, 589
1.6–7: 36
1.9: 211, 235, 238–39
1.10: 589
1.14: 465
1.22: 288
1.24: 223
1.26: 63, 286
1.27: 493
1.28: 573
1.29: 335, 393
1.31: 599
2.5: 334
2.6: 77, 476
2.9f.: 519, 597
2.10: 142, 143, 334, 453, 476
2.16: 324
2.17: 448, 470
2.18: 63, 286
2.19: 142, 334, 598
2.20: 589
2.23: 370, 446
2.24: 335, 425, 476, 600
2.25: 140, 282, 334, 540, 601
3.1: 553
3.2: 336
3.4: 335
3.5: 328, 522, 598
3.8: 328, 512, 596
3.10: 149
3.13: 149
3.14: 373, 473
3.14–17: 593
3.16: 335
3.17: 473
3.18: 149, 399, 452
3.19: 335, 473
3.22: 119, 467
4.1: 230, 603
4.2: 589
4.3–5: 487
4.4f.: 149
4.7: 141, 285, 427, 468
4.12: 335, 472
4.14: 116, 393, 476
4.16f.: 572
4.17: 221
4.19: 598
4.20: 593
4.22: 136
5.7: 138
5.24: 528
6.3: 149, 476
6.4: 334, 426, 593
6.6: 282
6.7: 63, 286
6.7f.: 489
6.8: 590
6.9f.: 605
6.11: 282
6.12: 376, 490, 591
6.13: 371
6.14: 466
6.17f.: 476
6.18b–19a: 460
6.20: 474

6.21: 465, 466
6.22: 493, 592
7.1: 592
7.2: 592
7.2f.: 592
7.4: 456
7.6f.: 606
7.7f.: 591
7.8: 591
7.13: 604
7.15f.: 591
7.15–16: 98
7.19: 394
7.19f.: 592
7.21f.: 494, 592
8.5: 590
8.8f.: 119, 607
8.11: 141, 526
8.12: 607
8.13: 502, 591
8.13f.: 590
8.16f.: 592
8.17: 415
8.18f.: 592
8.21: 335
9.3: 393
9.5: 335
9.6: 474
9.9f.: 476
9.9–11: 139
9.9–13: 393, 477, 580
9.11: 461
9.13: 457
9.15: 478, 607
9.16: 476
9.17: 393
9.18: 142, 598
9.21: 210
9.23: 141, 598
9.23b: 124
9.26–27: 243
9.27: 573
10.9: 335
10.12: 598
10.15–18: 146
10.18f.: 138
11.3: 589
11.4: 63, 103, 141, 286, 290
11.8f.: 593
11.29: 142, 598
11.30: 527
12.1f.: 153, 468
12.4: 142, 524, 598
12.6: 598
12.7: 210
12.8: 598
12.12: 398, 458, 471
12.15f.: 590
12.16: 138
12.19: 149
13.1: 598
13.1f.: 598
13.2: 143
13.5–7: 604
13.7: 107, 597
13.8: 288
13.9: 469, 470
13.11f.: 592
13.13: 143
13.14–18: 603
13.15f.: 475
14.7: 598
14.8: 598
14.10: 143, 590
14.12: 143, 597
14.13: 140, 143, 597
14.16: 590
14.17: 598
14.18: 143
14.19: 138
14.18–20: 551
14.22: 393, 503, 595
15.1: 604
15.2: 150, 336
15.3: 148
15.3f.: 528
15.5f.: 543, 601
15.5–6: 113
15.6: 149
15.10: 590
15.13: 475
15.13f.: 521, 598
15.15: 289
15.18: 393
16.1f.: 553
16.1–4: 244

16.2: 336
16.4: 149
16.6: 149
16.10: 335, 336
16.11: 588
16.13f.: 593
16.15f.: 598
16.16: 143
16.26: 286
17.1–2: 16, 133
17.2: 469
17.4: 474, 568
17.4f.: 478
17.5: 393, 476, 607
17.6: 136, 477
17.9: 568
17.10b: 99
17.12f.: 474
17.13: 150, 452
17.14: 474
17.15: 474
17.16: 464, 476, 477, 593, 594
17.17: 336
17.18: 324
17.19: 606
17.20: 335, 393, 477, 593, 594
17.20f.: 477
17.21: 335
17.23–25: 598
18.1: 140, 102, 597
18.2: 597
18.3: 288, 392, 468
18.6f.: 590
18.8: 140, 597
18.10: 140, 141, 597
18.11: 505
18.11f.: 149
18.12: 141, 394
18.14: 141, 335
18.15: 587
18.16: 140, 516, 597
18.18: 475
18.19: 132
18.21: 63, 286, 469, 470
18.22: 141, 597
18.27: 393
18.28: 335
18.30: 288
18.31: 393
18.33: 590
19.1: 141, 597
19.2: 465
19.2a: 120
19.3: 591
19.4f.: 603
19.6: 590
19.7: 288
19.9: 283, 336
19.9–11: 590
19.11: 149
19.15: 604
19.17: 239, 280, 583
19.19: 138, 147, 283, 467
19.20: 229
19.21: 393
19.22: 336, 593
19.23–25: 557
19.28: 591
19.32: 63, 286
19.34: 63, 286
19.37: 598
19.38: 598, 603
20.3: 150
20.7: 152
20.7a: 129
20.11: 149, 474, 606
20.12: 149
20.15f.: 590
20.16: 393, 588
21.1: 603
21.1f.: 138
21.7: 394, 595
21.9: 328, 596
21.13: 474
21.14: 595, 596
21.23–25: 112
21.24f.: 543, 601
21.30f.: 593
22.3: 118
22.5: 63
22.12: 394, 608

22.13: 511, 599
22.14: 290, 335
22.16: 393
22.17f.: 475
22.20–23: 590
23.2: 598
23.9: 152
23.10: 561, 605
23.11: 393
23.13: 393, 595
23.17–19: 146, 591
23.17–20: 100
24.1f.: 606
24.4: 466, 476
24.7: 476
24.8: 286, 288
24.10: 104, 141, 598
24.14: 63, 286
24.16: 145
24.17: 393
24.19: 374
24.20f.: 143, 597
24.21: 141
24.22: 525, 598
24.30: 141, 597
24.31: 150
24.33: 392
24.35: 99, 138, 283, 603
24.38: 476
24.40: 467, 475, 559
24.43: 147, 468
24.45: 141, 558
24.46: 590
24.48: 63, 281
24.49: 63, 153, 286
24.53: 590
24.57: 286
24.58: 286, 336
24.62: 143
24.62f.: 603
24.63: 597
25.1: 141, 598
25.6: 590, 598
25.7f.: 567
25.9f.: 496, 592
25.17: 138
25.17f.: 606
25.18: 592
25.19f.: 604
25.23: 473
25.24: 599
25.25: 149, 598
25.26: 103, 141, 149, 552, 598, 603
25.27: 596
25.28: 282, 597
25.29: 141, 598
25.30: 593
25.33: 151
25.34: 282, 603
26.3: 63, 153, 286, 469
26.3a: 227
26.4: 475
26.8: 517, 597
26.10: 394, 467
26.15: 138, 603
26.18: 283
26.22: 149, 457, 576
26.24: 474
26.26f.: 603
26.29: 138
26.33: 598
27.1: 215, 282
27.4f.: 597
27.5: 143
27.6: 319, 328
27.6–11: 603
27.9: 416, 286
27.9f.: 147
27.12: 467, 475
27.15f.: 590
27.30f.: 603
27.31: 239, 280
27.35: 594
27.36: 283, 592
27.44: 147, 466
27.45: 472
28.6: 283
28.7: 283
28.12: 588, 597
28.13: 474, 588
28.14: 475
28.15: 392, 474
28.19: 598

28.21f.: 477
28.22: 474
29.2: 141, 334, 526, 600
29.2–3: 121
29.3: 454, 476
29.8: 152
29.9: 604
29.9f.: 605
29.15: 473
29.18: 282
29.24: 111
29.27: 153, 469
29.31: 141, 598
29.33: 149
29.34: 592
29.35: 592
30.1: 468
30.3: 286
30.6: 283, 592, 594
30.13: 377
30.18: 594
30.27: 283
30.28: 153, 469
30.30: 284
30.31: 227, 286, 469
30.32: 286, 465
30.34: 288
30.36: 141, 597
30.38: 151, 334
30.39: 284, 589
30.40: 589, 607
30.42: 334
31.2: 599
31.3: 286, 469
31.5: 304
31.7: 139
31.8: 334, 471
31.8b: 438
31.9: 151
31.10: 599
31.19: 283
31.19–21: 604
31.25: 489, 590
31.26: 138
31.27: 145
31.27a: 115
31.33f.: 590
31.33–34: 220
31.33–35: 607
31.35: 335
31.39: 334, 600
31.40: 284, 394
31.41: 221, 509, 596
31.42: 394, 430, 469
31.43: 336, 474
31.44: 465
31.47: 590
31.48: 593
32.1–3: 551
32.2: 590
32.5f.: 283
32.7: 141
32.10: 153, 469, 595
32.11: 595
32.12: 147
32.13: 139, 475
32.18: 77, 334
32.18f.: 471
32.20: 77
32.20f.: 476
32.21: 336
32.22: 590
32.23f.: 138
32.25: 282
32.29: 283
32.30: 334
32.31: 283
32.32: 141
32.32f.: 537
32.33: 335
33.1: 141, 597
33.3: 603
33.4: 284
33.7: 476, 603
33.10: 152, 283, 477
33.13: 470
33.15: 286
33.16f.: 590
33.17: 590, 593, 603
34.3: 138
34.4f.: 590
34.4–7: 108
34.5: 149

34.7: 142, 144, 282, 591
34.8: 594
34.12: 153, 469
34.16: 459, 467
34.18f.: 607
34.21: 150
34.26: 603
34.27f.: 592
34.30: 470, 474
35.3: 284, 286
35.5: 607
35.6: 598
35.10: 322, 473
35.16: 138, 144, 282
35.18: 393, 590
35.19: 598
35.20: 598
35.27: 598
36.8: 598
36.22: 598
36.32: 141, 598
36.35: 598
36.39: 141, 598
37.2: 144, 284
37.2–4: 145
37.5f.: 138
37.7: 334
37.10: 286
37.11: 590
37.15: 77, 141, 334, 597
37.17: 594
37.17f.: 138
37.20: 147, 465
37.22: 288
37.24: 598
37.25: 597
37.27: 288
37.29: 599
37.35f.: 591
38.1: 141, 598
38.2: 141, 598, 601
38.5: 145, 544, 602
38.6: 141, 598
38.9: 323, 394, 471, 602
38.13: 587
38.16: 286, 336
38.20: 607
38.24: 594
38.25: 604, 605
38.26: 503, 595, 607
38.30: 603
39.1: 604
39.2: 282
39.3: 150, 597
39.4: 591
39.9: 150, 453
39.11: 598
39.13: 283
39.14: 594
39.15: 145
39.18: 145
39.22: 115, 591
39.22f.: 515
39.23: 143, 596
40.6: 597
40.10: 596
40.13: 473, 475
40.14: 392, 394, 467
40.18f.: 473
40.19: 122, 475
40.21f.: 590
40.21–23: 607
41.2–4: 588
41.6f.: 588
41.7: 599
41.8: 141, 598
41.10: 149, 604
41.11: 592
41.12: 473, 592
41.13: 592
41.17: 605
41.17f.: 563
41.18–20: 588
41.22: 597
41.23f.: 588
41.24: 598
41.27: 335
41.29f.: 148, 476
41.30f.: 478
41.31: 607
41.32: 588
41.33: 288
41.33f.: 466

41.34: 152, 239, 285
41.36: 128, 478, 607
41.41: 393
41.44: 473
41.46f.: 606
41.48: 592
41.50: 336, 603
41.51f.: 590
41.54: 590
41.56f.: 105, 591
42.1: 77, 334
42.2: 151, 286
42.3f.: 590
42.6: 473
42.8: 590
42.16: 468, 470
42.22f.: 591
42.27: 141, 599
42.28: 594
42.30: 138, 503
42.36: 393
42.37: 336
42.38: 470
43.1f.: 606
43.4: 469
43.5: 336
43.8: 151, 286
43.9: 393, 467
43.10: 379, 469
43.14: 152, 288, 372, 431, 465, 596
43.15: 590
43.20: 604
43.21: 216, 599
43.21f.: 590
43.25: 336
43.32: 335, 600
44.1: 336
44.2: 335
44.4: 466
44.8: 336
44.9: 477
44.12: 592
44.14: 142, 598
44.15: 324
44.16: 336
44.18: 289, 232, 608
44.19: 604
44.20: 215, 282, 589
44.22: 470
44.23: 428
44.26: 336
44.29: 470
44.30: 142
44.30f.: 472
44.33: 232
44.34: 142
45.5: 608
45.6f.: 149
45.8: 283
45.9: 466
45.9f.: 465
45.12f.: 456
45.14: 488, 590
45.15: 117, 146, 591
45.16: 502, 603
45.19: 150, 393, 465
45.20: 288
45.21f.: 592
45.28: 335
46.6f.: 592
46.12: 282
46.28: 604
46.31: 286
46.33f.: 471
47.4: 288
47.6: 392
47.13: 473, 606
47.16: 153, 469
47.19: 151, 153, 286, 336, 469
47.20f.: 590
47.20–22: 593
47.21: 594
47.23: 393
47.24: 477
47.25: 466, 594
47.26: 593
47.29: 288, 392, 465
47.30: 465
48.3: 138
48.4: 139, 564, 587
48.5: 473

48.7: 598
48.9f.: 591
48.14: 527, 595
48.17: 77, 230, 319
48.21: 587, 606
48.22: 393
49.1: 153
49.4: 273, 288
49.6: 197
49.7: 388
49.8: 273
49.9: 389, 506
49.11: 388
49.14: 328
49.15: 388
49.17: 18, 192, 275
49.18: 389
49.26: 273, 388
49.27: 290, 333
49.28: 592
50.3: 284, 335, 600
50.4: 392
50.5: 286, 288, 467, 474
50.8: 593
50.12f.: 138
50.23: 592
50.24: 475
50.25: 453, 476, 608

Exodus

1.7: 19, 603
1.10: 472
1.12: 142, 334
1.17: 607
1.18: 283
1.19: 335, 442
1.22: 474
2.5: 141, 597
2.7: 239, 280, 476
2.11: 283, 301, 596
2.13: 141, 334, 597
2.16: 566
3.1: 604
3.2: 597
3.3: 286
3.7: 136
3.8: 283
3.10: 153, 469
3.11: 336
3.12: 472
3.13: 148, 476
3.16: 465
3.18: 467
3.20: 149
3.20f.: 475
3.21: 472
4.7: 491, 591
4.11: 321, 335
4.12: 475
4.13: 233
4.14: 336, 472, 477
4.14f.: 148
4.15f.: 139, 475
4.18: 286
4.21: 415, 465, 477
4.25f.: 593
5.1: 146
5.4: 334
5.5: 474
5.7: 476
5.9: 582
5.10: 328
5.12f.: 597
5.13: 141
5.20: 596
6.3: 590
6.3–5: 589
6.6: 474, 569
6.6–7: 125
6.9: 607
6.11: 152
7.1: 393
7.2: 475
7.3f.: 475
7.6: 592
7.6f.: 598
7.9: 471
7.13: 607
7.15: 477
7.15–16a: 417
7.17: 148
7.17f.: 476, 478

7.21: 603
7.22: 607
7.23: 607
7.26: 466
7.27: 468
7.27f.: 139, 476
7.28f.: 478
8.4: 130, 152, 285
8.5: 140, 335
8.7: 478, 500, 593, 608
8.11: 607
8.12: 147, 464, 465
8.13: 592
8.15: 607
8.16: 466
8.17: 468
8.19: 478, 593, 594
8.20: 334, 537, 600
8.22: 335, 468
8.23: 148, 475
8.24: 152, 421, 475
8.25: 288, 476, 587, 606
8.27: 592
8.28: 607
9.1: 466
9.3: 468
9.3f.: 476, 579
9.4: 478
9.6: 590
9.7: 591, 607
9.8: 466
9.8f.: 147
9.10f.: 607
9.12: 607
9.13: 76, 466
9.15: 380
9.19: 449
9.23: 590
9.24: 141, 597
9.25: 590
9.25f.: 497
9.26: 593
9.28: 150, 153, 469
9.29: 472
9.30: 335, 594
9.30–32: 591
9.33: 590
10.4: 468
10.4f.: 476
10.5: 478, 607
10.7: 393
10.12: 223
10.13: 497, 591
10.14: 336
10.15: 607
10.17: 152
10.19: 494, 592
10.20: 607
10.21: 152
10.22f.: 592
10.23: 592
10.24: 336
10.25: 152, 467, 476
10.27: 607
10.28: 224
11.2: 152
11.3: 599
11.4f.: 476, 606
11.7: 335
11.7f.: 475
11.9f.: 591
11.10: 98, 607
12.4: 594
12.8: 478, 499, 594
12.11: 139, 476, 599
12.12: 478
12.13: 472, 478, 607
12.14: 478, 594
12.15: 474
12.16: 474
12.17: 476
12.19: 474
12.21f.: 147, 466
12.22f.: 577
12.23: 478, 608
12.28: 592
12.29: 591
12.32: 466
12.34: 140
12.34–36: 591

12.35: 283
12.36: 151
12.38: 590
12.39–42: 598
12.44: 336, 470, 474, 593
12.48: 285, 475, 475
12.51: 594
13.3: 466
13.4f.: 472
13.7: 335
13.12: 599
13.15f.: 150, 477
13.17: 147, 467
13.18: 490, 591
13.19: 476, 608
13.20f.: 143, 597
13.21: 141
13.22: 334
14.2: 152
14.2–4: 466
14.3: 595
14.5: 152
14.6: 590
14.7: 598
14.8: 141, 597
14.9: 513, 596
14.10: 597, 603
14.15: 152
14.20: 607
14.22: 598
14.27: 141, 597
14.28: 592
14.28f.: 590
14.30: 328, 596
15.1: 330
15:1–18: 270
15.5: 284, 331
15.6: 331
15.7: 330, 333
15.9: 237, 273, 286
15.12: 331, 333
15.13: 390
15.14: 318, 333
15.14–15: 314
15.16: 390
15.17: 330, 333, 390
15.19: 590
15.22: 607
15.23: 593, 607
15.26: 139
16.4: 476, 587
16.4f.: 606
16.5: 477
16.6f.: 444
16.7: 334
16.10: 591
16.12: 146, 475, 608
16.13: 590
16.14: 599
16.18: 607
16.19: 288
16.19f.: 607
16.20: 210
16.21: 284, 472, 546
16.24: 607
16.27: 594
16.31: 598
16.34f.: 591
16.35: 378, 394
17.1: 598
17.2: 77, 286, 320, 334
17.5: 150, 466
17.6: 476, 608
17.10: 590
17.11: 334
17.12: 149, 591
18.14: 141
18.15: 335
18.18: 336
18.19: 464, 465
18.21f.: 476
18.22: 465
18.23: 285
18.25f.: 547
18.26: 145, 334, 477, 594
19.1f.: 604f.
19.3: 145, 289, 291, 603
19.4: 280
19.5f.: 478
19.10: 466
19.18: 138, 603
19.19: 102, 319, 536

19.21: 147, 467
19.23: 150, 464, 465
19.24: 147, 465
20.3–9: 335
20.9: 139, 476
20.10: 473
20.11: 282
20.18: 605
20.19: 608
20.21: 590
20.24: 475, 476
20.25: 151
21.4: 123
21.5: 595
21.8: 594
21.11: 285, 434
21.12: 148, 467, 468
21.14: 285
21.15: 468
21.16: 468
21.17: 468
21.18: 581
21.19: 285, 478, 594
21.20: 285, 467, 468
21.22: 422, 468, 608
21.23: 285
21.26: 467
21.27: 285
21.28: 467, 468
21.29: 608
21.33: 285, 467
21.33f.: 148
21.35: 467, 478
21.36: 468
21.37: 148, 381, 394
22.1: 148, 467
22.2: 375, 393
22.4: 222, 275, 285
22.5: 152, 467, 468
22.6: 148, 468, 471
22.7: 393
22.9: 148, 599
22.9f.: 394
22.10: 336, 478, 608
22.11: 468
22.12: 336, 468
22.13: 148, 394, 468, 599
22.14: 393, 469, 596
22.15: 468
22.22: 469, 472
22.22f.: 475
22.23: 467
22.26: 600
23.4: 468
23.5: 285, 477, 594
23.7: 288, 335
23.8: 289, 291, 335
23.9: 150
23.10: 476
23.11: 336, 476
23.12: 289, 291
23.23: 335
23.23f.: 472
23.25: 150
23.27: 467, 475
23.29: 147, 467
23.30: 152
23.30f.: 475
23.31: 467, 475
24.1f.: 147, 466
24.2: 477
24.6: 590
24.7: 145, 289
24.10: 598
24.10f.: 591
24.12: 153, 469
24.13f.: 591
24.16f.: 598
24.25: 136
24.32: 591
25.2: 152
25.10: 530
25.10–14: 54
25.11: 478, 594
25.12: 599
25.14f.: 478, 594
25.17: 599
25.18: 478, 594

25.20: 598, 599
25.21: 477
25.23: 599
25.26f.: 594
25.27: 478
25.29: 478, 594
25.31: 478, 499, 594, 598
25.31f.: 597
25.36f.: 476
25.40: 152
26.3f.: 139, 476
26.5: 329
26.6: 466
26.7: 478, 594
26.9–11: 572
26.11: 152, 466
26.15: 328, 598
26.15–17: 599
26.17: 594
26.24: 289
26.24f.: 139, 476
26.31: 477, 594
26.35: 477
26.37: 599
27.1: 599
27.2: 477, 594
27.3: 477, 594
28.3: 476
28.4f.: 478
28.6f.: 477, 594
28.7: 152, 466, 476
28.9–11: 477, 594
28.13f.: 478, 594
28.15: 594
28.15f.: 477
28.20: 594
28.20f.: 477
28.25: 476
28.29f.: 476
28.32: 336, 478, 594
28.35: 151, 477, 607
28.37: 477, 594
28.39: 478
28.40: 323
28.42f.: 466
28.43: 150, 151, 475, 578
29.4: 476
29.8: 476
29.12: 477
29.13f.: 477
29.15: 476
29.17: 476
29.18: 599
29.25: 599
29.28: 478
29.31: 476
29.33: 600
29.34: 594
29.37: 478, 593, 594
30.1: 477, 594
30.7: 459, 594
30.8f.: 473
30.10: 477, 594, 599
30.12: 151, 471, 478, 607
30.20: 151, 472
30.21: 151, 607
30.25: 460, 501, 593
30.29: 478, 500, 593, 594
30.30: 476
32.34: 443
30.34f.: 147, 465
30.36: 478, 594
30.37: 474
31.3: 283
31.13f.: 476
31.14: 474, 600
31.15: 464, 468
32.7f.: 595
32.8: 283
32.9: 594, 595
32.10: 286
32.13: 286, 475
32.15: 598
32.15f.: 598
32.32: 336
33.1f.: 466
33.3: 607
33.7: 142, 147, 334, 454
33.8: 334, 472
33.9: 147, 334
33.10: 598

33.10f.: 147
33.11: 335, 477
33.13: 392
33.14: 475
33.15: 468
33.17: 214
33.19: 475
33.20: 336
33.21: 474
33.21f.: 569
33.23: 477
34.1: 147
34.1f.: 466
34.3: 231, 477
34.7: 335
34.9: 392, 468
34.10: 475
34.14–16: 423
34.25: 136
34.28: 592
34.30: 591
34.33f.: 600
34.33–35: 105
34.34: 334
34.34a: 443
34.34f.: 476
35.21: 591
35.22: 592
35.30: 594
35.31: 283
35.31–35: 595
36.3: 394, 591
36.3f.: 149
36.5: 304, 329
36.6: 288
36.6f.: 591
36.8: 592
36.8f.: 598
36.10: 590
36.11: 591
36.11f.: 592
36.12: 329
36.14: 592
36.17: 590
36.20: 328, 596
36.23f.: 590
36.24f: 590
36.29: 334, 335, 477
36.29f.: 145
36.30: 599
36.33f.: 591
36.35: 592
36.36: 598
36.37f.: 603
36.38: 599
37.1: 598
37.3: 526, 598
37.6: 598
37.7f.: 592
37.9: 592, 596
37.10: 598
37.14: 592
37.17: 592
37.23f.: 592
37.25: 592, 598
37.26f.: 590
38.1: 598
38.3: 592
38.7: 592
38.24: 282
38.27f.: 591
39.3: 603
39.8f.: 592
39.17f.: 590
39.21: 151, 539, 601
39.23: 336
39.32: 139, 592
39.43: 591
40.2f.: 476
40.9: 152, 466
40.14: 476
40.16: 592
40.17: 594
40.30f.: 548
40.31f.: 477, 594
40.32: 334
40.34: 590
40.34f.: 607
40.34–36: 600
40.36: 142, 334
40.37: 285, 334, 472
40.38: 334

Leviticus

1.2: 285, 466, 474
1.3: 335
1.13: 599
1.17: 530, 594

2.1: 285, 474
2.3: 599
2.4: 285
2.6: 466
2.9f.: 599
2.11: 474
2.12: 477
2.14: 285
2.15: 599
3.1: 471
3.9: 477, 594
3.16: 599
4.3: 471
4.7: 477
4.10: 335
4.11: 474
4.12: 477, 594
4.13: 467
4.17f.: 477
4.21: 599
4.22: 335
4.23: 394
4.24: 599
4.25: 477
4.26: 150
4.28: 394
4.30: 477
4.31: 150
4.32: 285
4.34: 477
4.35: 127
5.1: 285, 471, 599
5.2: 148, 471
5.3: 392
5.4: 392, 471
5.5: 469
5.6: 150
5.7: 285
5.8: 478
5.9: 477, 599
5.10: 150
5.11: 285, 594, 600
5.12: 599
5.12f.: 150
5.13: 476
5.18f.: 599
5.23: 471
6.4f.: 478
6.6: 594
6.8–10: 599
6.11: 336
6.14: 473
6.21: 393
7.5: 599
7.6: 336
7.7: 474
7.12f.: 594
7.14: 474
7.16: 336
7.19: 336, 474
7.24: 336
7.25: 464
7.27: 464
7.32: 477
7.32f.: 474
7.34: 219
8.10: 128, 151
8.15: 151, 590
8.16f.: 590
8.19f.: 590
8.20f.: 590
8.21: 598
8.25f.: 590
8.28: 598
8.29: 592
8.30: 151
8.35: 151, 607
9.4: 393
9.6: 151, 224
9.9–11: 590
10.6: 288
10.9: 288
10.12f.: 466
10.13f.: 477
10.16: 603
10.17: 285
10.18: 336
10.19: 470, 593
11.3: 336, 474
11.9: 336, 474
11.35: 148
11.39: 285
11.43: 146
11.44: 149, 474, 478, 607
12.2: 285, 477, 594
12.7: 150, 599
12.7f.: 467
13.2: 148

13.3: 393, 474
13.5: 393
13.6: 393
13.7: 285
13.8: 393, 599
13.11: 474, 594
13.12: 467
13.13: 393, 599
13.14: 472
13.15: 599
13.16: 285
13.17: 393, 599
13.20: 599
13.22: 285, 599
13.25: 393, 474, 599
13.27: 285, 599
13.30: 599
13.31: 285
13.32: 393
13.34: 393
13.35: 285
13.36: 336, 393
13.37: 393, 429, 596
13.39: 596
13.42f.: 474
13.45: 474
13.51: 393
13.53: 285
13.54: 152
13.55: 393
13.56: 393
13.57: 285
13.58: 474
14.3: 393
14.5f.: 477, 594
14.8: 146
14.18: 150
14.19: 146, 477
14.19b–20: 420
14.20: 150
14.34f.: 471
14.36: 146, 150, 151, 607
14.39: 393
14.44: 285, 393
14.46: 596
14.48: 393
15.2: 466
15.3: 381, 393, 508
15.11: 474
15.13: 472
15.15: 150
15.17: 474
15.19: 474
15.24: 275, 478
15.25: 285, 335
15.29: 146, 393, 477
15.30: 150
15.31: 150, 151, 478, 607
16.2: 151, 152, 285, 608
16.4: 149, 447
16.6: 150
16.11: 150, 455
16.13: 151, 476, 607
16.14: 478
16.18–20: 476
16.19: 150
16.25: 477
16.26: 146
16.28: 146, 336
16.31: 474
17.2: 466
17.6f.: 478
17.11: 148, 335
17.14: 149
17.15: 464
18.2: 466
18.4f.: 150
18.5: 474
18.7: 473
18.9: 474
18.10: 474
18.11: 474
18.15: 473
18.26: 477, 478
18.27: 149
18.28: 151, 607
18.29: 464
18.30: 151, 478, 607
19.2: 466
19.5: 472
19.12: 150
19.17: 151
19.20: 474

19.23: 471
19.29: 151, 152
19.33: 285
19.36f.: 150
19.37: 474
20.2: 468
20.7: 532, 600
20.8: 532
20.9: 468
20.12: 468
20.13: 375, 469
20.14: 151
20.15: 468
20.17: 467, 474
20.18: 393, 469
20.20: 393, 469
20.22: 151, 476, 478, 607
20.23: 149, 280
20.25: 474, 478, 607
20.26: 149, 218, 280
20.27: 468
21.1: 466
21.6: 151
21.7f.: 474
21.9: 468
21.10: 335
21.14: 474
21.15: 151
21.21: 473
21.23: 151
22.2: 150, 151, 152
22.6–7: 117
22.7: 146, 336, 472, 477
22.9: 466, 478
22.11: 336
22.13: 336
22.23: 336, 474
22.28: 474
22.29: 336
22.31: 476, 600
22.32: 600
23.2: 466
23.8: 473
23.10: 466, 471
23.11: 477, 594
23.15: 594
23.15f.: 477, 594
23.20: 478, 594
23.21: 593
23.22: 472
23.27: 473
23.29: 464
23.30: 464
23.32: 474, 477, 594
23.35: 473
23.36: 473
23.41: 594
24.2: 152
24.5: 477, 594
24.9: 600
24.10: 598
24.11: 598
24.14: 147, 466
24.16: 470, 472
24.17: 468
24.23: 591
25.2: 439, 466
25.6: 608
25.9: 477, 594
25.10: 290, 336, 474, 477
25.11: 290, 473
25.14: 468
25.25: 285
25.28: 393, 467
25.29: 478, 594
25.30: 594
25.35: 285, 467
25.36: 150
25.39: 285
25.40f.: 475
25.43: 150
25.46: 336, 477, 594
25.47: 285
25.49: 152, 381, 392, 394
25.52: 477, 594
26.5: 477
26.6: 531
26.11: 478
26.12: 477
26.16: 476, 522, 598
26.16b: 127

26.17: 600
26.20: 476
26.26: 472, 478, 582
26.29: 477
26.31: 478
26.33: 477
26.34: 605
26.36: 474, 600
26.37: 531
26.41: 334, 476
27.2: 285, 466
27.8: 477, 594
27.10: 285, 469
27.12: 477, 594
27.16: 285, 599
27.17: 285
27.18: 285
27.20: 393, 471
27.22: 285
27.26: 474
27.33: 469, 594

Numbers

1.18: 603
1.47f.: 604
1.54: 592
2.34: 394, 592
3.6: 414, 465
3.9: 599
3.10: 153
3.11: 393
3.17: 282
3.41: 465
3.45: 466
3.46f.: 475
3.47: 477, 594
3.49f.: 592
4.15: 466, 467
4.19: 150, 464, 607
4.20: 466
4.24f.: 139, 474
4.48f.: 592
5.2: 152
5.3: 151
5.4: 592
5.6: 474
5.12: 285, 466
5.13: 392, 393, 600
5.14: 393, 394
5.15: 594
5.19: 373, 392
5.20: 392
5.21f.: 466
5.26: 146, 477
5.27: 259, 393
5.28: 393
5.31: 477
6.2: 285, 466
6.7: 474
6.9: 285, 477, 594
6.16f.: 477
6.20: 146, 336, 477, 594
6.24–26: 137
7.1: 151
7.5: 465
7.6–9: 592
7.18f.: 504, 595
7.89: 596
8.2: 466, 472
8.3: 592
8.6: 466
8.7: 465, 466
8.10f.: 476
8.13f.: 151
8.15: 139, 336
8.19: 151, 334, 539, 601
8.20: 592
8.21f.: 491
8.26: 336
9.5: 592
9.10: 285
9.14: 285
9.15: 334, 600
9.16: 334
9.17: 474
9.17–23: 334
9.18: 334
9.19: 472, 478
10.2: 466
10.3: 472, 476
10.4: 437
10.5: 122, 472
10.6: 472, 478, 594
10.7: 472
10.9: 471

10.10a: 444
10.14–17: 602
10.14–28: 598f.
10.18: 599
10.21: 476
10.25: 598
10.29: 329
10.30: 323
10.31: 473
10.33: 141, 597
10.33f.: 598
10.36: 334, 472
11.4: 336, 603
11.5: 334, 595
11.7–9: 509
11.8: 394, 596
11.9: 142, 334
11.10: 328, 590, 596
11.13: 335
11.14: 335
11.15: 286, 608
11.16: 466
11.17: 151, 476, 478, 607
11.18f.: 593
11.19: 594
11.20: 283
11.21: 467
11.22: 421, 476
11.23: 322, 335
11.25: 607
11.26: 282, 598
11.32: 592
11.33: 606
11.35: 605
12.2f.: 598
12.6: 285, 335
12.8: 321, 335
12.10: 599
12.12: 213
12.14: 146, 336, 470
12.15: 590
12.16: 603
13.3: 598
13.12: 335
13.17–20: 147, 466, 598
13.18: 532
13.20: 476
13.22: 591, 598
13.23f.: 593
13.30f.: 590
13.33: 590
14.2: 380
14.3: 140
14.4: 596
14.9: 288
14.10: 591
14.12: 286
14.13: 470
14.13f.: 471
14.14: 470
14.14f.: 470
14.17: 288
14.20: 595
14.22: 284, 393, 394
14.24: 283, 445
14.31: 450
14.36: 283
14.38: 590
14.40: 474, 568
14.43: 150, 474
14.44: 591
15.18: 466
15.19: 472
15.24: 469
15.30: 477
15.33: 301, 596
15.34: 336
15.38: 153, 465, 466
15.39: 472
16.5: 466
16.21: 286
16.22: 153, 468
16.26: 608
16.27: 302, 590
16.29: 393, 469
16.34: 590
16.35: 603
17.2: 152, 225
17.3: 475
17.7: 591
17.10: 286
17.11: 595
17.12: 591
17.15: 591
17.20: 467, 474

17.23: 591
17.25: 151
17.26: 592
17.27: 393
18.5: 151, 478, 607
18.7: 335
18.13: 336
18.21: 393
18.21f.: 540
18.22: 151
18.26: 472
19.2: 152
19.2f.: 147, 466
19.5: 477, 594
19.7: 146, 336, 477
19.11f.: 477, 594
19.13: 393, 464, 469, 477
19.14: 285
20.2f.: 604
20.8: 147, 151, 466, 476
20.12f.: 598
20.16: 529
20.19: 285
20.26: 466
21.7: 152
21.8: 474
21.9: 471, 602
21.12f.: 605
21.13f.: 600
21.14: 335
21.21–23: 607
21.26: 283
21.34: 374
22.4: 598
22.7: 599
22.11: 213, 476
22.20: 474
22.22: 597
22.23: 328, 596
22.29: 394, 469
22.31: 596
22.33: 394, 469
22.34: 469
22.38: 335, 474
23.3: 474
23.4: 283
23.6: 141, 597
23.7: 330
23.8: 390
23.9: 77, 330
23.10a: 360
23.10b: 196
23.13: 336
23.17: 141, 597
23.19: 389
23.19a: 198
23.20: 362, 390
23.21: 389
23.23: 315, 333, 390
23.26: 474
23.27: 153, 468
24.1: 607
24.2: 328, 596
24.5: 388
24.6: 390
24.7: 273
24.9: 388
24.17: 330, 333
24.17–19: 199, 367, 389, 391
24.18: 141
24.19: 389, 391
24.24: 391
24.25: 590
25.6: 141, 587, 597, 606
25.11: 150
25.12: 587
25.17: 466
26.9–11: 591
26.10: 151
26.19: 283
27.8: 285
27.11: 467
27.13: 442
27:18f.: 466
28.2: 466
28.17: 473
28.18: 473
28.19: 594, 608
28.27: 608
29.7: 477, 594, 608
29.12: 608
30.6: 393
30.7: 285
30.9: 285

30.11: 381, 393
30.12: 393
30.13: 148
30.14: 336, 474
30.15: 285, 595
31.6: 599
31.7: 335
31.7f.: 591
31.9: 590
31.52f.: 593
32.1: 599, 604
32.5: 468
32.17: 392, 608
32.23: 393, 469
32.34–37: 590
32.40f.: 590
33.1f.: 606
33.3: 592
33.4: 141
33.9: 149, 598
33.14: 607
33.36: 598
33.38f.: 598
33.40: 141, 597
33.51: 466
33.51f.: 471
33.54: 477, 594
34.2: 466
34.6: 475
35.2: 465, 477
35.2a: 131
35.3: 477
35.5: 478, 594, 599
35.10: 466
35.10f.: 471
35.12: 151, 478, 607
35.16: 259, 393
35.17: 259, 393
35.19: 470
35.20: 471
35.21: 393, 468
35.22: 393
35.23: 141
35.27: 599
35.28: 336
36.3: 470
36.4: 285, 471
36.4a: 438

Deuteronomy

1.3: 594
1.11: 288
1.16: 281, 466
1.18: 211, 336
1.20: 594, 595
1.21: 146, 608
1.22: 277, 279
1.30–31: 16
1.31: 17
1.32: 64
1.41: 336, 475, 594, 595
1.44: 335
1.45: 607
2.4: 65
2.9: 146, 608
2.11: 335
2.12: 284, 334, 336
2.17–20: 600
2.17–21: 598
2.19: 146, 608
2.20: 334, 335, 394
2.25: 467
2.28: 420, 467
2.30: 65
2.31: 393
2.34: 592
3.3: 64
3.8f.: 600
3.9: 335
3.19: 506
3.21: 65
3.24: 64
3.25: 286
3.28: 77, 335
4.3: 65
4.5: 64
4.11: 64, 141, 277, 279, 597
4.12: 64, 514, 596
4.21: 603
4.22: 64, 476
4.25: 285
4.25f.: 596
4.26: 393, 469
4.28: 336
4.30: 471

4.33: 283, 328
4.36: 64
4.37: 64
4.38: 64
4.39: 476
4.42: 141
4.45f.: 63
4.46: 64
4.47–49: 63
5.12: 64
5.23: 141, 277, 279
5.25: 64, 65
5.27: 466
5.28: 64
5.29: 64
5.31: 153
5.32: 594
6.3: 64
6.10f.: 63
6.19: 64
7.1: 471
7.2: 594
7.10: 335
7.16: 286
8.3: 279
8.10: 393
8.16: 279
8.19: 393, 469, 596
9.7, 22, 24: 17
9.9: 394, 495, 592
9.14: 286
9.15: 597, 599
9.16: 595
9.18: 592
9.20: 603
9.23: 607
10.1f.: 466
10.1–3: 605
10.2: 286
10.5: 64
10.6: 603
10.12: 64
10.15f.: 548
10.16: 477
11.4–6: 64
11.8: 153
11.13: 64
11.16: 467
11.22: 64
11.26: 64, 65
11.29: 471
11.31: 476
12.3: 477
12.7f.: 594
12.15: 336
12.22: 336
12.23: 473
12.28: 465
12.28a: 131
12.30: 286
13.2: 285
13.6: 151
13.11: 466
13.12: 151, 240–41, 289
13.15: 595, 600
13.17: 593
14.24f.: 63
14.27: 474
14.29: 600
15.2: 64
15.3: 289
15.6: 392, 441
15.12: 477
15.12f.: 440
15.16: 336
16.1: 466
16.2: 64
16.7: 64
16.9: 473
16.19: 289, 291, 335
17.2–4: 63
17.4: 595
17.5: 466
17.12: 474
17.13: 151, 240, 289
18.9: 65
18.16: 336
19.1f.: 472
19.3: 65, 234
19.4: 475
19.8f.: 63
19.10: 151, 607
19.11: 467
19.16: 285
19.18: 393, 469
19.20: 240, 289

20.1: 472
20.5: 468
20.5f.: 393
20.6: 468
20.7: 468
20.8: 336
20.12: 285
21.3: 475
21.8: 151, 608
21.18: 608
21.21: 289, 466, 240
21.22: 285
22.6: 141
22.8: 151, 437, 607
22.16: 282, 605
22.20f.: 422
22.21: 466
22.24: 466, 467
23.12: 336, 472
23.24: 132
23.25: 471
24.9: 64
24.13: 466, 475, 476
25.3: 467
25.12: 498, 594
25.18: 599
25.19: 472
26.3: 394, 595
26.5: 606
26.10: 394
26.18f.: 64
27.5: 593
28.1: 64
28.7: 596
28.8: 465
28.12: 64, 477
28.22: 465
28.26: 599
29.4: 592
29.18: 472
30.1–3: 471
30.4: 17, 285
30.12: 233, 289, 291, 336
30.13: 289, 290, 291, 336
30.15: 378, 394
30.16: 477
30.17: 285
30.17f.: 508
30.17–18: 430
30.18: 394
30.19: 394, 595
31.6: 146, 608
31.12: 153
31.20: 328
31.26: 64, 466
32: 270, 284, 330
32.1: 273, 274
32.2: 273
32.6: 195, 390, 596
32.7: 198
32.8: 272
32.8–11: 193
32.8–20: 366
32.10: 331, 333
32.12: 331
32.13: 193
32.14: 142, 331
32.15: 359, 390, 596
32.16: 332
32.17: 363
32.18: 196, 390, 596
32.22: 194, 391
32.23: 333
32.25: 290
32.26: 389
32.29: 151, 285, 360
32.30: 390
32.35: 391
32.36: 390
32.37: 389, 596
32.38: 273, 274
32.39: 333
32.40: 330, 360
32.40–41: 361
32.41: 274
32.41f.: 333
32.43: 391
32.8–20: 363
33.3: 332, 333
33.4–5: 194
33.6: 273, 608
33.7: 332

33.8: 332, 333, 390
33.9: 145, 332, 388
33.10: 273
33.12: 328
33.20: 388
33.22: 290, 333
33.23: 390
33.24: 273
33.29: 390
34.4: 596
34.6f.: 598
34.9: 604

Joshua

1.7: 239
7.7: 394
9.24: 281
10.40: 281
18.2: 282
19.50: 281

Judges

1: 149
1.2: 393
1.8: 590
1.8f.: 146
1.9: 603
1.10: 525
1.11: 598
1.12: 148, 449
1.16: 284, 604
1.20f.: 591
1.21: 149, 217
1.22: 598
1.23: 598
1.24: 596
1.25: 590
1.26: 598
1.27: 603, 605
1.28: 590
1.29: 604, 605
1.30: 605
1.31: 605
1.33: 591, 605
1.35f.: 598
2.1: 281, 284
2.2: 607
2.3: 394
2.14: 607
2.16f.: 591
2.17: 595
2.18: 334, 394
2.18a: 441
2.19: 334, 472
2.23: 607
3.5f.: 604
3.6: 590
3.11: 282
3.16: 599
3.17: 598
3.19: 591
3.20: 141
3.23: 545, 603
3.24: 599
3.25: 141, 303, 597
3.26: 284
3.26f.: 604
3.27: 599
3.28: 607
3.30: 282
3.31: 604
4.1: 589
4.2: 143, 598
4.3: 591
4.4: 605
4.4f.: 143, 588
4.4–6: 562
4.5: 284
4.6: 466
4.11: 284
4.16: 590, 592
4.17: 604
4.20: 466
4.21: 282
4.22: 563, 587, 597, 606
5: 270
5.2: 274
5.3: 274
5.6: 332
5.8: 333
5.9: 274
5.10: 274
5.17: 388
5.21: 273
5.24: 197
5.25–27: 358

5.26: 143, 284, 313
5.26f.: 506
5.29: 330
5.30: 312, 334
5.31: 282
6.2: 394, 592
6.3: 394, 439, 602
6.4: 142, 284, 334, 601
6.5: 289, 334
6.8: 605
6.10: 607
6.11: 141, 597
6.13: 153, 283, 374, 427, 469
6.15: 336
6.18: 239, 280
6.19: 592, 604
6.21: 591
6.24: 598
6.25: 466, 477
6.25f.: 466
6.27: 371
6.28: 591
6.31: 468
6.33: 604
6.34: 604
6.35: 604
6.39: 286
6.40: 590
7.1: 591, 598
7.3: 468, 590
7.4: 474
7.5: 335
7.6: 590
7.7: 477, 605
7.8: 590, 591
7.10f.: 146
7.11: 477
7.11f.: 143, 518, 597
7.13: 141, 145, 545, 587, 588, 597, 603, 606
7.14: 505, 595
7.18: 476
7.19: 592
7.24: 604
7.25: 136, 590
8.1: 277
8.4: 303, 588, 597
8.7: 472
8.9: 472
8.9f.: 598
8.11: 279, 591
8.12: 590
8.16f.: 590
8.19: 380, 469
8.20: 607
8.28: 282, 607
8.29f.: 591
8.33–35: 607
9.2: 466
9.5: 282
9.7: 153, 469
9.9: 394, 424
9.11: 380, 468
9.13: 394, 468
9.15: 468
9.18: 590
9.19: 153, 469, 470
9.20: 468
9.25: 284
9.29: 336
9.43: 597
9.44: 604
9.45: 590, 605
9.48: 506
9.51f.: 591
9.56f.: 590
10.1: 143, 518, 597
10.4: 335, 599, 600
10.6: 607
10.10: 283
11.6: 466
11.10: 285
11.17: 590, 607
11.18: 277, 279, 607
11.19f.: 607
11.23: 336
11.24: 474
11.28: 607
11.29: 590
11.34: 141, 517, 597, 598

11.35: 335
11.36: 392
11.37: 238–39, 286, 465
11.39: 591
11.39f.: 600
11.39–40: 320
11.40: 334
12.1: 336
12.2: 558, 607
12.3: 281
12.5: 334, 602
12.6: 334, 601
12.9: 591
12.14: 596
13.2: 146, 598, 599
13.3: 477
13.4: 152, 285, 584
13.5: 478
13.7: 608
13.8: 289
13.9: 141, 516, 597, 598
13.14: 288
13.16: 285
13.18: 150
13.19: 143, 520, 588, 597
13.20: 141, 597
13.20f.: 607
13.23: 394, 469
14.3f.: 591, 597
14.4: 143
14.5: 143, 597
14.6: 599, 607
14.8: 599
14.9: 607
14.10: 334, 600
14.15: 152, 285
14.18: 394, 469
15.1: 607
15.2: 149
15.3: 595
15.7: 430
15.14: 605, 606
15.18: 148, 467
15.19: 593
16.2: 594
16.4: 599
16.5: 465
16.8f.: 143
16.9: 141, 607
16.10: 283, 336
16.12: 141, 597
16.13: 218, 336
16.16: 284, 394
16.18: 145, 542, 602
16.20: 286, 591
16.23: 594, 604
16.26f.: 598
16.31: 591
17.1: 599
17.3: 335, 377, 394
17.5f.: 598
17.6: 334, 473
17.7: 143, 597, 598
17.9: 77, 335
18.1: 143
18.1f.: 606
18.7: 141, 302, 513, 588, 596, 598, 599
18.9: 286
18.10: 472
18.12: 496, 593, 598
18.15f.: 597
18.17: 141, 507
18.18: 604
18.22: 284
18.22f.: 605
18.25: 467
18.27: 590, 604
18.28: 598
18.29: 598
18.30: 591
18.31: 282
19.2: 281, 282
19.3: 598
19.8: 602
19.9: 418
19.10: 524, 598
19.11: 237–38, 240, 566
19.13: 465
19.15: 599
19.16: 143, 587

19.16f.: 606
19.17: 77, 335
19.18: 329, 597
19.20: 288
19.22: 561
19.23–25: 607
19.27: 141, 597
19.28: 597
19.30: 602
20.4f.: 555, 605
20.12f.: 607
20.15: 592
20.16: 335
20.17: 604
20.27: 106, 598
20.28: 143
20.31: 595
20.32: 465, 590
20.33: 141, 597, 604
20.34: 138, 591
20.35: 599
20.37: 604
20.40: 591, 604
20.41: 604
20.42: 591
20.42f.: 595
20.46: 139, 282
20.48: 592, 604
21.1f.: 604
21.7: 126
21.8: 591
21.9: 599
21.10: 466
21.14: 607
21.15: 604
21.20: 466
21.21: 148, 476
21.22: 335, 336
21.24f.: 598
21.25: 334, 473

1 Samuel

1.10: 77, 600
1.11: 285
2.1: 388
2.4: 389
2.5: 389
2.6: 271
2.6f.: 136
2.29: 282
12.3: 238, 240
12.19: 240
13.17: 140, 334
14.28: 282
18.5: 140
25.25: 239

2 Samuel

1.27: 282
12.31: 603
13.12: 239
13.18: 602, 603
14.17: 240
19.38: 238, 241
22: 271, 330
22.2: 330
22.3: 334
22.4: 330
22.5: 140, 332, 390
22.5–20: 364–66
22.7: 313, 331, 390
22.8: 332, 390
22.9: 332, 390
22.14: 332, 390
22.15: 390
22.16: 76
22.20: 389
22.22: 363
22.29: 115, 145
22.33–46: 333
22.34: 332
22.37: 330
22.38: 331
22.40: 331
22.42: 331
22.43: 331
22.44: 389
22.47: 330
22.50: 274

1 Kings

7.8: 284
12.9: 238, 241
15.11: 342
15.19: 240–41
17.21: 289
18.4: 603
19.10: 282

19.13: 587
19.14: 271, 282

2 Kings

4.10: 238, 241
6.17: 240–41
6.27: 276
18.3f.: 75
18.29: 240
23.4: 603

Isaiah

3.16: 271
5.19: 290
9.2: 342
12.1: 284
24.6: 272
40.12: 277
41.1–5: 284
41.5: 279
41.28: 276
42.6: 284

Ezekiel

14.7: 276
16.11: 68
16.13: 68
44.8: 279

Hosea

6.1: 284
11.4: 284

Amos

3.6: 285
5.8: 272
6.3: 272, 277, 279
9.5: 272
9.6: 272
9.15: 608

Zechariah

1.3: 238
9.5: 240

Psalms

12.6: 238, 290
18.2: 330, 334
18.3: 290, 334
18.4: 330
18.4–20: 284
18.5: 140, 332, 390
18:5–20: 271
18.7: 314, 331, 332, 390
18.8: 332, 390
18.9: 332
18.14: 332
18.20: 389
18.22: 363
18.23: 145
18.26f.: 136
18:33–46: 271, 331, 333
18.34: 332
18.37: 330
18.38: 330
18.40: 331
18.42: 331
18.43: 331
18.44: 389
18.47: 330, 334
18.50: 274
37.36: 68
40.18: 289
44: 284
45.11f.: 275
45.12: 275
46.11: 238
47: 284
51.20: 240
55.3: 238
55.8: 238
59.17: 238
61.3: 290
68: 284
68.2: 240
71.16: 238
90: 284
90.16: 240
91.5: 290
95.2: 238
104.20: 275, 285
107: 284
121.3: 240
142.3: 238

Job

9.16: 259
34.29: 276

Ruth

1.17: 343

Daniel

5.10: 270
6.8: 270
8.12: 284

General Index

affix, 6, 75, 210–11, 384
anaphoric, 43, 390, 448–49, 516, 530
anterior, 8–10, 14, 19, 30, 48, 62, 139, 143–44, 157, 159, 167, 175, 182, 191, 195, 212, 214, 216–20, 245, 272–73, 283, 333, 337, 339–42, 344, 353, 356, 359, 362–63, 367, 369–70, 372, 374–75, 381, 383–87, 390, 392–93, 395, 400, 407, 429, 441, 445, 457, 462, 464, 469–70, 477, 505, 594–96, 603, 610
apodosis, 26–27, 45, 58, 94, 123, 133–34, 136–37, 139, 152–53, 179, 199, 227, 274–75, 288, 317, 335–36, 350, 354–56, 361–62, 371–73, 375, 379, 384, 386–89, 391–98, 402–8, 410–13, 422, 426–36, 439–40, 442, 450, 462–63, 467–70, 474, 477, 501, 508, 593–94, 596, 599, 608
apposition, 16, 19
Archaic Hebrew, 2–3, 20, 34, 57, 76, 101, 158, 191, 199–200, 228, 230, 242, 245, 284, 288, 300, 312, 325, 341, 358–59, 383, 386, 396, 398, 433, 463
aspect, 1, 10, 13–15, 17, 19, 21, 29, 43, 47, 62–63, 75, 109, 114–16, 124, 157, 195, 220, 249, 295, 298, 310, 314, 325, 362, 370, 374, 378–79, 382, 386, 393–94, 429, 441, 469, 482, 494–95, 499–500, 505, 507, 509–10, 527, 533–35, 538, 540–41, 546, 548–49, 562, 571, 574, 585–86, 594–95
assertion, 15, 43, 63, 379–80, 570, 574
asyndesis, 31, 41, 66, 76, 82, 101–2, 140–43, 151, 186, 196, 222, 224, 227, 230, 233–34, 243, 265, 285, 297, 299–301, 320, 333–35, 344, 362–63, 366–67, 372, 383, 387, 389–90, 404, 428–29, 440, 448, 468–69, 472, 480,

492, 495, 497–98, 501, 510–12, 514–16, 520, 523, 547, 554–57, 563, 565–67, 582–83, 586, 591–94, 596, 599–600, 604–5
attendant circumstance, 19–20, 67, 103, 107, 134
auxiliary, 10, 44, 326
background, 2, 15, 42–43, 52, 67, 73, 100, 104–14, 121, 139–45, 151, 155–56, 220, 244, 260, 284, 293, 295, 298, 332, 334, 337, 340, 363–64, 366, 377, 383, 394, 439, 455, 473, 475, 481, 484, 486–89, 492, 495, 505, 512, 514–15, 517–20, 523–24, 528–30, 533–38, 540–44, 547, 549–50, 552–58, 560–63, 565–66, 585, 588, 590–92, 595–98, 600–2, 604–7, 611
biclausal linking, 40–41, 148, 597
bleaching, 7–8, 12, 386
category, 2, 4, 6, 9–10, 13, 15, 40, 60–62, 158, 161, 170, 231, 247, 273, 327, 362, 385, 589
chaining, 21, 27–29, 79, 455, 587
chunk, 44–45, 58, 396–98, 414
chunking, 44, 396
circumstantial, 20, 27–28, 81, 89, 93–95, 100–4, 139–42, 144, 265, 271, 298–300, 302–3, 306, 308, 311, 314–15, 318–19, 325, 328, 331–32, 363, 389–90, 417, 489, 495, 511–12, 514–16, 518, 520–23, 525, 527–31, 533, 536, 540, 552, 559, 561, 588, 590, 592, 595, 597–602, 605
clause linking, 18, 38–41, 73, 134, 152, 199, 361–62, 438, 468, 472, 479
clause-initial, 29, 31, 65, 76, 92, 177, 193, 196–97, 200, 207, 222–23, 225, 228–30, 232, 234, 243, 263, 265, 272–73, 275–76, 288, 291, 303–4, 310, 312, 314–15, 330, 333, 363, 417, 429, 468, 594
clause-type, 4, 18–20, 35–36, 42, 49–50, 53, 57–59, 65, 71–72, 75, 93, 106–7, 109, 116, 134, 146, 155, 191, 195, 198, 201, 221, 229, 242, 245, 262, 279, 288, 291, 320, 325, 349, 354, 381–84, 395, 397, 399–400, 402, 404, 407–8, 410, 416, 419, 425–26, 428, 431, 433–34, 436, 450, 461–63, 470, 479–86, 490, 501, 510,

519, 541, 570–71, 574, 576, 580, 583, 588–89, 600, 610–11
cleft construction, 102, 258, 502, 591
clitic, 19, 129, 133, 151, 153, 158, 160–62, 180, 190, 207, 211–12, 225–27, 249, 251, 253–54, 274, 281, 284, 286, 290, 294, 327, 329, 400–1, 416, 466, 468–69, 608
cohortative, 15–16, 23, 63, 129–31, 133, 146, 151, 197, 210–12, 225, 227, 236–38, 274, 281, 290, 336, 400, 416, 468–69, 582, 607–8
comment, 19–20, 42, 56, 67, 139–40, 142, 149, 359, 425, 445–47, 450, 458, 460, 473–74, 478, 492, 495–96, 498, 500–1, 507–10, 523, 525, 530, 534, 536–37, 541, 547–49, 567–68, 591, 593, 596, 600
comparative, 2, 4–5, 19, 48–49, 51, 57, 72–74, 142, 156, 253, 258, 268, 300, 326, 334–35, 395, 397, 586
complement, 16–17, 25–26, 30, 40, 64, 93, 129–35, 151–52, 224–25, 285, 303–4, 335–36, 390, 414–15, 465, 490–91, 501, 504–6, 511–12, 517, 523, 526, 529, 532, 568, 584, 595, 597, 600, 608
conditional, 26–27, 43, 78, 122, 133, 136, 153, 178, 199, 222, 248, 269, 274, 276, 336, 350, 361–62, 372–73, 375, 379, 386, 389, 398, 400, 402–3, 407–8, 410–11, 413, 427, 433, 436–39, 442, 444–46, 449–51, 464, 468, 470–72, 474, 507–8, 546
conjugation, 2, 9–10, 15, 17, 30, 77, 92, 155–56, 158, 160, 162–63, 166–67, 169–71, 178–79, 183–84, 187–90, 200, 207, 226, 228, 247–48, 250, 252–53, 255, 257, 259, 261, 266, 269, 275, 285–86, 288, 293, 296, 305, 307, 310–11, 333, 337, 339, 341, 344, 348, 397
conjunction, 2–4, 17–18, 22–23, 28–31, 34–36, 41, 48–50, 54–59, 64, 68–72, 75–76, **79–153**, 164–65, 176, 182, 186, 191, 193, 214, 222–24, 229, 258, 266, 289, 319, 331, 336, 344, 347, 350, 354, 374, 381, 383, 387–88, 390, 397, 423, 437–39, 444–45, 471, 481, 486, 507, 532, 546, 564,

566, 570–71, 573, 588–89, 609
connective, 18–19, 21, 25, 29, 41, 59, 66, 78–79, 81–82, 85–86, 89, 91, 97, 101, 133, 135–37, 171, 193, 397, 428, 447–48, 479, 481–82, 484, 611
consecution, 37–38, 72, 82, 481
consecutive, 36–37, 46–47, 49, 58, 71–72, 94, 134, 155, 242, 252, 255, 259, 265, 268, 389, 435, 479–480, 482, 584, 611
  consecutive tense, 1, 3–4, 38, 43, 46, 58, 63, 66, 97, 134, 155, 246, 291, 293, 325, 384, 395, 399, 431, **479–608**, 609, 611
  consecutive *waw*, 1, 37, 46, 49, 54, 71–72, 75, 81, 97, 99, 104, 134–35, 139, 153, 265, 329, 391, 480–82, 611
construction, 1, 6–8, 20, 43–45, 58–62, 64, 78, 97, 102, 105, 109–10, 112, 115, 119–20, 142–43, 145, 147, 178, 187, 213, 230–31, 233, 259, 268–69, 275, 280, 294, 296, 300–4, 324, 326, 328, 333, 335, 337–39, 363, 374, 379, 381, 384–86, 390, 393, **395–478**, 479, 481, 502, 506, 509–10, 523, 525, 534, 561–62, 571, 587, 594, 600, 610
continuity, 3, 37–38, 47, 53–54, 72, 107, 109–10, 112–15, 117, 124, 128, 134–35, 145, 150, 242, 287, 356, 382–83, 399, 407–8, 426, 435–36, 451, 463, 479, 481–86, 491–92, 503, 511, 515, 519, 523, 535, 538–39, 541–42, 544, 549–51, 553, 556–59, 561, 570–71, 573–79, 582–85, 588, 610. *See also* discourse continuity
continuous, 14, 24, 334, 459, 463, 536, 552, 559–60, 572, 608
conversive *waw*, 45–47, 72, 74, 480
coordination, 40–41, 133, 285, 466
cross-linguistic, 5, 8–9, 13, 50–51, 61–63, 157, 294, 337, 341, 360, 385, 531
cursive, 10. *See also* durative
deictic, 15, 29, 67, 217, 283, 315, 484, 563–64, 568
dependency, 40
dependent, 7, 146, 512, 586
diachronic, 4–6, 16, 18, 51, 60, 66, 73, 75, 140, 161, 273, 284, 287, 296, 341, 369,

385–86, 395–97, 434, 453, 461, 480
diegetic present, 171, 317, 330, 334
directive, 21, 23–26, 28, 31, 33, 561
discontinuity, 3, 42, 48–49, 53, 104, 107, 110, 112, 115–17, 122–23, 126, 134, 150, 382, 399, 458, 461, 479–86, 492, 501–2, 504, 506–7, 511, 521, 523, 535, 549–50, 552–54, 556–57, 561, 573, 577, 584–86, 588–89, 591–92, 610–11. *See also* discourse discontinuity
discourse, 1, 15, 19–21, 33, 37–39, 41–42, 51–52, 67, 72–73, 89, 92, 118, 132, 135, 137, 177, 201, 242, 284, 323, 335, 388, 434, 445, 451, 470, 481, 483–84, 507, 533, 554, 556, 574, 584–87, 604, 606
discourse continuity, 35–38, 48–49, 53–54, 97–98, 104–5, 107, 109–10, 115, 118–20, 124, 126–27, 129–30, 133–34, 144, 195, 211, 218, 221–23, 229, 242–43, 246, 325, 376–77, 383–84, 399, 407, 414, 416, 419, 425, 452–56, 458, 461, 470, 479, 481–82, 484–85, 490, 534, 555, 561–62, 564, 566, 570, 574, 576, 583, 587–89, 608, 610–11. *See also* continuity
discourse discontinuity, 53–54, 97, 101, 104, 115–16, 123, 126, 459, 479, 482, 586, 610. *See also* discontinuity
discourse level, 100, 479
discourse type, 19–20, 33–34, 51, 67, 584
domain, 11–13, 21–33, 35–36, 58, 67, 70, 93, 96, 120, 147, 158, 175, 177–78, 196, 198, 242–44, 274, 299, 327, 373, 375, 392, 396, 407, 414, 418–19, 422–24, 432–33, 435–36, 588
domain type, 21, 158, 242, 419, 463
dream report, 334, 545, 560, 563–64, 587–88, 596, 606
durative, 10–11, 43, 159, 249, 282, 601
elaboration, 19, 31, 89–90, 97–99, 114, 134, 138–39, 144, 186–87, 196, 215, 222, 234, 265–66, 320, 334, 348, 394, 455, 458–60, 477–78, 481, 487, 490, 492–94, 497–99, 501, 504–5, 527, 547, 564, 591–95, 607–8
embedded, 23–24, 40, 63, 136, 297, 417, 443, 470, 489, 510, 525, 545

energic, 15, 46, 72, 144, 153, 190, 225–28, 233, 252, 254, 272, 286, 313, 329–32, 334, 359, 480, 594, 601–2
focal, 62, 86, 113, 122–24, 126, 146, 148, 150, 175, 177, 404, 417, 423, 446–47, 450, 455, 458–61, 463, 477, 487–88, 490, 493–95, 508, 523, 526–27, 559, 579, 607
focal result, 123–25, 148–50, 538–39, 577–78, 607
focus, 4, 38, 43, 50, 63, 72, 213–14, 216, 219, 370, 372–73, 481, 483, 493, 502, 517, 523, 526, 556, 563, 583, 585, 590, 606
focus marker, 102, 319, 502, 516, 594, 597
foreground, 1, 15, 42–43, 52, 73–74, 194, 377, 484, 488, 493, 501, 503–4, 517, 521, 533–34, 549–50, 552, 554–65, 567, 587, 590, 603–6, 611
freestanding, 2
future, 1, 9–12, 14, 17, 19, 24, 43–45, 47–48, 61, 70, 78, 112, 122, 125, 132, 139, 147–48, 179, 184, 194–95, 201, 214, 240, 256, 260, 271, 273–74, 285, 294–96, 300, 305–7, 309–12, 315–17, 321–25, 329, 333, 335–36, 340–44, 346, 348, 350, 352, 354–57, 359, 361, 366–67, 369, 372–75, 377, 386–87, 391, 393–98, 403, 406–7, 410–11, 413, 417–21, 424–26, 428–29, 431–33, 435–36, 438–41, 451–53, 455–57, 462–65, 469–70, 472, 475–77, 499–500, 510, 520–21, 541, 548, 554, 559–60, 564, 568–70, 577, 581, 588, 593, 596, 605
future anterior, 214, 341, 346, 357, 375, 393
future perfect, 356, 389
gemination, 34–36, 45, 54, 66, 68–71, 160, 242, 245, 314, 480, 609
general present, 271, 275, 305, 316–17, 321, 342, 451, 477, 519
generalisation, 7, 191, 220, 257, 295, 301, 328, 340, 386, 398
gram, 6–7, 10–11, 13, 20, 50, 60–63, 75, 77, 109, 156–57, 174, 191, 214, 220, 222, 293–96, 299, 304, 321–22, 340–42, 345, 369, 377, 382, 384–86, 392–93, 399, 417, 424, 427, 435, 462, 508, 586, 588. *See also* morpheme, grammatical; verbal form

gram type, 14, 62
grammatical, 6–7, 12–13, 21, 40, 60, 62–63, 69, 129, 131, 133, 158, 205, 225–26, 228, 255, 267, 327, 348, 384–85, 585, 611
  form, 11, 60
  function, 6
  meaning, 6, 9, 13, 44
  morpheme. *See* morpheme, grammatical
grammaticalisation, 5–9, 11, 45, 50–51, 60–62, 73, 156–57, 191, 213, 247, 293–95, 300, 337, 384, 392
habitual, 14, 19, 43, 47–48, 105, 113, 120–22, 139, 142, 147, 193, 212, 221–22, 271, 284, 293, 295–96, 298, 305, 307, 309, 314, 316–17, 320–21, 325–26, 331–32, 334–35, 363, 366, 369, 378–79, 394–96, 425–26, 432–33, 438–42, 451, 453–55, 457, 471–73, 476–78, 509–10, 537, 539, 542, 544, 546–47, 562, 586, 593–94, 599–602
historical linguistics, 4
homonymy, 13, 205, 228, 242, 296, 325, 425, 468, 610
homophony, 34–36, 70, 210, 244, 246, 609
hypotaxis, 41, 136
illocutionary, 40, 140, 195
imperative, 15, 23, 25, 32–33, 65–66, 96, 120, 130–31, 133, 147, 151, 197–98, 224–25, 238, 255–57, 261, 278, 280, 287, 335, 348, 394, 400, 408–9, 411, 415–17, 464, 468, 475, 486, 506, 570, 573, 582–83, 608
imperfective, 4, 9–11, 14–15, 17, 24, 43, 47–49, 57, 63, 65, 68, 74, 76–77, 109, 114, 142, 155–56, 160–67, 170, 178, 183–84, 187–91, 193, 200, 202–3, 207–9, 211, 226, 228–29, 246, 249–51, 253, 255–56, 258, 260–61, 266, 269, 272, 277, 279–80, **293–336**, 363, 381, 389–90, 395, 417–18, 424, 426, 435, 457, 461–63, 482, 514, 516, 519, 533–36, 538–39, 541, 544, 549, 558, 571, 584, 586–87, 589, 600–1, 609–10. *See also* long *yiqṭol*
indicative, 2–4, 11, 15, 21–22, 26–30, 32, 35, 43, 45, 55, 62, 71–72, 77, 157–58, 160, 166, 170, 174–75, 177, 179, 184, 186, 191, 196–97, 201, 207–9, 212, 214–15, 218, 240–43, 245–48, 253–54, 270, 280–82, 285, 287, 298,

326, 383, 480, 570, 588–89, 609–10
inductive *waw*, 46–47. *See also* conversive *waw*
infinitive, 16, 26, 64, 87, 99, 142, 255, 260, 264, 272, 275, 280, 311, 330, 377, 402, 411, 442, 463, 600, 602
inflection, 14–15, 60, 220, 327, 385
initial position, 37, 59, 65, 76, 110, 131, 174, 188–89, 191, 200, 202, 222, 224, 229–30, 245, 263, 276, 288, 291, 318–19, 325, 390, 417, 585
initial verb, 1, 196, 310
instruction, 19, 33, 37, 53–54, 96, 99, 120, 129, 136, 139, 234, 322, 400, 403, 409, 411, 413–20, 424, 436, 455, 459–60, 464–66, 481, 498, 530, 539, 559, 570, 572–73, 577–78, 582, 592, 597
interclausal, 41
interruption, 38, 108–9, 359, 366, 479–80, 482, 486–87, 492, 497, 509, 511, 515, 520, 523, 529–30, 532–36, 538, 541, 549, 571, 574–75, 586, 589, 593
intrusion, 30, 245, 247, 453, 455
invasion, 11, 17, 222, 382. *See also* intrusion
irrealis, 12, 52–54, 57, 69, 76–77, 122, 157–58, 160–61, 209, 212, 223–25, 229, 242, 247–48, 280, 285, 341, 344, 359–61, 379
jussive, 2–4, 23, 25–26, 33, 35–36, 45, 48–49, 55, 64, 69–72, 76, 89, 93, 129–31, 133, 151–52, 155–58, 160–63, 165–66, 168–72, 174–81, 183–84, 187–91, 196–200, 202–3, 207–8, 211–12, 222–33, 235–36, 238–48, 250–54, 256, 258–61, 263, 265, 269–71, 273–75, 277–78, 281, 284–86, 288–91, 296, 324, 329, 336, 391, 400–1, 406, 416, 418, 425, 465–69, 486, 570, 573–75, 582–84, 588, 603, 608–10
linked to, 41, 56, 80, 320, 456, 501, 504
locative, 80, 280, 294, 326
long *yiqṭol*, 1–4, 10, 16–17, 49, 53, 55, 57, 63, 65, 69, 76–77, 101–2, 104–5, 109, 112, 140, 142, 144, 152, 200, 204, 206, 211, 223, 228–30, 232–33, 235, 239–40, 246, 248, 272, 276, 278–81, 286–89, 291, **293–336**, 395, 417, 425, 431, 443, 463,

479, 536, 570–71, 609. *See also yiqṭol(u)*
macro-syntax, 3, 21, 53, 102, 107, 114, 145, 439, 469, 483
main clause, 16, 22, 28, 57, 96, 100, 102, 120, 136, 139, 147, 152, 198, 201, 223, 253, 294, 297–304, 306, 308, 312, 316, 318–19, 362, 376, 390, 399, 402, 436, 438–39, 441, 443, 445–46, 450, 462, 473, 489, 501, 504, 510–16, 518, 522, 525–27, 529–31, 535, 539–41, 546, 581, 599
main line, 37–38, 41, 53, 57, 97, 100, 103, 105, 109, 143, 159, 192–93, 265, 295, 311, 331, 334, 359, 363, 366, 377, 383, 389–90, 440–41, 451, 472, 475, 479, 482–84, 492–93, 501, 503–4, 511–13, 516, 520, 523–24, 530, 535–36, 538–41, 543, 546–47, 549–50, 552, 554–55, 559, 562–67, 569–71, 574–75, 582, 586–88, 593, 600–1, 605
marker, 10, 14, 21, 42, 63, 69, 82, 89, 102, 116, 135, 137, 146, 155, 158, 183, 217, 226, 249, 255, 294–98, 318–19, 326, 335, 445, 484–85, 502, 516, 594, 597
matrix, 103–4, 141, 502
modal, 1, 26, 31–32, 47, 57, 63, 77–78, 88, 93, 96, 120, 140–41, 147, 158, 175, 196, 198, 203, 226, 237, 242–43, 249, 322, 330, 334, 369, 399–400, 407–8, 413, 419, 451, 465, 582, 588
modal sequence, 32–33, 175, 198, 228, 237, 242–43, 257, 291, 384, 397, 400, 407–9, 411, 413–21, 424, 426, 432–33, 436, 450, 462, 464–66, 559, 570–71, 573–74, 582–84
modality, 10–13, 63, 223, 242, 559, 585
mood, 2, 13–15, 63, 69, 158, 198, 225, 248–49, 274–75, 336, 362
morpheme, 4, 6–9, 14–17, 22, 34, 44–45, 60–63, 69–70, 105, 147, 155, 216, 225–27, 229, 231, 233, 236, 247, 270, 272, 279, 286, 288, 297, 301, 325, 327, 340, 358–59, 382, 385, 396–97, 410, 428–29, 439, 441, 443, 462, 502, 504, 508, 511, 536, 541, 543, 549, 561, 571, 580, 584, 586, 589

grammatical, 6–10, 13, 21, 60, 71, 75, 157, 213, 220–21, 341, 385–86. *See also* gram; verbal form
lexical, 7
verbal, 3, 6, 8, 13, 20, 59, 73, 155–56, 213, 218, 295, 324–25, 339, 341, 385, 397, 462, 485, 502, 514, 533, 570, 574, 609–10
narrative, 10, 15, 19, 22, 28–31, 33, 37, 43, 50, 53, 71, 73, 75, 82, 84–87, 89, 92, 97, 103, 105, 107, 109–11, 114, 118, 120–21, 128, 136–39, 146, 158–59, 163–64, 167, 170, 177, 179–82, 184–87, 191–94, 201, 204–5, 214, 221–22, 242–47, 252, 261–63, 266, 268–69, 273, 282, 284, 286–87, 296, 311, 313, 315, 323, 327, 339–40, 342, 345, 352, 358–59, 363–66, 368, 382–83, 387, 390, 419, 473, 481, 488–89, 501, 504, 506–7, 509, 520, 523–24, 530, 533–36, 540–41, 543–45, 548, 554–55, 558–61, 563, 565, 567, 571, 574, 580, 584, 586–88, 601, 604–6
narrative chain, 28, 31, 86–87, 118, 164, 193, 282, 545
narrator, 39, 140, 263, 358, 495–96, 591
native speaker, 40, 155
non-consecutive, 1, 37, 480
non-initial, 1, 31, 110, 188, 191, 196, 228, 232, 274–75, 315, 319, 325, 440, 585
non-initial verb, 1
obligation, 12, 53, 132, 203, 218, 278, 289, 307, 310, 317, 321–23, 325, 329, 335–36, 350, 395, 403, 411, 414, 417–20, 424–25, 432–36, 439–40, 447, 451–53, 455, 457, 462–64, 466, 472–73, 475–77, 498–99, 510, 521, 541, 548, 559, 569, 573, 577, 597
oral, 17, 34, 68, 267, 533
orthoepy, 34–35, 480
paragogic *heh*, 15–16, 197, 225, 235–38, 283, 290
parataxis, 41
participle, 17, 57, 102, 106, 141, 143, 213, 271, 284, 300–1, 384, 456, 474, 492, 512–14, 519–20, 552, 586, 599, 605
active, 17, 77, 101, 107, 140, 295, 300, 304, 312, 315–16, 319, 325, 443, 453, 455–56, 522, 531, 563–64, 581. *See also qoṭel*
passive, 243, 334, 384

past, 1–3, 8–10, 12, 14, 17, 19, 24, 30–31, 34–36, 45, 47, 49, 55, 61, 66, 68–71, 73, 75–77, 85, 105–6, 109, 118, 121–22, 124, 140, 142–45, 147, 156–59, 163–67, 170–72, 174, 177, 179–82, 184–86, 191–96, 198, 200, 202–5, 211–12, 214–15, 217, 219–20, 222, 242, 245–50, 252–53, 255–56, 260–62, 264, 266, 271–73, 281–82, 284, 293–96, 298–99, 304–9, 311–15, 317–20, 323–26, 331–34, 336, 339–43, 345, 347–50, 352–56, 358–59, 363, 365–71, 373–76, 378, 384–85, 387–88, 390–92, 394–95, 400, 407, 426, 436, 438–39, 441, 451, 453–55, 462, 464, 470, 472–73, 476–78, 490, 504, 507, 509–10, 514, 517, 520, 533–36, 538–40, 542, 544, 547–50, 554–59, 561, 572, 588, 593–96, 599–602, 609–10

path, 5, 7–9, 51, 62, 156, 191–92, 213, 220, 247, 280, 293–96, 341, 369, 384–86, 392

perfect, 6, 10, 14, 16, 22, 26, 30, 49, 59, 78, 133, 145, 157, 159, 199, 256, 259, 263, 280, 315, 338, 359, 385, 387–89, 391–92, 601–3. *See also* future perfect; prophetic perfect

perfective, 2, 8–10, 14–15, 19, 28–31, 34–36, 43, 47–49, 55, 61, 63, 66, 68–69, 71, 89, 106, 118, 121, 124, 156–64, 167, 170–71, 178–82, 185–87, 191–96, 200–5, 211–14, 217, 220–22, 228, 230, 242–50, 253–54, 256, 258, 260–63, 266, 272, 277, 280–81, 284, 287, 294–99, 305, 313, 318, 324, 328, 333, **337–94**, 395, 400, 407, 441, 462, 470, 490, 495, 504, 507–10, 533–35, 541–42, 544, 548–50, 554–57, 562, 572, 584, 586, 595, 609–10. *See also qaṭal*

performative, 17, 65, 112, 335, 354, 359–61, 368–69, 377–78, 389, 391, 393, 429–30, 457, 464, 469, 502–3, 508, 543, 580–81, 594–96

pluperfect, 12–13, 109, 143–44, 159, 212, 219–20, 283–84, 341, 347, 351, 363, 369, 372, 376, 470, 489–90, 528, 549–50, 552–53, 557, 566, 591, 604–5

polysemy, 13

position, 2, 7, 17, 22, 25, 30–31, 37–38, 45, 52, 58–59, 61, 65–67, 69–70, 72, 74, 76, 109–10, 131, 137, 140, 160, 163, 174, 176–77, 188–89, 191, 193, 196, 200, 202, 222–24, 229–31, 245–46, 249–50, 257, 262–63, 267, 271, 276, 278–79, 286–88, 291, 293, 297, 300–1, 318–19, 325, 383, 390, 407, 410, 417, 420, 425, 440, 447, 455, 458–59, 488, 512–13, 515, 520–22, 585, 588, 609–10
syntactic, 7
pragmatic, 1, 59, 72, 81, 103, 111, 135, 139, 200, 242, 273, 449, 481–82, 484, 515–16, 518, 531, 535–36, 539, 543, 547, 571, 578–79
predication, 40, 139, 274, 338–39, 385, 512
prefix conjugation, 2, 15, 17, 77, 155–56, 160, 162–63, 166, 169–70, 178, 183, 187–90, 200, 226, 228, 247, 252–53, 255, 259, 266, 269, 275, 285–86, 288, 293, 296, 305, 310–11, 333, 348
prefix consonant, 35, 242, 245, 314, 609
present, 1, 8–11, 17, 19, 22, 40, 45, 57, 61, 65, 77, 137, 165, 171, 184, 191, 195, 212–15, 217, 248, 256, 259, 271–73, 282–83, 294–95, 299–300, 306–7, 310–12, 316–17, 321, 325–26, 330–31, 335, 340–45, 348–49, 351, 357, 359–60, 362, 369, 371–72, 378, 388, 393, 405, 426, 431–32, 442, 451, 454, 469, 476, 503, 529, 537, 580, 600. *See also* diegetic present; general present; progressive present
present anterior, 195, 216, 218, 283, 347, 366, 373, 378, 389, 392, 596
proclitic, 41, 54–55, 79, 82, 86, 89, 116, 156, 158, 163, 169–71, 180, 191, 200, 202, 208, 229, 242, 246, 249, 281, 313–14, 347, 359, 366, 390, 397
progressive, 6, 10–11, 14, 17, 19, 63, 77, 280, 294–95, 300, 304, 306, 310–21, 325–26, 329, 331, 334–35, 366, 390, 451, 453–54, 476, 512, 514, 516–17, 563, 600
progressive present, 57, 274, 307–9, 312, 315, 317, 320, 330, 334, 360, 389, 476–77
prophetic perfect, 194, 201, 273, 340, 367, 391

protasis, 19, 26–27, 63–65, 67, 122–23, 133, 139, 148, 150, 152, 178–79, 199–200, 222, 269, 274–77, 285, 310, 317, 335–36, 349, 354–56, 361–62, 371–73, 375, 379, 389–94, 398–99, 402–4, 406–7, 410–13, 421–22, 426, 428, 430, 433–37, 440, 442–43, 448, 464, 467–68, 470–71, 473–75, 501–2, 507–8, 546, 581, 593, 599–600, 608
prototypical, 11, 76, 157–58, 213, 247, 251, 301, 306, 311, 320, 325, 341, 363, 370, 372, 384, 386, 388, 399, 407, 462, 521–22, 570, 574
purpose clause, 25, 64, 91, 128–31, 152, 198–99, 211, 265, 276, 281, 285, 468
qaṭal, 1–4, 10, 17–19, 37, 42, 45–48, 52, 55, 57, 59, 64–65, 70, 72–74, 95, 97–99, 101, 103, 105–9, 111–13, 115–16, 118–19, 122, 124, 126, 131–32, 136, 138, 140–46, 148–53, 193–96, 199–201, 203–5, 207, 209, 213–22, 224–25, 242, 244–46, 271–74, 278–79, 281, 283–85, 299, 302, 306, 311, 313–16, 318, 321, 324, 326, 330–34, **337–94**, 395–97, 422, 424, 426–31, 433, 439, 441, 444, 446, 450, 457, 462, 469–73, 477, 479, 482, 486–97, 501–11, 515, 520, 527–29, 537–38, 540–41, 543, 548–61, 564, 566–68, 570–71, 574–76, 580–81, 584, 586–96, 599–607, 609–10
qoṭel, 10, 18, 64–65, 102–3, 106–7, 115, 121–22, 136, 139–43, 145, 147–48, 150, 192, 199, 213, 271–72, 284, 295, 300–4, 312, 314, 316, 318–21, 325, 328, 332, 334, 366, 371, 417, 433, 450, 453, 455–56, 470–71, 476–78, 483–84, 507, 511–22, 528, 535–37, 545, 549, 552, 555–56, 558–64, 571, 579–80, 586–88, 590, 595–99, 604–7. *See also* participle, active
realis, 36, 52–54, 69–70, 75–76, 122, 146, 157–58, 160, 182, 184, 186, 194, 209, 212, 220–22, 229, 242, 247–48, 250, 252, 258, 262, 269, 280, 282, 284, 287–88, 331, 379, 383, 589
reanalysed, 11–12, 288, 299, 301
receiver, 11, 112, 121, 239, 517, 519, 524, 548

reconstruction, 4, 246
reduction, 7, 61, 385, 397
phonological, 7
semantic, 8
reflexive-benefactive, 15
relative clause, 16, 23–24, 64–65, 77, 151, 192, 196, 213, 222, 230, 233, 283–84, 289, 300–2, 306, 316–18, 328, 333, 335–36, 344, 357, 363, 388–90, 393, 449–50, 464, 474, 501, 510–11, 525, 559, 591, 593, 596, 598–99
relative *waw*, 47
renewal, 10–11, 17, 300, 325–26, 382, 455
result, 7–8, 13, 24, 27, 31–33, 40, 64, 89–90, 94, 113, 119, 123–25, 128, 134–35, 138, 148–52, 156, 160, 184, 191, 214, 235, 246–47, 267, 270, 275, 281, 283, 289, 337–40, 370, 380, 384, 388, 397–405, 407, 411, 413–15, 418, 420–27, 431, 433, 435–36, 450, 462–63, 465–68, 481, 485, 490, 538–39, 572, 577–79, 582, 607
resultative, 8–9, 19, 156–57, 195, 212–14, 246, 280, 337–40, 346, 359–60, 363, 369–70, 372, 384–86, 388–89, 392, 399, 407–8, 462
rhetorical, 39, 64, 473
saliency, 42–43
semantics, 1, 13, 19, 51, 74, 92, 97, 113, 127, 130, 132, 134, 144, 150, 152–53, 212, 271, 408, 418, 425, 427, 435–36, 438, 452, 455, 487, 492, 494–95, 498–501, 512, 521, 523, 529, 535–36, 541, 576, 584, 591–92
sender, 11, 225
sequence, 12, 21–22, 24–25, 28, 30, 32–33, 44, 92, 118, 148, 175, 177, 194–95, 221, 228, 230, 235, 237, 257, 268, 291, 339, 383–84, 388, 396–97, 400, 407–8, 411, 413–16, 418–21, 424–26, 436, 462, 464, 466, 486, 514, 570, 573–74, 582–84, 587, 590
sequential, 1, 26, 28, 31, 40, 44, 50, 80, 82, 89, 99, 111, 116–17, 120, 122–23, 138, 147–48, 192–96, 271, 359, 364, 366, 396, 406, 455, 459–60, 470, 488, 528, 542–43, 576–77, 581, 585, 590, 596, 607
serial verb, 19, 64, 227
short *yiqṭol*, 2–4, 15–16, 34–36, 48–49, 55, 63–64, 69, 76, 118, 130, 147, **155–291**, 318, 324–25, 382–84, 468,

479, 481, 570, 589, 609–10. *See also yiqṭol(Ø)*
signal, 21, 31, 35–36, 49, 52–54, 72, 89–90, 104, 109–10, 114, 116–17, 120–21, 135, 143–44, 158, 174, 177, 207, 214, 217, 219–20, 223–24, 228–29, 232, 242–43, 246, 286, 296, 298, 315–16, 339–41, 347, 361, 364, 366, 369, 376–77, 379, 384, 407, 414, 416, 436, 439, 449, 458, 461, 479, 481–86, 488, 492, 506, 510–11, 517, 523, 533–34, 541–42, 544–45, 550–52, 554–57, 562, 566, 570, 573–74, 576, 585–87, 589, 592
sociation, 40
source construction, 9
stative, 9, 32, 48, 57, 175, 214, 271, 337–38, 343, 345, 348, 351–52, 359, 369, 388, 415
stativic, 109, 144, 170–71, 212, 214–15, 282–83, 326, 335, 338, 344, 359, 369–72, 388–89, 392, 429, 431, 470, 503, 516, 527, 549–50, 552, 556–58, 589, 595–97, 599, 604, 607
storyline, 72, 106–8, 111, 119, 146, 220, 382–83
stress, 7, 68–69, 167, 208–9, 248, 269, 279–80
subjunctive, 11, 15, 43, 62, 158, 160–61, 198, 249–50, 274, 298, 325
subordinate clause, 23, 63, 83, 136, 160, 198, 213, 266, 294, 296–99, 302, 304, 316, 318, 320, 374, 392, 398, 420, 446, 462, 475, 559
subordination, 30, 92, 198, 295, 298, 306, 326, 420, 445, 533
suffix conjugation, 30, 167, 170–71, 179, 184, 255, 257, 261, 339, 344, 397
synchronic, 4, 6, 13, 18, 46, 55–58, 60, 76, 155, 222, 242, 246
syndesis, 32, 41, 83, 97, 100–3, 105–6, 140–43, 150, 224–25, 265, 285, 311, 366, 397, 468–69, 515–16, 520, 523, 525, 527, 550, 554, 565, 591, 605
syntagm, 2, 12, 21, 40–41, 56, 70–71, 74, 77, 102, 139–40, 156, 189, 198, 231, 242, 244, 269, 274, 278–79, 330, 361–62, 388–89, 391, 485
telic, 43
temporal, 1, 13–14, 19, 21, 24, 29, 38, 43, 45, 47, 65, 74–75, 83, 85–86, 89, 93, 109–10, 116–17, 120–22, 124–25, 139, 142, 146, 158, 167,

199, 204, 215–21, 242–44, 247, 273, 276, 278, 289, 294, 298, 303, 305, 307, 309, 313, 319, 333–35, 348, 350–52, 359, 362, 366–67, 369–70, 372, 374, 379, 386, 388, 391, 394, 398–99, 402, 431, 436–44, 446, 450, 454, 458, 462, 468, 470–72, 475–76, 486–87, 491, 497, 500, 521, 523, 531, 533, 538, 540–41, 544, 546, 554, 559–60, 564, 566, 569, 571, 579, 581, 585, 589, 602–6, 608

temporal succession, 31, 39–40, 43, 80, 85–86, 95–96, 116–19, 122, 134, 138, 146, 148, 163, 184, 205, 265, 347, 377, 406, 446, 458, 481, 486–87, 491, 521, 523, 528, 538, 557, 572, 576, 590–91, 604, 607

tense, 3, 8–10, 12–15, 17, 40, 45–47, 54–59, 63, 65, 67, 69–70, 74–75, 155, 157, 159, 171, 180, 185–86, 214, 225, 246–50, 252–53, 255–56, 259, 261, 271, 283, 307, 310, 325, 327, 333–34, 344, 351, 362, 386, 388, 391, 393, 396, 462, 464, 481, 485, 533–34, 549, 580, 585, 611

text-linguistics, 37, 39, 42, 52, 479–80, 482, 484–85, 570, 574

Tiberian reading tradition, 34–35, 480

topic, 43, 72, 74, 152, 291, 445–48, 450, 473–74, 481, 483, 501, 507–10, 541, 548–49, 554, 567–68, 585–87, 592–93, 596, 603

typology, 5, 13, 47, 53, 56–57, 60, 294, 395, 476

unidirectional, 9

ventive, 15–16, 63, 129–31, 133, 141, 147, 151, 153, 197, 210–12, 225–28, 233, 235–41, 254, 274, 281, 283–84, 286, 288, 290, 295, 313, 327, 329–30, 336, 400–1, 416, 466, 468–69, 608

verbal category, 4, 10

verbal form, 1, 5, 8, 10–13, 15, 21, 29, 36–37, 40, 45–52, 54–57, 61, 71–72, 74–75, 77, 155, 162, 170, 174, 181, 197, 202, 207, 211, 222, 224, 226–27, 229, 233, 237, 242, 245, 253, 256, 260, 262, 273, 296, 298–300, 310, 314, 327, 337, 348, 383, 391, 417, 470, 486, 587. *See also* gram; morpheme, grammatical

verbal noun, 10, 105, 442–43, 448, 470, 472
verbless clause, 66, 103, 106, 121, 124, 126, 141–42, 187, 217–18, 244, 272, 406, 411, 443, 445, 447, 480, 483, 505, 509–11, 518, 523–25, 527–29, 531–32, 552–53, 559, 565–68, 570, 586, 599, 605
volitive, 16, 43, 70, 131, 139, 197, 223, 226–27, 230, 235–39, 243, 247–48, 271, 274–75, 287, 289–91, 317, 324, 332, 336, 346, 349, 369, 379, 386, 392, 394, 401, 404, 407, 415–16, 418–19, 468, 475, 559, 570–71, 574, 583
wa(y)-yiqṭol, 19, 36–37, 42, 47–48, 50, 52–55, 57, 63, 66, 72–76, 78, 95, 97–99, 101–11, 113, 115–16, 118–21, 124, 126, 128, 136, 138–46, 149–51, 155, 184, 192–96, 201, 203–5, 209, 211, 213–22, 229, 233, 243–46, 248, 271–72, 275, 278–79, 281–84, 287–88, 301–4, 313–14, 319–20, 322–23, 332, 334, 359, 364, 366, 368, 371, 376, 380, 382–83, 388, 390–91, 394–95, 444–46, 470, 473, 480–81, 485–97, 503, 507–9, 511–20, 523–29, 535–55, 557–67, 569–72, 575–76, 580, 584–93, 595–601, 603–7, 609–11
wa-qaṭal, 4, 36–37, 43, 45, 47–48, 50, 52–55, 57–59, 64–65, 74–78, 96, 99, 104–5, 107–9, 111–14, 116–17, 119–23, 125–28, 131–34, 136, 139, 142–53, 199, 203, 218, 222, 229, 234, 236, 275–76, 278–79, 284, 287, 289, 313, 323, 325, 332–34, 358–62, 366–67, 369, 380–81, 384, 388–94, **395–478**, 479, 481, 485–86, 492, 497–500, 508–10, 519–22, 529–32, 535, 541–49, 554, 559–60, 564, 567–73, 575–82, 584, 586–89, 593–94, 596–603, 605–11
waw-less, 1, 46, 284, 333
word order, 1–2, 17, 38, 52–54, 60–61, 65, 69, 72, 75–76, 82, 112–13, 136, 177, 189, 191, 193, 196–97, 200, 203, 228–30, 232–35, 240, 245–46, 287–88, 293, 296–98, 310, 313, 319, 325, 382, 440, 443, 493, 533–34, 549, 570, 585–86, 610
yaqtul, 2, 28–33, 36, 48–49, 54, 71–72, 89, 92–93, 118, 146, 155–58, 160–79, 181–89,

191, 197, 200, 206–7, 209, 225–26, 245–50, 252–54, 256, 258–59, 261, 264–66, 268–69, 279–80, 286, 294–99, 305, 308–9, 311, 318, 324–28, 339, 342, 348–49, 351–53, 382–83, 400–1, 405–6, 410, 412–13, 464, 534, 588–89, 610

yaqtula, 33, 248

yaqtulu, 4, 37, 49, 71–72, 77, 93, 162–63, 165, 170–71, 173–74, 184, 187–89, 206–7, 226, 248–50, 252, 255–56, 259, 266, 280, 286, 293–97, 299–300, 304–11, 324–25, 328–29, 350–51, 353–55, 382, 386–87, 402–6, 432, 435, 464, 467, 471, 534, 609

yiqṭol(u), 16, 18–20, 37, 63, 65–66, 71, 77, 101–2, 104–5, 111, 113–14, 116–17, 120–23, 126–28, 132, 136 37, 139–42, 144–53, 192–93, 195, 199–200, 202–5, 207–11, 214, 222–23, 226, 228–36, 239–40, 248, 271, 275–77, 281, 284–87, 289–91, 293, 295, 297, 299, 301, 303, 305, 307, 309, 311–27, 329–36, 358–66, 370, 374–75, 381, 389–90, 394, 399, 417–21, 423–28, 430–56, 458–61, 463–64, 466–78, 492, 497–501, 506, 508–10, 519, 521, 535–43, 547–49, 554, 558–59, 570, 574–83, 586–87, 589, 591, 593–94, 597, 599–601, 603, 605–8, 610. *See also* long *yiqṭol*

yiqṭol(Ø), 16, 18–19, 34–36, 63, 66, 68, 70–71, 96, 103, 118, 129–31, 133–34, 146–47, 150–53, 158, 192–93, 195–203, 205, 207–15, 218, 220, 222–25, 228–29, 231–33, 235–39, 242–46, 270–77, 279–80, 284–85, 288, 290, 313, 316, 318–19, 331–33, 336, 360, 363–64, 366, 382, 411, 416, 418, 420, 425, 427, 465–66, 468, 475, 486, 571, 573–75, 582–84, 588–89, 608, 610. *See also* short *yiqṭol*

About the Team

Alessandra Tosi was the managing editor for this book and provided quality control.

Anne Burberry performed the copyediting of the book in Word. The fonts used in this volume are Charis SIL and SBL Hebrew.

Cameron Craig created all of the editions — paperback, hardback, and PDF. Conversion was performed with open source software freely available on our GitHub page at https://github.com/OpenBookPublishers.

Jeevanjot Kaur Nagpal designed the cover of this book. The cover was produced in InDesign using Fontin and Calibri fonts.

Cambridge Semitic Languages and Cultures

General Editor Geoffrey Khan

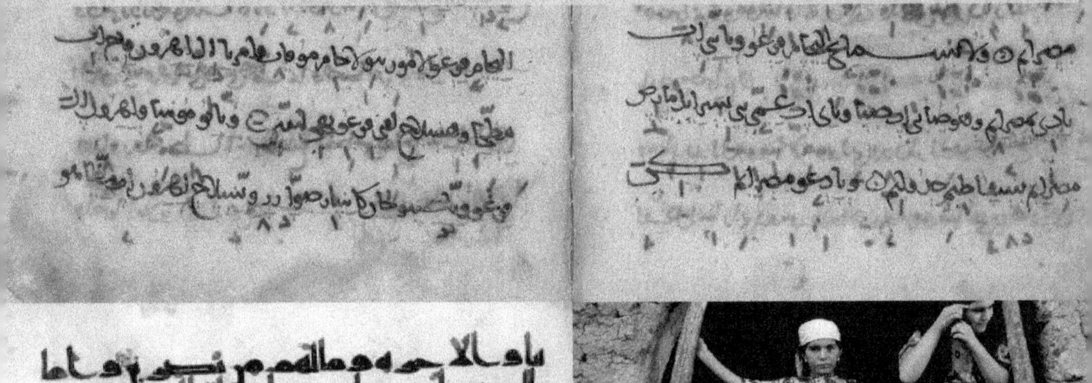

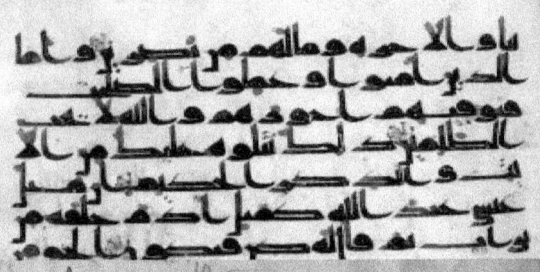

www.ingramcontent.com/pod-product-compliance
Lightning Source LLC
Chambersburg PA
CBHW070752300426
44111CB00014B/2384
* 9 7 8 1 8 0 5 1 1 3 5 0 8 *